S0-ADD-470

GLOBAL HISTORY

Volume Two:

The Industrial Revolution to the Age of Globalization

Jerry Weiner, Ph.D.
Professor, Kean University, NJ

Mark Willner, M.S.
Adjunct Faculty, Brooklyn College, NY

George Hero, M.A.
Director of Social Science Research, Midwood High School, Brooklyn, NY

Contributing Editor:
Bonnie-Anne Briggs, M.S.
Social Studies Department Head, Gates Chili High School, Rochester, NY
(retired)

Unless otherwise specified, all photos have been supplied by The Granger Collection, New York. Other images and photos were obtained from the following:

Ambient/Alamy: p. 386
David Wootton/Alamy: p. 637
dbimages/Alamy: p. 659
James Nesterwitz/Alamy: p. 507 (left)
Juergen Henkelmann Photography/Alamy: p. 387
Megapress/Alamy: p. 606
Mike Goldwater/Alamy: p. 523 (bottom)
NASA: p. 660 (bottom)
Petr Bonek/Alamy: p. 416 (bottom)
Philip Womuth/Alamy: pp. 369, 388
Photodisc: pp. 278, 456, 614 (top), 618, 632, 635, 646
POPPERFOTO/Alamy: p. 408
Robert Hading Picture Library Ltd/Alamy: p. 366
Reuters: pp. 494, 500, 551, 562
Sandra Baker/Alamy: p. 385 (bottom)
Shutterstock: pp. 611, 612
U.S. Marine Corps: p. 660 (top)
ullstein bild / The Granger Collection: pp. 352, 397, 400, 420, 425, 427, 459, 460, 461, 469, 471, 472, 482, 484, 492, 521, 522, 523 (top), 525, 531, 564, 653
United Nations: p. 347
vario images GmbH & Co. KG/Alamy: p. 385 (top)
Yvon Sauvé/Alamy: p. 507 (right)

Front Cover:
Photodisc: background image
The Granger Collection, New York:
    upper left-hand center image—Cleanup efforts on a French Beach after an oil spill
    lower left-hand center image—Ruins of Great Zimbabwe
Shutterstock:
    upper right-hand center image—helicopter landing in Vietnam during the Vietnam War.
    lower right-hand center image—Cathedral of Vasily the Blessed on Red Square Moscow Russia

Back Cover:
Shutterstock: background image—the Louvre pyramid
The Granger Collection, New York:
    upper left-hand center image—Soho Engineering Works at Birmingham, England, French engraving, 19th century
Oteri - ullstein bild/The Granger Collection
    lower left-hand center image—A crowd of people on top of the Berlin Wall, 1989
Nowosti - ullstein bild/The Granger Collection.
    upper right-hand center image—Auschwitz Survivors, 1945.
NASA:
    lower right-hand center image—International Space Station

Copyright © 2008 by Barron's Educational Series, Inc.

All rights reserved. No part of this book may be reproduced in any form, by photostat, microfilm, xerography, or any other means, or incorporated into any informational retrieval system, electronic or mechanical, without the written permission of the copyright owner.

All inquiries should be addressed to:
Barron's Educational Series, Inc.
250 Wireless Boulevard
Hauppauge, New York 11788
http://www.barronseduc.com

ISBN-13: 978-0-7641-6003-5
ISBN-10: 0-7641-6003-6

Library of Congress Catalog No. 2004057490

Library of Congress Cataloging-in-Publication Data
Willner, Mark.
    Global history / by Mark Willner, George Hero, Jerry Weiner.
        p. cm.
    Includes biographical references and index.
    ISBN 0-7641-5811-2
    1. World history. I. Hero, George. II. Weiner, Jerry III. Title.

D21.W735 2005
909—dc22   2004057490

Printed in China
9 8 7 6 5 4 3 2

About the Authors

Jerry Weiner, Ph.D. is a professor at Kean University in New Jersey where he coordinates Secondary Education Programs, teaches courses in secondary and elementary social studies education on the graduate and undergraduate levels, and supervises graduate thesis preparation. He is also responsible for the development and coordination of European Studies and Programs at Kean University. Dr. Weiner has had a long career in public and private education. He has taught classes on the university level in history and social studies education at Teachers College, Columbia University, and Hunter College and Medgar Evers College, CUNY. He has also taught global economics courses in Europe at the Ecole Superieure de Commerce in Pau, France and the Universidad de Deusto in San Sebastian, Spain. For many years, Dr. Weiner was an administrator and teacher in the New York City public school system. Among the numerous positions that he held, Dr. Weiner was a social studies supervisor at Boys and Girls High School and Louis D. Brandeis High School. He also served as President of the New York City Social Studies Supervisors Association (SSSA). He is a graduate of the Graduate Center, CUNY where he was awarded his doctorate in Latin American History with a specialization in Brazilian Studies in 1980. He has received a number of awards and fellowships throughout his academic career and as an educator. Among these honors were a Fulbright Fellowship for Study in Brazil in 1976–1977 and the John Brunzel award for outstanding social studies supervision in 1987. Dr. Weiner is the author of many books and articles dealing with history and social studies education. Among these works, he has participated in the writing of all Barron's "Let's Review World and Global History" editions.

Mark Willner was the assistant principal and chairman of the social studies department at Midwood High School in Brooklyn, NY from 1973–2005. He has also taught at Morris High School in the Bronx, Wadleigh (Harlem) Evening High School in Manhattan, and Temple Emanu-El Religious School, also in Manhattan. He was selected as the "Outstanding Social Studies Supervisor in the United States" for the year 2000. Similar outstanding supervisory honors were bestowed upon him in New York State (1991) and in New York City (1984, 1988). In 1997, New York State chose him as its "Distinguished Social Studies Educator." New York State also chose him, in 1995, to receive the "Louis E. Yavner Teaching Award for Outstanding Contributions to Teaching About The Holocaust and Other Violations of Human Rights." His most recent honor was as a winner of the 2004 "Spirit of Anne Frank Outstanding Educator Award" presented by The Anne Frank Center, U.S.A. Mr. Willner obtained a bachelor's degree in history from Queens College and a master's degree in social science education from Yeshiva University. As a recipient of Fulbright, N.E.H. and other grants, he has studied and traveled extensively in Asia and Europe. He has supervised in-service courses in conjunction with consulates, museums, and universities in New York City on China, India, Japan, Korea, the Middle East, and the Holocaust.

He is a past President of the New York City Social Studies Supervisors Association (SSSA), and has sat on the Executive Boards of the New York State SSSA and the New York City Association of Teachers of Social Studies/United Federation of Teachers (ATSS/UFT). He is currently one of the twelve members on the Executive Board of the NSSSA (National Social Studies Supervisors Association). Mr. Willner is the lead author of Barron's *Let's Review: Global History and Geography*. He has also contributed to Barron's *Regents Exams and Answers: Global History and Geography, Regents Exams and Answers: U.S. History and Government*, and *CLEP (How to Prepare for the College Level Exam Program)*. He has been a frequent presenter at social studies conferences on the national, state, and local levels.

George Hero has taught in the social studies department of Midwood High School at Brooklyn College in New York City since 1984. He is also the founder and director of the Social Science Research program at Midwood. A specialist in Eastern European History, he has also taught at Brooklyn College and Long Island University. Mr. Hero serves as the co-Chairperson of the Human Rights Committee of the World Federation for Mental Health. He is a co-author of Barron's *Global Studies, Volume II*. In recent years, he has worked on a new edition of American diplomat George Horton's account of the persecution of Christians in Turkey, *The Blight of Asia*. In 2003, he won an award for the "Outstanding Teacher of Social Studies" in New York City. Currently, he is an adjunct faculty member at Brooklyn College, and a consultant/education coordinator with the Gilder Lehman Institute of American History.

Bonnie-Anne Briggs is a graduate of Nazareth College of Rochester, with a B.A. in history with a minor in economics and the State University of New York at Brockport, with an M.S. in Education with concentration in Educational Administration. She retired in June 2002 from her position as a teacher and Teacher-in-Charge (Department Head) of Social Studies at Gates Chili High School in suburban Rochester, N.Y. Miss Briggs taught Global History and Geography, United States History and Government, Advanced Placement Economics, as well as an elective in Canadian and Russian Studies. She was an adjunct professor in social studies education at SUNY Brockport from 1988 until 2005. Miss Briggs is a past President of the Rochester Area Council for the Social Studies. She is also a past officer of both the New York State Council for Social Studies (NYSCSS) and the New York State Social Studies Supervisory Association. She chaired a variety of committees for these organizations and currently is the Chair of the NYSCSS Awards committee. She has been a frequent workshop presenter at local

and state conferences as well as a member and presenter at ASCD. In 1988 Miss Briggs was a recipient of the Rochester Area Council for the Social Studies Distinguished Service Award and the New York State Social Studies Supervisory Association Supervisor of the Year Award. In 1989 she received the NYSCSS Distinguished Educator Award. In 1977 she was the youngest person to that date to receive the Outstanding Alumni Award from Nazareth College of Rochester. In 1993 she was inducted into the Gates Chili High School Alumni Hall of Fame in its first year and was a semifinalist for the New York State Teacher of the Year Award. In 1992 Bonnie-Anne was nominated by a former student and included in Rochester Institute of Technology's Distinguished Teacher Recognition Program, for "outstanding dedication to students in their pursuit of education." She was the recipient of a NYS Multinational Scholarship given with Goethe House and the German government for study and travel in Germany. She participated in an NEH Advanced Economics study program. In 2000 she participated in a Colonial Williamsburg Teacher Institute. She has been a frequent writer on NYS Regents Examination committees. She was also an officer of the Rochester chapter of Phi Delta Kappa.

Miss Briggs is currently a very active docent and off-site presenter for the Susan B. Anthony House, a national landmark in Rochester. For several years she has also served as an educational consultant with the Education Department, Colonial Williamsburg, Williamsburg, Virginia. She also worked with National Evaluation Systems on the development of the NYS Social Studies Teacher Certification Test and subsequent scorings of that test. Miss Briggs is the co-author of *A Brief Review of United States History and Government*, Prentice Hall Publishing. She has traveled extensively in the United States, Europe, Canada, and the Caribbean.

Contents

ERA VIII

SOME CHALLENGES OF THE TWENTY-FIRST CENTURY

Introduction   **611**

Preface

FOR WHICH COURSE WAS THIS BOOK DESIGNED?

This book was designed to be used as the second volume of a basic two-volume high school text for a two-year, four-term study of the world—its history and its people. It can also be used in a one-year, two-term study. The material is presented in a manner that is appropriate for an introductory survey course. This volume covers the regions of Africa, Asia, Europe, and Latin America, from the early nineteenth century to the beginning of the twenty-first century.

WHAT ARE THE SPECIAL FEATURES OF THIS BOOK?

The information included here is mainly historical. It is a global history book. We begin with a general introduction to the social sciences. We then embark on a "trip through time" as we "travel" from ancient civilizations onward. Additional features of the book that you should know about include:

1. **A great deal of attention, more than is usual in a textbook, is given to the history of Eastern Europe and the former Soviet Union.** These areas of Europe have undergone crucial changes during your lifetime. A background historical knowledge is needed to understand these changes. Even with the publication of this book, historic events are occurring there that will have an impact in this century. Americans of your general need to be well-informed about these areas and how they have changed.

2. **All the authors of this book are high school social studies teachers.** This is very rarely the case with high school history textbooks. The authors have, combined, more than one hundred and ten years of successful experience in teaching global history classes. Much of this book is based upon that experience and therefore contains information that students such as you need to know. The authors also have traveled in the regions described, can speak several foreign languages, and have earned fine reputations for writing other instructional material on global issues.

3. **This book also explains, and has references to, various concepts and issues described in the global history and geography part of the social studies**

syllabus of New York State and that of other states. The fifteen key history concepts are change, choice, citizenship, culture, diversity, empathy, environment, human rights, identity, interdependence, justice, political systems, power, scarcity, and technology. The five key geography concepts are the world in spatial terms (places and regions), physical systems, human systems, environment and society, and the uses of geography. The eleven major world issues are population, war and peace, terrorism, energy resources and allocations, human rights, hunger and poverty, world trade and finance, environmental concerns, political and economic refugees, economic growth and development, and determination of political and economic systems.

4. **Each historical era in the book is broken into chapters and sections.** Enriching the text chapters are questions, maps, timelines, and charts.

5. **Significant attention is focused on Africa, Asia, and Latin America.** These are the areas where most of the world's people live and where the earliest known civilizations began.

SPECIAL MESSAGE TO HIGH SCHOOL STUDENTS OF THE TWENTY-FIRST CENTURY

In Volume I and this book, you will learn much about the past history of the four major world regions outside the United States—Africa, Asia, Europe, and Latin America. As a result, you will be able to understand the world that exists now and the world that will exist in the future years of the twenty-first century. The world of the 1990s and 2000s—during your lifetime—is different from the world of the twentieth century prior to your birth. During those earlier years, there were many changes on the world map, as well as crucial global events. There were, for example, two "hot" wars, a "cold" war, and several revolutions—some bloody and some peaceful. This was the world that your teachers, parents, and grandparents knew and studied about.

The present-day world is a different place, for reasons that you will learn about in this book. In addition, your generation probably knows more about the world than any earlier generation of American high school students. This knowledge has been acquired mainly from outside of school and may stem from one or more of the following reasons:

1. You or someone you know may have already traveled somewhere overseas, in Europe, Africa, Asia, or Latin America.

2. You may know somebody who works for a global company or someone who does business with people from around the world.

3. Television, movies, and advertising carry much information about people in other countries.

4. You may have something in your home that was made in a foreign nation.

5. Through the process of cultural diffusion and education, you may already be familiar with one or more languages other than English. You probably know something about music, sports, clothes, cosmetics, and food that are originated elsewhere.

6. The United States is a multicultural society. Throughout our nation, and probably right in your own community, are people who can trace their ancestry to different parts of the globe.

7. In each year of your lifetime, thousands of foreign tourists have traveled to the United States. Perhaps you have met some of them in your community.

SUMMARY

Although citizens of the United States, you, your family, and your friends are also "citizens of a global community." To understand this community, you are about to begin a study of it. Africa, Asia, Europe, and Latin America have strongly influenced our own nation's history. And of ironic historical interest, it is the United States that has greatly influenced the global community during the past two centuries. What will be the nature of the United States' relations with that community in the twenty-first century? Your generation's actions may well furnish the answer to this question. Upon reading this textbook, you will be well informed and well equipped to take your place as a citizen of the United States and of the world.

Good luck with this book. It will help you in your travels through the world—past, present, and future.

Mark Willner

Introduction to the Social Sciences

Social science is the term used for all or any of the branches of study that deal with humans in their social, economic, and political relations. These studies are referred to as the social sciences. Modern social sciences use the scientific method. The use of this organized and systematic way of research dates from the eighteenth century. Social sciences use quantitative methods and statistical techniques to analyze humans and their behavior with each other.

The social sciences are sometimes called the people sciences. Social sciences help us to understand how people lived and acted in the past as well as the present. The social sciences are anthropology, geography, history, political science, economics, sociology, and psychology. In all of these subject areas, scientists have their special interests and areas of expertise. The information that social scientists collect and analyze helps us to interpret how people behave and the reasons why events occurred.

History in its broadest sense is the story of all people and their past. History is closely related to the social sciences when it is studied and written about in a systematic and scientific way. History is the record of human accomplishments and failures. It is the story of how people have lived on our planet since the beginning of recorded events. Historians are people who study and write about human beings, events, and places in the world since the beginning of recorded civilization. To write about history, they use different records that tell them about our past. Historical records help the historian to analyze and explain how and why things happened the way they did so that we can learn from the past. Historians look for all kinds of evidence about why events happened. For this reason, the other areas of the social sciences are important to historians if they want to get a complete story. Sometimes historians write about situations in the hope that the same type of event will not happen again. This is particularly true of wars and situations in parts of the world where acts of genocide occurred.

THE METHODS AND SKILLS OF HISTORICAL ANALYSIS

Various methods can be used to study and analyze history. These methods of historical analysis and study require different types of skills.

- Interpretations of historical events are investigated. Developing perspectives or pictures and perceptions or understandings are the key skills in this type of analysis and study of history.

- Hypotheses about interpretations of historical events are investigated. The skill of constructing hypotheses that work is essential in this method of study and analysis.

- Examination of primary historical evidence leads to explanation and analysis. Finding differences and classifying types of evidence are crucial in this method.

- Concepts or ideas and themes are studied over a period of time. The skills in developing a conceptual or thematic framework are important in this method.

- Comparisons and contrasts are made concerning similar types of historical events. The skill to make proper comparisons and contrasts is essential in this method of analysis and study.

Economics is the study of how human beings use resources to produce various goods and how these goods are distributed for consumption among people in society. Throughout human history, people have lived and worked in different economic systems. These economic systems include barter, capitalism, fascism, socialism, and communism. Economists use complex mathematical techniques and statistical data in economic forecasting and analysis and management of resources.

Sociology is the scientific study of human behavior. As the study of humans in their collective or group aspect, sociology is concerned with all group activities—economic, social, political, and religious. Sociology tries to determine the laws governing human behavior in social contexts. Sociologists investigate a selected group of social facts or relations.

Psychology is the science or study of living things and their interactions with the environment. Psychologists study processes of how people sense other people, things, and their own feelings. They concentrate on the development of learning, motivations, personality, and the interactions of the individual and the group. Psychology is concerned with human behavior and its physiological and psychological basis.

Anthropology is the study, classification, and analysis of humans and their society—descriptively, historically, and physically. Its unique contribution to studying the links of human social relations has been the special concept of culture. Its emphasis is on data from nonliterate peoples and archaeological remains explorations. Anthropologists study the characteristics, customs, and cultures of people.

Political science is the study of government, political processes, institutions, and political behavior. Political scientists study and comment on fields such as political theory, national and local government, comparative government, and international relations. Political scientists are often called upon to make predictions about politics such as elections and people's reactions to different events.

GEOGRAPHY—THE PHYSICAL WORLD

Human beings and societies in all regions of the earth share a common global environment. This environment is a closed system consisting of a variety of physical features—land forms, bodies of water, vegetation and animal species, and climatic regions. These physical features are the result of several natural processes including the rotation and revolution of the earth, geological activity, the water cycle, and biological interactions.

The environment provides humans with a variety of renewable and non-renewable resources, which can be used to meet the needs of both individuals and societies. Though these needs are basic to all humans, the different ways in which these are met are determined by the differences in environments that exist from one part of the earth to another.

The land surface of the earth is generally divided into seven large land masses, called continents—North America, South America, Asia, Africa, Europe, Australia, and Antarctica. Large bodies of water, called oceans—Atlantic, Pacific, Indian, and Arctic—and smaller ones called seas cover about 70 percent of the earth's surface. The bodies of water separate some of the continents from one another.

In recent centuries, humans have improved their abilities to use more of the earth's limited resources, and technology has created closer contacts among peoples of different cultures. This global interdependence has made it increasingly important to understand the similarities and differences among cultures. Hopefully, such understanding will aid in solving shared problems and resolving disputes between peoples of different cultures.

MAPS AND THEIR USES

We can illustrate much information about the world with maps, but we must be aware of their limitations and distortions. Projecting the features of a sphere (the globe) on a flat surface (a map) can distort sizes and distances, especially when we attempt to show the entire world.

Attempting to illustrate the shapes of land masses correctly can distort the sizes of the land masses. On the other hand, trying to show size can distort shape, as in the Gall-Peters projection. Thus, maps can convey inaccurate impressions of the importance and influence of certain areas of the world.

Placement or location can give false impressions of the relationships among regions or the relative importance of an area. For example, in the Mercator projection, with the Atlantic Ocean in the middle, North America and Europe are located top center. This seems to illustrate both the importance and the closeness of their relationship. Compare the Mercator projection and the Japan Airlines map. The Japan Airlines map centers on the Pacific Ocean and therefore islands in the Pacific become important. If you look at the Macarthur Corrective Map, which was created by Australians, you will see a different story and emphasis in which land areas in the South Pacific are prominent.

Reading maps requires an understanding of their language. The scale provides a tool for determining distances. A map's legend or key provides information about the meanings of lines, symbols, colors, and other markings found on the map itself.

Modern technology has changed how we think about the size of the world. Actual (or absolute) distance has become less important than relative distance—how quickly communication and transportation can move ideas and people from one part of the world to another. Culture regions once separated by thousands of miles or formidable physical barriers now interact with one another.

Maps can present information in many ways. A topographical map attempts to show physical features, a political map focuses on the way humans divide up the world (the boundaries of nations), and economic maps illustrate the ways in which people use the environment and resources. Comparing specific maps, such as rainfall patterns and population distribution, can be useful in understanding ways of life and the relationships between humans and the world in which they live.

ERA V

AN AGE OF REVOLUTIONS, CONTINUED

(1826–1914)

INTRODUCTION

Although it is impossible to give an exact date when the first Industrial Revolution started, many of the early happenings associated with its beginnings started around the mid-1700s. This first phase of the Industrial Revolution lasted to the end of the 1800s. Today the Industrial Revolution has entered into a new phase in which there is a continuing development of technologies that have advanced and revolutionized telecommunications, medicine, transportation, finance, banking, investment, and manufacturing. These ongoing changes constantly affect and alter the way we live and will continue to do so.

To say that our lives have changed since the start of the first Industrial Revolution would be an understatement. We take a lot of things for granted today. When we walk into a room, we expect the light to come on when we flip a switch. Our food is kept fresh in the refrigerator, and we often go to school by bus, car, or train. We have hot and cold running water and can take baths and showers in our homes. Today we are used to the idea that we can send a shuttle up into space. A human being has walked on the moon, and we watched this historic event on television. Computers, cell phones, and digital video recordings are now everyday things. We are entertained and enlightened at home by a "magic box" that takes us around the world in seconds. We download music and listen to songs on our cell phones.

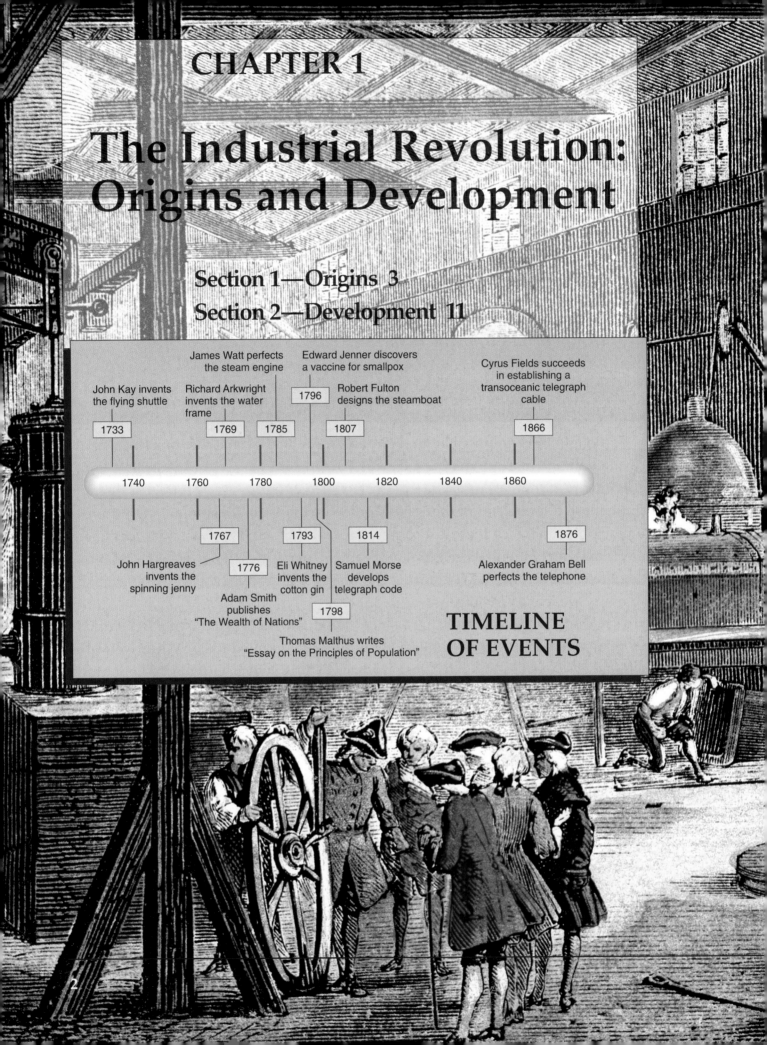

CHAPTER 1

The Industrial Revolution: Origins and Development

John Kay invents the flying shuttle

1733

Richard Arkwright invents the water frame

1769

James Watt perfects the steam engine

1785

1796

Edward Jenner discovers a vaccine for smallpox

Robert Fulton designs the steamboat

1807

Cyrus Fields succeeds in establishing a transoceanic telegraph cable

1866

1740   1760   1780   1800   1820   1840   1860

1767

John Hargreaves invents the spinning jenny

1776

Adam Smith publishes "The Wealth of Nations"

1793

Eli Whitney invents the cotton gin

1798

Thomas Malthus writes "Essay on the Principles of Population"

1814

Samuel Morse develops telegraph code

1876

Alexander Graham Bell perfects the telephone

TIMELINE OF EVENTS

Origins

Historians trace the origins of the **Industrial Revolution** to the agricultural changes that started in the fifteenth century. The **Agricultural Revolution** set the stage for the Industrial Revolution that took place in the following centuries. The long-term consequences of the changes in agriculture, such as the closing of lands to farming and the increased movement of people to the cities, were major factors that led to industrial development and growth in some Western European nations such as **Great Britain**, **France, and Holland**, and, later, elsewhere.

> **Main Idea:**
> The **Agricultural Revolution** set the stage for the Industrial Revolution that took place in the following centuries.

In pre-industrial times, most people lived in rural farming communities that had populations of several hundred people. In the countryside, life was harsh for peasants and their families who were employed in agriculture. Although feudalism had for the most part ended in Western Europe after the Middle Ages, the life of the rural peasantry hardly improved. The landlord still reigned supreme. The economic gap between rich, rural landowners and poor farmers, who made up the vast majority of the population in the countryside, remained very wide. After the Agricultural Revolution began in some Western European countries, the important changes in farming and livestock raising methods helped start the Industrial Revolution.

Other factors also led to the origins of the Industrial Revolution. The Age of Discovery led to a Commercial Revolution, which increased the availability of capital, trading opportunities, natural resources, and labor. The expansion of world trade and the establishment of colonial empires led to the creation of markets for finished goods and a need for raw materials. Technological advances made it possible to produce goods more efficiently and quickly. The development of machines and other types of technology made the production of goods and services much easier.

THE INDUSTRIAL REVOLUTION BEGINS IN GREAT BRITAIN

The Industrial Revolution began in Great Britain in the 1700s. Great Britain was the nation that combined all of the necessary political, economic, and social factors that led to a steady development of industrial production throughout the 1700s. By the nineteenth century, Britain was the leading industrial and trading nation in the world. The phenomenal rise of industrial production in Britain made the 1800s a time period when the British continued to expand their political and economic power throughout the world. During the nineteenth century, Britain greatly expanded its trading empire. Other nations of Europe and the United States spent the nineteenth century trying to catch up to Great Britain and duplicating the advances that made the British the world's first industrial trading empire.

Political Stability

The growth of industry in Great Britain was, in part, due to the nation's political stability. Starting in the 1700s, the British overcame political and social problems at home and developed a more democratic political system. During the unstable political times in the 1600s, the English beheaded one king and forced another to flee the country. In the eighteenth century, Britain did take part in the many wars, particularly against its rival France, but these international conflicts led to no battles on English soil. A nationalist political spirit gradually developed in Britain. British laborers believed that they were helping to build their nation. British industry was thus able to grow and prosper without the interruptions caused by destruction due to warfare and social conflict at home. The need for military preparedness even helped the growth of the British textile industry. Manufacturers benefited from government contracts for cloth to supply the nation's military forces with uniforms.

The ordinary citizen, who worked in England's factories and businesses, profited from the century of peace at home. Business investment grew in a political climate that supported and encouraged economic growth. The political influence that the increasingly powerful bankers, merchants, and other professional and business groups had in Parliament led to laws that stimulated new investment in industry. In Great Britain, the rise of a commercial and banking class that was politically powerful helped lessen the influence of the landowning class. The influence was more tied to agricultural and stock-raising pursuits.

The Agricultural Revolution

Another factor that helped to stimulate the growth of industry was the Agricultural Revolution. During the 1700s and 1800s, agricultural production increased in Europe because of innovations, new ways of doing things, which changed farming methods. A greater food supply was needed because of an increase in population, particularly in the urban centers that rose as the industrial economy developed. Rapidly growing urban industrial centers stimulated the increased production of food supplies and other farm products.

Small-scale farming declined, in part, because it became more profitable for landowners to push their tenants off the land and enclose it, fence it off, to raise sheep for wool. This **enclosure movement** led to the migration of farm labor to the cities, particularly in Great Britain. In addition, scientific and technological advances in farming equipment and methods led to the rise of large land holdings, which improved harvests and livestock production.

The impact of scientific and technological advances in agriculture also aided the development of industry in England. Crop rotation changed the method by which farmers kept fields fertile and resulted in increased yields. **Crop rotation**, perfected through experimentation by **Charles Townshend**, called for the planting of different crops to allow the soil to replenish or renew itself. Townshend's idea was to grow turnips and clover to replenish the soil with nutrients lost in the growing of such cereals as wheat. In addition, the turnips and clover helped provide feed for animals. Alfalfa, which restored nitrates to the soil, could be grown and fed to animals. The next season wheat

Cyrus H. McCormick's improved reaper of 1847.

could again be planted. Crop rotation revolutionized agriculture. It was no longer necessary to allow fields to lie fallow. More cattle and sheep could be raised for meat, wool, and other animal by-products. The diets of more people improved as meat became available at a lower cost.

Food production also increased because of the invention of machines and tools that improved farming methods. **Jethro Tull** symbolized the scientific farmer who used machinery in a well-planted field. Tull planted seeds in a straight row as opposed to scattering them at random. The seed drill was used by Tull to reduce seed loss and better control the weed problem. Other innovators perfected the iron plow that replaced less-efficient wooden plows. Still other inventions such as mechanical reapers led to further gains in the production of food supplies.

These new methods of farming dramatically changed agricultural production beginning in the early 1700s. The revolution in agriculture was a key to the success of the Industrial Revolution. There was a growing need to feed city workers and an increasingly urban population. The urban centers depended on greater farm production of traditional staples such as wheat and barley. The newly introduced American crops of corn and potatoes also improved the food supply as these staples became more popular.

The small farmer who was concerned with survival lacked the resources to expand food production for markets beyond the village. The harsh struggle to provide food for the family and pay rent and taxes prevented most farmers from taking advantage of increasing production by purchasing or renting more land. Instead the rich, rural landowners and other real estate investors purchased public and private lands and created large estates. The open-field system ended as more land was enclosed. The large landholders possessed the capital to farm by using scientific methods and thereby increased food production. The efficient farming methods made large-scale agricultural production more profitable. The raising of livestock also grew as a result of the enclosure movement. The enclosure movement had a negative impact on the need for

Main Idea: These new methods of farming dramatically changed agricultural production beginning in the early 1700s.

farm workers. The rural laborers were forced off the land and obliged to seek work in the urban centers. Many of the displaced farm workers became the labor force in the manufacturing of textiles and other products.

Changes in Manufacturing

In the 1600s into the early 1700s in Great Britain, the small-scale factory production that developed in textiles and other crafts increasingly converted to the domestic system of labor. In the domestic system, an entrepreneur, a person who engaged in a business, had greater control over the laborers who produced the goods. In the **domestic system**, workers were most often hired by entrepreneurs to produce woolens and other finished goods in their homes. Merchants supplied the raw wool, and paid spinners, weavers, fullers, and dyers to make a product that could be sold at market for the highest possible price. As the Industrial Revolution began to develop, entrepreneurs increasingly employed networks of workers, often groups of families. The use of the domestic system greatly helped in the development of Britain's woolens industry.

This more efficient labor system increased the profitability of manufacturing. The domestic system worked well during the 1600s. By the early 1700s, it could not keep up with the steady rise in demand for woolens, cotton cloth, leather goods, lace, and other goods. Starting in the 1700s, a series of technological advances revolutionized wool and cloth production. Cotton goods and woolens entrepreneurs found new ways to expand the textile industry.

Main Idea:
A number of inventions changed the method of producing textiles.

Technological developments in the textile industry also aided industrial growth. A number of inventions changed the method of producing textiles. The woolen industry had existed for centuries in Great Britain and the Netherlands. In Britain, woolens production was second to farming in the number of people employed and the volume of trade. In the 1700s, the demand for woolen goods increased. The need for raw wool was one reason for the enclosure movement. Advances in machinery changed cloth production. One of the first innovations that speeded the weaving of cloth was the flying shuttle. In 1733, **John Kay**, a British clockmaker, developed a weaving process that produced thread at a faster pace. Weavers could then produce wider fabrics using more materials. Weavers began to use spinner's thread faster than it could be made.

In 1767, **James Hargreaves** devised the spinning jenny. This machine enabled one person to spin up to seven threads at once. The spinning machine was steadily refined. Later models could produce up to 80 threads at a time. In 1769, **Richard Arkwright** invented a spinner called the water frame. This machine was capable of holding up to 100 spindles and used water power to continually run machines. The water frame also resulted in an increase in cloth production. In 1779, **Samuel Crompton** further improved the cotton business by utilizing the best features of the spinning jenny and water-powered frame to devise a machine known as the cotton mule. In a few short years, workers were able to produce high-quality cloth in larger quantities. Then, thread was being spun more quickly than cloth could be woven. However, in 1785, **Edmund Cartwright** developed a power-driven machine for weaving called the power loom. Weavers could now produce up to 200 times more fine cloth than before.

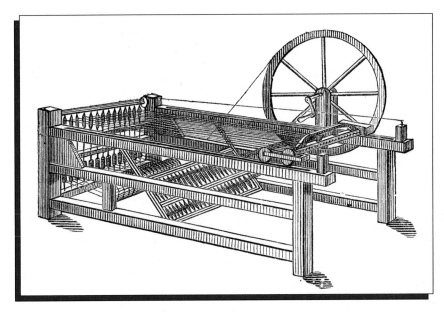

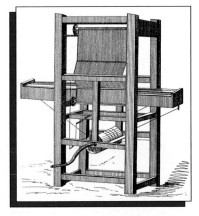

James Hargreaves' spinning jenny, invented c. 1764, patented 1770.

Dr. Edmund Cartwright's power loom of 1785, with vertical warp. Wood engraving, 1892.

James Watt's Steam Engine at an English coal mine in the 1790s: contemporary painting by an unknown artist.

The new problem in producing cloth concerned the raw cotton that weavers used in the spinning machines or power looms. The difficulty in separating out the seeds led to a shortage of cotton. However, by 1793, an American, **Eli Whitney**, invented the cotton gin. Whitney's laborsaving machine greatly aided the British cotton industry. The cotton gin cleaned the seeds from the fibers and the end result was a greater production of raw cotton, particularly in the United States during the 1800s. British importations of raw cotton in huge quantities enabled textile production to expand rapidly.

The Development of New Sources of Power and Transportation

Great Britain's rich supply of natural resources and excellent geographical conditions aided the start of the Industrial Revolution. Fine harbors and swiftly flowing rivers helped spur British trade. Access to raw materials and markets enabled British merchants and entrepreneurs to promote industrial growth. Shipment by water in a growing British merchant marine allowed overseas commerce to expand. Raw materials and finished goods flowed continuously on the nation's water transportation system. In addition, water provided the initial power for the development of industry.

James Watt (1736–1819). Scottish engineer and inventor: colored engraving after a painting by Sir William Beechy.

Great Britain also possessed large supplies of coal and iron that were accessible. These key raw materials were essential for industrial development. Coal was also used as a power source to fuel industrial machinery. By the 1760s, miners could use canals to ship coal more cheaply and easily to developing factories. Iron production also improved because of technological changes. In the 1700s, new processes were developed that increasingly made more efficient use of coke fuel to produce stronger iron. The ability to utilize coal instead of charcoal resulted in expanded iron production and more machinery for industry.

The early textile mills were built near flowing streams and rivers to take advantage of this source of water power. The ability to use the tremendous potential of steam finally became a reality when **James Watt** first developed the **steam engine** in 1785. By building upon earlier innovations, Watt made it possible for textile machines to be driven by steam engines. The harnessing of steam allowed entrepreneurs to build factories in more convenient locations. Freezing water during the cold winter was no longer a problem because of steam power.

Steam power also helped in coal mining. In 1698, Thomas Savery developed a steam-driven pump that helped in removing water from mines. By the 1700s, Savery's pump was improved upon by Thomas Newcomen. The innovative Newcomen pump was safer, but it often broke down and required lots of coal to generate the steam. Watt's steam engine greatly expanded the power of the earlier steam pumps, did not consume more fuel, and was safe to use.

The Development of Capital, Commerce, and Labor

The Commercial Revolution, which began earlier in the 1500s, led to an accumulation of money, or **capital**. Overseas trading empires that were financed by joint stock companies and banks created new wealth. This capital was reinvested and helped make the growth of industry possible. Fortunately for Great Britain, the nation's expanding overseas trading empire enabled British merchants and bankers to become more prosperous. More money became increasingly available for investment in industry.

Royal Exchange, London. Watercolor from Rudolph Ackermann's Microcosm of London, 1808–1810.

In addition, the wealthy land-holding aristocracy and gentry profited greatly from the new large-scale farming. Landowners also earned money in overseas commerce, including the slave trade. The aristocracy and landed middle class often took advantage of investment in the growing industries.

The English banking system also began to modernize by the early 1700s. More efficient financial services such as loans at reasonable interest rates spurred investment in industry. Money became more readily available to improve machinery, construct factories, and increase production. The British government assisted in this process by encouraging business investment with favorable laws passed by Parliament.

The Growing Supply of Labor in Great Britain and Western Europe

One of the crucial factors in the development of industry in Great Britain and elsewhere in Western Europe was the availability of a larger labor supply. The overall rise of the population in Western European nations was slow but steady. After the catastrophic demographic, or population, drop caused by the bubonic plague—a disease spread by black rats infested with fleas that carried a deadly bacillus—population growth resumed. By the mid-1700s, Western European population was approximately 135 million, or twice what it had been four centuries earlier. Within the next century, or by 1850, there was a phenomenal burst of population growth. For a variety of reasons, the number of Europeans rose to approximately 255 million. The new farming methods led to a rapid growth of food supplies to feed the expanding urban population.

Advances in medicine led to a declining death rate, particularly from the dreaded disease of **smallpox**. In 1796, **Edward Jenner** discovered a vaccine that was effective against smallpox. The control of this highly contagious disease, and other advances such as improved sanitation, resulted in people living longer. The survival of children through the perilous years from birth through early childhood reflected the better living conditions, more abundant food supplies, and improved health conditions of this period.

In 1798, **Thomas Robert Malthus**, a British economist, predicted that Europe was on the brink of another population catastrophe. In his "Essay on the Principles of Population," Malthus stated that European population was growing geometrically, while the available food supply was only increasing arithmetically. This prediction of dire consequences was based on Malthus's belief that European nations would soon outstrip their resources. Fortunately for Europe, the Industrial Revolution enormously expanded the productive capacity of Great Britain and other countries. It was now possible for the economies of industrial nations to support larger populations.

In Great Britain, it is estimated the population tripled from 1750 to 1850. By the mid-1800s, there were about 18 million people living in England. This rapid population growth in Great Britain spurred industrial progress by adding to the labor force. Other factors made it possible to absorb these extra workers into the new factories and businesses. The rising demand for manufactured products required a growing labor supply. Expanding retail businesses also employed more workers.

> **Main Idea:**
> The new farming methods led to a rapid growth of food supplies to feed the expanding urban population.

Thomas Robert Malthus (1766–1834). English cleric and economist. Stipple engraving, 19th century.

Development

THE SPREAD OF INDUSTRY TO OTHER NATIONS

Main Idea:
Individual and family businesses, partnerships, and corporations flourished in the expanding industrial world of the nineteenth century.

Industrialization spread rapidly to other countries. As was true in Britain, during the 1800s the factory system became the center of the industrial economy in **France**, **Germany**, the **United States**, northern **Italy**, **Belgium**, and the **Netherlands**. Industrial growth was characterized by large-scale manufacturing that took place in factories. After the 1870s, smaller scale industrial development began to spread to other global areas.

Improvements in transportation and communication helped industry to grow. The digging of canals in Great Britain, France, the United States, and elsewhere provided water links that made the shipment of raw materials and finished goods easier and cheaper. Private companies constructed roads linking urban areas. Steam-powered locomotives made railroad transportation possible in the industrializing areas of Western Europe. In the nineteenth century, a railroad boom began in the industrializing countries. Scientific inventions also led to the development of better communications. The telegraph, wireless, and telephone all assisted commerce and industry to expand and operate more efficiently.

The spread of industry was facilitated by the expansion of the capitalist system. The rise of big business in turn spurred the development of industrial capitalism. Mass production of cheaper goods resulted in higher profits but required greater investment in machinery. Individual and family businesses, partnerships, and corporations flourished in the expanding industrial world of the nineteenth century.

Great Britain

Great Britain sought to prevent the spread of industrial knowledge and technological advances to other countries. Parliament passed laws to prohibit the exportation of British industrial secrets. Laws making machinery export illegal and prohibiting British technicians and mechanics from moving to other countries were enacted. The English goal was to safeguard its position as the world's leading industrial and trading nation. Despite the severe restrictions enacted, however, Great Britain could not maintain its industrial monopoly.

France

In the 1800s, the French government pursued policies that encouraged industrialization. France at first promoted its textile manufacturing. From the 1830s to the mid-1860s, cotton textile production doubled. The invention of the silk loom by Joseph-Marie Jacquard led to the rise of a dynamic silk manufacturing industry. French industry tended to specialize in the fabrication of luxury items.

Carpets, tapestries, fashion clothing, excellent wines, and porcelains were not mass-produced in large factories. Artisans in limited-sized businesses manufactured these craft-oriented goods.

French railroad development aided industrial growth. A railroad network was built that radiated out of Paris in all directions. Banking and commercial interests influenced the French government to reduce high tariffs and other trade barriers.

Trade and commerce thereafter expanded. In the decades after the Revolution of 1848, French industry tended to remain as primarily small-scale, craft-oriented enterprises. Agricultural production also continued to be characterized by the traditional system of limited-sized family farms.

Germany

In Germany, an industrial economy began to develop in the period after the Congress of Vienna. British investment was the initial source for industrial capital in the German states. German industrial pioneers such as Krupp, Stinnes, and Mannesman later provided much of the national capital to finance industrial growth. The combination of government funding with national and international investment capital led to a boom in railroad development after 1840.

The German textile and metallurgy industries flourished by the mid-1800s. Advanced mining techniques led to the exploitation of the Ruhr and Saar iron and coalfields. After the 1840s iron production in Germany significantly

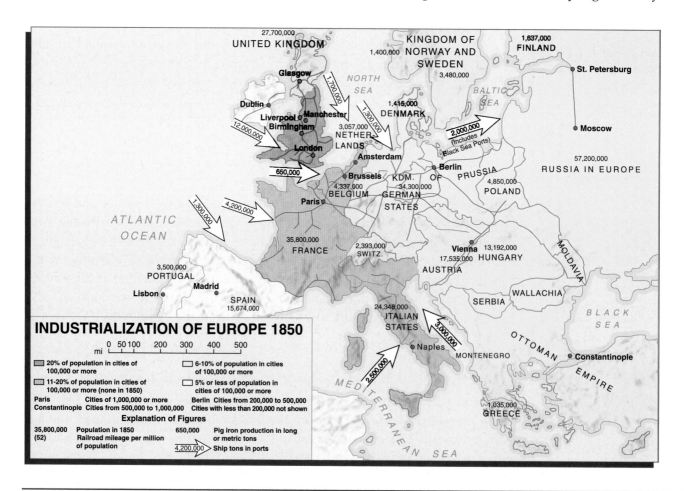

increased. Under the leadership of Prussia, the German states created a customs union called the **Zollverein** in 1834. This free-trade area included all the major German states. The removal of trade barriers encouraged industrial expansion. By the 1850s, Germany had the European continent's most powerful industrial economy. Within a generation, Germany would challenge Great Britain's industrial leadership.

Other European Countries

Industrialization spread elsewhere in Europe in the 1800s. Belgium profited from its commercial relations with the Netherlands and rich deposits of coal for fuel to build textile factories. In northern Italy, the combination of a skilled and urbanized labor force, plentiful deposits of coal and iron, and good transportation and communication links led to industrial growth. Later, the manufacturing of textiles on a large scale spread to Eastern Europe and Czarist Russia.

DEVELOPMENTS IN BUSINESS AND INDUSTRY

Industrial Capitalism Leads to Mass Production

The development of the capitalist system aided the rise of large factories and mass production. Capitalism was the economic system that made it possible for more individuals to invest in and own manufacturing enterprises. The possibility of earning more profits motivated people to invest in all types of manufacturing businesses. Capitalism contributed to the growth of bigger business enterprises and increased production.

> **Main Idea:**
> The possibility of earning more profits motivated people to invest in all types of manufacturing businesses.

Capital investment greatly aided the expansion of the factory system. Increased financial investment in new factories and equipment accelerated during the 1800s. In order to make very high profits, industrial capitalists sought control of all aspects of the means of production. Manufacturers exploited the labor force and determined the range of consumer choice.

Pre-industrial capitalism first led to the growth of a global trading economy. By the nineteenth century, the Industrial Revolution resulted in a manufacturing economy that incorporated gains made earlier during Europe's commercial expansion. **Investment capital** was utilized to purchase costly machinery that replaced more expensive and less efficient labor. The development of mass production technology enabled factory owners to produce large quantities of identical goods by using fast-working and precise machinery. The mass production of similar goods received a boost when the concept of interchangeable parts was introduced. By the early 1800s, Eli Whitney's contribution of replaceable parts made it easier to assemble machinery and change worn-out parts.

During the nineteenth century, the idea of industrial efficiency increasingly became popular because it led to more production at a cheaper cost and higher profits. In the later decades of the 1800s, factories adopted a division-of-labor system. Workers were assigned specialized tasks and took responsibility for a particular job. As the product moved down the assembly line, each worker was responsible for completing a task. The success of the assembly-line system

The world's first assembly line at the Ford plant in Highland Park, Michigan, 1913. Trained workers put together the flywheel magneto ignition system for the Model T.

increased the quantities of manufactured goods and lowered production costs. The industrialist had greater ability to sell at a cheaper price and thus expand the market for the particular product. Assembly-line production spread in Europe and the United States.

The American **Henry Ford** utilized the assembly-line system to **mass-produce** automobiles in 1908. A conveyor belt transported an auto body, and workers alongside all completed their specialized tasks to finish the car. The Model T Ford became the symbol of efficient assembly-line production

Business Organizations Modernize

The need to finance industrial development led to the growth of more complex business organizations. The expansion of industry and trade resulted in larger-sized businesses. Individual and family-owned enterprises continued to grow, but other types of business organizations became popular because they proved more capable of raising capital and limiting risk.

Partnerships were formed by two or more individuals who agreed to share management responsibility and work together to raise capital. Debt liability was thus limited for each partner, and more business could be taken on by a group of partners. The partnership form of business grew in the 1800s.

The corporation, or enterprise owned by many investors, became the favored form of business organization of larger companies by the mid-nineteenth century. Corporations or joint stock companies had played a pivotal role since the Commercial Revolution in financing expeditions and trading ventures. During the 1800s, entrepreneurs increasingly offered shares of stock or ownership in new companies to raise the necessary capital to launch a manufacturing enterprise. Investment in the stock of an enterprise made the holder of that company's shares a part owner of the business. Stockholders could earn income based on the number of shares that were held, if the company was profitable. In addition, a stockholder could also be relieved of the responsibility of risking his personal assets if the company failed and could not pay its debts.

The success of big business corporations in Great Britain, Germany, the United States, and elsewhere in Europe was often at the expense of smaller enterprises that could not compete on a larger scale. Corporations, when possible, bought out smaller companies and tried to establish a monopoly, or complete control, of the market for a particular product. The Standard Oil Company, organized and controlled by the American John D. Rockefeller, established total domination of the oil industry in the United States. In Europe and the United States, large corporations sought control of the companies that contributed to their final products. This form of monopoly was called vertical integration and was used in Europe and the United States to eliminate competition.

John D. Rockefeller (1839–1937). American oil magnate. Wood engraving, American, 1889.

Banks increasingly played a key role in financing industrial development. In Europe, the **House of Rothschild** based in Paris became one of the world's leading investment banks. The **Rothschild Bank** worked with other investment institutions to organize companies and finance overseas business ventures in transportation, mainly railroads, and communication systems. As the 1800s progressed, international investment ventures by private banks became more commonplace. Governments also became involved in helping protect investments and secure markets.

Fluctuations in the Business Cycles

In the era of the Industrial Revolution, business cycles increasingly determined the fate of entire national economies. The **business cycle** included periods of prosperity and boom times as well as recession and depression. Industrialization made related businesses increasingly dependent on each other. If the economy was expanding, one industry might contribute to the growth of another. For example, the railroad boom led to increased coal and iron production.

Main Idea:
Business cycles followed predictable sequences, although the length of time of each expansion and decline varied.

Business cycles followed predictable sequences, although the length of time of each expansion and decline varied. During a boom phase there was high employment, increased production, and more buying and selling; however, prosperous times did not last forever. Inevitably a period of recession or even bust followed. Decreased business activity and unemployment resulted. If the decline was severe enough, it was called a depression. Business fluctuations often led to widespread suffering.

Before the nineteenth century, most people in Europe lived in the countryside or small towns and farmed for a living. By the twentieth century, there was an enormous growth in the cities. The numbers of factory workers in the industrialized nations of Western Europe grew during this period. Agricultural employment and rural populations declined while industry expanded. The development of the industrial economy brought great changes for the urban factory worker. Workers were naturally dependent on their salaries to support themselves and their families. The arrival of hard times particularly hurt the urban industrial worker. Unfortunately, the capitalist system of production could not guarantee workers' jobs all of the time.

Scientific Advances Further Industrial Development

Industrial development benefited from advances in science and technology. Transportation and communication improvements made businesses easier to manage and more profitable. The harnessing of steam power revolutionized water and land transportation. In 1807, the American Robert Fulton perfected a steam-powered boat, which was able to travel on the Hudson River. By the late 1830s, steamships were crossing the Atlantic Ocean carrying passengers and goods.

> **Main Idea:**
> The pace of life quickened wherever the new technology spread.

Richard Trevithick, a British engineer, developed a **steam-powered locomotive** that ran on rails in 1804. A railroad boom took place first in Britain and later worldwide as design improvements made the steam locomotive workable. Railroads and steamships made it possible to move more goods and at a cheaper price. Transportation advances helped spur the growth of a world economy and led to increased overseas investment.

The late 1800s saw the development of a new type of engine that used gasoline, which came from petroleum oil, for fuel. This internal combustion engine ultimately replaced the steam engine in the 1900s because it was easier to operate and more dependable. The combustion engine eventually powered cars, trucks, ships, and locomotives. The increased production of land vehicles led to the building of better road networks.

Scientific advances also played an important role in speeding communication. The development of faster communication systems made the operation of businesses easier. **Samuel Morse**, an American inventor, is credited with developing the **telegraph** in 1844. Morse code, based on a system of dots and dashes, was transmitted over telegraph wire. Telegraph lines that carried information at speeds over great distances soon linked the industrial nations in Europe and the United States. In 1866, **Cyrus Field** completed a transatlantic cable that linked Europe to North America. In the 1870s, it became possible to send a cable around the world from New York to Tokyo and elsewhere in a matter of minutes.

Another communication advance was the invention of the telephone in 1876 by **Alexander Graham Bell**. The telephone used small electrical wire to

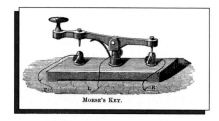

Morse's telegraph key, a brass lever mounted on a hinge: wood engraving, American, 1873.

The "Lion" locomotive, built by the firm of Todd, Kitson, and Laird of Leeds, England in 1838 for the Liverpool & Manchester Railway: photographed c. 1900.

carry the sound of people's voices and enabled people to speak over long distances. In 1895, **Guglielmo Marconi** perfected a system of transmitting electric signals without the use of cable or wire. Marconi's wireless was called the radio in the United States.

By harnessing electricity to power streetlights and provide electric current motors, electricity became more practical. Thomas Edison's invention of the incandescent light brought cheap lighting to factories, streets, and homes. By the early 1900s electricity began to replace coal as the primary source for industrial energy to power machines. Technological innovations in transportation, communication, and electricity led to dramatic changes in the ways people lived and worked. The pace of life quickened wherever the new technology spread. Industrialization brought an ever-increasing mechanization and modernization to the world economy.

LINK TO TODAY

The Industrial Revolution, which started in the 1700s, brought great changes to the nations of Western Europe and later the United States, Japan, and other parts of the world. In the twentieth century, the growth of industry and commerce in other areas of the world led to major changes in nations that only took part in the first Industrial Revolution as suppliers of raw materials or consumers of industrial-made goods. These goods were made primarily in European nations and the United States. The industrial supremacy of the United States and nations of Western Europe began to diminish in the decades after World War II. There was a shift of production to other areas of the world, particularly Asia in the last decades of the twentieth century.

Today, if we look at the growing areas of industrial production, it is evident that the world has changed in terms of production of goods and their consumption. For example, today Asian nations such as China, South Korea, Taiwan, and India have become major producers of industrial goods, which to a large extent are consumed in the countries where the first Industrial Revolution took place. This second Industrial Revolution has been accomplished with the aid of an ever more sophisticated telecommunications network. Computers have enormously added to the development of industry in other parts of the world.

The Industrial Revolution is no longer confined to the nations of Western Europe and the United States. Japan, China, India, Brazil, South Korea, and other nations have developed economies that are very industrial. In the future, the nations of the world that can produce the best quality goods for the least price will be the key industrial nations. Our world has become more competitive and smaller in terms of industrial production. Many of the economic and social ideas that brought about the first Industrial Revolution seem to belong to the industrial world of the past. Today Americans and Europeans can no longer be guaranteed that just because they live in the nations of the first Industrial Revolution they will live better than most people in other parts of the world.

CHAPTER SUMMARY

There was no single reason why Great Britain became Europe's leading industrial power by the nineteenth century. During the 1700s and 1800s, British industrial growth profited from many favorable conditions that encouraged its rapid development. Great Britain was ripe for the economic changes that transformed the nation into the world's first modern global political and economic power.

England was a politically stable nation whose government supported economic growth. The nation combined abundant natural resources, a favorable geography, and a business and scientific climate that encouraged new and innovative ideas. Most of the important inventions and innovative ideas that resulted in an increased capacity for industrial production in the 1700s and the first part of the 1800s originated in Great Britain.

The British also developed a banking system, which was capable of supporting industrial growth and handling the increased amount of financial transactions. Great Britain had a growing labor supply available for industry because of the movement of people to urban areas as a result of the agricultural enclosure movement and an increase in population.

The ideas advocated by Adam Smith in *The Wealth of Nations* about free enterprise and laissez-faire economics proved to be the correct formula for British industrial expansion. A noninterventionist government policy was an important factor in Britain's economic transformation.

Increased industrial production in Europe, the United States, and Japan was the result of a combination of factors. Great Britain served as a model for other European nations to follow. The growth of transportation and communication networks was also important for the growth of industry. The rise of big business concerns, particularly corporations, which were capable of raising large sums of capital for investment in factories and equipment, enabled manufacturing to expand. By the end of the nineteenth century, a number of nations in Western Europe, the United States, and Japan had launched their Industrial Revolutions.

IMPORTANT PEOPLE, PLACES, AND TERMS

KEY TERMS

Industrial Revolution	smallpox	Rothschild Bank
Agricultural Revolution	capital	business cycle
enclosure movement	Zollverein	steam-powered boat
crop rotation	investment capital	steam-powered
domestic system	mass production	locomotive
steam engine	House of Rothschild	telegraph

PEOPLE

Charles Townshend	James Hargreaves	Edmund Cartwright
Jethro Tull	Robert Fulton	Eli Whitney

James Watt	Adam Smith	Samuel Morse
Edward Jenner	Thomas Robert	Guglielmo Marconi
Alexander Graham Bell	Malthus	Thomas Edison
Cyrus Field	Henry Ford	

PLACES

Great Britain	Germany	Netherlands
France	Italy	United States
Holland	Belgium	

CHAPTER 1

MULTIPLE-CHOICE QUESTIONS

Select the number of the correct answer.

1. Place the following events in the correct chronological order:

   A. The Agricultural Revolution
   B. The Commercial Revolution
   C. The Age of Discovery
   D. The Industrial Revolution

   (1) C, A, B, D
   (2) C, B, A, D
   (3) A, B, C, D
   (4) B, A, D, C

2. Which of the following is the best example of an advancement made during the Agricultural Revolution?

   (1) James Watt developed the steam engine.
   (2) James Hargreaves devised the spinning jenny.
   (3) Charles Townshend perfected the idea of crop rotation.
   (4) Edmund Cartwright invented the power loom.

3. The development of the Agricultural Revolution in the eighteenth century made which of the following possible?

   (1) Most farmers sold their farms and moved to the cities.
   (2) Farm production increased to meet the needs of the growing urban areas.
   (3) Factory workers moved back to farming communities.
   (4) Quantities of surplus farm goods were sold in Africa and Asia.

4. The domestic system can best be described as

   (1) many workers on an assembly line.
   (2) families working to produce goods, especially textiles in their homes.
   (3) an advanced method of very fast woolen production.
   (4) children employed in factories working large spinning looms.

5. Which of the following Americans greatly aided the growth of the British cotton industry with his invention?

   (1) Eli Whitney
   (2) Thomas Edison
   (3) Henry Ford
   (4) Samuel Morse

6. Question 5 refers to an American invention that aided the growth of the British cotton industry. Which of the following inventions was it?

(1) Automobile
(2) Telegraph
(3) Phonograph
(4) Cotton gin

7. From the middle of the eigteenth century to the middle of the nineteenth century in Europe, the population almost doubled. What would be considered a major reason for this development?

(1) Millions of people relocated to European colonies.
(2) Birth control information was widely available.
(3) Most people lived by subsistence farming.
(4) Smallpox vaccinations and improvements in sanitation were available to more people.

8. Thomas Malthus predicted which of the following catastrophes for the early nineteenth century?

(1) widespread famine
(2) an increase in industrial accidents
(3) extended periods of global warming
(4) desertification in Africa that would cause food shortages

9. The Industrial Revolution originated in

(1) the United States
(2) France
(3) Great Britain
(4) Germany

10. What did Great Britain do to try to prevent the spread of industrial knowledge to other countries?

(1) forbade emigration of British citizens
(2) stopped all foreigners from traveling to Great Britain
(3) employed children in the factories
(4) passed laws to prohibit the exportation of industrial secrets

11. A natural resource that was most needed by all countries industrializing in the 1800s was

(1) uranium
(2) aluminum
(3) coal
(4) silver

12. Which technological development was vital to the success of every industrializing country in the 1800s?

(1) railroads
(2) automobiles
(3) airplanes
(4) canal boats

13. The creation of the Zollverein in Germany in 1834 encouraged industrial expansion because it

(1) developed advanced mining techniques
(2) removed trade barriers between German states
(3) increased hydroelectric production
(4) created a unified German government

14. Capitalism encouraged the development of new industries in which one of the following ways?

(1) It was a system that hired new inventors directly.
(2) It allowed individuals to invest in manufacturing enterprises.
(3) It guaranteed to make even poor people wealthy.
(4) It gave workers the opportunity to join unions.

15. When mass production replaced the domestic system, finished goods were almost always

(1) more attractive to the buyer
(2) of better quality
(3) more useful
(4) cheaper

16. By the 1800s businesses increasingly offered shares of their stock for sale to the public. They did this primarily to

    (1) interest consumers in their products
    (2) raise money for expansion of their business
    (3) take advantage of small business owners
    (4) limit their financial growth

17. Investors were willing to buy shares of stock in new businesses because they expected to

    (1) make a profit
    (2) own the business eventually
    (3) learn industrial secrets
    (4) travel to overseas markets

18. Which of the following inventors is correctly matched with his invention?

    (1) Alexander Graham Bell—telegraph
    (2) Robert Fulton—steam powered boat
    (3) Samuel Morse—gasoline engine
    (4) Cyrus Field—wireless radio

19. Which of the following statements expresses an opinion about the Industrial Revolution?

    (1) The Industrial Revolution began in Great Britain and spread to other countries.
    (2) Inventors during the Industrial Revolution developed time- and money-saving devices.
    (3) All workers benefited from the new factory system.
    (4) Urban populations increased as rural populations decreased.

20. The Industrial Revolution had a major economic impact because

    (1) workers decided that communism was an effective way to improve unsafe working conditions
    (2) although it began in a limited geographic area within a century it spread to many areas around the globe
    (3) business owners made efforts to slow the spread of new inventions
    (4) the Agricultural Revolution was able to develop new farm tools

THEMATIC ESSAY

Directions: Write a well-organized essay that includes an introduction, several paragraphs addressing the task below, and a conclusion.

Theme: Change

Change often occurs in cultures when humans develop new ideas in science and technology.

Task

Choose four individuals from this chapter and for each individual chosen

- identify a specific change that occurred as a result of the individual's ideas
- discuss whether the change was a positive or negative change

You may use any individual from this chapter. Some suggestions you might wish to consider include Charles Townshend, James Hargreaves, Eli Whitney, James Watt, Edward Jenner, Thomas Malthus, Henry Ford, and Alexander Graham Bell.

Guidelines

In your essay, be sure to

- develop all aspects of the *Task*
- support the theme with relevant facts, examples, and details
- use a logical and clear plan of organization, including an introduction and a conclusion that are beyond a restatement of the theme
- introduce the theme by establishing a framework that is beyond a simple restatement of the *Task* and conclude with a summation of the theme

This question is based on the accompanying documents (1–7). The question is designed to test your ability to work with historical documents. Some of these documents have been edited for the purposes of this question. As you analyze the documents, take into account the source of each document and any point of view that may be presented in the document.

Historical Context

The era of the Industrial Revolution was a time of great change.

Task

Using information from the documents and your knowledge of global history, answer the questions that follow each document in Part A. Your answer to the questions will help you write your Part B essay in which you will be asked to

- explain how the Agricultural Revolution led to the Industrial Revolution
- identify and describe two ways in which life was changed during the Industrial Revolution
- discuss why Great Britain was a likely place for these events to occur

Part A: Short Answer Questions

Directions: Analyze the documents and answer the short answer questions that follow each document.

Document 1

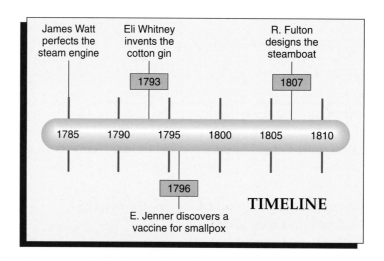

Question

Based on the events in this timeline, what are two generalizations that could be written about this time in history?

1.

2.

Document 2

2. a. According to this illustration, what would be one positive result of the Agricultural Revolution?

b. According to the illustration, what would be one negative result of the Agricultural Revolution?

Document 3

3. a. What is this type of production called?

b. Why was this type of production used?

Document 4

Question

4. Identify two types of commercial activity suggested in the document.
   a.
   b.

Document 5

Questions

5. a. Identify Point B and give one characteristic of this point.
   b. Identify Point D and give one characteristic of this point.

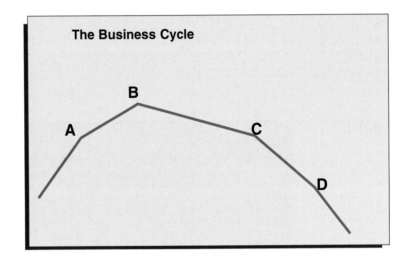

The Business Cycle

B

A

C

D

Document 6   "Such is the delicacy of man alone, that no object is produced to his liking. He finds that in everything there is need for improvement.... The whole industry of human life is employed not in procuring the supply of our three humble necessities, food, clothes and lodging, but in procuring the conveniences of it according to the nicety and delicacy of our tastes."

Adam Smith
Scottish philosopher and economist, 1723 –1790

Question   6. Explain how the statement above from Adam Smith might explain the development known as the Industrial Revolution.

Document 7

Agricultural Revolution in England 1500–1850

By Mark Overton

A second reason why we can claim an agricultural revolution in the century after 1750 is that as each agricultural worker produced more food, so the proportion of the workforce in agriculture fell. This falling proportion of workers in agriculture enabled the proportion working in industry and services to rise: in other words improved agricultural production made the industrial revolution possible, and many would regard the industrial revolution as the beginning of the modern world. By 1850 only 22 per cent of the British workforce was in agriculture; the smallest proportion for any country in the world.

> "The development of agrarian capitalism in England saw the development of better farm management and more efficiency in using the workforce."

Exactly how those working on the land were able to produce more food remains something of a mystery. More animal power was available to English farmers than to their counterparts elsewhere, and from the 1820s and 30s a wide variety of machinery was developed, which was particularly important for improving the efficiency of the cutting and threshing of grain. The improvement in labour productivity, however, had begun long before this.

The key probably lies in the way the English workforce was organised and employed. The development of agrarian capitalism in England, with those involved in agriculture divided into landowners, capitalist tenant farmers and labourers, saw the development of better farm management and more efficiency in using the workforce.

Question　　7. According to Mark Overton's article, what allowed more workers to be able to be employed in industrial jobs?

Part B: Essay

Directions: Write a well-organized essay that includes an introduction, several paragraphs, and a conclusion. Use evidence from *at east four* documents in the body of the essay. Support your response with relevant facts, examples, and details. Include additional outside information.

Historical Context

The era of the Industrial Revolution was a time of great change.

Task

Using information from the documents and your knowledge of global history, write an essay in which you

- explain how the Agricultural Revolution led to the Industrial Revolution

- identify and describe two ways in which individual lives changed during the Industrial Revolution
- discuss why Great Britain was a likely place for these events to occur

Guidelines

In your essay, be sure to

- develop all aspects of the *Task*
- incorporate information from *at least four* documents
- incorporate relevant outside information.
- support the theme with relevant facts, examples and details
- use a logical and clear plan of organization, including an introduction and a conclusion that are beyond a restatement of the theme

The Impact of the Industrial Revolution

TIMELINE OF EVENTS

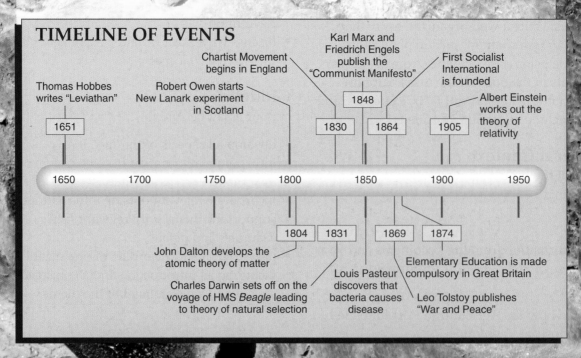

Thomas Hobbes
writes "Leviathan"

Robert Owen starts
New Lanark experiment
in Scotland

Chartist Movement
begins in England

Karl Marx and
Friedrich Engels
publish the
"Communist Manifesto"

First Socialist
International
is founded

Albert Einstein
works out the
theory of
relativity

1651

1848

1830   1864   1905

1650   1700   1750   1800   1850   1900   1950

1804   1831   1869   1874

John Dalton develops the
atomic theory of matter

Charles Darwin sets off on the
voyage of HMS *Beagle* leading
to theory of natural selection

Louis Pasteur
discovers that
bacteria causes
disease

Elementary Education is made
compulsory in Great Britain

Leo Tolstoy publishes
"War and Peace"

Changes in Social and Economic Conditions

THE LIVES OF PEOPLE CHANGE

How did the lives of people change when some European societies underwent the transformation from an agricultural to an industrial economy? Why did some people benefit from these changes while other people only exchanged one difficult existence for another? How did people live in the developing cities? What were the living conditions in the growing industrial centers? These are some of the questions that will be discussed in the following pages. In this chapter, you will read about how the lives of people were changed as urban centers developed and expanded in the Industrial Age. You will also read about what the cities were like in the 1800s as they rapidly grew.

The **Industrial Revolution** had an enormous impact on the way people lived and worked. The working and living conditions in the nations that developed industrial economies changed as cities grew larger. The shift from a rural agricultural economy to an urban industrial economy led to major changes in society that had important long-term consequences for many people. **Industrialization** completely altered the lives of those people who left rural agricultural areas for the urban centers where they could find factory work. In

> **Main Idea:**
> The **Industrial Revolution** had an enormous impact on the way people lived and worked.

Glasgow, Scotland. Old houses at the corner of George Street and High Street. Photograph, late 19th century.

the 1800s, the expansion of the industrial economy transformed the economic and social structure in **Great Britain**, elsewhere in Western Europe, and the United States.

For the most part, rural life on the farm had never been easy. A farmer's existence was often full of difficulties and problems. The farmer historically worked throughout the year from sunrise to sunset, in all types of weather, performing tiring agricultural tasks. Living conditions in farming villages were often harsh. Life was rustic and pleasures were few and simple. To quote **Thomas Hobbes** from his 1651 book *Leviathan*, rural life was "nasty, brutish, and short." Young children were called upon to help out with chores around the farm at an early age and later worked alongside their parents to do whatever had to be done to help their families survive. Marriage took place at an early age, and the newlywed couples were fortunate if they could farm their own land right away.

Prior to the Industrial Age, a person's position in life was determined at birth. Two positive aspects of rural farm life were that it created a sense of equality and a sense of sharing. In farming communities, most people shared the same lifestyle. **Rural** families lived and usually remained together or in the same general locality. There were many extended families of grandparents, parents, children, uncles, aunts, and cousins. Families were better able to take care of their older members when they ceased to be economically productive or were ill. The family provided a sense of ethics and morality, which included respect for one's elders.

Main Idea:
As a result of the migration to the cities, many people faced new and difficult economic and social problems.

The Industrial Revolution caused major changes for those people who gave up their traditional farming lifestyles. In the European nations, people left their rural farming homes and went to urban areas where they could find jobs in the factories that developed in the industrial centers. As a result of the migration to the cities, many people faced new and difficult economic and social problems.

The city served as an escape from the difficult rural life that most farmers faced. Many farming families who came to the city left because of the grueling agricultural work and the authoritarian rule of the landlord who dominated rural life. Despite its harshness, many farming families believed that the city offered more hope for advancement and a better life. They did not realize that the living conditions of the workers and their families in the cities were too often as miserable or even worse than the life they faced in the countryside. Coming to a city and adopting an **urban** city lifestyle was not very easy or without problems.

Industrialization contributed to the rapid growth of large cities. When people moved to larger towns and cities, their lives changed radically. They had to adapt to different ways of living and working. They came in search of new opportunities and jobs and hoped for a better life for themselves and their families. The city offered many new ways of making a living for those people who came to the urban centers from rural areas. The rise of the factory system created a need for more workers in the urban centers. Throughout the 1800s, despite the difficult working and living conditions, people continued to flock to the cities in search of work.

City living was often destructive for the unity of the working-class family. Working and living conditions led to a growing sense of individualism and need for personal survival. In contrast to farming life, urban family members increasingly often stopped functioning as a cohesive unit. Urban families had to adapt to patterns of labor and lifestyles that often ruined their health. Family members no longer spent large amounts of time together. Most often after returning from a hard and long day of work, people ate quickly and slept. There was hardly any time for social events.

Not everyone benefited from the opportunities available in the industrial urban centers. Although there were new opportunities for people to improve their economic situation and status in society, many people did not fare that well in the difficult urban environment. Poverty, long work hours, overcrowding, poor sanitary conditions, crime, and other socioeconomic problems overwhelmed many people and their families. In reality, for most industrial workers, there was little possibility to rise above the level of their families' industrial working status.

THE GROWTH OF THE MIDDLE CLASS

The growth of industrial centers resulted in the expansion of the **middle class**. The middle class was the social and economic class between the aristocracy, or very wealthy, and the workers, or less fortunate groups in society. During the Industrial Revolution, people in urban areas had more of an opportunity to use their initiative and talent to achieve material success and a higher status in a more flexible and fluid society. The middle class greatly grew in number and prospered as the result of many new opportunities that were now open to people who were educated and talented.

Social Life, England, 19th century. Cartoon by George du Maurier from "Punch," 1878.

The development of a sizable middle class in Western Europe and in the United States was not possible in the pre-industrial agriculture based economy. In the Pre-Industrial Era, the middle class was primarily made up of a small number of doctors, storeowners, lawyers, and others whose professions afforded them a reasonable sum of money. There was a natural limit to the number of these professionals and small businessmen in societies, which were primarily agricultural. There were not enough opportunities for advancement, particularly in European countries where farm ownership and agricultural employment began to decrease. The growth of industrialization and the rise of the urban centers gave more opportunities to an expanding middle class.

Main Idea:
The middle-class lifestyle led to changes in the family.

Industrialization enabled new groups of people to enjoy the benefits of middle-class life. Successful owners of mines, railroads, and factories gained upper-middle-class status. Increasing numbers of professional workers such as managers of companies and stores, teachers, clerks, and owners of small businesses achieved middle-class status. The middle-class lifestyle led to changes in the family. In the agricultural economy, men and women shared the responsibility of providing for the family. However, in the industrial economy, middle-class men increasingly became the sole providers for their families. In the growing cities, middle-class women devoted themselves to bringing up their children and maintaining the home. A husband's success was often measured by his ability to hire domestic help to relieve his wife's burdens at home. Servants were employed for low wages to perform the tedious household chores, enabling middle-class women to escape the drudgery of washing laundry, cleaning, and other unpleasant household tasks.

In the 1800s, few middle-class women worked outside of their homes. Nevertheless, many women who no longer had to work took the opportunity to improve their lives. Freed from the household chores, middle-class women used the time to educate their children and themselves at home. These women

"New School-Room, Boys' Home, Regent's Park-Road." A London, England, school for orphan boys. Wood engraving, 1870.

A bird's-eye view of the city of Manchester, England, during the Industrial Revolution: English engraving, 1876.

Main Idea: The middle class tried to copy the lifestyles of the aristocratic upper class.

taught their daughters how to embroider, sew, cook, and act like refined young ladies. In addition, some women instructed themselves in the natural sciences, geography, gardening, and ways to improve their homes. A small number of middle-class women even sought to obtain college degrees, which at the time was unusual.

The urban middle-class family was very conscious of its social position and economic status. It did not identify with the other growing social class, the industrial workers. The middle class tried to copy the lifestyles of the aristocratic upper class. Much of their wealth went into the purchasing of large homes and even estates that were lavishly furnished and decorated. Even those middle-class families who lived a more moderate lifestyle were conscious of their status in society. They sought to show their social position by dress and other mannerisms that set them apart from the working class. A respectable appearance and polite manners were among the expected social norms that the middle class displayed in society.

Middle-class boys had more opportunities than girls outside of the home. Boys were sent to school for the training needed to succeed at work and to maintain their family's social position. Higher education for young men from good families became increasingly possible. Some middle-class young men were educated to take over their fathers' positions in the family business. Girls and young women had limited job opportunities. Middle-class women were not expected to be wage earners or pursue professional careers.

LIFE AT WORK AND HOME OF THE GROWING URBAN WORKING CLASS

The largest growth of population in the industrializing nations of **Western Europe** and after the Civil War in the United States was in the number of urban industrial workers in the cities. This population explosion of urban workers began in Great Britain in the mid-1700s. It resulted in expanding urban centers where people flocked to find work. The majority of people who came to the cities ended up as industrial workers in factories and mills. Working conditions in the industrial plants were often extremely difficult and even dangerous and unhealthy in many workplaces. Workers labored twelve to sixteen hours daily, six days a week.

As the population increased, the living conditions that the workers confronted at home steadily worsened. Despite gains made in medicine and the improved food supply, the working class found it difficult to cope. They led a lifestyle that forced them to work long hours and raise their families in an urban environment where living conditions were often described as being horrible. The vast majority of workers and their families had a miserable home life. Workers were kept away from their homes by the long workday. After dark, the exhausted workers returned to their crowded, poorly constructed tenement buildings.

Often living space was limited to one or two rooms for a family of six to ten people. The lack of ventilation and adequate heating made these apartments too hot in the summer and too cold in the winter. The poor health conditions resulted in the spread of communicable diseases such as typhoid and cholera. The **tenements** were built out of either wood or brick and little attention was given to the common areas. Courtyards, halls, and alleyways were often dark. Large piles of garbage and other filth including excrement made these areas

Paying children for their labor in the brick-yards. Wood engraving, English, 1871.

unsightly and unhealthy. The stench that rose from these tenements was often overwhelming.

Street conditions were hardly any better. Most streets were unpaved and had no drainage facilities. When it rained, the mud combined with garbage and other filth, making walking in the streets difficult. Horse-drawn carriages and wagons added to the problem. The air was often heavy with black smoke from the coal-burning factories and mills. At times, there were attempts to clean larger avenues, but in general few cities did much to improve the quality of the streets. Crime became commonplace on dark and isolated city streets and alleys. Some changes were made with the introduction of gas street lamps, paved streets, and drainage systems, but the unhealthy conditions of the industrial city streets for the most part continued throughout the nineteenth century.

The increased supply of **skilled** and **unskilled workers** led to a favorable labor situation for those who owned industrial production facilities. The owners of factories and mills were able to keep wages very low. Poor salaries made it necessary for an entire family, including young children who often started working as early as age six, to search for employment. Finding a job for all of its members did make it easier for the family to survive. Nevertheless, family life suffered since everyone was out of the home most of the time working. Children and women were particularly sought after because they worked for lower wages than men. Young children who labored in mines and factories often did dangerous jobs. Many of them were your age or younger.

Much of the labor involved operating noisy machinery that lacked safeguards. The long hours of monotonous and repetitive labor often resulted in accidents that seriously injured working men, women, and children. There was no compensation for the loss of a finger, limb, or life of a worker. Medical care for sick or injured workers or their families was rarely available.

Workers followed their rigid schedules throughout the year. There were no vacations, sick leaves, or paid holidays. Ventilation and lighting were often very poor, and workers suffered in an atmosphere where the air was full of fumes and smoke. Horrible environmental conditions led to serious health problems for workers in factories, mills, and mines. For example, coal miners, particularly children, breathed in coal dust that blackened their lungs, thus shortening their lives. The crowded conditions in the factories and poor ventilation caused the easy spread of diseases such as tuberculosis and pneumonia, which killed many workers.

The lack of time to enjoy their lives was a dilemma for the industrial workers. In the agricultural lifestyle, the rhythms of the seasons and the sun's daily path determined the work cycle of farmers. There often was time after harvests, during religious festivals, and on Sundays to rest and enjoy life. Industrial workers, however, found that time ruled their lives in a more impersonal and structured manner. Workers were required to report to their jobs and follow rigid schedules that were designed to maximize production. The factory workers moved to the sound of the bell that signaled the beginning and the end to a shift as well as periods allowed for activities such as lunch. To a large measure, the workers became dehumanized as they lost their ability to function as independent human beings.

Main Idea:
Poor salaries made it necessary for an entire family, including young children who often started working as early as age six, to search for employment.

CONTRASTING LIVING CONDITIONS IN THE CITIES

The living conditions of workers and their families differed greatly from that of the upper- and middle-class city residents. The comfortable lifestyles of the upper-class families were shared by the increasingly well off middle class. Professionals such as lawyers and doctors and small business owners were better able to provide their families with conveniences and luxuries previously only available to the upper class. Even middle-class parents who were not very affluent had comfortable lives and offered their children the advantages of education, health care, and proper sanitation. Workers and their families, for the most part, did not share in these advantages of city life.

Prior to the 1800s, most cities developed in places that were convenient to land and water trading routes. The Industrial Revolution, however, led to an explosive growth of cities in areas that were not natural marketplaces. Cities grew near new sources of power, such as coal, and other raw materials. The building of factories or mills often led to a rapid rise in the surrounding population as people flocked in to find work. Factory owners and middle-class families took the best available housing and constructed new and more lavish homes on private estates. The workers and their families were forced to make due with whatever housing was offered to them or was available to rent.

Main Idea:
Some of the enlightened factory and mill owners sought to establish towns in which the living conditions of the workers were tolerable.

In the early stage of the Industrial Revolution, some of the enlightened factory and mill owners sought to establish towns in which the living conditions of the workers were tolerable. In factory towns such as Manchester and Sheffield in Great Britain, there were attempts to provide workers with better living conditions. As industrial competition heightened in the 1800s, however, less care and thought went into planning city growth. In fact, urban cities grew so quickly that housing, sanitation, and other conditions of life became increasingly dangerous and unhealthy. The owners of factories, mills, and mines were more concerned with profits and industrial competition than they were with the living conditions of the workers and their families. Even though some mill owners provided their laborers with housing and were instrumental in raising health standards, most industrialists opted not to improve the general living conditions of their workers.

The rapid growth of cities throughout the period of industrialization resulted in the construction of tenement-type housing for working-class families in the poorer city neighborhoods in **Great Britain**, **France**, **Germany**, **Belgium**, and the **United States**. The factory, mill, and mine owners operated with a free hand. Industrialists did not concern themselves with improving the conditions of city life. Essentially, they lacked a sense of social responsibility. Rivers that flowed through industrial cities were used to dump industrial and mining wastes. The water in rivers and streams became increasingly contaminated and unusable for drinking, cooking, and even washing.

Not surprisingly, the terrible living and working conditions in the cities had a negative impact on the average worker's life span. Disease was rampant in the factories and tenements. The ravages of pneumonia, tuberculosis, cholera, and typhoid reduced the life span of the working class. Children were particularly vulnerable and suffered greatly if they worked in the dark, damp, and poorly ventilated mines.

Provision shop for unemployed English textile mill workers during the "cotton famine" in Manchester resulting from the Union blockade of Confederate ports during the American Civil War: colored English engraving, 1862.

Workers had flocked to the cities in hopes of finding work and creating a better life for themselves and their families. Unfortunately, for most workers this did not happen. Although most workers did find jobs, their lives rarely improved. In rural areas, families were used to difficult and long hours of work on farms. In reality, the farming lifestyle often proved to be more humane than the working lifestyle in the industrial city. At least in rural areas people shared life as a family unit. However, in the city all the social conditions were different. Increasingly, the working-class family ceased to be a cohesive social unit. Industrial labor was more impersonal and dangerous. Accidents and sickness added to the miserable conditions. The harsh economic situation trapped most working families into a life of poverty.

THE GROWTH OF A CAPITALIST SPIRIT

As the 1800s progressed, the Industrial Revolution transformed the economies of Great Britain, other Western European nations, and the United States. Industrial capitalism was profit driven and totally unregulated. The idea of **laissez-faire** or lack of government regulation of industry was the rule. Materialism, or the tendency to be more concerned with money or luxury goods rather than spiritual or intellectual values became more prevalent. A materialist culture developed in the Industrial Age, which the manufacturing and business elite increasingly embraced. The upwardly mobile middle class supported this belief in materialism. The growing middle class sought status and prosperity. They overwhelmingly supported economic ideas that allowed entrepreneurs and industrialists to maximize their control over industry and capital without governmental interference. One result was that the urban worker and family suffered difficult lives.

New Economic Theories and Ideas

THE GROWING CALL FOR REFORM

Industrialization brought prosperity and benefits to some Western European nations and the United States. Some European economies, particularly those of Great Britain, France, Belgium, and the Netherlands were transformed, and many people, particularly the upper and middle classes, prospered. Nevertheless, the Industrial Revolution also created problems that were caused by the wide-ranging economic and social changes. There was growing criticism that the Industrial Revolution did not benefit everybody and had a negative effect on the lives of most people who lived in urban centers. These liberal and radical critics believed that the economic and social changes that took place only aided and profited the wealthy factory owners, rich merchants, and the middle class. The widespread poverty and harsh labor and living conditions of the working class spurred those interested in **economic** and **social reforms** to develop new ideas to change how the industrial society functioned.

> **Main Idea:**
> Liberal reformers and radical revolutionaries advanced new political, economic, and social theories and ideas about the organization of society.

During the 1800s in Europe, there were increasing demands for political, economic, and social reform. Liberal reformers and radical revolutionaries advanced new political, economic, and social theories and ideas about the organization of society. Political repression, however, became the rule in the post-Napoleonic Period. Under the leadership of Prince Metternich, at the Congress of Vienna, 1814–1815, the European powers sought to defend absolute monarchies, prevent liberal and radical reforms, and repress outbreaks of nationalist movements. The stable political, economic, and social climate that the Metternich system tried to establish and maintain did not last very long. By 1830, a number of revolutions took place in different European nations such as **Greece**, the **Netherlands**, **Poland**, **Italy**, and parts of the **Austrian Empire**. Although these first revolutions were for the most part put down and contained, they could not be permanently stopped.

Beginning with the revolutionary movements that took place in 1848, the deep divisions in the industrializing societies and elsewhere in Europe were again revealed. The revolutions that broke out by mid-century often separated the middle-class liberals, who wanted moderate reforms, and the workers and their intellectual supporters, who demanded more radical changes. Thereafter, there would be a marked split among those liberal reformers who wanted to bring moderate changes to the workings of the industrial society and those who proposed a revolution to overthrow the existing societies and create a worker-controlled state.

THE ECONOMIC IDEAS OF ADAM SMITH

The Industrial Revolution had its earliest impact in Great Britain. Industrialization led to material progress and higher social status for the British upper and middle classes. The upper classes of society, particularly the business leaders, believed in the ideas of **Adam Smith** about laissez-faire economics. Smith's *The Wealth of Nations* supported the capitalist viewpoint that government should not interfere very much in economic matters. He believed that the economy would regulate itself by an "invisible hand." Smith stated the value of labor should be determined in an economy in which workers had to sell their labor in a free and competitive market. According to Smith, labor, not money, was the true source of wealth, and a person's motive for labor was self-interest.

Adam Smith (1723–1790). Scottish economist. After a painting by Charles Smith.

Smith had been the first to explain the relationship between capitalism and laissez-faire economics. He theorized that competition and free-market pricing was best and would lead to resources being put to the most productive use. By allowing people to act in their own self-interest, Smith wrote that they would ultimately bring about economic progress and social harmony. He argued that the economy followed the law of supply and demand. Without governmental interference, the cheapest and best-made products would attract consumers. Efficient producers would make more profits, hire more workers, and expand their businesses, thereby benefiting everyone.

OTHER IDEAS CONCERNING THE INDUSTRIAL ECONOMY AND THE ROLE OF GOVERNMENT

Smith's ideas became very influential as the Industrial Revolution developed. However, there were many people who opposed his ideas about the proper relationship between government and business and what role the government should play in regulating the economy. Most reformers and radicals who were opponents of Smith's ideas argued that it was the lack of governmental business regulations that led to an industrial society of haves and have-nots in Great Britain and elsewhere in Western Europe and the United States. They believed that workers were exploited and often lived in miserable conditions. These proponents of an increased role of government in the economy believed more strongly in regulating the economy to prevent economic injustices and misery.

Malthus and Ricardo: The Influence of the Growth of Population and Food Supply

There were also other economic theorists who believed that the terrible working and living conditions that developed in industrial societies could not be avoided and were a direct result of overpopulation and an inefficient food

David Ricardo (1772–1823). English economist. Colored stipple engraving, 19th century.

supply. In 1798, **Thomas Malthus**, in his "Essay on the Principles of Population," took a gloomy view about the workings of the economy. Malthus wrote that misery and poverty were natural outcomes because population grew at a faster rate than the food supply. Malthus saw this as a law of nature and was against any interference in this process. He believed that nothing could be done to prevent natural disasters such as famine and disease. In Malthus's view, these unavoidable outcomes were the only real checks on unwanted population growth.

Another English economist and banker, **David Ricardo**, writing twenty years later, linked the persistence of poverty to what he referred to as the "iron law of wages." Ricardo, in his most famous work, *The Principles of Political Economy and Taxation*, theorized that as the population increased so did the labor supply. Wages tended to stabilize around the subsistence level. Any rise in the price of labor would cause the working population to increase to the point that it heightened competition because of a glut of workers whose market price, or wages, would fall back to the subsistence level. In other words, increased competition for jobs kept wages low. Ricardo also stated the value of almost any good was the function of the labor that produced it. Ricardo agreed with Adam Smith that government interference would only make matters worse. In addition, like Malthus, Ricardo theorized that poverty was inevitable.

Bentham and Mill: Ideas About Economic Reform

There were other people; however, who believed that poverty could be controlled if reforms were made. These early reformers attacked laissez-faire economic ideas. They argued that governments should be required to bring about changes to improve society. In Great Britain, many of these early reformers were religious figures or humanitarians who worked to have Parliament pass legislation to abolish slavery and regulate working conditions. These reformers sought to change ideas about government involvement in solving society's problems.

Jeremy Bentham, who developed the idea of utilitarianism, argued that the true test of any institution or action was its usefulness. Bentham and his pupil **John Stuart Mill** believed that a useful government should influence the distribution of wealth. Mill proposed a tax on income that would allow government to bring the greatest happiness to the largest number of people.

Bentham and Mill criticized laissez-faire economics. They were among those reformers who were concerned with correcting economic abuses such as monopolies and other business actions that brought harm to society. Utilitarians did not condemn the capitalist system. Instead, they sought

John Stuart Mill (1806–1873). English philosopher and economist. Photographed in 1865.

The Chartist riot at Newport, England, November 4, 1839: wood engraving, English, 19th century.

to reform it by means of corrective legislation. Bentham and Mill also supported the ideas of a good public education and the right to vote for men and women. Both men wanted to politically reform society to serve the needs of the many, as opposed to the few.

THE BEGINNING OF WORKER MOVEMENTS

Worker associations also tried to improve the harsh labor conditions and low wages through protests and strikes. In the 1800s, workers' associations began to transform into **labor unions**. Despite the opposition to unions by owners of large businesses and government laws against worker combinations, laborers continued to organize to fight for better hours and wages. In Great Britain, workers had to overcome the Combination Acts of 1799 and 1800 to keep their labor union cause alive. By the 1820s, British workers gained parliament's acceptance and were allowed to meet and discuss labor issues such as wages and hours. **Labor organizations** also sought to expand political rights of workers and called for reforms in the qualifications for voting.

In the 1830s, a workers' movement called the **Chartist Movement** developed in Great Britain. The Chartists wanted real political reform. They argued for universal suffrage for men, a secret ballot, annually elected Parliaments, and equal electoral districts. Chartists supported payments for members of Parliament and opposed property qualifications for office. The Chartists managed to continue as a force in Great Britain through the 1840s despite the fact that the movement failed to convince Parliament of the need for political reform.

SOCIALISM

Main Idea: Socialism called for a society in which workers own, manage, and control production.

There were some reformers, called socialists, who believed that the capitalist economic system itself was the real cause of society's problems. **Socialism** called for a society in which workers own, manage, and control production. These socialists argued that the Industrial Revolution led to a fierce competition by owners of businesses to make profits, thus causing misery for the working class. Some socialists believed that production should be only controlled, and not necessarily owned, by the government, whereas others argued for worker control and ownership. Many of these socialists believed in a political system in which there was a democratic means of gaining power and promoting their ideas. They respected the idea of individual values.

Other advocates of socialism argued that the government should control production and distribution so that more people, particularly workers, could share in society's abundance. These socialists were called radicals because they sought to bring about fundamental changes in the relationship between government and the economy and how the economy operated. These radical socialists argued for ideas that they believed were in the interest of the working class, the proletariat. They believed in government control and ownership of property and the means of production and distribution. Many of the radical socialists supported the idea of violent revolution.

UTOPIAN SOCIALISM

A number of the early socialists were often referred to as utopians. The **utopian socialists** envisioned the creation of an ideal society in which all people would

share equally in its benefits. One of the first of the utopian socialists was **Robert Owen**, a wealthy Scottish cotton manufacturer. Owen had experienced firsthand the misery of the working class in his youth. At the age of ten, Owen worked in the textile industry. However, by the time he was twenty-three, Owen had become a successful factory owner. Conscious of the workers' plight, Owen decided to create an industrial community where people could work in a more just and healthy environment.

In 1800, in a Scottish mill town called **New Lanark**, Robert Owen established his industrial community. Owen tried to give his workers better working and living conditions. Owen did not give the control of production to his workers, but he did pay higher wages, provided for education by constructing schools, and offered affordable and decent housing. The New Lanark experiment was a profitable success and encouraged other utopian socialists.

Robert Owen (1771–1858). Welsh socialist and philanthropist. Canvas, 1834, by W. H. Brooke.

In France, Charles Fourier also worked to create model communities in which cooperation would replace competition and improve workers' lives. Fourier's ideas resulted in the establishment of workers communities. The Fourier plan called for an organization of five hundred to two thousand workers in which each person would do the job for which he or she was best suited and share in the profits. All of the utopian communities set up in France and later in the United States that followed Fourier's ideas ultimately failed.

The utopian socialists did not adequately deal with the issue of who controlled the political system. These socialist reformers had no plan for workers to take control of political power from the traditional nobility, industrial elite, and middle class in Western European societies such as Great Britain and France. By ignoring the reality of actual power, these early socialists left government control in the hands of a combination of aristocrats and members of the bourgeoisie. These economic groups bitterly opposed the idea of giving real political power and authority over production to workers and their supporters.

KARL MARX AND SCIENTIFIC SOCIALISM

Karl Marx is credited with developing the theoretical basis for scientific socialism, the economic and political philosophy that came to be known as **Marxism**. Marx dismissed the earlier theories of socialism, particularly its utopian version, as impractical. Marx and his close friend and collaborator **Friedrich Engels** devoted their lives to the formulation of economic theories and political analysis based partly on the work of earlier theorists and historians. Nevertheless, Marxist philosophy was in many respects unquestionably original. Marx and Engels wrote that the exploited working class would rise up and ultimately gain control of society. Marx challenged the laws of economics that supported capitalism. He argued that capitalism was unstable and in the course of history would eventually self-destruct.

> **Main Idea:**
> Marx challenged the laws of economics that supported capitalism.

Karl Marx was the son of a prosperous German lawyer who had converted from Judaism to Christianity to further his career in the legal profession. In Germany, Marx earned a doctorate in history and philosophy. Beginning in his student years, Marx gained a reputation as someone with radical views who was deeply concerned with the miserable working conditions created by the factory system. In his early writings, Marx blamed industrial capitalism for society's political, economic, and social problems.

By the 1840s, Marx's political and religious views led to problems with the Prussian government. As a result, Marx left Germany and settled for a time in Paris, where he met and collaborated with Engels. In 1848, they published their socialist theories in a work entitled *The Communist Manifesto*. This critical historical analysis of society became the basis for scientific socialism or communism.

Karl Marx (1818–1883). German political philosopher.

Karl Marx spent the later part of his life in Great Britain. Marx's large and needy family was for the most part supported through the generosity of his friend, Friedrich Engels. The failed revolutions of 1848, in their attempts to promote political and economic reforms, did not end Marx's work to promote scientific socialism. In 1867, the first part of his major economic work *Das Kapital* was published. In Great Britain, Marx continued his activist role to promote scientific socialism. Increasingly, this type of socialism became known as communism. In the 1860s and 1870s, Marx worked and argued with other leading socialist and trade union activists. He helped found the First Socialist International in 1864. The International sought to promote the causes of the worker or proletariat in Europe and the United States. By the time of his death in 1883, Marx was the most prominent figure in European socialism.

MARX AND THE THEORY OF COMMUNISM

Marxism argued for a practical and scientific analysis of society's problems. Only then, Marx believed, would socialism become the path for the working class to follow. Essential to Marx's interpretation of history was the importance he placed on the idea of class struggle. Marx wrote that the historical process could be divided into different stages of a political struggle for control of society's economic benefits by competing social classes. Marx stated that the stages of history were really economic conflicts among the classes to determine ownership of the means of production, labor, and machinery. The social group that controlled production was the ruling class in the four different stages of history. Marx argued that in all societies throughout history, there had been power struggles between two economic groups, the haves and the have-nots.

In ancient society, Marx declared that production was based on slavery. In the medieval centuries in Europe, the principles of feudalism determined production. The industrial capitalist stage was based on the system of wage labor. In the present stage of industrial capitalism, the struggle to control society was between **capitalists**, or the **bourgeoisie**, and the **workers**, or the **proletariat**. Marx saw this division of society into classes as a natural result of existing economic forces. According to Marx, the ruling class never gave up control of society or production without conflict. Therefore, Marx believed that history only moved forward because of class struggle. Marx believed this conflict was inevitable and predicted that the working class would rise up in revolution. The proletariat would ultimately replace the bourgeoisie and take control of the means of production.

In his interpretation of history, Marx placed emphasis on economic conditions. According to Marx, society's laws, customs, religions, social systems, and art all developed in response to existing economic forces. Humanity's historical struggle for a better material life and living conditions could only be understood by using an economic analysis of the factors that determined political and social issues. Marx's economic interpre-

> **Main Idea:**
> According to Marx, society's laws, customs, religions, social systems, and art all developed in response to existing economic forces.

Wrapper of the first edition of Karl Marx's and Friedrich Engel's *The Communist Manifesto*, London, 1848.

tation of history was based on the idea that history followed scientific laws just as in nature.

In nineteenth-century industrialized societies, Marx stated the workers suffered because the bourgeoisie or capitalist class seeking to maximize its profits exploited them. Marxism stressed the idea that the worker had the right to earn a living wage. However, he believed that the worker, because of the owner's control of the means of production, labored more hours than he or she should in order to live. This extra work resulted in surplus value. Marx wrote that surplus value was the difference between the price of a good and the wage paid to a worker.

For example, according to Marx, if the workers needed to labor four hours a day in order to live, they were paid wages for their work during this working time. The money earned constituted a living wage, although it was basically a subsistence wage. The employer believed that this was the wage to which the worker was entitled. However, the factory owner wanted the worker to labor for more than four hours so that the owner could make profit. If workers wanted to keep their jobs, they had to labor ten or more hours a day. These extra hours were not really paid for and resulted in the owner stealing hours of labor from the workers. Marx believed that the worker was exploited in this unequal relationship between capital and labor.

According to Marx's surplus value theory, the capitalists sought to keep as much of the profit as possible. Marx wrote that this was wrong because the profit motive resulted in the industrial capitalist paying the workers low wages. On the other hand, Marx believed that this basic economic injustice was a natural and inevitable outcome of the present industrial capitalist stage of history. Marx regarded labor as the real source that created productive value or capital. Although he praised the bourgeoisie for having expanded the material basis of civilization by industrialization and urbanization, Marx also blamed this ruling class for the miserable working and living conditions of most of the population. Marx theorized that as capitalist competition continued to increase, profit margins would shrink. This competition would inevitably result in more people living in poverty. The contradiction of an industrial society based on the prosperous few and the poverty of the many would ultimately lead to revolution. Marx wrote, "workers of the world unite; you have nothing to lose but your chains."

Marx predicted the inevitability of violent revolution by the workers to seize economic and political power. He realized that the capitalists would never peacefully give up economic and political power. Marx saw a communist revolution first resulting in a dictatorship of the proletariat, or a government that would be more just and would rule in behalf of the working class. This workers' government would bring economic, political, and social justice. Eventually a classless society would emerge. There would be no need for governments. The government would wither away when it was no longer needed to protect the proletarian revolution.

Main Idea:
Marx believed that basic economic injustice was a natural and inevitable outcome of the present industrial capitalist stage of history.

FAILURE OF MARXISM IN WESTERN EUROPE

Marx's prediction that communist revolutions would occur in the Western European industrialized societies failed to happen. The socialist parties that followed Marx's ideology in Western Europe did not bring about the inevitable revolution that Marx predicted. In the decades after Marx's death, most of the industrialized countries initiated economic and social reforms. In Western Europe, the standard of living rose from the late 1800s into the early 1900s. Many of the worst abuses seen in the first stages of the Industrial Revolution were ended.

Governments began to initiate reform that led to improvements in working and living conditions. Public health improved, and public education became more commonplace. Labor unions were increasingly allowed to organize. This resulted in gains for workers in terms of health and accident insurance, unemployment insurance, higher wages, safer working conditions, and fewer hours. Child labor abuses were gradually ended in most countries.

Marx underestimated the workers' identification with their own countries. Nationalism was a strong force in the Western European industrialized societies. Marx's idea of an international community of workers did not appeal to the vast majority of industrial laborers. The workers slowly earned better wages and gained social protections. As a result of these reforms, workers were more willing to support their national governments. Most workers hoped to change the capitalist system through peaceful methods and not by overthrowing the established order.

Although Czarist Russia did not fit Marx's description of an industrial society where proletariat revolution was inevitable, the country had not completely shed traces of feudalism that had led to the assassination of Alexander II at St. Petersburg, March 13, 1881, which is depicted here in a contemporary drawing giving detailed information of the event.

COMMUNISM IN RUSSIA AND EASTERN EUROPE

Despite the failure of Marx's prediction that communist revolutions would ultimately occur in Western Europe's industrial societies, his ideas did eventually have a major impact on the course of human history. In the 1880s, a number of the socialist parties that formed in European nations adopted Marx's ideas.

In the early 1900s, a small group of communists used Marx's ideas to bring revolution to Russia. Czarist Russia did not fit Marx's description of an industrial society where proletarian revolution was inevitable. Russia was basically an agricultural society that had not completely shed the traces of feudalism. Nevertheless in 1917, a determined number of radical Russian Marxists seized power. The use of Marx's ideas to create a communist society had an enormous impact on the course of historical developments in the twentieth century.

> **Main Idea:**
> Marx underestimated the key and crucial role played by the capitalist class in the industrial economy.

In fact, Marx's prediction that industrial societies would ultimately become communist turned out to be wrong. However, in agricultural societies such as in Russia and later in Eastern Europe, Asia, and elsewhere, Marxism did achieve its goal of a communist-led revolution and the seizure of power. In part, this was due to certain weaknesses in Marx's analysis of the capitalist system. Marx did not foresee the ability of the capitalist system to change and adapt to new conditions. Marx wrote his theories when laissez-faire capitalism was the rule of the day. He thought that capitalism was a temporary stage and could not predict the different forms of state-sponsored capitalism, which developed in the twentieth century.

Marx underestimated the key and crucial role played by the capitalist class in the industrial economy. He failed to recognize the importance of the captains of industry in developing an economy that satisfied the demands of people who wanted to be consumers and have a more material life. He did not realize how much self-interest determined people's decision making. Marx could not predict that when his economic theories were put into practice they would be distorted. In the countries that became Marxist or communist in the twentieth century, a ruthless dictatorial and essentially nonproductive ruling class and bureaucracy gained power. They exploited the people while claiming to rule in their name in a dictatorship of the proletariat.

THE LEGACY OF SOCIALISM

In the twentieth century, democratic forms of socialism developed in Western Europe. In Britain, Sweden, and elsewhere, greater emphasis was given to the democratic means of gaining government control of important aspects of the means of production to benefit the public. The democratic socialists gained power through elections and were respectful of individual values and political rights. They were willing to give up political power if they lost the support of the electorate. In Western European countries and the United States, associations began to develop into labor unions. Slowly, unions became more commonplace, and their right to represent workers was gradually accepted. As the century progressed, workers benefited from these reforms, which improved their job and living conditions.

Changes in Medicine, the Sciences, and the Arts

The cultural, scientific, and medical achievements of any civilization can tell us much about the people in that society. This is true today and is also valid for society in the 1800s. In that time, the work of scientists, medical researchers, artists, musicians, and writers increasingly reflected the new scientific, social, economic, and political conditions brought on by the Industrial Revolution.

Prior to the nineteenth century, doctors had less knowledge of the causes and prevention of deadly diseases. For example, smallpox and diphtheria had killed millions of people over the previous centuries. New discoveries in medicine helped gain more control of these and other fatal diseases in Western Europe and elsewhere. During the nineteenth century, advances in medicine and science dramatically improved people's lives particularly in some Western European nations and the United States. Scientific discoveries in biology and chemistry led to the development of new medicines and the adoption of innovative medical techniques. People began to live longer and healthier lives because of medical breakthroughs.

There were also important improvements made in transportation and communication, based on a steady stream of scientific inventions and technological achievements. Discoveries in the fields of biology, chemistry, and physics unraveled some of the mysteries of science. Psychology and sociology rose in importance as a result of research.

The scientific discoveries and the achievements in the arts, literature, and music were in part related to a greater freedom to express new and controversial ideas. A society that encourages and welcomes new ideas in industry and science is also likely to foster and accept new ideas in the arts. Reason and natural law were combined with emotion, imagination, and intuition, that is, knowing something without reasoning. This led to major cultural advances and a new inspiration to the arts. European artists and composers sought to express the feelings of societies that were in the process of undergoing great changes. The Industrial Revolution spurred the growth of a middle class that provided a new and larger audience for the arts, literature, and music.

Main Idea:
During the nineteenth century, advances in medicine and science dramatically improved people's lives particularly in some Western European nations and the United States.

MEDICAL DISCOVERIES AND ADVANCES

In 1776, **Edward Jenner**, an English doctor, discovered a cure for one of the world's most dreaded diseases—smallpox. Jenner's discovery of a vaccine that would prevent smallpox was based on his observation of natural phenomena. He noticed that dairy workers in England who had contracted cowpox, a non-

Louis Pasteur (1822–1895). French chemist and microbiologist.

deadly disease, were immune from catching smallpox. Jenner theorized that there was a connection between the two diseases. By the later decades of the nineteenth century, the widespread inoculation, that is, the injection of a mild form of the virus into the body, of people in Western Europe with a smallpox vaccine practically wiped out the disease.

A French chemist, **Louis Pasteur,** conducted research that led to significant advances in medicine. Pasteur found that tiny organisms called bacteria caused infections. In the 1850s, Pasteur proved that people could prevent infectious diseases if they were properly immunized by means of a vaccination. He discovered that a weakened strain of anthrax bacteria could be injected into sheep to allow the animal to build resistance to a more deadly form of the disease. In the 1880s, Pasteur applied his methods to the organisms that caused rabies. By a series of inoculations, Pasteur was able to save the life of a young boy who was bitten by a rabid dog. Prior to Pasteur's discovery, rabies was a fatal disease. Pasteur also developed the process of heating a liquid to kill bacteria. The process is called pasteurization in his honor.

The German physician **Robert Koch** conducted experiments, which proved that bacteria caused infectious diseases. Koch found the specific bacteria that caused tuberculosis and cholera. Koch also collaborated with Pasteur in

A Ward in the Hampstead Smallpox Hospital. Wood engraving, English, 1871.

Changes in Medicine, the Sciences, and the Arts **47**

studying anthrax. The British surgeon **Joseph Lister** applied to surgery the discoveries of Pasteur and Koch about bacteria and germs. Despite advances in surgery made through the use of anesthesia, about half of all surgical patients died. The high death toll was caused by infectious diseases, which resulted from medical procedures. Lister connected the filthy conditions of hospitals to the spread of germs that caused people's deaths after surgery.

Lister began a program in the hospital where he operated to improve standards of cleanliness. He insisted on the use of clean medical instruments and a hospital environment that no longer tolerated the filthy conditions that had been considered normal up to this time. The survival rate of Lister's patients increased enormously. By the 1890s, other European nations as well as the United States adopted Lister's methods.

SCIENCE EXPLORES NEW IDEAS ABOUT LIVING THINGS

Major discoveries in biology resulted in new ways of looking at life. By using microscopes in the 1600s, scientists had observed that cells make up all life. However, it wasn't until the mid-nineteenth century that the cell theory was formulated. Scientists discovered that cells created other cells and had lives of their own. Previously, nonliving matter was thought to be the source of live cells. The use of improved lenses in microscopes made it possible to prove the theory that all living matter was composed of cells.

In the 1870s, scientists also studied the question of how living things passed on their biological characteristics. Research showed that reproductive-type cells transmitted people's biological characteristics to the next generation. A decade earlier, a scientist discovered that there was a pattern for the characteristics of traits that were inherited. **Gregor Mendel**'s experiments with plants led him to conclude that tiny particles, later called genes, were responsible for the transmission of traits. Although Mendel's ideas were not widely known until the twentieth century, his work laid the groundwork for genetics, the science of heredity.

DARWIN'S THEORIES CHALLENGE EXISTING IDEAS

The most controversial scientific ideas came from the work of the British naturalist and biologist **Charles Darwin**. Darwin believed that there was a need to explain the existence of the great variety of plants and animals, which resulted in the enormous diversity of life. He also wondered why some plants and animals became extinct while others lived on. Darwin's research thereafter sought answers to these challenging questions.

In 1831, Darwin set off on a world voyage on the HMS *Beagle*, a British naval vessel. During these travels, he studied a wide variety of plant and animal life. The research only increased Darwin's curiosity about why certain plants and animals survive whereas others die off and disappear.

Charles Robert Darwin (1809–1882): oil over a photograph.

Darwin's initial research led him to hypothesize that most animal groups increase more quickly than their food supply and therefore they are in a constant struggle for survival. Those plants and animals better adapted to their environment are the ones who survive. The survivors who lived on passed on these characteristics to their offspring. Darwin named this process of struggle natural selection.

Darwin wrote two groundbreaking books, *The Origin of the Species by Means of Natural Selection*, published in 1859, and *The Descent of Man*, published in 1871. They were considered radical because they challenged previously held ideas about how species arose and how human beings originated. Darwin rejected the idea that species arose spontaneously. In addition, his theory of evolution was viewed as an attack on the religious ideas of his day because it contradicted the biblical account of creation.

In his work, *The Descent of Man*, Darwin theorized that humans and apes had a common ancestor. The belief that human beings descended from an ancestor that was apelike led to a long and bitter controversy. Religious people who believed that God created man and woman heatedly challenged supporters of Darwin's theory of evolution. The scientific study of Darwin's theories gradually led to their acceptance and changed people's understanding about the origins of life and human evolution. Nevertheless, this controversy still exists today in such religiously based beliefs as "intelligent design," which emphasizes the role of God in the origin of living things.

SOCIAL DARWINISM

Darwin's theories were later utilized to explain economic and social issues. In the late 1800s, **Herbert Spencer**, a British philosopher, applied Darwin's ideas to develop a social theory about people's struggle for existence. This was called **Social Darwinism**. Spencer wrote that only the strongest humans survive. Social Darwinism justified aggressive business practices that enabled strong competitors to drive out weaker ones. Industrial leaders were involved in an economic competition for the survival of the fittest in the capitalist system.

Main Idea:
Social Darwinism justified aggressive business practices that enabled strong competitors to drive out weaker ones.

Social Darwinism also was applied to theories of racial superiority, extreme nationalism, and imperialism. Strong European nations justified their use of military power against weaker nations as necessary to protect their industrial trading economies. The Englishman **Rudyard Kipling** claimed that European nations, in practicing imperialism, had a responsibility to improve the lives of people overseas. Some European composers such as the German **Richard Wagner** created musical works that stimulated pride in a national and ethnic identity. It should be noted that many of these ideas, which are considered racist today, were considered in this time period to be the reality of the then existing world situation.

THE DEVELOPMENT OF THE SOCIAL SCIENCES

Main Idea:
Psychiatry and psychoanalysis gradually came to be accepted as proper methods of treatment for increasing numbers of people with mental problems.

In the mid-nineteenth century, the study of human behavior in society, or sociology, became more accepted in Europe. The French philosopher, Auguste Comte, applied scientific methods to theorize laws that governed human behavior. In Europe and elsewhere, those who wanted to bring a more scientific rationale to the organization and workings of government and society adopted Comte's ideas.

Another new social science that developed was psychology, or the study of human behavior. In Russia, **Ivan Pavlov** conducted experiments with dogs that proved that animals could be conditioned to act in certain ways. Pavlov's theory about unconscious responses to certain stimuli influenced other scientists. Other psychologists applied Pavlov's ideas to design training programs that could change a person's behavior.

The writings of **Sigmund Freud** greatly influenced the study of human behavior. Based on his work with mentally ill people, Freud theorized that an unconscious part of the mind governs much of human behavior. He believed that the unconscious at times masked the reasons for a person's behavior. Freud pioneered the development of a method of treatment to help people discover the motives for their actions and thoughts. Psychiatry and psychoanalysis gradually came to be accepted as proper methods of treatment for increasing numbers of people with mental problems.

ADVANCES IN PHYSICAL SCIENCES

In the early 1800s, the work of the British teacher John Dalton also helped to revolutionize the study of chemistry. Dalton theorized that invisible particles called atoms made up all matter. He concluded, in 1804, that atoms were the basic elements of all things and similar atoms were in fact identical. Later in the century, scientists worked out the theory that similar atoms had the same properties. A periodic table of the known elements, which was ordered according to each element's atomic structure, was developed.

Physicists also worked to discover other mysteries of the atom. In the 1890s, scientists conducted experiments with electromagnetic waves. Their work with high-energy electric waves led to the discovery of unknown emissions, thereafter called X-rays, that could penetrate the body tissue and other matter. Other physicists such as **Albert Einstein** furthered the study of the laws of physics. Einstein eventually developed the theory that energy and matter were interchangeable. He also theorized that all matter was in constant motion. Einstein's 1905 theory of relativity stated that matter could only be measured by comparing it to the motion of other objects or matter. The work of these and other early physicists led to an era of scientifically applicable ideas based on the laws of physics. The use of atomic energy for peaceful and military purposes in the twentieth century was made possible by this early pioneering work.

Albert Einstein (1879–1955). American (German-born) theoretical physicist. Photographed in 1921.

ART, LITERATURE, AND MUSIC TAKE NEW FORMS OF ARTISTIC EXPRESSION

In the 1800s, art and music were greatly influenced by the changes that transformed society. There was a creative reaction to the order and reason that the Enlightenment had brought to artistic and musical expression. This led to the presentation of new forms of art and music to a wider audience.

Romantic artists looked to nature, themes of the glorified past, and heroic rebellion for subjects to paint. **Romanticism** stressed imagination and human emotion instead of reason. The French painters' works, which mirrored the brighter colors and sweeping paint strokes, symbolized the romantic artists' emotional style of art.

In England, other romantic artists emphasized the love of nature in their works. British painters revolutionized landscape painting through the use of color. These artists reflected their sensitivities to the beauty of nature. The individual's awe in face of the power of nature was captured in their paintings.

By the mid-nineteenth century, some artists turned back to **realism.** Their canvases reflected real and concrete objects and rejected sentimentality. Realistic artists portrayed life honestly and sought out themes that reflected daily existence. The paintings of French artists depicted life objectively and did not hide its blemishes.

In the later decades of the 1800s, other forms of artistic expression developed. Some artists turned away from romanticism and realism. They looked to fleeting impressions for their ideas, as opposed to static forms. French Impressionists such as **Claude Monet**, **Auguste Renoir**, and **Edgar Degas** were inspired by the color spectrum and how light reflected the brilliance of the placement of colors. Their paintings showed the effects of light at a given moment.

> **Main Idea:**
> There was a creative reaction to the order and reason that the Enlightenment had brought to artistic and musical expression.

Claude Monet painting. Regatta at Argenteuil. Oil on canvas, 1872.

Edgar Degas: Le foyer de la Danse a l'Opera de la Rue le Peletier. Oil on canvas, 1872.

Natural light, which made the most of the pure colors of the spectrum—oranges, reds, yellows, and bright blues—inspired the Impressionist artists.

By the close of the 1800s, another group of painters called **Post-impressionists** even took the emphasis on bright light and color to greater extremes. The paintings of **Paul Cezanne**, **Vincent van Gogh**, and **Paul Gauguin** reflected an effort to experiment with new ways to show form. Shapes were used along with color to depict mood and express emotion.

LITERATURE REFLECTS ROMANTICISM AND REALISM

By the late nineteenth century, many writers' works reflected a literary style that valued emotion, imagination, and intuition. English poets such as **Percy Shelley** and **John Keats** glorified nature and a simpler life in their poems. **Henry Wadsworth Longfellow** expressed the romantic poet's belief that there was a universal spirit that united all things in nature. Romantic literature often reflected the theme that industrialization was to blame for the ugliness in society and the decline of traditional values.

Other writers stressed ideas of romance and adventure in their literary works. The German writer Johann von Schiller wrote about the legendary hero William Tell. The Frenchman **Victor Hugo** portrayed tales of human suffering in a powerful and moving manner in *The Hunchback of Notre Dame* and *Les Miserables*. The French writer George Sand depicted peasants and workers with compassion in her fiction.

The Scottish writer Sir Walter Scott wrote historic novels such as *Ivanhoe*, exciting the imagination of people who looked romantically back to the Middle

Ages as a time of adventure and heroism. Other nineteenth-century writers and poets expressed the romantic ideals of individual liberties and nationalism in their writings. The English poet Lord Byron mixed his poetry with a real-life involvement with the Greek fight for independence from the Ottoman Turks.

Literature also reflected realistic views of life by the mid-nineteenth century. The French writer Honore de Balzac in *The Human Comedy* realistically showed how aspects of French bourgeoisie life were based on greed and stupidity. Balzac was particularly critical of the failures and foolishness of the growing middle class.

English writers such as William Thackeray ridiculed the displays of wealth by the upper and middle classes in their novels. **Charles Dickens** wrote about the horrible conditions of the hospitals, prisons, and poorhouses. In his fictionalized account of urban life, *Hard Times*, Dickens realistically portrayed the evils that materialism and industrialism caused in the city.

The Russian writer **Leo Tolstoy** painstakingly recounted and analyzed social customs and peasant lives. Tolstoy's 1869 historical novel, *War and Peace*, depicted the lives of five families in the time of Napoleon's invasion of Russia. Another Russian writer, Theodor Dostoievskii, presented a clear view of the Russian judicial system in *Crime and Punishment*.

ROMANTICISM INFLUENCES MUSIC

In the 1800s, music reflected the romanticism that stirred the emotions of many composers. The romantic composers sought to express their feelings in a freer musical manner. They rejected the form and order that the Enlightenment brought to musical composition. The symphonies of the German **Ludwig van Beethoven** bridged the transition from a more classical to a freer romantic style. Beethoven used themes of freedom and liberty when he composed his revolutionary Third Symphony, the *Eroica*.

Other romantic composers, such as the Austrian **Franz Schubert**, the Russian **Pyotr Tchaikovsky**, and the Czech **Antonin Dvorak**, used melodies that gave vent to their powerful emotions. Nationalism found expression in the music of the romantic compositions of such artists as the German Richard Wagner. His cycle of four operas, *The Ring of the Nibelungen*, used a German epic of the Middle Ages to evoke strong feelings of nationalism.

Opera also flowered in the 1800s. The works of the Italian **Giuseppe Verdi** reflected the growing popularity of operatic music. Public concert halls in Italy and elsewhere were packed to hear Verdi's *Aida* and *Rigoletto*. The range of power of instruments grew during the 1800s. The piano became an important instrument in concert halls. A growing number of middle-class people

Ludwig van Beethoven (1770–1827). German composer. Oil, 1815, by Joseph Willibrord Mahler.

began to attend piano recitals featuring the works of Poland's **Frederic Chopin**. The size of orchestras increased, and attending a musical concert to hear the romantic works of Europe's great composers became almost commonplace.

THE LEGACY OF ADVANCES IN THE ARTS AND SCIENCES

The growth that took place in the areas of the arts and sciences carried into the twentieth century. People in industrializing European nations began to live longer and healthier lives. They had more time to enjoy a life that afforded them some leisure time. This was particularly true of the growing middle class, which could take advantage of the new opportunities for cultural enrichment and had the means to benefit from advances in science and medicine.

LINK TO TODAY

The Industrial Revolution led to new theories and ideas about political, social, and economic ideas. These new ideas had a significant effect on the political developments that took place throughout the nineteenth century and into the twentieth century. This can be clearly seen in the development of socialist theories and ideas and the rise of communism in the twentieth century. The openness to new political, social, and economic ideas also had a dramatic impact on the arts and sciences.

In the second decade of the twentieth century, a communist revolution took place in Russia. The aftereffects of the Russian Revolution of 1917 dominated the political, social, and economic events during the twentieth century. Thereafter the Soviet Union became the focal point of a battle, which was termed by the communists as the struggle between capitalism and socialism. For most of the twentieth century, particularly after the fall of fascism after World War II, the political, economic, and social events that took place between the nations supporting free enterprise and the capital system and those nations supporting communism, were a struggle over which system, capitalism or communism, would ultimately lead humankind into the twenty-first century.

Toward the end of the twentieth century, the communist system of government collapsed in the Soviet Union. Thereafter as the twenty-first century dawned, only capitalism had survived. Yet despite the success of the nations supporting the ideas of capitalism and free enterprise, a new economic philosophy, which is referred to as globalization, developed. Once again the nations of the world are in competition; only this time they are competing to see which type of capitalist system can best profit from the ideas of the on-going development of economic globalization.

CHAPTER SUMMARY

In this chapter, we have seen that industrialization and urbanization led to major changes in the way people lived. People came to the urban centers in search of work and a place to live. Some people benefited more than others from the changes that took place. Those who benefited were members of the upper class and the growing middle class. Most people, however, had more difficult lives. These people were the working class and their families.

Despite scientific and technological achievements that led to improvements in city life, most urban city residents did not benefit from these advances. Workers faced a number of problems that were not easily resolved. Housing and sanitation inadequacies, communicable diseases, industrial pollution, and rising crime continued to affect the overall quality of life for most city residents.

The Industrial Age also had an impact on European economic development. Industrial capitalism triumphed in the nineteenth century. Laissez-faire attitudes regarding industrial and business enterprises led to the acquisition of great fortunes. The middle class supported industrialization because it led to its prosperity. The working class benefited the least from the changed economic conditions.

Factory workers' lives were full of drudgery and poverty. The terrible conditions under which most workers lived led to demands for the reform of industrial capitalism and the political system that supported it. Residents of urban environments today, particularly those living in large crowded cities, might recognize many of the problems that plagued the earlier urban centers. In some modern-day cities, new issues would later be added to the earlier problems of city life. Concerning the developing life in the city, an often-quoted French saying, "the more that things change, the more they remain the same," applies to how city life evolved.

As change was taking place in the economic and political spheres, it was also taking place in the field of science and the arts. Scientific investigation provided us with the early vaccines that protect us against disease. We found that if we protect ourselves against bacterial infection, we would live longer and better lives. When Darwin proposed his natural selection and origin of the species theories, he created a storm that is still with us today over whether life as we know it was created by God. His theories were applied to the business and political worlds. Psychology and psychiatry looked into people's motivations and actions. Mental illness came to be treated like other illnesses. In the arts, romantic adventure and nationalism dominated. This was reflected in the works of a number of writers, artists, and musicians. Unfortunately, the worker had little time to enjoy all of this. In time, workers did benefit from many of these advances, but they did not occur until well into the twentieth century.

We see a clear connection between historical forces at work and philosophical thought and debate. Clearly the standard of living of most Europeans was increasing, but there were costs involved. These costs included poor living and working conditions for most people. Children worked long, hard hours in factories and mines. Wealth was being concentrated in a few hands. Thinkers asked a critical question in the 1800s: Was this suffering a necessary result of the capitalist system? There were thinkers who answered "no." A group of these were called utopians because they believed that the government had an obligation to intervene in order to create a better society. These utopians wanted to design what to them was a perfect community. Other thinkers were harsher in their condemnation of the capitalist system. They believed that change would only come through the workers rising up and overthrowing the present system and taking control. Karl Marx and his followers had an impact on Europe that we are still feeling today. His theories and ideas resulted in criticism of the existing political, social, and economic order and called for change.

Western European economic life heightened the differences between the middle class and the lower class. The gap between rich and poor widened and created new tensions. The development of industrial capitalism created unanticipated problems. Alongside the upper- and middle-class prosperity, there also existed widespread poverty among the working class. Large financial organizations such as banks and business corporations increasingly gained influence and power in the prospering industrial economies of Western Europe. The huge sums of money and great profits earned gave the wealthy upper and middle classes control of the political process. Political decisions almost always reflected the interests of the wealthy business class.

IMPORTANT PEOPLE, PLACES, AND TERMS

KEY TERMS

Industrial Revolution	social reforms	bourgeoisie
industrialization	*The Wealth of Nations*	proletariat
rural	labor unions	*The Origin of the Species*
urban	labor organizations	*by Means of Natural*
middle class	Chartist Movement	*Selection*
tenements	socialism	Social Darwinism
skilled workers	Marxism	romanticism
unskilled workers	*The Communist*	realism
laissez-faire	*Manifesto*	
economic reforms	*Das Kapital*	

PEOPLE

Thomas Hobbes	Edward Jenner	Claude Monet
Adam Smith	Louis Pasteur	Auguste Renoir
Thomas Malthus	Robert Koch	Edgar Degas
David Ricardo	Joseph Lister	Paul Cezanne
Jeremy Bentham	Gregor Mendel	Vincent van Gogh
John Stuart Mill	Charles Darwin	Paul Gauguin
Robert Owen	Herbert Spencer	Percy Shelley
Friedrich Engels	Rudyard Kipling	John Keats
utopian socialists	Richard Wagner	Henry Wadsworth
capitalists	Ivan Pavlov	Longfellow
workers	Sigmund Freud	Victor Hugo
Karl Marx	Albert Einstein	Charles Dickens

Leo Tolstoy	Pytor Tchaikovsky	Giuseppe Verdi
Ludwig van Beethoven	Antonin Dvorak	Frederic Chopin
Franz Schubert		

PLACES

Great Britain	Belgium	Poland
Western Europe	United States	Italy
France	Greece	Austrian Empire
Germany	Netherlands	New Lanark

CHAPTER 2
MULTIPLE-CHOICE QUESTIONS

Select the number of the correct answer.

1. Which statement best describes some positive aspects of rural life in the early stages of the Industrial Revolution?

   (1) It created a sense of equality and a sense of sharing.
   (2) It allowed older family members to live independently away from younger family members.
   (3) It offered children good educational opportunities.
   (4) It brought modernization to a more traditional lifestyle.

2. The majority of middle-class women in industrializing societies in the nineteenth century could best be described as

   (1) being accepted into colleges and universities in large numbers
   (2) spending most of their days on difficult household tasks
   (3) rarely working outside the home
   (4) taking active roles in politics

3. Which term describes the urban working class?

   (1) capitalists   (3) farmers
   (2) urban rich   (4) proletariat

4. The urban working class experienced which of the following situations?

   A. poor sanitation
   B. dangerous working conditions
   C. paid vacations
   D. crowded housing

   (1) A, B, C
   (2) A, B, D
   (3) B, C, D
   (4) A, C, D

5. *Laissez-faire* is a French term used in economics that means

   (1) a lack of government regulation of industry
   (2) a spirit of cooperation between labor and management
   (3) interest in society in consumer goods
   (4) the ability of a monarch to control trade

6. Adam Smith described his concept of laissez-faire in

   (1) *The Wealth of Nations*
   (2) *The Industrial Revolution*
   (3) *The Invisible Hand*
   (4) *An Essay on the Principles of Population*

7. Socialism was a new concept in the nineteenth century. One of its major beliefs stated that

   (1) big business owners could be depended on to care for workers
   (2) workers could never expect to rise above the problems of the working class
   (3) capitalism was the real cause of society's problems
   (4) middle-class managers would always come to the aid of the working class

8. Robert Owen as a Utopian was one of the first mill owners to

   (1) improve living and working conditions for his employees
   (2) encourage the hiring of mill workers younger than twelve years old
   (3) discourage his workers from being allowed to marry
   (4) require ten-hour work days six days a week

9. A basic belief of Karl Marx was that

   (1) managers and owners could be convinced to provide a living wage for workers
   (2) the capitalist class would ultimately agree to improve profits by improving working conditions
   (3) workers should be content to have steady employment in any situation
   (4) there would always be a class struggle between workers and owners of businesses

10. A major reason that Karl Marx's prediction of multiple revolutions did not occur is that

   (1) workers couldn't understand what Marx was teaching
   (2) governments in several industrialized countries passed legislation to aid the working class
   (3) Marx's ideas were never made public throughout Western Europe
   (4) Marx expected workers to unite in an international effort against owners

11. Karl Marx worked with

   (1) Robert Owen
   (2) David Ricardo
   (3) Friedrich Engels
   (4) Prince Metternich

12. During the first half of the nineteenth century, Great Britain was different politically from much of the rest of Europe because it

   (1) experienced violent revolutions
   (2) allowed an absolute monarch to limit Parliamentary powers
   (3) opposed nationalism as a concept
   (4) made reforms toward greater democracy

13. Louis Pasteur, Robert Koch, and Joseph Lister all made major contributions in which area?

   (1) safety for miners
   (2) urban planning
   (3) improved sanitation
   (4) speed of transportation

Base your answers to questions 14 and 15 on the drawing below and your knowledge of social studies.

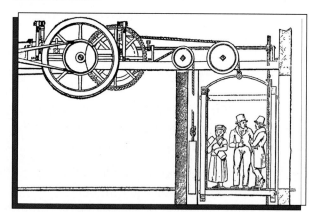

14. The invention illustrated in this drawing is an early example of

   (1) an oil drum
   (2) an elevator
   (3) a hot air balloon
   (4) an observation deck

15. This invention made which of the following possible in the growing urban areas of nineteenth-century Europe?

    (1) faster communications between cities
    (2) improved use of natural resources
    (3) safer employment for children
    (4) buildings several stories high

16. Charles Darwin's work was considered controversial in the nineteenth century because

    (1) it challenged previously held beliefs about how human life began
    (2) religious groups gave his work wide support
    (3) he based his work on things he had read about but not really seen himself
    (4) he expressed his ideas in two books he wrote

17. The development of laissez-faire capitalism was most influenced by which event?

    (1) The Age of Exploration
    (2) The Agricultural Revolution
    (3) The actions of the British Parliament
    (4) The Industrial Revolution

18. In a textbook chapter on the Industrial Revolution, which section title would be most likely?

    (1) Business Organizations Modernize
    (2) The Rule of King Henry VIII
    (3) The Rise of the Christian Church
    (4) The Results of the Crusades

19. Which person of the nineteenth century is most associated with the following statement?

    "The history of all hitherto existing society is the history of class struggles."
    (1) Leo Tolstoy
    (2) Charles Darwin
    (3) Karl Marx
    (4) Albert Einstein

20. A number of writers in nineteenth-century Europe frequently developed themes about

    (1) the difficulties of life for the working class
    (2) science fiction in the twentieth century
    (3) life in Ancient Greece and Rome
    (4) exploration in Africa

THEMATIC ESSAY

Directions: Write a well-organized essay that includes an introduction, several paragraphs addressing the task below, and a conclusion.

Theme: Economics

Throughout history people have found various ways to solve the problem of achieving their needs and their wants. Basic *needs* include food, clothing, and shelter; *wants* may include those things people think will improve the quality of their lives.

Task

Select two of the individuals in this chapter who are important for their ideas about economic development. For each of these individuals

- describe at least one major idea of the individual about economics
- explain how the person thought the idea should be developed and explain who specifically would benefit if a society adopted this idea
- discuss why the 1800s were a time of economic change

You may use any individual from this chapter. Some suggestions you might wish to consider include Adam Smith, David Ricardo, John Stuart Mill, Karl Marx, and Friedrich Engels.

This question is based on the accompanying documents (1–7). The question is designed to test your ability to work with historical documents. Some of these documents have been edited for the purposes of this question. As you analyze the documents, take into account any point of view that may be presented in the document.

Historical Context

The era of the Industrial Revolution was a time of great change. Inventions caused some people to become wealthy while others struggled just to survive. Lifestyles of almost everyone were changed; while some improved, many were not.

Task

Using information from the documents and your knowledge of global history, answer the questions that follow each document in Part A. Your answer to the questions will help you write your Part B essay in which you will be asked to

- discuss political, social and/or economic results of the Industrial Revolution
- discuss some of the positive and negative results of the Industrial Revolution

Part A: Short Answer Questions

Directions: Analyze the documents and answer the short answer questions that follow each document.

Document 1

Questions

1. a. What does this illustration show about working conditions in a mill in the nineteenth century?
   b. What is one invention that might have been used in a factory of this time period?

Document 2

"Society as a whole is more and more splitting up into two hostile camps, into two classes directly facing each other—bourgeoisie and proletariat."

Karl Marx, *The Communist Manifesto*

Question

2. When Karl Marx wrote about these two "camps," what was he predicting would happen between them?

Document 3

Question

3. The ironworks factory shown is typical of those found in European industrializing cities in the nineteenth century. Identify one problem that appears for factory workers in this illustration.

Document 4

Question

4. What is one possible reason for the women in the photograph to go on strike?

The photograph shows some of the hundreds of women who went on strike at a matchworks factory in England in the nineteenth century.

Document 5   The following is from *Hard Times* by Charles Dickens:

Day was shining radiantly upon the town then, and the bells were going for the morning work. Domestic fires were not yet lighted, and the high chimneys had the sky to themselves. Puffing out their poisonous volumes, they would not be long in hiding it; but, for half an hour, some of the many windows were golden, which showed the Coketown people a sun eternally in eclipse, through a medium of smoked glass.

Questions   5. a. What does Dickens say is about to happen to the view of the sun in this town?
   b. According to the passage above what industrial development is the cause of this?

Document 6

Over London–By Rail. Colored wood engraving after Gustave Dore from London: A Pilgrimage, 1872.

Question   6. Identify two problems that would likely be experienced by people living in the area pictured in this document.
   a.
   b.

Document 7

"There is always more misery among the lower classes than there is humanity in the higher."

Victor Hugo, *Les Miserables* 1862

Question	7. Identify two examples of "miseries" that the lower classes were suffering at the time that Victor Hugo wrote *Les Miserables*. a. b.

Part B: Essay

Directions: Write a well-organized essay that includes an introduction, several paragraphs, and a conclusion. Use evidence from *at least four* of the documents in your essay. Support your response with relevant facts, examples, and details. Include additional outside information.

Historical Content

The era of the Industrial Revolution was a time of great change. Inventions caused some people to become wealthy while others struggled just to survive. Lifestyles of almost everyone were changed; while some improved, many did not.

Task

Using information from the documents and your knowledge of global history, write an essay in which you

- discuss political, social and/or economic results of the Industrial Revolution
- discuss some of the positive and negative results of the Industrial Revolution

Guidelines

In your essay, be sure to

- develop all aspects of the *Task*
- incorporate information from *at least four* documents
- incorporate relevant outside information
- support the theme with relevant facts, examples, and details
- use a logical and clear plan of organization, including an introduction and conclusion that are beyond a restatement of the theme

CHAPTER 3

Political Change and Global Nationalism— Western Europe

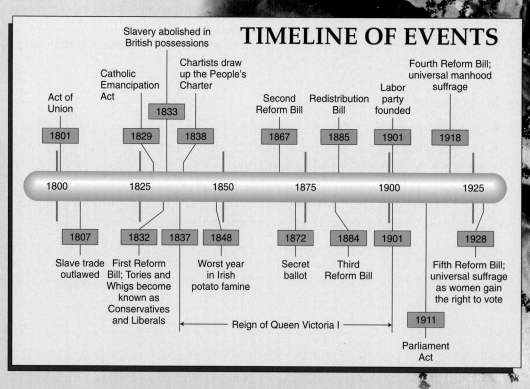

TIMELINE OF EVENTS

Act of Union — 1801

Catholic Emancipation Act — 1829

Slavery abolished in British possessions — 1833

Chartists draw up the People's Charter — 1838

Second Reform Bill — 1867

Redistribution Bill — 1885

Labor party founded — 1901

Fourth Reform Bill; universal manhood suffrage — 1918

1800 — 1825 — 1850 — 1875 — 1900 — 1925

Slave trade outlawed — 1807

First Reform Bill; Tories and Whigs become known as Conservatives and Liberals — 1832

1837

Worst year in Irish potato famine — 1848

Secret ballot — 1872

Third Reform Bill — 1884

1901

Fifth Reform Bill; universal suffrage as women gain the right to vote — 1928

← Reign of Queen Victoria I →

Parliament Act — 1911

Victor Emmanuel III, King of Italy, 1900–1946.

Advances in British Democracy

We have traced the growth of **democracy** in Great Britain through both revolutionary and evolutionary periods. At the beginning of the nineteenth century, Britain was the most democratic nation in Europe, yet the British political system had a long way to go to be called truly *democratic*, as we use the term today. A number of practices still had to change to allow Britain to become what it is at the present time. Let us now trace these further evolutionary changes that began about 1800. We will pay particular attention to the situation that existed in Ireland, a situation that was not resolved in the 1800s.

NONDEMOCRATIC CHARACTERISTICS IN BRITAIN

Our discussion will begin by reviewing our definition of democracy. As we noted on the first page of Chapter 16 in *Global History, Volume One*, democracy may be defined as a system of government that has two basic features: **popular sovereignty** and **equality and respect for the individual**.

The British system in 1800 had some characteristics that conflicted with these features and was therefore nondemocratic. These characteristics were as follows:

> **Main Idea:**
> The British system in 1800 had some characteristics that conflicted with the basic features of a democracy.

- *Open ballot:* People voted in the open, not in private or secretly. Thus, they did not always vote the way they may have wanted, and they may also have been subject to bribery and intimidation.
- *Voting restrictions:* The only citizens allowed to vote were those who owned a certain amount of property. Because of these restrictions, only 5 percent of the British population was eligible to vote in parliamentary elections. Women could not vote, and neither could those men who were middle-class merchants, workers, and farmers.
- *Officeholding requirements:* Very few people were eligible to hold public office. Eligibility requirements were based on property, religion, and gender (sex). You could hold office if you owned a certain amount of property, belonged to the Anglican Church or some other Protestant group, and were a man. Government positions were thus denied to women, Catholics, Jews, and poor people.
- *Unfair representation in the House of Commons:* An area of land on which many people lived was marked off with boundaries and was called a political district or borough. Each borough in Britain was allowed to elect representatives to the House of Commons. Because of the **Industrial Revolution**, big population changes occurred, with people leaving rural areas to live in urban areas. This meant that boroughs in rural areas lost population, while boroughs in urban areas such as Manchester gained population. However, the

number of representatives from all these boroughs remained the same! The "losing" boroughs should have had reductions made in their representatives. This was not done, and such boroughs became known as **rotten boroughs**. Some urban boroughs became underrepresented, whereas others weren't represented at all. And in some districts, wealthy landowners who were in the House of Lords were able to choose representatives to the Commons. These districts were called **pocket boroughs**. The political power in such districts was, figuratively, in the "pocket" of the wealthy landowners.

- *Power of the House of Lords*: Members of the House of Lords were not elected. Their seats were appointed, based on heredity; this process was not an example of popular sovereignty. In addition, since passage of laws needed agreement by both parts of Parliament, the House of Lords could vote down a bill favored by the House of Commons.

THE REFORM BILLS

The Reform Bill of 1832

A movement to change or reform some of the preceding nondemocratic characteristics began to grow, particularly among middle-class merchants and workers. Their efforts were stalled during the period of the Napoleonic Wars. But a few years after these wars ended in 1815, the movement gained strength. When the Whig party came to power in Parliament in 1830, its **cabinet** members wanted the House of Lords to agree to a bill passed in Commons that would provide for some political reforms. To make sure that the Lords, controlled by the Tory Party, would do this, the Whigs got King William IV (r. 1830–1837) to threaten to appoint more Whig nobles as Lords' members. The ultimate result was passage of the Reform Bill of 1832.

> **Main Idea:**
> By obtaining the right to vote (also called the **franchise**), people connected with the Industrial Revolution—bankers, merchants, factory owners—were going to have a greater role in the nation's political affairs.

This bill, also called the *First Reform Bill*, was a partial step along the path toward more democracy. It provided for the following:

- More than fifty rotten boroughs were abolished, as were many pocket boroughs. Urban, industrial boroughs got more seats in Commons.
- The right to vote (**suffrage**) was extended to middle-class males, as property qualifications were lowered.

By obtaining the right to vote (also called the **franchise**), people connected with the Industrial Revolution—bankers, merchants, factory owners—were going to have a greater role in the nation's political affairs. Many of these new voters became supporters of the Whig Party, because they were thankful for the liberal political changes it brought about. The Whig Party soon changed its name to the Liberal Party. The opposition Tory Party, consisting primarily of landowners, and not wanting to make sweeping political changes so quickly, changed its name to the Conservative Party.

Democratic Progress Between the First and Second Reform Bills

It would be thirty-five years later, in 1867, before a second major reform bill was passed in Parliament. But before we examine that legislation, we should consider some other early nineteenth-century democratic advances made in Britain. In 1807 slavery was abolished in all British possessions. Specific religious qualifications for serving in Parliament were done away with in 1829 and in 1858. With passage of the Catholic Emancipation Act in 1829, Catholics were permitted to serve in Parliament if they recognized the Protestant rulers as the true heads of the kingdom and denied the authority of the pope to interfere in the kingdom's affairs. In 1858, Jews were given the right to serve in Parliament.

A group of Englishmen concerned with making democratic changes were active in the 1830s and 1840s. In 1838, they wrote their proposals in a document called the *People's Charter*. Known as the **Chartists**, they wanted Parliament to provide for

Main Idea:
Although the Chartist Movement faded away in the 1850s, by 1918 all of their demands except annual elections had been adopted.

- ending property qualifications for service in Parliament.
- the secret ballot.
- universal manhood suffrage—giving the right to vote to all males.
- yearly elections of Parliament and.
- salaries for members of Parliament.

The Chartists held parades and meetings to publicize their demands. They were not successful, as these demands were considered too extreme for the times. Although the Chartist Movement faded away in the 1850s, by 1918 all of their demands except annual elections had been adopted.

The Reform Bill of 1867

Benjamin Disraeli (1804–1881). 1st Earl of Beaconsfield. English statesman and writer of Jewish descent. Steel engraving, 19th century.

By the 1860s, the desire for parliamentary reform had grown. The Tory (Conservative) Party, led by **Benjamin Disraeli** (1804–1881), wanted to gain the credit for fulfilling this desire. Accordingly, the conservatives obtained passage of the Reform Bill of 1867. Also known as the Second Reform Bill, this legislation lowered property qualifications for voting even further than did the 1832 bill. Almost all male workers in cities were enfranchised, given the vote or franchise, as were men who paid rent for or owned their homes in urban areas. Consequently, the number of men now allowed to vote was almost doubled what it had been. This newly enfranchised population, so hoped Disraeli, would not support the Conservative Party. This desired result did not come about, particularly as most city workers voted for liberals. Eventually, in 1901, workers and others would form a new party, the Labor Party.

Further Increases in Voting Rights

The issue of voting rights was the subject of additional legislation in the late nineteenth and early twentieth centuries. In 1872, the *secret ballot* system was adopted by Parliament. Also called the *Australian Ballot*, because it originated in Australia, it replaced the open ballot system. The bill providing for the new system was enacted under the leadership of the liberal Prime Minister William

Gladstone (1809–1898). In three additional reform bills, the franchise was again extended:

1. In the Reform Bill of 1884 (the Third Reform Bill) agricultural workers were given the right to vote.
2. Universal manhood suffrage was achieved with passage of the Reform Bill of 1918. This Fourth Reform Bill gave the franchise to all men over twenty-one years of age.
3. True popular sovereignty, an aspect of a complete democracy, came about with enactment of the Reform Bill of 1928. By this bill, the right to vote was given to all women over twenty-one years of age.

Emmeline Pankhurst (1858–1928). English woman-suffrage advocate.

Suffragettes arrested outside Buckingham Palace in May 1914.

The goal of **universal suffrage** was now achieved. This achievement was largely due to the efforts of several women who were active in leading a movement to improve the position of women in British society. These women were called **suffragettes**. Among their leaders were **Emmeline Pankhurst** and her daughters, Christabel and Sylvia. Their actions carried forward the hopes of **Mary Wollstonecraft**, an eighteenth-century pioneer in the struggle for equality for women in England.

Mary Wollstonecraft Godwin (1759–1797). English writer. Wood engraving, 1898, after a painting by John Opie.

Additional Parliamentary Reforms

The measures described so far did much to affect who could vote for members of Parliament; nevertheless, other laws were enacted that produced changes concerning Parliament. The *Redistribution Bill* of 1885 divided the nation into political districts that were approximately equal in population. Of historic importance for the functioning of Parliament were two laws that limited the power of the House of Lords. The House of Lords was not an elected body and was controlled by the conservatives. It could prevent a bill passed by the House of Commons from becoming law, as consent was needed by both houses for a bill to become a law. This situation did not seem right, as the House of Commons was a more representative body, elected by the people. The issue reached a head with the 1909 budget. Under Liberal Party leadership, the Commons passed a budget bill that the Lords defeated. In new elections for the House of Commons, the Liberals won. These results showed that voters supported the original budget bill. The House of Lords now agreed to pass it.

> **Main Idea:**
> Of added significance in 1911 were measures that required elections to the House of Commons every five years and that gave salaries to members of the Commons.

This incident set the stage for the famous Parliament Act of 1911. Again under Liberal Party leadership, the Commons passed a bill that would weaken the legislative power of the Lords. It was defeated in the House of Lords, and new elections were held for Commons. The Liberals won a majority of seats and claimed that they had the nation's support for the original bill. When the Lords still refused to consent to the bill, **King George V** (r. 1910–1936) threatened to appoint more Liberals to the House of Lords to ensure passage of the bill. In 1911, the bill was passed. It effectively weakened the power of the Lords over legislation by providing that

- any money bill passed by the Commons would become law, even if the Lords were against it, after thirty days.
- other bills passed by the Commons three times over a two-year period would become law, even if opposed by the Lords.

The House of Lords, therefore, had merely a temporary or *suspensive veto* over legislation. Of added significance in 1911 were measures that required elections to the House of Commons every five years and that gave salaries to members of the Commons. Finally, it should be noted that the Lords' suspensive veto over legislation was reduced to one year, as stated in the Parliament Act of 1949.

GROWTH OF CABINET POWER

The government of Great Britain can be described as a *constitutional monarchy* as well as a *parliamentary democracy*. The cabinet consists of members of Parliament who act as advisers or ministers to the monarch. They include the chief adviser or *prime minister* and other people, all of whom are chosen by the majority party in Parliament. The majority party is the party that has won a majority of seats in the House of Commons, through elections by the population. The practice of the cabinet being selected from and being responsible to the majority party is called *cabinet responsibility to the Parliament*. As we noted in Chapter 16 in *Global History, Volume One*, the practice of a ruler relying on advisers from Parliament

Victoria of England. Queen of Great Britain, 1837-1901.

began in the years following the **Glorious Revolution** of 1688–1689. The first two Hanoverian kings, George I (r. 1714–1727) and George II (r. 1727–1760), spoke English poorly and were content to trust the business of running the government to the cabinet. George III (r. 1760–1820) spoke English very well and was serious about his role as king. He frequently met with his cabinet. The role and prestige of the cabinet grew during these first hundred years after the Glorious Revolution and was to continue during the nineteenth century. This was particularly evident in the distinguished careers of two renowned prime ministers, **Benjamin Disraeli** and **William Gladstone**.

They were key figures in British politics from 1866 to 1894. In addition to their brilliance and popularity, they were trusted and respected by the **monarchy**. The British ruler during these times was **Queen Victoria** (r. 1837–1901). The granddaughter of George III, she reigned for the longest period of any British monarch. This period became known as the *Victorian Era* or *Victorian Age*, celebrated for its advances in social, economic, and political affairs, and Queen Victoria was careful to stay within the limits of her power, leaving her cabinet ministers, such as Disraeli and Gladstone, the freedom to push through the kind of reform legislation we have already described.

The expansion of cabinet responsibility and the passage of reform democratic legislation are very important parts of the British system of government. They came about over a long period of years, in a peaceful manner, and thus were achieved through **evolution** rather than through violence and **revolution**. The system has managed to combine continuity with necessary changes and has attempted to guarantee human rights to all its citizens. However, unlike the situation in the United States, no written **constitution** in Britain forms the basis of its democracy. What does pass for a British constitution is really a combination of the following:

- actual written documents and laws, such as the Magna Carta and the Reform Bill of 1832, and
- unwritten customs and traditions, such as cabinet responsibility.

From what we have now learned, it is clear that politics in nineteenth-century Britain led to significant democratic changes. However, one political issue grew more critical and controversial in the 1800s and early 1900s. Failure to resolve it peacefully in those times has led to problems even in our own era. This issue was the Irish Question.

> **Main Idea:**
> The role and prestige of the cabinet grew during these first hundred years after the Glorious Revolution and was to continue during the nineteenth century.

THE IRISH QUESTION AND THE GREAT IRISH FAMINE

The onset of problems between England and Ireland prior to 1800 has been described already. The English Protestants who settled in Northern Ireland (**Ulster**) were a minority, but they had dominated political and economic affairs. The majority of people, Irish Catholics, were very upset with the conditions

Daniel O'Connell (1775–1847). Irish Nationalist leader. Wood engraving, 19th century.

under which they lived. Under English rule ever since being conquered in the twelfth century, the Irish people had wished to become independent. As the nineteenth century opened, Britain tried to ease tension. By the Act of Union, passed in 1801, Parliament joined Ireland and Great Britain to form the United Kingdom of Great Britain and Ireland. The Irish were given representation in the British Parliament but were angry at the little real power they had in that body. There were also angry at having to pay taxes to the Anglican Church and high rents to absentee Protestant landlords. One of the leaders, **Daniel O'Connell**, the "Great Emancipator," organized people to demand reforms and some kind of **home rule** or independence.

Amidst this atmosphere, a terrible tragedy struck Ireland—the potato famine of the 1840s, with 1847–1848 being the worst year. Because of natural conditions, the potato crop, a mainstay of the Irish diet, was ruined. What was to become known as the **Great Irish Famine** proved to be a severe human catastrophe. It was mainly the result of a potato blight, a fungus that ruined the harvests of 1846, 1848, and 1849. As first reported in a Dublin newspaper in 1845, healthy green fields of potatoes became black. Accompanying this change was a horrible, sickening, rotten smell. As the Irish people relied on the potato as their chief food source, the failure of the crop was to have devastating consequences. The grim story can be seen in these statistics: the official population of Ireland fell from 8,175,124 in 1841 to 6,552,385 in 1851! This loss of over 1.6 million people was the consequence of famine-related deaths and also immigration to other parts of the world. These official numbers, however, probably do not tell the entire story. Many of Ireland's poorest people, on the west coast and in rural areas, were skipped over by census takers or avoided being counted. Tragically, it seems that approximately one person in every four disappeared between 1841 and 1851.

Historians who have studied the Great Irish Famine have considered a set of causes for the famine-related deaths and huge immigration. They have noted a food shortage, the inability to obtain food, and the failure of the British government to regulate market conditions for buying and selling food and to provide adequate support and assistance. A serious question has arisen over the availability of food. One Irish historian, Mary E. Daly, has used several calculations and determined that as of 1846 there was a major food shortage, and that provisions existed only for six million of Ireland's over eight million inhabitants. Other historians claim that starvation arose primarily from the inability of the poor to buy available food.

> **Main Idea:**
> A gruesome image in Irish memory is that of evicted tenants perishing from starvation or disease, with their homes destroyed.

Many of the poor were tenants who worked on large areas controlled by landlords. Those tenants who could not pay their rents were evicted from the land. The number of families evicted between 1846 and 1848 grew to an estimated 974,930 people. A gruesome image in Irish memory is that of evicted tenants perishing from starvation or disease, with their homes destroyed. Countless numbers of landless and homeless sought relief in shelters, ditches along the roads, and soup kitchens. One set of soup kitchens was established in 1846 by Irish Quakers, who formed the CRC (Central Relief Committee of the Society of Friends). They also secured help from their American counterparts.

Interior of a peasant's hut during the Great Potato Famine of 1846–1849 in Ireland. Colored engraving, 19th century.

The General Relief Committee (GRC) of New York City met in 1847. It sent $250,000 to Ireland, with money raised from New Yorkers all over the state. The British government also set up some temporary soup kitchens, but these were criticized for their poor nutritious content. By 1847, however, private soup kitchens were closed due to lack of funds and workers. The public soup kitchens were closed then also, as the British Treasury Under-Secretary Charles Trevelyan claimed that the famine was "over."

For many Irish, hope for a better life rested with emigrating (leaving) from their homeland for foreign shores. In the period of 1845–1851, for example, it is estimated that almost 20 percent of the population emigrated. Of these approximately one and one-half million people, the majority went to the United States. Others went mainly to Britain, Canada, and Australia. It was not easy to get passage overseas, nor to survive the trip itself. In their often weakened condition, many emigrants were sickened with and died of fever en route. Consequently, the vessels bearing them were called **coffin ships**. Several thousands passed away in a fever hospital in Quebec, Canada. Those Irish who left for the United States soon crowded into such urban areas as Boston, Philadelphia, and New York. They generally worked as unskilled laborers, while enduring anti-Irish and anti-Catholic prejudice. By 1850, the U.S. census showed that there were over 960,000 Irish-born residents. This accounted for 43 percent of the foreign-born American population.

The effects of the Great Irish Famine have been multiple and long-lasting. The course of Irish history was changed. The Irish Diaspora (places where people of Irish descent live that are outside of Ireland) altered world history, especially in America, Canada, Australia, and England. Irish immigrants and Irish Americans have had a major impact on every phase of American life, including

Main Idea:
Those Irish who left for the United States soon crowded into such urban areas as Boston, Philadelphia, and New York.

politics, labor, sports, religion, arts, entertainment, and business. In the 1990 U.S federal census, forty-four million Americans voluntarily reported their ethnicity as Irish. New York State is very proud of its Irish heritage. In 1855, 26 percent of the population of Manhattan had been born in Ireland. By 1900, 60 percent of the population was of Irish descent. Today, thousands of New Yorkers trace their ancestry to famine-era immigrants who made valuable contributions to the state's economy, cultural life, and political development.

Another long-lasting consequence of the Great Irish Famine was the growth of Irish nationalism. This was true of those who rejected the Union between Britain and Ireland as well as those who were angered by perceived British insensitivity to Irish suffering. Irish nationalists in the late nineteenth century pressed for land law reforms as well as home rule legislation. The British generally resisted these demands, fearful that the Protestant minority in Ireland would suffer. Nevertheless, legislation was enacted in 1869 that freed Catholics from paying taxes to the Anglican Church. The 1870 and 1881 land acts eased restrictions on evictions, rents, and purchases of land. Elected as an Irish representative to Parliament, Charles Parnell tried to gain the help of both liberals and conservatives in obtaining more benefits for Ireland. Critical moments came in 1886 and 1892 when Gladstone and the liberals introduced home rule legislation. These efforts were unsuccessful. In 1895, the Conservatives did get some land reform laws passed but stayed away from any home rule bills. A short-lived achievement occurred in 1912, when Parliament did pass a home rule bill. However, Protestants in Ulster were so alarmed at the passage that they set up an armed force of more than one hundred thousand men to resist the carrying out of the bill. The bill was never enforced. When World War I broke out in 1914, with Britain as one of the powers involved, the Irish Question faded into the background. Yet, when the war was over in 1918,

Main Idea:
Irish nationalists in the late nineteenth century pressed for land law reforms as well as home rule legislation.

Distribution of clothing to the starving during the Great Potato Famine of 1846–1849 in Ireland: contemporary colored engraving.

attempts were again made to "answer" this troublesome question. In Chapter 15 in this volume, we will look at these attempts to decide whether or not they were satisfactory.

SECTION SUMMARY

As this section ends, we see a far more democratic Britain that opened the century. This is generally true, but for the situation in Ireland. What is important to realize is that the changes in Britain took place over a long period of time in a fairly peaceful manner. Few changes that last are accomplished quickly. One has only to look at the French Revolution to realize that. It is also interesting to note that most of the demands of Chartists, a "third party," were incorporated. You will often find in history that when third parties have reasonable demands, existing parties "claim" these demands themselves in order to eliminate the third party. The monarch continued to reign but no longer ruled as power shifted to the House of Commons, the body that now represented the people. Even though there are many similarities between the United States and Great Britain, there are two important differences to remember. First, Britain does not have a written constitution. Second, the British parliamentary system is considerably different from our own presidential/congressional system. There are many arguments for the advantages of each. Can you think of some?

Charles Stewart Parnell (1846–1891). Irish Nationalist leader; at the Kilkenny election. Wood engraving from an English newspaper of 1890.

Changes in France (1815–1910)

TIMELINE OF EVENTS

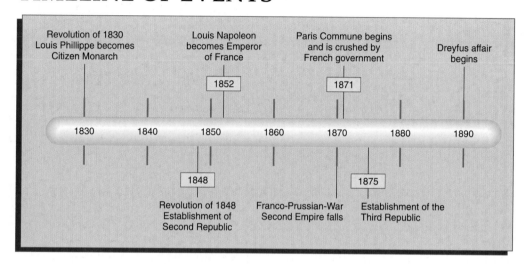

Napoleon's defeat at Waterloo in 1815 left France in chaos. The almost constant warfare during the French Revolution and Napoleon's reign had caused great damage to the French nation and its people. After the final defeat of Napoleon, the victorious Allies determined how France was to be treated at the Congress of Vienna, which met in 1814 and 1815 (see Chapter 22 in *Global History, Volume One*). During the Congress of Vienna, a number of important issues were settled concerning France's future government and land area. The French royal family was restored to power, and France's borders were reduced to those that existed in 1790. The leaders of Europe hoped to return to the past and erase the changes made after the French Revolution.

In this section, you will learn if the leaders of Europe were successful in determining the future of France. You will see if it is possible to turn back the clock once change has taken place. By the end of the section, you can evaluate whether the French Revolution and the Napoleonic Era brought lasting changes to France.

THE BOURBON RESTORATION

The restoration of **Louis XVIII** to the French throne in 1814 was a crucial test for postwar stability. In an effort to ensure peace and order at home, the restored king and his advisers designed a political compromise. The monarchy's compromise called for a balance between the restored political heritage of the old regime and the changes that followed the French Revolution. For example,

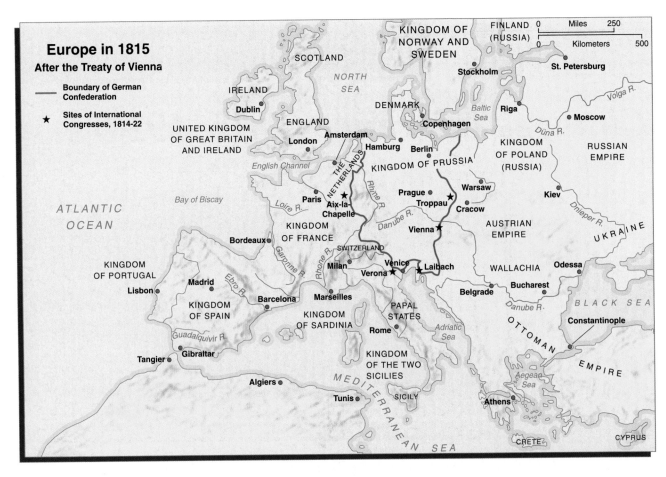

Europe in 1815

After the Treaty of Vienna

— Boundary of German Confederation

★ Sites of International Congresses, 1814-22

Louis XVIII granted a charter that called for a two-house legislature. Service in the Chamber of Peers was based on a person's noble status and was hereditary. The Chamber of Deputies was open to men who were not nobles, but it was limited to men of landed wealth.

During his reign, the king and his ministers sought to rule the French nation and its people with political restraint and administrative efficiency. Napoleon's centralized administration and tax system were enthusiastically maintained by the restored monarchy. At first, Louis's moderate policies proved effective in preventing a revival of radicalism in France. However, after the assassination of a member of the Bourbon family, the **Duke of Berry** in 1820, the King did impose political restrictions in an effort to smother radical ideas printed in the press and taught in universities.

After Louis XVIII died in 1824, the Count of Artois, the King's younger brother, succeeded to the throne. The new ruler adopted the name of King Charles X. Charles was different from his older brother in that he was an ultra-royalist who sought to revive the symbols of the

King Louis XVIII of France (1755–1824): engraving, 19th century, after a painting by Francois-Pascal-Simon Gerard (1770–1837).

privilege of divine right that the kings of France enjoyed before the French Revolution. During his reign, public criticism of the monarchy grew, particularly after the election of 1827, which brought a large number of liberals to the legislature. The liberals soon found themselves in conflict with the king and his conservative supporters.

Main Idea:
The French Bourbon restoration had provided political stability for fifteen years; however, by 1830, political instability once again came to France.

The liberals in France favored a republican form of government and were against the idea of a hereditary monarchy. They favored restrictions on the Catholic Church and supported an economic policy that called for free trade and other laissez-faire ideas. Charles X reacted to his increasingly hostile opposition with firmness. In 1830, the King's ministers issued a set of secretly drafted decrees. These decrees, which are known as the July Ordinances, dissolved the recently elected chamber, further restricted suffrage, and increased press censorship.

Public reaction to the July Ordinances was negative and soon turned violent. In Paris alone, seven hundred people died in three days during a popular uprising against the King's decrees. Seeking to prevent more violence and maintain political stability, Charles X tried to appoint a more acceptable ministry, but it was too late. Liberal leaders started to plan for a new regime. By August, Charles decided to give up his throne, or abdicate.

The French Bourbon restoration had provided political stability for fifteen years; however, by 1830, political instability once again came to France. During these years, ideas of liberalism began to sweep over Europe. A number of these ideas came from England where a liberal political system was gradually put into place. Under the English political system, the monarchy was preserved, but the power of the hereditary ruler was greatly reduced. The English system served as a model for France when a new monarch was called to the throne.

THE LIBERAL MONARCHY IN FRANCE

King Louis Philippe of France (1773–1850): line and stipple engraving, early 19th century.

The revolution that shook France in 1830 resulted in the establishment of a liberal monarchy. **Louis Philippe**, who traced his descent in the royal line to the House of Orleans, became the new king. Louis Philippe thought of himself as a citizen-king and chose the revolutionary tricolor as France's flag. Nevertheless, the king assured other monarchs that France would not export revolution, thereby heading off a possible European reaction.

Louis Philippe owed his throne to the growing influence and political power of the French middle class. The growing political influence of the middle class reflected this group's increasing economic power. Many members of the middle class were liberals who believed in an individual's right to liberty and property. They also wanted laissez-faire economic policies that favored their industrial and commercial interests. The liberals also supported constitutional government, basic individual freedoms, and the separation of Church and state.

THE JULY MONARCHY

Louis Philippe's regime is referred to as the July Monarchy. A new constitution was presented to the French people as a contract that could not be broken. The old aristocracy, which was influential during the previous two regimes, thereafter lost political power to the moderately liberal middle class. Despite opposition from the right (the conservative, pro-Bourbon legitimists) and the left (the liberals and radicals who were the advocates of a republic), the July Monarchy established itself as a symbol of political stability. Even those French citizens led by Louis Napoleon, the former emperor's nephew, who supported the Bonaparte legacy, could not stir up a serious revolt against the citizen monarch. Louis Philippe remained as king of France for eighteen years.

> **Main Idea:**
> Louis Philippe's rule in France concentrated on economic growth and an efficient and stable administration.

Louis Philippe's rule in France concentrated on economic growth and an efficient and stable administration. In 1833, a national system for public education was established, which greatly benefited the growing middle class. In addition, beginning in the 1830s, the July Monarchy enthusiastically supported the growth of railroads. The monarchy benefited from the stability and progress that it offered to the middle class. Visions of economic development and political order encouraged the expanding bourgeoisie, the French name for the middle class, to support Louis Philippe.

In the 1840s, political conflict in France essentially involved a struggle between two middle-class factions. The political differences separating the two groups led by Adolphe Thiers and Francois Guizot were not great and basically involved the interpretation of the existing constitution. Guizot, who was French premier from 1840 to 1848, emphasized the rule of law and parliamentary government in order to ensure stability and make progress. Louis Philippe supported Guizot's faction until the end of the July Monarchy in 1848. In that year, revolutionaries with more radical visions of democracy and social justice swept away the Guizot government. The faltering French economy enabled revolutionaries to attract support, and by 1848, the French people, particularly the working class, became increasingly discontent. They demanded political reforms, especially voting rights.

THE REVOLUTION OF 1848

Louis Philippe's attempt to use troops to control the demonstrations that broke out in February 1848 resulted in the weakening of the king's position and power in the eyes of the people. The French soldiers sympathized with the working-class protesters and joined them. Over the next number of days, bloody disturbances took place in Paris and other French cities. On February 24, the Parisian workers broke into the Chamber of Deputies and forced the proclamation of a republic. Louis Philippe fled into exile in Great Britain.

The February Revolution was at first led by the radicals and those liberals in favor of republican ideas and sympathetic to the growing problems that the working class faced in France. A provisional government was set up, and a new constitution was drafted. In the spring of 1848, an expanded electorate that

Barricade on the Boulevard Montmarte in Paris at the outbreak of the Revolution of 1848: contemporary colored engraving.

included all adult males elected a French government. The constitution enacted many democratic reforms, including a constituent assembly and a president elected by universal manhood suffrage.

THE SECOND REPUBLIC

Jean Joseph Charles Louis Blanc (1811–1882). French socialist and journalist: line engraving, French, 1845.

The idea of a republic was not new to France. During the period of the French Revolution, the First Republic was established, and it lasted until the creation of the Napoleonic Empire. The Second Republic did not last very long because of basic disagreements that divided the middle class and the workers. The social gulf separating the moderate middle class, who were the majority in the constituent assembly, and the working class could not be bridged. Class-oriented violence now marked the political strife in France.

The provisional government took power immediately after the proclamation of the Second Republic and represented some of the more radical and socialist factions. The socialist **Louis Blanc** was a member of the provisional government. Blanc outlined his ideal for a new social order based on the principle of "from each according to his needs, to each according to his abilities." In the first stage, Blanc argued for the immediate relief of the unemployed through a ministry of progress, which would establish his social workshops system.

Napoleon III (1808–1873). Emperor of France, 1852–1870. Contemporary French print.

The social workshops were to be controlled by the workers and supported by the state.

When the newly elected constituent assembly met on May 4, 1848, it immediately replaced the provisional government with a five-man executive council of its own containing no socialists or radicals. Discontent among the radicals and socialists led to an unsuccessful coup headed by the radical thinker and revolutionary **Louis Auguste Blanqui**. The government reacted by dissolving the Blanc-inspired workshop program. The workers' reaction was immediate and violent. A class war began in the streets of Paris. For three days, the government's troops were pitted against armed workers. An estimated ten thousand people were killed and wounded in a struggle without mercy until the French military regained control of the city.

The June Days of Terror frightened the wealthier bourgeoisie, nobility, and other middle-class citizens. In the December 1848 election for president of France, all four candidates who sought election campaigned as republicans. **Louis Napoleon Bonaparte** was the candidate who received the greatest overall support from the various classes who composed the electorate in French society. The electorate was disillusioned with the course of events in France and wanted a return to order, stability, and renewed economic progress. French people thought back to the glory days of Napoleon I and longed for a return to those times of national greatness. Louis Napoleon won 70 percent of the votes and became the first and only president of France's Second Republic.

LOUIS NAPOLEON BONAPARTE AND THE SECOND REPUBLIC

Main Idea:
When the Chamber of Deputies rejected a constitutional amendment that would have allowed him a second term, Louis Napoleon decided to take complete political power and engineered a coup d'etat.

Louis Napoleon's term as president of the Second Republic brought him into political conflict with the deputies in the Chamber of Deputies who favored a monarchy. Nevertheless, in his first years of office, Louis Napoleon's popularity grew as he continued to appeal to public opinion as a democratic reformer and increasingly gained the support of the powerful groups in France—the army, the middle class, the Church, and the peasants. The future **Napoleon III** also won the confidence of the largely Catholic French population. He helped the pope suppress an attempt by Italian nationalists to establish a republic in Rome and gave the Roman Catholic Church control over French education.

When the Chamber of Deputies rejected a constitutional amendment that would have allowed him a second term, Louis Napoleon decided to take complete political power and engineered a coup d'etat. On December 2, 1851, Louis Napoleon called the Second French Republic a failure and took complete control of the government. Victory was assured by the arrests of opposition deputies and other potential opponents. Louis Napoleon also used soldiers to take effective control of the Parisian streets. The concentration of both the executive and legislative powers in his hands was part of Napoleon's shrewd plan to use dictatorial authority to win popular support.

Louis Napoleon then used a plebiscite to have the people grant him the power to create a new constitution. In this first plebiscite, he boldly reestablished universal suffrage for all French men and received a strong show of support. In a second plebiscite held shortly thereafter, about 95 percent of the electorate approved of transforming France from a republic back to a hereditary empire. In 1852, Louis Napoleon became Napoleon III, Emperor of France, and established the Second Empire.

THE SECOND EMPIRE

Louis Napoleon modeled the Second Empire after the First Empire of his uncle Napoleon Bonaparte and sought to recreate its greatness. Under the rule of Napoleon III, France's Second Empire brought important changes to the nation in the following years. In the 1850s, Napoleon III benefited from an economic boom in France, which his government helped stimulate by encouraging economic growth. The state created special investment funds and tax incentives, and launched huge public works projects. The state support of entrepreneurs engaged in public works projects gave rise to rumors of political spoils and speculation. Paris changed enormously and gained a reputation as one of the world's most beautiful and increasingly important cities. The prefect, or appointed mayor of Paris, Baron **Georges Haussmann**, created broad boulevards and impressively decorated public buildings. He also rid the city's center of slums and designed the way the heart of Paris looks today.

Municipal renovation of a Paris neighborhood, ordered by Baron Haussmann. Line engraving, 19th century.

The court of Napoleon led by **Empress Eugenie** achieved a measure of brilliance. French prestige in the arts and sciences increased, and the talented artists and scientists received the emperor's rewards of honors and promotions. The emperor sponsored social and educational reform and publicly took credit for his works. During the Second Empire, French cultural achievements flourished, and Paris became a center of leadership in the arts and sciences.

Foreign Policy

Louis Napoleon's foreign policy was designed to increase his popularity. One way that Napoleon sought to prove his greatness was by becoming involved in foreign wars and risky overseas adventures. Napoleon saw the **Crimean War** as an opportunity to show the world that France was once again a military power to be respected and to increase his own stature. France opposed the Russian attempt to take advantage of the weakness of the Ottoman Empire and expand toward the warm water ports of the Mediterranean Sea. Joining with Great Britain, the French were soon involved in war. The French military, fighting as an ally of the British, achieved success in the Crimean War (1854–1856). The victory in the Crimean War brought the emperor great prestige when the Russians asked for peace after the fall of Sebastopol.

> **Main Idea:**
> One way that Napoleon sought to prove his greatness was by becoming involved in foreign wars and risky overseas adventures.

France also profited from actions and measures taken to protect its political interests, trade, and financial involvement in other parts of the world. In the Middle East, the French actions led to improved trade and protection of the nation's financial interests. France's intervention in Italy had less success because it resulted in the loss of papal territory. His support of Italy had antagonized French Catholics, and the emperor subsequently tried to strengthen his domestic popularity by an adventure in Mexico. Using the initial pretext (excuse) of a joint British, French, and Spanish intervention in the country to force payment of foreign debts, France kept its troops in Mexico after the other

The French military commander General Francois Certain Canrobert and his forces at the Siege of Sevastopol during the Crimean War, 1854. Wood engraving from a contemporary American newspaper.

nations withdrew because of an American warning. The emperor then sought to impose French control over Mexico. This led to a war in which the liberal Mexican government was defeated. France then installed Archduke **Maximilian** of Austria as emperor in Mexico. Unexpected strong Mexican resistance and U.S. opposition forced the French to finally withdraw and abandon Maximilian. Napoleon's prestige suffered greatly after Maximilian was defeated and then executed.

The Second Empire Falls

Main Idea:
The French public became concerned with the high cost of military glory.

The empire's changing fortunes caused it to lose support at home as the 1860s progressed. Even Louis Napoleon's successful colonial ventures in Indochina and Africa began to be regarded as a very expensive military burden. The French public became concerned with the high cost of military glory. Napoleon III sought to turn public opinion in his favor by taking measures to liberalize the empire. In 1868, freedom of the press and the right to assembly were once again permitted. Members of the legislature were also allowed to question ministers. Workers were allowed to organize and even strike. The government also established public secondary schools for girls. The emperor's belated attempts at liberalization did not satisfy his critics and even served to alienate some of his old supporters. In 1870, facing an increasingly difficult political situation at home and in Europe, the emperor permitted the establishment of a full-fledged parliamentary system and chose political leaders. The new prime minister was a supporter of returning France to a republic.

In foreign affairs, Louis Napoleon, looking to regain public favor and support in the legislature, took a nationalist stand regarding France's growing differences with **Prussia**. The main issues were France's concern over the growth

Siege of Paris, 1871. Burning the trees in the Bois de Boulogne, Paris, for charcoal during the Franco-Prussian War. Wood engraving from an English newspaper of 1871.

of German strength on its borders and competition over influence in Spain. The Prussians, led by **Otto von Bismarck**, were well prepared for battle and maneuvered the French into a declaration of war. The German military machine quickly crossed into France and in a period of six weeks decisively won the **Franco-Prussian War**. The German capture of Louis Napoleon soon led to the collapse of the Second Empire.

PEACE WITH PRUSSIA AND THE PARIS COMMUNE

Main Idea:
These unpopular measures led to increased unrest and a general uprising in Paris.

In early 1871, the newly elected French National Assembly made peace with Prussia. The peace treaty was humiliating for France, which lost the provinces of **Alsace** and **Lorraine** and agreed to pay Prussia the equivalent of one billion dollars in war reparations. A further humiliation for the French was the staging of a Prussian victory march in Paris. These concessions to Prussia angered many people in France and led to demonstrations and calls for a renewed war against the hated Prussians. The French legislature reacted to the increasingly violent demonstrations by seeking to restore order in Paris, but its actions had the opposite effect. The provisional government suspended payments to national-guard soldiers. The national-guard troops had played a prominent role in defending Paris during the German siege. There were many Parisians in the ranks, and the lack of payment turned many of them against the provisional government. In addition, Parisians were angered by the government's declaration that all debts and rents suspended during the siege of Paris now be paid. These unpopular measures led to increased unrest and a general uprising in Paris.

During the revolt, workers who wanted a socialist form of government established the **Commune of Paris**. The leaders of the Paris Commune considered themselves the legitimate government of the city. They began to operate as the city's governing officials. They were soon in conflict with the National Assembly because of their refusal to recognize its authority. The communards called for the conversion of France into a decentralized federation of independent cities. The Paris Commune also declared itself against the Roman Catholic Church and propertied classes.

A bitter and bloody civil war broke out in Paris. By the time that the troops loyal to the National Assembly regained control of the city, more than twenty thousand people

Barricades in front of the Hotel de Ville during the Paris Commune of 1871: wood engraving from a contemporary English newspaper.

Paris Commune, 1871. Burning the guillotine in the Place Voltaire. Wood engraving from a contemporary French newspaper.

had been killed and more than forty thousand arrested. That bloody week in May 1871 left a legacy of class bitterness and further polarized French politics. The intensification of the social divisions between the middle class and the workers continued into the twentieth century.

THE THIRD REPUBLIC AND CONTINUED POLITICAL CRISIS

After the destruction of the Paris Commune, a political struggle developed over what form the new government should take. Royalists and republicans fought over this vital political issue. Finally, in 1875, a constitution that gave France a third republican government was agreed upon. The Constitution of 1875 provided for a two-house legislature that elected a president for a four-year term. The real political power was in the hands of the legislature, which had to approve all acts before they officially became law. A cabinet of ministers was created with the post of premier to handle all executive business.

Main Idea: The Third Republic proved politically unstable and unpopular from its beginnings.

Unfortunately for France, the Third Republic proved politically unstable and unpopular from its beginnings. The political parties in France were really political groupings held together by immediate concerns. These political groupings constantly shifted their allegiances and alliances based on whatever the most important issues at the moment were. This political instability continued to the end of the nineteenth century. Royalist sentiment remained strong but was divided along Bourbon, Orleanist, or Bonapartist lines. Republicans were equally divided over issues related to liberalism. Radical republicans were stridently anticlerical and antiroyalist, whereas the moderates sought to compromise on key issues.

Georges Ernest Jean Marie Boulanger (1837–1891). French general. Photograph by Nadar.

The 1880s and 1890s were decades of political crises for the Third Republic. One of its greatest threats came from a popular war hero, General **Georges Boulanger** who became war minister in 1886. Boulanger championed the idea of revenge against the Germans. Royalists and other antirepublicans supported Boulanger in his desire to declare war. Boulanger called for a new legislature and constitution and began making plans for a coup d'etat. His goal was to establish a more authoritarian regime, but he lost his nerve and fled to Brussels. The Boulanger movement soon collapsed without the direction of its popular leader.

A second threat to the Republic in the 1890s involved the failure and bankruptcy of the company that had won the right to construct a canal through Panama to link the Atlantic and Pacific Oceans. The French Panama Company's loss of money invested by thousands of stockholders led to a scandal that shook the government. Charges of corruption, poor management, and dishonesty resulted in trials that further embittered the public. The socialist movement benefited from this scandal and won nearly fifty seats in the legislature for the first time.

THE DREYFUS AFFAIR

The Third Republic's gravest crisis in the 1890s was the Dreyfus affair. Captain **Alfred Dreyfus**, a Jewish army officer, was arrested and charged with treason for selling military secrets to the Germans. The French army was a known stronghold of **anti-Semitism**. The army's superior officers were monarchists and Catholics. As the case progressed, it became obvious to impartial observers that the officer corps knew that Dreyfus was innocent. Nevertheless, the French army was willing to sacrifice Dreyfus to cover up their general incompetence and to protect the real guilty party, who was linked to the general staff. Dreyfus was court-martialed and sentenced to loss of his military rank and deportation for life. He was sent to Devil's Island, a notorious prison off the northeast coast of South America. In general, public opinion applauded the conviction.

Dreyfus's family and many supporters continued to maintain his innocence. By 1897, growing evidence indicated that Dreyfus was convicted through the use of forged documents. The military, however, remained adamant and refused to go along with a reversal of Dreyfus's sentence despite new evidence indicating that a Major Esterazy was responsible for the treasonous acts. Esterazy was tried by court-martial and acquitted within minutes. Army leaders argued that military authority would be undermined if Dreyfus would be retried.

Emile Zola, a French writer and leading supporter of Dreyfus, sent an open letter to Felix Faure, the president of the French Republic, accusing the judges of acting on orders of the war ministry. The case became a major political and social issue in France. Catholics, monarchists, militarists, and conservatives joined together in patriotic indignation against socialists, republicans,

Main Idea:
The French army was willing to sacrifice Dreyfus to cover up their general incompetence and to protect the real guilty party, who was linked to the general staff.

Alfred Dreyfus (1859–1935). French army officer. Photographed c. 1894.

Emile Zola's denunciation of the French General Staff's handling of the Dreyfus Affair in a letter to President Felix Faure, as published in Georges Clemenceau's newspaper "L'Aurore," 13 January 1898.

anticlericals, and Jews, whom they accused of selling out the country and weakening the army.

The Dreyfus affair continued into the first decade of the twentieth century. Dreyfus was retried in 1899, but the military court, despite newly submitted evidence, refused to admit that an injustice had taken place. The military court once again found Dreyfus to be guilty. In the retrial, the military court officers ruled that there were extenuating circumstances and sentenced him to ten years. Faced with worldwide indignation, France finally issued a pardon to Dreyfus. In 1906, he was readmitted into the army with the rank of major and given the Legion of Honor after he was completely exonerated by the French Supreme Court of Appeals. The support that republicans, socialists, artists, and writers gave to Dreyfus at last proved successful, and justice was served.

The Dreyfus affair was an important test that demonstrated that the Third Republic could survive despite the deep split it caused among a generation of French citizens. After the Dreyfus affair, republican supporters began to demand reforms that were beneficial to the working class. The Dreyfus affair continues to influence France to our present day. The issue of anti-Semitism remains a serious problem for French society to resolve at the beginning of the twenty-first century.

Main Idea:
The Dreyfus affair was an important test that demonstrated that the Third Republic could survive despite the deep split it caused among a generation of French citizens.

SECTION SUMMARY

If we look at French society and politics during the nineteenth century, we see that there was often conflict among monarchists, republicans, liberals, radicals, conservatives, and socialists. Political stability was uncertain from the 1800s after the fall of Napoleon Bonaparte, to the twentieth century. Monarchies, an empire, and republics came and went. The Third Republic, which did last until 1940, was never able to fully stabilize the nation.

Unification of Italy

TIMELINE OF EVENTS

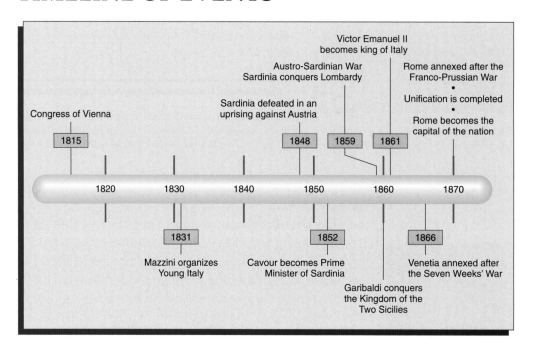

Do you know anyone who is Italian? If so, perhaps that person, or others of his or her family, was born in a nation that can be identified today on a map as Italy. Have you ever gone to an Italian restaurant? The food was prepared and named from traditions originating in a nation that can be identified today on a map as Italy. This nation occupies land in southern Europe, mainly on a peninsula surrounded by three seas. Although Italian people have lived on this land for centuries, the nation-state we locate today on a map as Italy came into existence only in the second half of the nineteenth century. The history of the creation of this nation at that time is the topic for this section.

The desire of the Italian people to form their own nation, free of rule by others, is an example of **nationalism**. Nationalism is the belief that a group of people who share a common **culture**, language, and historical tradition should have their own country in a specific area of land. Nationalism is also a feeling of pride in and loyalty to one's country. When people who were ruled by outsiders finally accomplish their nationalistic goals and form a nation-state, they can then make their own laws and have their own government. Such people are said to be **sovereign** and to have independence or **autonomy**.

The spirit of nationalism greatly influenced the political history of Europe in the nineteenth century, particularly with the unification movements that led to the births of modern Italy and Germany. And in the last years of the twentieth century, it was a factor in the breakup of the former Soviet Union. This spirit has been a force for both good and evil. Nationalism can be viewed favorably when it brings people together for common, shared peaceful purposes. It is also a force for good when a person becomes proud to do good things for his nation, or carries out peaceful responsibilities, or feels happy at the accomplishments of his fellow citizens. On the other hand, it can be a force for evil when it brings people together for the purpose of committing wrongful acts. This is also true when a person does things that cause harm to others under the name of nationalism. Extremely intense and passionate nationalistic pride, as shown by individuals who think their nation is always right and can never do anything wrong, is called *chauvinism*. Such intense nationalism can also be evident when a nation thinks its ways are superior and attempts to impose them on others or even destroy the ways of others. This may be called excessive **ethnocentrism**.

BACKGROUND TO ITALIAN UNIFICATION

The modern nation of Italy was formed by uniting several Italian-speaking regions. For this reason, our study of nationalism in Italy requires that we see how this process of unification occurred.

There was no united Italian nation in 1815 due to the decisions of the **Congress of Vienna**. As you may recall, this meeting was held at the end of the Napoleonic Wars in order to remake the map of Europe (see Chapter 22 in *Global History, Volume One*). The Austrian minister at this meeting, Prince Metternich, had no desire to promote unity in the Italian peninsula. For him, Italy would simply be a "geographic expression"—a place, not a free united nation. To guarantee this situation, this "place" was divided as follows:

> **Main Idea:**
> There was no united Italian nation in 1815 due to the decisions of the **Congress of Vienna**.

1. Lombardy and Venetia, two provinces in the north, were to be governed by Austria.
2. The **duchies** of Tuscany, Parma, and Modena, along with the Kingdom of the Two Sicilies, would be under local rulers controlled by Austria.
3. Rome and the Papal States would be under the authority of the Catholic Church.
4. Only the Kingdom of Sardinia (which included Sardinia and Piedmont) would be under Italian control. Therefore, the vast majority of Italian people were under some sort of foreign domination not of their own choosing.

The domination of Austria was the biggest obstacle to Italian unification. The Austrian military crushed uprisings against the rule in 1820, 1821, 1831, and 1848. Another obstacle was the Catholic Church. It feared that a united Italy would interfere with the **pope's** authority in Rome and the Papal States. Still another roadblock in the path to unification was a political disagreement among Italian nationalist leaders themselves. **Giuseppe Mazzini** and **Giuseppe Garibaldi** wanted an autonomous Italy to be set up as a democratic republic. **Camillo Cavour** preferred Italy to become a constitutional monarchy, similar to that in Great Britain.

As we will soon see, these three men were to play important leadership roles in promoting unity. Additional factors helping the cause of Italian nationalism were

- the influence of the French Revolution's ideals of liberty and nationalism.
- remembrance of the great achievements on the Italian peninsula during the Roman Empire and the **Renaissance**.
- growth of patriotic societies such as the **Carbonari** and **Young Italy** that spread ideas of unity in their speeches, writings, and other activities.
- the active role of Sardinia and its royal House of Savoy.

NATIONALIST LEADERS

Giuseppe Mazzini

Giuseppe Mazzini (1805–1872). Italian patriot.

Mazzini (1805–1872) was a thin man, who was fond of poetry and philosophy. He was more an idealist and a thinker than a doer and a man of practical affairs. His plan for Italy called for a democratic government led by and responsible to the people. These goals, along with his fear of **monarchy**, put him at odds with Cavour. He was a member of the Carbonari and was a founder of Young Italy (1831). He was active in the short-lived uprising of 1848 and spent several years in prison and exile. His propaganda efforts on behalf of unification were carried out both in Italy and abroad. More than anyone else, he inspired Italians with hopes for unity and autonomy. For these reasons, he has been called the "soul" of unification.

Giuseppe Garibaldi

Garibaldi (1807–1882) was an adventurous person, often unpredictable, very hot-headed, and willing to take risks. In dress, he was a nonconformist, known particularly for his famous red shirt. He had a reputation for military skill and daring, having escaped capture from both Austrian and French armies. He lived in exile for a number of years, working once as a candlemaker in Staten Island, New York. Although distrusted by Cavour, his bravery as a soldier in the cause of Italian nationalism made him popular as the "sword" of unification.

Camillo Cavour

Cavour (1810–1861) was a master statesman of the nineteenth century. A short man, his eyes and manner made him seem shrewd and clever. For this educated, well-traveled man, Mazzini was too much of an unrealistic dreamer, and Garibaldi was a good but reckless soldier. In 1852, Cavour became prime minister of Sardinia, a kingdom ruled by **Victor Emmanuel II** of the House of Savoy. It was Cavour's intention to have Sardinia lead the fight for Italian unity. A man of action and cool planning, he once remarked, "I cannot make a speech,

Conte di Camillo Benso Cavour (1810–1861). Italian Statesman. Mezzotint, 1860, by John Sartain.

but I can make Italy." The movement for Italian unity became known as the **Risorgimento**, the Italian word for resurgence or revival. It was also the name of a newspaper that Cavour had once edited. For his efforts as a diplomat in working with or against other European countries to aid Italy, he has been called the "brain" of unification.

STEPS IN THE UNIFICATION PROCESS

The years 1859 to 1870 were the crucial ones in which the various parts of the Italian peninsula and islands were united into one nation. During this time, Cavour's planning proved to be effective. He wanted Austrian power removed, while adding land to Sardinia, so that Victor Emmanuel would be proclaimed king of a unified country. These goals could not, he felt, be accomplished solely by the Italians. Foreign help was needed. Such help would be forthcoming if Sardinia showed it was a stable, prosperous kingdom with armed power. In other words, Sardinia wanted to get enough respect so that major powers, such as France, would be willing to take her side in future struggles. With Victor Emmanuel's help, Cavour built railroads, helped farmers, assisted banks, and made the army stronger. Although Sardinia's assistance to France and Britain was not needed in the Crimean War (1854–1856), Cavour sent troops. He was thus invited to the peace conference, where he made a brief but impressive speech about the need for Italian unification.

> **Main Idea:**
> With Victor Emmanuel's help, Cavour built railroads, helped farmers, assisted banks, and made the army stronger.

Having become friendly with Napoleon III of France, Cavour persuaded him to agree to a secret alliance against Austria. France wanted to weaken Austria's position as a European power and was willing therefore to see Austria lose land in Italy. Cavour, of course, wanted to see Austria out of Italy so that unification could be promoted. France would send forces to Sardinia if Sardinia could draw Austria into a war. On the assumption that the combined Sardinian-French forces would drive Austria out of Lombardy and Venetia, Sardinia would give France the territories of Nice and Savoy. When Sardinian protest provoked Austria into declaring war in 1859, the plan was hatched. With the promised French help, the Austro-Sardinian War lasted just two months. Having suffered severe defeats at the battles of Magenta and Solferino, Austrian forces left Lombardy. Italian nationalists gained inspiration from this and overthrew Austrian rulers in several states. As preparations were being made to invade Venetia, Cavour was shocked to learn that Napoleon III had dropped out of the war and signed a peace treaty with Austria.

Why had Napoleon done this? The answers rest upon what France now saw as its own best interests. In matters of foreign policy, a nation will usually act on the basis of its own self-interests. In this case, Napoleon feared that a long war with Austria would tempt mighty Prussia to come to Austria's side. This he did not want. Second, he did not anticipate armed Italian anti-Austrian uprisings in other parts of the peninsula. He was worried that a large united Italy would become a Mediterranean rival to France. Finally, Napoleon was pressured by French Catholics to get out of the war. They claimed that a united Italy under Cavour would lessen the power of the Roman Catholic Church and take away much of its property.

The Austro-Sardinian War of 1859 was now over. Sardinia kept its word and ceded (gave up) Nice and Savoy to France. Austria permitted Sardinia to annex, add, Lombardy to its Territory. Austrian rulers who had been overthrown in the states of Modena, Tuscany, Parma, and Romagna were restored. However, in the next year, 1860, the people in these states voted in a **plebiscite** to be annexed to Sardinia. (A plebiscite election in one in which a population votes yes or no on the issue of political self-determination.) So it was that in April 1860 an enlarged Sardinian **parliament** met. All of Italy except Venetia, the Papal States, and the Kindgom of the Two Sicilies were represented.

THE CRUCIAL YEARS OF 1860–1861

As notable as this meeting was, it was not the only reason that 1860 was a momentous year in Italian history; in May 1860 Garibaldi began a series of military conquests that led him to be called the "sword" of unification. With approximately one thousand armed men, wearing red shirts and slouch hats, he sailed from Piedmont to invade the island of Sicily. He had secret financial support from Cavour, even though Cavour's wish for an eventual monarchy in Italy conflicted with Garibaldi's preference for a **republic** without a king. Although the two men disliked each other, they did share a common dream of an autonomous Italy and realized that each could help the other. Garibaldi's Red Shirts easily defeated the Austrian-backed ruler of Sicily and then sailed to southern Italy, where they were again victorious. In these newly conquered areas, the former Kingdom of the Two Sicilies, people welcomed Garibaldi enthusiastically and joined his army.

> **Main Idea:**
> In May 1860 Garibaldi began a series of military conquests that led him to be called the "sword" of unification.

Garibaldi was now poised to move forth, to take Rome and the Papal States. This was of concern to Cavour, still fearful about Garibaldi's republican ideas and worried that an attack on the French troops protecting Rome might provoke France into declaring war. Aware that Garibaldi disliked him, Cavour cleverly advised Victor Emmanuel to lead Sardinian troops southward by himself, take some of the Papal States but not Rome itself, and meet with Garibaldi. Victor Emmanuel did all this, parading with Garibaldi through the streets of Naples to cheering crowds. In a plebiscite, people in the former Kingdom of the Two Sicilies agreed to be united with the Kingdom of Sardinia. Garibaldi, willing to give up his hope of a Italian republic, refused the many titles and honors Victor Emmanuel offered him and retired to his farm. In March 1861, the Kingdom of Italy was proclaimed with Victor Emmanuel as king.

THE IMPACT OF THE SEVEN WEEKS' WAR AND THE FRANCO-PRUSSIAN WAR

The only parts of Italy not under Victor Emmanuel were Austrian-controlled Venetia and French-controlled Rome. Based upon two events soon to happen outside of Italy, the new kingdom would add these parts in a bloodless manner. In the Seven Week's War of 1866 between Austria and Prussia, Italy joined the side of Prussia. Austria was defeated and ceded Venetia to Italy. By plebiscite, the Venetians became part of the nation of Italy. During the Franco-Prussian War of 1870, France withdrew her troops from Rome. In September, Italian forces entered the city. In a plebiscite, Rome's citizens voted 134,000 to 1,500 to join Italy. **Rome** now was designated as the capital of **Italy**—a "place" that was no longer a "geographical expression," but a unified nation destined to have an important role in European affairs.

A UNITED ITALY FACES PROBLEMS

A unified nation as it approached the last thirty years of the nineteenth century, Italy faced problems that were economic, social, and political. It was without large deposits of coal and iron and thus did not have a strong industrial base to compete with other countries. The south was much poorer than the north. The relationship between the Catholic Church and the new government was very controversial, becoming known as the *Roman Question*. Pope Pius XI had never agreed to the annexation of Rome and the Papal States and did not at first accept the legality of the new kingdom. He even went so far as to forbid Catholics from participating in politics. The Roman Question continued to pose a serious problem until 1929. In that year, an area in Rome, Vatican City, was set up as a sovereign state in an agreement between the pope and the dictator Mussolini.

Another source of irritation between the south and north was the dominance of northerners in the new government. The government was created as a constitutional monarchy, hopefully to function as Great Britain's did. These hopes were imperfectly realized, as Italy lacked a long tradition of representative self-government. The regional variations and frequent bad feelings between local areas held back a workable democratic central government. In addition, the growth of many political parties made compromises difficult to achieve and often led to instabil-

Modern-day Italy

ity and government crises. Finally, there were many Italians who felt that additional territory belonged to Italy for cultural and traditional reasons and therefore ought to be added to the new nation. This territory was called *Italia irridenta* (Italy unredeemed) and included Trieste, Trentino, and Istria. This issue was partially settled after World War I. Italy soon joined in the race by European countries for **colonies** overseas. In Africa, by 1900, Italy had obtained Eritrea, Italian Somaliland, and Libya while failing to conquer Ethiopia.

SECTION SUMMARY

By the close of the nineteenth century, there was a united Italy in southern Europe. It was a long time in the making but when a hardheaded practical man involved himself—Cavour—the job got done! It seems that dreamers are interesting in history but that you need practical people as leaders. Garibaldi was one of history's more colorful characters, ready for adventure at any time. He fought in both the Old and New Worlds, and a movie of his life would be fun to see. But the step-by-step planning of Cavour got the job accomplished. He "used" other nations, when he could, to help him toward his goal, but he was ready to step aside if necessary. He did not seek personal glory: The creation of Italy was his aim. Italy, however, had a number of continuing problems: the industrial north against the agricultural south; the opposition to the Church in many areas against the agricultural south; the opposition to the Church in many areas against the followers of the papacy; the monarchists against the liberals. We will look at these issues again.

Main Idea:
By the close of the nineteenth century, there was a united Italy in southern Europe.

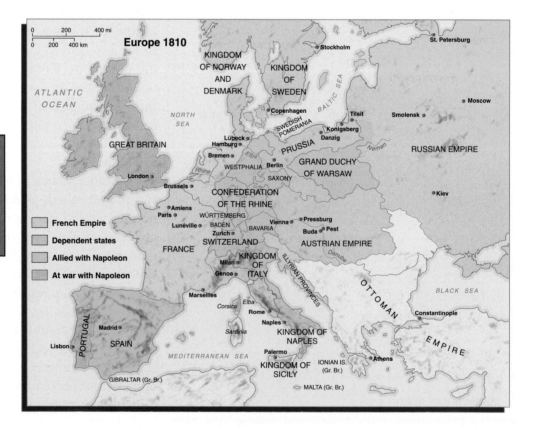

Unification of Germany

TIMELINE OF EVENTS

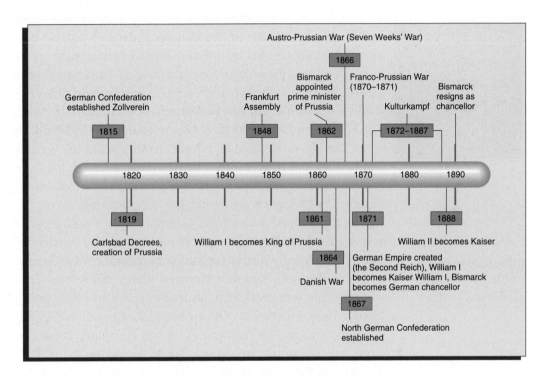

In the first half of the nineteenth century, Germany was, like Italy, a "geographic expression." There were several German states, but no unified country with a central government. The nation of Germany that we find today on a map did not come into being until 1871. It is located on land that for centuries prior to this time was inhabited by people who spoke a common language and who shared many common traditions. Until 1806, the German states were part of the Holy Roman Empire. The Napoleonic Wars had brought an end to that **empire**. But when Napoleon himself was defeated at Waterloo in 1815, the **Congress of Vienna** met to remake the map of Europe. Its plans regarding the German states included the creation of the German Confederation, under the authority of Austria. Fifty-six years later, by 1871, the confederation had passed out of existence, Austria's role was weakened, and a united Germany had arisen under the leadership of the state of Prussia. How did all this occur? Who was responsible? This section will provide the answers. German unification was similar to Italian unification in some ways, but it was also very different. Try to discover the similarities and differences as you read the section.

Main Idea:
Until 1806, the German states were part of the Holy Roman Empire.

OBSTACLES TO GERMAN UNIFICATION, 1815–1862

The presence of Austria as one of the thirty-nine states in the German Confederation was the main obstacle to unification of the *German* people in 1815 and in the years immediately thereafter. The word German in these times described an **ethnic group** and a **nationality**, not a **nation**. There were, for example, German people in both Austria and Prussia. Austria was ruled by Germans but was also an empire that included many other non-Germanic nationalities. Examples were Italians, Hungarians, Serbs, Croats, Czechs, Poles, and Romanians. Each of these nationalities, in fact, wanted to form its own nation. Austria sought to put down any nationalistic attempts by these groups, as we saw in the case of the Italians. Austria was also against any nationalistic or unification actions by other German states, such as Prussia and Saxony. If they were to unite, Austria would lose its commanding position over German people in Europe and would be faced with a rival power on its northern border. Therefore, we should not be surprised that Austrian Minister Metternich pressured the German Confederation to issue the **Carlsbad Decrees** in 1819. These were designed to silence people from speaking, writing, or teaching about nationalist and liberal ideas. Under these decrees, for example, newspaper editors and university professors could be jailed for expressing thoughts about unification. Such laws were examples of censorship.

> **Main Idea:**
> Austria sought to put down any nationalistic attempts by these groups, as we saw in the case of the Italians.

Opposition to a unified German nation was also held by France. France felt secure with having weak neighbors on its borders and would thus have been upset by any hint of nationalism shown by the German states. Even among some of the non-Austrian German states, there was concern about a unified nation. This was especially so in Bavaria and other south German states. The people here, who were outnumbered by the north German states, were mainly Catholic and mostly farmers. A united Germany would be under greater influence by the northern states. These areas, such as Prussia, were primarily Protestant and were more interested in commerce and manufacturing.

Factors Favoring German Unification

In spite of the many obstacles described above, a number of factors favored German unity in the first half of the nineteenth century. Curiously, the Napoleonic Wars were an indirect factor. Napoleon's conquests had provoked a cohesive, nationalistic reaction among Germans, as they fought against him. As you may recall, both Austria and Prussia had troops at Waterloo and were represented at the Congress of Vienna. That 1815 meeting created the German Confederation, as we have seen. However, the confederation was ineffective and disappointed German nationalists. They now considered other means of achieving unity.

> **Main Idea:**
> Napoleon's conquests had provoked a cohesive, nationalistic reaction among Germans, as they fought against him.

A form of economic unity was achieved by some German states with the formation of the **Zollverein** in 1819. This was a tariff or customs union that included Prussia and several states, but not Austria. Members of this union would not place tariffs (special taxes) on goods coming from other members. Before 1819, many states would tax goods highly from other states. This would make products more expensive and slow down trade. With the Zollverein in existence, prices were lower, trade grew, and manufacturers, workers, and merchants prospered. This free-trade association brought Prussia and the other member states closer together economically but had little immediate political effect. It was apparent to industrialists, however, that even greater prosperity would come about with unification under a national government. Existence of the Zollverein added to tension between Prussia and Austria.

Another factor encouraging a feeling of national unity as well as pride among Germans was the work of philosophers and historians. **Johann Fichte** (1762–1814) was a philosopher who declared the Germans to be the greatest of all people, with the need to unite and become the leader among civilized nations. Additionally, he claimed that German was superior to other languages. The philosopher **Georg Hegel** (1770–1831) was a strong supporter of the Prussian monarchy, emphasizing the value of a powerful central government. There arose a group of Prussian historians who claimed that it was Prussia's great mission in history to unite the German people. The most famous of these historians was **Heinrich von Treitschke** (1834–1896). Treitschke considered himself an intense patriot, believing that the Germans were the best of all peoples and that the Prussians were the best of all Germans.

The Importance of 1848

Very soon, we will meet those Prussian figures who shared these thoughts and were prominent in weaving together a fabric of nationhood from separate pieces of geographical cloth. Before we do so, we will talk about two events between 1815 and 1862 that were attempts at unification. One of these was the Revolution of 1848. In that year, German liberals pressed for certain goals that were similar to goals being sought in other parts of Europe:

The representatives of the Frankfurt National Assembly holding a meeting at Paulskirche, 1848.

- A written **constitution** to limit autocratic monarchs.
- Expansion of the right to vote.

Main Idea:
Frederick's actions sealed the doom of the Frankfurt Assembly and the Frankfurt Constitution.

And in the German states, there was a wish to create a nation from the German Confederation but without Austria. The movement's both liberal and nationalistic goals resulted in the election of the *Frankfurt Assembly* in 1848. The assembly drew up a constitution, modeled after features from the American and British political systems, and offered the position of **emperor** of a united Germany to King Frederick William IV of Prussia (r. 1840–1861). He refused the offer, afraid that Austria would go to war against him if he accepted the proposal. Also, as a believer in the **divine right** theory, he believed that any crown that he could accept "is not one created by an Assembly born of revolutionary seed [but] must be a crown set with the seal of the almighty." Frederick's actions sealed the doom of the Frankfurt Assembly and the Frankfurt Constitution. It was against his principles to "pick up a crown from the gutter," as he described the offer of the Frankfurt Assembly.

In 1850, however, Frederick William IV did try to unite several German states by speaking with the rulers of those states. He was told by Austria to stop doing this. While in the town of Olmutz, he made the decision to obey this command. This "humiliation of Olmutz" was yet another Austrian action that angered Prussia.

UNIFICATION LEADERS

Otto von Bismarck

The most important figure in the history of German unification was Otto von Bismarck (1815–1898). Standing more than six feet tall and possessed of a powerful build and a rough-looking face, Bismarck came from a rich, noble, landowning family in the Brandenburg section of Prussia. Such families formed the aristocratic class of people known as **Junkers**. A strong-willed person, he could not stand to be criticized and scorned those who he believed were his social and intellectual inferiors. He also looked down on the ideals of democracy and liberalism. For him, an elected parliamentary government was useless and ineffective; a written constitution was simply "a sheet of paper" and should never be allowed to limit royal power and governmental action. From 1851 to 1862, he held several political positions such as Prussian delegate to the German Confederation and Prussian spokesman to Russia and France. In 1862, King William (Wilhelm) I of Prussia (r. 1861–1888) appointed him to be the Prussian prime minister.

In this post, he moved to strengthen Prussia and make it the centerpiece around which other states would be added to create a German nation. In this respect, Prussia was to become a "German Sardinia." He proved to be bold, daring, and willing to lie and deceive and to use force when necessary to accomplish his goals. He denounced the democratic efforts of the

Prince Otto von Bismarck-Schonhausen (1815–1898). Prussian statesman.

Frankfurt Assembly, declaring that Germans do "not look to Prussia's liberalism, but to her power. The great questions of the day are not to be decided by speeches and majority resolutions—but by blood and iron."

King William I

William I of Prussia (1797–1888). King of Prussia (1861–1888) and Emperor of Germany (1871–1888).

King William I came to the throne of Prussia in 1861, as a member of the **Hohenzollern Dynasty**. As was true of some of his predecessors, he wanted Prussia to be a powerful, militaristic, and authoritarian kingdom. Under him, Bismarck became prime minister and enjoyed his support of the "**blood and iron**" policies.

Helmuth von Moltke

Von Moltke (1800–1891) became head of the Prussian army. He made it the best trained and most efficient fighting force in Europe. Unlike Garibaldi, he was a quiet, calm military planner. He was one of the first generals to use modern scientific methods of warfare, regarding careful use of new weapons, battlefield formations, and detailed strategies. His love for Prussia, his interest in the army, and his obedience to Bismarck and King William were unquestioned.

STEPS IN THE UNIFICATION PROCESS

The years 1862 to 1871 were the crucial ones in which various German states, under Prussia's leadership, were unified into a German nation. The steps involved in this process were carried out according to Bismarck's goals. These were to strengthen Prussia and then take appropriate measures against Austria and France. Pursuit of these goals led Prussia to fight in three wars; in 1864 with Denmark, in 1866 with Austria, and in 1870 to 1871 with France.

Strengthening Prussia

When Bismarck was appointed Prussia's prime minister in 1862, he found the kingdom to be enjoying economic prosperity. He wanted to maintain this, while increasing Prussia's military might. Accordingly, he frequently asked the Prussian parliament to raise taxes and approve funds for reorganizing the army and giving it more weapons. And just as frequently, parliament turned him down. Many of its members were liberals who distrusted Bismarck and opposed his obvious militaristic policies. Not to be outdone, Bismarck would often dissolve parliament, raise taxes with the king's consent, and call for elections to a new legislature. His collection and spending of monies violated the Prussian constitution, as did his censorship of newspapers and restrictions on anyone who criticized him. With the support of an expanding army, many of whose officers were Junkers, and with the cooperation of the king, Bismarck practically ruled Prussia as a dictator. Much of his success in ruling with a weak—sometimes without any—parliament was due to a strong public feeling of nationalism that made many overlook his autocratic behavior. In addition, his success in foreign policy overshadowed any concerns about domestic policy.

The Danish War (1864)

This brief war illustrated the shrewd and deceptive diplomatic maneuvering of Bismarck to achieve both short-term and long-range goals. In the short run, he wanted to obtain more land for Prussia and increase its prestige; in the long run, he wanted to reduce Austria's status. Strangely, this war began with Prussia and Austria as allies against Denmark in a dispute over the states of Schleswig and Holstein. Holstein was populated mainly by Germans and belonged to the German Confederation. Schleswig had a mix of both Germans and Danes. Although not actually part of Denmark, both sides had been ruled by the Danish King. Under a new constitution in 1863, the King claimed that the states belonged to him, and he announced that he was about to **annex** Schleswig first. He dismissed the protests about his intentions from Prussia and Austria, whereupon they both declared war against Denmark. Denmark was no match against their combined armies and surrendered after only three months of fighting.

> **Main Idea:**
> In the treaty ending the war, Denmark agreed to give up both Schleswig and Holstein.

In the treaty ending the war, Denmark agreed to give up both Schleswig and Holstein. Austria assumed that Prussia and Austria would jointly control the two states. Austria also moved to have both states combine into a single state and then become part of the German Confederation. Bismarck contested this, standing up to Austria. After bitter arguments, it was decided that Prussia would administer Schleswig and Austria would administer Holstein. This decision was not to Austria's liking, as Bismarck well knew, and was part of his anti-Austrian policy.

The Seven Weeks' War, or Austro-Prussian War (1866)

Bismarck's anti-Austrian policy was not aimed at destroying Austria, but at isolating it and reducing its power among the German states. He would then be free of Austria as an obstacle in his path toward establishing a Prussian-dominated German nation. He felt that war was bound to occur and that he had to be ready, both militarily and diplomatically. Military preparedness progressed well under von Moltke. Diplomatically, Bismarck made some wise arrangements. He signed a secret treaty with the new Kingdom of Italy, promising to give it Austrian-controlled Venetia if Italy helped Prussia in a war with Austria. Bismarck did this, aware that he was violating a rule of the German Confederation that prohibited one member from signing a treaty of alliance with a foreign nation against another member. Concerned that France might aid Austria in a war, Bismarck convinced France to stay out of any conflict. He vaguely suggested to France that he would not stand in France's way if it were to annex Belgium. France agreed, assuming that a German civil war would weaken both Prussia and Austria and thus leave France with limp, disunited neighbors on its eastern border. Bismarck had also paved the way to keep Russia out of any conflict, as he had previously signed a treaty with that country promising Prussian help if Russia had to put down a revolt in Poland.

Another dispute between Prussia and Austria arose over the Schleswig-Holstein Question. This dispute led to the Austro-Prussian War of 1866, in which most German states, afraid of Prussian might and sharing a common religious tie of Catholicism with Austria, took the Austrian side. A few states took Prussia's side. In what thus amounted to a German civil war, Prussia won a quick, stunning victory. The war was over so soon that it has also been called the Seven Weeks' War. Von Moltke's troops fought with advanced weapons, while making effective use for that time of such technology as the railroad and the telegraph. His forces were much better trained and organized than were those of Austria. The most crushing Prussian victory was the Battle of Sadowa. The *Treaty of Prague* ended the wars and contained these provisions:

Main Idea:
In what thus amounted to a German civil war, Prussia won a quick, stunning victory.

1. The German Confederation was dissolved. A new association was to be created of most German states, but without Austria and four south German states. (In 1867, the association became known as the North German Confederation.)
2. Schleswig-Holstein was to be added to Prussia.
3. Venetia would be added to Italy.
4. Austria was to pay Prussia a small **indemnity** (amount of money for losing the war).

Austria was treated leniently in this treaty. Such was Bismarck's intent, even though Prussian King William fiercely opposed him and wanted to humiliate Austria. Bismarck's generosity was not the result of any special kindness nor humanitarian gesture. He reasoned that Prussia might need Austria's help at some future time. And as the 1860s drew to a close, Prussia comfortably found itself as the leader of the twenty-one-member North German Confederation—a union of almost all the German states. Yet, it realized that the last obstacle remained on the path to a fully united nation.

The Franco-Prussian War (1870–1871)

In his book *Reminiscences*, written sometime after the 1870s, Bismarck says: "I assumed that a united Germany was only a question of time, and that the North German Confederation was only the first step in its solution . . . but I did not doubt that a war with France must take place before a united Germany could be realized." The war that Bismarck felt was inevitable would be important to him in two specific ways:

1. It would produce a patriotic feeling and a sense of nationalism among all Germans in a struggle against a common enemy.
2. It would persuade the four south German states, mainly Catholic and somewhat concerned about being part of a nation led by Protestant Prussia, that they would be better off, more prosperous, and safer in union with Prussia.

As much as Bismarck was edging toward a confrontation with France, he was aware that the French themselves were thinking about going to war. France was growing extremely worried about the growth of German unity and power to its east. Some Frenchmen even took up the cry "Revenge for Sadowa," angered at Prussia's defeat of Austria in the battle. Others believed that, during the 1860s, France had suffered a loss of prestige in foreign affairs. A war might now help to regain prestige and respect.

An air of tension was evident among French and Germans as the 1870s began. In newspapers and speeches, bitter words and accusations were exchanged. In such an atmosphere, Bismarck did not want to appear as the aggressor. He thought it would be better to make France look like the one responsible for a conflict. The opportunity to do this arose in a very unlikely manner, regarding the throne of Spain. With their throne vacant, the Spaniards offered it to Prince Leopold, a Hohenzollern relative of Prussian King William. If Leopold accepted this offer, it would anger France for fear of a possible Spanish-Prussian alliance. Leopold at first accepted the offer but then changed his mind. This would have ended the matter, but the French wanted to be sure that no Hohenzollern would ever become king of Spain. To achieve this goal, France wanted such a promise from the head of all the Hohenzollerns, Prussian King William. The French minister made this demand upon the king at the town

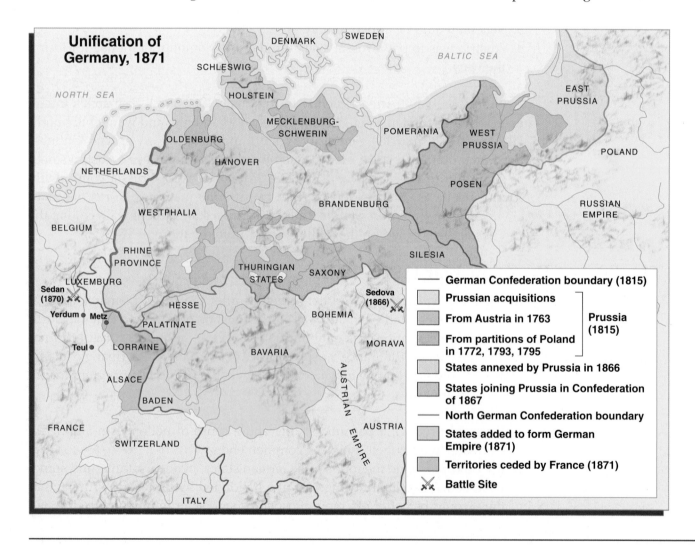

Unification of Germany, 1871

Legend:
— German Confederation boundary (1815)
Prussian acquisitions
From Austria in 1763 — Prussia (1815)
From partitions of Poland in 1772, 1793, 1795 — Prussia (1815)
States annexed by Prussia in 1866
States joining Prussia in Confederation of 1867
— North German Confederation boundary
States added to form German Empire (1871)
Territories ceded by France (1871)
✕✕ Battle Site

The Proclamation of the German Empire in the Galerie des Glaces at Versailles, January 18, 1871: oil on canvas by Anton von Werner.

Main Idea:
The mood in Paris was that French forces would easily cross the Rhine River and that the Catholic south German states would warmly welcome them. Tragically for France, these expectations proved to be completely unrealistic.

of Ems. The king refused to give in to the demand and sent a telegram to Bismarck describing the events at Ems. Bismarck now edited the telegram in such a way that it appeared as if the French minister and the Prussian king had insulted each other. Bismarck then released the telegram for publication by the press. It became known as the *Ems Dispatch* and had the effect of inciting both French and Germans. It was timed to be published July 14, 1870. As this was France's Independence Day, French patriotism was duly aroused, with crowds in Paris shouting for war with Prussia and screaming, *"A Berlin, A Berlin"* ("On to Berlin"). On the same day in Berlin, having heard about the dispatch, crowds emotionally spoke out for war with France. On July 19, 1870, France declared war on Prussia. The Franco-Prussian War had begun!

France boasted that its army was prepared, with its war minister stating that all was ready even "down to the last button . . . of the last soldier." The mood in Paris was that French forces would easily cross the Rhine River and that the Catholic south German states would warmly welcome them. Tragically for France, these expectations proved to be completely unrealistic. Its army was disorganized and was short of ammunition, food, and transportation. It never reached German soil. The south German states immediately sided with Bismarck, adding to his already impressive military forces. Under von Moltke, these well-equipped forces moved quickly to the French border and won several battles. One of the most significant was at Sedan in September 1870. A French army of 120,000 men was defeated, with Emperor Napoleon III of France taken as prisoner. Prussian forces soon thereafter surrounded Paris.

On January 18, 1871, with Paris facing starvation and collapse, a historical event occurred in the nearby Palace of Versailles. In its famous Hall of Mirrors, built and often walked through by King Louis XIV, the German Empire was proclaimed. Prussia's **King William I** became Emperor **William I (Kaiser Wilhelm)** in the presence of Bismarck and many German princes and statesmen. The North German Confederation was abolished. The new union, the German Empire, contained both northern and southern states. Unification had been achieved. The nation of Germany was a reality.

Less than two weeks later, on January 28, 1871, Paris surrendered. Negotiations for peace were concluded with the Treaty of Frankfurt in May. Its harsh provisions were dictated by Bismarck:

1. France would cede Alsace and Lorraine to Germany.
2. France would pay to Germany an indemnity of $1 billion.
3. France would support a German army of occupation until the entire amount of the indemnity was paid.

The treaty was a humiliation for France, stirring in its people a quest for revenge. The bitterness they felt went very deeply into their souls. Accordingly, tension between France and Germany continued right up to the moment of their next confrontation less than fifty years later, in World War I.

THE NEW NATION OF GERMANY

The Germany that was born with blood and iron in the second half of the nineteenth century began to build itself up as a major European power. It did things that had roots in the pre-1871 history of the German people, and also did things that would prove to be the basis for twentieth-century activities. We will now look at some of these things from 1871 to 1900 in terms of political, economic, and social policies.

Political Policies

The government was headed by Kaiser William I, who appointed Bismarck as chancellor (prime minister). A two-house parliament was created, consisting of the **Bundesrat** and the **Reichstag**. The Bundesrat was the upper house, whose members were appointed by the rulers of the twenty-five states. It had greater power than did the Reichstag, whose members were elected by the few people eligible to vote. Although there were several political parties in both houses, the kaiser and the chancellor controlled enough members to affect parliamentary decisions. Bismarck, in fact, was referred to as the **Iron Chancellor**. Both the kaiser and the chancellor had very few limits on their power; Germany was thus more an autocracy than a limited monarchy. In addition, because Prussia was more than half of the nation, it had enough representatives in both the Bundesrat and the Reichstag to influence legislation.

The government wanted Germany to be known as a great empire, or **Reich**. The kaiser was, therefore, the head of the Second Reich. (The Holy Roman Empire that had ruled the German people for centuries, until 1806, was considered to be the First Reich.) As we will see, the Second Reich was to last for forty-seven years, 1871 to 1918. During that time, the government adopted

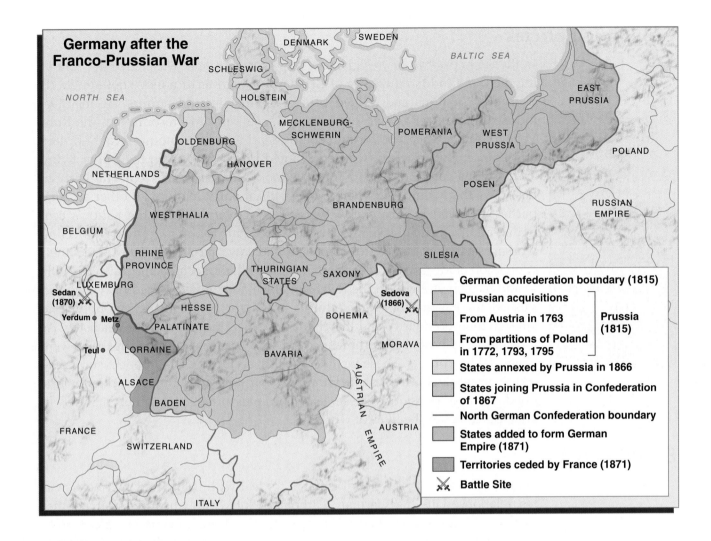

Germany after the Franco-Prussian War

Legend:
- German Confederation boundary (1815)
- Prussian acquisitions
- From Austria in 1763
- From partitions of Poland in 1772, 1793, 1795 } Prussia (1815)
- States annexed by Prussia in 1866
- States joining Prussia in Confederation of 1867
- North German Confederation boundary
- States added to form German Empire (1871)
- Territories ceded by France (1871)
- ✕ Battle Site

Main Idea:
Although William I had been content to let Bismarck act on his behalf, this was not true for his grandson.

policies that it felt were necessary for Germany to be regarded as a major power—militarism and imperialism. Militarism could be seen in the continued buildup of the army and navy. Imperialism referred to acquiring **colonies** overseas, something that several other European nations had begun to do in the nineteenth century. In Chapter 6 in this volume, we will examine Germany's role in the race for colonies. Both militarism and imperialism would be underlying factors for the terrible conflicts in 1914 and 1939 that became World Wars I and II.

In 1888, when William I died, his sickly son continued the Hohenzollern line as Frederick III. After Frederick's brief reign of three months, his son became Kaiser William II (r. 1888–1918). Although William I had been content to let Bismarck act on his behalf, this was not true for his grandson. William II and Bismarck did not get along very well. William was unwilling to let Bismarck continue to have a dominant role in affairs of state. Bismarck, in turn, was upset at this attitude. Both men disagreed on issues concerning Russia and laws dealing with the Social Democrat Party. Finally, in 1890, the Kaiser forced Bismarck to resign as chancellor.

Economic Policies

Main Idea: Bismarck now changed his views and pushed for passage of many reforms asked for by the socialists, hoping to weaken their popularity and thereby reduce their numbers in the Reichstag.

In the years prior to his resignation, however, Bismarck was active in promoting the rapid industrialization of Germany. A high-tariff policy kept out goods from other nations and helped protect German manufacturers. As the steel industry progressed, based upon the rich coal and iron resources in the Ruhr Valley, Germany became very prosperous and was an economic rival of Britain and France. Nevertheless, workers wanted improvements in their poor living and working conditions. Many of them looked to the Social Democrat Party to pass laws that would help them. This political party, along with other socialist parties, believed in greater involvement by government in the nation's economic affairs. Bismarck feared these parties and the many reforms affecting workers that they hoped to enact. He had laws passed that restricted their expression of ideas in speeches and in print. Still, the social democrats were able to add to their strength in the Reichstag. Bismarck now changed his views and pushed for passage of many reforms asked for by the socialists, hoping to weaken their popularity and thereby reduce their numbers in the Reichstag. As a result, the German government voted into law several measures that were beneficial to workers. These included health, accident, and old-age insurance—a kind of social security system. Other laws provided for limited working hours, holidays, and pensions. These laws became models for other nations, in attempts to better the lives of workers.

Social Policies

Main Idea: Citizens of non-German descent were often pressured to adopt German ways.

One of the bitterest issues for Bismarck to deal with in the new Germany was his relations with the German Catholics. Unlike the disputes that another German, Martin Luther, had with the Catholic Church, Bismarck's chief problems dealt more with political and economic issues rather than religious ones. Most German Catholics lived in the south and favored a weak central government. They formed a political party, the Center Party, which opposed Bismarck's wish to create a strong centralized government. The Catholics also had ties to the pope and felt that Church lands in Germany should be controlled by him rather than by the predominantly Protestant German government. For Bismarck, therefore, such attitudes by Catholics were threats to German unity and showed a lack of nationalism. He thus mounted a nonviolent attack on the Catholic Church, called the *kulturkampf* (struggle for civilization). In 1872, severe laws were enacted to control activities of Catholics: Priests were put under government authority and were not allowed to criticize the government, Catholic schools were closed, Jesuits were expelled from Germany, and only civil marriage ceremonies were permitted. In spite of these actions, Catholic resistance increased as did the number of Reichstag seats won by the Center Party. As was the case with the Social Democrat Party, Bismarck now began to change his views. Between 1878 and 1887, he had almost all the anti-Catholic legislation **repealed** (removed as laws). Even many Protestants had urged him to do this, alarmed at some features of the *kulturkampf*.

Although no *kulturkampf* was carried out against other minorities in Germany, there existed prejudicial and at times harsh attitudes toward such peoples. They included Germans who were of Danish, French, and Polish descent, as well as German Jews. Citizens of non-German descent were often pressured to adopt German ways. Jews were falsely accused as threats to the nation by an adviser to the kaiser, Adolf Stocker, while Bismarck tried to blame Jews for his problems with the *kulturkampf*. These examples of **anti-Semitism** were to reach ghastly levels in the **Nazi Holocaust** of the twentieth century (see Chapter 11 in this volume).

SECTION SUMMARY

We referred to Cavour as hardheaded in Section 3, but the term certainly also applies to Bismarck—if not more so! Here was a man who dominated European politics during the last half of the nineteenth century. Nations were not able to act without taking into consideration the position of Bismarck and of a new and powerful nation in the center of Europe—Germany. He was totally dedicated to the accomplishment of unifying the German states into a nation that would become a dominant force on the continent. Every action he took was dedicated to that goal. He was able to accomplish what he wished because the people followed him, because he was able to dominate a weak king, and because there were not strong democratic traditions to overcome. He was shrewd enough to defeat Denmark quickly and not punish this small nation so that it wouldn't hate him. He was also smart enough to realize that Austria wasn't much of a military power and gained it as a friend after defeat, and he tricked Louis Napoleon into declaring war on him! The legacy of hatred he earned in France would come back to cause problems in the future, after a jealous William II finally forced Bismarck to resign.

LINK TO TODAY

Nationalism on Parade in New York City

The nationalist feelings described in this chapter led to pride and strong feelings of ethnic unity among the British, Irish, French, Italian, and German peoples. These feelings and emotions have found expression as members of these nationalities immigrated to the United States and built up large communities here. Because New York City was the port of entry and eventual home for major numbers of Irish, Italian, and German immigrants, their presence is reflected, for example, in several annual parades along Fifth Avenue. In September, one can view the Steuben Day parade. This event honors Baron von Steuben, a German who was active in the American Revolution. In October, many Italian flags wave in celebration of Columbus Day. Every March witnesses a sea of green, as Irish Americans proudly walk in the St. Patrick's Day parade. It should be noted, though, that such ethnic-oriented parades occur not just in New York but in many places throughout the United States. Such cultural expressions underscore one of our own nation's enduring phrases: *E Pluribus Unum* ("Out of many, one people").

CHAPTER SUMMARY

The political changes and nationalistic advances explored in this chapter help us to understand much about Western Europe in the nineteenth century. Such understanding is a guide for recognizing the existence in our own century of the nation-states we can now label and locate such as Britain, Ireland, France, Italy, and Germany. In the next chapter, we move to Eastern Europe to investigate the political changes and nationalistic trends in that region.

IMPORTANT PEOPLE, PLACES, AND TERMS

KEY TERMS

democracy	Commune of Paris	ethnic group
popular sovereignty	anti-Semitism	nationality
ballot	nationalism	nation
Industrial Revolution	culture	Zollverein
rotten boroughs	autonomy	constitution
pocket boroughs	ethnocentrism	emperor
suffrage	Risorgimento	divine right
franchise	Congress of Vienna	Junkers
Chartists	duchies	democracy
suffragettes	Renaissance	liberalism
universal suffrage	Carbonari	Hohenzollern Dynasty
Glorious Revolution	Young Italy	blood and iron
evolution	monarchy	annex
revolution	republic	Ems Dispatch
home rule	plebiscite	Bundesrat
Great Irish Famine	parliament	Reichstag
coffin ships	colonies	*kulturkampf*
Crimean War	empire	repealed
Franco-Prussian War	Congress of Vienna	Nazi Holocaust

PEOPLE

Benjamin Disraeli	Louis Blanc	Camillo Cavour
Emmeline Pankhurst	Napoleon III	Pope
King George V	Georges Haussmann	Victor Emmanuel II
Charles Parnell	Maximilian	King William I
William Gladstone	Otto von Bismarck	Helmuth von Moltke
Queen Victoria	Georges Boulanger	Kaiser Wilhelm I
Daniel O'Connell	Alfred Dreyfus	Iron Chancellor
Louis XVIII	Emile Zola	Heinrich von
Charles X	Giuseppe Mazzini	Treitschite
Louis Philippe	Giuseppe Garibaldi	

PLACES

London	Papal State	Prussia
Ulster	Sicily	Alsace and Lorraine
Ireland	Crimea	Italy
Sardinia	Paris	Rome

CHAPTER 3

MULTIPLE-CHOICE QUESTIONS

Select the number of the correct answer.

1. In the early 1800s the British system of voting was considered undemocratic by some because only one of the following groups was allowed to vote. Which one group was it?

   (1) farmers
   (2) middle-class merchants
   (3) women
   (4) male property owners

2. The First Reform Bill of 1832 in Great Britain accomplished which action to make the government more democratic?

   (1) Rural areas were given more seats in the House of Commons.
   (2) Property qualifications were lowered to allow people like bankers and factory owners the right to vote.
   (3) More members of the Tory Party were appointed as members of the House of Commons.
   (4) Women who owned property were granted suffrage.

3. By 1860 which two minorities were specifically given the right to serve in Parliament?

   (1) Catholics and Jews
   (2) Catholics and Tories
   (3) Jews and Whigs
   (4) Tories and Whigs

4. Emmeline Pankhurst was a British leader of the suffragette movement. This meant that she specifically wanted

   (1) public education for girls
   (2) the right to vote for women
   (3) equal pay for equal work
   (4) improved conditions in prisons

5. The British constitution might be considered unusual because it

   (1) is both written and unwritten
   (2) is entirely based on historic documents
   (3) has not been changed since the Reform Bills of the 1830s
   (4) has been changed as a result of violent revolutions

6. Which statement expresses an opinion about the Great Irish Famine?

   (1) The Irish relied on the potato as their chief food source.
   (2) A fungus caused the potato crop to fail.
   (3) When Irish tenant farmers couldn't pay their rents, they were evicted from the land.
   (4) Most Irish impacted by the famine were happy to leave Ireland for other countries.

7. Charles Parnell is remembered for his efforts to

   (1) improve Irish trade with Europe
   (2) strengthen the power of the Anglican Church in Ireland
   (3) obtain more legal benefits for the Irish in the English parliament
   (4) solve the immediate food shortages of the Irish famine

8. Which headline below best describes the period in France known as the "Bourbon restoration"?

   (1) "King Charles X Successful in Restoring Absolute Power to the French Monarchy"
   (2) "French Bourbon Restoration Struggles with Political Instability"
   (3) "Monarchs Maintain Power While Dealing with Changing Political Views"
   (4) "Bourbon Monarchs Unable to Maintain Power in Struggles with Parliament"

9. The Dreyfus affair was an example of

   (1) ethnocentrism
   (2) anti-Semitism
   (3) imperialism
   (4) militarism

10. French government in the nineteenth century was most accurately characterized by which term?

    (1) monarchy
    (2) dictatorship
    (3) democracy
    (4) oligarchy

11. During the first half of the nineteenth century, Prince Metternich of Austria called Italy a "geographic expression." This meant that Italy was

    (1) a united nation under one leader
    (2) a Catholic Kingdom led by the pope
    (3) a place on a map with some common aspects of culture
    (4) a territory that belonged to Austria and was governed by it

12. "I cannot make a speech but I can make Italy." Who said the above statement about Italian unification?

    (1) Giuseppe Mazzini
    (2) Giuseppe Garibaldi
    (3) Camillo Cavour
    (4) Victor Emmanuel

13. A plebiscite is a vote to determine if citizens of an area will

    (1) annex other territories
    (2) show confidence in their leader
    (3) participate in a revolution
    (4) become independent

14. Rome became the capital of Italy in 1870. Almost sixty years later what Italian area became a separate sovereign state?

    (1) Sardinia
    (2) Vatican City
    (3) Sicily
    (4) Trieste

15. Before the German states worked on their unification, Germans felt common bonds of

    (1) language
    (2) occupation
    (3) religion
    (4) government

16. King Frederick William IV of Prussia would not accept "a crown from the gutter" for a united Germany because he believed in

    (1) Austrian superiority
    (2) democratic elections
    (3) the divine right theory
    (4) parliamentary appointments

17. One of Bismarck's major goals was to

    (1) establish a Prussian-dominated German nation
    (2) join Italy and Germany to increase military power
    (3) unite Germany and Austria as equal legal partners
    (4) keep Russia out of wars with Prussia

18. The proclamation of the German Empire in 1871 could be considered somewhat surprising in that it formally occurred in

(1) Berlin's Reichstag Building
(2) Westminster Abbey in London
(3) St. Stephen's Cathedral in Vienna
(4) the Palace at Versailles near Paris

19. Place the events that follow in the correct chronological order:

A. German unification
B. The Great Irish Famine
C. The death of Queen Victoria
D. Italian unification

(1) B, A, C, D
(2) B, D, A, C
(3) A, B, C, D
(4) D, A, B, C

20. Which conclusion would be appropriate to apply to nineteenth-century Europe?

(1) The century was characterized by major cultural and scientific advances with the wealthy paying little attention to government.
(2) Natural disasters caused major loss of life in several European nations.
(3) Most governmental leaders were slow to enact political changes.
(4) Ethnic differences were related to such events as regional wars and the formation of new countries.

THEMATIC ESSAY

Directions: Write a well-organized essay that includes an introduction, several paragraphs addressing the task below, and a conclusion.

Theme: Turning Points

Turning points are major events in history that have led to lasting change.

Task

Identify **two** major turning points in nineteenth-century European history and for each

- describe the historical circumstances surrounding the turning point
- explain how **each** turning point changed the course of a European nation's history

You may use any example from nineteenth-century European history. Some suggestions you might wish to consider include English reform bills, the Great Irish Famine, establishment of nineteenth-century French republics, Italian unification, and German unification.

You are not limited to these suggestions.

Do *not* use any turning points in United States History.

Guidelines

In your essay, be sure to

- develop all aspects of the *Task*
- support the theme with relevant facts, examples, and details
- use a logical and clear plan of organization, including an introduction and a conclusion that are beyond a restatement of the theme
- introduce the theme by establishing a framework that is beyond a simple restatement of the *Task* and conclude with a summation of the theme

DOCUMENT-BASED ESSAY QUESTION

This question is based on the accompanying documents (1–9). The question is designed to test your ability to work with historical documents. Some of the documents have been edited for the purposes of the question. As you analyze the documents, take into account the source of each document and any point of view that may be presented in the document.

Historical Context

Geographic and environmental conditions are often linked to the pursuit of nationalistic goals. In nineteenth-century Europe, Ireland, the German states, and the Italian states all struggled with geographic and/or environmental issues in their efforts to promote nationalism.

Task

Using information from the documents and your knowledge of global history, answer the questions that follow each document in Part A. Your answers to the questions will help you write the Part B essay in which you will be asked to do the following.

Select two areas (Ireland, Germany, **and/or** Italy) and for each area selected

- identify a geographic **and/or** environmental issue that caused problems for the area in its pursuit of nationalism
- describe how a leader **and/or** the people of the area worked to solve the problem identified above
- evaluate the outcome of the effort made to achieve nationalism

Part A: Short Answer Questions

Directions: Analyze the documents and answer the short answer questions that follow each document.

Document 1   Field Marshal Helmuth von Moltke: 1866

The war of 1866 [between Prussia and Austria] was entered on not because the existence of Prussia was threatened, nor was it caused by public opinion and the voice of the people; it was a struggle, long foreseen and calmly prepared for, recognized as a necessity by the Cabinet, not for territorial aggrandizement, for an extension of our domain, or for material advantage, but for an ideal end—the establishment of power. Not a foot of land was exacted from Austria, but she had to renounce all part in the hegemony of Germany. . . Austria had exhausted her strength in conquests south of the Alps, and left the western German provinces unprotected, instead of following the road pointed out by the Danube. Its center of gravity lay out of Germany; Prussia's lay within it. Prussia felt itself called upon and strong enough to assume the leadership of the German races.

Questions
     1. a. According to Field Marshal Helmuth von Moltke, why did Prussia enter into a war with Austria?
         b. Identify one geographic issue mentioned by von Moltke.

Document 2

"Why should Ireland be treated as a geographical fragment of England? Ireland is not a geographical fragment, but a nation."

Charles Parnell, Ireland (1846–1891)

Question

2. What was Parnell protesting about the treatment of Ireland?

Document 3

Question

3. What are two factors suggested by the map that might make German unification difficult?
   a.
   b.

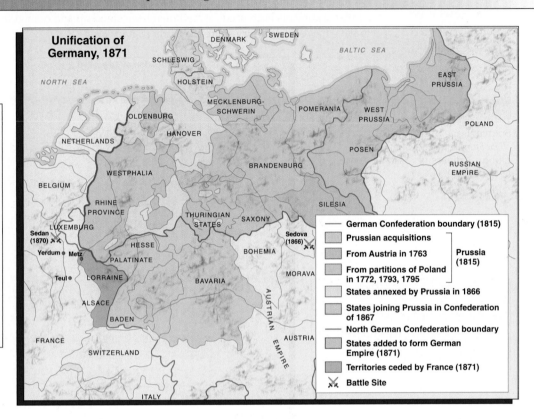

Unification of Germany, 1871

DENMARK, SWEDEN, BALTIC SEA, SCHLESWIG, HOLSTEIN, EAST PRUSSIA, NORTH SEA, MECKLENBURG-SCHWERIN, POMERANIA, WEST PRUSSIA, POLAND, OLDENBURG, HANOVER, NETHERLANDS, POSEN, WESTPHALIA, BRANDENBURG, RUSSIAN EMPIRE, BELGIUM, RHINE PROVINCE, THURINGIAN STATES, SAXONY, SILESIA, LUXEMBURG, Sedan (1870), Sedova (1866), HESSE, BOHEMIA, Yerdum, Metz, PALATINATE, MORAVA, Teul, LORRAINE, BAVARIA, ALSACE, AUSTRIAN EMPIRE, BADEN, FRANCE, AUSTRIA, SWITZERLAND, ITALY

Legend:
- German Confederation boundary (1815)
- Prussian acquisitions
- From Austria in 1763 } Prussia (1815)
- From partitions of Poland in 1772, 1793, 1795
- States annexed by Prussia in 1866
- States joining Prussia in Confederation of 1867
- North German Confederation boundary
- States added to form German Empire (1871)
- Territories ceded by France (1871)
- Battle Site

Document 4

Count Cavour

Speech to the Piedmont Chamber of Deputies, 1858:

Questions

4.
a. What is a problem Count Cavour recognizes in his efforts to achieve Italian unification?
b. What factor does Cavour say is already working to unite Italians?

After the disaster of Novara and the Peace of Milan [1849], two courses were open to us. We could, bowing to adverse fate, renounce all the aspirations which had guided King Carlo Alberto during the last years of his reign, seal ourselves up within our frontiers, think only of the material and moral interests of this country [Piedmont-Sardinia]. . . On the other hand, we could, while accepting all the hardships imposed by accomplished facts, keep alive the faith that inspired the great actions of King Carlo Alberto, and, while declaring our firm intention to respect treaties, maintain in the political sphere the enterprise which was defeated in the military sphere [Italian unification]. . . In recent years, therefore, we have tried to do away with the last hindrances to our country, and we have lost no occasion to act as the spokesman and defender of the other peoples of Italy. This policy found one such occasion in the Crimean War. . . .Our hopes were not disappointed in regard to the credit that Piedmont would acquire. As for the defense of the rights of Italy, that was our task in the course of the Congress of Paris. . . .it was an outstanding fact that the cause of Italy was for the first time supported by an Italian power.

Document 5

Question

5. According to Isaac Butt, what are two reasons why the Irish are dissatisfied with the English?
   a.   b.

Can we wonder if the Irish people believe that the lives of those who have perished have been sacrificed by a deliberate compact to the gains of English merchants and if this belief has created among all classes a feeling of deep dissatisfaction, not only with the ministry but with English rule. What can be more absurd, what can be more wicked, than for men professing attachment to an imperial Constitution to answer claims now put forward for state assistance to the unprecedented necessities of Ireland, by talking of Ireland being a drain upon the English treasury? If Cornwall (England) had been visited with the scenes that have desolated Cork (Ireland), would similar arguments been used? Would men have stood up and denied that Cornwall was entitled to have the whole country share the extraordinary loss?

Source: Isaac Butt, *"The Famine in the Land,"* Dublin University Magazine, XXIX, April 1847.

Document 6

Question

6. What are two geographic factors could hinder Italian efforts at unification?

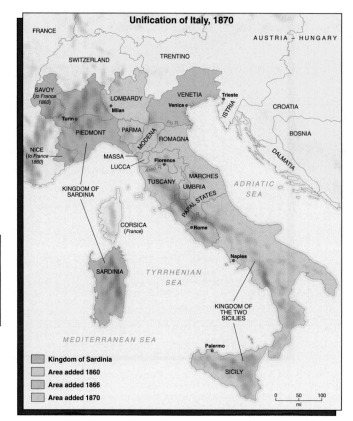

Document 7

Question

7. Why does Otto von Bismarck think that Germany must at some time fight with Austria?

Otto von Bismarck:

Letter to Minister von Manteuffel, 1856

Because of the policy of Vienna [the Congress of Vienna, 1815], Germany is clearly too small for us both [Prussia and Austria]; as long as an honorable arrangement concerning the influence of each in Germany cannot be concluded and carried out, we will both plough the same disputed acre, and Austria will remain the only state to whom we can permanently lose or from whom we can permanently gain. . . .I wish only to express my conviction that, in the not too distant future, we shall have to fight for our existence against Austria and that it is not within our power to avoid that, since the course of events in Germany has no other solution.

Document 8

The English government provided work for people who love it not. The government was required to prevent starvation, not to reward laziness. Its duty was to encourage the growth of industry in Ireland, not to prevent it. Its task was to stimulate others to give people jobs, not to outbid them, or drive them from the labor markets. The problem is that the Irish peasant tasted of famine and found that it was good.

The worst symptoms of the Irish famine are that the people may become rebellious. Fear and Rumor make the situation dangerous. The Irish people report the worst and believe the worst. England is blamed for making a disaster caused by Heaven even worse. Instead of accepting that the potato blight was an act of God, the Irish complain about the government. The potatoes were destroyed by a decree from on high. Such are the thanks that the government gets for attempting to relieve great suffering.

Edited for the purposes of *The Great Irish Famine Curriculum*.

Questions

8. a. What is the attitude of the editorial writer of the *London Times* toward the Irish people?
   b. According to this editor, what was the cause of the Irish Famine?

Document 9

"A Country is not a mere territory; the particular territory is only its foundation. The Country is the idea which rises upon that foundation; it is the sentiment of love, the sense of fellowship which binds together all the sons of that territory."

Guiseppe Mazzini
Italian propagandist and revolutionary, founder of the secret revolutionary society Young Italy (1832), 1805–1872

Question

9. What is Mazzini trying to encourage in his statement?

Part B: Essay

Directions: Write a well-organized essay that includes an introduction, several paragraphs, and a conclusion. Use evidence from *at least five* documents in the body of the essay. Support your response with relevant facts, examples, and details. Include additional outside information.

Historical Context

Geographic and environmental conditions are often linked to the pursuit of nationalistic goals. In nineteenth century Europe, Ireland, the German states, and the Italian states all struggled with geographic **and/or** environmental issues in their efforts to promote nationalism.

Task

Using information from the documents and your knowledge of global history, write an essay in which you will be asked to do the following.

Select **two** areas (Ireland, Germany, **and/or** Italy) and for each area selected

- identify a geographic **and/or** environmental issue that caused problems for the area in its pursuit of nationalism
- describe how a leader **and/or** the people of the area worked to solve the problem identified above
- evaluate the outcome of the effort made to achieve nationalism

Guidelines

In your essay, be sure to

- address all four aspects of the *Task* by accurately analyzing and interpreting *at least five* documents
- incorporate information from *at least five* of the documents in the body of the essay
- incorporate relevant outside information
- support the theme with relevant facts, examples, and details
- use a logical and clear plan of organization
- introduce the theme by establishing a framework that is beyond a simple restatement of the *Task* or *Historical Context* and conclude with a summation of the theme

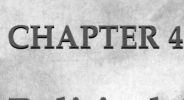

CHAPTER 4

Political Change and Global Nationalism— Eastern Europe

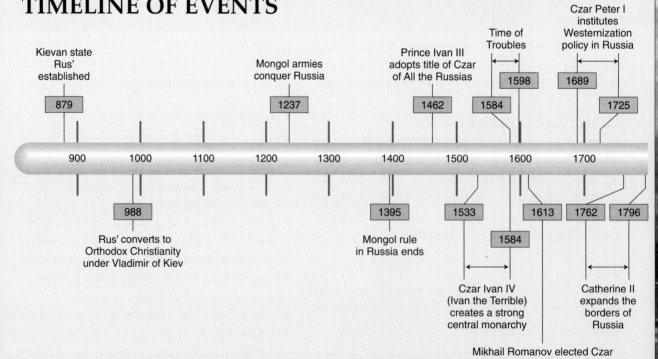

TIMELINE OF EVENTS

Kievan state Rus' established
879

Mongol armies conquer Russia
1237

Prince Ivan III adopts title of Czar of All the Russias
1462

Time of Troubles
1598
1584

Czar Peter I institutes Westernization policy in Russia
1689
1725

900 1000 1100 1200 1300 1400 1500 1600 1700

988
Rus' converts to Orthodox Christianity under Vladimir of Kiev

1395
Mongol rule in Russia ends

1533
1584
Czar Ivan IV (Ivan the Terrible) creates a strong central monarchy

1613
Mikhail Romanov elected Czar
Foundation of Romanov Dynasty

1762
1796
Catherine II expands the borders of Russia

Czarist Russia

The importance of **Czarist Russia** in European history, particularly in the nineteenth and twentieth centuries, was enormous. A vast empire that stretched from Eastern Europe to the Pacific, it produced a fascinating civilization full of contrasts and contradictions. A combination of many cultural influences, the Russian Empire created its own unique identity. The impact of Russia on Eastern Europe was especially important as it shaped the development of that region. Czarist Russia's influence politically, and its contributions culturally, had a great impact on modern Western Civilization.

EARLY HISTORY (600–1689)

Kievan Rus' (879–1237)

The earliest settlers in Russia were **Slavic tribes** who migrated there between 600 and 700. In developing trade (furs, beeswax, and honey) rather than agriculture, their settlements grew from towns to prosperous cities. These cities

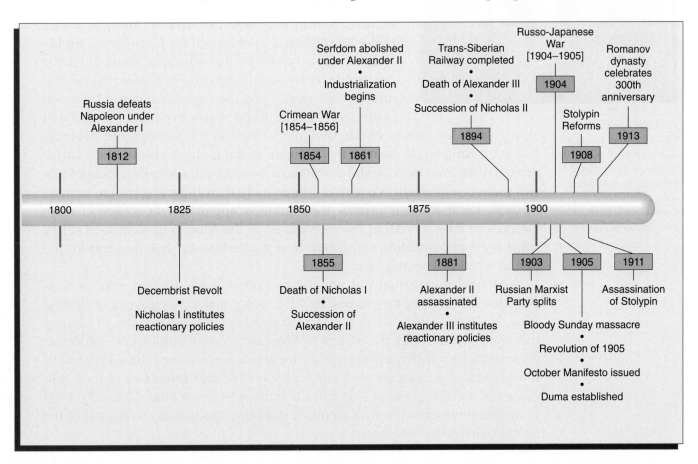

depended on **Scandinavian Vikings**, whom the Slavs called **Varangians**, to protect them and their trade routes. The Varangians became the ruling class, intermarrying with the Slavs, founding a new state, **Rus'**, and a royal dynasty, the **House of Rurik**. By 879, a loose union of **semiautonomous** (partly independent) city-states under the leadership of a prince at **Kiev** was established. The **Kievan state** became a center of trade. It was located in the **Ukraine**, the most fertile region of Russia, with excellent river transportation. It became powerful and wealthy, establishing a close relationship with the **Byzantine Empire** (see Chapter 5 in *Global History, Volume One*).

The Conversion of Rus'

Vladimir I (956?–1015). First Christian ruler of Kievan Rus', c. 978–1015. St. Vladimir the Great between his murdered sons, Saints Boris and Gleb. Detail of a Russian icon, Moscow School.

In 988, Prince Vladimir (r. 978–1015) was converted to Eastern Orthodox Christianity, bringing Kiev and all Rus' with him. With the adoption of the Byzantine faith came cultural, artistic, and social influences. Rus' was also brought into the political orbit of Byzantium and its Eastern European allies, known collectively as the **Byzantine Commonwealth** (see Chapter 5 in *Global History, Volume One*). Under Byzantine influence, Kievan culture attained a high level of sophistication, with a highly educated upper class.

Appanage Russia (1237–1480)

In 1237, Kievan Rus' was invaded by **Mongol** armies under **Batu Khan**, a grandson of the legendary **Genghis Khan**. Called **Tartars** by the Russians, these nomadic Asiatic horsemen conquered most of Russia and ruled it for over 200 years. Only the city of **Novgorod** (founded by the legendary Rurik) was able to remain independent by repulsing the attacks of the Mongols, as well as the **Swedes** and **Teutonic** (German) **Knights**. Known as the **Khanate** of the **Golden Horde**, the Mongol princes ruled from their capital city of **Sarai**, located in the **steppes**. Mongol rule was indirect and usually consisted of little more than collecting tribute from its subjects. Local Russian princes were granted **appanages** (a source of extra income) or they served as representatives of the Mongol government. They ruled their principalities with little, if any, interference. For this reason, the period is called Appanage Russia.

Mongol domination did not last as uprisings by Russian princes overextended Mongol military forces. By 1395, every major Mongol city, including Sarai, had been destroyed. Between 1450 and 1480, the last remains of Mongol rule were wiped out by the princes of **Moscow.** Mongol domination cut Russia off from contact with the West just as the Renaissance started, thus isolating it. It also made the Russians extremely conservative and protective of their religious and social traditions. This attitude is the reason that later rulers who tried to carry out reforms met with so much stubborn opposition on the part of the nobility, clergy, and peasantry.

The Moscovite State (1462–1689)

Ivan III (1440–1505). Called Ivan the Great. Grand Duke of Russia, 1462–1505. Color woodcut, 16th century.

Moscow soon rose to prominence among the Russian cities, especially after it became the seat of the **Russian Orthodox Patriarchate**. The Patriarch's presence enhanced the image of the city. When the Byzantine Empire fell to the **Ottoman Turks** in 1453, **Prince Ivan (John) III** (r. 1462–1505) declared Moscow to be the *Third Rome* or center of the Byzantine tradition and Eastern Orthodox Church (**Constantinople** took the title of Second Rome after the fall of the original capital city of Rome in 476). In 1462, Ivan married **Sophia Paleologus**, niece of the last Byzantine emperor, and adopted the imperial Byzantine coat-of-arms (the double-headed eagle), declaring himself **czar** or **caesar** (emperor) **of all the Russias**. The claim to be the sole ruler of Russia was a recognition of the power the princes of Moscow had in fact accumulated.

Under **Czar Ivan (John) IV "the Terrible"** (r. 1533–1584) the dream of the Moscovite princes to rule all of Russia was finally fulfilled. Always a person who brought out both admiration and fear in people, Ivan's reign was key to the establishment of a powerful central government and absolute monarchy. In the earlier part of his reign, he was a popular czar who regained much of European Russia from the Mongols. The later part of his rule was one of terror. Ivan used brutal and ruthless force against the local princes and **boyars** (nobles). By the end of his reign, he had ended their independent authority and made them subservient to the monarchy. He also created a new **"service nobility"** that was loyal to the czar. Suffering from depression and paranoia in his last years, Ivan killed his eldest son and heir in a fit of rage. This left Russia wih a weak and possibly mentally defective successor, **Czar Feodor (Theodore)** (r. 1584–1598) who died without an heir. This began a period of **anarchy** (disorder) known as the "Time of Troubles." Feodor's chief minister, the boyar **Boris Godunov**, became czar after his death. Rumors soon circulated, however, that he had murdered Feodor's younger brother **Dimitrii** in order to take the throne. Despite being

> **Main Idea:**
> Under **Czar Ivan (John) IV "the Terrible"** (r. 1533–1584) the dream of the Moscovite princes to rule all of Russia was finally fulfilled.

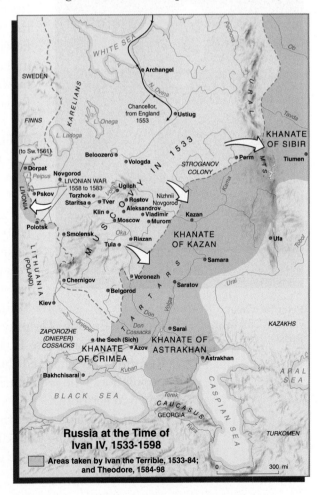

Russia at the Time of Ivan IV, 1533–1598

Areas taken by Ivan the Terrible, 1533–84; and Theodore, 1584–98

Michael Romanov
(1596–1645). Russian
czar, 1613–1645.
Colored engraving,
19th century.

an effective leader both in foreign and domestic affairs, Boris Godunov became unpopular and a target for ambitious nobles who wanted power. In 1604, Russia was invaded by a Polish army led by an individual pretending to be the dead Czarevich Dimitrii. This began a period of civil war during which Godunov died and Poland temporarily dominated Russia. This ended in 1613 with the selection of a new czar, **Mikhail (Michael) Romanov** (r. 1613–1645), by the **Zemskii Sobor** (Council of Nobles). The Romanov dynasty ruled Russia for the next 300 years.

CZARIST RUSSIA (1689–1917)

Westernization Under Peter the Great (1689–1725)

Under the first Romanovs, the monarchy grew strong, and Russia's borders expanded. The reign of **Peter (Piotr) I "the Great"** (r. 1689–1725) was a turning point in Russian history. Beginning a policy of "**Westernization**," Peter introduced Western European customs, technology, and industries to his nation. He even traveled to the West himself to learn Western technology firsthand, recruit craftsmen to bring back to Russia, and personally establish diplomatic relations with the rulers of Western Europe. Realizing that Russia had fallen behind the rest of Europe, the czar feared that it was in danger of being conquered by neighboring nations with modern armies, particularly **Sweden**. Peter modernized Russia's military and managed to defeat the Swedes, gaining the coastal regions along the **Baltic Sea** and the **Gulf of Finland**.

Peter the Great
(1672–1725). Czar of
Russia, 1682–1725. Oil
on canvas, 1717, by
Aert de Gelder.

Peter adopted the bureaucratic system of Western European monarchs to make government more efficient and absolute. When the Patriarch opposed these policies, the czar abolished the Patriarchate and established the **Holy Synod (Council of Bishops)**, tying the Church closer to the Autocracy. Peter built a new capital city, **Saint Petersburg**, on the shores of the Baltic, giving his new navy a limited sea route to Europe. He intended it to be a **"Window to the West,"** as it was modeled on the cities of Western Europe. Despite great opposition from the nobles and the Church, Peter did transform Russia into a modern power. However, the **Petrine Reforms** only changed the upper classes and the government. The bulk of the population, who were peasants, remained unaffected by the reforms, many tied down in serfdom.

Peter was a larger than life figure in many ways. He stood almost seven feet tall, possessing boundless energy and a violent temper. He was relentless in pursuing his goals and ruthless in putting down opposition. Like Ivan "the

The 12 colleges established in St. Petersburg by Peter the Great, beginning in 1722: contemporary engraving.

Terrible," he was responsible for the deaths of many, including his own son. His goal was to bring Russia "kicking and screaming" into the modern world. He did this at high cost to both his country and his family.

Russia's Expansion Under Catherine the Great (1762–1796)

Peter the Great was followed by a series of weak and incompetent rulers, yet the system he created continued to function. The reign of **Catherine (Ekaterina) II "the Great"** (r. 1762–1796) restored strong leadership. German by birth, Catherine married the weak and unpopular **Peter III** (r. 1762). Unlike her husband, her intelligence, energy, and personality made her popular with many in the Russian court. Catherine was well educated in the French language and culture as well as the ideas of the **Enlightenment** (see Chapter 20 in *Global History, Volume One*). She was also very ambitious and possessed a legendary appetite for power. With the assistance of the imperial guards, Catherine overthrew Peter and became czaritsa or empress.

> **Main Idea:** Catherine was well educated in the French language and culture as well as the ideas of the **Enlightenment.**

With many allies in both the military and nobility, Catherine established a strong and stable government. An **"enlightened despot,"** she addressed the need for domestic reform by attempting to change Russian law and abolish serfdom. The reforms were interrupted by the widespread and violent peasant revolt led by the Don Cossack **Emelian Pugachev,** which lasted from 1773 to 1774. Even though the rebellion was unsuccessful, it threatened the established order and put an end to any further reform.

Catherine was more successful in foreign policy. She renewed Russia's drive to expand its borders. In two successful wars against the Ottoman Empire between 1769 and 1792, she captured all the Turkish territory north of the **Black Sea** as far as the **Balkan Peninsula**. This included the **Crimea**, which gave Russia a limited warm water port. She also established Russia as the protector

Catherine II of Russia (1729–1796). Oil on canvas by Lampi.

of Eastern Orthodox Christians in the Ottoman Empire. This policy was aimed at gaining Constantinople in order to free access from the Black Sea to the **Mediterranean**. While Catherine's efforts fell short of this, she established it as a goal for her successors and made interference in Eastern Europe a traditional feature of Russian foreign policy (see Chapter 4, Section 2 in this volume). In addition, much of **Siberia** was explored and settled by the Russians in her reign. When Catherine died in 1796, Russia had become a vast empire and a major factor in world affairs.

Russia in the Napoleonic War (1801–1814)

After the brief reign of Catherine's incompetent son and successor **Paul (Pavel)** (r. 1796–1801), **Alexander (Aleksandr) I** (r. 1801–1825) carried on the Russian policy of expansion, gaining **Georgia** and **Finland**. In his early years, the czar made some attempts at internal reform, but he was forced to abandon them because they were too far-reaching for the time.

Alexander's fame rests in Russia's victory in the **Napoleonic Wars** (1799–1815). The Russian policy of the **"scorched earth"** (retreating and burning anything that could be used by the enemy), forced Napoleon to overextend his forces, resulting in his ultimate defeat. This brought both the czar and his nation great prestige (see Chapter 22 in *Global History, Volume One*).

Czar Alexander I of Russia (1777–1825). English stipple-and-line engraving, 1817.

The Decembrist rebels at Senate Square, St. Petersburg, Russia, 1825. Watercolor by Karl Kolman.

Reaction Under Nicholas I (1825–1855)

Alexander's brother and successor, **Nicholas (Nikolai) I** (r. 1825–1855) began his reign with the suppression of the **Decembrist Revolt**, an unsuccessful attempt by a group of reform-minded army officers to overthrow the autocracy and replace it with a constitutional monarchy. This made the new czar a **reactionary** (someone who is extremely opposed to change), with an exaggerated fear of revolution. He opposed any kind of internal reform and established a policy called **official nationality**, which promoted Russian nationalism and stressed its culture ("**Orthodoxy, Nationalism and Autocracy**"). A program called **Russification** was also followed, which forced non-Russian minorities to adopt the dominant culture or face discrimination. He ignored Russia's domestic problems, especially serfdom, which created great discontent among the population.

Nicholas also pursued the traditional policy of expansion and interference in Eastern Europe. Russia's disastrous involvement in the **Crimean War** (1854–1856) (see pp. 134–135) made it very clear that both modernization and internal reform were badly needed if Russia was to continue to remain a world power. Nicholas's death in 1855 brought an end to the conflict.

Nicholas I of Russia. Russian name, Nikolay Pavlovich (1796-1855): contemporary lithograph.

Reform Under Alexander II (1855–1881)

The reign of **Alexander (Aleksandr) II** (r. 1855–1881) brought much needed reforms to Russia. In 1861, he officially ended serfdom with the **Emancipation Edict**. Along with their freedom, the newly emancipated (freed) serfs received land, which they would pay for over a period of forty-nine years. The government also compensated the landowners for their losses. Full ownership of the land was given to village communes (*mir*), until the individual peasant paid his loan to the government. The land received by the peasants after emancipation was, however, insufficient to support their numbers while their loan payments placed a tremendous financial burden on them. Unable to compete with large landowners in a free market, many lost their farms and were forced into the cities, where they became factory workers.

The czar also established a system of elected rural assemblies (*zemstvo*), which were responsible for running local government (schools, orphanages, roads, bridges) and collecting taxes. This first Russian experiment in representative government was fairly successful. The legal system was also changed as the concept of equality before the law and trial by jury were adopted. Reforms were also made in education and the armed forces. The Russian military was modernized as well.

Czar Alexander II of Russia (1818–1881). American mezzotint, 1857.

Russian Village, 1861. Wood engraving, English, 1861.

The assassination of Alexander II at St. Petersburg, March 13, 1881. Contemporary drawing giving detailed information of the event.

Industrialization in Russia

Alexander began a program of industrialization in order to bring Russia's economy and technology up to date. With the benefits of industrialization, however, came its evils: slums, exploitation of workers, and urban unrest. The growth of

a **proletariat** (workers) class in Russia brought new support to the **revolutionary movement**, which had been growing since the 1870s. Beginning with the unsuccessful radical middle-class group called **S Narod** ("To the People") or **Narodniks**, the revolutionary movement turned to violence as fanatical intellectuals and students took charge. A new revolutionary organization, **The People's Will**, began committing acts of terrorism to force the government into further reforms. In 1881, terrorists assassinated Alexander.

Alexander III (1881–1894)

The Czar Liberator's successor, **Alexander (Aleksandr) III** (r. 1881–1894), was a determined autocrat who reacted to his father's assassination by crushing any revolt with force. With the **Okhrana** (Czarist Secret Police), he arrested, exe-

Czar Alexander III (1881–1894) with his family. The future Nicholas II, last of the czars, stands directly behind his father. Original cabinet photograph.

Count Sergei Y. Witte (1849–1915). Russian statesman.

cuted, or drove the bulk of the revolutionary movement into exile. The policies of Official Nationality and Russification were revived and increased as well. Censorship and controls on education and the arts were also tightened. There was a rise in persecutions of non-Russian minorities, especially against Jews. Bloody **pogroms** (anti-Jewish riots) caused many Jews to immigrate to the United States.

Alexander continued to develop the empire's industries. Under the guidance of Finance Minister **Sergei Witte**, Russia went on the **gold standard**, attracted foreign investment, expanded its industrial output, and completed the construction of the **Trans-Siberian Railway** (an engineering feat for that time), which connected European Russia with the Pacific.

Nicholas II (1894–1917)

Alexander III was succeeded by his well-intentioned, but weak son **Nicholas (Nikolai) II** (r. 1894–1917). Nicholas tried to pursue the policies of his father but lacked Alexander III's will and determination. His German-born wife, the **Czaritsa Alexandra**, was domineering and superstitious, often interfering in her husband's affairs and influencing his decisions. Their son, the **Czarevich Alexis (Aleksei)**, suffered from **hemophilia** (disease of excessive bleeding), which was kept a secret to maintain confidence in the continuity of the monarchy. This often resulted in behavior on the part of the royal couple that made them appear irresponsible and unfeeling. It also gave enormous influence to a corrupt and fraudulent "holy man," **Grigori Efimovich**, known as **Rasputin** (one who is given to immoral behavior), who was able to control the bleeding of the czarevich. He was often the cause of scandal and embarrassment for the royal family.

The Establishment of Marxist Revolutionary Parties

Nicholas was unable to repress the radical movements as effectively as his father. During his reign, revolutionary groups continued to develop. In 1898, Russian **Marxists** formed the **Social Democratic Party**, hoping to organize industrial workers into a revolutionary force. In 1903, they divided into two rival factions, the moderate Mensheviks, which means "minority," and the extremist **Bolsheviks**, or "majority." Ironically, the majority of Social Democrats were Mensheviks; while the Bolsheviks were few in number.

Led by **Vladimir Illich Ulianov**, known as **Nikolai Lenin** (1870–1924), the Bolsheviks were determined revolu-

Boys in a Russian shoe factory in 1888. Note the ubiquitous Singer sewing machine.

Grigori Efimovich Rasputin (1871?–1916). Russian monk.

tionaries who believed in using any means to achieve their goals. Lenin believed that the workers were not capable of revolution, which would ultimately be for their greatest benefit. It was therefore the duty of the Bolshevik Party to organize and lead them toward a complete overthrow of the existing order. In contrast, the Mensheviks believed that their duty was to represent the wishes of the workers. They worked toward peaceful change within the system, rather than advocate violent revolution. Unlike the Bolsheviks, who were a small and secret organization based on strict discipline, the Mensheviks were an extensive group divided into many disunified branches.

Despite the efforts of the government, these revolutionary groups were able to organize strikes and agitate workers in factories.

Bloody Sunday and the Revolution of 1905

In 1904, Russia went to war against Japan over possessions in Korea. Despite a superior military force, Russia was defeated because it overextended its supply lines. The loss in the **Russo-Japanese War** (1904–1905) aggravated the discontent that existed within the nation, especially in the cities. In January 1905, a peaceful demonstration to petition the czar for reforms was fired upon by troops. This resulted in a massacre, which became known as Bloody Sunday. The czar was blamed for the deaths (although he knew nothing about it until afterward), and given the name of Bloody Nicholas.

This event, combined with the humiliating defeat in Korea, discredited the monarchy and led to an uprising in Russia's cities known as the Revolution of 1905. The government was able to put down the rebellion, but with great difficulty. Hoping to stem the tide of revolution, the czar issued the October Manifesto of 1905, which established a parliament, the **Duma**, and granted a constitution. While the October Manifesto officially made Russia a constitutional monarchy, the Duma had limited powers and the nation continued to remain an autocracy.

The Stolypin Reforms

Fearful of future revolutions, Nikolai began to adopt reforms. Working with Prime Minister **Piotr Stolypin**, he passed several laws that encouraged the creation of independent farms and a conservative class of landowning peasants. Known as the **Stolypin Reforms**, these measures reduced revolutionary activity considerably. Stolypin's assassination in 1911 by revolutionaries prevented further reforms. The movement leading toward revolution reached a climactic moment in 1917 (see Chapter 8 in this volume).

Bloody Sunday. Troops (at bottom) firing on unarmed factory workers who had marched to the Winter Palace in St. Petersburg to petition the Czar, 22 January 1905. It is believed that this event sparked the Russian Revolution of 1905.

RUSSIAN SOCIETY:

Kievan Culture

Early Russian society was dominated by religion. The architecture, art, and music of the Kievan, Appange, and Pre-Petrine Russia were exclusively ecclesiastical in nature. The magnificent Russian Orthodox cathedrals, churches, and monasteries reflect the brilliant style of early architects. The secular buildings, such as the palaces in the **Kremlin** fortress of Moscow, also reflect this religious influence in its architecture and decoration. Literature consisted of theology, haigiography (the biographies of saints), and poetry. Historical writing was limited to monastic chronicles, the most famous of which was *The Russian Primary Chronicle*.

The Westernization of Russian Culture

After Peter the Great, Russian culture also developed along Western European lines. The quality of Russia's architects and artists was excellent, but their work was highly imitative of the West. Russia's greatest contributions were in literature and music. It was in these fields that the Russians showed the most originality and creativity.

Literature

The most famous of Russian poets was **Aleksandr Pushkin** (1799–1837), whose works of poetry and prose won him great distinction. Among his most famous works are the poems "Eugene Onegin," "The Bronze Horseman," and

"Poltava," and the stories "A Captain's Daughter" and "Boris Godunov." Many Russian novelists won great fame as well. The earliest was **Nikolai Gogol** (1809–1852), whose short stories and novels are known for both their humor and creativity in satirizing contemporary Russian society. Among his more famous tales are "Taras Bulba," "The Diary of a Madman," "The Inspector General," and "The Overcoat." His novel and greatest masterpiece is *Dead Souls*, which satirized the evils of serfdom. The two greatest Russian novelists were **Feodor (Theodore) Dostoyevskii** (1821–1881) and **Count Lev (Leo) Tolstoi** (1828–1910). Dostoyevskii was acclaimed for his psychological novels: *Crime and Punishment*, *The Idiot*, *The Demons*, and *The Brothers Karamazov*, which is considered by many to be the greatest novel ever written. Tolstoi's contributions are no less impressive including *Anna Karenina* and the massive work on Russia during the Napoleonic Wars, *War and Peace*. Russia also produced many outstanding playwrights, the best known of which was **Anton Chekhov** (1860–1904). His dramas and comedies have become classics, especially "The Cherry Orchard," "Uncle Vanya," "The Seagull," and "Three Sisters."

Music

Russian contributions to music are also of great importance. Russian composers often combined traditional church and folk music with Western European styles to produce some of the greatest pieces ever written. Among the most famous of these composers in the czarist period were **Aleksandr Borodin** (1833–1887), **Modest Mussorgskii** (1839–1881), **Piotr Illich Tchaikovskii** (1840–1893), and **Nikolai Rimskii-Korsakov** (1844–1908). These musical giants composed operas, choral works, symphonies, concertos, and chamber music. Some even composed traditional liturgical music for use in the Russian Orthodox Church.

SECTION SUMMARY

Czarist Russia was a brilliant civilization with many contrasts. The poetry, music, and literature existed next to serfdom and autocracy. The growth of the Russian Empire, which had an enormous effect on the development of European history, was initially motivated by a fear of invasion. The policies of the czars were often the result of a desire to "keep up" with Western Europe in order to be safe from attack. Yet, in its desire to imitate the West, Russia faced unique problems that made its leaders realize that it was different. Indeed, the failure to adopt Western-style democratic reforms was to have a shattering impact on Russia in the early and late twentieth century.

Russia's vast size and the strong conservative traditions of its people made change difficult. The population, which was basically peasants, was never affected by the changes until much later, if at all. It is not difficult to understand why Russia was never completely part of the Western European community. Its importance in that development, however, cannot be denied.

Discontent in the Austro-Hungarian and Ottoman Empires

TIMELINE OF EVENTS

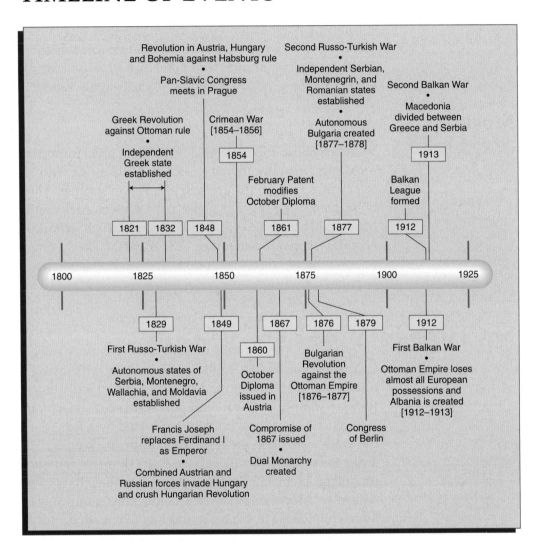

By the 1800s, there were separate nation-states in Western Europe. But in south-central and southeastern Europe, two prominent empires still existed. They were the Austro-Hungarian and Ottoman Empires. Even though they came to an end in the twentieth century, they were powerful in their times and were the sites of many nations that exist today.

THE AUSTRO-HUNGARIAN EMPIRE

The **Austrian Empire** of the **Habsburgs** was the largest in Europe outside of Russia. Its peoples were divided into three major geographical divisions: **Austria**, **Bohemia** (modern Czech Republic and Slovakia), and **Hungary**. The population was composed of different nationalities—**Germans**, **Czechs**, **Magyars**, **Poles**, **Serbians**, **Croatians**, **Slovenes**, **Slovaks**, **Ruthenians** (**Ukrainians**), **Romanians**, **Dalmatians**, and **Italians**. In some parts of the empire the nationalities lived in blocs, but in many regions, they were mixed together, often producing tension and conflict. The Germans occupied all of Austria and considerable parts of Bohemia. Yet, this ruling group was not a majority within this multinational empire.

The Sites of the Different Ethnic Groups

The Asiatic Magyars were dominant in Hungary, but only accounted for about half the population, which contained many **Slavs** and Romanians. The Italian population was limited to the parts of northern Italy controlled by the Austrians. The Czechs occupied Bohemia and the adjoining **Moravia**. In addition to the Czechs, the Serbians, Croatians, Slovenes, Slovaks, Dalmatians, Poles, and Ruthenians were the Slavic peoples of the empire, both united and divided by religious, cultural, and ethnic ties. The Serbians, Croatians, Slovenes, and Dalmatians were **Yugoslavs** or **Southern Slavs**, occupying the southeastern part of the empire. They were separated from their fellow Slavs in the north by the Germans, Magyars, and Romanians, who stretched across Central and Eastern Europe. The Romanians, who had religious, cultural, and ethnic ties to both the Latin and Slavic peoples, were extremely proud of their unique background. The empire was divided religiously as well as culturally. While most of the population was either **Roman Catholic** or **Eastern Orthodox Christian**, there were substantial minorities of **Protestant Christians**, **Muslims**, and **Jews**. Despite all the differences, the Habsburg Empire managed to stay together. Many of these subject nationalities (peoples under Austrian control), however, such as the Serbs and Romanians, hoped to break away from the empire and become independent nations.

> **Main Idea:**
> Despite all the differences, the Habsburg Empire managed to stay together.

The Austrian Revolution of 1848

In 1848, the Austrian Empire was ruled by the weak and incompetent Emperor Ferdinand I (r. 1835–1848) who had given the running of the government to the reactionary **Prince Clement (Klemenz) von Metternich** (1773–1859). Metternich was dedicated to preserving the established order and regarded both nationalism and democracy as threats to the empire (see Chapter 22 in *Global History, Volume One*). While ignoring the problem of dissatisfied nationalities, which had been raised in Austria since the beginning of the nineteenth century, he put down any attempts at political and social reforms. The **bourgeoisie** (middle-class) became impatient with government policy, which served the interests of the land owning aristocracy. Intellectuals and students were dissatisfied with the autocratic system and desired democratic reforms. The peasantry was discontented with the **Robot**, the system of obligatory peasant labor. Metternich's policies only made this resentment stronger.

Main Idea: Metternich was dedicated to preserving the established order and regarded both nationalism and democracy as threats to the empire.

Revolution in France in February of 1848, sparked a similar reaction in Austria a month later. Rioting forced Metternich, and later the emperor, to flee the capital of **Vienna**. In July, a constituent assembly met in Austria to write a new constitution. The group consisted of writers, editors, professors, and students, with few members of the bourgeoisie or the **proletariat** (workers), making it highly unrepresentative. The assembly abolished the Robot, which ended both the peasants' discontent and their interest in revolutionary reform. The disagreement between revolutionary leaders and the loss of widespread support resulted in the restoration of imperial power by October. In order to pacify the dissatisfaction created by the restoration of absolute monarchy, Emperor Ferdinand was replaced by his nephew, **Franz Josef (Francis Joseph) II** (r. 1848–1916), and a promise of future reform was made. In March of 1849, a demand was made for the establishment of a decentralized system, but this was suspended by the government on the grounds that a crisis with the national minorities of the empire existed.

The Hungarian Revolution of 1848

Revolution erupted in Hungary as well in 1848. In March, the radical Magyar journalist **Louis (Lajos) Kossuth** (1802–1894) led a revolutionary government that demanded independence. The Magyar leadership was divided, but moderates, such as the great landowner **Count Istvan (Stefan) Szechenyi** (1791–1860), favored the development of cultural and economic independence while remaining within the Habsburg Empire. The Magyars approved the **March Laws**, which established an elected Hungarian parliament and abolished serfdom. In the autumn of 1848, the Austrians tried to invade Hungary and restore imperial control. The nationalistic Magyars, despite disagreements among the leadership, successfully defended their land. In April of 1849, the **Magyar Diet** or parliament declared Hungary an independent republic, electing Kossuth as its first president. In June, Franz Josef enlisted the assistance of the Russians in suppressing the new Hungarian state. By August, the Austrians controlled Hungary, and Kossuth was forced to flee.

Main Idea: In June, Franz Josef enlisted the assistance of the Russians in suppressing the new Hungarian state.

The Czech Revolution of 1848

There was also revolution in Bohemia in 1848. The Czechs revolted in April seizing the capital city of **Prague**. The Austrian government promised them a constituent assembly and reforms to prevent them from establishing an independent kingdom. In June, the first **Pan-Slavic Congress** met in Prague, trying to establish Slavic solidarity against Austria. Only a few days after, however, Austrian forces invaded Bohemia and crushed the **Czech Revolution**, establishing a military government there.

The Compromise of 1867

Following the upheavals of 1848, the Austrian government reestablished centralized rule. Power was given by the distrustful emperor to loyal German-speaking officials. In an effort to regain popular support, Franz Josef experimented with decentralization by issuing the **October Diploma** in 1860. It created aristocratic assemblies in Hungary and Bohemia that would elect representatives to the **Imperial Diet**. The Magyars refused, demanding the restoration of the March Laws. In 1861, the emperor modified the October Diploma by issuing the **February Patent**, which established a parliament for the empire known as the **Reichsrat**. It consisted of an Upper House, which was appointed by the emperor, and the Lower House, which was elected by the Austrian upper-class and bourgeoisie. The Magyars also refused to participate in this new arrangement.

The Dual Monarchy

> **Main Idea:**
> Franz Josef was forced to agree to the **Ausgleich** or **Compromise of 1867**, which created the **dual monarchy** of Austria-Hungary.

In 1866, Austria's defeat by Prussia and the successful unification of Italy (see Chapter 3, Section 3 in this volume), greatly weakened the prestige of the Habsburg monarchy. The Magyars, led by **Istvan (Stefan) Deak** (1803–1876) and **Gyula (Julius) Andrassy** (1823–1890), demanded independence from Austria. Franz Josef was forced to agree to the **Ausgleich** or **Compromise of 1867**, which created the **dual monarchy** of Austria-Hungary. The compromise divided the Habsburg Empire in two: the **Austrian Empire** and the **Kingdom of Hungary**. Austria was governed under the February Patent of 1861, while Hungary followed the March Laws of 1848. Domestically, each state operated separately but was still ruled by the emperor nationally, who had control over the military and foreign affairs. More importantly, Austria and Hungary were bound by the need to keep the national minorities under control. The attitude toward the Slavs was especially hostile, creating a desire among them for unification with their fellow Slavs who were gaining independence from the Ottoman Empire. Slavic nationalism and Austro-Hungarian repression grew as the century progressed.

THE OTTOMAN EMPIRE

The Ottoman Empire ended its conquests in Europe in 1683 when the **Turkish** army was stopped by the Habsburgs outside of Vienna. Throughout the seventeenth and eighteenth centuries, they were slowly pushed back toward Asia. By the nineteenth century, the Ottoman Empire was known as the "Sick Man of Europe" due to its long process of territorial disintegration. Beginning with the **Greek Revolution of 1821**, in which southern and central Greece won independence, a rise in **Balkan** and **Slavic nationalism** started to eat away at the remainder of Ottoman possessions in Europe.

The Ottoman System

The internal system of the Ottoman Empire contributed to its disintegration. Unlike the other states of Europe, there was no strong central government. The **sultan**, who lived in the capital city of **Constantinople** (formerly the capital of **Byzantium**), ruled his empire like a feudal lord, exercising little control over regional areas. The local Turkish rulers usually did as they pleased, especially if they controlled areas where there was a sizable population or majority of non-

Turks. Treatment of non-Turkish peoples, especially Christians and Jews, was often extremely harsh. In the Balkans and Eastern Europe, the rise in Slavic nationalism created greater tension and hatred between the Turks and their subjects. Rebellions were answered with massacres and great destruction. This resulted in terrorism and equally violent responses from the local populations. In addition, the Russians had adopted a policy of assisting their fellow Slavs and Orthodox Christians (the Greeks and Romanians), in order to drive the Turks from Europe and secure a free route from the Black Sea to the Mediterranean. Russian ambitions in Eastern Europe and the Mediterranean created concern among the other Great Powers, especially the Austrians and British. This created a potentially explosive international scene.

The Greek War of Independence (1821–1832)

Main Idea:
In 1821, they rose up inspired by a new sense of nationhood led by young Greeks who had been educated in Western Europe and exposed to the concepts of nationalism and democracy.

The first people in the Ottoman Empire to rebel against Turkish rule were the Greeks. In 1821, they rose up inspired by a new sense of nationhood led by young Greeks who had been educated in Western Europe and exposed to the concepts of nationalism and democracy. Using the slogan "Freedom or Death" to rally the population, they were supported by the clergy of the Greek Orthodox Church and foreigners who were **philhellenes** or "friends of Greece," such as the English poet Lord Byron. Unsuccessful at first, they soon gained support by the British, French, and Russians who were hoping to gain influence in the region. Both Austria and Prussia opposed their support because they feared it would encourage the other Eastern Europeans to demand independence as well. This produced a conflict of interests that permanently ended the agreements made by the Great Powers at the Congress of Vienna to oppose revolution (see Chapter 22 in *Global History, Volume One*). The Greek cause also had support from famous writers, artists, and composers throughout Western Europe. By 1832, the southern part of the Greek peninsula had been freed from Ottoman control and formed the modern Greek state.

The First Russo-Turkish War (1829)

Lacking advanced European weaponry and scientific technology, the relatively backward armies of the Ottoman Empire were unable to prevent the **secession** (breaking away) of Slavic states. After the **First Russo-Turkish War** (1829), **Serbia**, **Montenegro**, and the Romanian provinces of **Wallachia** and **Moldavia** became **autonomous** (self-governing) states under the protection of Russia.

The Crimean War (1853–1856)

In 1853, the Russians began a campaign to drive the Turks out of Eastern Europe by occupying the Romanian provinces. Alarmed by the action, Great Britain and France went to war on behalf of Turkey. They wanted to prevent the Russians from succeeding in their traditional goal of capturing the **Dardanelles** (the water passage that connects the Black Sea with the Mediterranean). This conflict became known as the **Crimean War** (1854–1856) because the French and British forces concentrated on capturing the Russian fortress of **Sebastopol** in the **Crimea** on the northern coast of the Black Sea. The war is best remembered for the tragic charge of a British cavalry unit known as the Light Brigade (over 600 British soldiers were massacred in this unsuccessful attack). The fortress was finally taken in 1855, and Russia was forced to withdraw from both the Crimea and Romania. Nationalism and a desire for independence on the part of the Slavic and Orthodox Christian peoples in Eastern Europe continued despite the Russian loss. Even though they failed to achieve their goals, the Russians maintained a strong presence in Eastern Europe.

The Second Russo-Turkish War (1877–1878)

Main Idea:
The autonomous Orthodox Christian Balkan states of Serbia, Montenegro, Wallachia, and Moldavia, joined by Greece, responded to the slaughter by declaring war on the Ottoman Empire.

In 1876, a revolt against Ottoman rule broke out in **Bulgaria**. The Turks suppressed the uprising by slaughtering thousands of Bulgarians. The autonomous Orthodox Christian Balkan states of Serbia, Montenegro, Wallachia, and Moldavia, joined by Greece, responded by declaring war on the Ottoman Empire. Once again asserting themselves as protectors of the Slavs and Orthodox Christians, the Russians went to war on their behalf. The **Second Russo-Turkish War** (1877–1878) resulted in the complete defeat of the Ottoman Empire. The Turks were forced to sign the **Treaty of San Stefano**, which established the independence of Serbia, Montenegro, and Romania (Wallachia and Moldavia), as well as granting autonomy to an expanded Bulgaria. The substantial increase in Russian power as a result of the treaty alarmed the other nations of Europe, who refused to accept it. In order to avoid war, the Russians, French, Austrians, and Germans met at the **Congress of Berlin** (1878) in order to find an acceptable solution. The **Treaty of Berlin** replaced the Treaty of San Stefano. It confirmed the independence of Serbia, Montenegro, and Romania, but it reduced the size of the autonomous Bulgaria. In addition, the Serbian province of **Bosnia-Herzegovina** was given to Austria to "administer." This angered Serbia, who lost her access to the sea, and created a rivalry between the Austrians and the Russians in the Balkans, ending the traditional alliance between Russia, Austria, and Germany (see Chapter 7 in this volume).

The Balkan Wars (1912–1913)

Under Russian patronage, Bulgaria, Serbia, Montenegro, and Greece formed the **Balkan League** in 1912. In the **First Balkan War** (1912–1913), they easily defeated the Ottoman Turks. Under the Treaty of London (1913), the Ottoman Empire lost all its European possessions except the area adjacent to the Turkish Straits. Serbia, still angry over the division of its lands in the Treaty of Berlin, demanded access to the Adriatic Sea. To avoid giving Serbia territory, Austria created the new Balkan state of **Albania**. This further created tensions between Austria and Serbia. Having been denied access to the sea, Serbia demanded Bulgarian **Macedonia** (which had been divided between Greece, Serbia, and Bulgaria) as compensation. This resulted in a dispute between the two nations that led to the **Second Balkan War** (1913), in which Serbia, Montenegro, Romania, and Greece joined the Ottoman Empire to defeat Bulgaria. The **Treaty of Bucharest** (1913) forced Bulgaria to give up land to Romania and divided Macedonia between Greece and Serbia. The Balkan League, however, also ended. Serbia, Montenegro, and Romania and Russia turned their attention westward, to their fellow Slavic and Orthodox Christians under Austrian rule.

The Growth of Turkish Nationalism (1876–1912)

By the mid-1870s the weaknesses in the Ottoman system had made it clear that reform was needed if the Turkish Empire were to continue to exist. Under the influence of young Turkish intellectuals, who had been educated in Western Europe, the government allowed the creation of the **Ottoman Constitution** in 1876. Supported by the leaders of the non-Turkish minority groups, the reformers proposed the transformation of the Ottoman Empire into a constitutional monarchy with a freely elected assembly in which all ethnic and religious groups would be proportionately represented. **Sultan Abdul Hamid II** (r. 1876–1909) responded by revoking the 1876 Constitution and beginning a period of political repression in 1878. He ordered the massacre of over 200,000 **Armenians**, claiming this large Orthodox Christian minority was responsible for revolutionary activity. This began a tradition in the Ottoman Empire of **scapegoating** or blaming problems on others and persecuting them (see Chapter 11 in this volume).

Abdul Hamid's restoration of absolutism and repressive policies led to the creation of the **Committee of Union and Progress (CUP)** by the reformers. Popularly known as the **"Young Turks,"** they wanted to restore the 1876 Constitution and implement a democratic system that allowed political representation for all the nations in the Ottoman Empire. In 1908, the Young Turks led a military takeover that made the sultan a constitutional monarch, restored the Constitution, and began preparations for the first free elections for an Ottoman parliament. Strong opposition to the reforms by conservatives and the army, combined with the continued loss of Ottoman territory in Eastern Europe and Africa, resulted in the domination of the Young Turk leadership by extreme

> **Main Idea:**
> The policy of minority persecution reached its height in 1915 during World War I with the **Armenian Genocide** in which over 1½ million Armenians were slaughtered.

LINK TO TODAY
The Canonization of the Romanovs

If the Bolshevik regime thought they had wiped out the memory of the Russian royal family in 1918 with the murder of the czar and his family, they were quite mistaken. Almost immediately after the brutal executions of the Romanovs on July 17 and 18, the Ipatiev House in Ekaterinburg became a site of pilgrimage for the religious and curious. The Soviet authorities became very annoyed by the constant discovery of candles, small holy icons, and flowers left there by visitors. By the 1970s, the government decided to tear the Ipatiev House down. Despite this, the devout continued to visit the site.

In 1981, the Russian Orthodox Church Outside of Russia (the Synodal or Russian Orthodox Church Abroad) decided to canonize or declare as saints all the people killed by the Bolsheviks during and after the Russian Revolution. This included Czar Nicholas II and his family, who were prominently featured in the newly painted icons of the Holy New Martyrs and Confessors of Russia. Even though the Orthodox Church in Russia (Moscow Patriarchal) did not recognize the canonization, icons of the martyred Romanovs appeared throughout Russia. With the fall of the communists a year earlier, the New Martyrs and Confessors were canonized by the Church of Russia in 1992.

A year later DNA testing proved conclusively that the remains found by the White Army at Ekaterinburg in 1918 were the Romanovs. The remains of two of the children were missing, but further DNA testing of the various individuals who claimed to be them showed that they were imposters. These included Anna Anderson, who had made a career of claiming that she was the Grand Duchess Anastasia.

Today the Russian Royal Martyrs are venerated in Orthodox Christian churches throughout the world. Rather than erasing the Romanovs from history, the communists unintentionally assured that Czar Nicholas II and his family will be remembered throughout the centuries.

Turkish nationalists. They developed the ideology, **Pan-Turanism**, which proposed the creation of a strong, exclusively Turkish state.

The minorities of the Ottoman Empire became the targets of persecution, especially the Armenians, who were the victims of further massacres from 1894 to 1896, which took over 300,000 lives. This policy of minority persecution reached its height in 1915 during World War I with the **Armenian Genocide** in which over 1½ million Armenians were slaughtered.

CHAPTER SUMMARY

The discontent in both the Austro-Hungarian and Ottoman Empires had a great effect on the development of European history. In Austria-Hungary, it was evident in the growing desire of subject nationalities to become independent. The Compromise of 1867 was able to satisfy the Germans and Magyars; it also worked to the common disadvantage of the Slavs. The poor attitude of the ruling groups toward the Slavic population destroyed the fabric of the multinational Habsburg Empire. The dissatisfaction of the Serbians in particular, would have far-reaching consequences for Austria-Hungary, especially in 1914. In the Ottoman Empire, discontent meant the end of their European possessions. Outside of a small area surrounding Constantinople, the Turks were driven into Asia Minor. The inability of the Ottoman system to rule efficiently made it clear that great change was needed. Its poor performance as a world power made that clearer. Unlike the neighboring Russian Empire, the Austro-Hungarian and Ottoman Empires lacked any widespread internal unity, be it religion, culture, or ethnicity. The Austrians depended on a tradition (Holy Roman Empire) that was unknown or no longer important to the majority of the population. The Ottomans, who won their empire through conquest, ruled by force over an extremely diverse and often hostile population. The collapse of both after World War I, however, would have even greater consequences for the peoples living in them.

KEY TERMS

slavic tribes	anarchy	pogroms
Scandinavian Vikings	Zemskii Sobor	gold standard
Varangians	Westernization	Trans-Siberian Railway
House of Rurik	Holy Synod (Council	hemophilia
semiautonomous	of Bishops)	Marxist
Kievan state	Window to the West	Social Democratic
Byzantine Empire	Petrine Reforms	Party
Eastern Orthodox	Enlightenment	Mensheviks
Christianity	Czaritsa	Bolsheviks
Byzantine	"enlightened despot"	Russo-Japanese War
Commonwealth	Napoleonic Wars	Bloody Sunday
Mongol	"Scorched Earth"	Duma
Tartars	Decembrist Revolt	Stolypin Reforms
Swedes	reactionary	*The Russian Primary*
Teutonic Knights	Official Nationality	*Chronicle*
Khanate of the Golden	Russification	Austrian Empire
Horde	Crimean War	Slavs
appanges	Emancipation Edict	March Laws
Russian Orthodox	emancipated	Magyar Diet
Patriarchate	proletariat	Pan-Slavic Congress
Ottoman Turks	revolutionary move-	Czech Revolution
Czar	ment	October Diploma
Caesar of all the	S Narod	Imperial Diet
Russias	Narodniks	February Patent
boyars	The People's Will	Reichsrat
service nobility	Okhrana	

PEOPLE

Prince Vladimir	Peter III	Grigori Efimovich or
Batu Khan	Emelian Pugachev	Rasputin
Genghis Khan	Paul (Pavel)	Nikolai Lenin
Prince Ivan (John) III	Alexander	Piotr Stolypin
Sophia Paleologus	(Aleksandr) I	Aleksandr Pushkin
Czar Ivan (John) IV	Nicholas (Nikolai) I	Nikolai Gogol
"the Terrible"	Alexander	Habsburgs
Czar Feodor	(Aleksandr) II	Franz Josef (Francis
(Theodore) Dimitrii	Alexander (Aleksandr)	Joseph) II
Mikhail (Michael)	III	Louis (Lajos) Kossuth
Romanov	Sergei Witte	Count Istvan (Stefan)
Peter (Piotr) I "the	Nicholas (Nikolai) II	Szechenyi
Great"	Czaritsa Alexandra	Istvan (Stefan) Deak
Catherine (Ekaterina)	Czarevich Alexis	Gyula (Julius)
II "the Great"	(Aleksei)	Andrassy

PLACES

Czarist Russia	Baltic Sea	Finland
Rus'	Gulf of Finland	Kremlin
Kiev	Saint Petersburg	Austria
Novgorod	Black Sea	Bohemia
Sarai	Balkan Peninsula	Hungary
steppes	Crimea	Moravia
Moscow	Mediterranean	Vienna
Constantinople	Siberia	Prague
Sweden	Georgia	Prussia

CHAPTER 4

MULTIPLE-CHOICE QUESTIONS

Select the number of the correct answer.

1. Kievan Rus' became an Eastern Orthodox Christian area as a result of

   (1) the invasion of Batu Khan
   (2) the influence of the Scandinavian Vikings
   (3) the formation of the House of Rurik
   (4) the conversion of Prince Vladimir

2. The adoption of Eastern Orthodox Christianity increased the influence of

   (1) the Byzantine Commonwealth
   (2) the Teutonic Knights
   (3) the Khanate of the Golden Horde
   (4) the Varangians

3. Czar Ivan IV, "the Terrible" could be best described by which pair of adjectives?

   (1) beloved but brutal
   (2) admired but feared
   (3) honest but a murderer
   (4) fair but ruthless

4. Peter the Great was responsible for

   (1) forbidding the Westernization of Russia
   (2) building the new city of St. Petersburg
   (3) closing Russia to European trade
   (4) beginning the Romanov dynasty

5. What conclusion could be drawn about Catherine the Great's reign?

   (1) Catherine the Great was successful in ending Russian serfdom.
   (2) Catherine and her husband Peter III were trusted and respected monarchs.
   (3) Russia became a vast empire and a major factor in world affairs.
   (4) Russia experienced a severe economic decline.

6. What invader of Russia was ultimately defeated by the "scorched earth" policy of Alexander I?

   (1) Batu Khan
   (2) Genghis Khan
   (3) Boris Godunov
   (4) Napoleon Bonaparte

7. During the nineteenth century, Russia gradually became more

   (1) industrialized
   (2) isolationist
   (3) communist
   (4) agricultural

8. Which statement expresses an opinion about Czar Alexander III?

(1) Alexander became czar as a result of his father's assassination.
(2) Russia under Alexander constructed the Trans-Siberian Railway.
(3) Alexander was disliked by all Russians or increasing the persecutions of non-Russian minorties.
(4) The Okhrana was a group used by Alexander to stop revolutionary movements.

9. Place the following twentieth-century events in correct order.

A. Establishment of the Duma
B. Assassination of Prime Minister Stolypin
C. Russia went to war with Japan
D. Marxists divided into two political parties

(1) A, B, C, D
(2) D, C, A, B
(3) C, D, A, B
(4) D, C, B, A

10. Pushkin, Tolstoi, and Chekhov are all famous Russian

(1) composers
(2) writers
(3) generals
(4) architects

11. Nicholas II's son Alexis suffered from

(1) tuberculosis
(2) leukemia
(3) hemophilia
(4) lung cancer

12. The Romanov family kept from the Russian people the fact that Alexis had a disease

(1) to enable them to seek medical help in England
(2) to maintain confidence in the monarchy
(3) to allow Alexis to attend school
(4) to prevent fear of contagion

13. The best example of the term *bourgeoisie* is

(1) the middle class
(2) aristocracy
(3) peasant farmers
(4) military officers

14. The Austro-Hungarian Empire of the nineteenth century could be characterized as a

(1) unified population in religion and language
(2) dual monarchy with ethnic rivalries
(3) geographically compact area with a single form or government
(4) militaristic nation seeking to expand

15. The Ottoman Empire acquired the nickname the "Sick Man of Europe" because

(1) women were taking over the government
(2) it had a high rate of disease
(3) the sultan ruled like a feudal lord
(4) it was gradually losing territory

16. The modern nation of Greece was formed as a result of which event?

(1) a war with Hungary
(2) a rebellion against Turkish rule
(3) an order of the Russian czar
(4) a massacre of Slavic peoples

17. Britain and France entered the Crimean War against Russia with a goal of

(1) preventing Turkey from gaining more land
(2) liberating the Orthodox Christian people in the Crimea
(3) limiting Russian expansion in the Crimea and Eastern Europe
(4) expanding their own territories in Romania

18. Which statement would be correct about the Balkan states during the end of the nineteenth century and the beginning of the twentieth century?

(1) There were frequent changes in national borders.
(2) The Ottoman Turks maintained strong control.
(3) It was a time of peace and cultural advancement.
(4) Economic prosperity encouraged urban growth.

19. Which minority group suffered repeated persecution and massacres by the Ottoman Empire?

(1) The Armenians
(2) The Habsburgs
(3) The Bulgarians
(4) The Macedonians

20. The term *Magyar* is most closely associated with the history of

(1) Austria
(2) Greece
(3) Russia
(4) Hungary

THEMATIC ESSAY

Directions: Write a well-organized essay that includes an introduction, several paragraphs addressing the task below, and a conclusion.

Theme: Power and Decision Making

Leaders in Russia, Eastern Europe, and the Ottoman Empire made decisions that increased their power. In some cases these decisions also benefited their citizens, but in other cases citizens suffered.

Task

Identify two leaders from this chapter who used their political power to make decisions for their country. For each leader chosen

- describe a specific decision that the leader made
- discuss whether the decision intended to help his or her citizens or to maintain his or her own power
- evaluate the success of the decision

You may use any leaders from this chapter. Some suggestions you may wish to consider include Czsar Peter "the Great," Empress Catherine "the Great," Prince Clement von Metternich, and Sultan Abdul Hamid II.

Guidelines

In your essay, be sure to

- address all aspects of the *Task*
- support the theme with relevant facts, examples, and details
- use a logical and clear plan of organization, including an introduction and a conclusion that are beyond a restatement of the theme
- introduce the theme by establishing a framework that is beyond a simple restatement of the *Task* and conclude with a summation of the theme

DOCUMENT-BASED ESSAY QUESTION

This question is based on the accompanying documents. The question is designed to test your ability to work with historical documents. Some of the documents have been edited for the purposes of the question. As you analyze the documents, take into account the source of each document and any point of view that may be presented in the document.

Historical Context

The culture or way of life of a people includes many aspects of development such as government and politics, religion, economics, transportation, the military, geography, and the arts.

Task

Using information from the documents and your knowledge of European history, answer the questions that follow each document in Part A. Your answers to the questions will help you write the Part B essay, in which you will be asked to

- identify at least three events that impacted the cultures of Eastern Europe and/or Russia in the nineteenth and early twentieth centuries
- discuss each event chosen and describe the impact of the event on the area's cultural development

Part A: Short-Answer Questions

Directions: Analyze the documents and answer the questions that follow each document in the space provided.

Document 1   St. Isaac's Cathedral

The weighty mass of St. Isaac's Cathedral dominates the skyline of St. Petersburg. Its gilded dome, covered with 100 kg of pure gold, soars over 100 meters into the air, making it visible far out onto the Gulf of Finland. The Cathedral was commissioned by Alexander I in 1818 and took more than three decades to complete. Its architect, August Monferrand, pulled out all the stops in his design, incorporating dozens of kinds of stone and marble into the enormous structure and lading its vast interior with frescoes, mosaics, bas-reliefs, and the only stained glass window in the Orthodoxy. By the time the cathedral was completed in 1858, its cost had spiraled to more than twenty million rubles—as well as the lives of hundreds of laborers. Both the exterior and the interior of the cathedral deserve prolonged observation, and the view from the dome is stupendous.

www.geographia.com/russia

Question   1. Based on the text, what might be one reason that Alexander I ordered this Cathedral to be built?

Document 2

"Well Jack! Here's good news from home. We're to have a medal."

"That's very nice. Maybe one of these days we'll have a coat to stick it on."

THE BRITISH FORCES AND THE CRIMEAN WAR.

Question

2. According to the cartoon "Patient Heroes," what are two problems experienced by the British forces in the Crimean War?

Document 3

On the Death of Louis Kossuth

Count Albert Apponyi (b.1846)

Born in 1846; of a family long distinguished in public affairs in Hungary; for many years leader of the National party in Hungary; President of the Hungarian House of Representatives in 1903; Delegate to the Interparliamentary Conference in London in 1906.

WE[1] have to speak in the name of a mourning nation before a world filled with emotional sympathy. Who is the man who, after half a century's absence, holds just the same place in the heart of his people as when he was its ruler? Who is the man to whom all nations pay a tribute of respect such as no material power can command, poor outcast tho he was?

Who was Louis Kossuth?

This question is being answered now. The features of the living are obscured by the mist of controversy; in its shadows we perceive but the flickering lamplight of transient opinion. But there comes the sharp wind of death; it dispels the mist; it blows out the lamps; the sun of history is rising. In the clearness of that night-born day we begin to see who Kossuth was.

Behold this nation before his hand was put to the wheel of her destinies. Was she a nation at all? Was she independent? Was she free? Was she a member of the great European family? In legal fiction, yes; but how in fact? In fact we see before us a shapeless multitude, torn by the conflicts of privilege and oppression, almost secluded from the great currents and the noble competition of the civilized world, having no independent government of its own, made subservient to a foreign power, uncertain even in its national self-consciousness, which now and then flashes up lightning-like in the patriotic outbursts of individuals, but has no firm hold on the masses; and, tho this people has a parliament, the power of that parliament hardly goes beyond the privilege of issuing impotent complaints—a picture, indeed, of decay and dissolution.

And now behold the present state of the country.

God be praised for what we became since. Tho very far still from the fulfilment of our destiny, we are a free nation strong in her unity, in the equality of her citizens; in the recognized power of her representation, a not unworthy sister of the greatest among civilized nations; conscious of our independence, we are governing ourselves in the spirit of liberty and progress; no aim appears too

Question

3. According to Count Apponyi, what were two reasons that the people of Hungary had to be grateful to Louis Kossuth?
a.

b.

high for our legitimate ambition and undoubted possibilities. A picture, indeed, of hope and self-confidence.

Between these two states of a nation stands a man whose name was Louis Kossuth. Behold and compare: the difference says who he was; he found the former, he created the latter.

Not he alone; certainly not. It would be sin to be wanting in piety on that day devoted to piety, to express gratitude toward one great man by discarding gratitude due to other great men. There have been many of them as coworkers in the great work of regeneration; some with Kossuth, some against him, but animated all of them by the same holy spirit of patriotism.

Kossuth is one of the founders of our nation; he has made her secure of her independence and of her moral connection with the sister nations; he has made her an active agent in the great work of human progress and, by linking her destinies to the highest aspirations of our kind, has laid her future on a foundation of indestructible strength. His name is a symbol of our nation's worth to the world; of her racial individuality and of her task in universal history. There lies the secret of the veneration this name encounters throughout the world and of the gratitude and enthusiastic love it will never cease to pour forth from the hearts of our people.

END OF VOL. VII

Note 1. Delivered in the Hungarian House of Representatives, at Budapest, on March 23, 1894. At the conclusion of his speech, Count Apponyi moved a series of resolutions, providing for a public burial of Kossuth and for the erection of a statue to him. Translated for this collection by Count Apponyi himself in August, 1906, after his return to Hungary from the London Conference of the Interparliamentary Union.

Source: Count Albert Apponyi 1894 "On the Death of Louis Kossuth"

Document 4

Question

4. What is one geographic problem that this map suggests for the governing of the Austro-Hungarian Empire at the end of the nineteenth century?

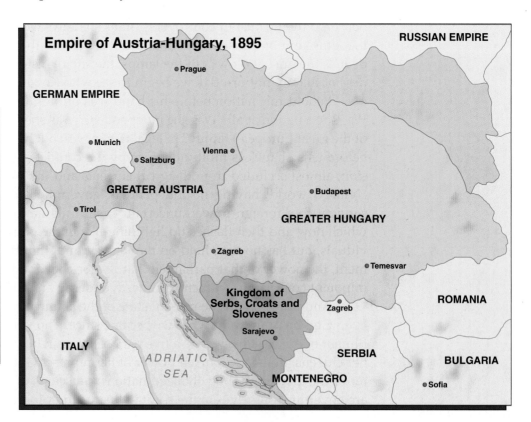

Empire of Austria-Hungary, 1895

RUSSIAN EMPIRE

GERMAN EMPIRE

Prague

Munich

Vienna

Saltzburg

GREATER AUSTRIA

Tirol

Budapest

GREATER HUNGARY

Zagreb

Temesvar

Kingdom of Serbs, Croats and Slovenes

Zagreb

ROMANIA

Sarajevo

ITALY

ADRIATIC SEA

SERBIA

BULGARIA

MONTENEGRO

Sofia

The Trans-Siberian Railroad

by Henry Michelsen, Secretary National Irrigation Congress

The results of the operations of the Trans-Siberian Railroad for the year 1898 are said to be encouraging to the Russian government. In its present unfinished state the traffic must be strictly local. An analysis of the government report shows that the country through which the line runs, though at present undeveloped and subject to the rigors of the climate on a prairie sloping to the Arctic Sea under the fifty-first degree of latitude, is still capable of producing great crops of grain; that it has fine forest resources, that live stock may flourish in it, and that coal has been found sufficient for the purposes of the railway and the population which may settle on the lands contiguous to it. Therefore, the railway may be expected, when finished, to become a factor in the commercial business of the world, even if its through traffic is not considered, by the opening up of the riches of the hitherto unknown continent which it is destined to make accessible.

The length of the road with its projected extensions is so great that even Americans, who are accustomed to deal with large distances, will have some difficulty in comprehending the scope of this undertaking. The longest continuous line on the North American continent is the Canadian Pacific Railway. Its main line from Montreal to Victoria is 2,990 miles in length. The located line of the Siberian railway, from Cheljabinsk to Vladivostock, is 4,776 miles; the branch through the recently acquired territory of Manchuria to Port Arthur will be 1,273 miles; so that the system will commence, before any feeders are built, with 6,000 miles of track. The distance from Vladivostock to St. Petersburg will be nearly 6,700 miles. The distance from Port Arthur to the harbors of the North Sea, on the estuaries of which the European trade with Eastern Asia is centered, is, approximately, 6,900 miles by the nearest route.

The watershed of the country east of the Ural Mountains is from south to north for more than 3,000 miles, which means a northern exposure entailing more severity of climate than is known on the railways of the United States and Canada. The rivers here are deep, full flowing streams, the alluvial bottoms of which necessitate large spans and make it desirable to have as few bridge piers as possible. Floating ice is in the rivers for about seven months of the year. The bridge at the Ishim has openings amounting to 700 feet, that at the Tobal 1,400 feet, that at the Irtish 2,100 feet; and the bridge over the Yenesei has a total length of just under 3,000 feet. Lake Baikal is traversed by a steam ferry for a distance of some forty miles. Forty bridges, each over 200 feet long, cross the tributaries of the Obi River between Omsk and Irkutsk. East of Baikal the road passes into the valley of the Amoor River, bridging waterways running from north to south. After spanning the Amoor at Khabarovka by a steel bridge some 5,000 feet in length, it turns abruptly to the south toward Vladivostock, running to the east of the rivers skirting the Khenden-a-Lin Mountains. The total length of water crossings between Cheljabinsk and Vladivostock is given at 301 miles exclusive of the forty miles of ferry; the snow sheds and fences at 565 miles.

This article originally appeared in
SCIENTIFIC AMERICAN for August 26, 1899.

Questions

5. a. According to Henry Michelsen, why was the construction of the Trans-Siberian Railroad considered such a major undertaking?
   b. Based on Michelsen's description, identify three problems faced in the construction of the Trans-Siberian Railroad.
      1.   2.   3.

The Treaty of Portsmouth, 1905–September 5, 1905.

The Conclusion of the Russo-Japanese War, signed at Portsmouth, New Hampshire.

(Text taken from Sydney Tyler, The Japan-Russia War, Harrisburg, The Minter Company, 1905, pp 564–568, quoted in There Are No Victors Here!: A Local Perspective on The Treaty of Portsmouth, Peter E. Randall, Portsmouth Marine Society, #8, Peter E. Randall, Publisher, 1985, pp 95–100)

The Emperor of Japan on the one part, and the Emperor of all the Russias, on the other part, animated by a desire to restore the blessings of peace, have resolved to conclude a treaty of peace, and have for this purpose named their plenipotentiaries, that is to say, for his Majesty the Emperor of Japan, Baron Komura Jutaro, Jusami, Grand Cordon of the Imperial Order of the Rising Sun, his Minister for Foreign Affairs, and his Excellency Takahira Kogoro, Imperial Order of the Sacred Treasure, his Minister to the United States, and his Majesty the Emperor of all the Russias, his Excellency Sergius Witte, his Secretary of State and President of the Committee of Ministers of the Empire of Russia, and his Excellency Baron Roman Rosen, Master of the Imperial Court of Russia, his Majesty's Ambassador to the United States, who, after having exchanged their full powers, which were found to be in good and due form, and concluded the following articles:

ARTICLE I.

There shall henceforth be peace and amity between their Majesties the Emperor of Japan and the Emperor of all the Russias, and between their respective States and subjects.

ARTICLE II.

The Imperial Russian Government, acknowledging that Japan possesses in Korea paramount political, military and economical interests engages neither to obstruct nor interfere with measures for guidance, protection and control which the Imperial Government of Japan may find necessary to take in Korea. It is understood that Russian subjects in Korea shall be treated in exactly the same manner as the subjects and citizens of other foreign Powers; that is to say, they shall be placed on the same footing as the subjects and citizens of the most favored nation. It is also agreed that, in order to avoid causes of misunderstanding, the two high contracting parties will abstain on the Russian-Korean frontier from taking any military measure which may menace the security of Russian or Korean territory.

ARTICLE III.

Japan and Russia mutually engage:

First.—To evacuate completely and simultaneously Manchuria, except the territory affected by the lease of the Liaotung Peninsula, in conformity with the provisions of the additional article I annexed to this treaty, and,

Second.—To restore entirely and completely to the exclusive administration of China all portions of Manchuria now in occupation, or under the control of the Japanese or Russian troops, with the exception of the territory above mentioned.

The Imperial Government of Russia declares that it has not in Manchuria any territorial advantages or preferential or exclusive concessions in the impairment of Chinese sovereignty, or inconsistent with the principle of equal opportunity.

ARTICLE VIII.

The imperial Governments of Japan and Russia with the view to promote and facilitate intercourse and traffic will as soon as possible conclude a separate convention for the regulation of their connecting railway services in Manchuria.

ARTICLE IX.

The Imperial Russian Government cedes to the Imperial Government of Japan in perpetuity and full sovereignty the southern portion of the Island of Saghalin and all the islands adjacent thereto and the public works and properties thereon. The fiftieth degree of north latitude is adopted as the northern boundary of the ceded territory. The exact alignment of such territory shall be determined in accordance with the provisions of the additional article II annexed to this treaty.

Japan and Russia mutually agree not to construct in their respective possessions on the Island of Saghalin or the adjacent islands any fortification or other similar military works. They also respectively engage not to take any military measures which may impede the free navigation of the Strait of La Perouse and the Strait of Tartary.

SUB-ARTICLES

In conformity with the provisions of articles 3 and 9 of the treaty of the peace between Japan and Russia of this date the undersigned plenipotentiaries have concluded the following additional articles:

SUB-ARTICLE TO ARTICLE III.

The Imperial Governments of Japan and Russia mutually engage to commence the withdrawal of their military forces from the territory of Manchuria simultaneously and immediately after the treaty of peace comes into operation, and within a period of eighteen months after that date the armies of the two countries shall be completely withdrawn from Manchuria, except from the leased territory of the Liaotung Peninsula. The forces of the two countries occupying the front positions shall first be withdrawn.

The high contracting parties reserve to themselves the right to maintain guards to protect their respective railway lines in Manchuria. The number of such guards shall not exceed fifteen per kilometre and within that maximum number the commanders of the Japanese and Russian armies shall by common accord fix the number of such guards to be employed as small as possible while having in view the actual requirements.

The commanders of the Japanese and Russian forces in Manchuria shall agree upon the details of the evacuation in conformity with the above principles and shall take by common accord the measures necessary to carry out the evacuation as soon as possible, and in any case not later than the period of eighteen months.

SUB-ARTICLE TO ARTICLE IX.

As soon as possible after the present treaty comes into force a committee of delimitation composed of an equal number of members is to be appointed by the two high contracting parties which shall on the spot mark in a permanent manner the exact boundary between the Japanese and Russian possessions on the Island of Saghalin. The commission shall be bound so far as topographical considerations permit to follow the fiftieth parallel of north latitude as the boundary line, and in case any deflections from that line at any points are found to be necessary compensation will be made by correlative deflections at other points. It shall also be the duty of the said commission to prepare a list and a description of the adjacent islands included in the cession, and finally the commission shall prepare and sign maps showing the boundaries of the ceded territory. The work of the commission shall be subject to the approval of the high contracting parties.

The foregoing additional articles are to be considered ratified with the ratification of the treaty of peace to which they are annexed.

In witness whereof the respective plenipotentiaries have signed and affixed seals to the present treaty of peace.

Done at Portsmouth, New Hampshire, this fifth day of the ninth month of the thirty-eighth year of the Meijei, corresponding to the twenty-third day of August, one thousand nine hundred and five, (September 5, 1905).

Questions

6. a. Based on this document, to what in the first Article are the Japanese and Russian governments agreeing?
   b. In Article IX, what is Russia giving up?
   c. In the Sub Article to Article III, what must both Japan and Russia do?

Document 7

Manifesto of October 17, 1905

We, Nicholas II, By the Grace of God Emperor and Autocrat of all Russia, King of Poland, Grand Duke of Finland, etc., proclaim to all Our loyal subjects:

Rioting and disturbances in the capitals [i.e., St. Petersburg and the old capital, Moscow] and in many localities of Our Empire fill Our heart with great and heavy grief. The well-being of the Russian Sovereign is inseparable from the well-being of the nation, and the nation's sorrow is his sorrow. The disturbances that have taken place may cause grave tension in the nation and may threaten the integrity and unity of Our state.

By the great vow of service as tsar We are obliged to use every resource of wisdom and of Our authority to bring a speedy end to unrest that is dangerous to Our state. We have ordered the responsible authorities to take measures to terminate direct manifestations of disorder, lawlessness, and violence and to protect peaceful people who quietly seek to fulfill their duties. To carry out successfully the general measures that we have conceived to restore peace to the life of the state, We believe that it is essential to coordinate activities at the highest level of government.

We require the government dutifully to execute our unshakeable will:

(1.) To grant to the population the essential foundations of civil freedom, based on the principles of genuine inviolability of the person, freedom of conscience, speech, assembly and association.

(2.) Without postponing the scheduled elections to the State Duma, to admit to participation in the duma (insofar as possible in the short time that remains before it is scheduled to convene) of all those classes of the population that now are completely deprived of voting rights; and to leave the further development of a general statute on elections to the future legislative order.

(3.) To establish as an unbreakable rule that no law shall take effect without confirmation by the State Duma and that the elected representatives of the people shall be guaranteed the opportunity to participate in the supervision of the legality of the actions of Our appointed officials.

We summon all loyal sons of Russia to remember their duties toward their country, to assist in terminating the unprecedented unrest now prevailing, and together with Us to make every effort to restore peace and tranquility to Our native land.

Given at Peterhof the 17th of October in the 1905th year of Our Lord and of Our reign the eleventh.

Nicholas
Translated by Daniel Field

Questions	**7.** a. What problem was Tsar Nicholas II trying to resolve by issuing his Manifesto of October 17, 1905?
	b. What are two guarantees that Nicholas made to the Russian people?
	1. 2.

Part B: Essay

Directions: Write a well organized essay that includes an introduction, several paragraphs, and a conclusion. Use evidence from *at least four* of the documents in the body of the essay. Support your response with relevant facts, examples, and details. Include additional outside information.

Historical Context

The culture or way of life of a people includes many aspects of development such as government and politics, religion, economics, transportation, the military, geography, and the arts.

Task

Using information from the documents and your knowledge of European history, answer the questions that follow each document in Part A. Your answers to the questions will help you write the Part B essay, in which you will be asked to

- identify at least three events that impacted the cultures of Eastern Europe and/or Russia in the nineteenth and early twentieth centuries
- discuss each event chosen and describe the impact of the event on the area's cultural development

Guidelines

In your essay, be sure to

- develop all aspects of the *Task*
- incorporate information from *at least four* documents
- incorporate relevant outside information
- support the theme with relevant facts, examples, and details
- use a logical and clear plan of organization, including an introduction and a conclusion that are beyond a restatement of the theme

CHAPTER 5

Political Change and Global Nationalism— Latin America

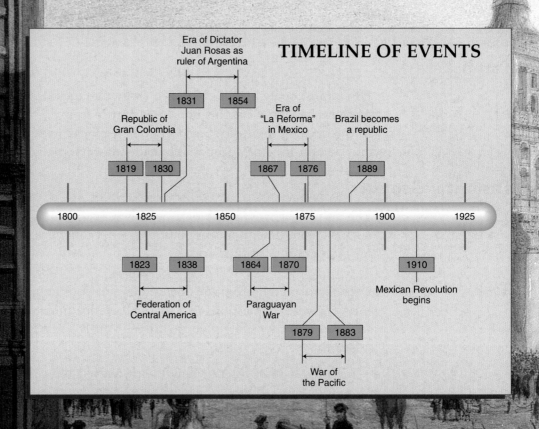

TIMELINE OF EVENTS

Era of Dictator Juan Rosas as ruler of Argentina
1831 **1854**

Republic of Gran Colombia
1819 **1830**

Era of "La Reforma" in Mexico
1867 **1876**

Brazil becomes a republic
1889

1800　1825　1850　1875　1900　1925

1823 **1838**
Federation of Central America

1864 **1870**
Paraguayan War

1910
Mexican Revolution begins

1879 **1883**
War of the Pacific

After the Wars of Independence were over, the viceroyalties in the Americas that had been for centuries ruled by Spain became free and independent nations. Only Cuba and Puerto Rico remained under Spanish colonial rule. The nations of Latin America were united in the sense that their Spanish colonial heritage gave them all some commonalities. Spanish continued to be the official language that was used in government, business, and daily life. Other local languages and dialects, however, did exist particularly among the lower classes and Native American peoples. The Roman Catholic Church remained the official religion of most of the people. Spanish culture and law continued to play major roles in society especially among the upper- and middle-class groups of society. A dominant Hispanic culture took root in all the new republics, but, eventually by the twentieth century, it became more genuinely Latin American as other influences developed within the individual republics.

In **Brazil**, independence came without the wars that were fought in the Spanish American republics. For almost a century Brazil was an empire ruled by descendants of the Portuguese throne. Brazil also inherited language, religious beliefs, and a cultural and legal heritage from Portugal. Brazil had a strong African and indigenous Native American influence, but the overall culture that developed was Luso-Brazilian reflecting the Portuguese heritage above all else.

> **Main Idea:**
> A dominant Hispanic culture took root in all the new republics, but, eventually by the twentieth century, it became more genuinely Latin American as other influences developed within the individual republics.

PROBLEMS DEVELOP AFTER INDEPENDENCE (1830–1850)

Conservative and Liberal Parties Compete for Political Power

Independence did not bring Latin America the political order, freedom, and prosperity the liberators had hoped for. In most of the new states, civil unrest followed the passing of Spanish rule. After winning their independence, the new Latin American nations began a long uphill struggle to achieve political unity and stability. In the new republics, **conservative** and **liberal** political parties competed, often violently, to rule their nation's government. The control of a nation's political power and authority brought those who were in charge important economic benefits.

Conservative or liberal political parties were active in most nations. The conservatives were generally the great landowners and the wealthier national merchants who sought to control and influence government institutions to pass laws or issue judicial rulings in their favor. They favored a highly centralized government, were strong supporters of the Catholic Church, and were interested in maintaining the existing social structure. The conservatives wanted to retain laws and customs relating to the Indians and the lower-classes that kept these groups under control.

The liberals were often provincial landowners, professional men, and other groups that had little political influence before independence. They were in favor of more regional autonomy, were against the Church's control of education, and wanted a federal type of government and guarantees of individual

> **Main Idea:**
> After winning their independence, the new Latin American nations began a long uphill struggle to achieve political unity and stability.

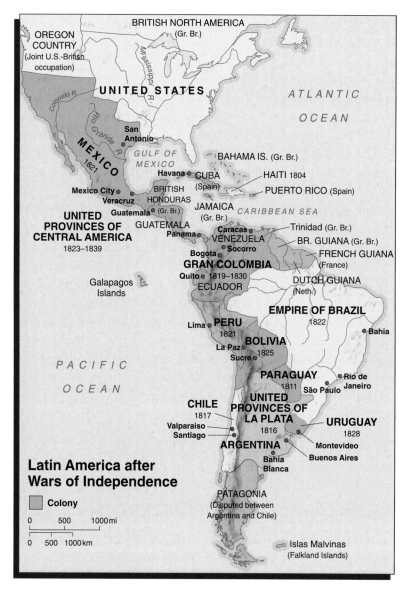

Latin America after Wars of Independence

Colony

0   500   1000 mi

0   500   1000 km

rights. The liberals were more in favor of integrating the Indian communities into the nation and changing the status of their communal landholdings to private property. Neither the conservative nor liberal political parties had genuine concern or interest in the well-being of the Indian population or the lower-class groups, unless a specific issue had an effect on their own economic or social interests.

Large Landowners Gain Political Power

The growth of regionalism within nations became a problem because of the great influence that powerful landowners had in the areas of the country far from the central government's authority and control. The leading roles that the large landowners played in military matters during the struggles for independence made them the most important men in their nations and local areas after the wars ended. During the decades after 1830, the political power and influence of these landowners increased. Often these owners of vast estates controlled private militias of armed men who would do their bidding. The powerful landowners were independent of government authority if it conflicted with their own self-interests.

The great landowners used their power and influence to increase their landholdings. They were owners of large estates, called **haciendas** and **estancias**, and often controlled the judicial system in their local areas. During the nineteenth century, Indian **communal property** often

Mexican hacienda owner and wife with their overseer: watercolor, early 1830s, by Don Carlos Nebel.

Main Idea:
Often the owners of vast estates controlled private militias of armed men who would do their bidding.

decreased in size if the communal land was adjacent to that held by a powerful landowner. When the land was desirable and ownership could be disputed, the owners of haciendas used armed force or took their claim to court and usually won the decision.

A large landowner who wielded great political power in his local area and controlled a private militia was called a **caudillo**. The caudillo's authority and power was based on his ownership of a large landed estate and use of armed men to enforce his decisions. The caudillos generally displayed some regard for republican ideas and institutions. Constitutional governments existed, but the constitution was usually only an effective legal document if the caudillo agreed to obey it. Very often this was not the case if a constitutional law conflicted with the caudillo's self interest. For the most part, caudillos ruled their local regions in a lordly manner. By means of regional political alliances, local caudillos worked together to ensure their rule of their local areas, the hacienda or estancia, without interference from the central government.

The Rise of National Armies and Military Officers

In the newly independent states, military officers who held positions of high command in the nation's army increasingly played a strong political role in the developing republics. This was one of the direct consequences of the years of destructive warfare and continuing postwar instability. In many of the republics, it became necessary to maintain costly national armies to guarantee peace and stability. Throughout Latin America, revolutionary uprisings were a continual threat. The military officers who controlled the national armies and great landowners who commanded private militias were the real holders of political power. In the new republics, the nation's military leaders generally supported the conservative landowning interests and their urban allies, wealthy local merchants, and government officials in political disputes.

The Social and Economic Structure of Latin American Societies

Social Issues

Independence left the existing economic and social structure intact. The only real change was that the Spanish merchants and government officials were no longer in charge of the government and economy. This was natural because the **Creole** upper class that led the independence movements had no intention of changing the existing social and economic order in a way that would offer the lower classes more political freedom and greater economic opportunities. They sought to replace the Spaniards in the positions of power, end mercantilist trade restrictions, and open their ports to the commerce of the world. They had no desire to change how the economy worked in terms of the labor or land systems. No agrarian reform took place, and the great landed estates not only remained intact but also often grew in size.

Nevertheless, the successful revolutions for independence led to a number of important social changes in the new republics. In many countries, constitutions or laws were written in a way to include some significant social reforms. Slavery was gradually abolished throughout Spanish-speaking Latin America.

Spanish-governed **Cuba** and **Puerto Rico** and Brazil were exceptions where the use of slave labor continued for most of the nineteenth century. Titles of nobility were done away with, and legal discrimination on the basis of race ended. There were also attempts to create public schools in some countries. However, education for the most part was only available for the male children of the wealthy landowners and children of middle-class professional families who lived in the larger urban centers.

Economic Issues

The revolutionary wars had a catastrophic effect on the economies of the new republics in the first years of independence. The new Latin American republics were faced with difficult problems that required immediate attention if their economies were to be revived. During the long years of war, there was a large loss of life and property. The death of many ordinary citizens who were workers and peasants and the serious damage to property had a negative impact on the economies of many nations. Sources of wealth were badly damaged or destroyed, and the needed labor, rural and city workers, was more difficult to find. The losses of human life and property destroyed were most severe in Mexico, Uruguay, and Peru where the fighting lasted for many years. The nation of Venezuela suffered the greatest loss in terms of human life.

The mine owners and mining industry suffered the greatest losses. Many of the working mines were flooded or otherwise badly damaged. Capital became scarce because of the chaotic wartime conditions and continued political instability in the new republics. Public debt rose during the wars as nations issued paper money to pay for soldiers and equipment. The new governments also issued currency that lacked the support of precious metals or foreign currency held as a reserve to bring confidence. Trade had almost come to a complete standstill between 1810 and 1826. Commerce with Spain stopped, and trade among the former colonies was also greatly reduced. Communication systems within and among the newly declared Latin American nations became very difficult and dangerous.

To restart their economies, the new Latin American nations first began to repair the damage caused during the wars for independence. At the same

Agricultural Products of Latin America

UNITED STATES

MEXICO
BELIZE
DOMINICAN REPUBLIC
CUBA
PUERTO RICO
GUATEMALA
JAMAICA
HAITI
LESSER ANTILLES
EL SALVADOR
COSTA RICA
VENEZUELA
GUYANA
SURINAME
COLOMBIA
FRENCH GUIANA
PANAMA
ECUADOR
BRAZIL
PERU
BOLIVIA
PARAGUAY
ARGENTINA
CHILI
URUGUAY

KEYS
Bananas
Beef Cattle
Cacao
Cassava
Coffee
Corn
Cotton
Fish
Potatoes
Soybeans
Sugarcane
Timber
Wheat
Corn Zone
Rice Zone
Wheat Zone

time, they pursued economic ideas that would ensure their continued independence and the financial well-being of their citizens, particularly the upper classes. The economies of the new nations had been overwhelmingly based and dependent on agriculture and mining. After the establishment of the new republics, agricultural products and raw materials continued to be the backbone of the export-oriented economies of all countries. Commercial agriculture brought in the most earnings in most countries. In some nations, notably Brazil and Cuba, slave labor was used to grow commercial crops that were exported.

Main Idea:
To restart their economies, the new Latin American nations first began to repair the damage caused during the wars for independence.

Between the years 1830 and 1850, Latin American exports to North Atlantic nations began to increase. Raw materials and foodstuffs were exported for sale in Europe and the United States. Examples of key primary export products were wheat and nitrates from Chile; tobacco from Colombia; hides, salted beef, and wool from Argentina; sugar from Cuba; **guano** (fertilizer) from Peru; coffee and sugar from Brazil; and cacao from Venezuela. These same countries were importing textiles and other consumer goods, thereby reducing their own manufacturing of goods and preventing local artisans from developing national industries. The failure to develop capitalist institutions and businesses in the new republics made the Latin American nations dependent on Great Britain and other industrializing countries.

The industrial manufacturers in Western Europe, particularly in England, produced almost all of the goods that Latin America imported in the first decades of independence. Latin American nations became part of the free-trade system that was developing in the nineteenth century in many parts of the world. In the 1800s, the economic ideas of Adam Smith greatly influenced the commercial policy decisions made in the new republics. Government involvement in matters of trade was restricted primarily to collecting customs revenues to pay for expenses such as salaries of officials.

Along with the growing flow of European imports came a group of European merchants. The European merchants were the representatives of the foreign trading houses and controlled the import-export business. They regulated the shipping of goods, the financing of shipping, and the insurance needed to maintain the commercial trading system. British bankers and merchants dominated and benefited most from the foreign investments made in Latin American trade throughout the nineteenth century. The wealthy landed class in Latin American nations cooperated with the European bankers and merchants since they too benefited from an export oriented agrarian based economy.

THE DEVELOPMENT OF LATIN AMERICAN NATIONHOOD (1826–1910)

After independence, the Latin American republics developed their own individual national histories. There were many similarities that linked the Latin American nations. They all had a common Spanish cultural and language heritage. Nevertheless, each nation had its own uniqueness, which separated it from its neighbor. In the sections that follow you will read and learn how many of the Latin American nations developed during the nineteenth century.

Mexico and Central American Republics

The Long Struggle for Independence

The viceroyalty of New Spain was very important economically to Spain because of its agricultural and mineral wealth. The monarchy, which was restored to the throne by the Congress of Vienna, tried very hard to hold on to what eventually would become the Mexican nation. The wars of independence were particularly deadly in terms of human life and property destroyed. They lasted from 1810 until independence was gained in 1821. At the time of its independence, Mexico was an enormous country in terms of land area. It included much of present-day southwestern part of the United States and almost all of Central America. The nineteenth-century national periods of Mexican and Central American history were oftentimes of political turmoil and warfare. **Mexico** was involved in wars that greatly reduced the size of its national territory. The Central American republics also experienced political instability and numerous violent revolutions.

The Central American Republics

> **Main Idea:**
> The economies of the Central American republics became increasingly dependent on a monocultural exportation of agricultural crops such as bananas.

In 1823, the future nations of **Central America** revolted against Mexican rule. Mexico never regained control of its most southern provinces, which became the Central American republics. The five provinces of Guatemala, Nicaragua, El Salvador, Honduras, and Costa Rica opted for separate nationhood and formed the Federation of Central America. Although this federation did not last beyond the 1830s, the nations of Central America became separate republics. During the nineteenth century, there were many violent revolutions and times when the Indian and peasant populations were brutally suppressed in the Central American republics.

Throughout Central America, caudillos and military officers fought among themselves to seize political power. Often they became dictators who used their positions of power for their own personal gain and interest. The large landowners supported powerful national caudillos as long as it furthered their own local situations. Conservative and liberal groups competed for political power and the right to benefit from the foreign-dominated export economy. The economies of the Central American republics became increasingly dependent on a monocultural exportation of agricultural crops such as bananas. Large landowners cooperated with the foreign export companies that controlled the economies of the dependent Central American nations.

Mexico

Mexico suffered greatly during the wars of independence. Political instability continued in the first decade of independence, the 1820s. Mexico lost more than half of its national territory between 1823 and 1853. First, it lost its southern provinces, which became Central America. Then from 1836 to 1853, the Mexican Republic lost approximately 40 percent of its national territory to an expanding United States. In 1836, the independence of Texas became a reality after a disastrous rout of the Mexican army. In 1847, the United States declared war on

Antonio Lopez de Santa Anna (1795?–1876). Mexican lithograph, 1849.

Mexico. Mexico's defeat led to the Mexican Cession, which resulted in a vast amount of Mexican territory becoming part of the United States.

During this period of more than three decades, Mexico was led by **Antonio Lopez de Santa Anna.** His disastrous leadership in the early decades of the new republic left the nation in ruin by the time of his exile in 1855. Santa Anna rose to power in the 1820s as a caudillo ally of Agustin de Iturbide who had defeated the Spanish forces and briefly became Emperor of Mexico. After Iturbide's fall, Santa Anna dominated the national political scene during the following decades by alternating between alliances with the conservative and liberal parties. It was only after three decades of disastrous political leadership that the Mexican people finally rid themselves of Santa Anna. This only happened after Santa Anna sold a part of Mexico to the United States, the Gadsden Purchase in 1853, to build a railroad.

Santa Anna's removal did not lead to political peace and stability. The conservatives and liberals continued their struggle for power. When the liberals seemed to be on the verge of military victory, the conservatives turned to foreign nations who intervened. The major European power who came to their aid

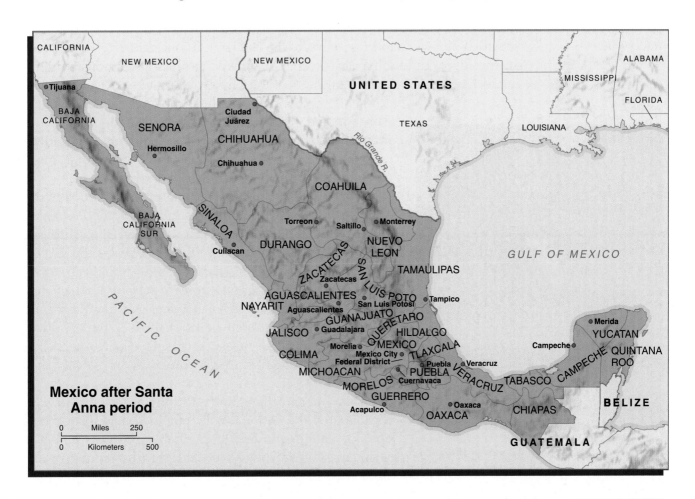

Mexico after Santa Anna period

Emperor Maximilian (1832–1867). Archduke of Austria and Emperor of Mexico (1864–1867). Photographed, c. 1865.

was France. Emperor Louis Napoleon was interested in restoring the glory that his uncle, Napoleon I, had earlier brought to the French nation. He sent French troops to Mexico to aid the conservatives. In 1863, Napoleon III used his influence with the conservatives, to have them invite Maximilian, a younger brother of the Austrian emperor, to be the ruler of Mexico. At first, largely due to the United States' involvement in the Civil War, Maximilian, supported by French troops and his conservative allies, was able to consolidate his rule in Mexico. However, after the Civil War, the United States warned France about its intervention, and the French soon withdrew their soldiers. Maximilian clung to power thinking he had the support of the Mexican people. In 1867, after his capture by the liberal army, Maximilian was tried and executed.

The liberals' return to political power is known as the era of the Reform, *La Reforma*. During the period of the restored republic (1867–1876), the liberals completed many of the reforms that they had started before being driven from power in the late 1850s. Under the leadership of President **Benito Juarez** and his successor Lerdo de Tejada, the liberal party enacted a number of important changes that made the nation more liberal regarding religion, education, and economic issues. The reform laws made the secular civil power superior to that of the Roman Catholic Church. The Church lost control of education, priests were not allowed to dress in religious attire in civil society, and much of the property of the Church was taken over by the government. In economic matters, modern capitalist ideas were adopted. It also became easier to buy and sell private property, particularly Indian communal land. Legislation made it easier for labor and business to act in their own self-interests without government interference.

In 1876, **Porfirio Diaz** became president of Mexico. The period from 1876 to 1910 is known as the *Porfiriato*. During this time, Porfirio Diaz pacified the Mexican nation and maintained his political power by the use of armed force. Diaz's goal was to guarantee political stability, and he used a rural police force to suppress Indian and peasant opposition to his land policies. Land became increasingly concentrated in the hands of the wealthy. Diaz also used harsh measures against city workers and allowed the Church to regain much of its wealth and influence.

Diaz opened the country to foreign investment. He consolidated the national debt, obtained new loans from abroad, and guaranteed a favorable business climate. Diaz gave foreign investors the right to own and profit from Mexico's subsoil wealth: petroleum and iron ore.

Benito Juarez (1806–1872). Mexican revolutionary and statesman. Colored steel engraving, American, 1870.

Porfirio Diaz (1830–1915). Mexican general and politician. Oil over a photograph, c. 1910.

Francisco Indalecio Madero (1873–1913). Mexican revolutionist and politician.

His economic policies increased foreign investment and led to the development of a railroad network. Diaz's political and economic actions were based on the ideas of positivism. Positivists sought to create a world of order and progress. In Mexico, the positivists were called *cientificos*.

By the first decade of the twentieth century, opposition to Diaz's dictatorial rule increased. By 1911, he was forced to leave the country and died in exile. In 1911, Francisco Madero became president; he was assassinated in 1913. This assassination was the spark that led to the long and violent Mexican Revolution.

Argentina, Paraguay, and Uruguay

Argentine Independence

Argentina, which was a part of the Viceroyalty of the Rio de la Plata, claimed its independence in 1816. Officially called the United Provinces of La Plata, Argentina was initially ruled by a junta, a group of political leaders based in the city of Buenos Aires. The political situation in the **Rio de la Plata** was very complicated. The population of Buenos Aires included a literate and liberal upper class of merchants, bankers, lawyers, and landowners

Argentina after independence in the late 19th century

BOLIVIA
PARAGUAY
BRAZIL
TUCUMAN
JUJUY
SALTA
FORMOSA
CATAMARCA
CHACO
MISIONES
SANTIAGO DEL ESTERO
LA RIOJA
SANTA FE
CORRIENTES
SAN JUAN
CORDOBA
ENTRE RIOS
URUGUAY
SAN LUIS
MENDOZA
Buenos Aires (city)
CHILE
PACIFIC OCEAN
LA PAMPA
BUENOS AIRES
NEUQUEN
RIO NEGRO
MAR ARGENTINO
CHUBUT
ATLANTIC OCEAN
SANTA CRUZ
ISLAS MALVINAS
TIERRA DEL FUEGO

with homes in the city as well as a large working class. The port of **Buenos Aires** provided the city and its inhabitants with revenues and salaries for its economic livelihood. Due to the strategic geographical position of its port and its facilities, Buenos Aires dominated the trade of the Rio de la Plata river system.

After declaring independence, the upper-class political leaders and merchants of Buenos Aires believed it was their right to rule in the place of the now eliminated Spanish monarchy. The upper class considered the city as the center of national unity and leadership. The junta, ruling group, representing the political and economic leaders of Buenos Aires, sought to gain control of the vast lands of the former viceroyalty. However, Buenos Aires faced strong resistance to its claim to political supremacy throughout the Rio de la Plata region. Paraguay, Uruguay, and Upper Peru, later called Bolivia, escaped the grasp of the United Provinces of La Plata and pursued their own paths to nationhood.

Paraguay

> **Main Idea:**
> Lopez was willing to open the country to outside influences, ideas, immigration, and technology.

In 1811, Dr. Jose Francia, a strong nationalist, was called upon to lead Paraguay's independence-minded landowners and merchants. Francia soon convinced the Paraguayans to declare independence and proclaim the nation a republic in 1813. By 1816, Dr. Francia became the nation's "perpetual dictator." He refused to follow the political lead of the Buenos Aires politicians and merchants and join the United Provinces. For a period of twenty-six years until his death in 1840, Francia, called *El Supremo*, ruled Paraguay with an iron hand and kept it isolated and free from foreign control. During this time, Paraguay developed a self-sufficient agriculture-based economy.

Carlos Antonio Lopez succeeded Francia. He ended the nation's long period of isolation and took it to its greatest heights. Lopez was willing to open the country to outside influences, ideas, immigration, and technology. When Lopez died in 1862, **Paraguay** was a prosperous and populous nation recog-

Buenos Aires, Argentina.
Line engraving, 1844

Catching cattle on the Argentine pampas. American engraving, 1853.

nized by the European powers. His oldest son, Francisco Solano Lopez, succeeded him and soon led Paraguay into a disastrous war with its neighbors. The war against the combined armed forces of Argentina, Brazil, and Uruguay was a tragic mistake for the Paraguayan people and the nation's territorial integrity. The Paraguayan War resulted in a huge loss of Paraguayan life and national territory. Paraguay remained an independent nation. However, thereafter, the republic continued to be ruled by dictators and generals who represented the wealthy white landowning class. The native Guarani population worked the land as exploited agricultural laborers. Paraguay remained a poor export-oriented agricultural economy into the twentieth century.

Uruguay

Main Idea: After years of intermittent battles, the British intervened and mediated a peace, which led to the recognition of Uruguayan nationhood in 1828.

Buenos Aires also failed in its attempt to gain control of the land that would ultimately become the nation of **Uruguay**. During the colonial period, the area to the east of the Uruguay River and south of Brazil was known as the *Banda Oriental* or Eastern Shore. This area had been claimed by both Spain and Portugal during the colonial period. After the declaration of its own independence in 1816, the Buenos Aires junta sought to take control of Uruguay. The inhabitants of the Uruguayan **pampas** (vast grasslands) met the Argentine military forces with fierce resistance. Many of the inhabitants of the pampas were **gauchos**, cowboys, who herded cattle during more peaceful times. However, the gauchos were also fierce fighters who were called upon when needed by landowners to defend their interests. The Uruguayans, led by Jose Artigas, demanded autonomy in a loose federal type of political arrangement with the United Provinces. Buenos Aires refused to negotiate, and the armed struggle continued.

In 1822, after declaring its own independence from Portugal, Brazil entered into the struggle and claimed that Uruguay was a part of its national territory. When the Brazilians sent soldiers to occupy Uruguay, they were met with armed resistance. The Uruguayans were aided by the Argentines who opposed the Brazilian claim and attempt to take over territory that they themselves wanted. After years of intermittent battles, the British intervened and mediated a peace, which led to the recognition of Uruguayan nationhood in 1828. Thereafter, Uruguay was able to retain its independence. Uruguayan politics were controlled by two political parties, which reflected the competing conservative and liberal political philosophies. Its agricultural and ranching economy remained primarily based on the exportation of meat and cereals, which continued into the twentieth century.

Argentina

The ruling junta in Buenos Aires not only had difficulty in controlling lands outside of the United Provinces of La Plata but also found its political authority challenged in its increasingly self-sufficient interior. Within the United Provinces, agricultural, ranching, and local business and manufacturing interests resented Buenos Aires's claim of political authority and supremacy. The wealth of these independent-minded landowners, businessmen, and manufacturers depended on the raising of livestock, production of cereals, particularly wheat, the manufacturing of textiles, and commerce. Ultimately, an armed conflict broke out between the Unitarians, the centralist-minded Buenos Aires political leadership, and the more federalist-inclined upper-class inhabitants living in the interior. By the 1820s, the federalist idea of national unity, supported by the large landowners, the owners of estancias, and other provincial interests, triumphed. A powerful caudillo landowner, **Juan Manual Rosas**, led the federalists. In 1829, Rosas became governor of the province of Buenos Aires.

By 1831, Rosas gained political control of the United Provinces after allying himself with the Buenos Aires upper-class merchants and local caudillos in the interior provinces. Rosas ruled the nation as a dictator and remained in power until 1852. During his dictatorial rule, the economy was based on the raising of livestock and agriculture for the export of hides and salted meat and grains, principally wheat, and the import of foreign goods. Rosas symbolized the caudillo dictator who ruled the nation through fear and armed force. The merchants of Buenos Aires and the large landowners of estancias benefited from his rule. He brought a measure of political stability to the nation, but the cost was the harsh suppression of dissent and liberties.

By the late 1840s, after an Anglo-French blockade of the La Plata, the anti-Rosas forces united in an effort to oust the dictator. With the help of a for-

Juan Manuel De Rosas (1793–1877): line drawing by an unknown artist, 19th century.

Bartolome Mitre (1821–1906). Argentine statesman, military leader, and historian. Wood engraving, American, 1865.

mer Rosas caudillo ally, Justo Urquiza, Rosas was defeated at the decisive Battle of Monte Caseros and forced to accept exile. Victory over Rosas led to the renewal of the dispute between Buenos Aires and the provinces, between unitarianism and federalism. Urquiza, the new caudillo strongman, failed to unite the provinces and Buenos Aires by armed force, and the two sides temporarily went their separate ways. Urquiza led the Argentine Confederation, and Buenos Aires became a separate and independent province.

In 1851, the economic superiority of Buenos Aires and the military leadership of **Bartolome Mitre** led to the defeat of Urquiza. The triumph of Buenos Aires in part reflected the need of the interior to use its port. It also signaled the rise of Argentine nationalism and decline of the caudillo strongman. Mitre became the president of the Argentine Republic and consolidated national unity. The economic progress of Argentina continued with Buenos Aires becoming the capital of a now more politically united and prosperous nation. The development of refrigerated ships greatly benefited Argentina, and the port of Buenos Aires became a meat packing capital for shipping beef and wheat to Europe.

For the remainder of the nineteenth century, presidents elected according to constitutional rules ruled Argentina. The Argentine electorate was basically the propertied landowning class, or oligarchy, which approved of presidential candidates if they supported their economic interests. Domingo Sarmiento, who greatly encouraged European immigration, followed Mitre in office. Hundreds of thousands of immigrants from Italy, Spain, and elsewhere came to Argentina and settled mostly in the capitol and other major cities. During the 1870s and 1880s, the interior of the nation, which was inhabited by Indian tribes, was conquered, and the land was distributed to the wealthy landowners.

Domingo Sarmiento (1811–1888). Argentine educator and statesman. Wood engraving, 1868.

As the decades passed, middle-class groups became increasingly resentful about their lack of political representation. By the 1890s, middle-class discontent led to the formation of the radical party. The ruling upper class of wealthy landowners and merchants eventually had to recognize the middle-class demand for political rights and compromise to avoid bloodshed. The rise of the middle class in Argentina led to the sharing of political power. By the turn of the century, Argentina was considered to be a positive and progressive exception to what was happening in most other Latin American nations. Argentina was seen as a nation whose future was bright due to its stable political system and prosperous economy.

The Andean Republics: Colombia, Venezuela, Ecuador, Peru, Bolivia, and Chile

Colombia, Venezuela, and Ecuador

Simon Bolivar (1783–1830). South American soldier, statesman, and revolutionary leader. Painting, 1824, by Jose Gil de Castro.

Simon Bolivar's dream of politically uniting all of the lands of the former Viceroyalty of New Granada, Colombia, Venezuela, and Ecuador into the Republic of Gran Colombia proved not to be a realistic idea. After independence was achieved, the reality was that the competing regional landowners, wealthy merchants, and other political interests worked against the idea of unification under a central government. By 1830, the republics of Venezuela and Ecuador went their separate ways. Despite his success as the liberator of the Andean republics, Bolivar died without ever achieving his idea of unifying the Andean nations and people.

During the nineteenth century, the republics of Colombia, Venezuela, and Ecuador experienced long periods of political instability. The upper-class groups divided themselves into the conservative and liberal political parties and fought for control of the national governments. Both parties wanted to control their nation's government to further the economic interests of the upper-class groups that they represented. Revolutions were frequent as the competing regional landowners, merchants, and other groups fought for power. The lower classes, mainly the mestizos, who were people of mixed blood, blacks, and Indians, were not thought of as being important. They were considered to be inferior and only valuable to the nation as peasants and laborers. Neither their needs nor interests were taken into account by the competing ruling upper class.

Bolivia

> **Main Idea:**
> In the 1890s, Bolivia became a major producer of tin. Nevertheless, as it entered the twentieth century, Bolivia remained a backward nation.

In 1776, when the Viceroyalty of the Rio de la Plata was established, Upper Peru became its mountainous northern corner. After the United Provinces declared independence, Buenos Aires was unsuccessful in its attempt to gain political control of this far-off province still under Spanish control. Buenos Aires sent two military expeditions to the future Bolivia, which were defeated by the Spaniards and their allies, the large landowners.

In 1825, General Antonio Andres de Sucre liberated Upper Peru from the Spaniards. After its independence, Upper Peru became the nation of **Bolivia**, named after the liberator, Simon Bolivar. For most of the nineteenth century, Bolivia was a nation ruled by caudillos and experienced numerous revolutions. Under the banners of the conservative and liberal parties, the caudillos fought among themselves for political power and control of large tracts of land. The Indians who made up the vast majority of the population of the nation were not participants in the political life of the nation. They were isolated from the Spanish-speaking population because they lived in a world where they used only their native languages, Quechua and Aymara. Indians either lived in their own separate village communities or worked as peasants for the large landowners. The ruling white upper class and mestizo, mixed racial blood, population exploited them and looked down upon them as being inferior.

In 1879, Bolivia's involvement with Peru in the War of the Pacific against Chile cost it its maritime province and outlet to the ocean. Twenty years later, Bolivia lost its eastern department of Acre to Brazil. In the 1890s, Bolivia became a major producer of tin. Nevertheless, as it entered the twentieth century, Bolivia remained a backward nation. In the mountainous highland plateau region, a wealthy Spanish-speaking upper class continued to exploit impoverished Indians who made up the majority of the population. In the lowland region bordering Brazil and Paraguay, a ranching and commercial agricultural economy began to develop.

Peru

Main Idea:
Going into the twentieth century, Peru remained a nation where the owners of large estates and merchants of the capital, Lima, exploited the lower classes who were the majority of the population.

In 1826, Peru emerged from the wars of independence economically bankrupt and politically divided. During the nineteenth century, the large landowners and wealthy merchants controlled Peru's political and economic life. This powerful group of upper-class landowners and wealthy merchants aided by the armed forces suppressed and exploited the mestizo and Indian lower classes. The upper class was divided into the conservative and liberal political parties. As elsewhere in Latin America, the conservative and liberal parties fought to gain political power to further their economic interests. After independence, military caudillos with the support of large landowners of haciendas and rich Lima merchants ruled the nation. Between 1826 and 1895, eighteen military caudillos governed **Peru** and took part in civil wars, revolutions, and several international conflicts.

In the 1840s, the exportation of guano, a potent fertilizer of bird droppings, bought some wealth and prosperity to the nation. By 1883, this period of prosperity ended after Chile defeated Peru in the War of the Pacific. The war was fought over the right to exploit rich nitrate deposits, which were based in Peruvian territory. The Chilean victory resulted in its takeover of the nitrate deposits and Peru's loss of national territory. The Chilean control and increase of nitrate exports, which were used as fertilizers, caused the decline of Peruvian guano exports. Going into the twentieth century, Peru remained a nation where the owners of large estates and merchants of the capital, Lima, exploited the lower classes who were the majority of the population. The vast economic and social divide would eventually lead to a political crisis in the twentieth century.

Chile

In 1817, **Chile** gained its independence. In the 1820s, the republic of Chile was approximately one-third its present size and was hemmed in by the Andes Mountains to its east and Pacific Ocean to its west. The Central Valley of present-day Chile was the core territorial basis of the nation at that time. At the time of independence, Chile had a very small population of about 500,000 people who were about one-third white and the remainder mestizo and Indian. About 100,000 unassimilated Indians lived in lands to the south.

Bernardo O'Higgins (1778–1842). Chilean soldier and statesman. English mezzotint, 1829.

In the first decade after independence, Chile experienced many of the same political problems that plagued the other Latin American republics. In 1823, **Bernardo O'Higgins** the hero of independence fell from power, and a decade of political instability began. However, in 1833, a constitution was adopted, and, thereafter, Chile began to progress politically and economically. Between 1831 and 1871, Chile had an established system of government with constitutionally elected presidents, each holding office in succession and serving for two five-year terms of office. Although the upper-class politicians, who as elsewhere controlled the political process, were split along the usual divide between conservative and liberal parties, Chilean political differences did not result in the types of violence and revolution that plagued other Latin American republics. Caudillo landowners had influence in their local areas, but they did not play a disruptive political role in Chile.

The political stability made economic development and progress more possible. In the 1840s, its rich copper mines made Chile the world's leading producer of the mineral. Chile's geopolitical situation with its port of Valparaiso on the Pacific served to stimulate agricultural growth. In the 1850s, agricultural production expanded as grain exports increased to feed the participants of the American California gold rush. More liberal trade policies were adopted, and banking institutions were developed. The favorable economic climate helped Chile to modernize. Santiago, the capital, installed gas lighting and opened public libraries. Railroads were built with the help of foreign investment, and the educational system was expanded.

In the 1870s, there was an economic downturn after Chilean copper lost its privileged position in the world market. However, in 1879, Chile engaged in a war with its neighbors, Bolivia and Peru, called the War of the Pacific over the issue of Chile's economic penetration of valuable nitrate deposits in Bolivian and Peruvian controlled territory. By 1883, the war resulted in a complete Chilean victory on land and sea. For the next forty years, revenues from export taxes on the foreign-run nitrate industry gave the Chilean government income to continue its modernizing efforts.

Chile entered the twentieth century as a nation that had made much progress after it politically stabilized and then economically developed in the 1800s. Chile became a magnet for European immigration and foreign investment. After 1895, Chile's population increased by over a million people in twenty years. The population of Santiago and Valparaiso expanded enormously as the capital city and the nation's major port continued to modernize. Foreign investment capital flowed into Chile and continued to stimulate the development of such public works as railways, docks, public buildings, and the expansion of education.

Main Idea:
Chile entered the twentieth century as a nation that had made much progress after it politically stabilized and then economically developed in the 1800s.

Brazil

Brazil gained its independence differently than the Spanish-speaking nations in Latin America. During the era of the Napoleonic Empire, the Portuguese monarchy sided with the English. When Napoleon invaded the Iberian Peninsula and his French soldiers marched on Portugal in 1807, the English navy came to the aid of the Portuguese royal family and court. The English navy transferred the royal family and many of the wealthy nobles and merchants across the Atlantic to Portugal's colony of **Brazil**. For the duration of the Napoleonic era, the king and his Portuguese court settled in Rio de Janeiro. The arrival of the king and his long-term residence in Brazil changed Brazil's position in the Portuguese Empire. Brazil was elevated to the status of a kingdom, which put it on a coequal political footing with Portugal.

Brazil's new political status as a kingdom and the residency of the royal family were very pleasing to the Brazilian upper class because of the growth of economic, cultural, and educational opportunities. Even though there was Brazilian resentment concerning the numerous Portuguese residents, nobles, merchants, and other hangers-on, the overall transference of the crown was well received and served as a dampening effect on any idea for an independent Brazil. Brazilian ports were opened, and an influx of cheap machine-made goods, mostly from England, entered the country and drove down prices. England particularly profited from Brazil's freedom from Portuguese control when it was granted major tariff concessions.

> **Main Idea:**
> Brazil's new political status as a kingdom and the residency of the royal family were very pleasing to the Brazilian upper class because of the growth of economic, cultural, and educational opportunities.

Brazil after independence

Al Alagoas
E.S. Espirito Santo
Pa Paraiba
Pe Pernambuco
R.J. Rio de Janeiro
R.N. Rio Grande de Norte
Se Sergipe

Dom Pedro II
(1825–1891).
Emperor of Brazil
1831–1889. Original
cabinet photograph.

After the fall of Napoleon, the political situation remained stable until a revolution took place in Portugal in 1820. The revolution led to a liberal Portuguese constitution. However, the Portuguese revolutionaries were reactionary about the issue of Brazil. They wanted the king, Dom Joao, to return to Portugal. The Portuguese merchants also were unhappy about the open ports and rights to manufacture that Brazil enjoyed. They wanted to reduce Brazil to its former colonial status and to revert back to the trading and manufacturing regulations in place prior to 1808. Joao returned to Portugal but left his son, Pedro, as regent of Brazil. In a private letter, he advised him that if the Brazilians demanded independence, he should head the movement.

In 1822, the Portuguese Cortes, the legislature, demanded that Pedro also return to Portugal. Pedro refused and followed the counsel of his Brazilian advisers to declare independence on September 7, 1822. Pedro I was formally proclaimed constitutional emperor later that year. The new empire of Brazil was the largest nation in Latin America and had a population of about four million people of whom perhaps half were slaves. The economy of Brazil was mostly based on the export agriculture of sugar and coffee. Minerals from mines in Minas Gerais also were exported.

Brazil achieved its independence with relative ease and did not suffer through the destructive wars of independence, as did the Spanish-speaking republics. Nevertheless, despite the unifying factor of the emperor, Brazil did experience regional revolts during its first two decades as a new nation. From 1822 to 1831, Dom Pedro I ruled Brazil as emperor in an increasingly autocratic and unpopular manner. In 1831, Pedro I abdicated and returned to Portugal. The country was governed until 1840 by a series of regents who ruled in the name of Pedro's underage son, the future Emperor Pedro II. In 1840, **Dom Pedro II** took his throne and ruled Brazil until 1889.

Brazil enjoyed four decades of domestic peace and a generally expanding economy once Pedro II was able to stabilize the nation politically. Pedro rotated the governments between the upper-class conservative and liberal politicians. He made alliances with the great rural landowners and used his royal power as a moderator of Brazilian politics to appoint cabinets and provincial officials. Pedro was a capable monarch who led his nation well in times of conflict and won the increasing admiration and respect of the Brazilian people.

The wealth of Brazilian economy increasingly shifted to the south of the country. During the nineteenth century, the sugar plantation economy in the north gradually declined as the price of sugar dropped due to oversupply. In its place, coffee became the nation's leading agricultural export. The growth of coffee agriculture signaled the rise of Sao Paulo and Minas Gerais and a shift of wealth and political power from the northeast to the south-central part of Brazil. In the extreme south, Rio Grande do Sul, a cattle-ranching economy developed. Later, during the Second Empire, rubber from trees in the Amazon also became a major export.

Main Idea:
Brazil enjoyed four decades of domestic peace and a generally expanding economy once Pedro II was able to stabilize the nation politically.

The shift to a coffee-based economy created problems in the north where most of the slaves were located on the sugar plantations. In Brazil, the use of slave labor continued after independence and lasted to the end of the empire. Starting in the 1850s, the slavery issue increasingly became a problem. The owners of large plantations sought to delay emancipation and looked for government compensation. After complete emancipation without compensation took place under the Golden Law of 1888, the monarchy lost the support of the rural landowning class. In addition, the monarchy lost the support of the Church, and the military, particularly the army officers, wanted a republican form of government. In 1889, the monarchy was overthrown, and a republic was declared. Pedro II went into exile, and the period of empire ended.

LINK TO TODAY

The Latin American republics have changed a great deal since the end of the nineteenth century. Today, the populations of all the Latin American nations are significantly larger. There has been an enormous expansion and modernization of the urban centers, particularly the capitals in all countries. In some nations, industrial centers have been created in the urban areas, and there are more manufacturing and service industry types of work. Many rural migrants have come to the cities to find work and look for a better life. In addition, many Latin Americans are immigrating north to the United States and Canada in search of great opportunities. The governments in Latin America have politically stabilized and democratic elections are held on a regular basis.

Nevertheless, despite the changes that have taken place in the Latin American republics, many of the economic and social conditions that existed during the first century of national independence still are in evidence today. Throughout Latin America, the wealth is still concentrated in the hands of the upper classes. Wealthy landowners still own and control most of the land. For the most part, the economies are still oriented toward agricultural products and raw materials export. In nations such as Brazil and Mexico, where national manufacturing and telecommunications industries exist, the beneficiaries of these new sources of wealth are aligned with the traditional landowner and rich merchant upper class. There has been little land reform anywhere in Latin America except Cuba.

The lower classes are still economically and socially deprived of many of the health and educational benefits enjoyed by the wealthy. Although there has been a gradual growth of the middle class, this bridge between the upper and lower classes does not exist on a significant scale as it does in the United States, Canada, and Western Europe. Much remains to be accomplished if societies in Latin America are to become republics where all citizens can aspire to have a better life.

CHAPTER SUMMARY

During the nineteenth century, most of the republics that were created in Latin America experienced difficulties in establishing political stability. The Spanish heritage left the wealthy Creole landowners and merchants in power. Regionalism became a problem in many republics because the great landowners, who were caudillos, wanted their own freedom of interference from the central government. On the national level, the upper classes competed among themselves under the banners of the conservative and liberal parties for political power to further their own economic interests. The lower classes of society, the mixed blood mestizo and mulatto, black and Indian populations, did not really gain very much economically or socially after independence.

Brazil was an exception because of its Portuguese heritage, and independence came relatively peacefully. Brazil was ruled as an empire from 1822 until a republic was declared in 1889. In its first decades, Brazil did experience some problems similar to those of the Spanish-speaking republics, but after 1840 during the Second Empire, Dom Pedro II was able to stabilize Brazil politically. However, in Brazil the issue of slavery ultimately undermined the emperor's political support and led to his downfall and the creation of a Brazilian republic.

IMPORTANT PEOPLE, PLACES, AND TERMS

KEY TERMS

conservative	communal property	gauchos
liberal	caudillo	Creole
hacienda	guano	
estancia	pampas	

PEOPLE

Antonio Lopez de Santa Anna	Profirio Diaz	Simon Bolivar
	Juan Manual Rosas	Dom Pedro II
Benito Juarez	Bartolome Mitre	Bernardo O'Higgins

PLACES

Cuba	Argentina	Brazil
Puerto Rico	Paraguay	Venezuela
Mexico	Uruguay	Ecuador
Central America	Bolivia	Colombia
Rio de La Plata	Peru	
Buenos Aires	Chile	

CHAPTER 5

MULTIPLE-CHOICE QUESTIONS

Select the number of the correct answer.

1. In what way was Brazil different from other Latin American colonies?

   (1) Roman Catholic was the major religion.
   (2) It had Portuguese heritage.
   (3) It gained independence last.
   (4) Rural areas had the most power.

2. A hacienda or estancia is best described as

   (1) a dairy farm
   (2) a textile mill
   (3) a small city
   (4) a large estate

3. A caudillo in Latin America in the 1800s was most like which of these roles in global history?

   (1) a Japanese samurai
   (2) a European medieval lord
   (3) a Buddhist monk
   (4) a Russian czar

4. What was generally true about education in the newly independent nations of Latin America?

   (1) It was primarily for sons of wealthy landowners and some middle-class families.
   (2) It was open to all children in urban areas.
   (3) Free public education was common throughout the new nations.
   (4) It was best organized and funded in rural areas.

5. Typical export items from the South American nations in the 1800s included

   (1) beef, sugar, coffee
   (2) rice, tea, apples
   (3) glass, rifles, carriages
   (4) fish, furs, lumber

6. Put the following events in the order in which they occurred in Mexican history.

   A. Texas won its independence
   B. Santa Anna was exiled
   C. Five southern provinces split with Mexico
   D. The United States gained land in the Gadsden Purchase

   (1) D, A, C, B
   (2) C, A, B, D
   (3) C, A, D, B
   (4) A, B, C, D

7. *La Reforma* is a period in Mexican history in which

   (1) the Roman Catholic Church gained power
   (2) modern capitalist ideas were adopted
   (3) Native Indians strengthened their control of land
   (4) the government took an increased role in private business

8. Which title below would best be used for an article about Porfirio Diaz after his death?

   (1) "Beloved Democratic Leader Diaz Mourned by Mexican Workers"
   (2) "Dictator Diaz Encouraged Foreign Investments but Died Beloved by Mexicans"
   (3) "Exiled Mexican Leader Diaz Dies Leaving Mixed Legacy"
   (4) "Diaz Assassinated by Wealthy Landowner"

9. Of the United Provinces of La Plata, which country was the most politically and economically important?

(1) Uruguay
(2) Peru
(3) Paraguay
(4) Argentina

10. Buenos Aires developed as a major commercial center as a result of its

(1) geographic location
(2) native Indian population
(3) silver mines
(4) close ties with Portugal

11. What nineteenth-century invention helped Buenos Aires to become a thriving meat packing export center?

(1) grain elevators
(2) refrigerated ships
(3) transatlantic cable communication
(4) canal boats

12. By the end of the nineteenth century, why was Argentina considered to be an exception to what was happening to most other Latin American nations?

(1) Native Indians had taken over the government.
(2) There was little or no immigration.
(3) It had a stable political system and prosperous economy.
(4) Middle-class discontent had caused a series of revolutions.

13. Simon Bolivar was known as the Liberator because he

(1) unified the Andean nations and people
(2) represented Spain in Latin America
(3) helped several Latin American nations gain their independence
(4) represented the concerns of the native peoples in Mexico

14. In the middle of the nineteenth century, Chile became the world's leading producer of

(1) copper
(2) gold
(3) uranium
(4) nickel

15. Place the following events in Brazil's history in the correct chronological order.

A. Golden Law enacted
B. Pedro II overthrown
C. Coffee replaced sugar as major export
D. King Dom Joao arrived to live in Rio de Janeiro

(1) A, B, C, D
(2) D, A, C, B
(3) C, B, D, A
(4) D, C, A, B

16. Which group in Latin America does not enjoy the benefits that the same group enjoys in the United States or Canada?

(1) the middle class
(2) the mestizos
(3) the Native Indian peoples
(4) the educated upper classes

17. Conservatives in most Latin American countries were generally from which group of people?

(1) peasant farmers
(2) great landowners
(3) small merchants
(4) mestizos

18. Frequently those most responsible for the actual production of nineteenth-century Latin American agricultural cash crops were

(1) the large landowners themselves
(2) village merchants
(3) slaves
(4) peninsulares

19. *Gaucho* was a Latin American term to describe a

(1) city dweller
(2) cowboy
(3) coffee picker
(4) copper miner

20. Of the Latin Amercan nations that gained independence in the nineteenth century, which one was named for the person who most helped it become independent?

(1) Peru
(2) Argentina
(3) Brazil
(4) Bolivia

THEMATIC ESSAY

Directions: Write a well-organized essay that includes an introduction, several paragraphs addressing the task below, and a conclusion.

Theme: Political Power

Various groups in Latin American history have struggled to gain, regain, maintain, or retain political power in their nations.

Task

Select two groups in Latin American history in the nineteenth century that struggled to gain, regain, maintain, or retain political power and do the following:

- Identify the group and the country with which it is associated.
- Describe its relationship with its pursuit of power.
- Evaluate the group's success with regard to political power.

You may use any example from this chapter, but do not use the same group or country more than once. Some suggestions you might want to consider include the liberals, the Native Indians, the conservatives, the merchant class, the Roman Catholic Church. Do not use any group from the United States in your answer.

You are not limited to these suggestions.

Guidelines

In your essay, be sure to

- develop all aspects of the *Task*
- support the theme with relevant facts, examples, and details
- use a logical and clear organization, including an introduction and a conclusion that are beyond a restatement of the theme
- introduce the theme by establishing a framework that is beyond a simple restatement of the *Task* and conclude with a summation of the theme

This question is based on the accompanying documents. The question is designed to test your ability to work with historical documents. Some of the documents have been edited for the purposes of the question. As you analyze the documents, take into account the source of each document and any point of view that may be presented in the document.

Historical Context

During the nineteenth century in Latin America there were many economic, social, and political changes occurring.

Task

Using information from the documents and your knowledge of global history, answer the questions that follow each document in Part A. Your answers to the questions will help you write the Part B essay, in which you will be asked to

- discuss three changes that occurred in nineteenth century Latin America that had economic, social, or political impact
- describe a positive or negative effect of each change that you identified

Part A: Short-Answer Questions

Directions: Analyze the documents and answer the questions that follow each document.

Document 1a

"The first duty of a government is to give education to the people."

Simon Bolivar (1783–1830)

Document 1b

"An ignorant people is the blind instrument of its own destruction."

Simon Bolivar (1783–1830)

Questions

1. a. Based on both of these documents, what is Bolivar saying is required for a people to have to survive?
   b. Who does Bolivar say should supply this need to the people?

Document 2

South America, 1790

Possessions
- British, Dutch, and French
- Spanish
- Potuguese

Unexplored

South America, 1828

Possessions
- British, Dutch, and French
- Independent

PATAGONIA (Unexplored)

Question

2. According to the two maps above, state two ways the area shown changed during the given time period.
   a.
   b.

Document 3

"Let us hope that after the lesson learned through the prolonged and painful experience undergone by our communities during the war, that we Mexicans will cooperate with the welfare and prosperity of the Nation, which may only be obtained through unfailing respect for the law, and with complete obedience to the authorities elected by the people."

"Mexicans: let us now pledge all our efforts to obtain and consolidate the benefits of peace. Under its auspices, the protection of the laws and of the authorities will be sufficient for all the inhabitants of the Republic. May the people and the government respect the rights of all. Between individuals, as between nations, peace means respect for the rights of others."

A statement by Benito Juárez who was reelected President of the Republic in October 1867.

Questions

3. a. According to these words of Benito Juarez, what was his major goal?
   b. How did Juarez expect to attain this goal?

Document 4

Question

4. What does the appearance of these buildings suggest to you about the lifestyle of some residents of nineteenth-century Argentina?

Document 5

Question

5. Based on this picture, describe two effects of the role of the Catholic Church on the people of Latin America.

a.

b.

Document 6

6 a.

a. Using both documents, identify two difficulties in transportation in nineteenth-century Latin America.

b. Identify one export product from nineteenth-century Latin America suggested by the pictures.

6 b.

Part B: Essay

Directions: Write a well-organized essay that includes an introduction, several paragraphs, and a conclusion. Use evidence from *at least four* documents in the body of the essay. Support your response with relevant facts, examples, and details. Include additional outside information.

Historical Context

During the nineteenth century in Latin America there were many economic, social, and political changes occurring.

Task

Using information from the documents and your knowledge of global history, answer the questions that follow each document in Part A. Your answers to the questions will help you write the Part B essay, in which you will be asked to

- discuss three changes that occurred in nineteenth century Latin America that had economic, social, or political impact
- describe a positive or negative effect of each change that you identified

Guidelines

In your essay, be sure to

- address all aspects of the *Task* by accurately analyzing and interpreting *at least four* documents
- incorporate information from the documents in the body of the essay
- incorporate relevant outside information
- support the theme with relevant facts, examples, and details
- use a logical and clear plan of organization
- introduce the theme by establishing a framework that is beyond a simple restatement of the *Task* or *Historical Context* and conclude with a summation of the theme

CHAPTER 6

Imperialism

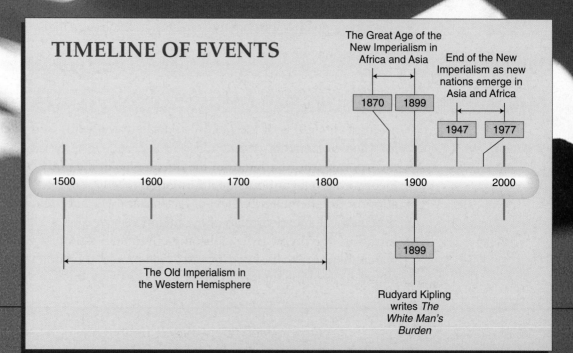

TIMELINE OF EVENTS

The Great Age of the New Imperialism in Africa and Asia

| 1870 | 1899 |

End of the New Imperialism as new nations emerge in Asia and Africa

| 1947 | 1977 |

1500   1600   1700   1800   1900   2000

The Old Imperialism in the Western Hemisphere

| 1899 |

Rudyard Kipling writes *The White Man's Burden*

The New Imperialism

Nations in Europe were eager for expansion, but they had no place to go on the continent without starting a war with a neighbor. This new nationalistic feeling led directly to the new imperialism. With the advances of the Industrial Revolution, even the smallest of nations could think about conquering large areas of Africa and Asia. These new colonies would then serve the Europeans' need for raw materials and markets for their products. The Europeans could feel good about taking them over because they could justify their actions as "humanitarian." Lessons had been learned from the older imperialistic period. New forms of control were soon developed.

Imperialism can be defined as the intentional control by a powerful nation over a weaker region or nation. This control is usually political, economic, and social or cultural. As many of the regions under this kind of control were colonies, the practice of imperialism can also be referred to as **colonialism**. Imperialistic policies have been carried out in history by European as well as non-European peoples. We will concern ourselves mainly with the imperialism of Western European nations and Japan.

THE OLD IMPERIALISM AND THE NEW IMPERIALISM

There have been two distinct periods of imperialism. The old imperialism lasted from about 1500 to 1800. It was a feature of both the Age of Exploration and the Commercial Revolution. It was concerned initially with establishing trade routes and obtaining resources, and soon thereafter with the actual acquisition of lands and control over the people in those lands. It was carried on by private individuals and companies, and also by nation-states. This older form of imperialism took place mainly in the **western hemisphere**—North America, South America, and the Caribbean region.

> **Main Idea:**
> Imperialistic nations desired to rule over other lands and people and to establish empires.

The **new imperialism** began in the second half of the nineteenth century and lasted a few years past the middle of the twentieth century. It was concerned with establishing trade routes and obtaining resources, but it also sought to create markets and to find places worthy of large financial investments. It was carried out mainly by governments as official policy and took place mostly in the **eastern hemisphere**—Africa and Asia. Imperialistic nations desired to rule over other lands and people and to establish empires for reasons that went beyond those characteristics of the older imperialism. Let us now see what the reasons were for the new imperialism.

REASONS FOR THE NEW IMPERIALISM

There were many reasons for the new imperialism. As with any historic development that affects large numbers of people in different global regions, we must examine reasons for imperialism from economic, political, and social viewpoints. It is also necessary to understand the particular time in history when a given development such as imperialism occurs. Two of the most important aspects of nineteenth-century European history that we have learned about—the Industrial Revolution and nationalism—have a connection with the new imperialism.

Economic Reasons

The increased supply of manufactured goods produced by the Industrial Revolution encouraged European nations to find new markets for these goods. A new market meant a part of the world where there would be an opportunity for people there to buy goods produced by the European nations. These nations would also seek out resource-rich regions in order to exploit, make use of, the region's raw materials. These raw materials would be turned into a finished, manufactured product. The Industrial Revolution also saw a rise in the number of wealthy business professionals, merchants, and large companies. With surplus capital available to them, they looked overseas for places to invest their money. As investors, they would hope to make a profit. They would also expect their own national governments to send soldiers to protect their investments, such as rubber plantations, from interference by natives of the region as well as by other imperialistic nations.

Political Reasons

Nations hoped to gain prestige and glory by expanding their power globally. These nationalistic desires sparked nations to seek a balance of power with other nations who were also trying to build colonial empires. New nations such as Germany and Italy wanted to achieve their own "place in the sun" and catch up with longtime colonial powers such as France, Great Britain, and the Netherlands. Imperialistic rivalries in some instances grew intense. Strong-willed leaders who urged the use of armed forces to pursue their nations' claims were engaging in **jingoism**. Nations also wanted overseas territories as places for military bases and coaling stations for their navies. In addition, a colony was a potential source of manpower for the imperialistic nation's army.

Social Reasons

European nations thought their way of life to be superior to other global areas. Consequently, they felt both an obligation and a right to spread their culture into these areas. These feelings of **ethnocentrism** can be seen in the 1899 poem, *The White Man's Burden*, by the Englishman **Rudyard Kipling** (1865–1936). It was about the obligation of carrying Western civilization to those people in other parts of the world, who were considered to be "backward" and less fortunate. These feelings were also the result of nineteenth-century notions of

Rudyard Kipling (1865–1936). English writer. Wood engraving, 1891.

white racial superiority and the theory of **Social Darwinism**. Such beliefs held that social progress depended on competition among human beings, resulting in the "survival of the fittest." And as Europeans saw themselves as more powerful and more advanced technologically, they regarded it as natural for stronger societies to conquer weaker ones.

Certainly, there were those European missionaries, educators, doctors, engineers, and scientists who went to Africa and Asia with such fixed, rigid views. Yet, among them were many who traveled overseas for purely humanitarian purposes, and with respect for the native peoples they met. Thus, for example, there were those missionaries whose emphasis was simply on seeking converts to Christianity; and there were those missionaries who were interested less with religion than with matters of health and living conditions. In addition, there were explorers who mainly wished to learn more about the physical geography of regions that were unknown to them.

FORMS OF IMPERIALIST CONTROL

The European nations that became imperialistic powers established their control and authority in different ways. The various forms or types of such authority and control are described in this section.

Sphere of Influence

By claiming a **sphere of influence**, a nation gained sole economic power in a region and had exclusive economic rights to trade, to invest, and to develop mines, factories, or railroads. Other nations could not interfere with its activities. This form of imperialism was used in China, where each foreign nation active there, such as Germany, had economic control in a specific region. In general, other foreign nations would respect this kind of arrangement.

Concession

A **concession** consisted of a foreign nation's obtaining special privileges. An underdeveloped region gave permission to a technologically advanced country to do something of economic value in the region. For example, the Arabs let the British drill for oil and build a railroad in the Middle East. Ultimately, while Arab rulers in the Arabian peninsula would gain part of the profits from the sale of the oil, it would be the British who would keep most of the profits and expand their economic and political control in the region.

Protectorate

Under a **protectorate** system, a colonial nation would allow the native ruler of a region to remain in office as a figurehead, while in reality the colonial power made all major decisions. The colonial nation, as a "protecting big brother power," would prevent other nations from coming into the region. For example, the French held Morocco and Tunisia as protectorates. Also, the Eastern European **satellite nations** controlled by the Soviet Union after World War II can be thought of as protectorates (see Chapters 9 and 12 in this volume).

Colony

To set up a **colony** an imperialistic nation would achieve total control over a region through settlement or conquest. The nation then would annex the region, or add it to its territorial belongings, with the region becoming part of a colonial empire. The colony would have the flag of the imperialistic power or mother country flying over it, just as if the colony were a piece of land situated in Europe within the boundaries of the mother country itself. French annexations of Algeria and Indochina, and Portuguese control over Angola are examples of colonial acquisitions.

Mandates

A **mandate** describes a region that is placed under the temporary control of a nation by an international organization. Such a situation is rare, but did occur after World War I. Turkey, a losing nation, was forced to give up its control of Palestine, Iraq, Syria, and Lebanon. The League of Nations, the forerunner of the United Nations, agreed to let Britain have a mandate over Palestine and Iraq, and to let France have a mandate over Syria and Lebanon. Britain and France were victorious nations in World War I, and gained control over the mandated territories for a limited amount of time.

SECTION 2

Imperialism in Africa

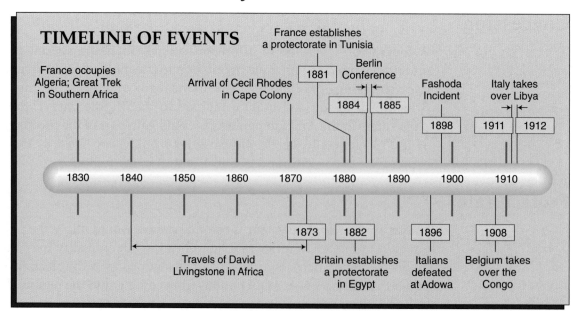

TIMELINE OF EVENTS

France occupies Algeria; Great Trek in Southern Africa

Arrival of Cecil Rhodes in Cape Colony

France establishes a protectorate in Tunisia — 1881

Berlin Conference — 1884 1885

Fashoda Incident — 1898

Italy takes over Libya — 1911 1912

1830 1840 1850 1860 1870 1880 1890 1900 1910

1873 — Travels of David Livingstone in Africa

1882 — Britain establishes a protectorate in Egypt

1896 — Italians defeated at Adowa

1908 — Belgium takes over the Congo

When the twentieth century began, over 90 percent of the African continent was controlled by Europeans. This control took the various forms that we learned about in the last section. The only parts of Africa that were not under European rule were the countries of Ethiopia and Liberia. And yet, just one hundred years earlier, at the start of the nineteenth century, there was no part of Africa under control by a European nation.

What then had brought on this historic change that saw European power extend into Africa? The general reasons are given in Section 1 of this chapter. In this section, we will see how this power was extended and how it was maintained. Several European nations became involved in the **"scramble for Africa,"** a competition for land and resources in this huge continent. The scramble for Africa was most intense from 1880 to 1910 and resulted in a **partition of Africa**, meaning a division of its land without any consent given by the African people.

There had been earlier contact between Europe and Africa, during the age of the old imperialism. In that period (1500–1800), however, Africa was not viewed as a target for conquest and takeover. The European interest in Africa at that time was focused on specific economic goals:

1. To trade for ivory, gold, and other items
2. To establish bases as stopovers for ships sailing to South and East Asia
3. To obtain slaves for work in the Americas, the "New World" of the Western Hemisphere.

Moreover, the European contact with Africa was limited mostly to coastal areas. The European nations that developed the largest colonial empires in Africa from 1880 to 1910 were Britain and France. We will look at the imperialistic roles they played in Africa's history as well as the roles played by Germany, Italy, Belgium, and Portugal.

<aside>
Main Idea:
The scramble for Africa was most intense from 1880 to 1910 and resulted in a **partition of Africa**, meaning a division of its land without any consent given by the African people.
</aside>

GREAT BRITAIN

In time, of all the European nations active in Africa, Britain came to rule over the largest number of African people. Britain's colonies were scattered all over the continent. In the north, Britain gained dominance in Egypt. Egyptian rulers in the mid-1800s borrowed much money from British banks. Unable to pay back all their loans, the rulers piled up large debts and were subject to pressure from bankers to follow various economic policies. Additional British interest in Egypt emerged with construction of the **Suez Canal** in 1869. A French company, headed by **Ferdinand de Lessep**s, had built the canal with the permission of the Egyptian government. The Egyptian government, in fact, was the biggest stockholder in this company. However, the head of the government, **Ismail Pasha**, had added to his country's foreign debt because of his excessive spending and fancy lifestyle. To pay off his debts, he sold large amounts of stock in the Suez Canal Company to the British government in 1875. Britain thus became a part owner of the canal. This was important to Britain, as it was the biggest user of the canal and considered it part of its "lifeline to India." In fact, the trade route from Britain through the Mediterranean Sea, the Suez Canal, and the Red Sea to

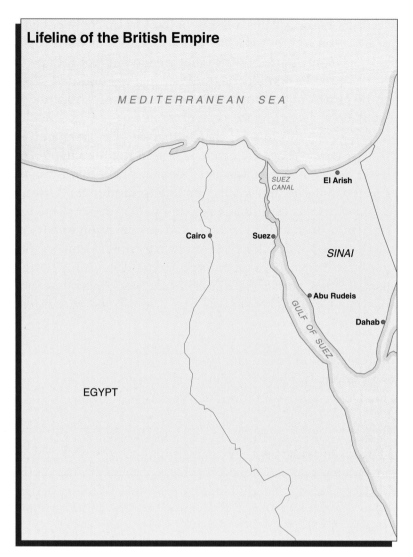

Lifeline of the British Empire

MEDITERRANEAN SEA

SUEZ CANAL

El Arish

Cairo

Suez

SINAI

Abu Rudeis

GULF OF SUEZ

Dahab

EGYPT

India and Britain's Asian possessions, became known as the **lifeline of the British Empire**.

With Egypt's financial problems growing worse, the British sent in troops in 1882. The reasons were supposedly to protect investments and the Suez Canal and to reorganize Egypt's monetary system. Although Egyptian officials remained in power, it was the British, who, by setting up a protectorate, really ruled the country.

British Involvement in Central and East Africa

British interests also reached south of Egypt, into the region known as the Sudan. Whoever controlled the Sudan, site of the upper Nile River, would be able to control the flow of the Nile waters into Egypt. In 1898, British forces in the Sudan defeated the forces of the **Mahdi**, the Islamic ruler, and captured Khartoum. Moving further south, the British reached the town of **Fashoda** only to find a French army that had recently arrived there. The French had raised their flag in this part of the southern Sudan, hoping to expand eastward from their empire in West Africa. The two European armies faced each other for almost two weeks, poised to begin a territorial war. However, since neither Britain nor France really wished to go to war, an agreement was signed that prevented fighting. It stated that France would recognize British authority over the Sudan, while Britain would respect France's colonization in West Africa.

This settlement of what became known as the Fashoda Incident, made without asking the Sudanese for their opinion, resulted in the addition of the Anglo-Egyptian Sudan territory to the British Empire. The Fashoda Incident also showed how overseas competition could lead to a war between colonial powers. It also demonstrated how great powers could compromise, under certain "face-saving" conditions. Finally, it signaled a growing friendliness between two former enemies—a friendliness that would be important in the world wars of the twentieth century.

In East Africa, another possible confrontation between colonial powers grew as England, Germany, and Portugal laid claims here. A settlement was reached in the **Berlin Conference** of 1884–1885. Recognition was given to a region labeled British East Africa and a region called German East Africa, and to Mozambique as a Portuguese colony. No Africans were involved in these agreements. Because British East Africa had much undeveloped land and a cooler climate than many other parts of Africa, it attracted many Englishmen to come and settle there. They were mainly from the poorer classes and saw an opportunity to better their lives at the expense of the native Africans. These Englishmen and their descendants came to look upon this territory as their homeland and thus developed a "settler mentality." This was to be a factor in their resistance to East African independence movements in the 1960s.

The British government's takeover in East Africa, as well as in some other regions, did come across some obstacles. One of these was the armed resistance of African people. Both the Shana and Matabele tribes, for example, fought two wars against the foreigners before being subdued. The British cause was helped by superior weapons, as well as general disunity among tribal groups. East African societies were also disrupted by a large slave trade, begun by Arabs, that lasted into the nineteenth century. Another factor that weakened these societies and made them vulnerable and open to a takeover was a famine caused by rinderpest. This is the name of cattle disease. The death of many cattle caused malnutrition and starvation for East Africans.

British Involvement in Southern Africa and the Influence of Cecil Rhodes

Southern Africa was another region that experienced British imperialism. The great attractions here were the rich deposits of gold and diamonds along with the geographically strategic locale of the tip of Africa. The tip of Africa had been settled by the Dutch in 1692 and was called Cape Colony. It was taken by the British in 1815, at the end of the Napoleonic Wars. In 1870, an Englishman whose activities were to shape the history of the region arrived in Cape Colony. This was **Cecil Rhodes** (1853–1902), as a financial investor who was to become a prime minister of Cape Colony and an empire builder. Rhodes acquired control of the diamond production in Southern Africa by the 1890s. The methods used to obtain land with diamond deposits included armed forces, bribery of local chieftains, and treaties.

Cecil John Rhodes (1853–1902). English administrator and financier in South Africa. Photographed c. 1895.

The use of treaties stirred controversy, because Europeans and Africans would view them differently. Controversy stemmed from a clash between English legal traditions and age-old African customs. A good example of this was the 1888 treaty signed by the Englishman Rudd, an agent of Cecil Rhodes, and Lobengula, chief of the Matabeles. By the terms of this document, **Lobengula** gave to Rudd (unknowingly) all the mineral rights of his tribal region. In return, he was to receive rifles, cartridges, a yearly income, and a steamboat. When Rhodes's company, the British South Africa Company, began to develop gold and diamond mines, Lobengula protested and even wrote a letter of complaint to Queen Victoria. The British position was that the 1888 treaty was a perfectly legal document that transferred title to and ownership of the land to them. In England, it was common for ownership of property to be exchanged by the signing of a con-

Cecil John Rhodes (1853–1902). English administrator and financier in southern Africa. "The Rhodes Colossus - Striding from Cape Town to Cairo." An English cartoon of 1892 hailing Rhodes' plan to construct a railroad extending from South Africa to Egypt.

tract. It was not so in Africa. From Lobengula's point of view, and that of tribal African societies, ownership of land was sacred and certainly could not be exchanged according to a piece of paper. Nevertheless, Lobengula lost his land. It soon became the English colony of Rhodesia, named after Cecil Rhodes.

Rhodes became an extremely wealthy man. He dreamed of a huge British Empire in Africa, hoping to complete a "Cape to Cairo" railroad. His dreams, if they had been realized, would have added to British power as well as to his own wealth. By the terms of his will, large sums of money, obtained from his gold and diamond mines, were left to establish scholarships at Oxford for Englishmen and Americans. Indeed, even now, it is an outstanding honor to be granted a Rhodes scholarship.

Although Rhodes was the key economic and political figure in the growth of British dominance in Southern Africa, this dominance could not have been achieved without the deployment of British soldiers. They were needed to win over the **Zulus**, a tribal people who were highly disciplined warriors who fought courageously. In 1879, however, at the Battle of Ulundi, the Zulus suffered a crushing defeat. By 1887, the entire Zulu nation fell to the British. British military power was also needed to fight against the **Boers**. The Boers were descendants of the Dutch settlers who had come to Southern Africa in 1652. They resented the British takeover of Cape Colony in 1815 and migrated northward. This migration, known as the **Great Trek**, resulted in the establishment of the Republics of Transvaal and the Orange Free State. Tension between the Boers and Britain was aggravated when more Englishmen came to these areas following the news of the discovery of valuable gold and diamond deposits. This tension resulted in the **Boer War** (1899–1902). Upon winning the war, Britain promised the Boers some form of self-government. In 1910, the Transvaal and the Orange Free State were combined with the British territories of Cape Colony and Natal to form the Union of South Africa. The region now became a self-governing dominion within the British Empire.

The colonial policy Britain followed in most of its African settlements as well as in most of its Asian colonies was called **indirect rule**. This policy permitted local rulers to maintain some power in their region, although they actually followed the directions given by the British. A good example of British colonial rule can be seen in Nigeria. Under the British administrator of this colony, **Sir Frederick Lugard**, local tribal chiefs were allowed to retain their authority as long as they obeyed general guidelines concerning such items as prohibitions on slavery and on warfare among themselves. (England had abolished its own transatlantic slave trade in 1807.) Native Nigerian laws, religion, and traditions could be maintained insofar as they did not sharply conflict with British standards. The British sought to build railroads, improve commerce and agriculture, fight disease, and educate selected natives. Because the British believed that their values and ways of life were superior to those of Africans and should be spread, the British even brought some Africans to school in Britain in order to educate them. The hope was that these individuals would plant British political and social ideas in Africa.

British Explorers

David Livingstone (1813–1873). Scottish missionary and explorer. Wood engraving, 1867, published on a premature account of Livingstone's death.

A great deal of interest about Africa grew from the travels and publications of British explorers. Businessmen, missionaries, and government officials gained knowledge about what they previously thought was an unknown or "dark" continent. Among the famous explorers were the following:

1. Mungo Park was the first Westerner to travel along the Niger River in West Africa.
2. **David Livingstone**, a physician and missionary, was the best-known European explorer of the nineteenth century. Between 1840 and 1873, he traveled extensively in Central Africa. His writings received wide publicity in Europe. He came across a magnificent waterfall in 1855, naming it **Victoria Falls**, in honor of **Queen Victoria**. In 1869, a New York newspaper reporter, **Henry Stanley**, traced down Livingstone near Lake Tanganyika. They then jointly explored areas of East Africa.
3. Richard Burton and John Speke journeyed south along the Nile River and throughout East Africa, helping to establish British claims to the region.

Victoria Falls, Africa.

The maps drawn by these explorers provided new information about Africa. Their books described several well-organized and developed native civilizations. Similar information appeared in the writing of some missionaries. However, there were also prejudiced accounts by Europeans, which pictured Africans as "savages" and were the basis for negative myths and stereotypes.

FRANCE

During the nineteenth century, France was able to build a colonial empire in Africa that covered more territory than Britain's. The first major French penetration was in North Africa. Upset with actions taken by the Barbary pirates from North African Islamic regions, France sent a military force in 1830 that arrested the ruler and took over the region.

In neighboring **Tunisia**, the ruler, known as the Bey, was a poor financial manager. He lived beyond his means, and borrowed heavily from French bankers and the French government. In 1881, wanting to reform Tunisia's monetary system, protect its investments, get repayment of loans, and expand its role in North Africa, France established a protectorate in Tunisia, and expanded its role in North Africa. France improved transportation and education and built up several industries.

With the acquisition of Algeria and Tunisia, France then felt it was necessary to protect these holdings by taking over **Morocco**. A dispute with Germany, which also desired a foothold in Morocco, was resolved in 1911. France secured a protectorate in Morocco, while Germany gained land in West Africa.

GERMANY

As a latecomer to national unity (see Chapter 3, Section 4 in this volume), Germany was also a latecomer to imperialism. Even though Chancellor Bismarck himself was not very interested in gaining colonies, Kaisers William I and William II, along with other Germans, believed that colonial acquisitions were necessary for Germany to be considered a great power and to enjoy a "place in the sun" with other European nations. The four scattered German colonies in West Africa covered very little land. These were Togoland, Cameroon, German East Africa, and Southwest Africa. Unlike Britain and France, which were able to strengthen their colonial empires well into the twentieth century, Germany never really had a chance to do this. It lost all its possessions after its defeat in 1918 in World War I.

ITALY

As was true of Germany, Italy was a latecomer both to national unity (see Chapter 3, Section 3 in this volume) and the race for colonies. As a result, there was very little land left for Italy to gain. It was thwarted in its efforts to take Abyssinia (Ethiopia), suffering a crushing defeat by the forces of **Emperor**

Menelik II (1844–1913). Emperor of Abyssinia (Ethiopia). Wood engraving, English, 1896.

Menelik II at **Adowa** in 1896. Italy did obtain the small desert lands of Eritrea and Somaliland near the **horn of Africa**. With the gradual weakening of Ottoman Turkish rule in North Africa, Italy was able to send in troops and acquire Libya in 1911–1912.

BELGIUM

Another latecomer to the scramble for Africa was Belgium. Its "empire" consisted of only one region—the **Congo**. Nevertheless, it was, and still is, one of the most resource-rich parts of the continent. Eager to obtain rubber and ivory from this part of Central Africa, Belgian **King Leopold II** (r. 1865–1909), acting as a private citizen, formed a company with several Belgian capitalists in 1876. The company made huge profits but did little to improve the lives of the people of the Congo. The native population was terribly mistreated. Many were forced to work on rubber plantations amid harsh conditions, and they were often subjected to torture. The company looked upon the Congo simply as an investment and followed a policy of **exploitation**. This meant that the company took unfair advantage of its position and cared only for itself.

News about the inhumane treatment of natives along with news of financial scandals resulted in the Belgian government taking formal control of the Congo in 1908. From that point on, the region was known as a colony, the Belgian Congo. Under the Belgian government, exploitation was somewhat reduced, and an attempt was made to copy the British system of indirect rule. The Belgians also followed a policy of **paternalism**. With this attitude, the Belgians viewed the Congolese as if they were children needing to be led and instructed, unable to care for themselves. Such an attitude was demeaning and racist, and was a factor in causing problems for the Congo when it became independent in 1960.

> **Main Idea:** Under the Belgian government, exploitation was somewhat reduced, and an attempt was made to copy the British system of indirect rule.

Leopold II
(1835–1909). King
of the Belgians,
1865–1909.

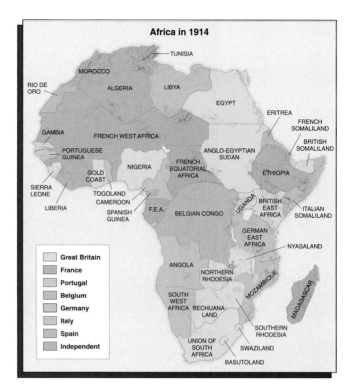

Africa in 1914

TUNISIA
MOROCCO
RIO DE ORO
ALGERIA
LIBYA
EGYPT
ERITREA
FRENCH SOMALILAND
BRITISH SOMALILAND
GAMBIA
FRENCH WEST AFRICA
PORTUGUESE GUINEA
GOLD COAST
NIGERIA
FRENCH EQUATORIAL AFRICA
ANGLO-EGYPTIAN SUDAN
ETHIOPIA
SIERRA LEONE
TOGOLAND
CAMEROON
LIBERIA
SPANISH GUINEA
F.E.A.
BELGIAN CONGO
UGANDA
BRITISH EAST AFRICA
ITALIAN SOMALILAND
GERMAN EAST AFRICA
NYASALAND
ANGOLA
NORTHERN RHODESIA
MOZAMBIQUE
MADAGASCAR
SOUTH WEST AFRICA
BECHUANA-LAND
SOUTHERN RHODESIA
UNION OF SOUTH AFRICA
SWAZILAND
BASUTOLAND

Great Britain
France
Portugal
Belgium
Germany
Italy
Spain
Independent

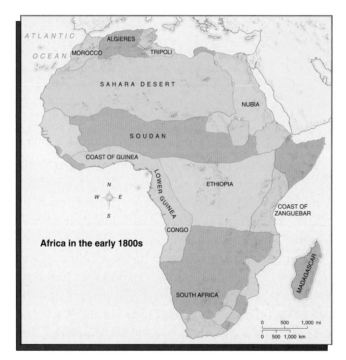

ATLANTIC OCEAN
ALGIERES
MOROCCO
TRIPOLI
SAHARA DESERT
NUBIA
SOUDAN
COAST OF GUINEA
LOWER GUINEA
ETHIOPIA
CONGO
COAST OF ZANGUEBAR
MADAGASCAR
SOUTH AFRICA

Africa in the early 1800s

0   500   1,000 mi
0 500 1,000 km

Main Idea:
Portuguese sailors on the way to Asia would stop along the east and west coasts of Africa to trade and to set up supply bases.

PORTUGAL

Portugal was one of the earliest European nations to have commercial contacts and settlements in Africa. Using its advanced navigational skills in the fifteenth and sixteenth centuries during the Age of Exploration, Portuguese sailors on the way to Asia would stop along the east and west coasts of Africa to trade and to set up supply bases. Eventually, these stopovers became the Portuguese colonies of Angola, Mozambique, and Portuguese Guinea. In the late nineteenth century, Portugal was fortunate in being able to have its colonial status in Angola and Mozambique recognized by the other European powers. By this time, it was a weak nation and could not have competed for land with England, France, and Germany. Yet, because all of these other nations feared each other, with each wanting to prevent the other from gaining land in Southern Africa, Portugal was allowed to retain Angola and Mozambique. This was one of the decisions reached concerning the partition of Africa at the Berlin Conference of 1884–1885.

Portuguese colonial policies were examples of both exploitation and paternalism. As was generally true of France's attitudes toward its colonies, Portugal viewed its African possessions as if they were, like Lisbon, part of Portugal itself. With such attitudes, as we will see in discussing the end of imperialism (see Chapter 15 in this volume), Portugal was very reluctant to grant independence to its colonies.

LINK TO TODAY
Nollywood and Literature

It is no secret to recognize that Nollywood rhymes with Hollywood, and that the former term has something to do with movies. Indeed, that term refers to the movie industry in Nigeria, and in a broader sense to the movie industry in many African countries. Even though the term is derived from the United States, the fact that some films are in English or have English subtitles is due essentially more to the British colonial influence in Africa. The same is true for films made in Africa which are in French or another former colonial power's language. Of course, there are also films made in some native African languages. This linguistic diversity in the film industry is also evident in literature produced in the African continent. And yet, a serious linguistic question remains about the two forms of cultural expression described here in this paragraph. The question aroused much debate, for example, in a 1952 writers' conference in Uganda. This was the question: "What is African literature?"

1. Is it literature written by Africans in an African language?
2. Is it literature written by Africans in a foreign language?
3. Is it literature about Africa written by foreigners in their own languages?

These are questions that are still being asked today and that are part of the legacy of European imperialism. Scores of well-educated African writers and film directors can speak one or more European languages and have traveled abroad. The Uganda conference could not agree on a specific definition of African literature. Can you?

Imperialism in Asia

As we now turn to Asia, we see very similar patterns to those in Africa. The military might of Europe due to the Industrial Revolution allowed it to take advantage of a militarily weaker area. The British flag was seen around the globe. The saying, "The sun never sets on the British Empire," was certainly accurate. The French were also active in their imperialistic goals, with holdings in many parts of the world. The Spanish, Dutch, and Portuguese held on to their small pieces. Germany and Italy were forced to play a smaller game due to their later arrival on the scene. A new player, the United States, obtained the Philippines after defeating Spain. The European nations also took advantage of the fact that there was little unity in the areas where they took control. The peoples that lived there were culturally intermixed and so a feeling of true nationalism did not really exist.

The Middle East was divided between Britain and France after World War I. The League of Nations gave over this area to these two nations in the belief that the area would be prepared for independence. The area that was Palestine was promised as a homeland to the Jewish people by the British, who then

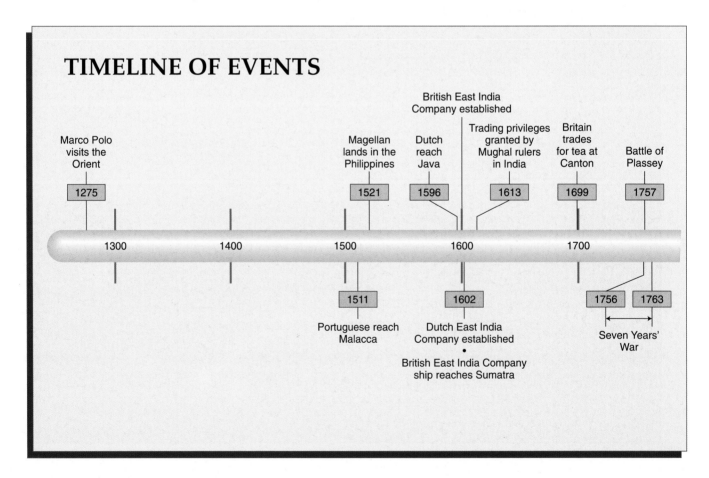

TIMELINE OF EVENTS

Marco Polo visits the Orient — 1275

Magellan lands in the Philippines — 1521

Dutch reach Java — 1596

British East India Company established / Trading privileges granted by Mughal rulers in India — 1613

Britain trades for tea at Canton — 1699

Battle of Plassey — 1757

1300   1400   1500   1600   1700

Portuguese reach Malacca — 1511

Dutch East India Company established — 1602

British East India Company ship reaches Sumatra

Seven Years' War — 1756 to 1763

reneged on that promise. It was not in the British interest to anger the Arabs who had the oil. This area saw four wars after the State of Israel was created in 1948, as the Arabs failed in their attempt to destroy the Jewish state.

SOUTH ASIA

Who was **Lord Cornwallis**? Most Americans know him as the English general who surrendered to George Washington in 1781, at the Battle or Yorktown. This surrender marked the end of the American Revolution and thus the end of British control over its thirteen colonies in North America. As you know, these thirteen colonies went on to form the United States of America. You also know that George Washington went on to become the country's first president. But do you know what happened to Lord Cornwallis after the Battle of Yorktown?

Most Americans cannot answer this question, probably because U.S. history textbooks usually do not mention him after the chapter on the Revolution.

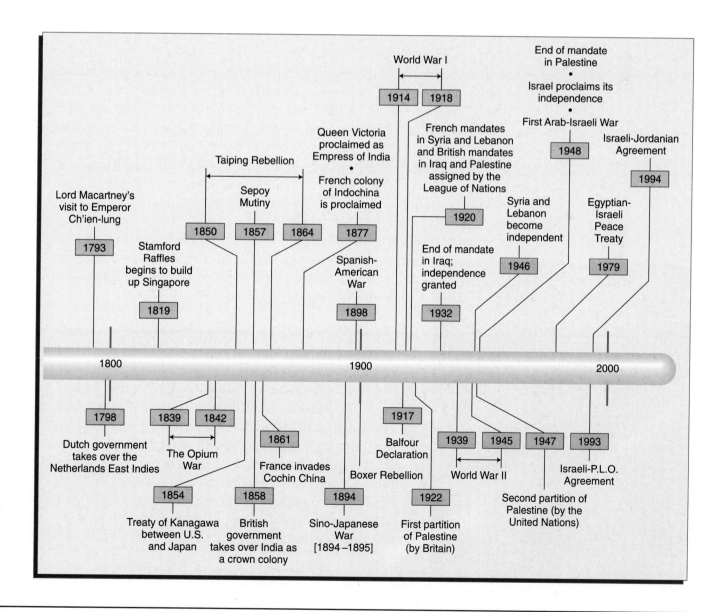

However, people in England and India know about him. This is because he had an important position in India, having gone there on behalf of the **British East India Company**. He was a governor-general there as well as a military commander, at a time in the late 1700s when the British were slowly gaining power in South Asia. Although today, with the British no longer in control of India, it is of interest to find a Cornwallis Road in downtown New Delhi—India's capital city!

The India that Cornwallis saw was not an independent united nation-state. It was a geographic expression, a place, just like Italy was prior to becoming a unified nation. British authority in this place called India reached a point where India became the largest colony in the British Empire. It was even termed the "Jewel of the Empire" as well as the "**jewel of the crown**." It covered a huge area in South Asia, geographically called the Indian Subcontinent, from which the present-day nations of India, Pakistan, and Bangladesh were carved.

Early British Involvement (1600–1858)

The British East India Company was formed as a private company in 1600, under a charter granted by Queen Elizabeth I. In 1613, it received permission to trade in India from the ruling **Mughals**. From this time until 1858, the company exercised powers usually associated with a government. It had, for example, its own private army. One of its employees, **Robert Clive**, led military forces to victories against both French and native armies. The French had competed with Britain for influence in South Asia, just as was the case in North America. The victories over the French came during the Seven Years' War (1756–1763), a true world war, as fighting occurred in both America and Asia. The most famous of these victories in India was at **Plassey** in 1757. Consequently, the British became the dominant and unofficial political power in the subcontinent. It was soon thereafter that Lord Cornwallis came to India.

Under his leadership, up to 1793, and that of succeeding governors-general, into the 1800s, the East India Company expanded its control in South Asia. It was able to do this for a number of reasons:

1. The region had hundreds of small states and no central government. The Mughal rulers controlled much, but not all, of the vast region.
2. There was religious divisiveness among the Indians. Tension existed between the two major groups, Hindus and Muslims, thereby restricting any cooperation among them against the British.
3. Linguistic divisiveness also existed. There was no common language; several languages and hundreds of dialects were spoken in the region.
4. Militarily, the Indians were unable to stand up to superior British arms and organizations.

Robert Clive (1725–1774). Baron of Plassey. British soldier and colonialist. Line-and-stipple engraving, English, 19th century.

The Sepoy Mutiny

Sepoy mutineers attacking the redan battery at Lucknow, India on July 30, 1857. Contemporary English colored engraving.

In 1857, a key event took place in India that was to affect sharply the relationship between the British and the Indians. This was the **Sepoy Mutiny**. Also known as the Sepoy Rebellion, it was fought against the British for both religious and political reasons. It began when Indians in the British army (**sepoys**) suspected that the grease used on bullet cartridges came from cows and pigs. If so, to bite into these cartridges, as was necessary when loading them, would have violated Hindu and Muslim beliefs: **Hindus** believe cows are sacred, and **Muslims** are forbidden from eating pork. These beliefs led to a mutiny that gradually spread beyond the armed forces and grew into an anti-Western movement. It attracted Indian princes and peasants. (In fact, some Indian historians view the Sepoy Mutiny as a war of independence.) Eventually, it was severely put down. Nevertheless, the East India Company was abolished. In 1858, it was replaced as a governing body by the British crown along with Parliament. India then became a crown colony.

The British Government's Colonial Policy in India

British authority following the Sepoy Mutiny covered almost 70 percent of the subcontinent. The **British Raj** (rule) expanded, using a variety of methods. In some instances, outright military subjugation, forcible takeover, occurred. Treaties and alliances were often made between the British and a prince of a state, who was an enemy of another prince. Special favors were also given to "cooperative" princes. These were successful examples of "divide and conquer" tactics.

Main Idea:
Indirect rule was the general policy in India, as had been the case with British possessions in Africa.

Indirect rule was the general policy in India, as had been the case with British possessions in Africa. In London, a minister from Parliament was given responsibility for Indian affairs. Under the minister was a viceroy in India who carried out directives. And under the viceroy were several British officials, or advisers, who watched over local matters but also left a large measure of control with the local rulers or princes. All of these people, British and Indian, were indirectly responsible to Queen Victoria. In 1877, she was recognized by Parliament as Empress of India.

For Britain, India was viewed as a source of economic wealth. Manufacturers of textiles, machines, and other products looked upon India as a vast market for their goods. This development of a market, however, harmed those Indian producers who could not compete with the British. Many local Indian industries suffered as they did not have the technology of the foreigners for mass production, nor could they sell items at competitive prices. British investment helped build up tea plantations as well as the steel and cement industries. The colonial government improved transportation by constructing railroads, bridges, and roadways. The number of hospitals and schools increased. A civil service system that provided for efficient government operations was introduced.

In social and cultural matters, the British sought to impose their own ways. They introduced the English language, wanting Indians to learn it. Those who mastered it could aspire to positions in the civil service system. The growth of churches was evidence of missionary activity. British style in architecture and gardens was soon apparent. The British attempted to make "**brown Englishmen**" out of selected Indians, who would be given a British-style education in England. It was hoped that they would adopt British cultural customs and values and return to India and spread them in the population. The British also acted to stamp out Indian cultural practices such as **suttee**. This was a Hindu custom whereby a widow would burn herself on the funeral pyre of her dead husband. To the British, such an act was considered to be suicide and contrary to Christian ideals and, therefore, was outlawed. Attempts were also made to end the Indian custom of killing unwanted baby girls (female infanticide).

British involvement in India grew rapidly, especially after completion of the Suez Canal in 1869. The trip there by ship was still, however, long and difficult. Life in India, with different climate and health conditions from those of Europe, could be challenging. British tombstones, for example, found as far north as Peshawar (in present-day Pakistan) and as far south as Madras (in present-day India), tell of English men, women, and children who died of cholera, malaria, and other diseases. Some of these tombs in Madras can be found in a historic building, St. Mary's Church, built by the British. It still stands today, with a sign outside proclaiming it as "the oldest Anglican church east of Suez." Inside the church, among several paintings, is a portrait of a famous member of the British East India Company, **Elihu Yale** (1649–1721). This is the same person for whom Yale University in New Haven, Connecticut, in the United States is named.

Thus, we can see how British imperialism brought a connecting link between three continents. Elihu Yale, a man from England, part of *Europe*, traveled to British India, in *Asia*, and is remembered for being a benefactor at a great university in a British colony in *North America*. The final note in this tri-continental historical drama occurred in the 1950s when Chester Bowles, a Yale graduate and the American ambassador to India, went to St. Mary's Church to place a plaque near the portrait of Elihu Yale. Thus, a citizen of the United States of America (a nation whose roots were as

Main Idea:
The British attempted to make "**brown Englishmen**" out of selected Indians, who would be given a British-style education in England.

BRITISH GROUP PORTRAIT.
Left-to-right: 2nd Duke of Devonshire (William Cavendish), Lord Cavendish (James Cavendish, standing), Elihu Yale, Mr. Tunstal, and page. Oil, c. 1708.

British colonies) traveled to India (a nation that was once a British colony) to honor a native of the former mother country of both colonial settlements. The connecting link involving Chester Bowles in the twentieth century had roots in the connecting link involving Lord Cornwallis in the eighteenth century, whom we mentioned at the start of this chapter.

EAST ASIA

When people gather to have big, fancy dinners, they may do this at home or in a large restaurant, or a catering hall. The occasion may be a happy family event, or a celebration of a holiday, or an important event such as a wedding or graduation. The food that is eaten may very well be served on expensive and beautiful dishes called china. This name was originally used by Englishmen over two hundred years ago to describe the skillfully designed porcelain and pottery made in China. Such items were much in demand by Europeans at the time. The desire to obtain these and other items was one of many reasons for European interest in China. This interest was eventually to grow into imperialistic activities.

China, along with **Japan** and **Korea**, is in a part of the world referred to as East Asia, the Orient, but it is better known as Southeast Asia. European imperialism was to affect this part of the world also. In this section, we will trace the European contact with East Asia.

CHINA

The major European imperialistic involvement in China occurred primarily in the nineteenth and twentieth centuries. However, interest in China goes back much earlier. In 1275, for example, Marco Polo's trip to the Orient stirred much excitement among Europeans. During the Age of Discovery, ships of Portugal were able to sail to China. They reached there in 1514 and set up a trading station at Macao in 1557. In 1699, the British were purchasing tea at the port of Canton (known today as Guangzhou). The British East India Company was very active in the tea trade, as the demand in London and elsewhere in the British Isles for tea increased enormously.

For the Chinese, trade with the British and other Europeans in the eighteenth century was very profitable. Along with tea, the chief Chinese exports to Europe were silk, sugar, and ginger. Yet, the Chinese did not want Europeans to trade outside of the Canton area. This restriction, as well as the many regulations imposed upon the European traders by the Chinese government, aroused resentment. The Chinese looked down upon the Europeans, considered them to be barbarians, and had little desire for European goods.

These kinds of Chinese ethnocentric attitudes were evident in the reaction to a visit in 1793 by **Lord George Macartney**, a representative of **King George III** of Britain. Macartney had come to see the **Emperor Ch'ien-lung**, of the **Ch'ing (Qing) Dynasty**, hoping to get increased trade and better contacts for British businessmen. He was shocked and saddened by the Emperor's response.

Marco Polo (1254–1324). Venetian traveler: line engraving, Italian, 1820.

The Emperor refused the foreigner's requests, noting that China had no need "to import any product produced by barbarians." This refusal, conveyed in a letter to King George, was upsetting to the British. Another reason for their discontent with the Chinese was the fact that they had to pay for Chinese goods with large amounts of silver. This form of payment was necessary, as the Chinese did not want to buy British products. For the British, an outflow of silver was considered harmful to their economy.

The Opium War (1839–1842)

This commercial relationship began to change dramatically in the early 1800s. The British realized that there was a market for opium in China. This narcotic drug was mass produced in India and sold by British merchants to the Chinese. Payment for the opium was made in goods and in ever-increasing amounts of silver. This drain of silver, as well as the injurious effects of opium-smoking on the Chinese population, angered the Chinese government. Accordingly, it banned all commerce in opium. Unable to enforce the ban, the government destroyed a stockpile of opium at a Canton warehouse in 1839. The British responded by sending warships to China. The **Opium War** (1839–1842) had begun!

The Chinese forces were no match for the British. Superior weaponry and organization led to a British victory. The resulting Treaty of Nanking in 1842 completely changed China's relations with the Western world. The chief provisions were as follows:

Chinese emperor (1736–1796). Emperor Ch'ien-lung attending an archery contest. Detail of scroll painting by Lang Shih-ning (1688–1766).

The bombardment of Canton, China, by the British fleet in 1841 during the First Opium War. Wood engraving, 19th century.

1. China consented to open five ports for trade, including Canton and Shanghai.
2. The British were given the island of Hong Kong.
3. China was to pay an **indemnity** (an amount of money for wrongdoing) to Britain to make up for destroyed opium.
4. British merchants and government officials could live in the five "treaty ports."
5. The British were granted the right of **extraterritoriality**. This meant that a British person in the treaty ports would be subject to British law, not Chinese law. In addition, if such a person was accused of committing an offense, he or she would be tried in British courts, not Chinese courts.

Main Idea:
The Treaty of Nanking was the first of what would be called **the unequal treaties**, for other nations forced China to sign treaties granting them the same trade rights Britain had gained.

These provisions were humiliating for the Chinese. The Treaty of Nanking was the first of what would be called **the unequal treaties**, for other nations forced China to sign treaties granting them the same trade rights Britain had gained. These other nations included France, Russia, and Germany. During the remainder of the nineteenth and into the early twentieth centuries, each of these four nations acquired a sphere of influence in different areas of China. They forced the Manchu rulers (leaders of the Ch'ing Dynasty) to give them economic privileges in these areas. These privileges included the right to build mines, factories, and railroads and to search for minerals. They also obtained land on which to build military bases to protect their spheres of influence.

The Sino-Japanese War

Non-European nations were also active in China. These were the United States and Japan. The United States was granted commercial privileges, although it did not acquire a sphere of influence. It did propose an "**Open Door Policy**," whereby all foreign nations would enjoy equal trading rights in China. The other nations accepted this idea in theory but did not really honor it in practice. One of these, an Asian newcomer to imperialism, was Japan. Having built up its economic and military power in the late 1800s, Japan was able to defeat China in the 1894–1895 **Sino-Japanese War**. Japan took over the island of Taiwan along with other Chinese territory.

A "Boxer" of the Boxer Rebellion in China, 1900. Drawing by H.W. Koekkoek.

The Boxer Rebellion

China's inability to defend itself against imperialism caused unrest among its people. The government, headed by the Empress Tz'u-hsi (r. 1898–1908), was also perceived to be corrupt and incapable of improving the lives of the people. Consequently, violence broke out in 1900, led by a secret Chinese society called the "Society of Harmonious Fists" or Boxers. This **Boxer Rebellion**, secretly supported by the empress, was aimed mainly at driving out foreigners from China. Many foreigners were killed by the Boxers before a combined army from six nations put an end to the fighting. Further agony followed for China, as the Manchu government was forced in a 1901 treaty to pay large indemnities and to let foreigners have expanded military and commercial powers. The United States returned most of its indemnity money to China, thereby earning some measure of goodwill.

The End of Dynastic Rule: The Nationalists Overthrow the Emperor (1911–1912)

Sun Yat-sen (1866–1925). Chinese statesman and revolutionary leader on a U.S. postage stamp, 1961.

In light of the events happening in China during the 1800s, as we have now seen, it is not surprising to find China ripe for dramatic revolutionary change in the early 1900s. Change did indeed occur with the weakening of the Manchu Qing (Ch'ing) emperor and the increasing strength of those Chinese committed to the modernization of their nation. On October 10, 1911, a successful rebellion broke out against the emperor. On this day, known to Chinese as "double ten" (10/10), a nationalist government rose to power. The emperor abdicated, removed himself from the throne; the dynasty that had ruled China for over 260 years, since 1644, came to an end. The people leading this revolution declared China to be a republic. They chose as president, **Sun Yat-sen** (Sun Yixian). Trained as a medical doctor, Sun admired Western ways and had traveled in Europe and the United States to gain support for his movement. Along with his political party, the Kuomintang or Nationalist Party, he hoped to make his nation, now called The Republic of China, established under a modern government. This new government would be based upon the **Three Principles of the People**. These were

1. *Nationalism*: Creating pride and unity among the Chinese people and pressing for the removal of foreign control.
2. *Democracy*: Establishing a means of giving the people a voice in choosing the government. There would be popularly elected executive, legislative, and judicial branches called yuans.
3. *People's Livelihood*: Ensuring economic prosperity, mainly by a program of land reform. Tenant farming would be eliminated, and land would be redistributed to the peasants. Major industries such as communication and transportation would be controlled by the government.

Even though Sun's ideas were noble and certainly looked very good on paper, they would not be easy to put into practice. The changes he described could not happen quickly and would take a long time to become real. Furthermore, Sun was not a strong leader. He did not have widespread authority and the military strength to support his program. Accordingly, he turned over the presidency to a general who was a major warlord, **Yuan Shih-kai**. Yuan was not a believer in democracy and soon became a military dictator. When he died in 1916, civil war broke out among other warlords and regional military leaders. The central nationalist government could not bring unity to the country. Disunity would continue, becoming more intense after the death of Sun Yat-sen in 1925. His successor, **Chiang Kai-shek** (also known as Jiang Jieshi) became worried about a threat to his rule from **Mao Zedong** and the Chinese Communist Party. Mao was one of the founders of the party in 1921. Fighting between Chiang's Nationalists and Mao's communists broke out in 1927. It would last until 1949 (as described in Chapter 16 in this volume), with historical consequences for the world's largest nation.

Chiang Kai-shek (1887–1975). Chinese general and statesman. Photographed c. 1931.

Why Did China Become a Victim of Imperialism?

As a result of all the imperialistic activity described here, China appeared to be a humiliated and partially dismembered country at the start of the twentieth century. It became a victim of imperialism for several reasons. For example,

1. its mineral resources attracted investors.
2. foreigners visualized its large population as both a market for the sale of goods and a source of cheap labor.
3. a great demand existed in the West for China's silk and tea.
4. the Manchu rulers did not have sufficient military power to repel the foreigners. Their rule was inefficient and corrupt. The country lacked the unity and centralized control necessary to protect itself.
5. the **Taiping Rebellion** (1850–1864), the longest and bloodiest war anywhere in the world during the nineteenth century, caused great devastation in China. It was led by Southern Chinese, who, for economic, political, and religious reasons, wanted to overthrow the government. Although the Ch'ing Dynasty was able to put down this revolt, the dynasty was severely weakened. Its inability to protect foreign citizens during the fighting gave yet another excuse for foreign troops to come to China and take advantage of the country. Military skirmishes took place, followed by more "unequal treaties," and more acquisitions of land and economic privileges.
6. the broadest and most profound reason contributing to China's victimization was, indirectly, its strong sense of pride and ethnocentrism. For centuries, China had been an advanced and prosperous country. Its achievements in science, politics, literature, and the arts were notable. It saw itself as the most powerful and civilized region on earth and isolated itself. It looked down upon others, not wanting to be affected by any outside "barbarian" customs. Such attitudes, however, prevented it from learning from others and caused it to be hostile rather than open to contact with foreigners.

Main Idea:
The broadest and most profound reason contributing to China's victimization was, indirectly, its strong sense of pride and ethnocentrism.

A section of the Great Wall of China. Photograph, 1901.

How Did Japan Avoid Becoming a Victim of Imperialism?

China's neighbor Japan, however, adopted a different attitude toward relations with Westerners in the nineteenth century. Prior to discussing this difference, we will briefly examine Japan's physical geography.

Japan is an island nation. It is made up of a string of islands located off the northeast coast of Asia in the Pacific Ocean. This kind of island formation is called an **archipelago**. These islands, numbering approximately 3,400, are sepa-

Main Idea:
As was true of China, Japan also viewed Westerners as barbarians. As was different from China, however, Japan recognized the Westerners' superiority in weapons, transportation, and technology.

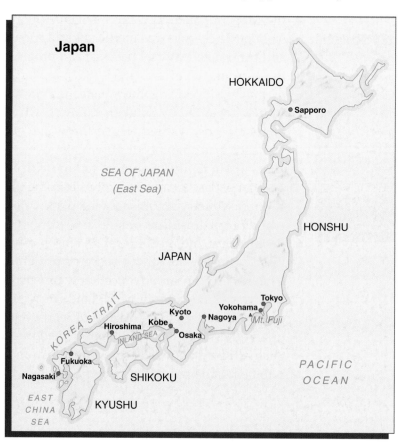

rated from the rest of Asia by two large bodies of water. These are the Sea of Japan (also known as the East Sea) and the Korean Strait (also known as the Tsushima Strait). Japan's physical detachment from the Asian mainland has had an important effect upon its people and history. The Japanese people have been able to develop their own culture and set of customs, while accepting some ideas and traditions from other countries.

They thus have much in common with each other, for example, in terms of race, language, religion, and values. The most distinctive land feature of the Japanese islands is its mountains. They take up almost 80 percent of the total land surface. The remaining 20 percent of the land is good for farming, but must be used carefully as it is such a small proportion in area. The great majority of people live on four main islands. These are Hokkaido, Honshu, Shikoku, and Kyushu.

Commodore Matthew Perry (1794–1858). American naval officer. Oil over a photograph.

As was true of China, Japan also viewed Westerners as barbarians. As was different from China, however, Japan recognized the Westerners' superiority in weapons, transportation, and technology. The Japanese further realized that there was much they could learn from these foreigners from across the seas.

In addition, Japan was fearful that hostility to foreigners and a refusal to open commercial contacts with them might subject it to the kind of victimization that China had suffered in The Opium Wars. Accordingly, in 1854, it signed the **Treaty of Kanagawa** with American **Commodore Matthew Perry**. Perry had been sent to Japan by President Millard Fillmore in 1853. The purpose of the trip was to obtain trading privileges with Japan and to ensure that any shipwrecked member of American sailing ships would find a refuge in Japan.

The Kanagawa Treaty opened up two Japanese ports for trade, and was soon followed by similar treaties with Britain, France, Holland, and Russia. The first U.S. Ambassador to Japan came form New York. His name was Townsend Harris.

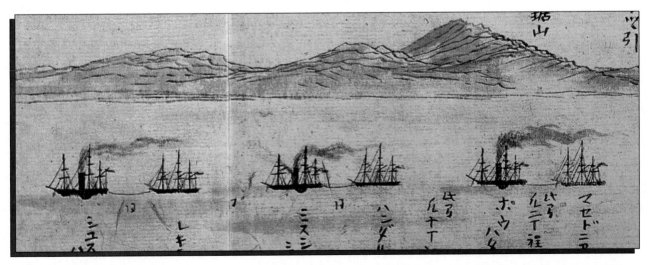

American naval vessels anchored in the harbor at Uraga, Japan at the time of Commodore Matthew C. Perry's expedition. Detail of color drawing, Japanese, 1854.

Emperor Mutsuhito of Japan, 1867–1912. Reign name: Meiji. Wood engraving, American, 1875.

Many Japanese saw the shogun's actions with the United States and other foreign nations as signs of weakness and feared increased contact with foreigners. Others welcomed the opportunity to engage in commercial activities overseas but felt that the Tokugawas did not command the respect and hold on the country's populace as had been true in earlier years. Furthermore, the Tokugawa Shogunate was not seen as ready to help Japan modernize and throw away the older feudalistic and isolationist policies. In 1867, the shogun was forced to resign under the pressure of several nobles. A young member of the royal family, **Mutsuhito,** became the emperor. He chose the reign name Meiji, which means "enlightened rule." (For the rule of every person who is an emperor, a name is chosen to describe the particular reigning time.) With the end of control by a shogun, and an increased emphasis on the role of the emperor, starting in 1868, this turning point in Japanese history has been referred to as the **Meiji Restoration**. The period of time in which Mutsuhito ruled (1868–1912), is called the Meiji Era.

With the Meiji Restoration of 1868, Japan embarked on a policy of modernization. It had avoided becoming a victim of imperialism. Its economy improved, and it sent young men overseas to learn Western ways in arms, government, and technology. Countries such as Germany and England were greatly admired. New machinery and transportation and communications systems were established. Men and women began to wear Western-style clothing. In 1889, the first Japanese constitution was written. A diet, parliament, was set up.

Japan Becomes an Imperial Power

Japan soon became the strongest industrial and military power in East Asia. During the Meiji Era, it began to embark on a policy of imperialism. One reason was its lack of natural resources, a lack that could be remedied by taking raw materials from neighboring countries. Also, as a matter of pride, Japan wanted to be seen by others as a powerful nation and to show that it was the equal of Western nations. It wanted to have "a place in the sun." Finally, the same sort of excessively ethnocentric feelings of cultural superiority that Europeans had felt toward Africans could be seen in Japanese attitudes toward other East Asians. These were strong motivations for the growth of a colonial empire. Accordingly, Japan viewed neighboring Korea and China as targets. A dispute with China over trading rights and influence in Korea led to a war in 1894–1895. This was to become known as the first Sino-Japanese War. Most of the fighting took place in Korea, where Chinese troops had been previously stationed. Because the Chinese were no match for the powerful Japanese armed forces, they were easily defeated. As the result of a peace treaty of Shimonoseki, Japan gained its first colonies, Taiwan and the Pescadores Islands.

Japan's victory over China sent shock waves throughout the world, most particularly in Russia. Russia saw itself as an Asian power and sought to have dominant economic and political influence in China and Korea. As these goals clearly conflicted with Japan's own foreign policy goals, a clash seemed immi-

> **Main Idea:**
> Japan wanted to be seen by others as a powerful nation and to show that it was the equal of Western nations.

Russo-Japanese War. Naval action involving a Russian cruiser, foreground, probably at Port Arthur, China, in 1904.

nent as the nineteenth century drew to a close. The clash occurred in 1904, when Japan sprung a surprise attack on Russian ships near the coast of China. In the ensuing **Russo-Japanese War** of 1904–1905, Japan emerged victorious. It destroyed the Russian navy, and crushed Russian forces in Korea and the Manchurian area of China. Peace negotiations, under the auspices of U.S. President **Theodore Roosevelt**, led to a treaty signed in **Portsmouth, New Hampshire**. The treaty gave Japan control over Manchuria and part of Sakhalin Island and recognition of its influence in Korea. Beyond these specific written treaty provisions stemming from the Russo-Japanese War, there was a much greater psychological and political unwritten result of the war. This was the fact that for the first time in world history, an Asian nation had defeated a European power in a major conflict. This sent a greater global shock wave than had been the case after the 1894–1895 Sino-Japanese War. Along with the tremendous increase in Japanese pride and nationalism, the Western world now saw Japan as a formidable power.

That power was further reflected in the occupation and annexation of Korea. In 1905, with Korea in a weakened condition, and without any possible interference from China or Russia, Japan began to increase its role in Korean affairs. The Koreans were helpless with the continued movement of Japanese officials and military figures onto its territory. In 1910, Japan officially annexed Korea and made it a colony. This condition would last until 1945, when Japan

was finally defeated in World War II. During its thirty-five-year period of occupation, Japan treated Koreans very terribly. Shinto became the official religion; land and resources were plundered; Koreans were forced to learn and speak Japanese; schools were controlled by the Japanese; and many Koreans were made to work for the Japanese both in Korea and Japan under harsh conditions. The occupation was yet another sad consequence in Korea's long history of being geographically near and thus being abused by three stronger powers. Accordingly, it has been said that "when China, Japan, or Russia sneezed, Korea caught cold."

Japan's subsequent desire to extend its colonial domains to all of East and Southeast Asia would bring it into conflict with the United States and other Western nations. This conflict was a cause of World War II (see Chapter 9, in this volume).

Theodore Roosevelt (1858–1919) in the White House: oil over a photograph, 1903.

SOUTHEAST ASIA

The name "Southeast Asia" is a relatively recent one. Prior to the twentieth century, various parts of the region had been known by other names (i.e., the **Spice Islands**, the East Indies, and Indochina). Some parts of Southeast Asia are on the Asian mainland, while others are islands in the form of archipelagoes. The best known of the latter are the present-day nations of Indonesia and the Philippines. Most mainlanders of Southeast Asia live on either the Malay or Indochina peninsulas.

European nations were initially interested in the spices from the region. One of the aims of Christopher Columbus in 1492 was to reach the Spice Islands in the "Indies." In later years, European interest was focused on mineral deposits such as tin and oil, and agricultural products such as rubber, tobacco, tea, and coffee. During the age of the new imperialism, Europeans also sought to control land in Southeast Asia in order to protect and have better access to their holdings in other parts of Asia. While Portugal and Spain were the first

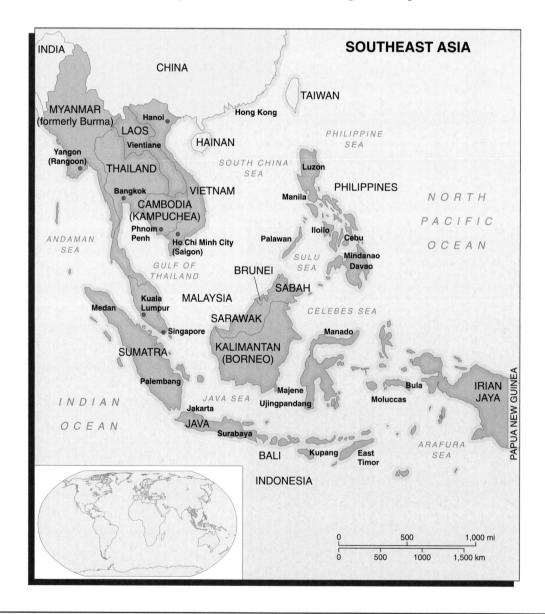

European nations to establish contact here, the major colonization was done by the Dutch, British, and French. Among non-European nations, the United States and Japan were colonial rulers for short periods of time.

There are ten independent nations today in Southeast Asia. With the exception of Thailand, every one of these was colonized at one point in its history. The colonizers were, as we have just seen, from different nations. This is one reason why this corner of Asia is sometimes described as a cultural "**patch-work quilt**." The sequence and pattern of involvement by European nations in Southeast Asia is similar in some ways to their involvement in the Americas, Africa, and other parts of Asia.

Portugal and Spain

Marco Polo's writings about his trip to Asia in the second half of the thirteenth century excited readers with accounts of both East and Southeast Asian lands. The Portuguese, navigational leaders in the Age of Exploration, reached India in 1498 as a result of Vasco da Gama's historic voyage. They soon moved on to the East Indies, reaching the Malay Peninsula in 1511 and some other areas shortly thereafter. They were able to put down resistance by Muslims who had controlled the sea routes, and were able to profit handsomely from the trade in spices such as nutmeg, cloves, pepper, and mace. The Portuguese had then pioneered an all-water route eastward from Europe to the Indies. Although they gained some small amounts of land, they were unable to construct large-scale colonial settlements.

> **Main Idea:**
> The Portuguese, navigational leaders in the Age of Exploration, reached India in 1498 as a result of Vasco da Gama's historic voyage.

The Spanish also wished to establish an all-water route to the region. They did so, thanks to the voyage of Magellan. Sailing westward across the Pacific Ocean, he landed in what is now the Philippines in 1521 and claimed the islands for Spain. The Spaniards were to rule here for over three hundred years, spreading Christianity and Spanish customs. Spanish governance over the Philippines was made chiefly from Mexico, Spain's major colony in the Americas. Following its pattern of colonial rule in the New World, the king of Spain gave large amounts of land to religious orders and other Spaniards. Natives who worked these lands endured much exploitation and hardship. Spain lost the Philippines to the United States as a result of the Spanish-American War of 1898.

The Netherlands

The first Dutch sailors to reach Southeast Asia arrived in 1596. They landed on the island of Java, part of present-day Indonesia. Their trade in spices was profitable and grew quickly. To conduct these commercial transactions, the **Dutch East India Company** was formed in 1602. The Dutch were able to keep away Portuguese and Spanish competition. However, because of severe mismanagement, the company went bankrupt in 1799. The Dutch government then took over control in Java, Sumatra, and neighboring islands, thus creating the colony called the Dutch East Indies or Netherlands East Indies.

The Dutch then introduced a practice known as the culture system. It was designed as an economic policy whereby crops would be cultivated for export. It required native farmers to grow export crops such as tea, quinine, coffee, and sugar on portions of their land. Local chieftains would assign quotas as ordered by the Dutch and gather the crops for sale. The Dutch would pay very low prices, some money then going to the chieftain and hardly anything to the farmers. The Dutch would then sell the crops on the world market for high prices and thus make tremendous profits. The system really became a policy of forced labor. In addition, it denied farmers the opportunity to use the land as they wished. They were not able to produce sufficient crops for their own local markets nor much food for themselves.

At the start of the twentieth century, Dutch colonial administrators sought to improve the lives of Indonesians by creating the ethical policy through which they planned to make certain welfare services available. Better schools and health facilities were built, along with paved roads and irrigation projects for rice cultivation. Politically, the Dutch pursued a policy of direct rule. Indonesians were given little say in the affairs of their land. Dutch rule was interrupted in 1942, during World War II, when the Japanese occupied the colony. The Japanese exploited the land for its resources and left in 1945, upon their defeat in the war. The postwar developments in Indonesia will be examined in Chapter 16 in this volume.

Great Britain

In 1969, the nation of Singapore, near the Malay Peninsula, had huge celebrations of what it labeled its one hundred fiftieth anniversary. Although this island nation became independent in 1963, Singapore dates it birth to the year 1819. This was when Sir Stamford Raffles, an employee of the British East India Company, established the site as a trading post. The site was strategically vital, as it commanded the Straits of Malacca. This waterway was part of the sea route to China.

Singapore and Malysia showing Strait of Malacca

MALAYSIA

● Kuala Lumpur

STRAIT OF MALACCA

INDIAN OCEAN

SINGAPORE

Singapore

Thomas Stamford Raffles (1781–1826). British East Indian administrator. Oil on canvas by George F. Joseph, 1817.

However, the British had already been in Southeast Asia for over two hundred years prior to Raffles's presence. A British East India Company ship had reached Sumatra in 1602. The British competed with the Dutch for domination of the spice trade. Eventually, they focused their attention on the region of the Malay Peninsula and left Sumatra and Java to the Dutch.

The nineteenth century witnessed significant British colonial advances in the region. Singapore and former Dutch Malacca became the Straits Settlement in 1824. In the 1870s, four sultans who ruled small areas on the Malay peninsula, fearful of attacks from Siam (current-day Thailand), entered into agreements with the British. The British agreed to give them protection, while obtaining greater commercial privileges. This action by the British was similar to the divide-and-conquer patterns that had occurred in India. In 1895, the sultans agreed to unite their areas as the Federated Malay States under British authority. Other sultans did not join the federation but agreed to some form of British control while retaining their powers. Thus, another form of indirect rule was established. In a short period of time, the Straits Settlement, the Federated Malay States, and the unfederated states became known as Malaya. The total British effort in the region—political, economic, and military—yielded rewards. The tin and rubber produced in Malaya led to much prosperity.

The other British possession in Southeast Asia was Burma. The western part of Burma was subdued with military force in 1826, in order to protect India's border. The rest of Burma was taken over in 1885, as the British were concerned about possible French penetration into the area and wanted to further shore up protection of eastern India. A British governor administered Burma, with hereditary rulers keeping some control over local affairs.

Main Idea:
The British had already been in Southeast Asia for over two hundred years prior to Raffles's presence.

France

As was the case with Britain and Holland, France organized an East India Company in the 1600s. Early on in that era, France was active in Cochin China. This is in present-day **Vietnam**. Both traders and missionaries were on the company's ships. In 1627, Alexandré de Rhodes, a French missionary, adapted the Vietnamese language to the Roman alphabet. With his knowledge of the region, he paved the way for further French influence. Both commercial and missionary activities slowly increased until the early 1800s. However, persecution by the Vietnamese emperors of both missionaries and their converts rose alarmingly. In the 1850s, the Emperor Tu-duc refused France's request for religious liberty and a trading post at Hue. As a result, in 1861 French forces invaded Cochin China, captured the main city of Saigon (now Ho Chi Minh City), and established a colony. In 1863, France announced itself to be the protector of Cambodia as well as other parts of what is now Vietnam.

Imperialistic activity then quickened with the designation of a French civilian governor in Cochin China in 1879, and the creation of a protectorate over Annam and Tonkin (other parts of present-day Vietnam) and Laos. In 1887, France declared all these regions together to be the colony of Indochina. As was true in its African colonies, France pursued a policy of direct rule in Indochina. The powerful French governor-general followed directives from superiors in

Paris, and made sure that these were carried out by French subordinates. Rice and rubber cultivation enriched the Frenchmen who came to Indochina, while very little of the wealth reached the native workers. France considered Indochina to be an actual part of French territory and even built parts of Saigon to make it look similar to Paris. This colonial attitude of the French was to spell trouble for it in the 1950s.

France had thoughts about moving into Siam, as did Britain. The Siamese recognized this and would frequently alternate their favoritism toward one nation and then toward the other. Because of this clever maneuvering, and because neither France nor Britain wanted the other to dominate the region, Siam was able to remain independent. It was the only part of Southeast Asia to escape colonization.

The growth of European power in East and Southeast Asia was similar in several ways to what we saw happen in Africa and South Asia. The scramble for land in the Orient occurred over a long period of time, for a host of reasons. Although major wars did not erupt there between the European powers themselves, those powers nevertheless did have to confront a non-European power in the 1940s who also sought land there—Japan. The nature of that struggle and its consequences for independence movements will be studied shortly (see Chapter 16 in this volume).

LINK TO TODAY

The Sports of Soccer and Cricket

When A colonizes B, much of the colonizer's culture affects the colonized people. When the colonizer leaves, the colonized people, now newly free, may or may not retain some parts of the culture of the former. Sports are cultural items. Ironically, two sports brought to colonized areas by Europeans, soccer and cricket, became enormously popular in the colonized areas even when these areas became independent. Of further irony is that teams from these new nations at times have bested the colonizer and have achieved fame and recognition. Cricket teams, for example, from India and Pakistan have defeated British teams. In **World Cup** soccer competition as of 2002, African teams have continued to improve. Although none had won the championship, teams from Cameroon (in 1990), Nigeria (in 1994), Senegal (in 2002), Cote d'Ivoire (in 2006), and Ghana (in 2006) have nevertheless performed well against European teams. Additional recognition of soccer's popularity in Africa came with the announcement in 2004 that the 2010 World Cup competition will be held in South Africa. That will be the first time that an African nation will host the tournament.

The first time that the tournament was held in Asia was in 2002. Japan and South Korea were cohosts. Although neither of these nations was ever colonized by Europeans, it is of historical significance that a European sport brought about cooperation between one Asian nation that had colonized another one.

CHAPTER SUMMARY

As we stated at the start of this chapter, the key terms in our definition of imperialism are "control," not "own"; "powerful," not "big"; "weaker," not "smaller." The prestige of the European nations was connected to this new movement. There is no doubt that the Europeans felt superior to their "newly conquered peoples," and considered the Asians and Africans inferior in culture and advancement. The fact that these centuries-old societies had their own cultures and own ways of doing things did not matter. To the Europeans, their ways were the only ways. Their drive was primarily economic, but there were those who truly did believe that they should, as Kipling wrote, "take up the White man's burden" and "send forth the best ye breed."

As we look at maps of Africa over the centuries, we see changes. At the beginning of the nineteenth century, there were a few outposts along the coastline but little else. One hundred years later, almost the entire continent was divided up. Great Britain and France got the major share with the newcomers, Germany and Italy, having to settle for what was left. Belgium and Portugal were allowed to keep their colonies because it was not in the interest of the other European countries to take them away. Each of the European countries ruled its area as it saw best. Boundaries were drawn by the Europeans without taking into consideration what was good for the Africans or what the Africans wanted.

It was also a period of high adventure. We should not diminish the accomplishments of the brave men and women who risked their lives in opening new lands. They often had little idea where they were going or if they would come back alive. They went through hardships that would stop all but the bravest. Some, like Rhodes, went for fortune; most went for fame.

If any lesson should be learned from the section on Asia, it is that a nation cannot stand still. As you know, China at one time was way ahead of Europe in intellectual development, but at a certain point decided that further advancement was no longer necessary. So China stagnated while the Europeans went through their Renaissance and Industrial Revolution. If you stand still, you go backward in relation to others; a nation cannot afford to do that. It is interesting that Japan exists as a model for us to observe. The Japanese had also closed themselves off to Western influences. After Perry arrived, they soon adopted the ways of the West and became imperialists on their own. Their history during the late nineteenth and twentieth centuries was very different from that of their neighbors.

We can also see possible problems starting to develop. There were jealousies among nations as France was envious of Britain, Germany was envious of France and Britain, and Japan wanted to have sole control over what it saw as its area. Nations seemed not to care about the people's welfare in the areas they controlled. These people were pawns in a nationalistic power play. As we move ahead in our study, this will become more evident.

KEY TERMS

imperialism	Boer War	extraterritoriality
old imperialism	indirect rule	unequal treaties
new imperialism	direct rule	"Open Door Policy"
colonialism	dark continent	Boxer Rebellion
jingoism	"civilizing mission"	Three Principles of the
ethnocentrism	assimilation	People
Social Darwinism	exploitation	Taiping Rebellion
sphere of influence	paternalism	archipelago
concession	British East India	Treaty of Kanagawa
protectorate	Company	Meiji Restoration
satellite nations	"divide and rule"	Russo-Japanese War
colony	"jewel in the crown"	"patchwork quilt"
mandate	Sepoy Mutiny	Dutch East India
partition of Africa	Ch'ing (Qing) Dynasty	Company
scramble for Africa	British Raj	culture system
lifeline of the British	"brown Englishman"	Treaty of Shimonoseki
Empire	suttee	World Cup
Berlin Conference	Opium War	
Great Trek	indemnity	

PEOPLE

Rudyard Kipling	Henry Stanley	King George III
Ferdinand de Lesseps	Emperor Menelik II	Emperor Ch'ien-lung
Ismail Pasha	King Leopold II	Manchus
Mahdi	Lord Cornwallis	Emperor Tu-duc
Cecil Rhodes	Mughals	Sun Yat-sen
Chief Lobengula	Robert Clive	Yuan Shih-kai
Boers	sepoys	Commodore Matthew
Zulus	Hindus	Perry
Sir Frederick Lugard	Muslims	Mutsuhito
David Livingstone	Elihu Yale	Theodore Roosevelt
Queen Victoria	Lord George Macartney	Stamford Raffles

PLACES

western hemisphere	Adowa	Asia
eastern hemisphere	"horn of Africa"	Nanking
Suez Canal	Plassey	Africa
Fashoda	China	Spice Islands
Victoria Falls	Japan	Portsmouth, New
"bulge of Africa"	Korea	Hampshire

CHAPTER 6

MULTIPLE-CHOICE QUESTIONS

Select the number of the correct answer.

1. The period known as old imperialism differed from that of new imperialism in that it

   (1) was concerned with establishing trade routes
   (2) was a time to search for raw materials and resources
   (3) lasted for approximately three hundred years
   (4) never attempted to control the peoples in foreign lands

2. Place the events below in the correct chronological order

   A. Commercial Revolution
   B. New Imperialism
   C. Age of Exploration
   D. Industrial Revolution

   (1) C, A, B, D
   (2) A, B, C, D
   (3) B, A, D, C
   (4) C, D, A, B

3. Social Darwinism is best described as

   (1) the opportunity for a nation to gain sole trading rights in another area
   (2) the conquest of a region rich in natural resources
   (3) the temporary control of one nation by another
   (4) the belief that human beings compete and the survival of the fittest occurs

4. The term *sphere of influence* was primarily used to establish exclusive economic rights in

   (1) India
   (2) China
   (3) Japan
   (4) Saudi Arabia

5. Kipling's poem *The White Man's Burden* is best associated with which concept?

   (1) concession
   (2) mandate
   (3) exploration
   (4) ethnocentrism

6. Europeans were involved in the "scramble for Africa" because they saw the continent as a source of

   (1) new religious ideas
   (2) raw materials
   (3) advanced technology
   (4) a well-educated workforce

7. The "lifeline of the British Empire" included which three geographic features?

   (1) English Channel, Suez Canal, Pacific Ocean
   (2) Mediterranean Sea, Red Sea, Atlantic Ocean
   (3) Mediterranean Sea, Suez Canal, Red Sea
   (4) Suez Canal, Nile River, Indian Ocean

8. Which headline below could have correctly been printed when Cecil Rhodes died?

   (1) "Developer of 'Cape to Cairo Railroad' Rhodes Dead at 49"
   (2) "Cecil Rhodes Leaves Gold and Diamond Fortune to Oxford University"
   (3) "Hero of the Napoleonic Wars, Rhodes, Dies in Cape Colony"
   (4) "Cecil Rhodes, Developer and Prime Minister in West Africa, Dies Suddenly"

9. A European country paired correctly with its land holdings in nineteenth-century Africa is

   (1) France—Algeria
   (2) Germany—Tunisia
   (3) Italy—the Congo
   (4) Portugal—Nigeria

10. What conclusion would be most accurate about European imperialism in nineteenth-century Africa?

    (1) The Africans overwhelmingly gained more power than they lost.
    (2) Europeans were welcomed by most Africans as religious symbols.
    (3) Europeans showed little concern for African cultures or heritage.
    (4) Africans were generally treated on an equal basis with Europeans.

11. The statement, "The sun never sets on the British Empire," meant that

    (1) the British controlled land only around the equator
    (2) the British favored development in hot desert climates
    (3) the British Empire was only in the Southern Hemisphere
    (4) the British controlled land all around the globe

12. The phrase "Jewel of the British Empire" described

    (1) Hong Kong
    (2) South Africa
    (3) India
    (4) Rhodesia

13. Among the positive actions of the British in India were

    (1) the building of railroads, bridges, and roadways
    (2) the encouragement of the Hindu practice of suttee
    (3) the development of competitive markets against local producers
    (4) the military takeover of some parts of the subcontinent

14. For centuries, the Chinese viewed European traders as

    (1) intelligent and humanitarian
    (2) barbarians
    (3) superior to the Chinese
    (4) violent invaders

15. Which of these factors did the Boxer Rebellion in China and the Sepoy Mutiny in India have in common?

    (1) Both opposed Hindu traditions in their countries.
    (2) Both actions protested European imperialism.
    (3) Both groups wanted foreign control of trade.
    (4) Both were inspired by Christian missionaries.

16. In the nineteenth century, enthnocentrism was a concept that is best seen in the actions of

    (1) the Chinese toward foreigners
    (2) the Indians toward Pakistanis
    (3) the Japanese toward the Chinese
    (4) the Chinese toward their own people

17. The American Commodore Matthew Perry is most closely associated with his activities in

    (1) China
    (2) Korea
    (3) Japan
    (4) Indonesia

18. In Southeast Asia, the only country never to have been colonized by Europeans was

    (1) Vietnam
    (2) Cambodia
    (3) Laos
    (4) Thailand

19. Zionists in the Middle East were people who were most interested in

(1) producing oil in Kuwait
(2) making part of Palestine a homeland for Jews
(3) gaining trading rights for the British
(4) securing Palestine as an Arab state

20. A lesson to be learned from the Age of Imperialism is

(1) areas that became colonies were encouraged to develop their own cultures and resources
(2) European powers felt justified and obligated to take control of less-developed areas
(3) Africa benefited much more than Asia from the Age of Imperialism
(4) European rivalries kept their competitive efforts within Europe

THEMATIC ESSAY

Directions: Write a well-organized essay that includes an introduction, several paragraphs addressing the task below, and a conclusion.

Theme: Cultures and Cultural Diffusion

The culture or way of life of a group of people may be enriched or damaged by its contact with other cultures. Cultural diffusion is the exchange of ideas between cultures.

During the Age of Imperialism in the nineteenth century, many African and Asian cultures had contacts with European cultures. These contacts had a variety of results.

Task

Identify two pairs of cultures who had contacts during the Age of Imperialism and for each

- explain one reason for the contact between the cultures
- discuss two results of the contact
- evaluate whether the results of the cultural diffusion were positive or negative

You may use any cultures from this chapter, but do not repeat reasons or results used in the discussion of one pair in the discussion of the other. Some pairs you may wish to consider include: the British in South Africa, the Belgians in the Congo, the Chinese and the Europeans, the Dutch and the Indonesians, the French in IndoChina, and the British in India.

You are not limited to these suggestions.

You may *not* use the United States in your answer.

Guidelines

In your essay, be sure to

- develop all aspects of the *Task*
- support the theme with relevant facts, examples, and details
- use a logical and clear plan of organization, including an introduction and a conclusion that are beyond a restatement of the theme
- introduce the theme by establishing a framework that is beyond a simple restatement of the *Task* and conclude with a summation of the theme

This question is based on the accompanying documents. The question is designed to test your ability to work with historical documents. Some of the documents have been edited for the purposes of the question. As you analyze the documents, take into account the source of each document and any point of view that may be presented in the document.

Historical Context

During the second half of the nineteenth century, many European countries expressed an interest in Africa. This interest would have both positive and negative effects.

Task

Using information from the documents and your knowledge of Global History, answer the questions that follow each document in Part A. Your answers to the questions will help you write the Part B essay, in which you will be asked to

- define the meaning of the word imperialism
- discuss three reasons why the Europeans were interested in Africa
- discuss at least two positive and two negative results of the European presence in Africa

Part A: Short-Answer Questions

Directions: Analyze the documents and answer the questions that follow each document.

Document 1

"The White Man's Burden" (excerpt)

Take up the White Man's Burden
In patience to abide
To veil the threat of terror
And check the show of pride:
By open speech and simple
An hundred times made plain
To seek another's profit
And work another's gain
Take up the White Man's Burden—
And reap his old reward:
The blame of those ye better
The hate of those ye guard—

Source: (adapted) Rudyard Kipling, "The White Man's Burden:.....1899"

Questions
1. a. Based on the poem above, what did Kipling mean by the phrase, "White Man's Burden"?
   b. What did he think was to be gained by this "Burden"?

Document 2

Questions

2.
a. What two European nations controlled the most land in Africa by 1914?
b. How many European countries were involved in Africa at this time according to the map?

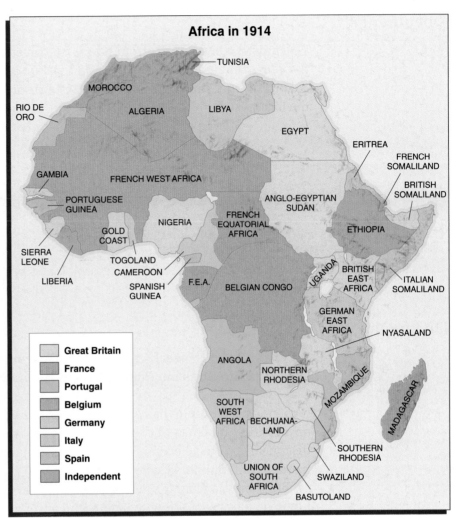

Africa in 1914

TUNISIA
MOROCCO
RIO DE ORO
ALGERIA
LIBYA
EGYPT
ERITREA
FRENCH SOMALILAND
BRITISH SOMALILAND
GAMBIA
FRENCH WEST AFRICA
ANGLO-EGYPTIAN SUDAN
PORTUGUESE GUINEA
NIGERIA
FRENCH EQUATORIAL AFRICA
ETHIOPIA
GOLD COAST
SIERRA LEONE
TOGOLAND
CAMEROON
LIBERIA
SPANISH GUINEA
F.E.A.
BELGIAN CONGO
UGANDA
BRITISH EAST AFRICA
ITALIAN SOMALILAND
GERMAN EAST AFRICA
NYASALAND
ANGOLA
NORTHERN RHODESIA
MOZAMBIQUE
MADAGASCAR
SOUTH WEST AFRICA
BECHUANA-LAND
SOUTHERN RHODESIA
UNION OF SOUTH AFRICA
SWAZILAND
BASUTOLAND

	Great Britain
	France
	Portugal
	Belgium
	Germany
	Italy
	Spain
	Independent

Document 3

Question

3. What are two ideas about Cecil Rhodes and Africa that the cartoonist is trying to show in his cartoon?
1.
2.

Document 4

"We must find new lands from which we can easily obtain raw materials and at the same time exploit the cheap slave labor available from the colonies. The colonies would provide a dumping ground for the surplus goods produced in the factories."

Cecil Rhodes, British Statesman (1853–1902)

Question	4. According to this statement by Cecil Rhodes, what were three reasons that imperialistic nations were interested in Africa? 1. 2. 3.

Document 5

An extract from a speech entitled "The True Imperialism" made by Lord Curzon at Birmingham, England Town Hall in 1907 follows:

"Wherever the Empire has extended its borders ... there misery and oppression, anarchy and destitution, superstition and bigotry, have tended to disappear, and have been replaced by peace, justice, prosperity, humanity, and freedom of thought, speech, and action......

But there also has sprung, what I believe to be unique in the history of Empires, a passion of loyalty and enthusiasm which makes the heart of the remotest British citizen thrill at the thought of the destiny which he shares, and causes him to revere a particular piece of coloured bunting as the symbol of all that is noblest in his own nature and of best import for the good of the world."

Question	5. According to Lord Curzon, what were two positive results of the British Empire's expansion around the world?

Document 6   SAMPLE OF A NATIVE TREATY

- We, the undersigned Chiefs of .... , with the view of bettering the condition of our country and people, do this day cede to the Royal Niger Company (Chartered and Limited), for ever, the whole of our territory extending from ....

- We also give to the said Royal Niger Company (Chartered and Limited) full power to settle all native disputes arising from any cause whatever, and we pledge ourselves not to enter into any war with other tribes without the sanction of the said Royal Niger Company (Chartered and Limited).

- We understand that the said Royal Niger Company (Chartered and Limited) have full power to mine, farm, and build in any portion of our country.

- We bind ourselves not to have any intercourse [i.e., transactions or communications] with any strangers or foreigners except through the said Royal Niger Company (Chartered and Limited).

- In consideration of the foregoing, the said Royal Niger Company (Chartered and Limited) bind themselves not to interfere with any of the native laws or customs of the country, consistently with the maintenance of order and good government.

- The said Royal Niger Company (Chartered and Limited) agree to pay native owners of land a reasonable amount for any portion they may require.

- The said Royal Niger Company (Chartered and Limited) bind themselves to protect the said Chiefs from the attacks of any neighbouring aggressive tribes.

- The said Royal Niger Company (Chartered and Limited) also agree to pay the said Chiefs .... native value.

- We, the undersigned witnesses, do hereby solemnly declare that the .... Chiefs whose names are placed opposite their respective crosses have in our presence affixed their crosses of their own free will and consent, and that the said .... has in our presence affixed his signature.

Done in triplicate at .... this ....day of .... , 188. .

Declaration by Interpreter.

I, ... of .... , do hereby solemnly declare that I am well acquainted with the language of the .... country, and that of the ....day of .... , 188. , I truly and faithfully explained the above Agreement to all the Chiefs present, and that they understood its meaning.

Question

6. Based on this document, identify three limits placed on the tribes who signed this document with the British Royal Niger Company.
   1.
   2.
   3.

Document 7

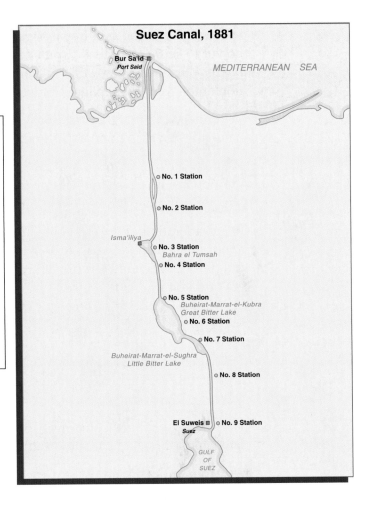

Suez Canal, 1881

Questions

7.
a. According to this nineteenth century map of the Suez Canal, what two bodies of water did the Canal connect?
b. In addition to connecting these two seas, what benefits did the builders of the Canal expect to gain?

Part B: Essay

Directions: Write a well-organized essay that includes an introduction, several paragraphs, and a conclusion. Use evidence from *at least four* documents in the body of the essay. Support your response with relevant facts, examples, and details. Include additional outside information.

Historical Context

During the second half of the nineteenth century, many European countries expressed an interest in Africa. This interest would have both positive and negative effects.

Task

Using information form the documents and your knowledge of Global History, answer the questions that follow each document in Part A. Your answers to the questions will help you write the Part B essay, in which you will be asked to

- define the meaning of the word imperialism.
- discuss three reasons why the Europeans were interested in Africa.
- discuss at least two positive and two negative results of the European presence in Africa.

Guidelines

In your essay, be sure to

- develop all aspects of the *Task*
- incorporate information from *at least four* documents
- incorporate relevant outside information
- support the theme with relevant facts, examples, and details
- use a logical and clear plan of organization, including an introduction and a conclusion that are beyond a restatement of the theme

ERA VI

A HALF CENTURY OF CRISIS AND ACHIEVEMENT

(1900–1945)

INTRODUCTION

War and upheaval marked the first half of the twentieth century. Ironically and fortunately, in the century's second half, the lifetime of your parents and grandparents, nations were more at peace than they were at war. The fifty years, from 1900 to 1950, witnessed the world immersed in two horrible wars, World War I and World War II. The peace that occurred after the Second World War has been generally maintained, primarily because of the fear of a third and more deadly conflict. Another factor rested with the desire among most nations to settle disputes without resorting to bloodshed on the battlefield.

Both of these world wars, along with the Holocaust brought on by Nazi Germany, revealed the darkest side of human nature. A much brighter side was seen in the creation of the United Nations and the realization by the Western democracies that they must play a crucial role to prevent the spread of tyranny and war.

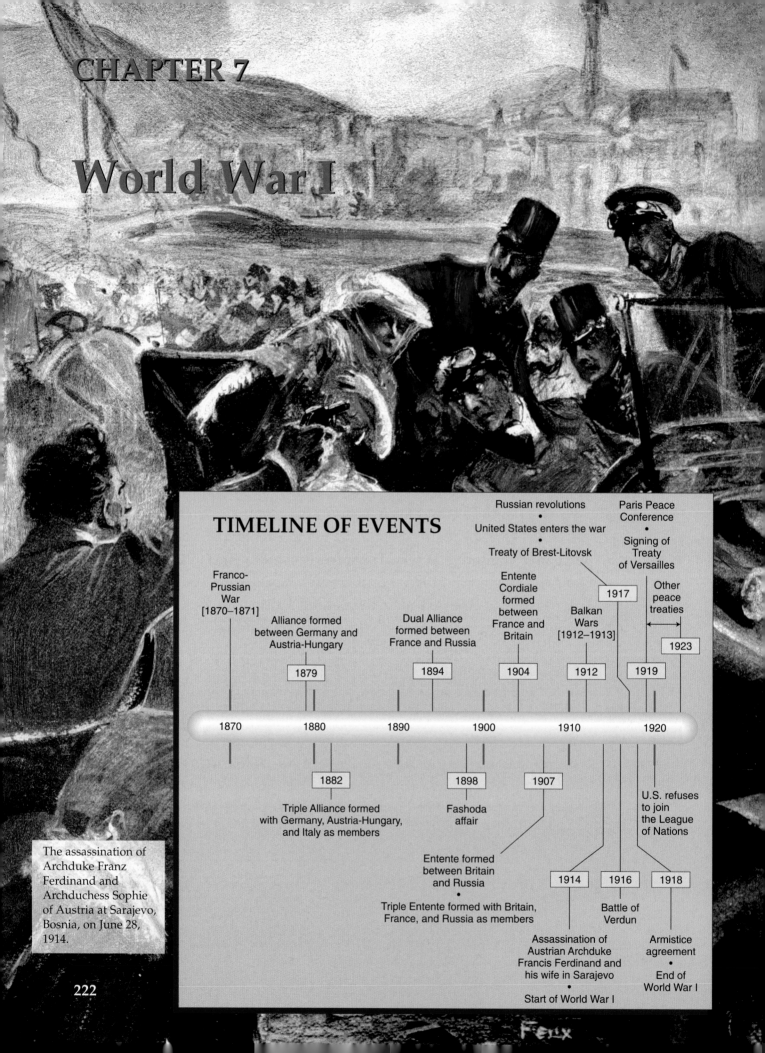

World War I

The assassination of Archduke Franz Ferdinand and Archduchess Sophie of Austria at Sarajevo, Bosnia, on June 28, 1914.

TIMELINE OF EVENTS

Russian revolutions
•
United States enters the war
•
Treaty of Brest-Litovsk

Paris Peace Conference
•
Signing of Treaty of Versailles

Franco-Prussian War [1870–1871]

Alliance formed between Germany and Austria-Hungary

Dual Alliance formed between France and Russia

Entente Cordiale formed between France and Britain

Balkan Wars [1912–1913]

Other peace treaties

1917

1879

1894

1904

1912

1919

1923

| 1870 | 1880 | 1890 | 1900 | 1910 | 1920 |

1882

1898

1907

Triple Alliance formed with Germany, Austria-Hungary, and Italy as members

Fashoda affair

U.S. refuses to join the League of Nations

Entente formed between Britain and Russia
•
Triple Entente formed with Britain, France, and Russia as members

1914

1916

1918

Battle of Verdun

Assassination of Austrian Archduke Francis Ferdinand and his wife in Sarajevo
•
Start of World War I

Armistice agreement
•
End of World War I

CAUSES OF WORLD WAR I

Why do nations go to war? This is a question that is not easily answered. Indeed, there may be many answers. Historians themselves may disagree on the answers and often disagree on the chief reason that led to a particular war. Perhaps each war should be examined separately, as the reasons for one conflict may indeed be very different from the reasons for another. This section will examine the reasons for the conflict that became known as World War I (1914–1918).

After learning about these reasons, you may wish to think about whether or not this war was inevitable, bound to happen. Viewed against the background of the preceding years, however, its outbreak in 1914 seemed surprising.

There had not been a major European war involving so many nations in almost 100 years. With the end of the Napoleonic Wars in 1815, the **Congress of Vienna** laid the foundation for a near-century of peace. This "**Pax Europa**" was broken only by a few brief and local wars (the Austro-Prussian, Franco-Prussian, Russo-Turkish, and Crimean Wars). Beginning in the 1870s, however, a series of forces and events combined to move Europe toward a major war. These included a growing spirit of **nationalism**, increasingly dangerous colonial conflicts, a complex system of entangling alliances, and a rising tide of **militarism**.

The war that was to sweep across Europe, and even draw in the United States, would last for four years. It was far more destructive of lives and property than any previous conflict and was the first so-called total war. Civilian populations became military objectives and targets along with soldiers. Terrifying weapons were used for the first time. It is no wonder that this terrible conflict was originally called the **Great War**. After it was over, President Woodrow Wilson of the United States hoped that the world would see it as "the war to end all wars."

Woodrow Wilson (1856–1924).

It is time now for us to see why this war occurred. In doing so, we will look at both underlying and immediate causes. Many factors contributed to the start of World War I. All of the major European powers shared some blame, although historians disagree on whether one nation was more at fault than any other.

Underlying Causes

Causes that build up over a long period of time, leading to an argument or dispute, can be called **underlying causes**. They can also be described as basic or fundamental causes.

Imperialism

The desire to control overseas regions (i.e., imperialism) led to sharp competition and rivalry among the nations of Europe. Examples included the following:

1. *Britain and Germany in East Africa*: Their colonies bordered on each other.
2. *Britain and Germany in the Middle East*: Germany wished to construct a Berlin-to-Baghdad railroad. For the British, this would pose a threat to their "lifeline to India" through the Suez Canal.
3. *France and Germany in Morocco*: Germany had contested France's establishment of a **protectorate**.
4. *Austria-Hungary and Russia in the Balkans (southeast Europe)*: Russia's support of Serbia was seen as a threat to the unity of the Austro-Hungarian Empire.

Nationalism

Strong ties to a nation and/or ethnic group (i.e., nationalism) stirred deep emotions. Many groups of people wanted to be free of control by other nations. For example, Bosnia and Herzegovina, where many Slavic people lived, wanted to be free from **Austria-Hungary** so they could be unified with **Serbia** and thus be with others of their own kind. Russia was a Slavic nation, so it backed the nationalist wishes of Bosnia, Herzegovina, and Serbia. Obviously, this angered Austria-Hungary. Austria-Hungary and the Ottoman Turks ruled over many different **nationalities**, who wanted to break free and form their own nations. Some of the other subject nationalities were Czechs, Slovaks, Poles, and Arabs.

Nationalism was also a source of anger and antagonism (opposition to someone or something) between France and Germany. Ever since France's defeat in the Franco-Prussian War (1870–1871), France had resented Germany. French pride was especially hurt by the loss of Alsace-Lorraine to Germany at the end of the war. France's passionate desire to regain this territory was reflected in the often-heard cry for *revanche* (revenge). This wish was ingrained in students your age and younger in schools throughout France in the late nineteenth and early twentieth centuries.

Alliances

Otto von Bismarck, chancellor of Germany, was well aware of France's antagonism toward Germany. Accordingly, to assist Germany in case of a French attack, and also to isolate France, he formed an alliance with Austria-Hungary in 1879. In 1882, Italy allied herself with these two nations because she was upset with France's seizure of Tunisia in North Africa. Thus was born the **Triple Alliance** of Germany, Austria-Hungary, and Italy. Known as the **Central powers**, these nations stated that their alliance was purely defensive and that they would not start a war. The parties to a defensive alliance, however, usually promise to help each other if any one of them is attacked by someone else. Formation of the Triple Alliance shows how a nation's self-interest influences its dealings with other nations. Anti-French feeling brought Italy and Germany together; then, as Germany was already allied with Austria-Hungary, Italy found herself an ally of that nation. This was ironic, however, as Italy had long feared Austria-Hungary and had wanted to get Austrian land that was inhabited by Italians. Italy may have thought that it was more in her interest to ally herself with the two German-speaking nations than to stay isolated.

The French and British were aware of the linkages put together in the Triple Alliance and became disturbed. France's wish to regain Alsace-Lorraine, along with her fear of being alone in a possible showdown with Germany and that nation's allies, prompted France to seek allies of her own. An opportunity arose when the czar of Russia faced economic troubles. France lent him money for both industrial and military projects, and the two nations also signed a treaty, forming the Dual Alliance in 1894. For reasons of self-interest, each felt good about this alliance: It gave France, to Germany's west, an ally on the eastern side of Germany, and it gave Russia an ally against Austria-Hungary, a competitor with Russia for influence in the Balkans.

Main Idea:
Only six years earlier, in 1898, Britain and France had almost gone to war over the Fashoda Affair in Africa, but now both nations were more afraid of Germany than of each other.

Although Britain had a long history of warfare with France, Britain was now growing much more alarmed about Germany. German naval power was seen as a threat on the seas, while German industries were challenging British products on the world market. Also, as we have seen, the two countries had clashing imperialistic ambitions in both East Africa and the Middle East. For these reasons, and because the British feared being alone in case of conflict with the Triple Alliance, it entered into an entente (understanding) with France in 1904. This Entente Cordiale, although not a strictly military alliance, nevertheless brought these two historic enemies closer together. It was also another instance of how self-interest affects a nation's foreign policy. Only six years earlier, in 1898, Britain and France had almost gone to war over the Fashoda Affair in Africa, but now both nations were more afraid of Germany than of each other. Also, the Anglo-French Entente of that year settled another colonial issue in Africa. It provided that Britain would recognize French control in Morocco in return for French recognition of British control in Egypt.

In 1907, Britain and Russia entered into an "understanding." Russia, weakened and shocked by her defeat in the Russo-Japanese War (1904–1905), was willing to smooth over with Britain the conflicting imperialistic claims of both nations in central Asia (i.e., Afghanistan and Persia). Britain saw in Russia another counterweight to Germany, geographically. Indeed, the agreement with Russia in 1907, and that with France in 1904, reflected a traditional British foreign policy goal in dealings with other European nations—to maintain a **balance of power**. As a country lying apart from the European continent, Britain would traditionally stay out of the disputes among continental countries. She would act differently, however, when events might, in her opinion, appear threatening to her interests. Thus, in the Napoleonic Wars, Britain sided with Prussia to stop General Napoleon. Less than one hundred years later, however, Britain found that her self-interest lay in aligning herself with France and Russia against Germany, the nation united by Prussia!

Main Idea:
Although these alliances were supposedly formed to keep peace, we have to wonder whether their creation provided a balance of power or a balance of terror. We can also ask, in general, whether alliances tend to promote peace or war.

This 1907 agreement between Britain and Russia, along with the Dual Alliance of 1894 and the Entente Cordiale of 1904, now aligned Britain, France, and Russia as the **Triple Entente**. The result was that, fewer than ten years into the twentieth century, Europe had become an armed camp. Two powerful alliances, representing six nations, had emerged. Although these alliances were supposedly formed to keep peace, we have to wonder whether their creation provided a balance of power or a balance of terror. We can also ask, in general, whether alliances tend to promote peace or war. In the early 1900s, the danger existed that the slightest dispute between any two nations in opposing alliances could expand into a confrontation among all six nations. This is what happened in 1914.

Militarism

Because the alliance system divided Europe into opposing groups, each member nation began to increase its military strength. Indeed, one German officer had said, "In time of peace, prepare for war." The growth of armies and navies, as well as the development of advanced weaponry, added to the **belligerent** (warlike, get-tough) mood. Belligerent and hostile nations have a tendency to settle arguments by fighting. As governments sought to build up their military arsenals, arms manufacturers such as Krupp in Germany and Schneider in France increased production.

Lack of Any World Peacekeeping Machinery

Prior to World War I, no strong global organization existed to foster peace or to settle disputes during the tense period from the 1870s to 1914, which was one of international anarchy. (The term *anarchy* refers to the absence of any overriding political organization, able to set and enforce rules.)

Immediate Cause

The **immediate cause** of World War I was the assassination of **Francis (Franz) Ferdinand**, Archduke of Austria, on June 28, 1914. He was killed in **Sarajevo**, the capital city of Bosnia and Herzegovina, by **Gavrilo Princip**. Bosnia and Herzegovina were Balkan parts of the Austro-Hungarian Empire and had Slavic

people who wished to be free. Princip was from nearby Serbia, an independent Slavic nation, which wanted unification with Bosnia and Herzegovina and was opposed to rule by Austria-Hungary. Although Princip was not a Serbian government official, Austria-Hungary nevertheless blamed Serbia for the killing. Although Serbia claimed it was not responsible, its government had known of the assassination plot beforehand.

The shots fired by Princip not only killed the archduke and his wife, but also would indirectly cause the deaths of almost ten million other people during the next four years. The event of June 28 has been likened to a "spark setting off the Balkan powder keg." The term *powder keg* referred to the crisis that had been smoldering in the Balkans for several years prior to 1914. Tension had existed since the 1870s, when Serbian nationalists with Russian backing strove to create a Slavic state from parts of Austria-Hungary and the declining Ottoman Turkish Empire. Subject nationalities under Austria-Hungary protested the treat-

Francis Ferdinand (1863–1914), Archduke of Austria.

ment they received. Austro-Hungarian opposition to these movements was intense. In 1912–1913, two Balkan wars were fought over land claims in the area. These wars would prove to be mere preludes to what would take place all over Europe from 1914 to 1918.

Archduke Franz Ferdinand and Archduchess Sophie of Austria moments before they were assassinated in Sarajevo, Bosnia, on June 28, 1914.

The arrest of Gavrilo Princip after the assassination of Archduke Franz Ferdinand, June 28, 1914.

EVENTS FOLLOWING THE ARCHDUKE'S ASSASSINATION

In the six weeks between the assassination on June 28 and the outbreak of war on August 4, 1914, events developed in a way that showed how jealousies, rivalries, bitterness, and underlying causes discussed previously would destroy the Pax Europa. The key events that saw the firing of a revolver in June and led to the blasting of guns in August were as follows:

Main Idea:
In the six weeks between the assassination on June 28 and the outbreak of war on August 4, 1914, events developed in a way that showed how jealousies, rivalries, bitterness, and underlying causes discussed previously would destroy the Pax Europa.

1. Between June 28 and July 23, Austria-Hungary decided to take action against Serbia. However, knowing that Russia might aid Serbia, Austria-Hungary wanted to be sure that Germany would stand behind her. Germany indicated her willingness to do so. The German agreement to support any policy to be pursued by Austria-Hungary has been interpreted as Germany giving her ally a "**blank check** to be filled in for any amount."

2. On July 23, Austria-Hungary sent Serbia an **ultimatum** (a set of demands that must be accepted). This required Serbia to put down all writing, teaching, and demonstrating that was against Austria-Hungary. The ultimatum also demanded that Serbia fire any officials opposed to Austria-Hungary, and that Austria-Hungary be allowed to send her own judges to Serbia to conduct a trial of those involved with the archduke's shooting. If the ultimatum was not answered positively within forty-eight hours, war would be declared on Serbia.

3. On July 25, France assured Russia of support in the crisis.

4. On July 26, Serbia, having received some assurance of support from Russia, responded affirmatively to all parts of the ultimatum except the last part.

5. On July 26, Britain called for an international conference.

6. On July 27, Germany rejected the invitation to attend.

7. On July 28, Austria declared war on Serbia and bombed the City of Belgrade, having begun **mobilization** (getting ready for war) during the summer.

8. On July 29, Russia began to mobilize. Germany tried to soften and moderate Austria-Hungary's reactions to the ultimatum's response.

9. On August 1, France announced that she would do what her interests dictated.

10. On August 2, Germany declared war on Russia.

11. On August 3, Germany declared war on France and invaded Belgium in order to attack France. Britain, not legally bound by her entente with France to assist that nation, pondered a decision to go to war.

12. On August 4, Britain declared war on Germany. What finally swayed Britain's declaration was the invasion of Belgium. In a treaty signed in 1839, Britain, the German State of Prussia, and other European powers had agreed to respect and guarantee the neutrality of Belgium. Germany's actions in 1914 were seen as a violation of this treaty. The fact that Germany was indifferent about Belgium's status and Britain's reaction was evident in the sarcastic statement made by Chancellor Bethmann-Hollweg of Germany. He dismissed Britain's action by stating that Britain had gone to war simply for "a scrap of paper." This remark, printed by presses all over the world, was a major reason for the charge of war guilt made against Germany after the war.

13. On August 6, Austria-Hungary declared war on Russia.

By the first week of August, all members of the two alliances had gone to war except Italy. That nation did not consider itself bound by the Triple Alliance agreement, and had always been uneasy about aligning itself with Austria-Hungary. In May 1915, Italy joined the Allies (Britain, France, Japan, Russia, and Serbia), having signed a secret agreement with them for a promise of land. Japan joined the Allied side in 1914, while the United States would join in 1917. By the time the war was over, other nations, as well as colonies of nations, had become involved as belligerents (participants in a fight).

In *Origins of the World War*, a book about World War I written in 1928, the American historian Sidney Fay states, "None of the Powers wanted a European War. Their governing rulers and ministers, with few exceptions, all foresaw that it must be a frightful struggle in which the political results were not absolutely

> **Main Idea:**
> What finally swayed Britain's declaration was the invasion of Belgium. In a treaty signed in 1839, Britain, the German State of Prussia, and other European powers had agreed to respect and guarantee the neutrality of Belgium.

Troops of the American 42nd Division firing from their trenches on the French battlefront, 1918.

certain, but in which the loss of life, suffering, and economic consequences were bound to be terrible." Since then, some other historians have supported Fay's thinking. Others have laid the blame on one or more of the major belligerents. All of them, however, have agreed on how shocking and unprecedented were the human and economic consequences. In the next section, we will see why these tragedies occurred as we survey the conduct of war.

CONDUCT OF WORLD WAR I

The terrible loss of life and property during World War I can explain why this conflict was originally called the Great War. New weapons and technology were used that made warfare more deadly than it had ever been before. With almost thirty nations and colonies involved, World War I had more participants, both military and civilian, than any prior war on our planet. The actual conduct of the war will concern us in this section.

New Weapons

The warfare from 1914 to 1918 produced unprecedented numbers of casualties as innovative (new) weaponry was employed on land and in sea and air. Ground forces were equipped with machine guns able to fire many bullets in quick succession over a wide area. The use of machine guns eliminated the traditional stand-up-and-charge tactics. Tanks were armored vehicles that contained lethal guns and were maneuvered by soldiers seated inside. These fierce-looking vehicles could easily break through enemy lines and move over different kinds of terrain (land). Exploding canisters released poison gas that caused injuries never experienced in prior conflicts between nations. The threat of gas warfare required infantry units to carry gas masks and to learn how to use them within seconds of an attack.

Naval warfare expanded with the construction of faster and more powerful battleships. Besides engaging in combat and troop transport, these ships

American soldiers in France learning how to use gas masks during World War I.

Germany used U-boats in both World Wars. This U-boat is returning from Scapa Flow, northeast of Scotland, where it sank the British battleship HMS Royal Oak on 14 October 1939.

Women machinists in the turning shop of a German state artillery factory, 1917.

were effective in maintaining blockades of water routes. An innovation was the submarine, first used by Germany. Also called U-boats, from the German word *unterwasser* (underwater), submarines inflicted enormous damage throughout the war.

Warfare in the air was introduced as belligerents on both sides sought to use the newly invented airplane. Aircraft were initially utilized to observe troop movements. Pilots also engaged in bombings and "**dogfights,**" but on a very limited scale. Aerial combat here was in its infancy and had little impact upon the course of the Great War.

The management and care of these new weapons called for extensive training. The training had to be given not just to professional soldiers but also to the thousands of civilians who were drafted to fight for their countries. The drafting of civilians for combat had been relatively rare in previous wars. Most fighting had been done by individuals who had voluntarily chosen military careers and were thus professional soldiers. World War I, with so many civilians in uniform and so many others at work in factories and at home in the war effort, became known as the first total war.

Military Aspects

The war was fought almost entirely in Europe and surrounding waters, although there was some action in the Middle East. From 1914 to 1916 the fighting resulted in a **stalemate**, with neither side gaining much ground. In 1917, even though Russia dropped out of the war, the entry of the United States helped the remaining Triple Entente nations to secure victory in 1918. In Europe, the war was fought on two fronts, the western and the eastern, described in relation to the geographical position of the Central powers. The major battles resulting from military strategic planning are listed here in chronological order, as are other key events of the war.

1. *Marne River (1914):* Lying to the southeast of Paris, the Marne River was the site of a strong defense effort by French forces against the Germans. After overrunning Belgium, Germany had hoped to score a quick victory against France by taking Paris. At the Marne River, both sides dug trenches in the ground, trying but unable to advance against each other. This kind of **trench warfare** was common along the western front.

2. *Tannenberg (1914):* This battle, fought on the eastern front, in Germany, proved to be a crushing defeat for the Russian army.

> **Main Idea:**
> In Europe, the war was fought on two fronts, the western and the eastern, described in relation to the geographical position of the Central powers.

3. *Gallipoli (1915):* In 1914, the Ottoman Turks, fearing Russia, joined with the Triple Alliance powers. Turkey was in a geographical position to prevent Russian ships from reaching the Mediterranean Sea. Britain and France landed troops on Turkey's Gallipoli peninsula in an attempt to capture the capital of Constantinople and connect with Russia. After eight months of combat, the Allies withdrew. They could not break through the Turkish lines, commanded by Turkish and German officers.

4. *Jutland (1916):* This was the largest naval battle of the war, occurring off the coast of Denmark in the North Sea, between Britain and Germany. Although neither belligerent could claim complete victory, the German attempt to break the British blockade remained unsuccessful.

5. *Verdun (1916):* The scene of the bloodiest battle of the war, this area in northeastern France locked France and Germany into an indecisive struggle. A famous example of dangerous, dirty, and at times boring trench warfare, the six-month-long encounter at Verdun saw almost 600,000 men killed.

6. *Russian Revolution of March (1917):* Russian forces had suffered disastrous losses in the war. The resulting discontent, along with other factors, led to the overthrow of **Czar Nicholas II**. However, the new provisional government, led by **Aleksandr Kerensky**, wanted Russia to stay in the war.

7. *United States Entry into the War (April 1917):* Although the United States had declared itself neutral at the outbreak of the war in 1914, and wished to follow a policy of **isolationism**, it changed its mind during the next three years—for a number of reasons dealing with economics, politics, geography, cultural ties, and **propaganda**. Congress sided with the British and French and declared war on the Central powers. This was done at the request of President Woodrow Wilson.

8. *Capture of Jerusalem by British Forces (1917):* This victory in Palestine by British **General Edward Allenby** helped protect British interests in the Middle East and was a severe blow against Ottoman Turkish rule in the region. It laid the basis for the British Mandate in Palestine, to begin after the war (see Chapter 15 in this volume).

American World War I poster by James Montgomery Flagg, 1918.

9. *Russian Revolution of November (1917):* In the second Russian Revolution of 1917, the provisional government was ousted by Vladimir Ilyich (Nikolai) **Lenin** and the Communists. Lenin had stated that he wanted to take Russia out of the war. This was accomplished with the signing of peace treaties with the Central powers at Brest-Litovsk in 1918.

10. *Chateau-Thierry and the Argonne Forest (1918):* One result of the Brest-Litovsk treaties was that Germany was now free to take troops from the eastern front to the western front. She did this, mounting a large offensive push in France. However, she was stopped at the battles of Chateau-Thierry and the Argonne Forest and was pushed back all the way to her own borders. These battles saw American forces under General **John Pershing** fighting with the French troops of General **Ferdinand Foch**.

End of the War

The skies were darkening for the Central powers in the fall of 1918. In September, the Turks requested peace. Austria-Hungary was coming apart, as some subject nationalities had declared their independence from the empire. On November 9, Kaiser William II of Germany abdicated (quit his office) and fled to Holland. A new German government was established and agreed to stop fighting the war. Accordingly, an armistice was signed in a railroad car in France on November 11, 1918, between Germany and the Allied forces. The armistice stated that all combat would cease at the eleventh hour of the eleventh day of the eleventh month of 1918. There was rejoicing then in many parts of the world. In the United States, November 11 has since been a national holiday, referred to also as Veteran's Day or Armistice Day.

Signing of the armistice between the Allied forces and Germany aboard a railroad car at Compiegne, France, November 11, 1918. From left: Ernst Vanselow, Alfred von Oberndorff, Detlev von Winterfeldt, John Arthur Ransome Marriott, Matthias Erzberger, Rosslyn Wemyss, Ferdinand Foch, and Maxime Weygand.

With peace now on the horizon, the world could breathe easier. In November 1918, nobody had yet called this war World War I. That title came later in the century, for reasons we will discuss in Chapter 9. The key problems for consideration in the winter of 1918–1919 were how to arrange a suitable peace, what to do with the defeated countries, and how to prevent another "great war" from occurring. These problems were on the agenda at the peace conference that took place in Paris in January 1919. The resolution of these problems, as well as the general results of the war, will be the next topic for us to examine.

RESULTS OF WORLD WAR I

What is the purpose of a peace conference? This is an important question to ask as we prepare to study the peace conference that took place after World War I. Delegates to this kind of conference may agree on its purpose but may disagree on how to achieve that purpose. They may not even agree on the purposes. Some other questions to consider are those raised at the end of the last section: How can a suitable and just peace be arranged? How should the defeated countries be treated? How can another war be prevented?

In this section, we will see how each of these questions was answered by delegates at the Paris Peace Conference of 1919 and also learn the general results of World War I.

The Delegates and Their Goals

The **Peace Conference** in Paris opened in January 1919, with delegates from almost all the victorious Allied powers. Russia was not present, as she was involved in a civil war (see Chapter 8, in this volume, "The Rise of Totalitarianism in Russia, Italy, and Germany"). Other absentees were the defeated nations. (It had been decided to call in Germany and her allies only after treaty terms had been drawn up.) The major participants in the Paris talks were the four most powerful Allied victors, known as the **Big Four**: France, Great Britain, Italy, and the United States. They were represented by their

Prime Minister David Lloyd George, Prime Minister Vittorio Emanuele Orlando, Premier Georges Clemenceau, and President Woodrow Wilson at the Versailles Palace during the Treaty Negotiations in 1919.

The "Big Four" (Premier Georges Clemenceau, President Woodrow Wilson, Prime Minister David Lloyd George, and Premier Vittorio Emanuele Orlando) at the signing of the Treaty of Versailles, June 28, 1919. Illustration by Edouard Requin.

respective leaders: Premier **Georges Clemenceau** of France, Prime Minister **David Lloyd George** of Great Britain, Premier **Vittorio Orlando** of Italy, and President **Woodrow Wilson** of the United States.

Each of these men came to the conference with specific goals and objectives. So did delegates from other nations, such as Belgium. Every delegate's goals represented the foreign policy desires of his nation. As we said previously, the foreign policy of a nation is influenced by its own self-interests. Foreign policy is also influenced by geography and a nation's past relations with other nations. These factors must be kept in mind in order to understand why there were disagreements among the Big Four at the 1919 Peace Conference.

France

Premier Clemenceau spoke for a nation that had been seriously hurt by Germany in this most recent war, as well as in the Franco-Prussian War some 47 years earlier. France wanted revanche for the loss of Alsace-Lorraine, and security against possible German **aggression** in the future. France hoped to severely weaken Germany by making that nation limit her military, give up land in Europe and overseas, and pay for damages during the war.

Great Britain

Although Britain was further away from Germany than was France, and although British soil had not been trod upon by German troops, Britain nevertheless wanted to see a weakened Germany. For Lloyd George, this would mean a reduced German navy, loss of colonies, and German reparations (payments) for the war. These goals would benefit British self-interests. Prime Minister George would be less harsh on Germany than would France. He may have remembered a slogan about Germany from a fellow countryman: "Hang the Kaiser, but preserve a balance of power."

Italy

Italy hoped to add to her territory in Europe, particularly with acquisitions from Austria-Hungary. It also wanted land overseas and claimed that many areas had been promised to it in secret treaties. Premier Orlando argued with Lloyd George about some of these claims and left the conference in anger. The Big Four then became the Big Three.

United States

President Woodrow Wilson arrived in Paris with goals that were entirely different from those of his fellow delegates. Much more idealistic than they, and coming from a nation whose soil was untouched by the war and was furthest from the Central powers, he did not seek punishment. His overall goal was a "peace without victory." His specific goals were outlined in a speech he gave to Congress in January 1918 that contained the famous **Fourteen Points**. Eight of these points concerned specific regions and nations, but the remaining six dealt with broad issues and spelled out objectives that Wilson hoped to see adopted at the peace conference:

1. Freedom of the seas
2. Self-determination for all people
3. Open diplomacy and the end of secret treaties
4. The end of tariffs and other economic barriers
5. Limitations on weapons
6. The establishment of a League of Nations to settle international disputes peacefully

It would almost seem that Wilson viewed war as a disease. And with a disease, doctors hope to cure it and ultimately find the reasons for it. If the reasons are known, then perhaps sufficient methods can be created to prevent its recurrence. Did the other "doctors" at the Paris Peace Conference agree with Wilson? Let us turn now to the provisions of the peace treaty that was put together and eventually signed at the Palace of Versailles in June 1919.

Provisions of the Versailles Peace Treaty

After much arguing and many compromises among the delegates, the Treaty of Versailles was drawn up in May 1919. At this point, representatives from the new German republic were summoned to appear and told to sign the treaty. Viewing the document as too harsh, the Germans at first refused to sign it. But when the Allies threatened to renew the war, the representatives had no choice. They signed the treaty on June 8, 1919, precisely five years after the assassination of Archduke Francis Ferdinand in Sarajevo! Another event from the past was called to mind at the signing ceremony. In the Hall of Mirrors, site of the ceremony, almost fifty years earlier after the Prussian victory in the Franco-Prussian War, the Prussian leader Bismarck had proclaimed the birth of the German Empire.

Although the treaty was a long document, its chief provisions can be summarized as follows:

1. *Creation of a League of Nations.*
2. *Loss of German territory in Europe:* Alsace-Lorraine would be returned to France. The resource-rich Saar Valley would be under League of Nations authority for fifteen years. During that period, France could have all the coal mined in the region as part payment for German war damages. The re-created nation of Poland received much German territory, including a strip of land that would give Poland a seaport on the Baltic Sea. This strip of land, known as the Polish Corridor, separated German East Prussia from the rest of Germany; **Danzig**, formerly a German city, would be a free city administered by the League of Nations for Polish use.
3. *Loss of German territory overseas:* All German colonies would be held as **mandates** by the League of Nations.

> **Main Idea:**
> After much arguing and many compromises among the delegates, the Treaty of Versailles was drawn up in May 1919. At this point, representatives from the new German republic were summoned to appear and told to sign the treaty.

4. *Military restrictions on Germany:* Germany was restricted to an army of 100,000 volunteers and prohibited from practicing **conscription** (drafting people into the armed forces). The Rhineland was to be demilitarized, and the navy limited to a few ships. Germany could not build submarines, military aircraft, or other instruments of war.
5. *War guilt and reparations:* Germany was forced to admit guilt for the war, and therefore required to make huge monetary payments called reparations.

Other Peace Treaties and Territorial Changes

Separate treaties were signed with the other Central powers.

> **Main Idea:**
> See the contrasting maps of Europe on this page to locate the major territorial changes after World War I.

1. *With Austria in 1919, the Treaty of St. Germain; with Hungary in 1920, the Treaty of Trianon.* In the last year of the war, the Austro-Hungarian Empire under Habsburg rule had ceased to exist. In its place were the independent nations of **Austria** and **Hungary** and the new nations of **Czechoslovakia** and **Yugoslavia**. Both consisted of subject nationalities that had long clamored for independent nationhood, free of Habsburg domination. The new Yugoslavia contained both Serbia and Sarajevo. Limitations were placed on the armies of both Austria and Hungary. They also had to pay reparations, though not as severe as those imposed on Germany. Also, Austria was forbidden from any future union (*anschluss*) with Germany.

2. *With Turkey in 1923, the Treaty of Sevres.* This treaty officially reduced the once powerful Ottoman Empire to the sole nation of Turkey. Non-Turkish areas in the Middle East were taken away and became mandates; two examples were **Palestine** and **Syria**. Turkey did not have to pay reparations, nor was her army restricted.

Other territorial arrangements saw Poland reestablished as a nation. It had undergone several partitions since 1795. The three Baltic regions of **Lithuania**, **Latvia**, and **Estonia** became free. They had been taken by Germany from Russia in the Treaty of Brest-Litovsk, which was canceled after the war.

A summary of major territorial changes after World War I is given below. Also, see the contrasting maps of Europe to locate these changes.

MAJOR TERRITORIAL CHANGES AFTER WORLD WAR I	
Change	**Nation from which land was taken**
Poland was recreated with a "corridor" to the sea	Germany and German-conquered areas of Russia
Romania was enlarged	Austria-Hungary
Yugoslavia and Czechoslovakia were created as new nations	Austria-Hungary
Austria and Hungary became separate nations	Austria-Hungary
Finland, Estonia, Latvia, and Lithuania were created	Russia
Alsace-Lorraine was returned to France	Germany
Syria, Lebanon, and Palestine became mandates under the League of Nations	Turkey

General Results of World War I

As we have seen, World War I was labeled the Great War for many reasons. An additional reason lies in the fact that the war changed the course of world history. It brought short-range results as well as long-range outcomes that affected future events and generations. The economic chaos and radical social changes in its wake were accompanied by historic political developments. Some of the most powerful European nations lost their influence and began to decline. Many monarchs lost their thrones. Some empires came to an end, while others expanded. A Communist government came to power in Russia. The general results, seen from economic, social, and political perspectives, are discussed next.

Economic

The war was very costly to the participants. Costs were estimated at close to $400 billion. In all belligerent nations, taxes had to be raised while living standards fell. The losers became debtor nations, some of them finding it difficult to make reparation payments while rebuilding their economies. Many of the economic problems arising from the war were partly responsible for the worldwide Great Depression that began in 1929.

Social

Casualties were heavy. Estimates are that ten million soldiers were killed and another thirty-one million were wounded. Civilian population losses were also in the millions, caused to a large degree by the deadly weapons used for the first time in warfare. Most Europeans failed to understand the destructive power of these weapons until they had been used, and to realize how horrible modern warfare had become. Displacement of people as refugees and changes in boundaries brought resentment. This was true, for example, in western Poland and Czechoslovakia, where large numbers of Germans now found themselves living. Ethnic tensions also existed, for a variety of reasons, between Turks and Greeks and between Turks and Armenians. Between 1915 and 1922 almost two million Armenians were killed by the Ottoman Turks in a campaign of genocide.

The Armenian Genocide

One of the most horrifying aspects of the First World War was the use of genocide (the planned annihilation or destruction of a people because of its religion, race, or nationality) as part of a war strategy. This was done by the Ottoman Empire to the **Armenian** people in 1915. Frustrated by constant losses during World War I, the Ottoman government made the Armenians scapegoats (people who are blamed for others' problems and failures) and claimed they were responsible for the empire's poor military performance. The leaders of the government, a group of army officers known as the **Young Turks**, adopted this policy as a means of shifting the population's anger and dissatisfaction with the war effort away from themselves. The Armenians, who were a large and prosperous Orthodox Christian minority in the Ottoman Empire, were an ideal scapegoat as most of their population lived in the traditional Armenian lands in northwestern Asia Minor near the Russian border. Accusing them of working with the Allies against the Ottoman Empire, the government began a systematic

Widowed Armenian women and their children in Turkey at the time of the Turkish genocide of Armenians, September 1915.

extermination of Armenians on April 24, 1913. Armenian men were rounded up and massacred, while the women and children were taken on death marches into the desert. Armenian political and religious leaders were publicly executed, often by impaling (driving the victim through a large stake) or beheading. Armenian churches and institutions were destroyed, and their confiscated homes were given to Turkish people. Some Armenians were able to escape into Russia (where a new Armenian state was later established), but the majority were slaughtered or died of starvation in forced marches across the desert into Syria. Out of a population of only three million, over half were killed or died.

The surviving Armenians established a republic in the Soviet Union after the war. The Young Turk leaders, who had fled Ottoman Turkey after the defeat of the Central powers, were found guilty of war crimes by an Ottoman military court, but they were never legally punished. After the modern nation of Turkey was established in 1922, the new government, under the **Turkish Nationalist Party**, denied that the Armenian genocide ever occurred. This policy of official denial has been continued by successive Turkish governments until the present day.

Main Idea:
After the modern nation of Turkey was established in 1922, the new government, under the **Turkish Nationalist Party**, denied that the Armenian genocide ever occurred. This policy of official denial has been continued by successive Turkish governments until the present day.

Political

New nations arose, and boundaries changed, as shown in the preceding table. Ownership of some colonies changed. The long-standing Ottoman and Austro-Hungarian Empires were no more. The League of Nations was formed in an effort to secure world peace and to watch over specified areas as mandates. Three traditional royal dynasties saw their centuries-long rule ended: the Hohenzollerns in Germany, the Habsburgs in Austria-Hungary, and the Romanovs in Russia. The world's first Communist government came to power in Russia as a result of a revolution. Germany was about to embark on her first experience as a democracy. The United States was now viewed as a major world power.

The Establishment of Modern Turkey

Main Idea:
The Nationalists set up a rival government in the city of Ankara in 1920, proclaiming it the Turkish Republic and rejecting the authority of the Sultan. Kemal was elected president of the new republic as well as commander-in-chief.

The Ottoman Empire was divided after World War I. Britain and France took over parts of the former Ottoman lands in the Middle East as mandates under the League of Nations. Western Asia Minor, which included the city of Constantinople, was given to Greece. (Constantinople's name was changed to Istanbul in 1930.) Yet, the victorious Allies did nothing to restore the Armenian people to their traditional lands in eastern Asia Minor. Angered by the Allied division and the weakness of the Ottoman government, the Turkish Nationalist Party was formed by a group of army officers under the leadership of war hero **Mustafa Kemal.** The Nationalists set up a rival government in the city of Ankara in 1920, proclaiming it the Turkish Republic and rejecting the authority of the Sultan. Kemal was elected president of the new republic as well as commander-in-chief.

Gaining the support of the army, the Nationalists invaded western Asia Minor. Kemal's forces took advantage of the war-weariness of the Allies (upon whom the Greeks, newly established in western Asia Minor, depended) and drove the Greek army back into Greece by 1922. Claiming that atrocities had been committed against the Turkish population while under Greek occupation, the Nationalist forces massacred the Greek population. The ancient city of **Smyrna**, for example, was burned to the ground. This began a policy of persecution to drive out some non-Turkish populations (i.e., Kurds) in order to create an exclusively Turkish state.

The victory of the Nationalists made Kemal a national hero. In the Turkish Constitution of 1923, he was given almost dictatorial powers. This enabled him to make radical changes that transformed Turkish society:

- There was a separation of the state from traditional Islamic law and custom.
- Traditional Islamic clothing, in particular the wearing of the veil by women and the fez (tall, brimless red cap) by men was replaced by Western clothing.
- The Latin alphabet replaced the Arabic.
- Mandatory (state-controlled) public education was established.
- Women were given the right to vote (1929) and encouraged to participate in public life.
- Sunday replaced the traditional Islamic Friday as the state "day of rest."
- Western technology was introduced to Turkish society.
- The Turkish army was modernized.

Kemal's role as the "Father of Modern Turkey" earned him the title of **Ataturk** or "Head Turk." His close relationship with the army gave the military enormous influence over succeeding governments after his death in 1938. Seeing themselves as the protectors of the established order, the military have exercised a strong and conservative influence over Turkish politics until the present day.

Kemal Ataturk (1881–1938), Turkish general and statesman, reviewing his troops.

LINK TO TODAY
Driving Through Europe on Armistice Day

In the United States and its World War I allies, November 11 has been observed and celebrated as Armistice Day ever since the Great War. In our country and only in our country, it is also known as Veterans' Day. To drive a car on that day through some parts of Europe, you would see some noteworthy contrasts. A driver going northeastward from France, into Belgium and Holland on November 11 would not be surprised to see some parades, or hear speeches or see wreaths being laid at cemeteries or at World War I battlegrounds. Yet, once you cross the border into Germany, you would not see those things. Why not? Does the answer lie in the chapter you have just finished reading? Here are some other challenging questions: How should nations preserve historical memory? Should they do this in similar ways? What will be the result if certain memories are not preserved?

CHAPTER SUMMARY

Europe would never be the same after World War I. The results left the world uncertain about the continent's future. As coming events would suggest, it may have been easier to achieve a victory on a battlefield than to gain a lasting peace at a conference table. The League of Nations was the first large international forum to design a peace plan for Europe since the 1815 Congress of Vienna. As we will see, however, the League of Nations lacked powers of enforcement and did not have the United States as a member. (In 1920, the U.S. Senate refused to let the United States join the League.)

The Treaty of Versailles stirred controversy. Critics claimed that it was too harsh on Germany and thereby planted the seeds of World War II. The Germans certainly were bitter about it, claiming that its provisions amounted to a *diktat* (dictated peace). Adolf Hitler and the Nazi Party were able to use this issue as an effective argument in their rise to power in 1933. Treaty critics in Germany and elsewhere believed that all of Wilson's Fourteen Points should have been incorporated into the treaty. In their view, the failure to do so created a peace with vengeance rather than with justice.

Whether or not we accept these opinions, we should pause to consider a situation that, although simplistic, nevertheless raises a fundamental issue of human nature. Assume that two longtime enemies, A and B, have a fistfight. A wins decisively. To make sure that B will never again bother A, how should A act toward B? Should A continue to beat up B, inflicting additional punishment? Or should A treat B kindly, helping him up and shaking hands? Critics of the Versailles treaty would probably choose the second course of action, and proponents of the treaty, the first.

Those who favored the treaty felt that Germany deserved what she received. For them, Germany was seen to have been a hostile, militaristic nation for decades that needed to be taught a lesson now that it was defeated in war.

German land in Europe was taken mainly on the basis of nationality; lands taken overseas were to be administered as mandates under the League of Nations with the promise of eventual independence. The treaty by itself cannot be blamed for the rise of Hitler and the Nazis. And if all the treaty provisions had been fully enforced, particularly the military one, argued the proponents, Germany would have been unable to engage in another world war.

You have now seen the answers to the questions posed on the first page of this chapter. These answers make us realize how troubling these questions are. Indeed, some of the decisions respecting territorial changes, as well as some other changes occurring in the World War I era, have become undone in our own times. The first few years of the 1990s, for example, witnessed a new Germany, a disunited Czechoslovakia, a surprisingly reformed Russia, and a dismembered Yugoslavia facing a bitter civil war. The twentieth century began with trouble in the Balkans, and ended with additional troubles. Yet, fortunately, no major war emerged from the Balkan crisis of the 1990s.

From the upheavals and discontent immediately after World War I, however, there did emerge totalitarian dictatorships in Russia, Italy, and Germany. This emergence will concern us in the next chapter.

IMPORTANT PEOPLE, PLACES, AND TERMS

KEY TERMS

Congress of Vienna	Central powers	propaganda
Pax Europa	League of Nations	armistice
nationalism	Dual Alliance	Paris Peace Conference
militarism	balance of power	Big Four
Great War	immediate cause	aggression
underlying cause	"blank check"	Fourteen Points
protectorate	ultimatum	mandate
nationalities	mobilization	conscription
revanche	dogfight	Armenian genocide
Triple Alliance	stalemate	dynasties
Triple Entente	trench warfare	Young Turks
belligerent	isolationism	Turkish National Party

PEOPLE

Archduke Francis Ferdinand	Ferdinand Foch	David Lloyd George
Gavrilo Princip	Woodrow Wilson	Mustafa Kemal (Ataturk)
John Pershing	Vittorio Orlando	
	Georges Clemenceau	

PLACES

Austria-Hungary	Sarajevo	France
Balkans	Gallipoli	Russia
Serbia	Verdun	

CHAPTER 7

MULTIPLE-CHOICE QUESTIONS

Select the number of the correct answer.

1. The Triple Alliance was composed of which set of countries?

   (1) Germany, Austria-Hungary, and Italy
   (2) Germany, Russia, and France
   (3) Italy, Great Britain, and Austria-Hungary
   (4) Great Britain, France, and Russia

2. The period from the 1870s to 1914 was known as one of international anarchy. This means that

   (1) there was constant fighting around the world
   (2) a few dictators had gained complete control
   (3) there were no recognized worldwide organizations that could set and enforce rules
   (4) most countries in the world had become increasingly warlike

3. Nations generally enter into alliances with other nations as a result of

   (1) a desire to conquer the other nation
   (2) a nation's self-interest
   (3) a goal to assist the other nation
   (4) an international law

4. The phrase, "the spark setting off the Balkan powder keg" is most directly linked to which event?

   (1) the formation of the Triple Alliance
   (2) the British goal of a balance of power in world relationships
   (3) the assassination of Archduke Francis Ferdinand and his wife
   (4) the growth of militarism in Germany and France

5. Which event can be most directly described as the cause of Britain's entry into World War I?

   (1) the assassination of Archduke Francis Ferdinand
   (2) the German declaration of war on Russia
   (3) the Austrian bombing of the city of Belgrade
   (4) the invasion of Belgium by Germany

6. Which statement expresses an opinion about weapons in World War I?

   (1) New weapons used in World War I included machine guns, submarines, and airplanes.
   (2) The use of machine guns eliminated the traditional tactics of "stand-up and charge."
   (3) The new weapons were easy to use and required little training.
   (4) Battleships were used to blockade water routes.

7. Between 1914 and 1917, the United States changed its foreign policy with regard to World War I from

   (1) containment to imperialism
   (2) intervention to colonialism
   (3) conquest to nationalism
   (4) isolationism to involvement

8. Between 1914 and 1918, unemployment declined in several world nations. This might be explained by

   (1) the use of new technology that eliminated some jobs
   (2) the need for production of war materials
   (3) the decrease of international trade
   (4) the desire of consumers to have more free time

9. Put the following events related to World War I in correct chronological order:

A. The Triple Entente was formed
B. Archduke Francis Ferdinand was assassinated
C. Czar Nicholas II abdicated in the first Russian Revolution
D. The United States entered the war

(1) A, B, C, D   (3) B, A, D, C
(2) A, D, B, C   (4) C, B, A, D

10. Which were the four victorious nations that participated in the Peace Conference?

(1) France, Russia, Belgium, United States
(2) Russia, Great Britain, England, United States
(3) France, Great Britain, Italy, United States
(4) Germany, Austria-Hungary, Russia, Italy

11. How was the United States different from the other nations that attended the Peace Conference?

(1) No battles had been fought on American soil.
(2) It was attempting to increase its size with territories won in the war.
(3) It sought to punish the losing nations.
(4) It wanted repayments for war debts.

12. The treaty that formally ended World War I and gave detailed provisions for Germany was known as the

(1) Treaty of Paris
(2) The Versailles Treaty
(3) The Fourteen Points Treaty
(4) The Berlin Treaty

13. Which world leader most encouraged the formation of a League of Nations?

(1) David Lloyd George
(2) Vittorio Orlando
(3) Georges Clemenceau
(4) Woodrow Wilson

14. Which nation was forced to admit guilt for World War I and forced to make large monetary payments to the victors?

(1) Russia
(2) Austria-Hungary
(3) Germany
(4) Italy

15. What would be the best title for the list of events that follows:

• Poland was created with a "corridor" to the sea.
• Yugoslavia became a new nation.
• Austria was separated from Hungary

(1) Goals of Germany for World War I
(2) Accomplishments of the United States in World War I
(3) Failures of the New League of Nations
(4) Changes that Occurred as a Result of World War I

16. During World War I, which ethnic group was specifically eliminated in a campaign of genocide?

(1) Russian Jews
(2) Armenians
(3) Bavarians
(4) Belgians

17. Which royal dynasty was the only one to survive after World War I as a ruling monarchy?

(1) The Windsors in Great Britain
(2) The Hohenzollerns in Germany
(3) The Romanovs in Russia
(4) The Habsburgs in Austria-Hungary

18. Which ethnic group took advantage of the political and economic changes following the official end of World War I to form its own country?

(1) Greeks   (3) Ukrainians
(2) Turks   (4) Spanish

19. The formation of the League of Nations and membership in it could be considered unusual because

(1) every world nation was anxious to belong to it
(2) it had the power to enforce international laws
(3) it was an effort to end international alliances
(4) the country that proposed it did not belong to it

20. World War I is considered a turning point in global history because of its

(1) major impact on the most powerful countries in the world at that time
(2) success in ending attempts to establish Communist governments
(3) very low loss of life and limited destruction of property
(4) ability to solve a world crisis at a very minimal cost to all involved

THEMATIC ESSAY

Directions: Write a well-organized essay that includes an introduction, several paragraphs addressing the task below, and a conclusion.

Theme: National Self-Interest

Nations have always acted toward other nations based on their own self-interests. This was true of nations before, during, and at the end of World War I.

Task

Identify one nation that had a major role in World War I and, for that nation,

- describe what specific self-interests motivated the nation to become involved in the conflict
- describe two actions taken by the nation before or during the war that supported this self-interest
- evaluate the degree of success the nation had in protecting its self-interests at the end of the war

You may select any European nation that played a major role in World War I. Some nations you might wish to consider include Austria-Hungary, France, Germany, Great Britain, Italy, and Russia.

You are not limited to these suggestions.

Do *not* use the United States in your answer.

Guidelines

In your essay, be sure to

- develop all aspects of the *Task*
- support the theme with relevant facts, examples, and details
- use a logical and clear plan of organization, including an introduction and a conclusion that are beyond a restatement of the theme
- introduce the theme by establishing a framework that is beyond a simple restatement of the *Task* and conclude with a summation of the theme

DOCUMENT-BASED ESSAY QUESTION

This question is based on the accompanying documents (1–7). The question is designed to test your ability to work with historical documents. Some of the documents have been edited for the purposes of the question. As you analyze the documents, take into account the source of each document and any point of view that may be presented in the document.

Historical Context

The time period of World War I witnessed the development of new ideas, new weapons, and new wartime strategies and was concluded by new types of peace-time efforts.

Task

Using information from the documents and your knowledge of global history, answer the questions that follow each document in Part A. Your answers to the questions will help you write the Part B essay in which you will be asked to

- discuss at least two ways in which the conduct of World War I was different from previous wars
- describe the impact of these changes on soldiers in World War I
- evaluate how the events involved in the conduct of World War I impacted the Treaty of Versailles

Part A: Short-Answer Questions

Directions: Analyze the documents and answer the short-answer questions that follow each document.

Document 1

Development of the tank began in the summer of 1915. The idea was to combine the caterpillar tracks of an American tractor with an iron-clad machine that could straddle the enemy's trenches. By spring of the following year a working model was available for testing. Manned by a crew of four, the 30-ton weapon's armament consisted of two cannons mounted on its sides. It lumbered along at three miles an hour. Encased in an unlit steel box, the crew suffered in an atmosphere that was only one step removed from Hell—unbearably hot, dusty, noisy, the air filled with the nauseating stench of gas fumes.

Source: "The Battlefield Debut of the Tank, 1916," EyeWitness to History, www.eyewitnesstohistory.com (2005).

Questions

1. Using the excerpt from a description of the first use of a tank answer the following questions:
   a. What problems are described for the crew of the tank?
   b. For what specific purpose was the tank invented?

Document 2

a.

"We were eighteen and had begun to love life and the world; and we had to shoot it to pieces. The first bomb, the first explosion, burst in our hearts. We are cut off from activity, from striving, from progress. We believe in such things no longer, we believe in the war."

—Erich Maria Remarque, *All Quiet on the Western Front*, Ch. 5

Question

2a. According to Remarque how did the war change an 18-year-old?

b.

"But now, for the first time, I see you are a man like me. I thought of your hand-grenades, of your bayonet, of your rifle; now I see your wife and your face and our fellowship. Forgive me, comrade. We always see it too late. Why do they never tell us that you are poor devils like us, that your mothers are just as anxious as ours, and that we have the same fear of death, and the same dying and the same agony."

—Erich Maria Remarque, *All Quiet on the Western Front*, Ch. 9

Question

2b. What specific problems of warfare does Remarque cite in this quotation?

Document 3

Question

3. What specific German threat is the cartoonist suggesting?

Document 4

"National sovereignty and economic sovereignty are together cardinal principles of true independence."

Mustafa Kemal Ataturk (1881–1938)

Question 4. According to Kemal Ataturk, what does a truly independent country need?

Document 5

"If one seeks to analyze experiences and reaction to the first postwar years, (World War I), I hope one may say without being accused of bias that it is easier for the victor than for the vanquished (defeated) to advocate peace."

Gustav Stresemann (1878–1929)
German politician, statesman, writer, and winner of
the Nobel Peace Prize in 1926

Question 5. Why would Stresemann say that peace was easier for a victorious country after World War I than for a defeated nation?

Document 6   Selected Articles from the Treaty of Versailles:

ARTICLE 11.

Any war or threat of war, whether immediately affecting any of the Members of the League or not, is hereby declared a matter of concern to the whole League, and the League shall take any action that may be deemed wise and effectual to safeguard the peace of nations. In case any such emergency should arise the Secretary General shall on the request of any Member of the League forthwith summon a meeting of the Council. It is also declared to be the friendly right of each Member of the League to bring to the attention of the Assembly or of the Council any circumstance whatever affecting international relations which threatens to disturb international peace or the good understanding between nations upon which peace depends.

ARTICLE 12.

The Members of the League agree that if there should arise between them any dispute likely to lead to a rupture, they will submit the matter either to arbitration or to inquiry by the Council, and they agree in no case to resort to war until three months after the award by the arbitrators or the report by the Council. In any case under this Article the award of the arbitrators shall be made within a reasonable time, and the report of the Council shall be made within six months after the submission of the dispute.

Question 6. How the does the Treaty of Versailles try to stop the threat of war in the future?

Part B: Essay

Directions: Write a well-organized essay that includes an introduction, several paragraphs, and a conclusion. Use evidence from *at least four* of the documents in the body of the essay. Support your response with relevant facts, examples, and details. Include additional outside information.

Historical Context

The time period of World War I witnessed the development of new ideas, new weapons, and new wartime strategies and was concluded by new types of peacetime efforts.

Task

Using information from the documents and your knowledge of global history, answer the questions that follow each document in Part A. Your answers to the questions will help you write the Part B essay in which you will be asked to

- discuss at least two ways in which the conduct of World War I was different from previous wars
- describe the impact of these changes on soldiers in World War I
- evaluate how the events involved in the conduct of World War I impacted the Treaty of Versailles

Guidelines

In your essay, be sure to

- address all aspects of the *Task* by accurately analyzing and interpreting *at least four* documents
- incorporate information from the documents
- incorporate relevant outside information
- support the theme with relevant facts, examples, and details
- use a logical and clear plan of organization
- include an introduction and a conclusion that are beyond a simple restatement of the *Historical Context*

CHAPTER 8

The Rise of Totalitarianism in Russia, Italy, and Germany

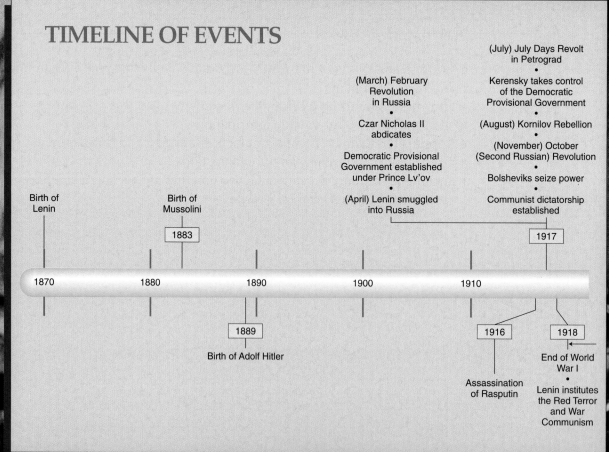

TIMELINE OF EVENTS

(July) July Days Revolt
in Petrograd

(March) February
Revolution
in Russia

Kerensky takes control
of the Democratic
Provisional Government

Czar Nicholas II
abdicates

(August) Kornilov Rebellion

Democratic Provisional
Government established
under Prince Lv'ov

(November) October
(Second Russian) Revolution

Bolsheviks seize power

Birth of
Lenin

Birth of
Mussolini

(April) Lenin smuggled
into Russia

Communist dictatorship
established

1883

1917

1870   1880   1890   1900   1910

1889   1916   1918

Birth of Adolf Hitler

End of World
War I

Assassination
of Rasputin

Lenin institutes
the Red Terror
and War
Communism

The world had little time to breathe after the Treaty of Versailles before it seemed that trouble was again on the horizon. Profound changes in three nations would affect the rest of the world for the remaining years of the century. It is interesting that in Russia, Italy, and Germany three men used similar tactics to rise to power and solidify their positions. Joseph Stalin, Benito Mussolini, and Adolf Hitler were different in many ways, but they also had much in common. They came from unimpressive backgrounds, but they were shrewd about human nature. Seeing a political vacuum, they filled it and then eliminated the opposition. Promises were made to people who were suffering economic hardships and welcomed the hope of a better future. All three leaders were single-minded men who used a small band of dedicated followers to frighten the masses of people. Each had a simple, easily understood plan. Each appealed to the nationalistic spirit of his nation's people and was successful because, among other reasons, good people did nothing. As a result of the actions of these three men, millions died.

COMMUNISM IN RUSSIA

The rise of **totalitarianism** in **Russia** began a trend that was to be followed throughout many parts of Europe in the twentieth century. Totalitarianism is a form of government in which one person or group, usually a political party, has

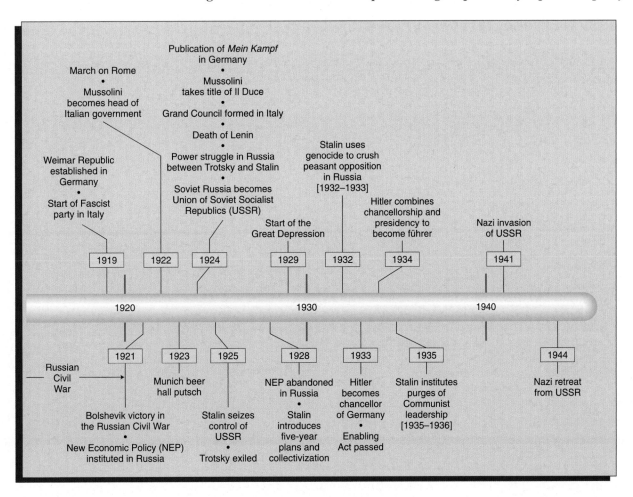

complete control and does not tolerate (allow) any opposition. With World War I, the traditional Russian czarist system collapsed and left a vacuum in its place. It was the **Bolsheviks**, or **Communists**, who seized the opportunity to take its place.

When the war began, the czarist government was trying to correct the many problems and widespread unrest created by Russian industrialization. The inability of the regime to fight a modern war made the faults and weaknesses of the **monarchy** even more apparent, and the lack of any democratic experience left the nation vulnerable to any group ruthless enough to seize power. Throughout the nineteenth century, the czars had failed to respond adequately to the need for political reform. That failure was about to doom the Russian monarchy.

Russia in World War I (1914–1917)

The Last Years of the Czarist System

For Russia, World War I was a devastating experience. It was the worst possible time for Russia, still trying to industrialize and solve many internal problems, to go to war. The magnitude of World War I, which destroyed many stable gov-

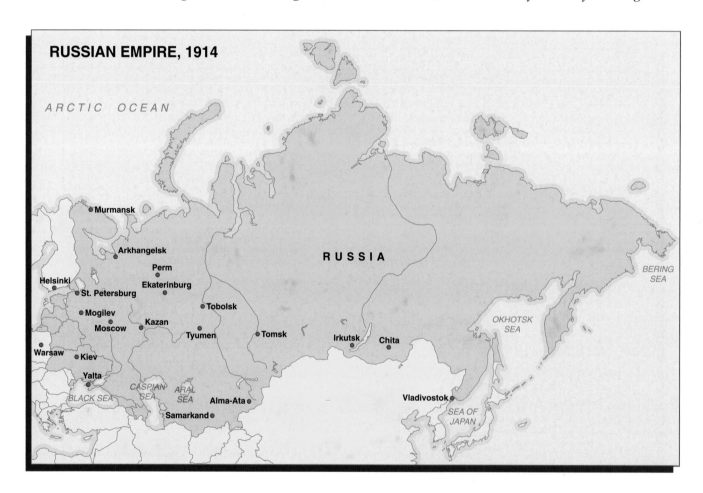

RUSSIAN EMPIRE, 1914

Main Idea:
Russia's limited industry, agriculture, and communications could not sustain a major war effort.

ernments, was even more damaging for the czarist regime. Russia's limited industry, agriculture, and communications could not sustain a major war effort. Despite advice to the contrary, Czar Nicholas (Nikolai) II (1868–1918) took personal command of the army in the autumn of 1915. The retreating Russian forces, demoralized (discouraged) by more than a year of terrible defeats, expected the czar's leadership to turn the tide of battle. Instead, the continuing losses undermined the image of the Russian ruler, who had left his unpopular wife, Czarina Alexandra (Aleksandra) (1872–1918), in charge of the government while he was away (see Chapter 4 in this volume). The civilian population also was demoralized by defeat and began to blame the German-born Alexandra for Russia's poor military performance. Russia was hopelessly unable to supply the troops with weapons or food. The fragile industrial structure was near collapse. Revolutionaries encouraged workers to strike, creating even greater shortages for the army. As hunger, suffering, and humiliation grew, soldiers refused to follow orders, revolted against the commanders, or simply deserted.

The February Revolution of 1917

By February 1917, the czar's army was either retreating or deserting, and riots were erupting in Russian cities. Returning to the capital city of Petrograd (St. Petersburg had been renamed at the start of the war), Czar Nicholas was captured. The **Duma** (Russian parliament) had already declared a new government, under the leadership of the liberal nobleman Prince Georgii Lv'ov (1861–1925). In March 1917, when Nicholas abdicated (resigned) as the czar of Russia, 300 years of rule by the **Romanov Dynasty** came to an end. He also abdicated for his son and thereby ended the centuries-old autocratic monarchy that had ruled Russia. The well-meaning but weak and incompetent czar never fully understood what had happened or why. He merely observed that the date on the letter of abdication was March 15, or the Ides of March, the day on which Julius Caesar had been assassinated in the Roman Senate (czar means "caesar" in Russian). He accepted his fall from power as fate.

The Provisional Government (March–October 1917)
THE PROGRAM OF THE PROVISIONAL GOVERNMENT

The Democratic provisional government, as the new administration was called, declared that Russia was a democracy and announced plans to hold elections. It consisted, however, of the **bourgeoisie** (middle class), liberal nobles, and intellectuals and did not end Russia's involvement in the war. The defeats continued. The leadership showed that it did not understand how desperate and tired the Russian people were from the war. The provisional government's goal to transform Russia into a **democracy** by allowing elections and freedom of speech was well intentioned, but impracticable during a major war. Also, the program of democratic reform was unfamiliar to most Russians, who had known no other form of government than **autocracy**.

Vladimir Ilich Ulyanov Lenin (1870–1924). Russian Communist leader.

In the meantime, the workers, soldiers, and sailors in the cities responded to the leaders of worker's parties, in particular the Socialists (see Chapter 4 in this volume). These parties formed their own councils, called **soviets**. In April, the leader of the Bolsheviks, or Communists, **Vladimir Lenin** (1870–1924), returned to Russia from exile in Switzerland and presented his radical program of **proletarian** (worker) Socialist **revolution** called the April Theses. Despite the program's appeal to the masses (it called for "bread, land, and peace"), the extremist Bolsheviks did not attract a majority of workers.

THE JULY DAYS

In July came a revolt against the unpopular provisional government. Known as the July Days, the uprising in Petrograd was the result of frustration over Russia's continued participation in the war. In an attempt to appease the populace, Lv'ov was replaced by **Aleksandr Kerenski** (1881–1970), a member of the Socialist Revolutionary Party. In September, General Lavr Kornilov (1870–1918), commander of the Russian army, attempted to seize power from the provisional government and establish a military dictatorship. Desperate for troops, Kerenski was forced to free all the revolutionaries, including many Bolsheviks who had been imprisoned during the July Days.

The October Revolution of 1917

Realizing that the Bolsheviks did not have enough support to win in the December elections, Lenin organized the Bolshevik armed forces to seize power. On November 7, 1917, the Bolsheviks overthrew the provisional government.

Aleksandr Feodorovich Kerenski (1881–1970), Russian revolutionary leader, photographed in the summer of 1917 while he was the prime minister of the provisional government.

Bolshevik troops led by Leon Trotsky making the crucial attack on the Winter Palace, October 26, 1917. Photographed by Ivan Kobozev.

The date was October 25 on the Julian calendar that Russia was still following. Therefore, the event was celebrated by the Communists as the **October Revolution**, but it is also known as the Second Russian Revolution.

The Russian Civil War (1918–1921)

The Establishment of Soviet Russia

After the October Revolution, Lenin and his followers made peace with Germany and removed Russia from the war. In the humiliating **Treaty of Brest-Litovsk** (1918), Russia gave up much territory in order to end her involvement in the conflicts. The new government claimed that the workers' parties, or soviets, were in control, and the nation was renamed Soviet Russia. The Bolsheviks then called on the peasants to seize landowners' property and the workers to take control of the factories. Religion was prohibited as a **reactionary** institution. All property of the Russian Orthodox Church was confiscated or destroyed. Lenin organized the **Cheka** (Bolshevik secret police) to fight **counterrevolutionary** (opposed to the revolution) activity.

The Victory of the Red Army

Before long, active opposition to the Bolshevik dictatorship broke out throughout Russia. The Russian Civil War (1918–1921) that followed was both destructive and bitter. The Bolsheviks, or Communists as they began to call themselves, created the **Red Army** to combat the counterrevolutionary armies, which were called the **White Army**. Atrocities were committed on both sides (Czar Nicholas and his family were brutally murdered in 1918 by the Bolsheviks). Despite greater support on the part of the populace, the Whites did not have strong lines of supply or communication. Also, the Bolsheviks had Russia's remaining industry under their control, whereas the White Army was dependent on assistance from the British and Americans. At the beginning, the anti-Communist forces captured large areas of Russia. However, as the conflict dragged on, overextension and lack of unity among the diverse leadership resulted in the loss of territory to the Reds. The Red Army, under the leadership of the ruthless Bolshevik Lev Bronstein, known as **Leon Trotsky** (1879–1940), became an effective fighting force. By 1921, the Whites had been defeated, and the Communists controlled Russia.

Leon Trotsky (1877–1940). Russian Communist leader, c. 1920.

War Communism

During the civil war the Bolsheviks established a policy known as **war communism**. Major industries, banks, and all utilities were nationalized. Private trade was prohibited, and food was seized from the peasants. The transportation and communication systems broke down. As the economy declined and fuel shortages followed, opposition to the Bolshevik government arose. To control the population, Lenin instituted the **Red Terror**, a systematic brutalization of the population. The Bolsheviks arrested and executed thousands of innocent people to promote an atmosphere of terror. Spies were planted to create mutual suspicion and to divide the populace, thus preventing unified opposition.

Soviet Russia Under and After Lenin (1921–1925)

Marxism-Leninism

Karl Marx (1818–1883). German political philosopher.

Lenin had adopted the ideas of **Karl Marx** into his own system (**Marxism-Leninism**). He believed that the Communist Party was the vanguard or forefront of the Russian Revolution. There had to be a period, the **dictatorship of the proletariat** (workers), when the party ruled without opposition in order to create the conditions for a Communist society. The government had this power because the Bolsheviks represented the proletariat, who were the majority. The ultimate goal was to create a society of workers all sharing equally the burdens and the profits of their labors.

The New Economic Policy

After the civil war, Russian discontent with Communist rule began to grow. Fearing the collapse of his newly established government, Lenin introduced the **New Economic Policy** (NEP) in 1921. This allowed a partial restoration of **capitalism** on a local level to avoid the disintegration of the economy.

"Crush capitalism or be crushed by it!" Soviet poster, 1919, by Viktor Deni.

Lenin justified this radical departure from communism as "one step backward to go two steps forward." He also imported foreign capitalists to provide technical expertise in rebuilding Russian industry. During this period, Soviet Russia invaded and occupied **Ukraine**, Belarussia, and the nations of the Transcaucasus. In 1924, under a new constitution, Soviet Russia became the **Union of Soviet Socialist Republics (U.S.S.R.)**. That same year, Lenin died, leaving no successor in the Soviet leadership.

The Struggle Between Trotsky and Stalin

Joseph Stalin (1879–1953). Russian Communist leader.

A struggle for power developed between Trotsky, who was Lenin's designated successor, and **Joseph Stalin** (Iosif Dzhugashvili), called the Man of Steel (1879–1953). Although less well known than Trotsky, Stalin had held several key positions in the Soviet regime and was able to take over the leadership of the Communist Party and Soviet Russia. By 1925, Stalin had forced his rival into exile. Trotsky was later assassinated in Mexico by Stalin's agents.

The U.S.S.R. Under Stalin (1925–1941)

The Purges

Stalin proved to be one of the most brutal and ruthless **dictators** in modern history. He was responsible for millions of deaths, starting with the elimination of all possible rivals. Creating his own secret police (the **NKVD**, which eventually became the **KGB**), Stalin spied on, arrested, tortured, and executed party members, government officials, artists, writers, clergy, workers, and even peasants whom he suspected of not supporting his policies. In time, he became subject to paranoia (fear and suspicion of others, often without cause), and even close friends and relatives were killed. From 1935 to 1936, Stalin conducted a series of **show trials** (hearings where the verdicts were predecided), known as the purges. Hundreds of leading Communists were arrested, forced to confess to crimes they had never committed, and executed.

The Five-Year Plan

In 1928, dissatisfied with the slow growth rate of Soviet industry, Stalin abandoned Lenin's NEP in favor of centralized economic planning. Goals for agriculture and industry (often unrealistically high), as well as the means for achieving them, were laid out in a series of **five-year plans**. These were designed to enable the U.S.S.R. to catch up with the other industrialized nations by emphasizing the development of steel, iron, coal, and oil. The population was expected to sacrifice and do without consumer goods until the Soviet Union could reach the level of industrial development attained by capitalist nations. Opposition to these plans was quickly and brutally put down.

Collectivization and Genocide

Homeless children dying during the Soviet engineered famine and mass killings in the Ukraine designed to undermine Ukrainian resistance to Communist rule. Photograph, winter 1933.

To pay for the imported technology needed to institute the five-year plans, farms were collectivized. **Collectivization** was the policy of forcing peasants to farm on state land and allowing the government to decide on the distribution of profits. Many peasants were opposed to this policy and refused to surrender their land. To end the opposition, Stalin began a series of mass killings between 1932 and 1937. He claimed that he was eliminating the **kulaks** (wealthy peasants who supposedly exploited their neighbors). In fact, few of the at least 4.5 million peasants who died by execution, perished in Siberian labor camps, or starved in Stalin's government-created famine in Ukraine (1932–1933) were kulaks. Other groups who opposed Stalin were also crushed.

In spite of these harsh measures, the peasants did not fully cooperate, and the collectivization program failed to achieve its goal. When World War II inter-

rupted the Third Five-Year Plan in 1941, only heavy industry had made any progress. The loss of life and the human suffering that these modest gains had cost were enormous. It is understandable that many Russians, especially the Ukrainians, first saw the invading German armies as liberators.

The U.S.S.R. in World War II (1941–1945)

Main Idea:
The only advantage the Soviets had was that the Germans had stretched their supply lines.

When Nazi Germany invaded the Soviet Union in 1941, the government was completely unprepared (see Chapter 9 in this volume "World War II"). Stalin's purges had eliminated most of the U.S.S.R.'s best generals. Also, despite all the suffering, Soviet industry was unequal to that of Nazi Germany. The only advantage the Soviets had was that the Germans had stretched their supply lines. Once again, the population was forced to resort to the "scorched earth" policy that had been used so effectively against Napoleon (see Chapter 4 in this volume "Czarist Russia"). By 1944, overextension of supply lines, the harsh Russian winter, and stiff military resistance by the Russians, despite heavy losses, had worn down the German forces. By 1945, the Red Army had pushed the Nazis out of Russia and Eastern Europe back into Germany and had occupied the eastern portion of that nation. The decision to enter World War II was disastrous for Russia. Not fully industrialized, the Russians were unable to fight a modern war on such a large scale. Even though Czarist Russia had adopted industrialization from Western Europe, the democratic system of government was absent. Russia's attempt to adopt the Western economic model without the political reforms that should come with it brought great problems. The nation's involvement in a conflict that strained fully industrialized nations resulted in revolution.

Once in power, the Communists encountered the same problems. They were able to rule only through force and terror. The Soviet regime's achievements were modest when the death and human suffering involved are considered. Much greater progress could have been achieved with far less loss of life if democratic reforms had been made. The actions of Lenin and Stalin were as bad as, if not worse than, those of the cruelest czars in Russian history. The Communist attempt to put "old wine in new bottles" produced an era of suffering for the Russians and other peoples of the Soviet Union.

FASCISM IN ITALY

From 1922 to 1943, **Italy** experienced totalitarian rule under a **fascist** government headed by **Benito Mussolini**. The word *fascist* comes from the Latin *fasces*, an axelike weapon that was a symbol of the Ancient Roman Empire. Mussolini wanted Italians to feel a strong sense of **nationalism** and to remember the glory of the Roman Empire. It is necessary for us to examine these reasons.

Reasons for the Rise of Fascism in Italy

1. *Economic:* Although considered a victor in World War I, the costs of the war for Italy had been staggering. After the war, there was much unemployment,

many strikes, and severe inflation. Along with city workers, farmers grew more and more dissatisfied with the hard economic conditions.

2. *Political:* The weak and divided parliamentary government of King Victor Emanuel III was unable to provide leadership or to inspire confidence in its ability to solve post-World War I crises. The multiple-party system in the legislature often caused a deadlock in the passage of laws. No one political party had a majority. Also, there was no strong democratic tradition in Italy. Moreover, the fear of communism and of a Communist–led revolution was exploited (used to advantage) by Mussolini, who promised to defend Italy and thereby won many followers. The failure by Italy to gain all the land it wanted at the Paris Peace Conference contributed to annoyance with the government. In short, many Italians hoped for a strong leader who could bring stability and pride to the nation.

3. *Social:* Italy was suffering from low morale and was saddened by the almost 700,000 deaths incurred in World War I. Pensions for families of those killed, as well as for wounded veterans, were frequently delayed, causing aggravation and anger. Mussolini promised the Italian people security, order, and economic progress in exchange for their liberties and freedom.

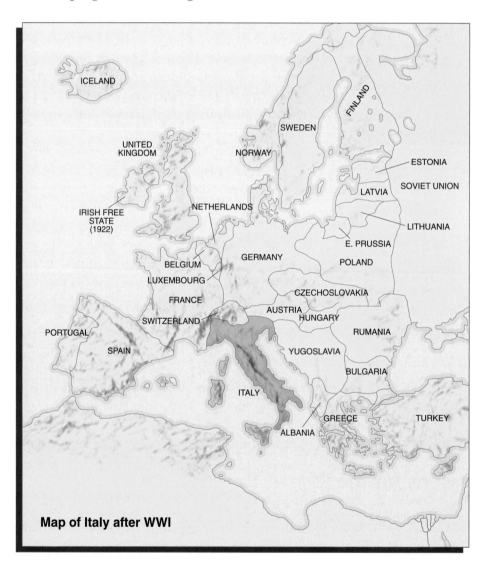

Map of Italy after WWI

The Role of Benito Mussolini

Benito Mussolini (1883–1945), Italian political leader, speaking in Rome in the 1930s.

Benito Mussolini (1883–1945) was born in central Italy. He worked as an elementary school teacher and as a journalist before being drafted to fight in World War I. Formerly he had favored **socialism** and atheism, while being opposed to the Italian monarchy and all forms of nationalism. These views and many others were to change as he ultimately came to champion private property, make his own peace with the monarchy and the Catholic Church, and advocate (call for) a chauvinism that made people proud to be Italian. This frequent shifting of viewpoints was common with him. He was an opportunist, someone without any really consistent beliefs who would change his views whenever it appeared advantageous to do so.

In 1919, Mussolini founded the *fasci di combattimento* (groups for combat). This organization was to become a powerful political and terrorizing force, tripling its membership to 300,000 between 1920 and 1922.

The Rise to Power of the Fascists

Mussolini's party attracted unhappy people from various segments of Italian society. Businessmen and the middle class were willing to give him financial support. His promise of full employment and calls for patriotic pride won him many city workers and army veterans. The fascists wore black shirts as uniforms, and became known by this clothing. The **blackshirts** began to engage in violent tactics and street demonstrations. Property and officials of other political parties, certain newspapers, and labor unions were attacked. Police often looked away from these incidents, and judges were pressured to release any fascists who had been arrested for violent behavior. These patterns were similar to those used in later years by Hitler in Germany.

Main Idea:
The **blackshirts** began to engage in violent tactics and street demonstrations.

In 1921, the fascists won some seats in the Italian parliament and expanded their activities. Mussolini felt encouraged to put added pressure on the government and to organize his supporters for a bold step. In the fall of 1922, the **March on Rome** took place. Fascist followers, claiming that they wanted to save Italy from a Communist takeover, went to Rome by railroad, car, carriage, and foot. King Victor Emmanuel III, fearing a coup (a quick, nonviolent takeover of government) sent a telegraph message to Mussolini in Milan on October 29, 1922, asking him to form a new government. The next morning, having taken a sleeping-car train, Mussolini arrived in Rome. He thus became the premier of Italy, without having been elected to the office or even thinking about it three years earlier.

Mussolini in Power

In short order, the premiership became a dictatorship. Although the king remained in office, Mussolini was given emergency powers. A law was passed that made sure the fascists would control the weakened parliament. Other laws restricted freedom of the press and civil liberties. Critics were silenced, usually by threats and terror. Giacomo Matteotti, publisher of a book exposing Mussolini and his tactics, was murdered. In 1924, Mussolini took the title **Il Duce** (the leader). He established himself as head of the Grand Council of the Fascist Party, the most powerful group in Italy. His picture could be seen in many places. So could signs that urged Italians to *credere, combattere, obbedire* (believe, fight, obey).

In the area of economics, Italy became a **corporate state**. This was a system in which most of the important industries, such as manufacturing and transportation, were formed into organizations known as syndicates. Each syndicate was like a corporation. From each syndicate, managers and workers came to meet with government officers chosen by Mussolini to decide on issues such as wages, prices, and working conditions. Private property was allowed in keeping with Mussolini's strong anticommunism stance.

> **Main Idea:**
> Each syndicate was like a corporation. From each syndicate, managers and workers came to meet with government officers chosen by Mussolini to decide on issues such as wages, prices, and working conditions.

Political power had now become authoritarian. This situation was not what those who helped to unify Italy in the nineteenth century had struggled for (see Chapter 3 in this volume).

Mussolini had little respect for democracy. Dictators such as he often use other means, such as force, fear, and fabrication to gain power. They will be successful if three conditions exist:

1. Discontent is widespread.
2. Those in power are weak and also insensitive to the nation's problems.
3. The majority of people are apathetic and do nothing to oppose the seizure of power.

To preserve power, dictators resort to some of the same means used to acquire that power. This was true, as we have seen, of Joseph Stalin in the Soviet Union. Other leaders who were cut from similar cloth in post-World War I Europe were **Marshal Pilsudski** in Poland (1926), **Antonio Salazar** in Portugal (1932), **Adolf Hitler** in Germany (1933), **John Metaxas** in Greece (1936), **King Carol** in Romania (1938), and General **Francisco Franco** in Spain (1939).

The use of armed forces at home was a strong thread in this cloth. The international community of the 1930s stood still while force was used domestically. When its use crossed international boundaries, however, force eventually led to severe conflict that broke out in the 1930s, something that will soon concern us (see Chapter 9 in this volume). However, we will first learn about the totalitarianism that arose in the nation most responsible for the war—Nazi Germany.

NAZISM IN GERMANY

Totalitarianism is a political philosophy that has emerged in the twentieth century. The term *totalitarianism* describes a government in which one political party, or a single group of like-minded persons, monopolizes all power and exercises complete authority over the masses of people and their activities. This system involves total control of all features of an individual's life by the government, with both civil and political rights being curtailed. Although various

Munich Conference, 1938. Cartoon by David Low showing the Munich Conference to partition Czechoslovakia: English, 1938.

forms of totalitarianism exist in parts of the world today, the earliest examples were evident in three European nations during the twenty-year period after World War I. These nations were the Soviet Union (under communism), Italy (under fascism), and Germany (under Nazism). Totalitarian societies look down upon individual human rights and civil liberties. The values of democracy are not found in such societies. Totalitarian states emphasize four factors:

1. Glorification of the whole community (i.e., the state)
2. Authoritarian rule by a dictator or by selected members of the one political party allowed to exist
3. Control of the individual citizen's life
4. Belief that the individual should serve the state and exists solely to promote the state's interests

In Western Europe, these features of totalitarianism were most characteristic of **Germany** under the control of Adolf Hitler and the Nazi Party, from 1933 to 1945. This government, known as the **Third Reich**, arose after the period of the **Weimar Republic**.

Germany Under the Weimar Republic (1919–1933)

The Weimar Republic was the German government established after World War I. It was a democratic government, with a constitution drawn up in the city of Weimar. There were many political parties that would campaign for seats in the government, which was headed by President **Friederich Ebert**. This was the government that had sent representatives to sign the Treaty of Versailles. However, this experiment with democracy in Germany faced many problems. These included economic chaos, street violence, and political threats from the left and right.

The five main reasons why the Weimar government was unsuccessful follow:

> **Main Idea:**
> This experiment with democracy in Germany faced many problems. These included economic chaos, street violence, and political threats from the left and right.

1. In the early 1920s, the Weimar government printed paper money with little hard currency to back it, resulting in severe inflation. (Inflation occurs when there is such a great amount of money in circulation that its value decreases.) This situation devastated the German economy and resulted in severe unemployment and street violence.
2. When Germany was unable to meet her reparation payments in 1923, France sent troops to occupy the **Ruhr Valley**, Germany's chief industrial area. Ill will grew against the French. The Weimar government's response was simply to print more money, which, of course, added to the inflationary crisis.
3. The terrible unemployment in Germany in the 1920s and again in the 1930s caused severe suffering and unrest.
4. The German economy was restored somewhat after 1923, and conditions temporarily improved. However, in 1929, a worldwide economic depression that threatened the stability of democratic governments everywhere

again brought much suffering to Germany. Unemployment rose to six million in 1932, and Germans lost faith in their political leaders. This further fueled the anger that had been caused by the Treaty of Versailles.

5. The government was unstable because no one single party was able to achieve a majority in the **Reichstag**, the more powerful of the two legislative houses created by the Weimar constitution. As a result, German political leaders seemed helpless to deal with the challenging economic problems.

These problems led many Germans to conclude that democracy was ill suited to their nation, and that a strong, bold autocracy would be preferable. The desire for such a political system grew as people remembered that it had brought Germany, under Bismarck's leadership, political unification, economic growth, and respect as an international power. Furthermore, a strong democratic tradition did not exist in German history. The evolution of representative elected government and respect for human rights, which over the centuries had taken place in such countries as Britain and France, had not occurred in Germany.

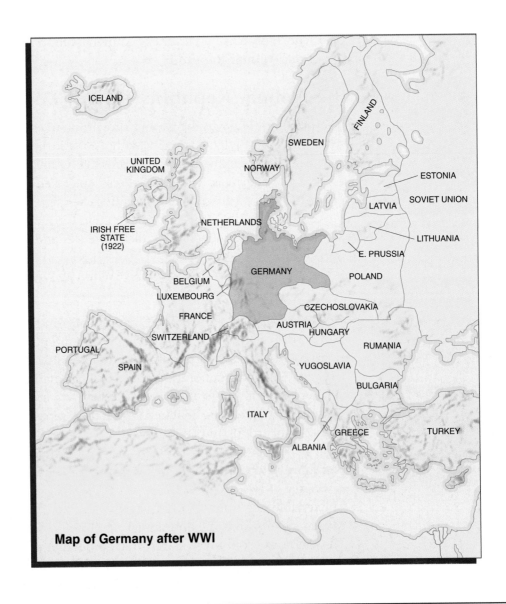

Map of Germany after WWI

The Role of Adolf Hitler

Adolf Hitler (1889–1945) was born in Austria and served in the German army during World War I. Afterward, he joined the **Nazi** (National Socialist German Workers) Party. He spoke out against the Weimar government and was arrested for his role in the Munich beer hall putsch of 1923, an unsuccessful attempt to overthrow the government. While imprisoned, he wrote the book *Mein Kampf* (My Struggle), which was not immediately popular in Germany. It explained Hitler's ideas for a stronger and more powerful German nation. It also revealed his racist beliefs concerning the alleged superiority of **Aryans** as a "master race" and the need to eliminate all groups he considered inferior, such as Jews, Slavs, gypsies, and blacks. Hitler was released from prison in 1924 and resumed efforts to expand support for his ideas and those of the Nazi Party. He showed himself to be a stirring and charismatic (appealing) speaker when addressing large crowds, thereby attracting many people to the party.

The Rise of the Nazis to Power

The Nazis began to run candidates for seats in the legislature and were able to win some, although they never gained a majority of seats. In addition to the problems of the Weimar government and the powerful role played by Hitler, a number of other factors also led to the eventual rise of the Nazis to power in Germany.

Swastika. The Persian-Indian symbol of good luck. In the West, it is more widely known as a symbol of Nazism.

1. *Economic problems:* The Nazis offered simple explanations for both the causes of and the cures for Germany's economic problems. These problems, as described earlier, affected millions of Germans (six million workers were unemployed in 1932). Reparations demanded by the Treaty of Versailles were condemned as unjust and were blamed for causing the economic crisis.
2. *Patriotic appeals:* The Nazi program stirred German nationalism by emphasizing several points. Some of the measures it called for include:

- A large increase in the armed forces
- Expansion of the German fatherland to include territory in Europe where people of German descent lived (i.e., **Austria** and parts of **Poland** and **Czechoslovakia**)
- Control over educational and cultural institutions in order to teach Nazi principles of **racism** and physical fitness for the glory of the state
- Ignoring the Treaty of Versailles and refusing to accept the war-guilt clause
- Regaining land that Germany had held in Europe prior to World War I and its overseas colonies
- Use of violence as a legitimate means to achieve domestic and international goals
- Glorification of the mythical German race (the so-called *Volk*) as the source of all strength and power.

The Nazis also claimed that Nordic Germans were destined to rule the world and to eliminate undesirable people. This attitude was an example of excessive **ethnocentrism**. Hitler and his followers blamed the Weimar government for accepting the Treaty of Versailles, and said it had been forced to do so by Jews, Communists, and others. Finally, the Nazis stated that German forces had not been defeated in World War I but rather had been "stabbed in the back."

3. *Anti-Semitism:* The term **anti-Semitism** refers to prejudice and hatred directed toward Jews only because they are Jews. Prejudiced attitudes toward Jews had existed in Germany and Austria for hundreds of years, resulting in persecution, exile, and loss of life and property. However, Hitler's prejudice against Jews was fanatical. He used them as **scapegoats** for his own personal failures in Vienna and elsewhere, and also for Germany's problems. These false ideas became persuasive parts of Nazi **propaganda**, especially when they were blended with **master race** theories. Hitler claimed that the Aryans (Germans of Nordic descent) were a master race and were naturally entitled to control and rule people of less "pure" blood, such as Slavs and Jews. (The **Holocaust**, in which six million Jews were systematically and intentionally murdered after Hitler came to power, was the tragic consequence of these misguided ideas (see Chapter 11 in this volume).

> **Main Idea:**
> Hitler's prejudice against Jews was fanatical. He used them as **scapegoats** for his own personal failures in Vienna and elsewhere, and also for Germany's problems.

4. *Fear of communism and of the Soviet Union:* The Nazis played upon these fears with great success, and portrayed themselves as the only ones capable of protecting Germany from foreign beliefs and potential aggressors. In this way, they were able to win the support of large segments of the German population, including such influential groups as bankers and industrialists. In addition, because Karl Marx was of Jewish origin, Hitler was able to link his own anti-Semitic propaganda with his anticommunism position.

5. *Use of private, illegal armed groups:* Many of Hitler's followers were organized into private armies. One such group was the **storm troopers**, or **brown shirts**. They employed scare tactics and violence to terrorize Jews and other opponents of the Nazis. Many were thugs and gangsters who took matters into their own hands and beat up people for little or no reason.

6. *Lack of meaningful opposition:* Few strong voices inside Germany spoke out against the Nazis. Many Germans came to gradually support Hitler, while others were apathetic. A third group feared to speak against him; indeed, many who did were later intimidated. Internationally, there was little awareness of or concern about the Nazi Movement.

The Nazis Come to Power

The formal takeover of Germany by the Nazis occurred in January 1933, when the president of the Weimar Republic, **Paul von Hindenburg**, appointed Hitler as chancellor. By this time, the Nazis had become the largest political party in Germany and formed the single largest block in the Reichstag, the German parliament. Yet they had never won a clear majority in any national election. (In 1932, for example, they won slightly less than 40 percent of the seats in the Reichstag. To control the government, a party had to win a majority of the seats.) At first, Hitler promised to preserve the Weimar constitution with all its democratic features and protections. However, he soon instituted (set in place) policies that ended the experiment in democracy that had been introduced in 1919 under the Weimar Republic.

In February 1933, he began to transform himself from a chancellor to a dic-

Paul von Hindenburg (1847–1934), German general and politician. Photographed at Berlin, Germany.

tator. He called for new elections to the Reichstag for March 4. However, on February 28, a fire of unknown origin destroyed the Reichstag building. Hitler blamed the Communists, predicting that they were about to lead a revolt. He then persuaded President von Hindenburg to issue orders ending freedom of speech and assembly. A mentally retarded Dutch Communist was eventually brought to trial and convicted of setting the fire. It is generally assumed, however, that the Nazis themselves had done so. To falsely and maliciously hold others responsible for acts they did not do is to use them as **scapegoats** and to employ the "**big lie**" technique. Both of these notorious tactics are frequently used by dictatorial and totalitarian governments.

In the March elections, the Nazis won only 44 percent of the seats. Nevertheless, with Hitler's followers applying various kinds of intimidation, almost the entire Reichstag voted to pass the **Enabling Act**. This act suspended the constitution and gave Hitler dictatorial powers. He shortly thereafter abolished all opposition parties. Labor unions and opposition newspapers were banned. Radio stations were placed under government control, with **Joseph Goebbels** as minister of propaganda. To carry out all these policies, Hitler established a secret police force called the **Gestapo**. People arrested by the Gestapo would often be sent to large prison areas called **concentration camps**. These, however, were not the **death camps** that were built in the 1940s.

Hitler's Government Becomes Known as the Third Reich

With the death of President von Hindenburg in 1934, Hitler became president as well as chancellor, adopting the tile of **der Führer** (the leader). He proclaimed his government as the Third Reich and predicted that it would last for 1,000 years. For Hitler, the Third Reich was the successor to both the Holy Roman Empire (*First Reich*) and the German Empire begun by Bismarck (*Second Reich*).

The rules and policies of the Nazis now were spread throughout Germany, in schools, churches, social clubs, sports programs, and a special Hitler youth organization. Young children were encouraged to wear the swastika, the twisted-cross symbol for the Nazi Party, and to inform authorities about their parents and any friends who were not following Nazi rules and regulations or who did anything else that could be regarded as against the government. Books that contained writings of Jews or any others who were deemed "undesirable" were burned. Large meetings and rallies were held where Nazi followers made emotional speeches praising Hitler and condemning Jews and the Treaty of Versailles, and where hundreds would shout approval of Hitler and give the Nazi salute. This situation was a far cry from the hopes of those who had brought forth the Weimar Republic, a chance for Germany to become a democratic nation.

Nazis burning books, May 1933, over a banner reading "German students march against the un-German spirit."

LINK TO TODAY

Paintings by Hitler: Should They Be Sold, Bought, or Destroyed?

In September 2006, a British auction house announced that in the near future it was going to have an auction of artwork by Hitler. The auctioneer had twenty-one watercolors and sketches done by Hitler during the years from 1916 to 1918, prior to his becoming active in the Nazi Party. The artwork was of rural scenes, showing houses and landscapes. The auctioneer predicted that some of them would sell for up to $8,000 each. It was not made clear how the auction house acquired the paintings. Nevertheless, a controversy arose. There are questions that were raised about this situation: Should the auction house destroy the paintings? Is it appropriate for the paintings to be put up for auction? If the paintings are sold, what should be done with the proceeds? If you were a British citizen who lost family members during the German air raids over London in World War II, or if you were a Holocaust survivor or had relatives killed in Nazi death camps, what would you do about this situation? How would you answer these questions?

CHAPTER SUMMARY

Hitler's coming to power resulted in a totalitarian dictatorship that eventually resulted in World War II and brought devastation to Germany and to most of the rest of Europe. His distorted ideas, along with his antidemocratic beliefs and tactics unfortunately found a receptive audience in post-World War I Germany.

In that audience were those who genuinely believed in him. Many other Germans tolerated him without much enthusiasm, assuming that he would not stay in power. For those who were apathetic, we are reminded of a famous comment by the eighteenth-century British statesman Edmund Burke: "All that is necessary for evil to triumph is for good men to do nothing."

The same comment would also be applicable, in various ways, to events in Russia and Italy that we have described. The dictatorial power that had become characteristic of Russia, Germany, and Italy by the 1930s was a threat to the citizens of those nations. The antidemocratic features of the totalitarian regimes in Italy and Germany also proved to be a menace to their neighbors and, indeed, to the world at large. This danger became apparent when these regimes, for a variety of reasons, attempted to expand beyond their borders. It took a world war to hold this expansion and to bring these regimes to an end.

In the 1930s, the world stood on the brink of another disaster. Europe was divided between the driving ambitions of the dictators of Germany, Italy, and the Soviet Union and the lethargy of the democracies of Britain and France.

The Russian people had traded the cruelties of the czars for the far greater oppression of Stalin, who stood out as one of the greatest mass murderers in modern history. Millions died because of his cruelty. Mussolini proved to be a pompous leader of little merit. Hitler became infamous as one of history's greatest villains.

Yet should we blame these three men alone, or do the people who stood by and allowed them to proceed share the responsibility? We keep asking the same question in this study of European history: Are there lessons to be learned, or are we destined to continue to repeat the same mistakes? What do you think?

IMPORTANT PEOPLE, PLACES, AND TERMS

KEY TERMS

totalitarianism	revolution	Marxism-Leninism
Bolsheviks	proletarian	dictatorship of the
Communists	October Revolution	proletariat
monarchy	Treaty of Brest-Litovsk	New Economic Policy
Duma	reactionary	capitalism
Romanov Dynasty	Cheka	Union of Soviet
provisional	counterrevolutionary	Socialist Republics
government	Russian Civil War	(U.S.S.R.)
bourgeoisie	Red Army	dictator
democracy	White Army	NKVD
autocracy	war communism	KGB
soviets	Red Terror	show trials

five-year plans	Reichstag	master race
collectivization	Nazi	Holocaust
genocide	Weimer Republic	storm troopers
kulaks	*Mein Kampf*	brown shirts
blackshirts	Aryans	big lie
fascist	racism	Enabling Act
March on Rome	ethnocentrism	Gestapo
Il Duce	anti-Semitism	concentration camp
corporate state	scapegoat	death camps
Third Reich	propaganda	der Führer

PEOPLE

Joseph Stalin	Vladimir Lenin	King Victor Emmanuel
Benito Mussolini	Aleksandr Kerenski	III
Adolf Hitler	Leon Trotsky	Friederich Ebert
Nicholas II	Karl Marx	Paul von Hindenburg

PLACES

Russia	Petrograd	Union of Soviet
Italy	Ukraine	Socialist Republics
Germany	Ruhr Valley	(U.S.S.R.)

CHAPTER 8

MULTIPLE-CHOICE QUESTIONS

Select the number of the correct answer.

1. Totalitarianism can best be described as a form of government

   (1) in which one person or group has complete control and does not allow any opposition
   (2) where a monarch has limited control while working within a parliamentary system
   (3) that was popular in ancient Greece and Rome and experienced a revival in the twentieth century
   (4) that encourages total freedom of expression by politicians, journalists, and artists

2. Place the following events in Russian history in correct chronological order

   A. Czar Nicholas abdicates
   B. Alexander Kerenski becomes head of the Duma
   C. Bolsheviks overthrow the provisional government
   D. The Communists defeat the Whites in the Civil War

   (1) A, C, D, B
   (2) B, C, D, A
   (3) A, B, C, D
   (4) B, A, D, C

3. Vladimir Lenin, in developing his policies, was most influenced by

   (1) Aleksandr Kerenski
   (2) Leon Trotsky
   (3) Josef Stalin
   (4) Karl Marx

4. Which series of terms all refer to the same topic?

   (1) Russian Orthodox, Red Terror, Red Army
   (2) Cheka, NKVD, KGB
   (3) Five-Year Plans, Duma, Proletariat
   (4) Communism, Capitalism, Dictators

5. Josef Stalin enacted a series of show trials in an attempt to

   (1) regain political power
   (2) eliminate his enemies
   (3) restore order to Russian courts
   (4) prove the actions of Lenin were wrong

6. Which generalization best describes the U.S.S.R. during the Stalinist period of the 1930s?

   (1) Citizens willingly gave up some rights to support the successful economic improvement plans enacted by the government.
   (2) Stalin encouraged individual ownership of large and small businesses to advance foreign trade.
   (3) Most citizens were deprived of rights that they had previously enjoyed while the government strengthened its totalitarian control.
   (4) The U.S.S.R. managed to avoid the worldwide depression and allowed its citizens to develop large private farms.

7. Benito Mussolini became premier of Italy as a result of

   (1) a coup d'etat
   (2) an election won by the fascists
   (3) direct assistance from Stalin
   (4) an invitation from King Victor Emmanuel III

8. Fascism became popular in the 1920s in Italy primarily as a result of

   (1) economic, political, and social problems caused by Italy's role in World War I
   (2) the Italian interest in the success of fascism in Germany at the same time period
   (3) the strong tradition of democracy that encouraged totalitarian governments
   (4) the desire of Italians to recover from being punished by the Treaty of Versailles

9. As a believer in fascism, Mussolini also was

   (1) in favor of a free press
   (2) a believer in a strong anti-communist government
   (3) against authoritarian rule
   (4) opposed to Italians having private property

10. Which phrase was most associated with Mussolini's rise to power?

    (1) "Peace, land, and bread"
    (2) "Freedom and equality"
    (3) "Believe, fight, obey"
    (4) "Work will set you free"

11. What did European leaders in the 1930s such as Antonio Salazar, John Metaxas, Francisco Franco, and Marshal Pilsudski have in common?

    (1) They encouraged freedom of expression by their journalists.
    (2) They used armed forces at home to control their citizens.
    (3) They were influenced by the Enlightenment thinkers on practices of government.
    (4) They worked together to improve their images in the world community.

12. Which statement best expresses an opinion about totalitarianism in Europe after World War I?

(1) Given the economic difficulties of the nations that adopted its theories, it was the only practical solution for true progress.
(2) Totalitarian governments emphasize the belief that the individual exists to serve the state.
(3) Germany under Adolf Hitler and the Nazi Party was most characteristic of totalitarian practices.
(4) Totalitarianism is a political philosophy that emerged in the twentieth century.

13. After World War I, the first type of government to be established in Germany was

(1) a monarchy   (3) a dictatorship
(2) an oligarchy   (4) a democracy

14. In which areas did Germany suffer the most serious problems during the 1920s and 1930s?

(1) military occupations by foreign troops
(2) severe inflation and high unemployment
(3) a powerful and autocratic government
(4) prolonged starvation due to a widespread drought

15. Adolf Hitler's role in the Munich beer hall putsch of 1923 was an example of

(1) a college prank of little consequence
(2) an effort to limit alcohol consumption
(3) an unsuccessful attempt to take over the government
(4) a planned effort to promote his new book

16. The Nazi program encouraged German nationalism by calling for

(1) acceptance of the Treaty of Versailles
(2) the practice of peaceful means to achieve national goals
(3) a decrease in the armed forces to allow Germans to work in factories
(4) expansion of Germany to include places where people of German descent lived

17. Which foreign term or phrase is given with its correct meaning?

(1) Volk—automobile
(2) Fasces—a mask
(3) Il Duce—to gamble
(4) Mein Kampf—my struggle

18. Which statement below was a basic belief of the Nazi Party in Germany in the 1930s?

(1) Aryans or Germans of Nordic descent were superior to other peoples.
(2) German enthnocentrism was an unacceptable concept.
(3) Jewish people made many positive contributions to society.
(4) All peoples practicing fascism were more culturally advanced.

19. A scapegoat is a person or group who

(1) shows remarkable leadership ability
(2) exhibits exceptional kindness to animals
(3) is often blamed falsely for economic or social problems
(4) revolts against the established government

20. King Victor Emmanuel III of Italy and Paul von Hindenburg, president of the Weimar Republic, had which of the following in common?

(1) Both appointed leadership positions to men who would become feared dictators of their countries.
(2) Each man strongly supported democratic governments for his nation.
(3) As leaders, they sought to work with the rest of the international community for world peace.
(4) They respected each other and agreed to work to prevent totalitarianism in their nations.

THEMATIC ESSAY

Directions: Write a well-organized essay that includes an introduction, several paragraphs addressing the task below, and a conclusion.

Theme: Change (in Form of Government)

During the first part of the twentieth century, many European nations sought to change their form of government. The changes occurred for a variety of reasons and caused a variety of results.

Task

Select a major European nation that experienced governmental change in the first half of the twentieth century. For the nation chosen

- describe the type of governmental change that occurred
- explain one reason why this change occurred
- identify one positive and one negative effect of this change on the nation

You may use any major European nation. Some nations you may wish to consider include Russia/the U.S.S.R., Italy, and Germany.

You are *not* limited to these suggestions.

Guidelines

In your essay, be sure to

- develop all aspects of the *Task*
- support the theme with relevant facts, examples, and details
- use a logical and clear plan of organization, including an introduction and a conclusion that are beyond a restatement of the theme
- introduce the theme by establishing a framework that is beyond a simple restatement of the *Task* and conclude with a summation of the theme

DOCUMENT-BASED ESSAY QUESTION

This question is based on the accompanying documents. The question is designed to test your ability to work with historical documents. Some of these documents have been edited for the purposes of the question. As you analyze the documents, take into account both the source of the document and the author's point of view.

Historical Context

Totalitarian governments of the early and middle twentieth century were developed by dictators in response to conditions in society, politics, and the economies of the time.

Task

Select one country and one leader that adopted a totalitarian form of government and

- identify a situation that caused the leader of that country to adopt totalitarian methods
- describe at least one tactic used by the leader to promote totalitarianism
- describe a short-term and a long-term result of the practice of totalitarianism on that country

Part A: Short-Answer Questions

Directions: Analyze the documents and answer the short-answer questions that follow each document.

Document 1

a.
"Only the mob and the elite can be attracted by the momentum of totalitarianism itself. The masses have to be won by propaganda."

—Hannah Arendt

Question	**1a.** According to Hannah Arendt how was propaganda to be used by totalitarian governments?

b.
"Totalitarianism is never content to rule by external means, namely, through the state and a machinery of violence; thanks to its peculiar ideology and the role assigned to it in this apparatus of coercion, totalitarianism has discovered a means of dominating and terrorizing human beings from within."

—Hannah Arendt

Question	**1b.** How do totalitarian governments control their citizens according to Hannah Arendt?

Document 2

"The workers and the peasants are wiping out the lords and barons, while the workers on the home front help till the land. Long live the alliance of the working class and peasants". Soviet poster, 1920 by Alexander Apsit.

Questions
2. a. Whose alliance were the Soviets celebrating in this poster?
   b. Why would that alliance be important to the Soviets at that time?

Document 3

Question

3. What does this picture of one of the palaces of Nicholas II of Russia suggest about the lifestyle of the Romanovs?

Document 4

"A lie told often enough becomes the truth."

—Vladimir Lenin

Question

4. According to this quote, how did Lenin feel dishonesty could be used?

Document 5

"In inner-party politics, these methods lead, as we shall yet see, to this: the party organization substitutes itself for the party, the central committee substitutes itself for the organization, and, finally, a 'dictator' substitutes himself for the central committee."

—Leon Trotsky

Question

5. According to Leon Trotsky how does a dictator come to power?

Document 6

"It is enough that the people know there was an election. The people who cast the votes decide nothing. The people who count the votes decide everything."

—Joseph Stalin

Question

6. What do Stalin's comments about elections say about his attitude toward a country using a democratic process in an election?

Document 7

7a.

"It is humiliating to remain with our hands folded while others write history. It matters little who wins. To make a people great it is necessary to send them to battle even if you have to kick them in the pants. That is what I shall do."

—Benito Mussolini

Question 7a. What did Mussolini think that it was necessary to do to make a "people great"?

7b.

"This is the epitaph I want on my tomb: 'Here lies one of the most intelligent animals who ever appeared on the face of the earth.'"

—Benito Mussolini

Question 7b. How did Mussolini hope to be remembered?

Document 8

8a.

"The great masses of the people will more easily fall victims to a big lie than to a small one."

—Adolf Hitler

Question 8a. What did Hitler mean when he referred to a "big lie"?

8b.

"When an opponent declares, 'I will not come over to your side,' I calmly say, 'Your child belongs to us already. . . What are you? You will pass on. Your descendants, however, now stand in the new camp. In a short time they will know nothing else but this new community.'"

—Adolf Hitler

Question 8b. How can you explain this statement of Hitler's?

Part B: Essay

Directions: Write a well-organized essay that includes an introduction, several paragraphs, and a conclusion. Use evidence from *at least five* documents in the body of the essay. Support your response with relevant facts, examples, and details. Include additional outside information.

Historical Context

Totalitarian governments of the early and middle twentieth century were developed by dictators in response to conditions in society, politics, and the economies of the time.

Task

Select one country and one leader that adopted a totalitarian form of government and

- identify a situation that caused the leader of that country to adopt totalitarian methods
- describe at least one tactic used by the leader to promote totalitarianism
- describe a short-term and a long-term result of the practice of totalitarianism on that country

Guidelines

In your essay, be sure to

- develop all aspects of the *Task*
- incorporate information from *at least five* documents
- incorporate relevant outside information
- support the theme with relevant facts, examples, and details
- use a logical and clear plan of organization, including an introduction and a conclusion that are beyond a restatement of the theme

CHAPTER 9

World War II

TIMELINE OF EVENTS

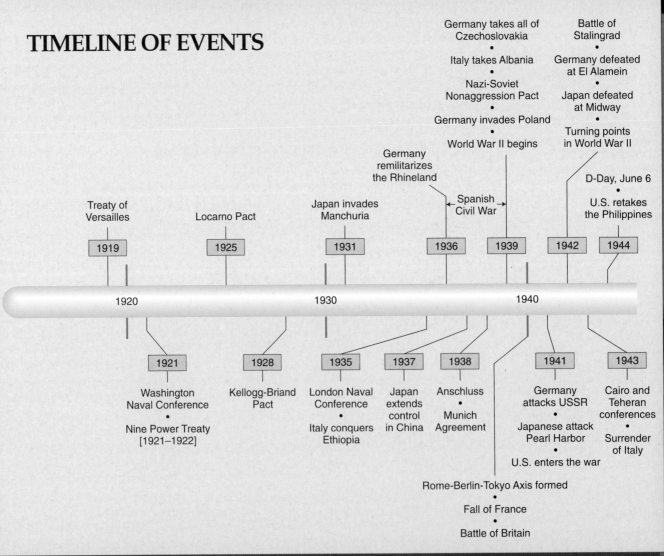

Germany takes all of Czechoslovakia
•
Italy takes Albania
•
Nazi-Soviet Nonaggression Pact
•
Germany invades Poland
•
World War II begins

Battle of Stalingrad
•
Germany defeated at El Alamein
•
Japan defeated at Midway
•
Turning points in World War II

D-Day, June 6
•
U.S. retakes the Philippines

Germany remilitarizes the Rhineland

←Spanish Civil War→

Treaty of Versailles

Locarno Pact

Japan invades Manchuria

| 1919 | | 1925 | | 1931 | | 1936 | 1939 | | 1942 | 1944 |

1920   1930   1940

| 1921 | | 1928 | | 1935 | 1937 | 1938 | | 1941 | 1943 |

Washington Naval Conference
•
Nine Power Treaty [1921–1922]

Kellogg-Briand Pact

London Naval Conference
•
Italy conquers Ethiopia

Japan extends control in China

Anschluss
•
Munich Agreement

Germany attacks USSR
•
Japanese attack Pearl Harbor
•
U.S. enters the war

Cairo and Teheran conferences
•
Surrender of Italy

Rome-Berlin-Tokyo Axis formed
•
Fall of France
•
Battle of Britain

Tragedy and international conflict strike the world again! Less than a generation has passed since the Treaty of Versailles marked the end to the "war to end all wars," and nations are once more on the march. We must ask the question, "Why?" As we look at the attempts at peacekeeping during the 1920s and 1930s, what weaknesses will we see? How could a Hitler get the world involved in another war, and how could he almost win? Was there a certain point at which, if the democracies had said, "Stop," Hitler would have retreated?

This time we have two new major players in the game—the United States and Japan. Japan will play the bully in the East, while the United States will attempt to use the oceans on her borders to stay out of the conflict. Japan will force the United States into action and will eventually pay a high price for doing so. New and more terrible weaponry that has the capacity for mass killing will be developed by both sides. Hitler will make the same mistake that Napoleon did, and the Soviet Union will make him pay for it.

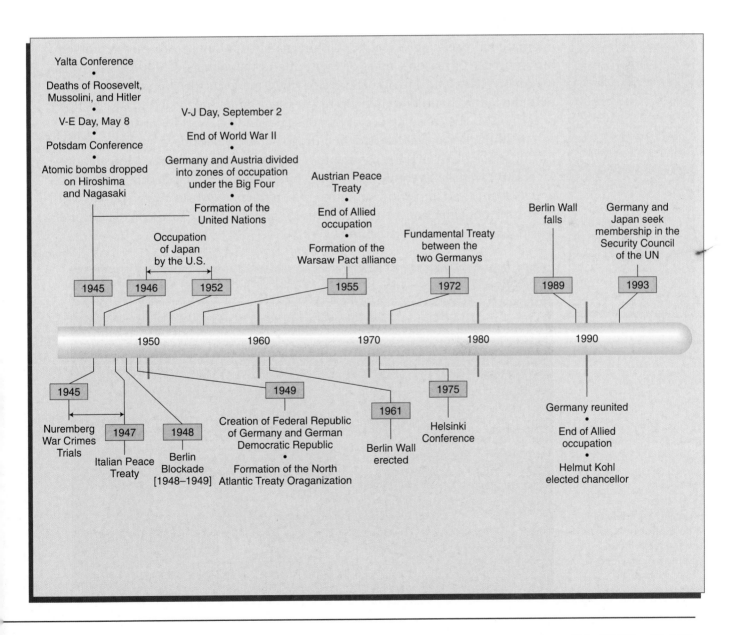

The saying "Politics make strange bedfellows" comes true when the democracies of the United States and Great Britain join with the totalitarian Soviet Union against a common enemy. Finally an exhausted world will see the destruction of two entire cities with the atomic bomb. The years from 1939 to 1945 will be a terrible period with terrible results.

CAUSES OF WORLD WAR II

If you stand before a house and look at it carefully, you will see its front and its top. What you cannot see is the foundation. If the foundation is sturdy and supports the house well, then the house will be stable. If, on the other hand, the foundation is weak, then the house is in danger of crumbling and cannot fulfill one of its chief purposes—to provide shelter. Indeed, the house may become unsafe for those who dwell within it.

After World War I, many nations hoped to prevent another war by building what could be called a house of peace. The foundations of this house were the Treaty of Versailles, the **League of Nations**, disarmament conferences, and international pacts (agreements). Unfortunately, the house of peace crumbled for a number of reasons, most of them due to the actions of the **Axis powers** (Germany, Italy, and Japan). The cracks they made in the foundations, along with the failure of other nations to repair them immediately, led to destruction of the house. The consequence of this destruction was World War II.

Although the war started in Europe, it soon became a global conflict. Fighting took place on three continents—Europe, Africa, and Asia. More nations (over fifty) were belligerents than in any other war in history. In this section, we will look at the attempts to maintain peace in the post-World War I era. We will then turn our attention to the underlying and specific causes of the second world war in the twentieth century.

Main Idea:
After World War I, many nations hoped to prevent another war by building what could be called a house of peace. The foundations of this house were the Treaty of Versailles, the **League of Nations**, disarmament conferences, and international pacts (agreements).

The 5th assembly of the League of Nations in the Hall of the Reformation, Geneva, Switzerland, September 1924.

Attempts at Peace in the Post-World War I Period

In the period between the two world wars, the major powers tried to create firm foundations to preserve peace and thereby reduce the chances of another huge conflict. These foundations were built with noble efforts, but, as we now can see, they had weak spots.

1. *The Treaty of Versailles (1919):* This treaty (see Chapter 7 in this volume) produced bitterness that Hitler and the Nazis were able to exploit. Germany felt that she had not been defeated, that she had voluntarily surrendered, and that the provisions of the treaty were very harsh. Also, because the treaty did not indicate specific means of enforcing its restrictions, its impact became meaningless.

2. *The League of Nations:* The League of Nations was not created to be, nor did it act as, a world government. It met in Geneva, Switzerland, and did record some achievements in its brief history. It resolved crises involving Sweden

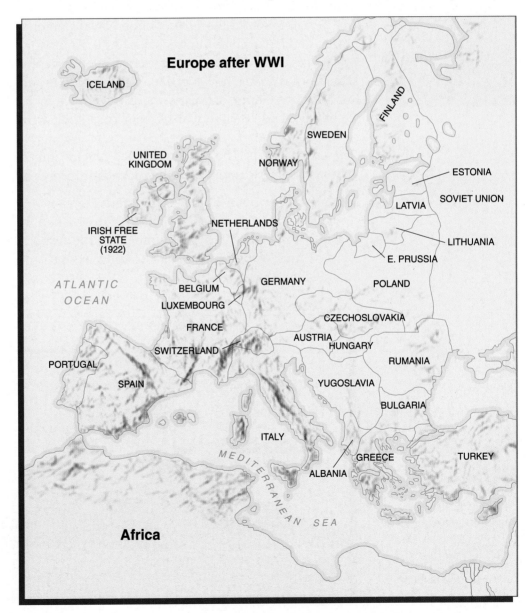

Europe after WWI

and Finland, and Greece and Bulgaria. Issues of health, trade, and labor were addressed; for example, it sponsored the International Labor Office. However, it was never a truly universal organization. It did reach a membership of fifty-seven nations by 1933, but the fact that the United States never joined was a blow to the organization's prestige. When the League first convened in 1920, none of the defeated nations from World War I were members. Germany was admitted in 1926 but withdrew, along with Japan, in 1933. Italy withdrew in 1936. The League was without power to tax, raise an army, or enforce its decisions. Its inability to respond effectively to Axis aggression in the 1930s signaled its doom. The requirement that all decisions receive the unanimous consent of its members hindered its functioning.

Main Idea:
Recognition of arms competition as a factor leading to World War I led to a series of conferences that attempted to limit armaments.

3. *Disarmament conferences:* Recognition of arms competition as a factor leading to World War I led to a series of conferences that attempted to limit armaments. At the Washington conference (1921–1922), Britain, the United States, Japan, France, and Italy agreed to halt construction of capital (large) warships for ten years. They also promised to maintain capital ships in a ratio of 5:5:3:1.67:1.67. At the 1930 London Naval Conference, Britain, the United States, and Japan compromised on a 10:10:7 ratio for a five-year period. This was to cover destroyers and cruisers as well as capital ships. At the London Conference of 1935, however, Japan's request to Britain and the United States for a 10:10:10 ratio, or **parity**, was turned down by the Western powers. The conference ended without an agreement, and Japan soon expanded its navy.

4. *International Pacts:* The 1920s witnessed several agreements among groups of nations hoping to strengthen their idealistic resolve for peace.

   - Nine-Power Treaty at the Washington Conference (1921–1922): The United States, Britain, Japan, and other nations wished to avoid any imperialist conflict in China. They therefore agreed to respect an **Open Door Policy** in China, providing equal trading rights and respecting China's independence.

HMS Iron Duke, launched in 1912 and scrapped in 1946, the super-dreadnought that was Sir John Jellicoe's flagship from the outbreak of World War I until after the Battle of Jutland.

Conference room during the final sitting of the Pact of Locarno, 16 October 1925. Middle table: Gustav Stresemann, Carl von Schubert, Robert Kempner, Wilhelm Gaus, Dr. Kiep, Dino Grandi, and Benito Mussolini. Foreign ministers: Austen Chamberlain, Aleksander Skrzynski, Eduard Benes, Aristide Briand, and Émile Vandervelde.

- Locarno Pact (1925): This was an agreement signed by the Western European Allies with Germany. It provided for Germany to accept permanently its boundaries on the west with Belgium and France and to seek a peaceful settlement of any disputes regarding its Polish and Czechoslovakian boundaries in the east.

- Kellogg-Briand Pact (1928): Also known as the Pact of Paris, this document was signed by more than sixty nations, including the United States, France, Germany, Italy, and Japan. They promised to resolve disputes in a peaceful manner, outlawing war "as an instrument of national policy." Although the pact was not backed by any threat of force, the signers hoped that world moral influence would make it work.

These pacts gained global attention, as they reflected noble aspirations for a better world. The mood they evoked in the 1920s contrasted sharply with that of ten years earlier.

Underlying Reasons for World War II

If the 1920s were a time for hope and optimism, the 1930s proved to be otherwise; a series of movements and events were to plunge the world into a second major conflict. The underlying causes of this tragedy, which included **militarism**, **nationalism**, **racism**, and **appeasement**, were both similar to and different from those that brought on World War I.

> **Main Idea:**
> A series of movements and events were to plunge the world into a second major conflict.

1. *Militarism:* Large amounts of money continued to be spent on weapons. Military strength was seen as a source of nationalistic pride. The leaders of the Axis nations always appeared in military dress, and they glorified war as necessary and just.

2. *Nationalism and Racism:* The Axis nations saw themselves as superior to others (the German "master race" theory, the Italian wish to revive the Ancient Roman Empire, Japanese self-pride based on Shinto teachings and the necessity to establish a "new order" in Asia) and therefore as having the right to extend their cultures and their borders.

3. *Imperialism:* The Axis nations sought to take over other lands for political, racist, and economic reasons. Japan moved into China (1931, 1937), Italy conquered **Ethiopia** (1935), and Germany annexed **Austria** (called the *anschluss*, or union, 1938) and **Czechoslovakia** (1938, 1939).

4. *Economic tensions:* Economic problems, brought on mainly by the worldwide depression of the 1930s, contributed to the rise of aggressive dictators. Germany also experienced difficulty in making reparation payments and in trying to overcome severe inflation.

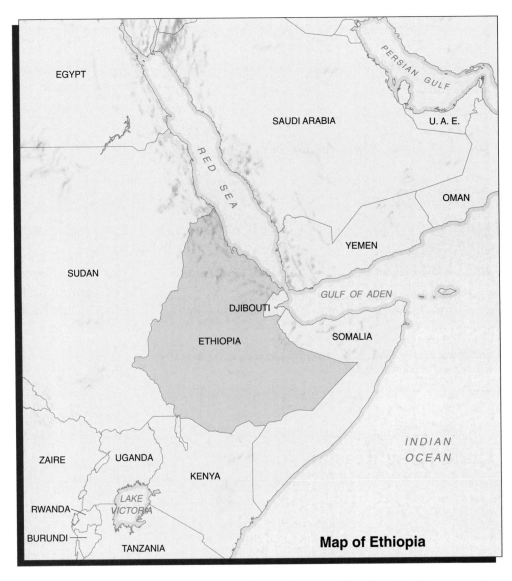

Map of Ethiopia

5. *Failure of collective security:* No united stand was taken by the democracies when the Axis powers took their imperialistic action. Little was done to curb the aggressive policies of Germany, Italy, and Japan. The League of Nations condemned some of these actions but was unable to take any other measures.

6. *Appeasement:* To give in to a potential aggressor, hoping that the aggressor will then be content and not commit any further harmful acts, is called appeasement. During the 1930s, the term came to mean the policy of accepting territorial **aggression** against small nations in the hope of avoiding a general war. The Munich Agreement of 1938 was an example of this meaning. It will be discussed later, along with other specific events leading to war.

Specific Events Leading to War in Europe

The 1930s saw the house of peace that some nations had hoped to build fall apart. It was not strong enough to withstand the many "rocks and projectiles" that were thrown at it by the three Axis aggressors. We will now examine the destructive acts of each one of them.

Italy

Even though **Benito Mussolini** stirred his countrymen's pride by frequent references to the Roman Empire, little available unoccupied land overseas was left for him to conquer. He saw an opportunity in Ethiopia in 1935, when he took advantage of a border dispute to send in an invasion force. Ethiopian soldiers under Emperor **Haile Selassie** were no match for the Italian army and were easily defeated. The League of Nations branded Italy as an aggressor and voted for sanctions (economic restrictions), but it had no way to enforce them. The League's actions were ignored by Mussolini, who proclaimed Ethiopia to be part of the Italian Empire. Additional **belligerent** actions taken by Mussolini were his aiding General **Francisco Franco** in the Spanish Civil War (1936–1939) and his annexation of Albania in 1939.

Benito Mussolini (1883–1945), Italian political leader, speaking in Rome in the 1930s.

Haile Selassie (1891–1975), Emperor of Ethiopia, pleading his cause at the League of Nations in Geneva in 1936 following the Italian invasion of Ethiopia.

Germany

The most serious acts of destruction aimed at the so-called house of peace were carried out by the **Third Reich**, Hitler's Nazi government. As did Mussolini, **Adolf Hitler** engaged in actions that went directly against both the spirit and the letter of the documents signed in the 1920s that aspired toward a peaceful world. The following is a chronology of his actions:

1935

Germany had begun to remilitarize. Factories were building war-related products. "Hunting clubs" were teaching people how to use weapons. **Conscription** (a draft of soldiers) was reintroduced. These activities were in violation of the Treaty of Versailles.

Adolf Hitler (1889–1945), Chancellor of Germany from 1933–1945.

1936

Flexing his muscles and stating his right to control all German territory, Hitler ordered troops into **the Rhineland**. Although such action also violated the Treaty of Versailles, and sparked an angry reaction from the French prime minister, nothing was done to stop Hitler.

1936–1939

The Spanish Civil War presented Hitler with an opportunity to test some of his newly trained soldiers and newly developed weapons. He used these to help General Franco in his revolt against the Spanish government. A republican government had been elected in **Spain**, including socialists, Communists, and liberals. The monarchy, the army, and the Catholic Church had lost some of their status and prestige in the nation. To remedy this situation, and to strike against what he feared was a possible growth of **communism**, General Franco and his followers, the Nationalists, struck against the government. Russia supplied the

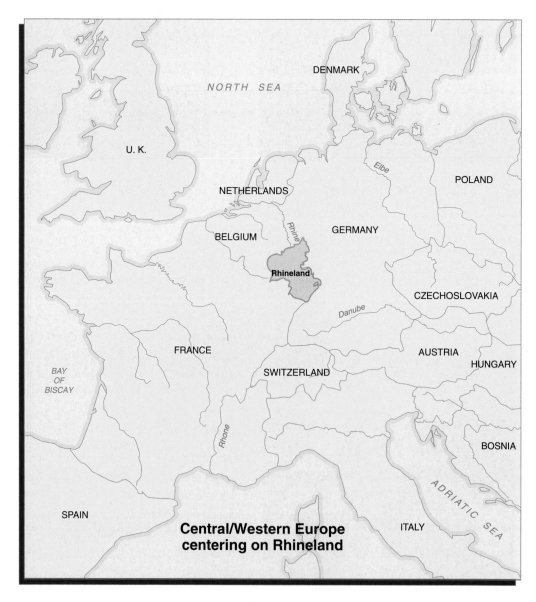

Central/Western Europe centering on Rhineland

Francisco Franco (1892–1975), Spanish soldier and dictator shortly after his investiture in 1936 as chief of the Spanish state and commander in chief of the insurgent forces.

Loyalists, those on the government side, and Mussolini and Hitler helped the Nationalists. Ultimately the Nationalists triumphed, with Franco establishing a fascist dictatorship in Spain.

The fact that no democratic nation stepped in to fight Franco and try to prevent his dictatorship was a sign of encouragement to Hitler. Perhaps he too could strike at some region without fear of resistance. The early cooperative efforts by Hitler and Mussolini in 1936 led to their forming a military alliance known as the Rome-Berlin Axis. The term *Axis* was introduced by Mussolini, from his theory that the world of the future would turn on an imaginary line drawn from Rome to Berlin. Soon after this agreement, Germany signed the Anti-Comintern Treaty with Japan. Endorsed also by Italy, this treaty aimed at cooperation against the expansion of Russian communism. From this moment on in 1936, Germany, Italy, and Japan would be known as the **Axis powers**.

1938

In March 1938, Hitler again violated the Treaty of Versailles by achieving *anschluss* with Austria. In the 1920s, a Nazi Party was started in Austria. It gained strength through terror, assassination of opponents, and other means similar to those used by the Nazis in Germany. By 1938, Austrian Chancellor Kurt Schuschnigg, pressured to include Nazis in his cabinet, had intended to hold a **plebiscite** (a nationwide yes or no vote) on the issue of *anschluss* with Germany. But before he could do this, Hitler sent German troops into Austria, had Schuschnigg arrested, and installed a Nazi as chancellor. As a sign of expanding Nazi policies, Hitler's storm troopers forced elderly Jewish men and women to clean the streets of Vienna. Again, nothing was done by Western nations in response to the events of March 1938.

Hitler next turned his attention to Czechoslovakia. Approximately one half of this new nation, formed after World War I, was surrounded by the Third Reich on three sides. Over three million Germans lived in the western region, called the Sudetenland. Hitler declared that it was only natural for the Sudeten Germans to be united with other Germans. The same theme was trumpeted by the Nazi Party that had been organized in the Sudetenland. The call for German unity provoked riots and demonstrations against the Czech government in May and June of 1938. The Czechs placed the region under martial law, sending troops to quell disorders. Hitler then maintained that the Sudeten Germans needed "protection" by the Third Reich. Nazi **propaganda** told of alleged Czech atrocities against these Germans. Hitler also described Czechoslovakia as a "dagger aimed at the heart of Germany" and asserted that Germany needed to expand its own borders to acquire *lebensraum* (living space). In light of these events and statements, tension grew in Europe during the summer of 1938. On September 22, 1938, Hitler announced that Germany would occupy the Sudetenland. Fear gripped Czechoslovakia, even though it had a defensive military alliance with the Soviet Union. This agreement stated, however, that the Soviet Union would offer assistance only if France did so. France consulted with

Main Idea:
Hitler sent German troops into Austria, had Schuschnigg arrested, and installed a Nazi as chancellor.

Britain, hoping for its support if matters came to a head. On September 29, a meeting to resolve the Sudeten crisis was held in the German city of Munich. Attending were Hitler, British Prime Minister **Neville Chamberlain**, French Premier **Edouard Daladier**, and Italy's Benito Mussolini. Czechoslovakia was not represented. Toward midnight, an agreement was reached.

The Munich Agreement provided for a **partition** of Czechoslovakia. Hitler would be allowed to annex **the Sudetenland** without interference. The other delegates to the Munich Conference agreed to the annexation, based upon Hitler's promise that he would not make any other territorial demands. Britain and France decided not to defend Czechoslovakia, and were thus willing to sacrifice the Sudetenland, in the hope of avoiding a full-scale war. Their decision was an act of appeasement. When Neville Chamberlain arrived back in London after the conference, he said that the Munich Agreement meant there would be "peace in our time." In October, German troops moved into the Sudetenland. The Axis powers had secured control of central Europe without having fired a shot.

> **Main Idea:**
> The other delegates to the Munich Conference agreed to the annexation, based upon Hitler's promise that he would not make any other territorial demands.

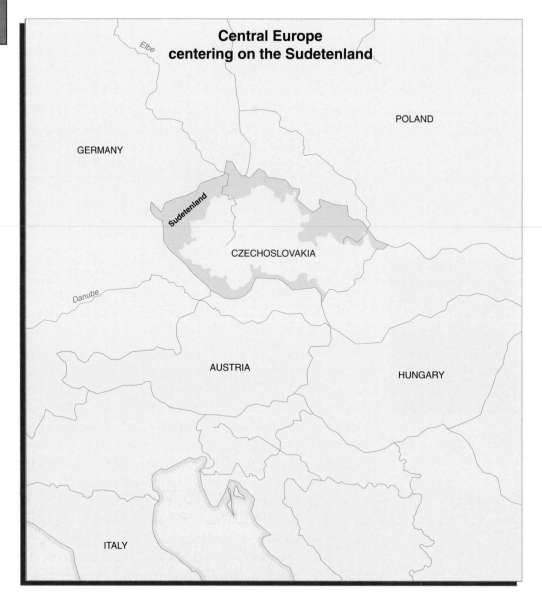

Central Europe centering on the Sudetenland

Delegates to the Munich Peace Conference of September 1938. From left: British Prime Minister Neville Chamberlain; French Prime Minister Edouard Daladier; German Chancellor Adolf Hitler; Italian Prime Minister Benito Mussolini; and, Italian Minister of Foreign Affairs Count Galeazzo Ciano.

1939

In March 1939, Hitler, disregarding his prior statements about Czechoslovakia, sent in troops to occupy the rest of the country. Thus another addition was made to the lands held by the Third Reich. Chamberlain's policy of appeasement had been a failure. Hitler's boldness increased as he grew more and more certain that the Western powers were too fearful and too weak to put up any show of force against him. This boldness was apparent in the threats he began to make to Poland in the spring and summer of 1939.

German soldiers goose-stepping in Berlin, Germany, September 1939.

1939

In August 1939, to the world's amazement, Hitler announced the signing of a treaty with the Soviet Union, the Nazi-Soviet Nonaggression Pact. It came as a surprise because Hitler detested communism, disliked the Soviet leader Joseph Stalin, had often talked about taking over the soil-rich Soviet region of Ukraine, and considered Slavs to be an inferior race of people. Nevertheless, he put aside these sentiments and thoughts, temporarily, in order to prevent the Soviets from fighting him over Poland. If Britain and France were to resist him, he did not want to worry about waging a war on two fronts.

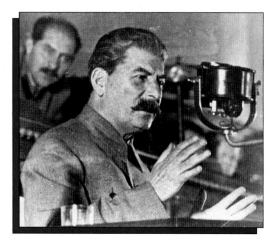

Russian Communist leader, Joseph Stalin, reporting on the draft of a new Soviet constitution from the Kremlin in Moscow, 1936.

France and Britain were surprised and upset over the treaty. Along with the rest of the world, they knew that Hitler and Stalin were antagonists and therefore felt that the two dictators could not possibly agree on anything. The two Western nations had now lost a potential ally, as they had assumed that they could count on Soviet help against Hitler if a war broke out. They also feared that Poland would be a likely target for Hitler's army, with the Soviets promising not to fight him.

By the terms of the treaty that were disclosed publicly, Germany and the Soviet Union promised not to attack each other and to remain neutral if the other was involved in a war. The secret parts of the treaty provided that the Soviets would not interfere with Hitler's move into western Poland in return for Hitler's not interfering with Soviet moves into eastern Poland and the Baltic nations of Finland, Lithuania, Latvia, and Estonia. Unknown to the world, Poland was about to undergo partition, and much of Eastern Europe was to be carved into German and Soviet zones of occupation.

In April 1939, prior to the Nazi-Soviet Nonaggression Pact (also called the **Molotov-Ribbentrop Pact**, named for the foreign ministers from the U.S.S.R. and Germany), Britain and France had signed a mutual assistance pact with Poland. They had thus let Hitler know that they were prepared to use force should he continue his moves eastward. Hitler's awareness of this pact (although he probably still doubted British and French resolve to fight) was a factor prompting him to sign the nonaggression pact with the Soviets in August.

Immediate Cause of War in Europe

On September 1, 1970, an American tourist in Warsaw, the capital of Poland, woke up to find Polish soldiers standing quietly at attention in several parts of the city. There was a small monument where each soldier stood, and a strange silence prevailed that had not been present on the previous day. The tourist soon learned the reasons for what he saw. These scenes were part of the Polish government's annual observance of the horror that had occurred thirty-one years earlier, on September 1, 1939. On that day, Germany invaded Poland, marking the start of World War II in Europe. In each part of Warsaw, where a soldier stood, some German atrocity against Polish people had occurred in September 1939.

German Panzer tanks advance during the invasion of Poland at the beginning of World War II. German army photograph, October 1939.

The buildup to the German invasion had begun a number of years earlier, but it intensified in the summer of 1939. Germany had been outraged at the 1919 Versailles treaty's award to Poland of the city of Danzig as well as a strip of German territory for access to the Baltic Sea. This territory, known as the **Polish corridor**, separated most of Germany from its region of East Prussia. Ever since 1933, Hitler had seized upon these issues as one of his appeals to German nationalism. A Nazi Party had been established in Danzig, and it campaigned for linkage with the fatherland (Germany). Now, in the last week of August 1939, with the ink barely dry on the nonaggression pact with the Soviets, Hitler demanded the return of Danzig and protection for Germans living in the Polish corridor. The Nazi propaganda machine had turned out stories of atrocities against these Germans. On August 19, Hitler requested the presence in Berlin of a Polish official to discuss a "German solution" to the "Polish question." No representative appeared. On August 31, during the night, German soldiers, masquerading as Poles, attacked a German radio station on the German-Polish border. Hitler, stating that Poland had attacked German forces, ordered the German army into Poland the next day, September 1. By breakfast time, German troops were on Polish soil, while German planes were bombing Warsaw and other parts of Poland.

On September 3, Britain and France demanded German withdrawal. Upon Hitler's refusal, they backed up their guarantees to Poland and declared war on Germany. World War II had begun.

At first, the United States was not a direct participant, although it gradually came to support the British and French. It was not until late 1941, two years after the invasion of Poland, that America entered the war. The immediate reason why it became a belligerent in the third year of the war is explained in the next section.

Main Idea:
On August 31, during the night, German soldiers, masquerading as Poles, attacked a German radio station on the German-Polish border.

Specific Events Leading to War in Asia

In Asia an aggressive, militaristic Japan moved to destroy the European "house of peace" during a ten-year period beginning in 1931.

1. *1931–1932:* During this time, Japan invaded parts of Manchuria, in northern China, wanting to possess the region's coal, iron, and fertile soil. With few resources on its crowded islands, and with a growing population, Japanese imperialists looked down upon China as a natural target. Japan's action was a violation of the Nine Power Treaty of 1921–1922. Japan ignored criticism from the League of Nations and withdrew from the organization. The United States, wanting to maintain an Open Door Policy in China, issued the

Stimson Doctrine, which stated that no recognition would be given to land taken by force. This had little effect on Japan, as it experienced no attempt by the United States to enforce the doctrine. Japan excluded all foreigners and exploited the mineral resources of Manchuria for its own use. The Chinese were unable to stop this from happening.

2. *1937:* Japan sought to invade other areas in China in 1937. Many historians regard these invasions as the opening battles of World War II in Asia. Although Japan's military might brought much suffering to the Chinese, by 1939 Japan had not been able to conquer the entire nation.

3. *1940:* With the fall of France and Holland to Germany in 1940, Japan took over French Indochina and claimed "protective custody" over the Dutch East Indies. With these advances in Southeast Asia, Japan was on the way to establishing its East Asian coprosperity sphere and a "new order." In truth, these were simply masks for Japan's expanding colonial empire. In September 1940, Japan signed a military alliance with Germany and Italy, officially creating the Rome-Berlin-Tokyo Axis.

Henry Stimson (1867–1950), American statesman, photographed in 1927 while governor general of the Philippine Islands.

Map of Japan and Manchuria

GOBI DESERT

Manchuria

MONGOLIA

SEA OF JAPAN

Sapporo

JAPAN

Tokyo
Yokohama

KOREA

Osaka

Seoul

Beijing

CHINA

YELLOW SEA

Hideki Tojo (1885–1948), Japanese general and prime minster, photographed in 1941.

4. *1941:* With Britain now struggling in Europe as the only remaining Western power against Germany, and unable to send reinforcements to Asia, it appeared likely that Japan would be able to take over such British colonies as Hong Kong and Malaya. The United States, having bases in Hawaii and the Philippine Islands, was the sole power left in the way of Japanese expansion in East Asia. When General **Hideki Tojo** became prime minister of Japan in October 1941, tension increased between Japan and the United States. Japan refused American requests to leave China, even though the United States stopped exports to Japan and moved its Pacific Fleet to Pearl Harbor in Hawaii.

On December 7, 1941, Japan launched a surprise attack against U.S. forces in **Pearl Harbor**. More than 2,000 Americans were killed, and many battleships and planes were destroyed. On December 8, 1941, U.S. President Franklin D. Roosevelt asked Congress to declare war on Japan, predicting that December 7, 1941, would become "a date that will live in infamy." Congress honored the president's request, and on the same day Britain declared war on Japan. In the following week, Germany and Italy declared war on the United States, while Congress answered with a war declaration against them. Less than twenty-five years after the end of World War I the world was engulfed in a second major conflict.

By 1939, as we have seen, there was no longer a house of peace. One may argue that its foundations should have been made more secure by its builders or even that it should have been constructed in a different manner. On the other hand, its destroyers acted in ways that were not fully anticipated. And even if these ways had been anticipated, what should the builders have done as "preventive maintenance" or "repairs"?

> **Main Idea:**
> By 1939, as we have seen, there was no longer a house of peace.

Three U.S. battleships stricken during the Japanese attack on Pearl Harbor, December 7, 1941. Left to right: USS *West Virginia*, severely damaged; USS *Tennessee*, damaged; USS *Arizona*, sunk.

32nd President of the United States, Franklin Delano Roosevelt, addressing the joint session of Congress, December 8, 1941, asking for a declaration of war against Japan.

> **Main Idea:**
> Never did one imagine that these leaders—heirs to cultures that had produced great writers, artists, and scientists—would pursue goals that would result in a world war.

In the period between the two world wars, the victorious nations in World War I, as democracies, were committed to goals other than preparing for war. They were attempting to improve the economic and civil well-being of their populations. The Great Depression, beginning in 1929, had produced serious setbacks to these attempts. The totalitarian governments of Germany, Italy, and Japan were less interested in the material well-being of their citizens, and more inclined to focus money and energy on "guns" than on "butter." Without any long tradition of democracy, they were able to use their people as instruments of their own policies and grandiose ambitions.

The Western democracies also found it difficult to understand the ugly proportions of totalitarian aggression. To average British, French, and American citizens, people such as Hitler and Mussolini seemed to be apart from the mainstream of humane and intellectual progress that Western Europe had been achieving ever since the Renaissance and the Enlightenment. Never did one imagine that these leaders—heirs to cultures that had produced great writers, artists, and scientists—would pursue goals that would result in a world war.

That war was fought in even more horrible fashion and in more locales than was World War I. The conduct of World War II will now concern us.

CONDUCT OF WORLD WAR II

While it was being fought, World War I had been called the Great War. Although World War II produced more casualties and was fought in wider geographical areas than the First World War, it was never called the greater war. Yet it may go down in history as, to borrow terminology from President Woodrow Wilson, the war that ended all wars. Perhaps we may, at the very least, call it the last great war of the twentieth century. One reason for this hope is the terror evoked by the new weaponry used in the war's final phases. Another reason is the peace-keeping machinery that was created at the war's end. The actual conduct of the war will be our topic in this section.

The War in Europe (1939–1941)

A 1940 painting of Winston Churchill (1874–1965) by Captain Cuthbert Orde.

This early part of the war saw many German successes. Poland surrendered on September 27, 1939. The German victory was marked by a new kind of warfare, called *blitzkrieg*, or lightning war, that involved coordinating swift, simultaneous attacks by air and land. The land forces included tanks, artillery, and infantry. In accord with the Nazi-Soviet Nonaggression Pact, the U.S.S.R. moved to seize "its areas" of eastern Poland, along with Estonia, Latvia, and Lithuania. In November 1939, Soviet forces attacked Finland and ultimately took it over in March 1940. For several months after the conquest of Poland, German forces were busy building up their strength without engaging in any major hostilities. A lull was apparent on the western front, as the Germans dug in behind their fortified position in the Rhineland, the **Siegfried line**. France amassed forces at the Maginot line, along its eastern border. The lack of any action in this part of Europe led to the name the "phony war." No one used this term after April 9, 1940, however, when Germany began to launch a series of successful blitzkrieg attacks. By May 1940, Denmark, Norway, Luxembourg, the Netherlands, and Belgium had fallen. These victories gave Hitler greater access to the North Sea and to Britain and afforded him the opportunity of attacking France without going through the Maginot line. They also led to the resignation of British Prime Minister Neville Chamberlain, a symbol of the failed policy of appeasement. His place was taken by **Winston Churchill**.

The Fall of France

By the end of May 1940, the German strategy of invading France through Belgium, north of the Maginot line, became clear. Avoiding the temptation to move immediately toward Paris, Hitler's troops sought to secure all of northeastern France by splitting the main French army in the south from a combined Belgian, British, and French force in the north. This was accomplished by moving quickly against the combined armies and forcing them to evacuate France at the English Channel seaport of **Dunkirk**. The evacuation of over 300,000 soldiers from Dunkirk in late May and early June of 1940 was astonishing. British ships, small boats, yachts, and other kinds of vessels rushed across the English Channel to save the soldiers. The Dunkirk evacuation of so many men, although a sign of a clear military gain for the Germans, proved to be a powerful morale builder for the British.

A study of German documents after the war reveals that Hitler had purposely held back from crushing the Allied forces, overwhelmingly British, at Dunkirk. He had the power to do so, but may have thought that Britain was no

Soldiers of the British expeditionary force are evacuated from Dunkirk, France, on an English battleship. World War II photograph, May–June 1940.

longer a threat to him and may have wanted to save his tanks, infantry, and air force for conquering France. The conquest became a reality with the Fall of Paris in June 1940, and on the same day the French signed an **armistice** with the Germans in a railroad car in the French village of Compiegne. To the shame of the French, this was the same car in the same village where the Germans had signed the armistice that ended World War I. Further shame was heaped upon France when Italy declared war on it in June. With France already on its knees, the "stab in the back," from its southeastern neighbor shocked public opinion in Britain and the United States. Italy now became a belligerent in World War II.

By the terms of the armistice, France was divided into two parts. Northern France was to be governed by the Germans, as occupied France. The southern region was to be under German supervision, but administered by a French government located in the city of Vichy and headed by Marshall **Philippe Pétain**. Vichy France, as this region was called, had in its government several collaborators. These were French citizens who were willing to work with the Nazis and carry out their wishes. Other French people continued to secretly fight the

The German army celebrates the entry into Paris, France, June 14, 1940, with a victory parade on the Champs Elysees. The Arc de Triomphe is in the background. World War II German army photograph.

Henri Philippe Petain (1856–1951),
a French soldier.

President de Gaulle, French soldier
and statesman, photographed at
the Arc de Triomphe in Paris,
France on November 11, 1960.

Germans as part of the resistance forces; they acted in small groups to sabotage German installations. Frenchmen who escaped to Britain after Dunkirk formed the Free French forces, under General **Charles de Gaulle**. They refused to have anything to do with the Vichy government and prepared for the day when they could return to France and drive out the Germans.

The Battle of Britain

With the surrender of France in June 1940, Britain stood alone. It was the only remaining anti-Axis belligerent. The United States, though alarmed at the fall of France and willing to give material aid to the British, wanted to continue its policy of **isolationism** rather than commit itself to fighting. Hitler now assumed, in these circumstances, that Britain would be willing to make peace, thereby leaving him in control of the European continent. He is even alleged to have sent out some peace feelers to London, promising to leave Britain alone, along with her colonial empire, if she dropped out of the war. The British would have none of this. Throughout its long history of trying to maintain a **balance of power** in Europe, Britain had often gone to war to prevent the kind of dominance by a single nation that Hitler achieved after defeating France.

In August 1940, Hitler and his Air Marshal, **Hermann Goering**, decided to bomb the British Isles as prelude to an invasion. Thus began the Battle of Britain, which was to last until November 1940. Under Prime Minister Winston Churchill, the mood of the population was defiant. He told the nation he would offer his "blood, toil, tears, and sweat." On June 4, 1940, after the evacuation from Dunkirk, Churchill set a courageous tone with an emotional speech that included these words:

We shall go on to the end . . . we shall fight with growing confidence and with growing strength in the air, we shall defend our Island, whatever the cost may be. We shall fight on the beaches, we shall fight on the landing grounds, we shall fight in the fields and in the streets, we shall fight in the hills; we shall never surrender.

Later in the month, he pleaded with his fellow citizens to "stand up to" Hitler. Otherwise, "the whole world . . . will sink into the abyss of a new Dark Age." With a ringing voice he further said: "Let us therefore brace ourselves to our duties, and so bear ourselves that, if the British Empire and its Commonwealth last for a thousand years, men will say, 'This was their finest hour.'"

Such Churchillian oratory strengthened the people for the frightening warfare to be waged by the Luftwaffe (the German air force). Day and night, mostly from August to November in 1940, German planes bombed airports, military bases, and industrial centers. The most terrifying moments came whenever there were attacks, referred to as the "blitz," often in the night, on heavily

Ruins flank the facade of St. Paul's Cathedral in London, England, after a German air raid during the London Blitz in 1940–1941.

populated civilian centers. This kind of total war was worse than what had occurred in World War I. However, Britain's civilian defense procedures during the bombing raids of 1940 proved reasonably effective in protecting people. Thousands slept in underground shelters, subways, and basements. Many fled their city homes for the countryside; parents in targeted urban areas such as **London** and Coventry evacuated many of their children to the country.

The most crucial factor in Britain's successful defense against the German onslaught was its air force. Royal Air Force (RAF) planes dueled with German pilots in the skies all over southern England. Britain's air war was significantly assisted by the use of **radar**. Invented in the 1930s, this scientific device could detect aircraft miles away. Its use was instrumental in the destruction of more than 1,700 German aircraft; British losses numbered approximately 1,000. As the air war continued, the Germans were preparing for an invasion along the French coast. Called Operation Sea Lion, the invasion could not begin as long as the RAF was still flying. With the Luftwaffe encountering unexpectedly high losses, Hitler called off Operation Sea Lion, the planned invasion of Britain, on the advice of Air Marshal Goering on September 17, 1940.

Although the Germans were to continue occasional bombing raids until 1941, the Battle of Britain was a defeat for them. In a glowing tribute to RAF pilots, Churchill proclaimed, "Never in the field of human conflict was so much owed by so many to so few."

Aggression in the Balkans and the Soviet Union

With a stalemate in the West, Hitler now turned his attention to the Balkans and to Eastern Europe. Although Mussolini had failed to take Greece in the fall of 1940, German forces put down strong resistance there and finally occupied the country in May 1941. Prior to this advance, Hitler had added Romania, Bulgaria, Hungary, and Yugoslavia to his domain. He had hoped to reach the Suez Canal, to disrupt British commerce, and to seize nearby oil fields. Unable, however, to go through neutral Turkey, he failed in an attempt to seize Egypt by attacking through Libya. Elsewhere in the Middle East, the Axis suffered a loss when British and Free French troops took over areas held by Vichy France, such as Syria.

The other military goal of Hitler in mid-1941 was the conquest of the Soviet Union. Unworried about his western front, with a weakened Britain and an isolationist America, he eyed with envy the rich soil of eastern Poland and the Russian oil fields in Ukraine and other areas, all essential to the fulfillment of his *lebensraum* policy. He was certain that Russia could be taken quickly,

Members of a German military police battalion enter a village in the Soviet Union protected by an armored tank. World War II German army photograph, c. 1942.

before the winter months. Willing to ignore the 1939 nonaggression pact and to risk the possible danger of a two-front war, Germany attacked Russia on June 22, 1941. The code name for the invasion was **Operation Barbarossa**, named for a Germanic king. The attack startled the world. Both Britain and the United States said they would try to send supplies to the Russians. Although they distrusted Soviet leader Stalin and feared communism, they considered it important to help any nation that was fighting Hitler.

The fighting by Soviet forces against the almost three million German troops did not go well at first. Retreating on several fronts, the Russians sought desperately to hinder enemy advances by following the scorched earth policy. Accordingly, they destroyed farm and industrial equipment, blew up roads, and burned crops. The strategy was partially successful, because the **Wehrmacht** (German defense forces) was unable to get any further than the approaches to Leningrad and Moscow by the end of 1941. With winter now setting in, and a successful counterattack near Moscow by Soviet General **Georgi Zhukov**, Hitler's war machine was forced to hold its lines.

Zhukov's attack on December 5, 1941, gave a welcome boost to Soviet morale, as did the events of the next several days. Japan's attack on the American naval base at Pearl Harbor on December 7, 1941 led to a declaration of war by the United States on Japan on December 8, 1941. On December 11, Germany and Italy, honoring their agreement with Japan, declared war on the United States. With its own declaration against these two nations, the United States became an active participant in the struggle against Axis aggression. As 1942 began, events in Europe were about to take a different turn.

Victory in Europe (1942–1945)

Some of the most horrible combat ever seen on our planet occurred in the years between 1942 and 1945. This was true in Europe, as well as in Africa and Asia. For Hitler, the war in Europe now, with America's entry, had two fronts. This situation, with reminders of World War I's tragedy for Germany, was just what he had wanted to avoid. Throughout 1942, therefore, he increased the pressure on the U.S.S.R. in the hope of quickly closing down the eastern front in order to meet the expected thrust from the Americans, British, and Free French on his west. Additional troops were sent to besiege Leningrad, while a major offensive was launched against Stalingrad.

Stalingrad

The battle for **Stalingrad** lasted six months. It became exceptionally brutal as German soldiers penetrated into the city and faced hand-to-hand combat with the Russians. Fierce weather, starvation, and disease took a terrible toll on both armies as well as on the civilian population. At Stalingrad, the Russians lost more men than the United States lost in the entire war! In late 1942, "**General Winter**," the same foe that had contributed to Napoleon's defeat in Russia in 1812, was to spell disaster for the Germans. This factor, along with continuing counteroffensives by the Soviets, resulted in the surrender of a German army of almost 350,000 men on January 31, 1943. Spurred by this victory, Soviet forces pushed the Germans out of their land by early 1944. The siege of Stalingrad had ended. With Hitler's battered soldiers retreating, the Russians seized previously Nazi-controlled territories in Eastern Europe—Latvia, Poland, and Hungary. The drive toward Berlin now gained momentum, and the Soviets began to envision an end to what they were to call the Great Patriotic War.

Allied Summit Meetings

On the western and southern fronts, the United States and its Allies became active. In 1941, President **Franklin D. Roosevelt** and Prime Minister Churchill signed the Atlantic Charter. This was an idealistic document, similar to President Woodrow Wilson's Fourteen Points, describing the war aims of the two major Atlantic democracies. Among other things, they pledged to do the following:

1. Seek no territories
2. Respect the right of people to practice self-determination and choose their own governments
3. Insure freedom of the seas
4. Provide access to equal economic opportunity
5. Work for an end to aggression by all nations

U.S. President Franklin Delano Roosevelt and English Prime Minister Winston Churchill meet on the HMS *Prince of Wales* off Newfoundland on August 14, 1941, to establish the Atlantic Charter. Standing are U.S. General George Marshall, left, and British General John G. Dill.

Soviet Premier Joseph Stalin, U.S. President Franklin D. Roosevelt, and British Prime Minister Winston Churchill at the Teheran Conference, November 1943, to discuss war plans.

In January 1942, twenty-six nations, as Allies fighting the Axis powers, sent delegates to a meeting in Washington, D.C. They promised to work together, not sign separate peace treaties, and adhere to the principles of the Atlantic Charter.

At another international meeting, held in Teheran, Iran, in December 1943, the **Big Three** (Roosevelt, Churchill, and Stalin) discussed plans for dealing with Germany. Stalin was emphatic that Germany must be divided and kept divided. His additional wish for a second front to be opened in the west with an invasion of occupied France was agreed to by Roosevelt and Churchill. However, Churchill, fearing Stalin's future designs on Eastern Europe, proposed a major offensive by American and British forces from the Mediterranean into the **Balkans** and then northward. Stalin's opposition to this proposal, supported by Roosevelt, prevented it from being carried out, with troublesome consequences after the war. The leaders at the Teheran Conference agreed to meet again.

North Africa and Italy

On the military scene, a combined American and British force under U.S. General **Dwight D. Eisenhower** landed in North Africa in 1942 and inflicted heavy losses on German units. A momentous victory that prevented the Germans under General **Erwin Rommel**, "the Desert Fox," from reaching the Suez Canal occurred in November 1942 at **El Alamein**. This was accomplished by British troops led by General **Bernard Montgomery**. The first significant Allied military venture in Europe occurred on July 10, 1943. Deciding to strike at the European Axis powers through their "soft underbelly," a combined American, British, and Canadian force landed in Sicily to begin an invasion of Italy. At this point, Marshal **Pietro Badoglio** took over the Italian government from Mussolini, who fled and was taken to the north of Italy by German parachutists. Badoglio supported the Allied nations, surrendered to them, and welcomed their landing on the Italian mainland in September 1943 to fight the remaining German soldiers. After heavy fighting at such places as **Anzio**, the Allies marched into **Rome** on June 4, 1944.

> **Main Idea:**
> The first significant Allied military venture in Europe occurred on July 10, 1943.

D-Day

With the victories in Italy by 1944, Germany was being hurt on her southern front, and the Russians were advancing on the east. What now remained to be done was a drive on Germany's western front. Such a drive, known as Operation Overlord, had been planned for months, under the overall command of General Eisenhower. It culminated in an immense show of force on June 6, 1944, D-Day, with an invasion on the beaches of **Normandy**, France. Thousands of ships transported American, British, Canadian, and Free French soldiers across the English Channel. In France, they met determined resistance from

General Eisenhower, Commander in Chief of the allied forces in western Europe, meeting with a member of an American Airborne unit just prior to the June 6, 1944 Invasion of Normandy (D-Day) during World War II.

American troops wade ashore at Utah Beach during the invasion of Normandy, France on June 6, 1944.

entrenched German forces but were able to take the beaches and march inland. Allied warplanes successfully battled German aircraft. Other Allied landings in France were made in August 1944, and the Wehrmacht began retreating eastward from these onslaughts. Finally, on August 25, 1944, Paris was liberated. Amidst cheers and prayers, General Charles de Gaulle led a victory parade into the city. The Allies were now ready for a drive to Berlin. One last major German stand took place in Belgium, in December 1944, at the **Battle of the Bulge**, but after a bitter ten-day struggle, the victorious Allies were able to set foot on German soil. As 1945 approached, it was evident that this would be the final year of the war.

Winston Churchill, Franklin D. Roosevelt, and Joseph Stalin at the Yalta Conference at Livadia Palace, Yalta, Crimea in February 1945. Standing left to right: Anthony Eden, Edward Stettinius, Alexander Cadogan, Vyacheslav Molotov, and W. Averell Harriman.

The Yalta Conference

In February 1945, the three main Allied leaders—Roosevelt, Churchill, and Stalin—met at **Yalta** to make postwar plans. They represented the most important members of the Grand Alliance of nations fighting the Axis powers. At this meeting, held in the Crimea region of the Soviet Union, the Big Three agreed on six points:

1. Germany should be demilitarized and divided into zones of occupation after the war.
2. Trials for war criminals should be held.
3. Arrangements would be made for a new international peacekeeping organization.
4. Poland was to be restored with new boundaries, getting some German land for her west while letting Russia have some of Poland's land to her east.

5. The U.S.S.R. would permit free elections in the Eastern European regions it had taken from the Germans.
6. The U.S.S.R. would enter the war in Asia against Japan once Germany had surrendered. In return, Stalin would get control of some northern Japanese islands, the **Kuriles**.

The agreements reached at the Yalta Conference were to cause problems after the war (see Chapter 12 in this volume "The Cold War"). Roosevelt was more willing than was Churchill to reach accord with Stalin. One reason was the U.S. President's strong wish to have the Soviets enter the war against Japan. As it happened, Roosevelt never lived to see the war's end; he died on April 12, 1945. He was succeeded in office by Vice-President **Harry S. Truman**.

V-E Day

> **Main Idea:**
> The date May 8, 1945, has since been proclaimed as **V-E Day**, the day of victory in Europe. To the relief of millions, the war in Europe had come to an end.

In that same eventful month of April 1945, the German army in Italy gave up. Mussolini was captured and killed by Italian guerrillas. He was then taken to Milan, where his corpse was shot five times by a mother who had lost five sons in the war. He was then hung by the ankles in front of a small shop. Later that month, American soldiers met their Soviet counterparts in eastern Germany. On April 30, Hitler committed suicide in his Berlin underground bunker. His body was then soaked with gas and burnt. Even though his remains were never found, there is no serious disagreement about his death. The Russians were attacking Berlin at the time and were permitted to march into the city first on May 2, 1945. On May 7, U.S. General Eisenhower received a formal unconditional surrender by German forces; on May 8, a formal surrender was also made to Soviet General Zhukov. The date May 8, 1945, has since been proclaimed as **V-E Day**, the day of victory in Europe. To the relief of millions, the war in Europe had come to an end.

One unanticipated horror of the war shocked the Allies as they marched through Europe while attacking German soldiers. This was the discovery of the torture and death inflicted on innocent civilians by the Nazis in **concentration camps** and **death camps**. The most seriously targeted of these civilians were Jews, victims of the **Holocaust**. This word refers to the intentional persecution and murder of European Jews by the Germans from 1933 to 1945. Six million were exterminated,

General Dwight D. Eisenhower, on a tour of the Third Army front, walks around a cluster of corpses representing the remains of many of the inmates of the German concentration camp at Gotha, Germany at the end of World War II on April 12, 1945.

mostly in camps such as Auschwitz, Dachau, and Treblinka. The planned extermination of a group of people because of their religion, race, or ethnicity is called **genocide**. The genocidal tactics of the Nazis were a horrible extension of Hitler's anti-Semitic attitudes. Although there were instances of Jewish resistance, such as the uprising of 1943 in the Warsaw Ghetto, the outside world stood by and did nothing while these deadly tactics—gas chambers, ovens, firing squads—were being used. Among other groups who suffered in the camps because the Nazis had labeled them as inferior human beings were homosexuals, Jehovah's Witnesses, gypsies, Slavs, and mentally retarded persons (see Chapter 11 in this volume).

Victory in Asia and the Pacific (1942–1945)

United States Marines raising the flag over Mount Suribachi, Iwo Jima on February 23, 1945.

From December 7, 1941, the date of the Pearl Harbor attack, until mid-1942, Japan achieved major success in Asia and the Pacific. Among its conquests during this time were **Hong Kong**, **Malaya**, **Singapore**, **the Philippines**, the **Dutch East Indies**, and **Burma**. Having already taken **Korea** and parts of eastern **China** and **French Indochina**, Japan seemed destined to carve out its so-called **co-prosperity** sphere in Asia. However, from May to August 1942, Japan was defeated in three major engagements that were to limit its imperial expansion:

1. The Battle of the Coral Sea, where American and Australian naval forces prevented an invasion of Australia.
2. The Battle of Midway Island, where the U.S. Navy broke Japanese codes, destroyed four carriers, and thereby prevented an attack upon Hawaii. This battle proved to be the turning point in the Pacific.
3. The Battle of Guadalcanal, where, at the most southerly point gained by the Japanese, American marines achieved a bitter and costly victory.

Main Idea:
They pledged to continue fighting Japan until that nation made an unconditional surrender.

U.S. forces were now ready to take the offensive and began to mount an "**island-hopping**" campaign. The goal was to slowly capture Japanese-held islands in the Pacific, on the way to attacking Japan itself. Meanwhile, on the Asian mainland in 1942 and 1943, Japanese troops began to retreat under pressure from the Americans, British, Chinese, and several native resistance groups. At the **Cairo** Conference of November 1943, Roosevelt, Churchill, and Chinese nationalist leader **Chiang Kai-shek** signed the Cairo Declaration. They pledged to continue fighting Japan until that nation made an unconditional surrender. Japan would lose all territories it had taken, with Korea to become independent.

Another major American success was gained in 1944 at the Battle of Leyte Gulf, near the Philippines. In October, U.S. General **Douglas MacArthur** was able to recapture the Philippines. He had escaped from there in 1942 with the promise "I shall return." Combined U.S. land, sea, and air forces now edged

Chiang Kai-shek (1887–1975), Chinese general and statesman, photographed c. 1931.

Douglas MacArthur (1880–1964), American army officer, photographed in the southwest Pacific in 1943.

closer to Japan with fiercely fought encounters at Iwo-Jima in February and March of 1945, and at Okinawa in April through June of 1945. In **Tokyo** itself, a single bombing raid took the lives of more than 80,000 people. These advances did much to weaken Japan's fighting ability and boost Allied morale. The cry "Remember Pearl Harbor" was a stimulus for American forces. So were the grim discoveries about indescribable Japanese treatment of soldiers and civilians of all ethnic backgrounds in prisoner-of-war camps.

The Potsdam Conference

In July 1945, with Germany and Italy out of the war, and Japan's defeat a virtual certainty, American, British, and Russian leaders met at Potsdam, a town near Berlin. Attending this meeting were Truman, Churchill, and Stalin. (During the Potsdam Conference, held from July 17 to August 2, **Clement Attlee** became British Prime Minister and replaced Winston Churchill.) The three Allies issued a declaration concerning the future control and occupation of Germany, while calling for Japan's unconditional surrender. Much distrust was evident at Potsdam, as Churchill and Truman were upset at Stalin for not keeping his Yalta promises concerning free elections in Eastern Europe. Because of this feeling, Truman did not want to tell Stalin about the successful testing of an American atomic bomb.

Atomic Bombs and V-J Day

The Potsdam Conference ended on August 2. Although the United States warned Japan about suffering terrible destruction if it did not surrender, the Japanese turned down the **ultimatum**. On August 6, 1945, unwilling to risk untold numbers of American lives in invading Japan, President Truman ordered that an atomic bomb be dropped on the city of **Hiroshima**. Loss of life and property from this

Hiroshima shortly after the explosion of the first atomic bomb on August 6, 1945.

Harry S. Truman (1884–1972), 33rd President of the United States, photographed at his White House desk in 1945.

Hirohito (1901–1989), Emperor of Japan, photographed in 1935 on his favorite horse, Shirayuki.

bomb was greater than the casualties and damage in any city ever bombed previously in wartime. On August 8, 1945, the U.S.S.R. declared war on Japan and raced to fight dwindling Japanese forces in northern China. As Japan still refused to surrender, the United States dropped a second atomic bomb on August 9, 1945, on the city of **Nagasaki**. The additional losses from this bombing finally compelled the Japanese to surrender. Speaking for the very first time to his people on the radio, Japanese Emperor **Hirohito** told them of his decision. The formal surrender took place on September 2, 1945, on board the battleship USS *Missouri*. The Japanese surrender was accepted by Supreme Allied Commander General Douglas MacArthur. World War II had finally come to a close. To this day, September 2, 1945, is remembered as **V-J Day**, the day of victory over Japan.

This section on the conduct of World War II is much longer than its counterpart on the conduct of World War I (see Chapter 7 in this volume "World War I"). This is due to the greater numbers of belligerents, weapons, combat zones, and deaths, as well as the sheer length of time involved. The results of the Second World War were staggering and historic, as will be seen in the next section. Only twenty-one years elapsed between the end of one world war and the start of the second. More than sixty years have now elapsed since the end of World War II without any significantly similar global confrontations. Let us hope that the absence of widespread strife will continue.

RESULTS OF WORLD WAR II

The world of 1945 bore little resemblance to the world of the 1930s. Europe was shattered and lay in ruins, its peoples facing an uncertain future. Japan's reign as an imperial power was over. Some of the questions that faced the victors of World War II were: How should the defeated nations be treated? Could any kind of machinery be established that would prevent another world war?

The answers to these questions will be discussed as we describe the general results of the Second World War. We will then focus on matters related mainly to Europe.

Economic Results

World War II proved to be the most costly war ever fought. The loss of life and property far surpassed that in any previous conflict. Military costs alone were said to range into hundreds of billions of dollars. The economies of many European nations were destroyed. The industrial productivity necessary to support warfare provided jobs to many, but did not really add to the economic wealth of nations. Indeed, resources such as rubber, steel, oil, and wood had to be used for military purposes rather than for consumer goods. The money and material needed to transport, equip, clothe, and feed the armed forces of a belligerent nation were staggering. Civilians who were drafted or who volunteered for military duty had to leave their jobs and learn new skills.

Communism spread into Eastern Europe because of the occupation of this region by the Soviet Union. The Communists promised high standards of living and a better distribution of goods and services than had existed under capitalistic systems prior to the war.

Social Results

More people—soldiers and civilians—were killed than in any other war. Much of this high casualty rate was due to refined and newer weapons, as well as to the racist policies of the Axis powers. Another factor was the wide-ranging fighting in the war, taking place on three continents—Africa, Asia, and Europe. More than twenty-two million died in both civilian and military populations; more than thirty-four million survived the war with wounds. At war's end, millions of people had become refugees and displaced persons. Homelessness, broken families, and poverty were constant reminders of the upheaval caused by the war. As a total war, involving all groups in a nation, the Second World War was of greater scope than World War I.

Scientific Results

By the end of the war, the use of radar had become much more sophisticated. Faster and more complex airplanes were built as knowledge of the science of aeronautics increased. Successful warfare at sea required advances in battleship and submarine design, as well as newer navigational equipment.

Main Idea:
The most lethal weapon to come out of the war was the atomic bomb.

Weapons research resulted in newer, more deadly products. German scientists were able to manufacture a pilotless, jet-propelled bomb, and a rocket-propelled bomb. These brought much suffering to British civilians in urban areas. The most lethal weapon to come out of the war, however, was the atomic bomb. Its development reflected the pioneering work done by many scientists in discovering aspects of nuclear reactions. Chief among them were **Enrico Fermi** (an Italian who fled to the United States in 1938), **Niels Bohr** (from Denmark), **Leo Szilard** (a refugee from Hungary), and **Albert Einstein** (a German Jew who came to the United States in 1932). Fearful of an atomic bomb's destructiveness, but also worried that the Germans might produce one during the war, U.S. President Roosevelt committed much money and other resources to a secret project to develop the bomb. The **Manhattan Project**, as it was called, resulted in the production of two atomic bombs. Their use in World War II ushered in the nuclear age.

The war also saw the development and application of new medicines to help save lives on the battlefields. These included sulfa drugs and penicillin. Along with better use of blood plasma, they reduced the number of combat-related deaths from what it had been in World War I.

Political Results

These results were the most dramatic and had consequences that have continued to our own times. Some will be discussed here; others will be considered in later chapters as indicated here.

1. The United States and the Soviet Union became the two leading **superpowers** and eventually clashed on many issues in what became known as the **Cold War** (see Chapter 12 in this volume "The Cold War").
2. The totalitarian systems of Germany, Italy, and Japan ended with the complete defeat of these nations.

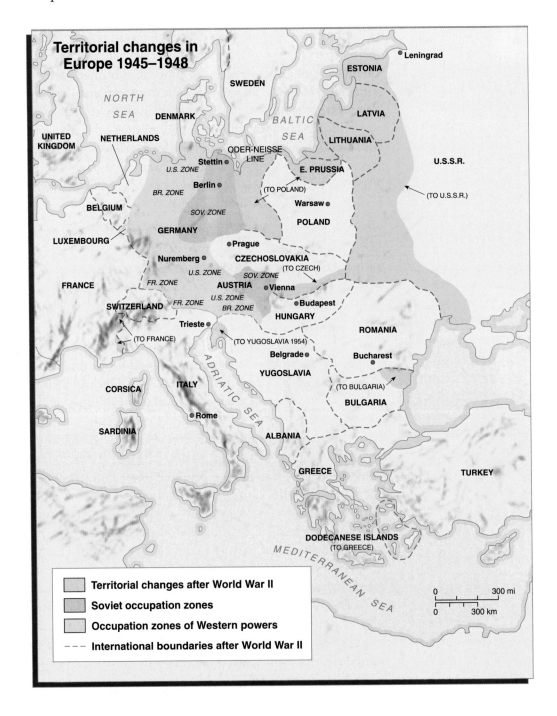

Territorial changes in Europe 1945–1948

Legend:
- Territorial changes after World War II
- Soviet occupation zones
- Occupation zones of Western powers
- --- International boundaries after World War II

3. Colonized peoples in Africa and Asia quickened their desires for independence. Their nationalistic movements were factors that would usher in the end of Western imperialism and the age of **decolonization** (see Chapter 15 in this volume, "The End of European Imperialism: Independence and Decolonization").

4. France and Britain, although victorious nations in the war, gradually gave up their empires and declined as world powers.

5. To maintain peace and address issues that could lead to conflicts, as well as issues affecting global social and economic concerns, the Allies established the United Nations (see Chapter 10 in this volume "The United Nations and Postwar Western Europe").

6. Peace treaties and territorial changes involved several nations. As agreed to in the 1945 Potsdam Conference, a Council of Foreign Ministers was created to draw up the peace treaties on behalf of the five major victorious Allies: the United States, the Soviet Union, France, Great Britain, and China. In 1947, a treaty was signed with Italy whereby she was to pay some reparations and to lose any colonies she had acquired. In other treaties, Bulgaria, Finland, Hungary, and Romania also had adjustments in their boundaries, losing some land acquired during the war.

> **Main Idea:**
> Many Soviet actions were in violation of the Yalta agreements.

7. Most Eastern European countries became **satellite nations** in a sphere of influence controlled by the Soviet Union (see Chapter 12 in this volume). Many Soviet actions were in violation of the Yalta agreements. The Soviet Union kept the Baltic states of Estonia, Latvia, and Lithuania, having annexed them in 1940. It also obtained an eastern region of Czechoslovakia and substantial territory from Poland. The Soviet border was now moved further west. Poland's border, named the Oder-Neisse line for the two rivers, was also moved further west with land taken from Germany. Germans who lived in what were now new parts of Poland, the U.S.S.R., and the Sudetenland area of Czechoslovakia, were expelled and forced to go to Germany.

8. Austria, which had become part of the Third Reich in 1938, was divided into four zones of occupation, administered by the United States, France, Great Britain, and the U.S.S.R. This situation continued until 1955, when the four Allies signed a formal peace treaty with Austria. By the treaty's terms, Austria became an independent nation with its pre-1938 boundaries. It was forbidden to have any political or economic union with Germany.

9. Germany was also divided into four zones of occupation—American, British, French, and Russian. However, Germany's postwar history and status were to be different from those of the other defeated Axis powers.

10. Japan was occupied until 1952 by the United States. Emperor Hirohito was allowed to stay in power. War crimes trials were held for key figures in Japan's military, such as Admiral Tojo, responsible for planning the Pearl Harbor attack. Convicted as a war criminal, he was subsequently executed. Under U.S. General Douglas MacArthur, the Japanese put together a new constitution modeled on a democratic structure. The United States also aided Japan in its industrial recovery from the war.

The Nuremberg War Crimes Trials

From 1945 to 1947, the Allied powers held a series of trials for several Nazi officials. Conducted at the German city of **Nuremberg**, these were known as the Nuremberg **War Crimes Trials**. The judges formed an international tribunal; the prosecutors were from the victorious nations. The defendant Nazis were permitted to have lawyers and to defend themselves, rights that they had never granted to the millions whose deaths they caused. Among the charges against the Germans were these three:

Nuremberg Trials (1945–1946). Hermann Goering, standing, with Rudolf Hess at the far left. Photograph, 1945–1946.

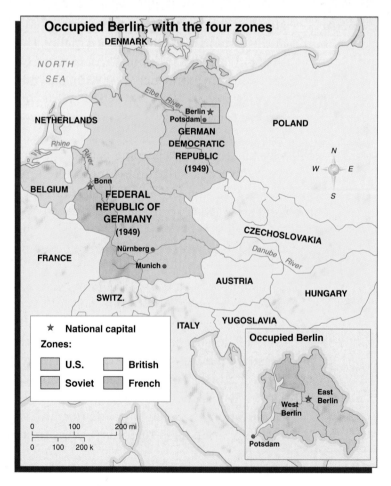

Occupied Berlin, with the four zones

1. "Crimes against the peace"
2. "Conspiracy to wage aggressive war"
3. "Crimes against humanity"

The first two charges related to the aggression that Germany had unleashed toward other nations. The third charge was based specifically on the atrocities committed by Germans against Jews and others considered to be "inferior human beings."

Main Idea:
The Allies wanted the trials to serve as a warning to potential aggressors and as a means of encouraging respect for international law.

The trials exposed the terrible actions taken by the Nazis, with evidence and testimony that shocked a war-torn world. Of the twenty-two defendants tried, nineteen were found guilty and three were acquitted. Twelve of the guilty were sentenced to death; seven, to life imprisonment. The Allies wanted the trials to serve as a warning to potential aggressors and as a means of encouraging respect for international law. They also hoped to promote the growth of democratic political organizations in Germany.

In addition to the Nuremberg trials, many other trials were held throughout Germany into the late 1940s. Among hundreds who were prosecuted as war criminals were doctors and nurses who had conducted outrageous "medical experiments" on concentration camp prisoners, camp guards, and officials in various war-related activities. These trials were part of a policy of **denazification**, which sought to cleanse Germany of Nazism by banning the Nazi Party and not allowing any former Nazi to hold positions in government, education, or industry. Some former Nazis escaped detection by changing their names and hiding or by secretly leaving Germany. A few others, who were accomplished scientists, may have been helped to leave Germany by Western officials, with the expectation that these scientists would be helpful in the research and development of weapons systems in the growing Cold War against Communist nations.

Occupation of Germany (1945–1990)

The division and occupation of Germany soon became a source of tension among the four occupiers. Three-fourths of the country, in the west, was controlled by the three Allied democracies—the United States, Britain, and

France—while the eastern part was occupied by the Communist Soviet Union. The city of Berlin was in the eastern part of Germany. Although this entire area of Germany was under Soviet control, **Berlin** was to be a divided city separated into four zones of occupation. The three zones held by the United States, Britain, and France were known as West Berlin; the Soviet zone, as East Berlin. The Berlin Blockade of 1948–1949,

A crowd at Checkpoint Charlie (sector border at Friedrichstrasse in Berlin). In the background a burning control house of the East German police on June 17, 1953.

Children at the Berlin Wall on Sebastianstrasse, Berlin, c. 1964.

imposed by the Soviets, challenged Western rights in West Berlin. Access to the city from the western parts of Germany was denied. The subsequent Berlin airlift by the United States and an Allied military buildup persuaded the Soviets to back down and end the blockade.

The Two Germanys

With the four World War II Allies unable to agree on a plan for German reunification, the Western nations permitted their zones in western Germany to come together in 1949 as the Federal Republic of Germany (West Germany), with its capital at **Bonn**. West Berlin was part of this new nation. The eastern part of Germany, under the Soviets, became the German Democratic Republic (East Germany); its capital was **East Berlin**. Thus, as the 1950s began, a strange, tense, and unexpected atmosphere engulfed central Europe. Even though Germany itself was no longer a military threat, those who had defeated her as friendly Allies were now at odds. The emerging hostile attitudes between the United States and the rest of the free world on the one hand, and the Soviet Union and the rest of the Communist world on the other, made for a very uneasy post-World War II peace. The division of Germany, of course, was an example of the attitudes that existed between the two sides in this confrontation known as the Cold War.

Tension increased with a strengthening of military forces. Both Germanys were allowed, with restrictions imposed by their occupiers, to build up their armies. The Allied nations also maintained troops in the two Germanys. The creation of two military alliances, the **North Atlantic Treaty Organization (NATO)** in 1949, and the Warsaw Pact in 1955, along with the crisis over the Berlin Wall in 1961, added to a mood of belligerence (see Chapter 12 in this volume "The Cold War").

Fortunately, from the 1970s onward, the bitterness in and over divided Germany eased somewhat. Normalization between the two Germanys was achieved in 1972 with the signing of the Fundamental Treaty, whereby West Germany and East Germany recognized each other and established formal diplomatic relations. Both nations were admitted to the United Nations in 1973, and the United States recognized East Germany in 1974. At the Helsinki Conference of 1975, thirty-three European countries, along with the United States and Canada, signed the Helsinki Pact. By its terms, the signers recognized all post-World War II boundary changes in Germany and elsewhere in Europe. They also agreed to recognize the importance of promoting human rights throughout Europe and to investigate any governmental actions that violated these rights. A Helsinki Watch Committee was established to conduct such investigations. This historic meeting in **Helsinki** was the largest gathering of

> **Main Idea:**
> The division of Germany, of course, was an example of the attitudes that existed between the two sides in this confrontation known as the Cold War.

George C. Marshall (1880–1959), American army officer, photographed in 1945.

European nations since the 1815 **Congress of Vienna**. The meeting's primary goals can be seen in its official title—the Conference on Security and Cooperation in Europe.

West Germany slowly began to function as a democracy, while enjoying great economic growth. It adopted a constitution providing for elections to a two-house parliament and protection of civil liberties. Political parties emerged, the most popular being the Christian Democrats and the Social Democrats. Some of the important heads of the government, known as the chancellors, have been **Konrad Adenauer**, **Willy Brandt**, **Helmut Schmidt**, and **Helmut Kohl**. West German industries expanded, particularly in automobiles and machinery. Its business leaders utilized technological advances and a well-educated labor force, while benefiting from the financial aid provided by the United States under the Marshall Plan. Over the years, a true "economic miracle" took place in West Germany.

East Germany, as a satellite of the U.S.S.R., became a Communist dictatorship. Its economy lagged behind that of West Germany, while its political system denied civil liberties and created a police-state atmosphere. Hundreds of its citizens tried to escape from the country, with several being shot as they tried to cross the border into West Germany. From 1946 until 1989, its only leaders were Communist party chiefs **Walter Ulbricht** and **Erich Honecker**. Starting in 1989, however, East Germany's history was to change drastically.

Reunification of Germany

Main Idea:
Once a blatant (conspicuous) symbol of divided Germany, having been built in 1961 to restrict free movement of people and ideas, the wall now lost its significance as a political, economic, and social barrier.

In 1989, the unhappiness and displeasure of East German citizens toward their government reached alarming proportions. During the summer months, thousands fled into **Czechoslovakia**, **Hungary**, and **Austria** in attempts to travel from these countries into West Germany. **Pro-democracy** demonstrations and confrontations with police broke out in **Leipzig** and other large cities. These actions forced the leader, Erich Honecker, to resign; **Gregor Gysi** replaced him. Gysi, in turn, was replaced by **Hans Modrow**, who suggested that some aspects of *capitalism* be introduced into East Germany. The ban on political parties was lifted, with new groups then challenging the Communists for control of the government and demanding free elections. In October, the celebration of East Germany's fortieth anniversary stirred little enthusiasm. Ironically, it provoked further antigovernment demonstrations. These were signs that historic events would soon occur. Less than a month later, on November 9, 1989, the hated Berlin Wall was opened! This was done by the East German authorities. Once a blatant (conspicuous) symbol of divided Germany, having been built in 1961 to restrict free movement of people and ideas, the wall now lost its significance as a political, economic, and social barrier. Throngs poured through the many openings in the wall, past the East German guards who previously would have prevented such movement by using force. It now seemed that the reunification process would be speeded along.

In March 1990, East Germany held it first-ever free and open elections. A government was chosen that promised to work for unity with West Germany. In

Young people removing concrete pipes from the Berlin Wall on December 22, 1989.

May, a series of crucial meetings, known as the **four-plus-two negotiations**, took place. These talks involved the four occupying powers (Britain, France, the Soviet Union, and the United States) plus the two German states. The delegates deliberated on the future of a united Germany. In July, an economic merger occurred when the West German mark became the unit of currency in East Germany. This meant that, even though the German people were still living in two separate nations, all Germans would use the same money. East Germans were allowed to move into West Germany; West German companies were permitted to set up capitalist-style businesses in East Germany.

A degree of economic unity had now been achieved, and the talks planning for political unity were continuing. Poland wanted to be included in the four-plus-two negotiations because it had suffered more from German occupation in World War II than any other European nation. Poland wanted assurance that a reunited Germany would respect Polish sovereignty and would not seek to retake any land given to Poland after the war. Specifically, Poland wanted to be sure that the Oder-Neisse boundary line between East Germany and Poland would remain intact. A promise to maintain this boundary was made by West German Chancellor Helmut Kohl in mid-1990, on the assumption that he would be the first head of a united German nation.

Unity talks proceeded now at a fast pace. The Big Four Allied nations of World War II agreed to end their status as occupiers. The talks culminated with the formal act of reunification on October 3, 1990. As that day began, at the stroke of midnight, near the Reichstag building in Berlin, a ringing sound came from a replica of the American Liberty Bell—a gift from the United States. The black, red, and gold flag of West Germany was raised as the flag of the reunited nation. The president of what up to that moment had been West Germany, **Richard von Weizsacker**, read a proclamation of unity. When he had finished, a crowd of more than one million sang the West German—now the national—anthem. They sang from the third stanza of what had been the prewar national anthem, the first verses of which had been banned in the postwar period.

> **Main Idea:**
> Poland wanted assurance that a reunited Germany would respect Polish sovereignty and would not seek to retake any land given to Poland after the war.

Divided for forty-five years, Germany was now reunited. Although the Germany of 1990, with a population of seventy-eight million, was now the largest nation in Western Europe, it was the smallest German nation in the 119 years since Bismarck had completed the first movement for unification.

The All-German Elections

In December 1990, the first all-German elections were held. The winners were the Christian Democratic Union (CDU) coalition party and its leader, Helmut Kohl. Kohl had campaigned on hopes for a new prosperity for all and a promise not to raise taxes to pay for reunification. By June 1991, however, the economic picture in the new Germany had darkened, and Kohl was forced to break his promises. Taxes had to be raised to finance the cost of reunification and to fight the economic depression that was engulfing the eastern part of the new nation. Many of the former Communist-state-controlled industries there had now closed down, leaving thousands unemployed. Untold numbers of these unemployed traveled westward, hoping to find jobs. This migration led to tensions between westerners and easterners. There has even been talk of a "wall in the head" that still divides the country.

> **Main Idea:**
> Kohl had campaigned on hopes for a new prosperity for all and a promise not to raise taxes to pay for reunification.

These predicaments caused trouble for Chancellor Kohl and his ruling coalition. Demonstrations were staged against him, with the CDU losing some local elections in 1991. Kohl was plagued by his hesitancy to send German soldiers to assist in the 1991 Persian Gulf War. In 1992–1993, he also faced domestic unrest that saw violence directed against new immigrants and long-time non-German residents in eastern Germany, as well as scattered outbreaks of anti-Semitism. As his popularity declined, that of the chief rival political party, the Socialist Democratic party (SDP), increased. Some commentators even predicted that the SDP would win control of the nation in the elections scheduled for 1994. They were wrong, as Kohl and the CDU emerged victorious. In light of this peaceful election, the world at the time had good reason to assume and hope that the two main postwar developments in Germany—its unity as a nation and its democratic structure—would continue into the twenty-first century. One unification change agreed to in 1994 was finally accomplished by 2000. This was the movement of the government from Bonn back to Berlin.

Entrance to the Reichstag (seat of the German Parliament). Photograph, 2001.

LINK TO TODAY
War Crimes Trials Held Once Again

It was after World War II, as we have seen in this chapter, that major War Crimes Trials were held in Germany and Japan. Certainly, the world hoped at the time that such judicial actions would never again be warranted nor needed. Sadly, these hopes were dashed as a result of atrocities occurring in the Balkan conflicts of the 1990s. (The history of these conflicts are described in Chapters 13 and 15 in this volume.) In 1993, the United Nations saw fit to create the International Criminal Tribunal for the Former Yugoslavia (ICTY). This was the first international war crimes court established since the prosecutions that took place in Nuremberg and Tokyo after World War II. The ICTY's initial charges and indictments were made in 1994, with full-scale trials beginning in 1996. Over the next ten years, as of summer 2006, according to ICTY documentation, indicted were "161 persons for serious violations of international humanitarian law in the territory of the former Yugoslavia." Among the charges, as was true in the post-World War II trials, were those of genocide and crimes against humanity. Information about the trials, even as they continued beyond 2006, can be obtained at this website: *http://www.un.org/icty/*.

CHAPTER SUMMARY

Over sixty years have passed since World War II. For the first time in this century, a generation of Europeans has grown up without being involved in warfare on the continent. This generation has benefited from the postwar peace. As its members move into leadership positions, it will try to learn from the past and to ensure the continued absence of war. Nevertheless, the impact and the memory of the Second World War linger, as two incidents in 1992 attest.

Early that year, a ceremony was held in London at the unveiling of a statue to Sir Arthur Harris. Known as "Bomber Harris," he was head of the British Bomber Command in World War II and directed the intensive bombing of the German city of Dresden in February 1945. This saturation bombing killed 135,000 people and is remembered to this day with horror by all Germans. Consequently, there was anger in Germany when the monument to Harris was dedicated. Upon learning that members of the British royal family had attended the dedication, a German newspaper in Munich protested the erection of the statue as "unnecessary and tasteless."

In September 1992, the German aerospace industry planned to celebrate in October the fiftieth anniversary of a major scientific achievement—the development of the V2 rocket. Development of this rocket at the German city of Peenemunde represented a tremendous breakthrough in space technology. The V2 could carry a warhead for a distance of 200 miles and reach an altitude between sixty and seventy miles. The V2 was unlike any previous weapon of

Main Idea:
The impact and the memory of the Second World War linger.

war and was used in German aerial attacks on British cities from 1942 to 1945. Almost three thousand people were killed in 1944 and 1945 alone. With memories of the V2 attacks, as well as the German bombings during the Battle of Britain, British protests about the upcoming October 1992 celebration spread. A strong voice of condemnation came from Winston S. Churchill, a member of the British Parliament and a grandson of the wartime prime minister. Even some Germans criticized the celebration, as it reminded them of the Nazi Era and the fact that the underground factories in Peenemunde had been built with slave labor. The celebration was ultimately canceled.

These incidents concerning the Harris statue and the V2 rocket are signs that the past is remembered. Another issue that has made headlines concerns Germany and its future. When the United Nations opened its forty-seventh session in September 1992, Germany's foreign minister let it be known that his nation would like a permanent seat on the Security Council. As we will see in the next chapter, the Security Council is a very powerful and prestigious group in the United Nations. Germany's request was based upon its strong economic position in world affairs. Ironically, its plea came just one day after Japan's foreign minister suggested that his nation be given a permanent seat on the same council. That the two major aggressors in World War II should, toward the end of the twentieth century, seek stature in a peacekeeping organization shows how much the world changed since 1945! We will now move on to learn about that organization and the ways that it functions.

> **Main Idea:**
> That the two major aggressors in World War II should, toward the end of the twentieth century, seek stature in a peacekeeping organization shows how much the world changed since 1945!

IMPORTANT PEOPLE, PLACES, AND TERMS

KEY TERMS

League of Nations	Open Door Policy	ultimatum
lebensraum	Siegfried line	V-J Day
Axis powers	imperialism	Manhattan Project
partition	collective security	superpowers
Munich Agreement	Maginot line	Cold War
aggression	armistice	decolonization
belligerent	collaborators	satellite nations
Third Reich	Wehrmacht	denazification
conscription	Big Three	Berlin Blockade
plebiscite	Battle of the Bulge	remilitarization
propaganda	isolationism	Battle of Britain
Molotov-Ribbentrop Pact	balance of power	War Crimes Trials
	radar	North Atlantic Treaty Organization (NATO)
Stimson Doctrine	Operation Barbarossa	
blitzkrieg	General Winter	Congress of Vienna
parity	V-E Day	four-plus-two negotiations
militarism	concentration camps	
nationalism	death camps	D-Day
racism	Holocaust	Atlantic Charter
appeasement	genocide	Spanish Civil War
anschluss	island hopping	

PEOPLE

Benito Mussolini	Hideki Tojo	Pietro Badoglio
Haile Selassie	Winston Churchill	Franklin D. Roosevelt
Francisco Franco	Philippe Pétain	Dwight D. Eisenhower
Adolf Hitler	Charles de Gaulle	Chiang Kai-shek
Neville Chamberlain	Georgi Zhukov	Hirohito
Edouard Daladier	Erwin Rommel	Albert Einstein
Joseph Stalin	Bernard Montgomery	Konrad Adenauer

PLACES

Germany	Poland	Midway Island
Japan	Manchuria	Guadalcanal
Washington	France	Danzig
London	Pearl Harbor	Polish corridor
United States	Dunkirk	Cairo
Czechoslovakia	Vichy	Tokyo
Ethiopia	Stalingrad	Potsdam
Rhineland	El Alamein	Hiroshima
Austria	The Balkans	Nagasaki
Spain	Paris	Iwo Jima
Sudetenland	Yalta	Nuremberg
Munich	Singapore	
Soviet Union	The Philippines	

CHAPTER 9

MULTIPLE-CHOICE QUESTIONS

Select the number of the correct answer.

1. The Axis nations were made up of

(1) Germany, Italy, and Russia
(2) U.S.S.R., Italy, and France
(3) Great Britain, Italy, and Spain
(4) Italy, Japan, and Germany

2. Which conference or pact most directly attempted to limit arms buildup after World War I?

(1) The Washington Conference
(2) The Treaty of Versailles
(3) Locarno Pact
(4) Kellogg-Briand Pact

3. The Munich Agreement of 1938 is an example of

(1) collective security
(2) appeasement
(3) ethnocentrism
(4) belligerent nation status

4. During the 1930s, which world leader directly aided Francisco Franco of Spain?

(1) Benito Mussolini
(2) Joseph Stalin
(3) Neville Chamberlain
(4) Franklin Roosevelt

5. The word *anschluss* specifically refers to the union of Nazi Germany with

(1) Japan   (3) Austria
(2) Italy   (4) U.S.S.R

6. Germany justified taking land beyond its own borders based on its claim of a need for *lebensraum*. This meant its need for

(1) military weapons
(2) seaports
(3) industrial development
(4) living space

7. In August 1939 Hitler surprised the world community by signing a nonaggression pact with

(1) Great Britain
(2) Czechoslovakia
(3) U.S.S.R.
(4) France

8. The specific event that caused the actual start of World War II in Europe was

(1) Japan's invasion of Manchuria
(2) The Molotov-Ribbentrop Pact
(3) The United States issuance of the Stimson Doctrine
(4) The German invasion of Poland

9. The specific event that caused the United States entry into World War II was

(1) the election of Hidecki Tojo as Prime Minister of Japan
(2) the Japanese attack on Pearl Harbor
(3) the formation of the Rome-Berlin-Tokyo Axis
(4) Japan's withdrawal from the League of Nations

10. To enable their march toward France, by May of 1940, Germany successfully occupied countries in which part of Europe?

(1) Northwest   (3) Southwest
(2) Southeast   (4) Northeast

11. The Vichy government headed by Marshal Pétain represented

(1) French citizens who were willing to work with the Nazi occupiers
(2) French resistance leaders
(3) sympathizers of democratic interests in France
(4) Frenchmen who escaped to Britain after the Dunkirk evacuation

12. "Never in the field of human conflict was so much owed by so many to so few."
—Winston Churchill

When Churchill spoke these words he was referring to

(1) the Munich Agreement
(2) the Battle of Britain
(3) Operation Barbarossa
(4) the Battle of Stalingrad

13. Which season of the year proved to be a help to the Russian army against the Germans just as it had been a help against the French about 130 years earlier?

(1) spring
(2) summer
(3) fall
(4) winter

14. Which country experienced a change of leadership during the war and also switched "sides"?

(1) Great Britain
(2) U.S.S.R.
(3) Italy
(4) United States

15. The Big Three were composed of which set of leaders?

(1) Hitler, de Gaulle, Mussolini
(2) Stalin, Churchill, Roosevelt
(3) Hirohito, Chaing Kai-shek, Pétain
(4) Franco, Churchill, Clemenceau

16. May 8, 1945, is known in history as V-E Day which stands for

(1) Victory in England Day
(2) Complete Victory for the Allies
(3) Victory in Europe Day
(4) Victory in the Pacific

17. President Truman justified the dropping of two atomic bombs on Japan on the fact that

(1) Japan bombed Pearl Harbor, Hawaii, first
(2) the Japanese continued to attack mainland China
(3) the United States possessed the bombs so that it made sense to use them
(4) he was unwilling to risk large numbers of American lives in a land invasion of Japan

18. During World War II the Manhattan Project was a code name for which event?

(1) the development by the United States of nuclear weapons
(2) the great sea invasion force that landed on the beaches of Normandy
(3) the surrender of the Japanese on the battleship *Missouri*
(4) the liberation of the Nazi-run concentration camps

19. War Crimes Trials were held at the end of World War II in an effort to

(1) blame all Germans for the miseries of the war
(2) force specific individuals responsible for the most violent of wartime actions to answer for their deeds
(3) show the defeated nations that no wars would be tolerated in the future
(4) bring the victorious nations together and to emphasize their powerful new role in world affairs

20. Place the following events in twentieth-century German history in correct chronological order:

A. Germany's reunification is completed.
B. Germany invades Poland.
C. The Berlin wall is torn down.
D. Germany is divided into four sectors.

(1) B, C, D, A
(2) C, B, A, D
(3) B, D, C, A
(4) D, B, A, C

THEMATIC ESSAY

Directions: Write a well-organized essay that includes an introduction, several paragraphs addressing the task below, and a conclusion.

Theme: Decision Making

When nations decide to begin wars and ultimately to try to end wars, decision making by a nation's leaders may impact many other nations.

Task

Using only the period of World War II, identify any two nations and/or leaders and for each

- identify the role played in either beginning, furthering, or ending World War II

- describe a national goal of each leader or country in the decision making process
- evaluate the ultimate success or failure of each goal

You may use any examples from your study of World War II *except* the United States. Some suggestions you might wish to consider include Benito Mussolini, Adolf Hitler, Joseph Stalin, Japan, and Great Britain.

You are *not* limited to these suggestions.

Guidelines

In your essay, be sure to

- develop all aspects of the *Task*
- support the theme with relevant facts, examples, and details
- use a logical and clear plan of organization, including an introduction and a conclusion that are beyond a restatement of the theme
- introduce the theme by establishing a framework that is beyond a simple restatement of the *Task* and conclude with a summation of the theme

DOCUMENT-BASED ESSAY QUESTION

This question is based on the accompanying documents (1–7). The question is designed to test your ability to work with historical documents. Some of these documents have been edited for the purposes of this question. As you analyze the documents, take into account the source of each document and any point of view that may be presented in the document.

Historical Context

World War II was a period of violent conflict between nations. There were great losses for both the aggressors and the victims, both the winners and the losers.

Task

Using information from the documents and your knowledge of global history, answer the questions that follow each document in Part A. Your answers to the questions will help you write the Part B essay in which you will be asked to

- identify at least two of the aggressor nations *and* two of the nations that were attacked during World War II
- describe two different situations where citizens of a nation under attack suffered
- discuss how at least two different world leaders reacted to developments during World War II
- develop at least one conclusion about the overall impact of World War II on humanity

Part A: Short-Answer Questions

Directions: Analyze the documents and answer the short-answer questions that follow each document.

Document 1

The guns did not make a constant overwhelming din as in those terrible days of September. They were intermittent—sometimes a few seconds apart, sometimes a minute or more. Their sound was sharp, near by; and soft and muffled, far away. They were everywhere over London.

Into the dark shadowed spaces below us, while we watched, whole batches of incendiary bombs fell. We saw two dozen go off in two seconds. They flashed terrifically, then quickly simmered down to pin points of dazzling white, burning ferociously. These white pin points would go out one by one, as the unseen heroes of the moment smothered them with sand. But also, while we watched, other pin points would burn on, and soon a yellow flame would leap up from the white center. They had done their work—another building was on fire.

The greatest of all the fires was directly in front of us. Flames seemed to whip hundreds of feet into the air. Pinkish-white smoke ballooned upward in a great cloud, and out of this cloud there gradually took shape—so faintly at first that we weren't sure we saw correctly—the gigantic dome of St. Paul's Cathedral.

Source: "The London Blitz, 1940," EyeWitness to History, www.eyewitnesstohistory.com (2001).

Question	**1.** What were two problems for citizens of London during the Blitz of 1940 as described by war correspondent Ernie Pyle?

Document 2

What follows is an excerpt from the Atlantic Charter of 1941:

Joint Statement by President Roosevelt and Prime Minister Churchill, August 14, 1941(1):

The following statement signed by the President of the United States and the Prime Minister of Great Britain is released for the information of the Press: The President of the United States of America and the Prime Minister, Mr. Churchill, representing His Majesty's Government in the United Kingdom, being met together, deem it right to make known certain common principles in the national policies of their respective countries on which they base their hopes for a better future for the world.

First, their countries seek no aggrandizement, territorial or other;

Second, they desire to see no territorial changes that do not accord with the freely expressed wishes of the peoples concerned;

Third, they respect the right of all peoples to choose the form of government under which they will live; and they wish to see sovereign rights and self government restored to those who have been forcibly deprived of them;

Fourth, they will endeavor, with due respect for their existing obligations, to further the enjoyment by all States, great or small, victor or vanquished, of access, on equal terms, to the trade and to the raw materials of the world which are needed for their economic prosperity;

Fifth, they desire to bring about the fullest collaboration between all nations in the economic field with the object of securing, for all, improved labor standards, economic advancement and social security;

Sixth, after the final destruction of the Nazi tyranny, they hope to see established a peace which will afford to all nations the means of dwelling in safety within their own boundaries, and which will afford assurance that all the men in all the lands may live out their lives in freedom from fear and want;

Seventh, such a peace should enable all men to traverse the high seas and oceans without hindrance;

Eighth, they believe that all of the nations of the world, for realistic as well as spiritual reasons must come to the abandonment of the use of force. Since no future peace can be maintained if land, sea or air armaments continue to be employed by nations which threaten, or may threaten, aggression outside of their frontiers, they believe, pending the establishment of a wider and permanent system of general security, that the disarmament of such nations is essential. They will likewise aid and encourage all other practicable measures which will lighten for peace-loving peoples the crushing burden of armaments.

Signed by: Franklin D. Roosevelt & Winston S. Churchill

Footnote: (1) The copy in the Department files is a press release which indicates signature by President Roosevelt and Prime Minister Churchill. Apparently, however, there was no signed copy.

| Questions | 2 a. What two world leaders signed the Atlantic Charter according to the excerpt above?
b. What is an economic goal that is specifically mentioned?
c. What specific enemy is identified in the excerpt? |

Document 3

Major Lozak, a staff officer in the Soviet Army:

"In those days there was something in a man's face which told you that he would die within the next twenty-four hours...I have lived in Leningrad all my life, and I also have my parents here.

They are old people, and during those famine months I had to give them half my officer's ration, or they would certainly have died. As a staff officer I was naturally, and quite rightly, getting considerably less than the people at the front: 250 grams a day instead of 350.

I shall always remember how I'd walk every day from my house near the Tauris Garden to my work in the centre of the city, a matter of two or three kilometres. I'd walk for awhile, and then sit down for a rest. Many a time I saw a man suddenly collapse on the snow. There was nothing I could do. One just walked on. And, on the way back, I would see a vague human form covered with snow on the spot where, in the morning, I had seen a man fall down.

One didn't worry; what was the good? People didn't wash for weeks; there were no bath houses and no fuel. But at least people were urged to shave. And during that winter I don't think I ever saw a person smile. It was frightful. And yet there was a kind of inner discipline that made people carry on. A new code of manners was evolved by the hungry people. They carefully avoided talking about food. I remember spending a very hungry evening with an old boy from the Radio Committee. He nearly drove me crazy—he would talk all evening about Kant and Hegel. Yet we never lost heart. The Battle of Moscow gave us complete confidence that it would be all right in the end. But what a change all the same when February came and the Ice Road began to function properly!"

Source: "The Siege of Leningrad, 1941–1944" EyeWitness to History, www.eyewitnesstohistory.com (2006).

Question

3. Using Major Lozak's statement, identify three conditions of life in Leningrad during the Siege.

Document 4

Questions

4. a. Who is the cartoonist showing as "marching across Europe"?
b. Identify one county this person has "marched over."

Document 5

"Never, never, never believe any war will be smooth and easy, or that anyone who embarks on the strange voyage can measure the tides and hurricanes he will encounter. The statesman who yields to war fever must realize that once the signal is given, he is no longer the master of policy but the slave of unforeseeable and uncontrollable events."

—Sir Winston Churchill

Question

5. What warning is Winston Churchill giving about beginning a war?

Sources:
Gregory Frumkin,
Population Changes in Europe Since 1939 (European estimates)

B. Urlanis, **Wars and Population** (Soviet Union and the Far East)

Singer and Small, **Wages of War** (the Americas and Ethiopia)

I.C.B. Dear, editor, **The Oxford Companion to World War II** (British Commonwealth)

AXIS	MILITARY	CIVILIAN	TOTAL
Germany	3,500,000	700,000	4,200,000
Japan	2,000,000	350,000	2,350,000
Romania	300,000	160,000	460,000
Hungary	140,000	290,000	430,000
Italy	330,000	80,000	410,000
Austria	230,000	104,000	334,000
Finland	82,000	2,000	84,000
Axis Total	**6,582,000**	**1,686,000**	**8,268,000**

ALLIED	MILITARY	CIVILIAN	TOTAL
Soviet Union	10,000,000	10,000,000*	20,000,000
China	2,500,000	7,500,000	10,000,000
Poland	100,000	5,700,000	5,800,000
Yugoslavia	300,000	1,400,000	1,700,000
France	250,000	350,000	600,000
Czechoslovakia	200,000	215,000	415,000
United States	400,000	—	400,000
United Kingdom (England, Scotland, Wales, and Northern Ireland)	326,000	62,000	388,000
Allied Total	**14,076,000**	**25,227,000**	**39,303,000**

*The majority of Soviet Union civilian casualties were Ukrainian.

Questions

6. Use the chart above, Estimated War Dead, World War II, to answer the following questions:
   a. What Axis nation lost the largest total number of people?
   b. What Allied nation lost the largest total number of people?
   c. Identify any Allied nation that had fewer military deaths than the United States.

Document 7

Press release by the White House, August 6, 1945

THE WHITE HOUSE
Washington, D.C.

IMMEDIATE RELEASE

STATEMENT BY THE PRESIDENT OF THE UNITED STATES

Sixteen hours ago an American airplane dropped one bomb on _____ and destroyed its usefulness to the enemy. That bomb had more power than 20,000 tons of T.N.T.; it had more than two thousand times the blast power of the British "Grand Slam" which is the largest bomb ever yet used in the history of warfare.

The Japanese began the war from the air at Pearl Harbor. They have been repaid many fold. And the end is not yet. With this bomb we have now added a new and revolutionary increase in destruction to supplement the growing power of our armed forces. In their present form these bombs are now in production and even more powerful forms are in development.

It is an atomic bomb. It is a harnessing of the basic power of the universe. The force from which the sun draws its power has been loosed against those who brought war to the Far East.

We are now prepared to obliterate more rapidly and completely every productive enterprise the Japanese have above ground in any city. We shall destroy their docks, their factories, and their communications. Let there be no mistake; we shall completely destroy Japan's power to make war.

Questions	7. a. What does the excerpt from the White House Press release of August 6, 1945 state about the specific power of the bomb that had been dropped?
	b. Why does the White House blame Japan for what happened?
	c. What does the President now intend to do to Japan according to the press release?

Part B: Essay

Directions: Write a well-organized essay that includes an introduction, several paragraphs, and a conclusion. Use evidence from *at least four* documents in the body of the essay. Support your response with relevant facts, examples, and details. Include additional outside information.

Historical Context

World War II was a period of violent conflict between nations. There were great losses for both the aggressors and the victims, both the winners and the losers.

Task

Using information from the documents and your knowledge of global history, answer the questions that follow each document in Part A. Your answers to the questions will help you write the Part B essay in which you will be asked to

- identify at least two of the aggressor nations and two of the nations that were attacked during World War II
- describe two different situations where citizens of a nation under attack suffered
- discuss how at least two different world leaders reacted to developments during World War II
- develop at least one conclusion about the overall impact of World War II on humanity

Guidelines

In your essay, be sure to

- address all aspects of the *Task* by analyzing and interpreting *at least four* documents
- incorporate information from the documents in the body of the essay
- incorporate relevant outside information
- support the theme with relevant facts, examples, and details
- use a logical and clear plan of organization
- introduce the theme by establishing a framework that is beyond a simple restatement of the *Task* or *Historical Context* and conclude with a summation of the theme

CHAPTER 10

The United Nations and Postwar Western Europe

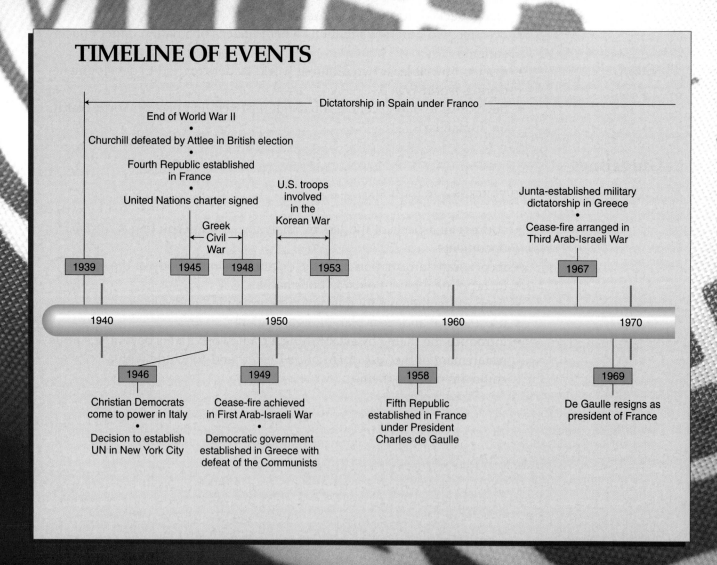

TIMELINE OF EVENTS

Dictatorship in Spain under Franco

End of World War II

Churchill defeated by Attlee in British election

Fourth Republic established in France

United Nations charter signed

Greek Civil War

U.S. troops involved in the Korean War

Junta-established military dictatorship in Greece

Cease-fire arranged in Third Arab-Israeli War

| 1939 | | 1945 | 1948 | | 1953 | | | 1967 | |

1940   1950   1960   1970

1946

Christian Democrats come to power in Italy

Decision to establish UN in New York City

1949

Cease-fire achieved in First Arab-Israeli War

Democratic government established in Greece with defeat of the Communists

1958

Fifth Republic established in France under President Charles de Gaulle

1969

De Gaulle resigns as president of France

We will look at two different themes in this chapter during the period between 1945 and 2000. For our first theme, we will view the development of the United Nations. It came into being as a result of World War II. The founders hoped that this body would be a more effective world forum than the League of Nations was and that it would be able to settle international differences before a major war started. They hoped also that certain reasons for war would be eliminated. From 1945 until 2000, there were a number of localized wars but no global conflicts such as World Wars I and II. Can the United Nations take credit for this situation?

In the second half of the chapter, we will trace the development of certain nations in Western Europe from 1945 until 2000. The devastation caused by World War II was enormous. The people involved in the conflict had to rebuild their lives and their nations. They had to do this with the threat of Soviet domination hanging over them. With the aid and protection of the United Nations, each proceeded along its own path to develop a sound political and economic system.

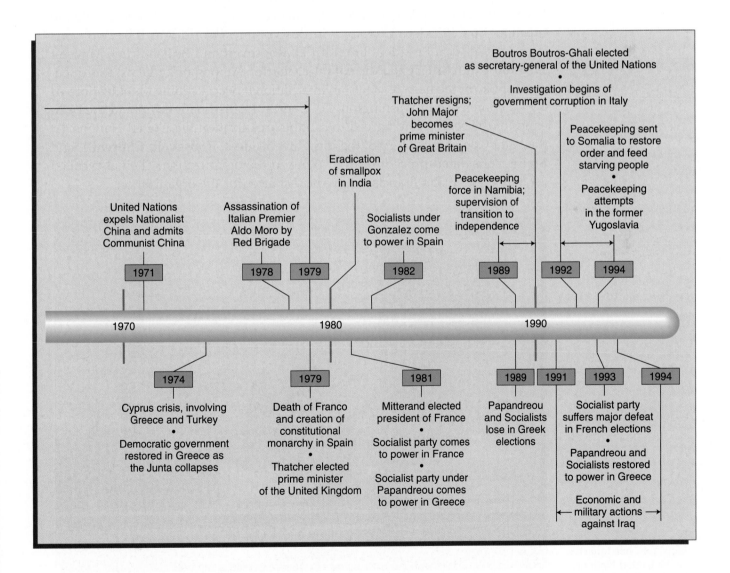

THE UNITED NATIONS

The year 1945 is very significant in the history of our planet. It marks the end of World War II, which may have been the war that ended all wars. It also marks the birth of the United Nations (UN). The fact that, from 1945 until 2000, there were no large-scale global wars such as World War II is due in part, but not solely, to the work of this organization. Although the United Nations has not always been able to prevent conflicts, it has had some success in bringing them to a halt and in curbing aggressive tendencies. Examples have been the Arab-Israeli wars, the Korean War, and the Persian Gulf War. Today, almost all the world's nations are members of the United Nations. They look to that organization as a place to attempt to settle disputes as well as a source of help in solving difficult social and economic problems.

Historical Background

The League of Nations, founded after World War I, was the predecessor of the United Nations. The League proved, however, to be very weak, and it failed to function after 1939 (see Chapter 9 in this volume "World War II"). Two years later, in 1941, U.S. President **Franklin D. Roosevelt** and British Prime Minister **Winston Churchill** signed the **Atlantic Charter**. Among other items, this document spoke of the need to create an international peacekeeping organization. At a 1942 conference in Washington, D.C., several Allied nations upheld the principles of the charter and agreed to call the organization the United Nations. At the Yalta Conference of 1945, the Big Three leaders, **Roosevelt**, **Churchill**, and **Stalin**, considered procedures for voting in the organization. They also called for a meeting in San Francisco to write a charter for the organization.

New York headquarters of the United Nations.

At the San Francisco Conference, held from April to June 1945, delegates from fifty nations drafted the UN charter. The same year, in sharp contrast to its refusal to join the League of Nations in 1920, the United States became the very first nation to approve the UN charter. This contrast reflected a change in American foreign policy from isolationism to internationalism. In addition, the United States consented to the establishment of UN headquarters in **New York City**. The UN came into actual existence on October 24, 1945, and October 24 has since been recognized as United Nations Day.

Purposes and Organizational Structure

The general purposes of the **United Nations** are stated in its charter: to maintain peace and to construct friendly relations among nations. In addition, the organization has these specific goals:

1. To put down acts of **aggression** by using collective force
2. To encourage respect for human rights
3. To improve social and economic conditions through international cooperation

In order to achieve these noble aims, the United Nations is organized into six major bodies and several specialized agencies.

The General Assembly

> **Main Idea:**
> The General Assembly considers international problems and can make recommendations to other UN bodies.

The **General Assembly** consists of all member nations, the total having reached 191 by 2006. Each member has one vote. The General Assembly meets once a year for about three months, starting in September. On occasion, it can be called into special session. It considers international problems and can make recommendations to other UN bodies. Although most matters are decided by a majority vote, on issues considered to be "important questions" a two-thirds vote is required for any decision. The General Assembly elects the secretary-general and other heads of the various UN bodies. It also determines the UN budget and spreads the expenses among the member nations. Also, it has the power to admit and expel members. For example, in 1971 the Communist People's Republic of China, which was in control of mainland China, was admitted to take the UN seat previously held by the Nationalist Republic of China, which controlled only Taiwan. In 1992, Yugoslavia was expelled because of the bitter fighting in that former country. Prior to Yugoslavia's expulsion, General Assembly membership had reached an all-time high of 179 nations.

In its early years, the General Assembly was dominated mostly by northern hemisphere nations; the **Western bloc** (the United States and allies) and the **Soviet bloc** (the U.S.S.R. and allies). By the mid-1990s, however, the General Assembly's configuration has now shifted dramatically. With the end of the Soviet Union and the collapse of communism in many parts of the world, the Soviet bloc ceased to exist. In fact, the majority power in the General Assembly today rests with the nations of Africa, Asia, and Latin America, lying primarily in the southern hemisphere and containing most of the world's population. This

Third World bloc consists of several nations that were colonies at the time the United Nations was founded. Although they do not always vote together on issues, their combined strength would account for more than 120 votes.

The Security Council

The **Security Council** has fifteen members. Five are permanent; the remaining ten are nonpermanent. The 1945 UN charter listed the five permanent members as the **United States, Great Britain, France,** the **U.S.S.R.,** and **China**. These **Big Five** were the original Security Council permanent members because they had been the chief victorious Allies in World War II. Since that time, two significant changes have occurred among these five members. In 1971, as stated in the preceding section, the China seat was given to the People's Republic of China. In January 1992, as a result of the dissolution (breakup) of the U.S.S.R., its seat was given to Russia. Further changes may take place in the twenty-first century, as Germany and Japan have indicated a desire to sit on the Security Council. In addition, some Third World members have begun to question whether Britain and France should be allowed to retain their memberships on the Council. That such changes should even be considered shows how much the world has evolved between the end of World War II in 1945 and today. During that time, Germany and Japan have risen from war-torn devastation to become major economic powers. Ironically, Britain and France have declined from the major status they once held.

> **Main Idea:**
> The Security Council functions as the UN's executive body.

The Council's ten nonpermanent members are elected by the General Assembly for a two-year term. They can be reelected, but not immediately after completing a term.

The Security Council functions as the UN's executive body. This means that it can do the following:

1. Investigate problems
2. Take action to maintain international peace (e.g., it has the power to call for UN members to take measures, military or economic, against an aggressor nation or nations)

The council meets continuously in order to resolve serious international disputes. It cannot, however, force members to agree with its decisions. Resolutions for action in the Security Council require nine votes, including the votes of all five permanent members. Therefore, each permanent member has veto power over Security Council proposals.

The Secretariat

The **Secretariat** is the organization responsible for all the administrative work of the United Nations. With a staff of several thousand workers, including experts and advisers, it assists in carrying out the decisions reached by the Security Council and the General Assembly. The head of the Secretariat, who is the most important UN official, has the title of **Secretary-General**. He or she is nominated by the Security Council, is voted on by the General Assembly for a five-year term, and can be reelected immediately. The secretary-general presents an annual report on UN activities to the General Assembly and attends all its meetings, as well as all meetings of the Security Council. He or she can act as a mediator in crises and is often assigned specific diplomatic activities. Eight people have served in this post:

1. **Trygve Lie** of Norway (1946–1953)
2. **Dag Hammarskjold** of Sweden (1953–1961)
3. **U Thant** of Burma (1961–1971)
4. **Kurt Waldheim** of Austria (1972–1981)
5. **Javier Perez de Cuellar** of Peru (1981–1992)
6. **Boutros Boutros-Ghali** of Egypt (1992–1997)
7. **Kofi Annan** of Ghana (1997–2006)
8. **Ban Ki-moon** of South Korea (2007–)

These individuals, like all other people who work in the Secretariat, act as international civil servants. They are not to take partisan, self-interested roles as representatives of their home nations, but rather to function as neutral figures in fulfilling the goals of the UN charter. This is the primary reason why each of the secretaries-general in UN history was chosen from a nation that was not directly allied with either of the Cold War superpowers. Indeed, Boutros-Ghali's election was meaningful in that he was the first secretary-general from the Arab world as well as from the continent of Africa.

The International Court of Justice

The **International Court of Justice** considers questions of international law. The fifteen judges, coming from different nations, decide cases by a majority vote. Countries that consent to have the International Court hear a case must agree in advance to accept its decision.

The Trusteeship Council

The Trusteeship Council was created to control and safeguard areas under UN trust or supervision. Such areas at times may have contained colonial people or may have been in transition from colonial rule to independence. In recent years, some Western Pacific islands have been under administration by the Trusteeship Council. The five Security Council members make up the Trusteeship Council.

The Economic and Social Council

The fifty-four members of the Economic and Social Council (ECOSOC) are elected by the General Assembly and serve for three years. They are concerned with achieving progress in economic, social, cultural, and health-related conditions. This organization works with groups such as the UN Commission on Human Rights to improve the status of people whose poor standard of living may lead to tension and wars.

The Specialized Agencies

The specialized agencies are bodies in the United Nations that carry out specific social and economic tasks. Six of these agencies are as follows:

1. UNESCO (United Nations Educational, Scientific, and Cultural Organization)
2. WHO (World Health Organization)
3. FAO (Food and Agriculture Organization)
4. UNICEF (United Nations International Children's Fund)
5. The World Bank (also known as the Bank for Reconstruction and Development)
6. The IAEA (International Atomic Energy Agency)

Successes and Failures of the United Nations

The United Nations has been more successful in dealing with social and economic issues than with political issues. Examples of success can be seen in eliminating smallpox, fighting famines, protecting the environment, and drawing attention to women's rights and the status of young children. In October 1993, for example, the United Nations reported that it had made significant progress in meeting health goals, such as immunization programs.

On political matters, the United Nations has had mixed results. Most of its effectiveness has been due to U.S. involvement. Six examples of positive actions are the following:

> **Main Idea:**
> The United Nations is not, and was not set up to be, a world government.

1. Imposing economic sanctions against Rhodesia (1966) and Iraq (1990–1994)
2. Pursuing armed intervention in the Korean War (1950–1953) and the Persian Gulf War (1991)
3. Sending peacekeeping units to Lebanon (1980s), Arab-Israeli borders (1949, 1973), and Cyprus (1963)
4. Overseeing the transition to independence in Namibia (1989–1990)
5. Supervising free elections in Angola (1992)
6. Sending a peacekeeping force to restore order and feed starving people in Somalia (1992–1994)

In other instances, however, UN decisions and resolutions have been disobeyed or defied. Here are six examples of nations that flouted UN resolutions:

1. Arab nations by attacking Israel (1948)
2. The U.S.S.R. by refusing to remove troops from Hungary (1956) and Afghanistan (1979–1980)
3. India by not honoring a cease-fire in its war with Pakistan (1971–1972)
4. Israel by annexing the Golan Heights (1981)
5. Iraq and North Korea by interfering with UN nuclear weapons inspectors (1991–1994)

Both proponents and critics of the United Nations recognize some of its limitations. It does not have its own military force and must depend on requests for help from member nations. It has a huge budget and often runs short of money when some members refuse to pay assessed expenses. Countries may simply refuse to heed UN resolutions and decisions when these conflict with what the parties involved perceive to be their own national interests. During the Cold War, the two major superpowers bypassed the United Nations or otherwise frustrated UN policy attempts when they so wished.

Nevertheless, it is important to remember that the United Nations is not, and was not set up to be, a world government. Rather, it serves as a place where crucial world issues can be raised and discussed. Nations and individuals come to it when in need, valuing its role as a forum and its influence on public opinion. Ultimately, it will be effective to the extent that its member nations want it to be.

POSTWAR WESTERN EUROPE

World War II left Western Europe devastated. The devastation was physical, economic, and emotional. The combined problems of rebuilding shattered nations and meeting the threat of Soviet domination from Eastern Europe made the task of preserving a stable democratic order even more difficult. Although economic, technical, and military assistance from the United States was a great help, the new Western European governments had to face strong opposition from the many left-wing (pro-Socialist/Communist) political parties that sprang up. The creation of the **North Atlantic Treaty Organization (NATO)** and the constant threat of military, possibly nuclear, confrontation with the U.S.S.R. made the task of political reconstruction even more challenging. All Western European nations had to face this complication, and each had to first tackle its own particular domestic political and economic problems.

Great Britain

After World War II, Great Britain had the dual problem of rebuilding an exhausted economy while dismantling its vast empire. This was exceedingly difficult because those colonial possessions had been vital sources of that island's great wealth in the nineteenth and early twentieth centuries. In addition, Britain had been willing to accept many immigrants from those possessions. They came from such diverse areas as East Africa, Southeast Asia, and the West Indies, seeking economic improvement or fleeing the chaos that independence had brought to their native lands. In some instances, these migrants added an even greater burden to an already weak economy.

Movement Toward a Welfare State

The elections in 1945 led to the replacement of Winston Churchill's Conservative Party wartime coalition with a liberal Labour Party government led by Clement Attlee. The conservatives lost because of voter concern with the economy, which was rapidly deteriorating. It was this new administration that negotiated the **partition** of India in 1947 and began a process of **decolonization** that removed Britain's primary source of wealth. The result was a reduction of the military, further contributing to the mass unemployment created after the war.

Domestically, the Labour government followed a policy of **socialism** that made Britain a welfare state, that is, a political system in which a government provides for the total care of its citizens. In the belief that the economy could not be dependent on **capitalism**, the Bank of England, coal mines, gas and electric companies, and the iron and steel industries were **nationalized** (put under the control of the government). However, as most British industries were still privately owned, a mixed economy (combination of socialism and capitalism) was created. The Labour government also extended insurance coverage for unemployment, old age, and sickness and set up a national health care program to provide free medical treatment for all Britons. These extensive reforms, however, necessitated a sharp increase in taxation, and the high cost for these social programs resulted in popular dissatisfaction and the Labour Party's loss to the Conservatives in the 1951 elections.

The Conservative government, which remained in power until 1964, restored some industries to private control and modified the health insurance program. Nevertheless, the cost of maintaining the welfare state was a further strain on the British economy, which was having great difficulty rebuilding because of the loss of its colonies and the competition in its domestic market from American and Japanese products. Inflation and the rise of trade unions demanding higher wages for workers also contributed to the problem. From 1964 to 1979, alternating Conservative and Labour governments were unable to create a strong and stable economy.

Thatcher and Major Move Away from the Welfare State

Margaret Thatcher (1925–), English politician and prime minister from 1979–1990. Photographed at the wheel of the "Melita," August 17, 1975.

In 1979, a Conservative government led by **Margaret Thatcher**, Britain's first woman prime minister, began a program of radically reducing the **welfare state**. This policy, known as Thatcherism, restricted the power of unions, cut government spending, lowered taxes, dismantled many welfare programs, and returned a number of industries to private ownership. Although these measures improved the growth of the British economy, they could not reduce the high rate of unemployment that had long been a great problem for many Britons. It was, however, Thatcher's opposition to increased British participation in the **European Community** that led to a split in the Conservative Party and her resignation in 1990. Her successor as Prime Minister, **John Major**, continued her domestic policies, but supported a role for Britain in the movement for European unity. Narrowly winning the 1992 elections, the Major government faced continued economic problems and strong opposition from both the Labour Party and extremely nationalist Conservatives.

France

After the collapse of the Nazi-controlled Vichy government and the liberation of France in 1945, a democratic coalition government was established under the presidency of General **Charles**

Charles de Gaulle (1890–1970),
French soldier and statesman.

de Gaulle. The new government, known as the *Fourth Republic*, consisted of three leftist parties: the Socialists, the Communists, and the Popular Republic Movement (MRP), which was a Roman Catholic progressive (favoring reform) party. The *Fourth Republic* was, however, politically divided and ineffective. Disgusted with the disunity and angry over the lack of power of the presidency, de Gaulle resigned in 1946. In 1947, the Communists were expelled from the coalition government after they had encouraged a series of strikes.

The Fall of the Fourth Republic

Although the Socialists and the MRPs remained divided over many issues (there were twenty-five different cabinets between 1946 and 1958), they did manage to create a mixed economy. Despite the political instability, the French economy grew. It was the strain of trying to maintain the old colonial empire that eventually caused the downfall of the *Fourth Republic*. After twelve years of unsuccessful fighting to preserve French possessions in North Africa and Southeast Asia, popular dissatisfaction with the Fourth Republic led to civil unrest. Amid fears of a complete breakdown of order, a new government was formed in 1958 under the leadership of de Gaulle.

The Fifth Republic

The *Fifth Republic*, as the new administration was called, gave President de Gaulle final authority over foreign policy and national defense, as well as the right to name the prime minister, dissolve the National Assembly, call for new elections, and assume emergency powers. This new arrangement reflected the popular anger over the disunity and instability of leadership in the Fourth Republic. De Gaulle ruled until 1969, restoring political stability and creating economic prosperity. He settled the colonial question by granting independence to all former French possessions. By 1960, France had become a nuclear nation as well. In 1968, however, student riots and strikes by workers devastated the French economy. Despite an overwhelming victory by de Gaulle in the 1969 elections, voter rejection of reforms later in that year led to his resignation.

Socialism Under Mitterand

De Gaulle's successors, **Georges Pompidou** and **Valery Giscard d'Estaing**, concentrated on building up the French economy and industry. The worldwide economic crisis of the 1970s crippled these efforts. In 1981, a Socialist government under **Francois Mitterand** was elected. Mitterand nationalized major industries and banks as well as increased taxes for new social programs. Those measures, however, created high inflation and forced Mitterand to cut spending, resulting in popular discontent. Support for increased participation in the European Community further hurt the government, resulting in a Socialist Party defeat in the 1993 elections. Opposition to a greater French role in the movement for European unity, especially from farmers, will present future governments with great challenges.

Italy

Modern-day Italy

The fall of the Italian fascist government in 1943 resulted, as in France, in the rise of leftist parties. In the 1946 elections the nations narrowly voted to abolish the *monarchy* and establish a *democracy*. Despite strong showings by the Socialists and Communists, the Christian Democrats emerged as the dominant party under the leadership of **Alcide de Gaspari**. Under a series of coalition governments, Italy's economy was rebuilt and expanded. Despite strong opposition by the Communists, who were excluded from the government in 1947, the Christian Democrats continued to lead coalitions after de Gaspari's retirement in 1953. There was, however, division within the party after its leader left.

Terrorism in Italy

In the 1960s, the Socialists and Communists gained strength. Although the leftist parties often won election to local positions, the Christian Democrats continued to control the national government. Italy's economy, which had grown until this time, experienced a slowdown because of high inflation and strikes by trade unions. The result was a period of political and economic instability. Adding to Italy's problems was the rise of **terrorism** in the 1970s by a leftist group known as the Red Brigade. This crisis reached its height with the assassination of former Prime Minister **Aldo Moro** in 1978. By the 1980s the terrorist activities had subsided as a result of strong countermeasures by the Italian government.

The War on Organized Crime

The 1980s and 1990s brought new political instability as the government mounted an attack on organized crime. Known as the Mafia, organized crime became the target of public criticism especially in regard to its influence over both local and national government. This situation forced the Italian political leadership to take legal and military action against leading criminal figures. Despite attempts by crime bosses to intimidate and assassinate government officials, the government has had some success in limiting the Mafia's power.

Criticism of Government Corruption

Despite many elections and changes of leadership in Italy since World War II, little changed in the way the Italian government operated. During the 1990s public criticism of the traditional corruption in government resulted in scandals that created further political instability. Committed to increased participation in the European Community, the Italian government faces great challenges from both internal criticism of traditional problems and a changing world economy. The 1994 elections saw the dominance of a coalition of right-wing parties, including a few Neo-Fascists, under a new prime minister, **Silvio Berlusconi**.

Greece

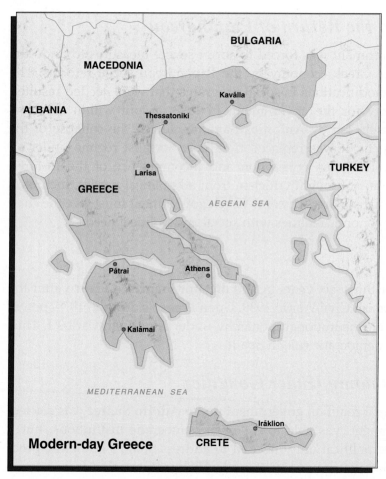

Modern-day Greece

Following World War II, Soviet-supported Greek guerillas attempted to overthrow the constitutional monarchy and establish a Communist regime in Greece. After the devastating civil war in 1945–1948, the Greek government faced both economic and political challenges. The Greek constitutional monarchy, led by a Conservative government, made great economic progress during the 1950s. By 1967, however, popular dissatisfaction with the traditional corruption in the Greek government and the rise of leftist parties had led to the overthrow of the monarchy, exile of the king, and establishment of a dictatorship by a group of generals in 1967.

Greece Under the Junta

The **Junta**, as the military regime became known, brought economic growth and internal stability to the nation. In 1974, however, it became involved in an unsuccessful attempt to reunite the predominantly Greek island of **Cyprus** with Greece through a military invasion. This resulted in a counterinvasion by **Turkey**, in which that nation took over 40 percent of the island, massacring and displacing much of the Greek population in the name of the Cypriot Turkish minority. The corrupt Junta, having sold much of its arms to foreign powers, was unable to mount an adequate military response. The Cyprus debacle resulted in the collapse of the military regime and the restoration of a democratic government under the conservative New Democracy party led by **Konstantinos Karamanlis**.

Karamanlis and Papandreou

Under Karamanlis, Greece enjoyed new economic growth and political stability. In 1981, the nation joined the European Community. Greece's lack of social programs and the traditional government corruption led, however, to the election of a Socialist government under **Andreas Papandreou** later that year. The Socialists nationalized key industries and created a social welfare program. Fearing popular discontent if taxes increased, Papandreou illegally used European Community funds intended for building Greek industry to offset the costs of his social reforms. This action led to charges of corruption that toppled his government in 1989. A new government was formed by the New Democracy party under **Konstantinos Mitsotakis**.

The Reforms of Mitsotakis and the Return of Papandreou

The Mitsotakis government was forced to adopt severe measures to undo the damage done to the Greek economy by the Papandreou social reforms. The spending cuts and modifications in social programs that were needed resulted in great unpopularity for the government. In 1993, a split within the New Democracy Party itself, led by **Antonios Samaras**, forced the collapse of the Mitsotakis government. It was replaced by a new Socialist regime under an aging Papandreou. The open corruption and incompetence of the restored Papandreou government brought criticism from all political parties, including many within the Socialist Party. The new Greek government must face the challenge of balancing economic realities with social and political needs.

Spain

Spain was ruled for thirty-six years by the **dictator Francisco Franco** after the fascists won the Spanish Civil War in 1939. Upon Franco's death in 1979, power was transferred to a constitutional monarchy under King Juan Carlos I. Thus began a new era of democratic rule in Spain.

Spain's Success as a Mixed Economy Under Gonzalez

In the 1975 elections, a coalition government under **Adolfo Suarez** was elected. The Suarez government was able to establish democratic institutions, but it could not create the political unity needed to address Spain's economic problems. In 1982, a Socialist government under **Felipe Gonzalez** was elected. Establishing a mixed economy, the Gonzalez government was able to balance the creation of a social welfare system with a market economy. Spain's entrance into the European Community in 1986 further strengthened the growth of the Spanish economy. In fact, Spain's economic strategy was so successful that it was viewed as a model by many Eastern European nations after the collapse of communism in 1989.

Terrorism and Basque Independence

A major problem faced by the Spanish government has been terrorism by the **Basques**, an ethnic group in Spain fighting for independence. Despite attempts by King Juan Carlos to grant measures of Basque self-rule, separatist extremists have continued attacks against both government officials and civilians.

Challenges for the Spanish Government

Despite this problem, the economic recovery of Spain has helped that nation to become a force on the European scene, as became evident when Spain was selected as the site of the 1992 Olympic Games. Nevertheless, challenges still face the Spanish government, both in dealing with internal problems and in connection with its increased participation in the European Community.

The rise of European unity and the collapse of communism have changed the goals of European governments. As the Cold War becomes a memory, new challenges await the nations of both Western and Eastern Europe. Experiments with socialism have left many people skeptical about the modern welfare state. Yet, with the growing concern over population size, economic growth, and environmental pollution, the role of government in solving these problems cannot be ignored. Discontent with traditional corruption in many European governments has created a movement for reform. Finally, the role of each nation in the new European Community, which now includes some nations of Eastern Europe, must be determined. The growing *nationalism* within many countries may prove a formidable (causing doubt or fear) obstacle to this goal. However, the transformation of most Western European nations from imperial powers to individual countries had made unity an economic necessity. In short, at the beginning of the twenty-first century, the nations of Europe are discovering new possibilities and facing new problems.

LINK TO TODAY
Diplomacy, Safety, and Gridlock

A nation's top diplomat is its leader or head of state. That person could be called by one of several names: president, prime minister, chancellor, and so on. When that person travels in a city, he or she usually has advisers and bodyguards and one or more cars. Traffic would often come to a halt as he or she passes. Can you imagine what would happen if several leaders were in one city at the same time for a few days? Well, if you were in New York City last September, or in any given September, you would not have to imagine. September is the month when the UN officially opens its sessions each year. Consequently, many heads of state come to address the General Assembly. September 2007, for example, witnessed scores of government leaders who traveled to New York City. While there, they traveled around the city, shopped, went to restaurants, stayed in hotels, and did the kinds of things that any visitor to "The Big Apple" might do. What did New Yorkers think of all this? Reactions were mixed. Most people felt pride in knowing that their city was of such global importance. Owners of hotels, restaurants, gift and clothing stores, and the like beamed happily as they knew that their businesses would greatly prosper. Also, during this time,

New York City was probably one of the safest places on earth. This was due to the heavy security presence provided by the local police department, national guard, FBI personnel, and private bodyguards. Dignitaries were made to feel comfortable and at ease, even if this meant redirecting of traffic and closing off streets, roadways, buildings, and other places. Yet, the result of all this was massive gridlock. People in cars, trucks, and buses could not travel easily along their accustomed routes. They also needed extra time to reach their destinations. Such was the price to pay for New York to be the site of the United Nations and to be considered "the capital of the world."

CHAPTER SUMMARY

Obviously, the United Nations has not lived up to all that its founders expected. In certain political situations, it has been unsuccessful, but in others there has been a degree of accomplishment. In the humanitarian area, the United Nations has brought hope to many parts of the world by fighting disease and hunger. Peacekeeping forces have kept small conflicts from getting larger. The organization also remains an important forum for the discussion of world issues. Without real police power, however, it will be only as effective as its members want it to be. How would you evaluate the United Nations?

Despite the seeming removal of the threat of Soviet domination, the Western European community still faces problems of expanding populations, inadequate economic growth, and environmental pollution. What should be the role of government in attempting to solve these problems? Even though there are forces within each nation moving the UN toward a real "community" of states, a nationalistic spirit still exists. Since it is obvious that a return to the "good old days" of imperialism is not possible, each nation must find a new role for itself in a new world.

IMPORTANT PEOPLE, PLACES, AND TERMS

KEY TERMS

Atlantic Charter	Secretariat	capitalism
United Nations	Secretary-General	nationalization
aggression	International Court of	welfare state
General Assembly	Justice	European Community
Western bloc	NATO	terrorism
Soviet bloc	partition	Junta
Security Council	decolonization	dictator
Big Five	socialism	Basques

PEOPLE

Franklin D. Roosevelt	Trygve Lie	Margaret Thatcher
Winston Churchill	Kofi Annan	King Juan Carlos I
Joseph Stalin	Ban Ki-moon	

PLACES

Yalta	France	Greece
San Francisco	U.S.S.R.	Cyprus
New York City	China	Turkey
United States	Norway	Italy
Great Britain	Ghana	Spain

CHAPTER 10

MULTIPLE-CHOICE QUESTIONS

Select the number of the correct answer.

1. After World War I, the United States refused to join the League of Nations. After World War II, the United States was a leader in organizing the United Nations. These statements illustrate the change in American foreign policy from

   (1) colonialism to imperialism
   (2) militarism to nationalism
   (3) ethnocentrism to patriotism
   (4) isolationism to internationalism

2. Why is it sometimes difficult for the Security Council of the United Nations to take action on a particular issue?

   (1) The General Assembly must approve all Security Council resolutions.
   (2) The Secretary General of the United Nations is not always available to preside over their meeings.
   (3) Any of the five permanent members of the Security Council can veto a resolution of the Council.
   (4) Some Third World member countries question the role of Britain and France at the Security Council.

3. The specialized agencies of the United Nations deal with such topics as

   (1) world health, food, and agriculture
   (2) mining and mineral rights
   (3) local town courts and crime concerns
   (4) humane treatment of animals

4. "Arab Nations Attack Israel" 1948
   "USSR Continues to Leave Troops in Hungary" 1956
   "India Refuses to Honor Cease-Fire with Pakistan" 1971–1972

   The headlines above are examples of

   (1) successful attempts by the United Nations to impact the world community
   (2) deliberate defiance of United Nations resolutions by certain nations
   (3) crises in which the United Nations was unable to suggest peacekeeping solutions
   (4) efforts by member nations to follow the resolutions of the United Nations

5. A limitation on the effectiveness of the United Nations is that

   (1) it has no military force of its own
   (2) it has no permanent meeting location
   (3) it cannot make resolutions suggesting a course of action
   (4) it has very little respect among the world community of nations

6. Where and when was the United Nations Charter drafted?

   (1) Washington, D.C., 1942
   (2) Yalta, 1945
   (3) San Francisco, 1945
   (4) New York City, 1950

7. What do the countries of Norway, Sweden, Burma, Austria, and Peru all have in common?

   (1) All belong to the Security Council of the United Nations.
   (2) Each was the home of a Secretary General of the United Nations.
   (3) All are located in Europe.
   (4) All were neutral during World War II.

8. The International Court of Law of the United Nations is able to function because

   (1) it is funded by the United States
   (2) it works with the Trusteeship Council
   (3) its fifteen judges come from five different countries
   (4) participants must agree in advance to accept the ruling of the Court

9. European countries had the most major rebuilding effort after World War II in which particular area?

   (1) The arts   (3) Religion
   (2) Economy   (4) Education

10. A socialist government is one in which

    (1) free enterprise exists in the economic sector
    (2) citizens must earn a set amount of money to qualify for government services
    (3) there are limits in freedom of speech, the arts, and business
    (4) the government provides for the total care of its citizens

11. In 1979, Margaret Thatcher made history in Great Britain by

    (1) encouraging British participation in the European Community
    (2) being appointed as a lady in waiting to Queen Elizabeth
    (3) becoming Britain's first female prime minister
    (4) introducing a number of popular welfare programs

12. When a country announces that it has "nationalized" a business, it means that

    (1) the business has been closed permanently
    (2) the government has taken control of the business
    (3) the business is run privately but the government claims all profits
    (4) the business will be used solely for international trade

13. After World War II, France was faced with fighting in its possessions in Southeast Asia and in North Africa. This ultimately led to

    (1) those colonies being granted complete independence
    (2) additional fighting between France and former European allies
    (3) economic gain for France with newly acquired oil resources
    (4) the reason for the development of nuclear power in France

14. The period after World War II through the 1990s was characterized in Italy by

    (1) peaceful economic growth
    (2) domestic terrorism and attacks on organized crime
    (3) a takeover by the Communist Party
    (4) a strong monarchy with the respect of Italians

15. Unlike other European countries after World War II, Greece experienced

    (1) political corruption
    (2) a powerful monarchy
    (3) a civil war
    (4) expansion of social welfare programs

16. Spain was unlike any other European nations in post-World War II in that

    (1) it joined the European Community to bolster its economy
    (2) it combined a social welfare system with a market economy
    (3) it allowed for a constitutional monarchy under King Juan Carlos
    (4) its World War II era dictator continued to rule the country until his death in 1979

17. The Basques are an ethnic group in Spain who want

  (1) independence
  (2) recognition of equal status for gypsies
  (3) Islamic religious tolerance
  (4) unity with France

18. Which economically recovering European country benefited by being chosen to host the 1992 Olympics?

  (1) Great Britain   (3) Greece
  (2) France   (4) Spain

19. What generalization would be true about Western European countries following World War II?

  (1) The victorious nations each emerged from the war with much more stable economies.
  (2) Monarchies survived the difficulties of the wartime era and became stronger at its conclusion.

  (3) The Communist parties in many Western European nations continued to play an active role.
  (4) Several countries adopted a new form of government and have maintained it now since the war.

20. "The United Nations is only as effective as its members will allow it to be."

This statement most accurately means that

  (1) member nations of the United Nations voluntarily follow the agreements established for belonging to the UN
  (2) the International Court of Justice will deal directly and forcefully with any member nation who does not cooperate with the directives of the UN
  (3) some members of the General Assembly force the Security Council to take certain actions
  (4) Communist nations are not allowed to belong to the United Nations

THEMATIC ESSAY

Directions: Write a well-organized essay that includes an introduction, several paragraphs addressing the task below, and a conclusion.

Theme: National Concerns and Goals

Immediately after World War II, Western Europe was a place where several nations experienced situations that required changes in national and governmental interests and concerns.

Task

Select two Western European countries and, for each,

- describe a national concern within that country
- discuss how the nation dealt with the concern and explain how the nation tried to meet a national goal
- evaluate the success of the country in dealing with the concern and in meeting its goal

You may use any two examples from Western Europe. Some suggestions you might wish to consider include Great Britain, France, Italy, Greece, and Spain.

You are *not* limited to these suggestions.

Guidelines

In your essay, be sure to

- develop all aspects of the *Task*
- support the theme with relevant facts, examples, and details
- use a logical and clear plan of organization, including an introduction and a conclusion that are beyond a restatement of the theme
- introduce the theme by establishing a framework that is beyond a simple restatement of the *Task* and conclude with a summation of the theme

DOCUMENT-BASED ESSAY QUESTION

This question is based on the accompanying documents (1–7). It is designed to test your ability to work with historical documents. Some of the documents have been edited for the purposes of the question. As you analyze the documents, take into account the source of each document and any point of view that may be presented in the document.

Historical Context

During and immediately after World War II, many world nations took a new interest in forming an international organization. That interest has continued and grown into the twenty-first century.

Task

Using information from the documents and your knowledge of global history, write an essay in which you

- identify three goals of the United Nations
- describe how the United Nations works to achieve these goals
- discuss how the United Nations attempts to bring together all of its member nations and give one example of its success in achieving that effort

Part A: Short Answer Questions

Directions: Analyze the document and answer the short answer questions that follow each document.

Document 1

PREAMBLE

WE THE PEOPLES OF THE UNITED NATIONS DETERMINED

- to save succeeding generations from the scourge of war, which twice in our lifetime has brought untold sorrow to mankind, and
- to reaffirm faith in fundamental human rights, in the dignity and worth of the human person, in the equal rights of men and women and of nations large and small, and

- to establish conditions under which justice and respect for the obligations arising from treaties and other sources of international law can be maintained, and
- to promote social progress and better standards of life in larger freedom,

AND FOR THESE ENDS

- to practice tolerance and live together in peace with one another as good neighbors, and
- to unite our strength to maintain international peace and security, and
- to ensure, by the acceptance of principles and the institution of methods, that armed force shall not be used, save in the common interest, and
- to employ international machinery for the promotion of the economic and social advancement of all peoples,

HAVE RESOLVED TO COMBINE OUR EFFORTS TO ACCOMPLISH THESE AIMS

Accordingly, our respective Governments, through representatives assembled in the city of San Francisco, who have exhibited their full powers found to be in good and due form, have agreed to the present Charter of the United Nations and do hereby establish an international organization to be known as the United Nations.

Question   **1.** Using the Preamble to the United Nations, identify two of the stated goals of the United Nations.

Document 2

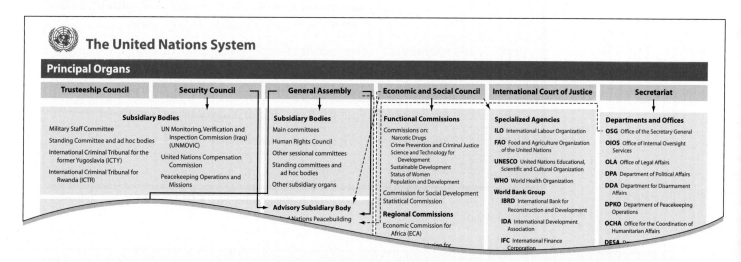

Question   **2.** According to the list of Principal Organs of "The United Nations System" chart, what are two topics that the United Nations deals with specifically?

Document 3

GROWTH IN UNITED NATIONS MEMBERSHIP
1945–2006

1945	51 Members	Argentina, Australia, Belgium, Bolivia, Brazil, Byelorussia, Canada, Chile, China, Colombia, Costa Rica, Cuba, Czechoslovakia, Denmark, Dominican Republic, Ecuador, Egypt, El Salvador, Ethiopia, France, Greece, Guatemala, Haiti, Honduras, India, Iran, Iraq, Lebanon, Liberia, Luxembourg, Mexico, Netherlands, New Zealand, Nicaragua, Norway, Panama, Paraguay, Peru, Philippines, Poland, Saudi Arabia, South Africa, Syrian Arab Republic, Turkey, Ukraine, Union of Socialist Republics, United Kingdom of Great Britain and Northern Ireland, United States of America, Uruguay, Venezuela, Yugoslavia
1955	76 Members	Albania
1956	80 Members	Japan, Morocco, Sudan, Tunisia
1957	82 Members	Federation of Malaya, Ghana
1958	82 Members	Guinea
1960	99 Members	Benin, Burkina Faso, Cameroon, Central African Republic, Chad, Côte d'Ivoire, Cyprus, Gabon, Madagascar, Mali, Niger, Nigeria, Republic of the Congo, Senegal, Somalia, Togo, Zaire
1991	166 Members	Democratic People's Republic of Korea, Estonia, Federated States of Micronesia, Latvia, Lithuania, Marshall Islands, Republic of Korea
2000	189 Members	Federal Republic of Yugoslavia, Tuvalu
2002	191 Members	Switzerland, Timor-Leste
2006	192 Members	Montenegro

Based on "Basic facts about the UN," DPI, 2004, Sales No. E.04.I.7, and Press Release ORG/1469 of 3 July 2006.

Questions

3. a. How many original members of the United Nations were there in 1945?
   b. What was the most recent country to join the United Nations?
   c. Of the years shown, which year had the most new members?

Document 4

MEMBERSHIP OF PRINCIPAL
UNITED NATIONS ORGANS IN 2006

General Assembly

The General Assembly is made up of 191 Member States. The States and the dates on which they became Members are listed in Press Release ORG/1360 issued 4 October 2002.

Security Council

The Security Council has 15 members. The United Nations Charter designates five States as permanent members and the General Assembly elects 10 other members for two-year terms. The term of office for each non-permanent member of the Council ends on 31 December of the year indicated in parentheses next to its name.

The five permanent members of the Security Council are China, France, Russian Federation, United Kingdom and the United States.

The 10 non-permanent members of the Council in 2006 are Argentina (2006), Congo (2007), Denmark (2006), Ghana (2007), Greece (2006), Japan (2006), Peru (2007), Qatar (2007), Slovak Republic (2007) and the United Republic of Tanzania (2006).

Questions

4. From your review of the "Membership of Principal United Nations Organs in 2006" answer the following:
   a. How many permanent members of the Security Council are there?
   b. Identify two of the permanent members.
   c. Identify two members whose terms end in 2007.

Document 5

Questions

5. a. What is the title of the poster Mrs. Roosevelt is holding?
   b. Why might many people in many nations be interested in what she is holding?

Document 6

The following is an excerpt from Secretary General Kofi Annan's remarks on the appointment of the Eighth Secretary General of the United Nations, October 13, 2006.

Let me extend my warmest congratulations to my successor, Mr. Ban Ki-moon.
Let me also congratulate all of you, the Member States, on this choice.

Mr. Ban, I am delighted that your election turned out this way—early and orderly.
Surely this is the way we would wish all Secretaries-General to be elected.

I would presume to give you only one piece of advice for when you take over next year: try to make full use of the unparalleled resource you will find in the staff of the Organization. Their commitment to the UN is the UN's greatest asset, and has been the surest source of strength for me in my work as Secretary-General.

More than 50 years ago, the first Secretary-General of the United Nations, Trygve Lie, used the following words in greeting his successor, Dag Hammarskjöld [and I quote]: "You are about to take over the most impossible job on Earth." [End quote.] While that may be true, I would add: this is also the best possible job on Earth.

Questions

6. a. How did Mr. Annan say that Trygve Lie described the job of Secretary General?
   b. What attributes does Mr. Annan himself think that his successor will need to have?

Document 7

The following is an excerpt from a speech by Ban Ki-moon as he accepted his appointment as Secretary General of the United Nations:

"My tenure will be marked by ceaseless efforts to build bridges and close divides. Leadership of harmony not division, by division not instruction, has served me well so far. I intend to stay the course as Secretary-General.

Asia is also a region where modesty is a virtue. But the modesty is about demeanour, not about vision and goals. It does not mean the lack of commitment or leadership. Rather it is quiet determination in action to get things done without so much fanfare.

This may be the key to Asia's success, and to the UN's future. Indeed, our Organization is modest in its means, but not in its values. We should be more modest in our words, but not in our performance…

...As Secretary-General, I will make the most of the authority invested in my office by the Charter and the mandate you give me. I will work diligently to materialize our responsibility to protect the most vulnerable members of humanity and for the peaceful resolution of threats to international security and regional stability..."

Source: http://www.un.org/apps/news/story/asp?NewsID=20255&Cr=ki-moon&Cr1=

Question	7. Describe two goals that Ban Ki-moon states in this acceptance speech.

Part B: Essay

Directions: Write a well-organized essay that includes an introduction, several paragraphs, and a conclusion. Use evidence from *at least four* documents in your essay. Support your response with relevant facts, examples, and details. Include additional outside information.

Historical Context

During and immediately after World War II, many world nations took a new interest in forming an international organization. That interest has continued and grown into the twenty-first century.

Task

Using information from the documents and your knowledge of global history, write an essay in which you

- identify three goals of the United Nations
- describe how the United Nations works to achieve these goals
- discuss how the United Nations attempts to bring together all of its member nations and give one example of its success in achieving that effort

Guidelines

In your essay, be sure to

- develop all aspects of the *Task*
- incorporate information from *at least four* documents
- incorporate relevant outside information
- support the theme with relevant facts, examples, and details
- use a logical and clear plan of organization, including an introduction and conclusion that are beyond a restatement of the theme

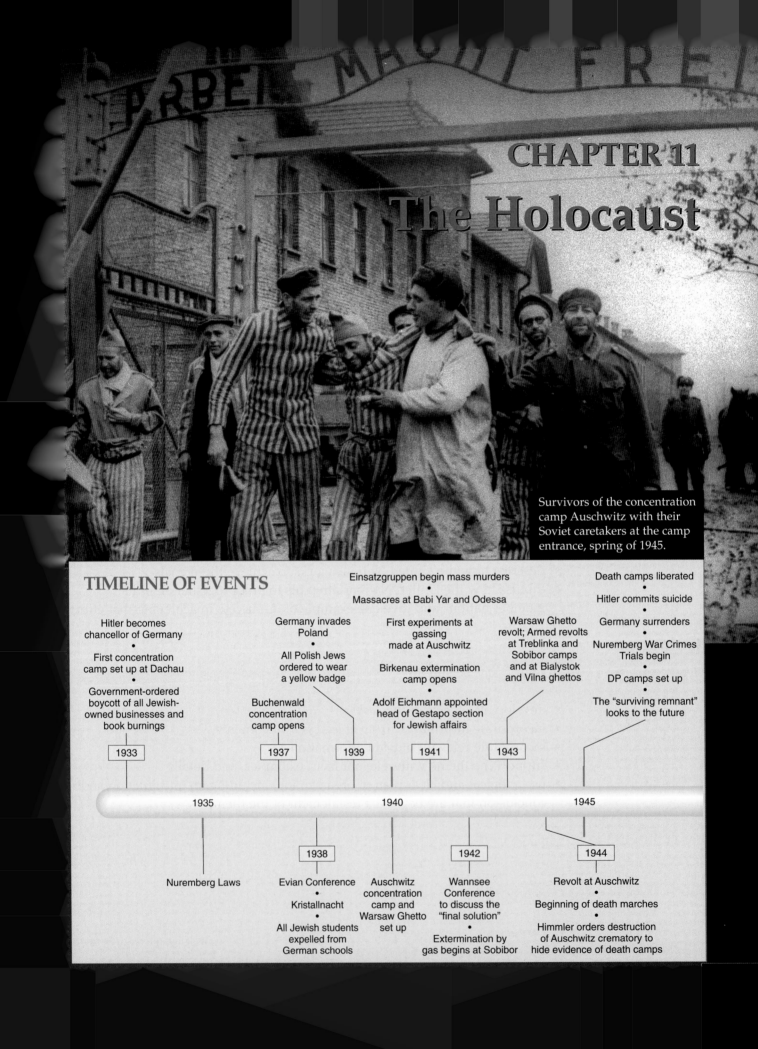

CHAPTER 11
The Holocaust

Survivors of the concentration camp Auschwitz with their Soviet caretakers at the camp entrance, spring of 1945.

TIMELINE OF EVENTS

Einsatzgruppen begin mass murders

Massacres at Babi Yar and Odessa

Death camps liberated

Hitler commits suicide

Hitler becomes chancellor of Germany

Germany invades Poland

First experiments at gassing made at Auschwitz

Warsaw Ghetto revolt; Armed revolts at Treblinka and Sobibor camps and at Bialystok and Vilna ghettos

Germany surrenders

First concentration camp set up at Dachau

All Polish Jews ordered to wear a yellow badge

Birkenau extermination camp opens

Nuremberg War Crimes Trials begin

Government-ordered boycott of all Jewish-owned businesses and book burnings

Buchenwald concentration camp opens

Adolf Eichmann appointed head of Gestapo section for Jewish affairs

DP camps set up

The "surviving remnant" looks to the future

1933   **1937**   **1939**   **1941**   **1943**

1935   1940   1945

1938   **1942**   **1944**

Nuremberg Laws

Evian Conference

Auschwitz concentration camp and Warsaw Ghetto set up

Wannsee Conference to discuss the "final solution"

Revolt at Auschwitz

Kristallnacht

Beginning of death marches

All Jewish students expelled from German schools

Extermination by gas begins at Sobibor

Himmler orders destruction of Auschwitz crematory to hide evidence of death camps

The worst international tragedy to affect Europe in the 20th century was World War II. In Chapter 9, we saw how Nazi Germany, under the leadership of **Adolf Hitler**, was responsible for the conflict that tore apart that continent from 1939 to 1945. Hitler and the Nazis were also responsible for another tragedy that shocked the world's conscience, one that lasted from 1933 to 1945, during the lifetime of the **Third Reich**. This was the **Holocaust**. In its simplest definition, the Holocaust refers to the intentional murder of six million **European Jews**. It also included the attempt by the Nazis to destroy Judaism as a religion. Approximately five million more people who were not Jewish also were victims of the Nazis. They included Poles, Gypsies, homosexuals, Roman Catholics, and other Christians, including clergy, the mentally and/or physically disabled and those who resisted Nazism of any nationality.

Main Idea:
While *holocaust* could refer to any one of a number of terrible acts of destruction, *Holocaust*, with an uppercase *H*, refers solely to the *very specific* destruction of a *specific* group of people by another *specific* group of people and its government at a *specific* time in history.

The proper noun *Holocaust* must be distinguished from the word *holocaust*, with a lowercase *h*. The latter can be used to describe *any* great, massive destruction, usually by fire. It is actually a Greek translation of a word used in the Bible, a word that means a total burning and describes a sacrifice. Today, the reduction to ashes of several large skyscrapers filled with people, such as the murderous attack by Arab terrorists on New York City's World Trade Center, could be termed a holocaust, as could the destruction caused by the dropping of atomic bombs on Hiroshima and Nagasaki during World War II. People also speak of a nuclear holocaust, fearful of the growth of nuclear weapons throughout the world today. So while *holocaust* could refer to any one of a number of terrible acts of destruction, *Holocaust*, with an uppercase *H*, refers solely to the *very specific* destruction of a *specific* group of people by another *specific* group of people and its government at a *specific* time in history. What happened to the Jews of Europe at the hands of the Nazis and their collaborators from 1933 to 1945 was not just "a holocaust," but is referred to as "The Holocaust."

The Holocaust was a unique event in world history. It was the most cruel and bloody attempt by a government to carry out a policy of **genocide** (a word coined after World War II to mean the planned **annihilation** or destruction of a people because of its religion or race or nationality). The usual aspects of the Holocaust can be seen in a portion of a report made in the United States by the President's Commission on the Holocaust in 1979:

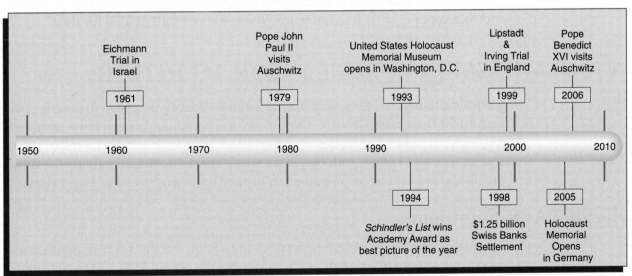

Timeline:

Eichmann Trial in Israel — 1961

Pope John Paul II visits Auschwitz — 1979

United States Holocaust Memorial Museum opens in Washington, D.C. — 1993

Lipstadt & Irving Trial in England — 1999

Pope Benedict XVI visits Auschwitz — 2006

1950 — 1960 — 1970 — 1980 — 1990 — 2000 — 2010

Schindler's List wins Academy Award as best picture of the year — 1994

$1.25 billion Swiss Banks Settlement — 1998

Holocaust Memorial Opens in Germany — 2005

The Holocaust was the systematic, bureaucratic extermination of six million Jews by Nazis and their collaborators as a central act of state during the Second World War; as night descended, millions of other peoples were swept into this net of death. It was a crime unique in the annals of human history, different not only in the quantity of violence—the sheer numbers killed—but in its manner and purpose as a mass criminal enterprise organized by the state against defenseless civilian populations. The decision was to kill every Jew everywhere in Europe; the definition of Jew as target for death transcended all boundaries.

The concept of the annihilation of an entire people, as distinguished from their subjugation, was unprecedented; never before in human history had genocide been an all-pervasive government policy unaffected by territorial or economic advantage and unchecked by moral or religious constraints.

The genocide practiced by the Nazis was a war. Indeed, a book about the Holocaust by the historian Lucy Dawidowicz calls it *The War Against the Jews*. In this chapter, we will try to understand why and how that war was carried out. We will also learn about the world's reaction, acts of resistance by Jews and non-Jews, and implications for our own times.

REASONS FOR STUDYING THE HOLOCAUST

The period of the Holocaust was one of the ugliest and darkest moments in the history of mankind. One reason for studying this topic is to prevent a tragedy like the Holocaust from ever happening again, to any group of people anywhere on earth. We can also learn about the danger of **apathy** (not caring) and about the consequences of hateful behavior toward people because of religion, race, or nationality. Knowledge of the Holocaust exposes us to an evil side of human beings, a side that we have to be aware of in order to prevent it from influencing harmful behavior toward other human beings.

Study of the Holocaust also makes us aware of how precious and fragile life can be. A threat to the life, well-being, and freedom of one of us is a threat to all of us. As was said by **John Donne**, a sixteenth-century English poet, "No man is an island, entire of itself; every man is a piece of the continent, a part of the main. . . . Any man's death diminishes me, because I am involved in mankind; and therefore never seek to know for whom the bell tolls; it tolls for thee."

ANTI-SEMITISM IN EUROPE PRIOR TO HITLER

Anti-Semitism can refer to any hostile actions taken against Jewish people only because of their being Jewish. These actions throughout history have included religious **prejudice**, separation and expulsion, economic and social restrictions, and attacks and killing. Anti-Semitism was a constant theme, perhaps the most prejudiced one, throughout European history for almost two thousand years.

Religious Anti-Semitism

The earliest and longest-lasting form of anti-Semitism has been religious anti-Semitism. Its origins rested in Christian beliefs about Jews. (Happily, these beliefs were declared false by Church authorities in the twentieth century and are no longer taught as Christian doctrine.) Among these beliefs were that Jews were responsible for the death of Jesus Christ (**deicide**), and that they used the blood of Christian children in ceremonies (the **"blood libel"** accusation). The earliest recorded charge of deicide against the Jews was made by **Melito**, Bishop of Sardis, in 167 C.E. Jews were also singled out because they refused to accept Jesus as the Messiah and to convert to Christianity, and because they practiced rituals different from those of Christians. Both before and during the Middle Ages, Jews were denied many civil rights and positions granted to other Europeans. Since the Catholic Church prohibited money lending, banking and commerce therefore became two of the few occupational fields that Jews were allowed to enter. This situation, however, would create a **stereotype** of Jews as greedy financiers and would often lead to persecution of them in times of economic distress.

> **Main Idea:** The earliest and longest-lasting form of anti-Semitism has been religious anti-Semitism.

Some examples of Church actions against Jews and their striking similarity to some of Hitler's actions are indicated below:

- In 309, the Church forbade marriages between Christians and Jews. (In 1935, the Nuremberg Laws said that Jews could not marry non-Jews. These laws were also known as the Laws for the Protection of German Blood and Honor.)
- In 1215, Jews were required to wear special badges on their clothing, and in some regions, to wear pointed hats. (In 1941, Jews in Nazi-occupied territories were forced to wear yellow stars with the word *Jew* on them.)
- In 1267, the Church ordered that Jews in cities must live in separate sections, which came to be known as **ghettos**. The word *ghetto* is derived from the Italian word *geta*, an iron factory in the neighborhood where Jews were forced to live in Venice in 1516. (In 1939, the Nazis began to force Jews to live in ghettos throughout Europe, with one of the biggest being the **Warsaw Ghetto** in Poland.)

Secular Anti-Semitism

> **Main Idea:** Secular anti-Semitism was not based on religious reasons; instead, it was a prejudice against Jews based on economic and social factors.

Although religious anti-Semitism was a main factor for hostility toward Jews prior to the twentieth century, two other forms of anti-Semitism began to take shape in the eighteenth and nineteenth centuries: *secular* anti-Semitism and *racial* anti-Semitism. **Secular** anti-Semitism was not based on religious reasons; instead, it was a prejudice against Jews based on economic and social factors. They were seen as a minority group who did not deserve all the rights and privileges of other groups. They might be perceived as objects of fear and resentment. Accordingly, they were discriminated against in housing, schools, and certain occupations. From the seventeenth century on, in parts of central and Eastern Europe, Jewish communities in both urban and rural areas were often subject to bloody attacks called **pogroms**. These violent attacks resulted in murder, rape, and the destruction of property. They were carried out by unruly mobs of non-Jews and would last from a few hours to several days. Examples were those conducted by Bogdan Chmelnitzki in **Poland** (1600s) and by Cossacks in **Russia** (1800s).

These examples of secular anti-Semitism were fueled by scapegoating, myths, distortions, and superstitions. One such false notion about Jews was described in a book titled *The Protocols of the Elders of Zion*. Written in the late nineteenth century in Eastern Europe, it claimed that Jews were involved in a world-wide conspiracy to take over the governments of Christian nations. It became a popular book in Europe in the 1920s and 1930s, even though it was proved to be a forgery and without factual basis. Diabolically, Hitler and the Nazis made use of the myths created by both religious and secular anti-Semitism.

Racial Anti-Semitism

As wrongful as was secular anti-Semitism, it did not have the potential for inde-scribable evil that was true of racial anti-Semitism. Also known as *scientific* anti-Semitism as well as eliminationist anti-Semitism, this belief emerged in the nineteenth century and would be used by Hitler to support Nazi genocide. As unproven theory, it held that, because of heredity and gene structure, Jews were an inferior and dangerous race of people. Considered to be as dangerous to society as bacterial and viral infections would be to the human body, such a race, said Hitler's propagandists, should be removed from society and eventually be done away with. Because of this false notion, as well as other beliefs we have discussed, six million Jews would be killed on orders from the leaders of the Third Reich between 1933 and 1945.

We have now examined three forms of anti-Semitism. A summary of the harsh messages communicated in these forms is described by the American professor Raul Hilberg in his book *The Destruction of the European Jews:* religious anti-Semitism—you may not live among us as Jews; secular anti-Semitism—you may not live among us; racial anti-Semitism—you may not live.

ANTI-SEMITISM IN GERMANY PRIOR TO HITLER

Throughout the long history of the German people, some great figures have emerged. In music, we know of Bach, Beethoven, Brahms, Handel, Mendelssohn, Schubert, and Wagner. In science and technology, we learned about Gutenberg, Roentgen, and Einstein. And in religion and politics, we know about the accomplishments of Martin Luther and Otto von Bismarck (see Chapter 3 in this volume). Yet, German society also brought forth Hitler and the Holocaust. Why? Is it possible to explain why a particular people has produced individuals who made noteworthy contributions to culture and progress as well as those who were responsible for evil and despicable acts? This is a difficult question to answer. Nevertheless, we can point to a lengthy record of anti-Semitism in German territory prior to Hitler's rise to power in 1933.

The Black Death

For example, the most notorious instance of fourteenth-century German anti-Semitism focused on the spread of a disease known then as the *Black Death*. A deadly, highly contagious illness, it killed hundreds of thousands of people from 1348 to 1350. Modern medical science has determined that these deaths were caused by the bubonic plague. The plague was probably spread by infected rats and fleas, amidst the common unsanitary conditions found in many towns and villages. However, fourteenth-century Europe was ignorant of the germ theory of disease as well as ways by which infections could be transmitted.

This ignorance, combined with an understandable fear of the unknown, provided a ripe setting for seeking a **scapegoat** for the plague. The Jews were blamed, even though there was no scientific evidence for this. One reason for heaping blame upon them was that they did not suffer as much from the plague as did others. This was probably due to the strict dietary and hygienic laws observed by many Jews, as well as to the fact that they often lived apart from and had little contact with their Christian neighbors.

The Impact of Martin Luther and Richard Wagner

Richard Wagner (1813–1883), German composer. American lithograph, 19th century.

Less than two hundred years after the ravages of the Black Death, another instance of anti-Semitism occurred. Although it did not lead to any deaths, it provided further fuel for the flames of prejudiced thinking. It took the form of sermons and writings by **Martin Luther**, the leading figure in the Protestant **Reformation**. Luther had hoped to convert German Jews to Protestantism, having admired them in his early years as a priest. Upon the refusal of Jews to convert, Luther's admiration turned to hatred. He now termed Jews as "children of the devil." In a widely read publication of his in 1543, he condemned Jews for their religious and economic practices. Ironically, this publication was reissued by the Nazis almost four hundred years later, even though they officially were against religion in general and religious leaders.

In addition to Luther, another revered German figure from the past who was used by the Nazis in their anti-Semitic propaganda was the composer **Richard Wagner**. Gaining fame in the nineteenth century, Wagner wrote operas that had stirring music and that pictured the German people as superior to all others. He was also known for his outspoken anti-Semitic views. Shortly before his death in 1883, he wrote of the Jewish race as "the born enemy of true mankind and of everything that is noble." Although he died six years before Hitler was born, Wagner's music along with his theories (now considered erroneous) about Germans and about Jews were to have enormous influence on Hitler and all of Nazi philosophy.

HITLER'S WAR AGAINST THE JEWS (1933–1939)

Hitler's anti-Semitic attitudes were well-formed by the time he became chancellor of Germany in 1933. He blamed Jews for his personal failure early in life to become a successful painter and also felt that Jews were responsible for Germany's defeat in World War I. Although neither of these charges was true, he nevertheless wrote about them in his autobiography ***Mein Kampf*** *(My Struggle)*, published in 1924. In 1919, he joined a political party that was against the democratic Weimar government and preached anti-Semitism. This was the German Workers' Party. Soon thereafter he rose to become party leader, with the name changed to the National Socialist German Workers' (**Nazi**) party. Eventually, he and his party would come to rule Germany as the **Third Reich** (see Chapter 8 in this volume "The Rise of Totalitarianism in Russia, Italy, and Germany").

Aryan Supremacy

Nazi philosophy became the philosophy of the Third Reich. Central to this way of thinking was the belief that the German people formed a **master race**, whose destiny was to rule the world and whose members were of "pure Aryan blood." By **Aryan**, the Nazis meant a superior, white, Nordic, heroic person, having a particular brain size and certain facial features. This doctrine of Aryan supremacy, although biologically false, had no room for Jews, blacks, or other groups who were deemed to be of "impure" or "mixed" blood. This racial theory added a new and tragic dimension to European anti-Semitism. Up to this

Boycott propaganda against Jewish shop owners. SA guard in front of a department store in Berlin on April 1, 1933.

point in the long and sad history of anti-Semitism, Jews could usually avoid persecution by converting, and by assimilating into the Christian world. But under Nazism, these possibilities no longer existed. German Jews would remain Jews and non-Aryan no matter how long they and their ancestors had lived in Germany and no matter how much they had contributed to German society. Mistreatment of Jews began soon after Hitler became chancellor on January 30, 1933. In April, for example, a **boycott** against Jewish stores and businesses was staged by Nazi Party members. They would stand outside these places with signs, urging people not to enter and buy things. The chief organizer of the boycotts was Julius Streicher, editor of the notorious anti-Semitic newspaper *Der Sturmer*. Later in April, the government passed a series of laws that did the following:

- Expelled Jews from civil service jobs
- Prohibited Jews from practicing law
- Denied payments from the national health service to patients who had gone to Jewish doctors
- Restricted Jewish enrollment in high schools

Book Burnings

On May 10, 1933, an event took place in Berlin, and in other cities as well, that was directed more toward Judaism as a religion and as a culture than against individuals. This was a public book burning. Thrown into the flames before cheering crowds were Jewish holy books as well as books written by Jewish authors. Delighted with such devastation, **Josef Goebbels**, Hitler's minister of propaganda, stated that "these flames not only illuminate the final end of an old era, they also light up the new." An ironical contrast to this statement is one made by **Heinrich Heine**, a German-Jewish poet whose works were among those consumed in the fires. Almost one hundred years ago, he had said: "Where they burn books, so too will they in the end burn human beings." The horror of this prophecy would come true during the Holocaust.

German Nazi party leader, Joseph Paul Goebbels, speaking at an SA roll call in Berlin in 1934.

Reichsführer-SS and Gestapo chief, Heinrich Himmler, welcomes members of a Waffen SS cavalry regiment. July 25, 1941.

All book burnings were supervised by members of the **SS**. This was an abbreviation for the *Schutzstaffel*, a small specially picked armed group created by Hitler in 1925 to protect him. It was to grow into a powerful political and military organization in the Third Reich, headed by one of Hitler's friends **Heinrich Himmler**.

Originally having only two hundred men, the SS rose to more than four million by 1940. It was to have direct responsibility for the concentration, labor, and death camps. Specially trained to hate and take action against all "enemies of the Reich," especially Jews, the SS included a feared secret police unit known as the **Gestapo** (*Geheimnis Staats Polizei*). Gestapo agents would frequently drag people from their homes in the middle of the night and also engaged in kidnapping and murder. The Gestapo became a law unto itself, with the SS becoming practically a government within the government.

The Nuremberg Laws

The attempt to isolate Jews from German society took a major step forward in 1935. In a mass rally and meeting in September, Nazi Party leaders enacted the **Nuremberg Laws**. These measures effectively stripped from Jews their rights as citizens and transformed them into mere subjects. Jews could not, for example, enjoy the rights, privileges, and protections of other Germans. They could not marry non-Jews nor employ Aryans in their households. Prohibitions were placed on their entering public places such as parks, owning dogs, and going to swimming pools and health spas. By the end of the year, it was common to see the sign "Juden Verboten" ("No Jews") in restaurants, villages, and towns throughout Germany. The Nuremberg Laws made Nazi racism part of the government's legal system and thus made possible the passage of much more anti-Semitic legislation. Such state-sponsored prejudicial decrees widened the psychological gap between Germans and Jews. German society looked upon Jews as aliens or even worse, whereas Jews felt severely handicapped and shamed by being singled out for unfair treatment. Lifelong relationships between Jews and non-Jews—in business, in school, and among families—were now being shattered.

In German-occupied Poland, a street sign, in German and Polish, reads that Jews are not allowed in Lindenallee. World War II German army photograph.

The Year 1938 as a Turning Point

The year 1938 was a critical one for the Third Reich, in regard to both its expansionist and its anti-Semitic policies. In March, Hitler achieved *anschluss* with Austria, followed by acquisition of the Czech Sudetenland in September as a result of the Munich Agreement (see Chapter 9 in this volume "World War II"). Austrian and Sudetenland Jews would now be subject to the restrictive and harsh laws of the Nazi Reich. For these Jews, as well as for those in Germany, however, these developments would prove to be overshadowed by others that made 1938 a bitter year.

The Evian Conference

In July, an international conference was convened at the French city of **Evian**. The purpose of the Evian Conference was to deal with the problem of growing numbers of people wanting to flee from the Nazis. The majority of these refugees were Jews. Many nations at the conference, including France, Canada, Australia, the United States, and Great Britain, deplored Nazi actions against Jews and stated that safe havens should be found for them. However, most of the nations, for a variety of reasons, either refused to open their doors or were willing to accept only a small number of refugees as immigrants. Holland, Denmark, and the Dominican Republic were more willing than others to accept refugees.

Main Idea:
Although the Evian Conference gave little hope for Jews suffering under the Nazis, it could not be described as a definite case of anti-Semitism.

Although the Evian Conference gave little hope for Jews suffering under the Nazis, it could not be described as a definite case of anti-Semitism. Such a description, however, clearly applies to three other events in 1938, brought on by German authorities. The less harmful of these were two decrees issued in October that, in effect, were additional ways of treating Jews as subjects and outcasts rather than as German citizens. The first decree ordered that, from then on, Jews would have to add another "identifying" name, such as Israel or Sarah, to their names. The second decree directed that their passports be stamped with the letter *J* for *Jude*, the German word for Jew. As dehumanizing as these rules were, they would be a far cry from the vicious physical attacks on Jews, their homes, and their holy places that took place nationwide on the evening of November 9, 1938. That date has since been referred to as **Kristallnacht** (night of the broken glass). As the worst anti-Semitic action since Hitler's rise to power in 1933, as a shocking sign of the genocide yet to come, and finally as a terrifying example of a totalitarian government's group-directed violence, the details surrounding Kristallnacht must be carefully examined.

Kristallnacht

What happened on Thursday night, November 9, 1938, and continued on through November 11, 1938, was an *aktionen* (a planned action) against German Jews that really became a pogrom. All over Germany, Nazi gangs, Gestapo members, and masses of citizens killed ninety-two Jews, set fire to almost two hundred synagogues while destroying seventy-six of these, broke into and looted more than seven thousand Jewish shops and businesses, and attacked untold numbers of people in their homes and in the streets. The local police did nothing during the attacks. More than thirty-five thousand Jews were arrested and sent to concentration camps. The breaking of so much glass, most of which had been made in Belgium, is the reason the *aktionen* is called Kristallnacht. Indeed, so much glass was broken that it would supposedly have taken all the plate glass factories in Belgium almost two years to make replacements!

Reinhard Heydrich (1904–1942), German Nazi officer and chief of the Gestapo. Photographed in the uniform of an SS-Obergruppenfuhrer, 1941.

Why did Kristallnacht occur? Nazi officials such as Propaganda Minister Joseph Goebbels claimed that the violence was a spontaneous outpouring of anger based on the killing of a German official in Paris by a Jewish teenager. This was a lie, and Goebbels knew it was a lie. In fact, it was a **"big lie."** From documents shown at the Nuremberg Trials in 1945, it is clear that the events of November 9–11, 1938, had been well planned. Secret notices had been sent before and during these dates from Gestapo headquarters all over Germany, under direct orders from **Reinhard Heydrich** and Heinrich Himmler, two Nazi officials close to Hitler. Use of the big lie technique, however, was a common feature of the Third Reich and has been characteristic of all totalitarian governments. The true background and aftermath of Kristallnacht are as follows.

During the early years of the twentieth century, thousands of eastern European Jews had come to Germany. In his wish, however, to make Germany *Judenrein* (free of Jews), Hitler gave an order to expel these people. In October 1938, more than eighteen thousand were forcibly taken to the German-Polish border, beaten, robbed, and sent into Poland. In this group were Zindel Grynszpan and his family. They wrote about their expulsion to their seventeen-year-old son, **Herschel Grynszpan**, who was studying in Paris. Angered at learning of his family's ordeal, Herschel went to the German embassy in Paris on November 6, 1938, where he shot Ernst von Rath, an embassy official. The Nazis claimed that this assassination was part of an international plot against Germany, blaming all Jews for the killing. This accusation of "collective guilt," holding all Jews responsible for the actions of one of them, was an example of the big lie technique. A cry for revenge arose from German newspapers, Nazi officials, and even some Church leaders. This revenge became the violence that allegedly occurred "spontaneously" a few days later on November 9, 1938. This allegation was of course another part of the big lie. To add insult to injury, the Nazis now claimed that because Jews were responsible for causing the violence and resulting damage, they would have to pay a penalty of more than one billion German marks!

The terror unleashed on November 9, 1938, does not deserve to be called Kristallnacht because the literal translation of this word refers to crystal, something pleasing, delicate, and refined. Clearly, none of these adjectives applies to what the Nazis and their followers did on that night. The collective guilt that the Germans laid upon the Jews was to be repeated in far more horrific form in the years after 1938. This is why the organized terror in November of that year has now been considered as the first act of the Holocaust.

HITLER'S WAR AGAINST THE JEWS (1939–1945)

With Germany's attack on Poland in 1939, World War II began. The conquests of Poland and other nations in Europe made the Jews in these areas subjects of the Third Reich. The Nazis were now to extend their anti-Semitic policies to these areas. They would also adopt practices that would be more shocking than those they had carried out between 1933 and 1938 in the territories they occupied in that time. To understand these practices more fully, we will examine events mostly in Eastern Europe. It was here, particularly in Poland, that Hitler's war against the Jews was more ferocious than in Nazi-occupied areas of western and southern Europe.

The Ghettos

Jewish children of the Warsaw Ghetto, 1941.

The ghettos were sealed-off, restricted areas of cities, into which Nazis forced Jews to live. These areas were different from Jewish ghettos in earlier centuries. In those ghettos, people could still get on with their lives in a limited manner. In the Nazi-imposed ghettos, however, the aim was not to create a permanent setting, but to have a temporary arrangement for people prior to sending them away as slave laborers or on to **death camps**. Isolation of Jews from non-Jews was another reason for the ghettos.

Heavily populated ghettos were established in **Lodz** and **Krakow** in Poland, **Vilna** in **Lithuania**, and **Bialystok** in Poland. The largest was Poland's Warsaw Ghetto, created in 1940 in a run-down neighborhood and surrounded by a newly built wall topped with barbed wire and cut glass. It was to have a population of almost 450,000 people. The buildings, food, water, and sanitary services here were inadequate to take care of so many people. Fully aware of this, however, the Nazis forced Jews there from other sections of Warsaw as well as from outlying rural villages. This overcrowding, often with several people confined to one room, created very harsh living conditions. Contributing to this inhuman existence were additional measures dictated by the Germans:

- Rationing of food and water below minimum health standards
- Removal of radios and telephones in order to cut off Jews from the outside world
- Stationing of armed guards to prevent people from leaving the ghetto
- Reducing heat in the winter
- Requiring all Jews to buy and wear a six-pointed yellow star on their clothing

At unpredictable moments, there might be roundups and arrests for no legitimate reasons, as well as beatings, rapes, and shootings.

The Judenrat

In each ghetto, the Nazis set up a Jewish council known as the *Judenrat*. In most instances, this council would consist of Jews who were respected leaders in Jewish communities. The *Judenrat* in a ghetto would have several functions:

- To act as an administrative government in obeying and carrying out Nazi regulations

- To be responsible for basic services such as employment, sanitation, health, and education and to establish a police force and jails
- To represent Jews in dealings with the occupation authorities

Jews who were *Judenrat* members had mixed feelings about their roles. On the one hand, they feared the shame of collaborating with the Nazis and worried about being seen by their fellow Jews as tools and puppets. On the other hand, they stood to obtain benefits and protection for themselves and their families, gain status, and do what they could to aid their fellow Jews. Clearly, they faced a dilemma.

The "Final Solution"

The word *solution* does not often appear when you study history. You are most likely to encounter it in a science or mathematics class. Math teachers will use the word in trying to answer a problem. This kind of thought process was diabolically applied by the Nazis in their treatment of Jews. Jews were seen as a "problem" that needed a solution. Consideration of just what to do with them became known as the *Jewish Question*. This anti-Semitic phrase, the Jewish Question, first crept into the minds of Europeans in the nineteenth century. For Hitler, from 1933 to 1939, in the areas making up the Third Reich—Germany, Austria, and Czechoslovakia—the three answers or solutions to this question were humiliation, separation, and expulsion. After 1939, with the German occupation of other parts of Europe, a fourth and final solution was agreed upon—the total annihilation of European Jews. The final solution to the Jewish Question would thus be mass murder or genocide.

> **Main Idea:**
> Jews were seen as a "problem" that needed a solution.

When was this incredible decision made? It is difficult to point to a specific date or document with instructions. However, historians believe that sometime in 1941 Hitler spoke to Heinrich Himmler, head of the SS, about the extermination of the Jews of Europe. In July 1941, the SS second-in-command to Himmler, Reinhard Heydrich, was placed in charge of planning this extermination, this final solution. On December 8, 1941, the day the United States entered World War II, the first extermination camp was opened at **Chelmno** in Poland. It is possible that Hitler had thoughts about genocide prior to coming to power in 1933. Yet, it was only in the early 1940s that exact plans were made to carry out this gruesome policy. By 1941, for example, the war had been going well for Germany and the other Axis powers. Any human restraints inside the Reich had weakened; there were also no concerns now about reactions from democratic nations. These countries had been very reluctant, as we have seen, even to admit fleeing Jews into their lands.

The Wannsee Conference

In January 1942 at Lake Wannsee, outside of Berlin, a conference was held to determine various ways of achieving the final solution. Heydrich, known for his fiery anti-Semitism, presided. Among others attending were **Adolf Eichmann**, a Gestapo officer who was assigned now as supervisor of Jewish Affairs and Evacuation Affairs. All participants in the Wannsee Conference were shown

charts and maps by Heydrich, indicating the numbers and nationalities of Jews who were to be included in the final solution. Basic logistical (behind-the-scenes) items were discussed, such as the locations of death camps, the cheapest and most efficient means of transporting Jews there from all over Europe, who would be responsible for the roundups and deportations, what should be done at the camps, how to identify "half-Jews" and what should be done with them, and so on.

Adolf Eichmann (1906–1962), German Nazi leader and SS officer. Photographed during his trial for crimes against humanity at Jerusalem, enclosed in a bulletproof booth and guarded by Israeli soldiers, 1961.

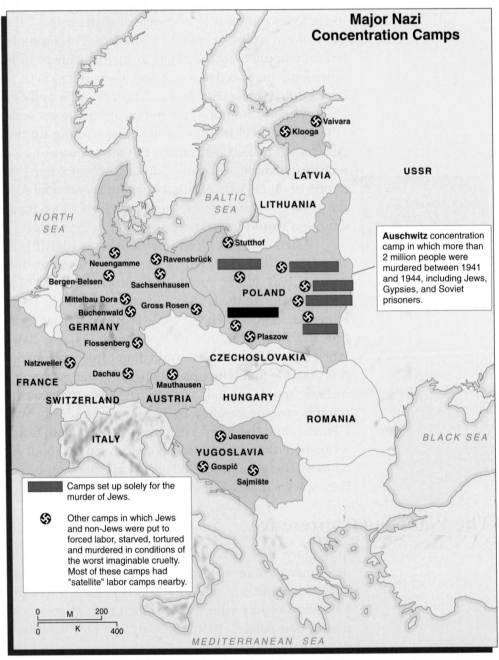

Major Nazi Concentration Camps

Auschwitz concentration camp in which more than 2 million people were murdered between 1941 and 1944, including Jews, Gypsies, and Soviet prisoners.

Camps set up solely for the murder of Jews.

Other camps in which Jews and non-Jews were put to forced labor, starved, tortured and murdered in conditions of the worst imaginable cruelty. Most of these camps had "satellite" labor camps nearby.

It is astonishing to realize that Heydrich and his colleagues were discussing very matter-of-factly the destruction of millions of human beings. The Wannsee Conference could just as well have been a meeting of the board of directors of a corporation, considering the transportation costs and other business issues connected with the manufacture and sale of a product. All the Nazis present at Wannsee considered themselves to be refined, cultured, and well-educated individuals. At the conference, they listened to classical music and enjoyed a fine meal. And yet, not one of them protested against the diabolical overall plan of wiping out a whole group of people from the face of the earth!

The implementation of the final solution would lie in the hands of the SS, not the regular German army. The latter, known as the Wehrmacht, was a well-trained professional military force.

The Einsatzgruppen

One of the most feared components within the SS was the **Einsatzgruppen** (Special Duty Groups). Eventually known also as "mobile killing units," their members were handpicked for "special actions" primarily in Poland and Russia—areas containing the great majority of European Jews. Among the many anti-Semitic lies put forth by Heydrich was that Jews were responsible for the rise of communism and must therefore be liquidated (killed) in accordance with Hitler's wishes. The Einsatzgruppen were given three specific tasks:

1. To encourage local peoples to stage pogroms against Jews
2. To transfer Jews to ghettos that were being created
3. To commit mass murder by shooting and other means

These tasks were usually not difficult to achieve. Large numbers of native people in areas taken by the Germans would often do the bidding of their occupiers. This was due in part to their fear of the Germans and willingness to accept German propaganda but was mainly due to their own feelings and traditions of anti-Semitism. Thus, for example, there were hundreds of Poles, Latvians, Lithuanians, Ukrainians, and other eastern European people who contributed to the final solution. They carried out Nazi requests regarding pogroms, transports, and shootings. Collaborators in Eastern Europe made the work of the Einsatzgruppen easy. Certainly not all people in this region aided the Germans, but there were more than sufficient numbers who pulled triggers, performed unspeakable acts of torture and humiliation, or stood by when bloody actions occurred. Such actions would take place in a number of ways. One

Naked and shaven inmates of Auschwitz on their way into the gas chambers, c. 1944.

such incident, typical of many others, was described by Otto Ohlendorf, an Einsatzgruppen commander:

> [A unit assigned to kill Jews] would enter a village or town and order the prominent Jewish citizens to call together all other Jews for the purpose of resettlement. They were requested to hand over their valuables to the leaders of the unit, and shortly before the execution to surrender their outer clothing. The men, women and children were led to a place of execution which in most cases was located next to a more deeply excavated anti-tank ditch. Then they were shot kneeling or standing, and the corpses thrown into the ditch.

The victims of this kind of brutality might often be forced to dig their own ditches/graves and would then be shot in the back of the neck. Administering what the Germans called "neck shots" became so sickening and frightful for some of the executioners that they asked to be "excused." Their places would be taken by the Trawnikis, those non-Germans trained at the Polish camp for such tasks. The largest single massacre committed by an Einsatzgruppen squad was by machine gun at **Babi Yar**. At this site, near the city of Kiev in the former Soviet Union, more than thirty-five thousand Jews met death.

The Death Camps

In 1942 in Poland, the Nazis finished building six large sealed and guarded facilities, chiefly for the purpose of killing Jews. They were located at **Chelmno**, **Treblinka**, **Maidanek**, **Sobibor**, **Belzec**, and **Auschwitz** and can be referred to as death camps or extermination camps. There were many other camps where Jews were killed, although they were not originally intended to be places for mass murder. These were called **concentration camps**, as their purpose was to concentrate enemies of the Reich in one place. The first of more than one hundred of these was opened at **Dachau**, Germany, in March 1933. Most of its original inmates were non-Jews and included supporters of the Weimar Republic, Socialists, Communists, and others who spoke out against the Nazis. Some other large concentration camps that were opened between 1933 and the start of World War II in 1939 were **Belsen**, **Buchenwald**, and **Ravensbruck** in Germany and **Mauthausen** in Austria. Many of these had subcamps, with increasing numbers of Jews and other imprisoned populations that included homosexuals, the mentally retarded, the physically handicapped, gypsies, and Jehovah's Witnesses. Along with Jews and Hitler's political enemies, all these groups were considered "unfit" and "undesirable" by him. Some concentration camps, such as

Entrance gate with lettering "Arbeit macht frei," Auschwitz Concentration Camp.
© Robert Harding Picture Library Ltd.

Mauthausen, became slave labor camps for the purpose of helping the German war effort. Hundreds of thousands perished there, from outright killing as well as from overwork under inhuman conditions.

Planet Auschwitz

Main Idea: Many of the things that happened on "planet Auschwitz" happened at other camps, but not with as much grotesque intensity nor with the large numbers of affected people as at this site in southwestern Poland. It is thus necessary for us to focus on Auschwitz to understand what all the camps were like.

Of all these horrible places, Auschwitz was the worst. In March 1941, after Auschwitz had already been opened as a concentration camp, Himmler chose it as the primary site for the murder of Europe's Jews. The world inside this camp would become so far removed from ordinary human existence that one inmate described life there as being on another planet.

Auschwitz was actually divided into thirty-nine camps within a radius of fifty miles. There were three main camps, each one capable of housing thousands of prisoners and having a separate function. Auschwitz I was a concentration camp; Auschwitz II was known officially as Birkenau and was a death camp that claimed the lives of three million people; Auschwitz III, known as Monowitz, was a slave labor camp. From 1942 on, transports, mainly railroad freight cars, would arrive daily. They were crowded with Jews, jammed in tightly, without food, water, or toilet facilities. Some transports took days to complete their journeys. The occupants, with only the belongings they could carry, had no idea where they were going. They were deported from almost all the European nations, from as far west as France and as far south as Greece; the greatest number of deportations were from parts of Poland and the former Soviet Union. With cool-headed efficiency, Nazi "desk-murderers" such as Adolf Eichmann routinely planned time schedules, made sure that transports were in good working conditions, assigned train engineers, and acted in a businesslike fashion as if they were arranging for shipments of cattle rather than human beings.

The Selection Process

Untold numbers of people did not survive the transports' journeys to Auschwitz. At the camp's entrance was a sign in German, *"Arbeit Macht Frei"* (Work will make you free). As yet another example of the big lie technique, this sign was supposed to inspire camp inmates with hope and make them feel welcome. What really happened upon arrival of the transports was very unwelcome and frightening. Their doors would be flung open by SS guards with dogs. Exhausted, tired, hungry, and thirsty, the surviving Jews were yelled at and forced to line up on a long railroad platform. Without knowing where they were nor what awaited them, they now underwent the "selection process." This hideous procedure was carried out by SS officials and medical doctors, among them the notorious Dr. **Josef Mengele**. They would look at the deportees and decide which ones seemed capable of work and which would be "nonproductive." As a result of this selection process, usually made with a casual flick of the thumb, nod of the head, or pointing with a cane, two columns of people were formed. On the right of the German officials might be healthy-looking males, from perhaps the late teens to 45 years of age, and some women; on the left would be children, the elderly, the sick, and the infirm, and the remainder of the transport's women. Mothers clutching babies would be on this line. Members of a family were often separated, while screaming, crying, and desperately reaching out to each other. Their anguish had no impact on their status. SS guards would beat them, while dogs would bark and threaten to bite; the two columns would be moved further apart. This moment would be the last time that those who survived the selection process, such as healthy teenagers, would ever see any parents and other relatives who were placed on the "nonproductive" line. Those placed on this line were sent immediately, unknowingly, to gas chambers. Here, they would be killed. Inmates needed by the SS, such as physicians, engineers, or carpenters, might be spared from some of the dirtier jobs. Among the dirtier jobs were those performed by the *Sonderkommando*, special units of prisoners who were assigned to take dead bodies from the gas chambers and elsewhere to be burned in a **crematory**. Auschwitz had four crematories, containing forty-six ovens.

Main Idea:
On the right of the German officials might be healthy-looking males, from perhaps the late teens to 45 years of age, and some women; on the left would be children, the elderly, the sick, and the infirm, and the remainder of the transport's women.

Daily life for inhabitants of Auschwitz was nightmarish, both emotionally and physically. They were isolated from all features of a normal society. When deportees entered Auschwitz, as well as any other camp, they were stripped of their humanity; they lost their names, employment, social status, friends, family, and identity. Each of them would be recognized only as a number, burned into an arm as a never-to-be removed tattoo. Inmates would wear ragged uniforms, be watched constantly, and be beaten and punished for any reason, and sometimes for no reason. They lived in crude, unsanitary barracks, crowded together with as many as four hundred other prisoners. They were purposely underfed, often with unfit and rotten food. SS physicians had determined a specific number of calories to be consumed. Food was rationed in such a way that prisoners would rarely survive for more than three months. These conditions often resulted in savage behavior among inmates and a breakdown of any civilized contact between them. Some might steal food from others, fight for scraps and crumbs, and rummage through garbage heaps for something to eat.

Medical Experiments

Another unique horror visited upon selected prisoners at Auschwitz was medical experiments. Never before had human beings been forced to undergo sadistic tests and experiments by medical professionals under official governmental authority. On planet Auschwitz, however, the SS did not consider inmates to be human or worthy of life. Accordingly, Himmler, and SS doctors such as Mengele, saw nothing wrong in "advancing scientific knowledge" by using Jews and other "subhumans" as guinea pigs. In one experiment, designed to help the German air force learn about the effects of high altitudes on pilots, inmates were placed in a decompression chamber. Here, they were subjected to air becoming so thin that their eardrums would often burst. It was common for many subjects to die from these tests.

Some other tortuous experiments were conducted to find out how people could endure cold—for example, having them standing naked in ice water or outdoors in bitter snow. Mengele, hoping to learn what caused eye color in twins, would kill them and then dissect the eyes. Various viruses, cancer cells, and typhus germs would be injected into prisoners to observe the effects. Newly developed drugs would then be administered to test their effectiveness. Surgical experiments, often without anesthetics, were carried out on sex organs. In addition, a group of healthy prisoners might be subjected to heavy doses of radiation, making them sterile. Specimens would then be taken from their affected tissues for laboratory analysis. Probably more for sports entertainment than for medical knowledge, prisoners would be tested to see how fast they would run when being chased by starving dogs.

The Gas Chambers

Gas chambers, such as those at Auschwitz, Belzec, Treblinka, and other extermination sites, were used mainly for two reasons: they were the least expensive and the most efficient means of mass murder. Experimentation with gassing at Auschwitz took place in September 1941, with large-scale exterminations underway by the summer of 1942. Gas had been used even earlier by the Nazis, as part of their **euthanasia** (mercy killing) program. In 1939, Hitler had ordered that "imperfect Aryans" (i.e., German children who were physically handicapped or mentally ill) should be put to death. It is not surprising that such methods would soon be employed against Jews on a massive scale, as part of the final solution.

By 1942, German scientists, having experimented with different gases, decided upon using **Zyklon B**, an insecticide. It was discovered that cans with pellets of the gas, when dropped through windows in the chambers' roofs, would soon poison the air inside the chambers. Death would occur within three to five minutes, upon inhalation of the gas. Between ten thousand and fifteen thousand people would be killed this way at Auschwitz, in any given day. The events occurring on such a day, carefully arranged by the SS, would unfold in a deceptive yet gruesome manner.

Jews selected for the gas chamber were never told the truth about what was going to happen. They would be marched to a sealed, harmless-looking building, where they were instructed to remove their clothes and place them on numbered hooks. They were given bars of soap and told that they would be taking a shower in order to be disinfected. These "instructions" were designed to comfort both the people who had just come off transports after days of traveling and the camp inmates who had been living in dirty barracks. Prior to being herded, with hundreds of others, into a large room with shower heads, the unaware victims would be told to remember their numbers so as to reclaim their clothing. They might also be spoken to reassuringly by guards, and even be accompanied by musicians, who, at a distance, would play soft and melodious music. Once the room was full, guards would lock the doors and drop the gas pellets into ventilation shafts. The resulting hissing sound from the pellets' bursting was quickly drowned out by the cries, screams, vomiting, and pounding on walls by the trapped Jews. SS officers would maliciously look

> **Main Idea:**
> Gas had been used even earlier by the Nazis, as part of their **euthanasia** (mercy killing) program. In 1939, Hitler had ordered that "imperfect Aryans" (i.e., German children who were physically handicapped or mentally ill) should be put to death.

Empty Zyklon B canisters on display in the Auschwitz Museum. Zyklon B gas was used to murder prisoners at the Auschwitz Birkenau death camp. © Philip Wolmuth/Alamy.

through peepholes. When they were satisfied that no one was left alive, they would order Sonderkommandos to open the doors, remove the bodies, and get the chamber clean and ready for its next victims!

The Crematory

The bodies would then be taken to the crematory, for burning in ovens and furnaces. Two thousand bodies could be incinerated every twenty-four hours. So many burnings took place at Auschwitz that, periodically, several inches of human fat had to be scraped from the chimney walls of the crematory. The ashes would be discarded. At times when the camp's furnaces were inoperative, the bodies would be burned in open pits. The stench of burning flesh would often spread for miles, thereby producing complaints from nearby townspeople. These complaints were at odds with statements by these same townspeople after 1945 that they "did not know" what was happening at Auschwitz.

A heartbreaking partial summary account of extermination processes at Auschwitz is contained in the 1979 report issued in the United States by the President's Commission on the Holocaust:

> At Auschwitz was a [company], a division of I. G. Farben. This . . . petrochemical complex brought human slavery to its ultimate perfection by reducing human beings to consumable raw materials, from which all mineral life was systematically drained before the bodies were recycled into the Nazi war economy; gold teeth for the treasury, hair for mattresses, ashes for fertilizer. In their relentless search for . . . [extermination methods], German scientists discovered Zyklon B, which could kill 2,000 persons in less than 30 minutes at a cost of one-half cent per body. Near the end of the war, in order to cut expenses and save gas, "cost-account considerations" led to an order to place living children directly in the ovens or throw them into open burning pits. The same type of ingenuity and control [used in] modern industrial development was . . . applied to the process of destruction.

The horrors perpetrated on the Jews of Europe, as we have now seen, were shameful, revolting, and inexcusable. While many of these horrors were also perpetrated on other groups, such as gypsies and Slavs, none suffered as much nor were intended for as much suffering as Jews. As Elie Wiesel, an Auschwitz survivor, has stated, "While not all victims were Jews, yet, all Jews were victims."

Did the Jews do anything to resist being victimized? Were they able to do anything? The complex answers to these questions will now be examined.

JEWISH RESISTANCE

Yes, there were many instances of Jewish resistance to the Nazis. In fact, these instances were some of the most heroic in human history. They occurred under conditions never experienced by other groups facing oppression, let alone the uniqueness of intended mass annihilation. These conditions, described here, made any decision to offer resistance a very difficult one:

- The physical, armed strength of the Germans and their collaborators was overwhelming. The Jews had no weapons of their own.

- Amidst the frightening quality of life imposed by the Germans in ghettos and camps (starvation, disease, forced labor, overcrowding, random shootings, and separation of families), mere survival from day to day became the chief goal. It required all of one's energy just to stay alive. Physical weakness and emotional demoralization had devastating effects on peoples' ability and will to survive.
- A small number of Jews felt that their suffering was God's will and that they should accept their fate.
- Attempts to have any organized leadership among Jewish communities were impossible, given the lack of means of communication and transportation.
- The Jews were alone, all alone. No help could be expected from anybody. No nation fighting the Germans during World War II offered aid to Jews. Most, as we have seen, did not even want to accept Jews as refugees fleeing Hitler. While the French and Dutch underground resistance groups were linked with sovereign nations fighting the Germans and could expect help from the surrounding native population and even from the United States and its allies, the position of Jews in European countries during the war years of 1939 to 1945 was completely different. There was no Jewish nation, as Israel was not yet in existence. Who then would aid the Jews, protect them, and give them weapons with which to fight?
- Deception and the big lie technique were used often by the Germans to mask their goal of genocide. Not wanting to publicize the truth about the camps, the Germans would state that the camps were merely labor camps, that life there would be more healthy and free than in crowded ghettos. Jews in Western European countries were often told, for example, that they were going to be "resettled in farmland to the east." Very few of them were aware of or could even imagine the horrors of the camps.
- Psychologically, human beings recoil from the unthinkable and the unknown. For Jews to believe that Germans, who were considered to be highly cultured and civilized, would now seek to kill off a whole people was difficult if not impossible to grasp. Most of those killed in the Holocaust could not conceive that innocent people would be murdered just because they were Jewish.

> **Main Idea:**
> Given all these facts, there were still several instances of resistance by Jews. These occurred in ghettos and camps and were both violent and spiritual.

Given all these facts, there were still several instances of resistance by Jews. These occurred in ghettos and camps and were both violent and spiritual. All of them were examples of bravery, courage, and heroism.

The Warsaw Ghetto Uprising (1943)

Of the many armed revolts by Jews against Germans, the most famous was in Warsaw, Poland. Sealed off from the rest of the city in 1940 by construction of an encircling wall, the Warsaw Ghetto became a terribly overcrowded area by 1941. Its peak population of 450,000 Jews in that year dwindled to 70,000 by April 1943. The drop was due primarily to the deportation of more than 300,000 Jews to the Treblinka death camp, where almost all were sent to the gas chambers.

Countless other thousands had died in the ghetto itself, either from hunger, from the cold, from disease, or in massacres by the Germans and their collaborators. The final deportation of Jews was to begin on April 19, 1943. The date was significant for two reasons:

Polish Jews crouch in fear as Nazi soldiers sift through the rubble of the Warsaw ghetto, c. 1943.

1. The evening of this day would mark the start of the Jewish holiday of Passover. The Nazis were aware of this and, fully knowing the dates of Jewish holidays, would often carry out sadistic and deadly actions at such times.

2. As April 20 was Hitler's birthday, SS head Himmler had hoped to present Hitler with a "birthday gift" on that day—an announcement that the Warsaw Ghetto was free of Jews and had been burned to the ground.

Hitler did not receive any "gift" on his birthday. What he did receive was news about a violent and bloody struggle that broke out when German forces entered the streets of the ghetto. These forces were met with gunfire from members of the **ZOB** (*Zydowska Organizacja Bojowa*, Jewish Fighting Organization). Led by 23-year-old Mordechai Anielewicz, the ZOB killed six SS soldiers and six Ukrainian guards. Such action by armed Jews shocked SS General **Jurgen Stroop**—he was surprised to learn that "inferior people" could and would offer resistance to the "master race." He was also unaware that some sort of revolt against Germans had been planned by Jews for the past few months. The ZOB had obtained a small number of weapons from the Polish underground, almost one hundred rifles and small quantities of pistols, hand grenades and explosives, along with three light machine guns. Numbering no more than fifteen hundred young men and women, ranging in age from 10 to the early 20s, the Jewish fighters were poorly trained, suffered from diseases, and had limited amounts of food, water, and medicine. In a David vs. Goliath contest, they were up against thousands of highly trained professional soldiers from the strongest European armed forces at the time. These soldiers were healthy and well-supplied and had access to modern means of warfare. These means, all of which were used against Jews in the ghetto, consisted of armored trucks, heavy machine guns, tanks, aircraft, artillery, flamethrowers, and chlorine gas. Facing such overwhelming superiority in weaponry and manpower, the Jews were able, astonishingly, to hold off the Germans and battle them for almost one month (April 19 to May 16, 1943).

German SS units deporting the Jewish population from the Warsaw Ghetto prior to the uprising. This picture was part of the report "There is no Jewish residential district in Warsaw anymore" from May 16, 1943, written by the SS and police captain of Warsaw Jürgen Stroop.

As the battle for the Warsaw Ghetto was in an urban setting, fighting took place in apartment buildings, on rooftops and street corners, from windows, and in sewers, basements, and underground bunkers. Stroop found gas and fire to be his most effective weapons in flushing out Jews from hidden areas above and below ground. Nevertheless, the ZOB continued to inflict heavy casualties on the Germans and to capture weapons from fallen soldiers. In the first week of fighting, more than 150 Germans had been killed and wounded. Yet the ZOB leadership, with its command bunker at #18 Mila Street, realized that, militarily, it could not exist for long. With no outside assistance, decreasing ammunition, buildings and bunkers destroyed, ZOB resistance began to crumble in the second week of May. Surrounded in their bunker, most leaders died from suffocation by gas, while others committed suicide. A scant few were able to escape through infested, dangerous sewers out of the city and then to nearby forests. On May 16, 1943, upon blowing up the unoccupied Warsaw synagogue, Stroop was able to inform Himmler that the Warsaw Ghetto "is no longer in existence."

Uprisings in Other Ghettos

Armed resistance occurred in many other ghettos, notably in Bialystok (**Poland**) and Vilna (Lithuania). In 1943, Jews in both cities attacked Nazi forces. The attackers had little ammunition and were eventually defeated. Most were hunted down and killed. A few were able to escape to the forests, where they formed partisan units and continued to fight the Germans. One of these was the famous partisan group led by Tuvia Bielski.

Uprisings in the Camps

It was much more difficult for Jews to offer armed resistance in the camps than was the case in the ghettos. Because the ghettos were sections of cities, there was always the possibility of obtaining smuggled weapons and food and of establishing some contact with local anti-German forces. The situation in the camps was much different, as these were usually built in the countryside and were completely cut off from the outside world. In addition, the frightening physical and emotional hardships in the camps made any coordinated resistance practically impossible. Yet, there were revolts in the camps. Three of these courageous episodes occurred in Treblinka, Sobibor, and Auschwitz.

Spiritual Resistance

The resistance efforts just described were aimed at violently hurting the Nazi oppressors and their collaborators, escaping from them, and rescuing other Jews. Another form of resistance, not using armed weapons, sought to preserve a sense of human dignity and identity. We may describe this form as **spiritual resistance**. Amidst environments of isolation, deprivation, and death imposed by the Germans, conditions under which human beings could not live or exist, Jews nevertheless found many ways to express this powerful manner of fighting back and maintaining their cultural heritage. This was true in both the ghettos and the camps.

In ghettos such as those of Warsaw and Vilna, examples of underground and illegal activities were as follows: self-help organizations to aid the weak and the poor; secret gatherings to recite prayers, hold religious services, and observe religious holidays; schools that taught both secular and religious subjects; poetry readings, dramatic presentations, and art exhibits; lectures and concerts; libraries, study groups, and various publications. One of the most important publications in Warsaw was organized by the historian **Emmanuel Ringelblum**. Under the code name *Oneg Shabbat* (Pleasure of the Sabbath), the publication's aim was to compile documentation about Jewish life in the ghetto under German occupation. These documents included diaries, posters, announcements, photographs, jokes, and other material gathered by a large staff, hidden in crates and milk cans and discovered after World War II.

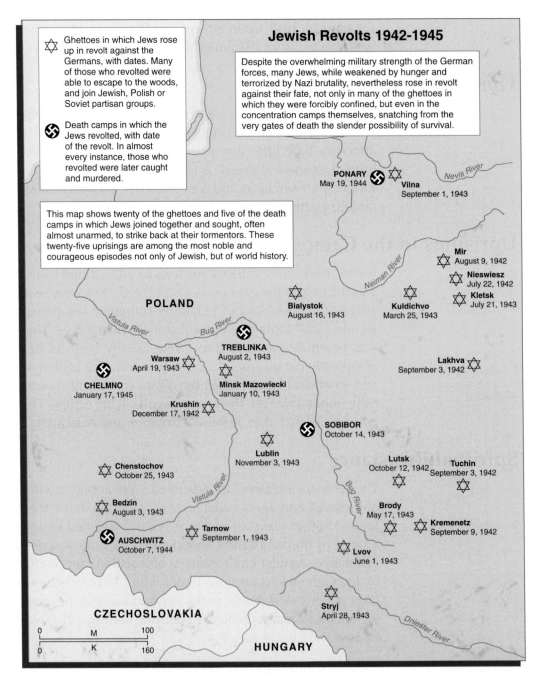

Jewish Revolts 1942-1945

Ghettoes in which Jews rose up in revolt against the Germans, with dates. Many of those who revolted were able to escape to the woods, and join Jewish, Polish or Soviet partisan groups.

Death camps in which the Jews revolted, with date of the revolt. In almost every instance, those who revolted were later caught and murdered.

Despite the overwhelming military strength of the German forces, many Jews, while weakened by hunger and terrorized by Nazi brutality, nevertheless rose in revolt against their fate, not only in many of the ghettoes in which they were forcibly confined, but even in the concentration camps themselves, snatching from the very gates of death the slender possibility of survival.

This map shows twenty of the ghettoes and five of the death camps in which Jews joined together and sought, often almost unarmed, to strike back at their tormentors. These twenty-five uprisings are among the most noble and courageous episodes not only of Jewish, but of world history.

PONARY
May 19, 1944

Vilna
September 1, 1943

Nevis River

Mir
August 9, 1942

Nieswiesz
July 22, 1942

Kletsk
July 21, 1943

POLAND

Bialystok
August 16, 1943

Kuldichvo
March 25, 1943

Neiman River

Vistula River

Bug River

TREBLINKA
August 2, 1943

Warsaw
April 19, 1943

Lakhva
September 3, 1942

CHELMNO
January 17, 1945

Minsk Mazowiecki
January 10, 1943

Krushin
December 17, 1942

SOBIBOR
October 14, 1943

Chenstochov
October 25, 1943

Lublin
November 3, 1943

Lutsk
October 12, 1942

Tuchin
September 3, 1942

Vistula River

Bug River

Bedzin
August 3, 1943

Brody
May 17, 1943

Kremenetz
September 9, 1942

Tarnow
September 1, 1943

AUSCHWITZ
October 7, 1944

Lvov
June 1, 1943

CZECHOSLOVAKIA

Stryj
April 28, 1943

Dniester River

0   M   100

0   K   160

HUNGARY

In the camps, where it was obviously impossible to do what was done in the ghettos, spiritual resistance was evident, nevertheless. Each day of survival in a place like Auschwitz, just by washing one's hands and doing the simplest of things, was an act of resistance. If anything, it signified a way of holding back the Nazi genocide. Preserving religious faith and traditions in any way possible was another means of opposing the dehumanization process in the camps. Examples, always done secretly and at great risk, were as follows:

- Reciting portions of the Bible to each other
- Writing down or scratching on discarded scraps of paper stories about Jewish heroes and procedures for observing holidays
- Staging mock religious services and whispering the spoken parts for events such as the Passover Seder

Frequently, according to German documents captured after the war, Jews prayed, sang, and comforted each other in the gas chambers. Mothers were known to calm their children, to smile at them and speak softly. Many Nazi officials were surprised at how such "inferior people" could die with dignity.

Januscz Korczak

One of countless acts of spiritual resistance, attempting to maintain some dignity and delay new news of the inevitable, involved Dr. **Januscz Korczak**. A famous Jewish pediatrician in Warsaw, he was the founder and director of an orphanage for very young Jewish children in the ghetto. His care and love for these children was boundless. This was probably why, at the age of 64, he accompanied them when they were ordered by the Germans, in August 1942, to leave the orphanage for the **Umschlagplatz** (the central train station in Warsaw). Even though, as a physician, he could have been exempt from this deportation order, Korczak chose to stay with "his" children. He did not tell them the truth about the journey they were to take. Rather, he had them dress up in their best clothes and told them they were going to enjoy a day of sunshine in some open, green fields.

What an astonishing sight this was to see, amidst the ugliness and misery of German-occupied Warsaw—an orderly march of two hundred small boys and girls, led by an old man carrying a sick child! One eyewitness noted that the children were

> emaciated, weak, shriveled and shrunk. They carry shabby packages; some have schoolbooks, notebooks under their arms. No one is crying. Their little eyes are turned toward the doctor. They are strangely calm; they feel almost well. The doctor is going with them, so what do they have to be afraid of? They are not alone, they are not abandoned.
> Dr. Korczak busies himself with the children.... He buttons the coat of one child, ties up the package of another, or straightens the cap of a third.

At the Umschlagplatz, another observer sadly watched the children remove their yellow stars as ordered. He remarked that the procession was like a "field of buttercups." The children were last seen boarding the train with Dr. Korczak. From the Umschlagplatz, as would be true for hundreds of thousands of Jews, they went on to Treblinka, to face death in the gas chambers.

Did Januscz Korczak act wisely? Is *spiritual resistance* an accurate term to describe what he did? Should he have told the children the truth? What would you have said to a child, younger than yourself, in such a situation? And further, on another day when a deportation was carried out, what should a mother and father have told their little son when he asked this question: "Why does Hitler hate me when he doesn't even know me?"

The agony of trying to answer these questions makes us more sensitive, today, about the horrors associated with the Holocaust. But we must also ask how sensitive was the world itself, from 1933 to 1945, when these horrors were being perpetrated against the Jews of Europe. The possible answers, neither easy nor satisfying, follow.

World Reaction to the Holocaust

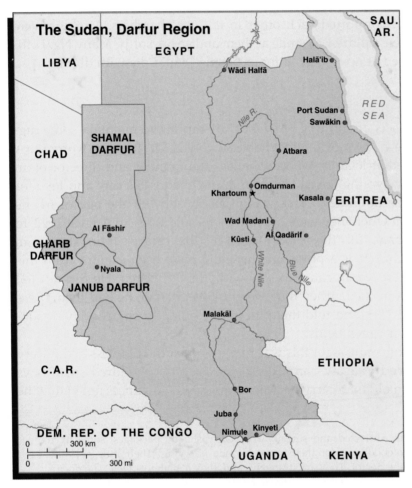

In the 2000s, the world learned about the mass killings in Darfur, **The Sudan**, believed what it learned, and tried to end the slaughter. In the 1990s, the world learned about mass killings in the former **Yugoslavia**, believed what it learned, and tried to end the bloodshed. In the 1980s, the world learned about mass killings occurring in **Cambodia** (formerly Kampuchea), believed what it learned, and tried to end the bloodshed. In the 1940s, the world learned about the mass killings of Jews, hesitated to believe initially what it learned, and did nothing to end the bloodshed. And even when convinced that the reported slaughter of innocent millions was true, the world still failed to take strong action. Recognition of its failure in the dark days of the 1940s may explain why the world was willing to do something about the mass murders of the 1980s, 1990s, and 2000s.

Reports about the worst of the Nazi atrocities began to leak out from Germany and German-controlled lands in 1941, but they were not fully accepted until 1942. On December 18, 1942, the *New York Times* carried a story about a joint declaration by eleven nations fighting Hitler in which they acknowledged and condemned his "bestial policy of cold-blooded extermination" of "the Jewish people in Europe." Among those signing the declaration were the United States, Britain, France, Greece, and Russia. Their willingness to issue this declaration was based upon information from several sources.

Why didn't the Allies mount any specific military action to stop the Nazi persecutions and mass killings between 1942 and 1945? Clearly, as we have seen, increasing evidence had led to increased awareness. In the Allied nations, Jews and others had requested that bombing raids be made. And in July 1944, British Prime Minister Winston Churchill himself labeled the Holocaust as "probably the greatest and most horrible single crime ever committed in the whole history of the world." The failure by the Allies to take any collective military action is generally explained by one or more of the following reasons:

> **Main Idea:**
> Even when convinced that the reported slaughter of innocent millions was true, the world still failed to take strong action.

- Many people thought that the best way to rescue the Jews and stop the mass killings was to win the war against the Germans. Accordingly, it would be more advantageous to use weapons and manpower against military targets than to destroy camps and railroad lines.
- Some government officials who learned of the atrocities simply refused to believe that such inhuman acts took place. Many ordinary private citizens, both Jewish and non-Jewish, initially refused to accept as true the reports of massacres and other beastly crimes.
- There were officials who, because of their own prejudices toward Jews, held back information and refused to take any action.
- The Nazis were fairly successful in practicing both delay and deception. From time to time, for example, the Gestapo would fake a willingness to enter into negotiations to save Jews. Meanwhile, the murders would continue. Nazi propaganda, rather than make any mention of gas chambers, would point out the benefits for Jews of being transported from grimy ghettos to camps "in the countryside." The camp at **Theresienstadt** (also known as *Terezin*) in Czechoslovakia was set up as a "model showcase," where newsreels and pictures were made by the Nazis to show Jews living freely and eating well. Invited visitors from such groups as the International Red Cross were able to observe pleasant scenes, without ever realizing or being told that the camp was built as a deception and as a stopover for inmates on their way to Auschwitz.

These Nazi "successes" should not, however, excuse the failures of the Allies. Those failures, as summarized by historian Martin Gilbert in his book *Auschwitz and the Allies*, "were those of imagination, of response, of intelligence, of piecing together and evaluating what was known, of coordination, of initiative, and even at times of sympathy."

Denmark, Sweden, and Raoul Wallenberg

Two nations that did take specific measures to show solidarity with Jews, by making heroic rescue efforts, were Denmark and Sweden. Having occupied Denmark since 1940, the Germans decided to send the small number of Danish Jews to Auschwitz in September 1943. SS troops had to be sent from Germany to arrange this because the Danish police, armed forces, and **King Christian X**, refused to cooperate with the Germans and become collaborators. The Wehrmacht commander in Denmark also refused to cooperate, claiming that rounding up Jews was not a military matter.

Christian X, King of Denmark, 1912–1947.
Photographed at the beginning of his reign.

Denmark and Sweden

NORTH SEA

NORWAY

SWEDEN

FINLAND

GULF OF BOTHNIA

Lulea
Skelleftea
Sundsvall
Falun
Västeras • Uppsala
Örebro
Stockholm
Norrköping
Linköping
Göteborg
Janköping
Alborg

GULF OF FINLAND

ESTONIA

LATVIA

LITHUANIA

DENMARK

Vejle
Copenhagen
Malmö

BALTIC SEA

RUSSIA

BELARUS

GERMANY

POLAND

Main Idea:
With the roundup scheduled for October 1943, the Danes made a secret agreement with neighboring Sweden for the transfer of Jews. Sweden promised to give **sanctuary** (a safe place) to Danish Jewish refugees.

With the roundup scheduled for October 1943, the Danes made a secret agreement with neighboring Sweden for the transfer of Jews. Sweden promised to give **sanctuary** (a safe place) to Danish Jewish refugees. In what was to become one of the most extraordinary rescues in history, the Danes helped more than seven thousand Jews to escape secretly over the fifteen-mile waterway separating Denmark from Sweden. Danish people from all walks of life hid Jews in their homes, drove them to coastal areas, posted lookouts to watch for Germans, provided stimulants to keep people awake, and smuggled them into all kinds of fishing boats and pleasure crafts for the trip to Sweden. After the war, the Danes welcomed back their former fellow citizens.

As a neutral country in World War II, Sweden could offer refuge to anyone claiming Swedish citizenship. One of its diplomats in German-occupied Hungary was **Raoul Wallenberg**. From 1944 to 1945, he worked brilliantly and courageously to place thousands of Jews under Swedish government authority in order to protect them from both the Nazis and their Hungarian collaborators. His main method was to issue "protective passports," certificates containing the Swedish embassy stamp and his signature. He had given out twenty thousand passports by January 1945 and had at times handed them directly to Jews who were about to be transported to Auschwitz. In addition, he was known to bring food and medicine at night to needy people. Wallenberg's efforts were truly humanitarian, yet when Hungary was freed of German occupation by the

Russians in 1945, he was taken prisoner by the Russians for unknown reasons and never seen again. Humanitarian actions similar to those of Wallenberg were also performed by other diplomats: **Sempo Sugihara** of Japan in Lithuania and **Aristide de Susa Mendes** of Portugal in France.

The year 1944 also had impact in New York State. Almost one thousand refugees, primarily Jewish, were evacuated from Europe and relocated to Fort Ontario. This site was in Oswego, New York. For further information, go to www.oswegohaven.org.

The Role of the Churches

Another person helpful to some Hungarian Jews was the Budapest representative of the pope, Angelo Roncalli. Roncalli, who later became **Pope John XXIII**, was one of the countless Christian clergymen who provided assistance to entrapped Jews. Nevertheless, the general attitudes of the churches in Europe (Catholic, Protestant, and Orthodox) to the plight of the Jews were varied and complex. **Pope Pius XI**, the Catholic leader at the time of Hitler's rise to power, wrote that myths of "race" and "blood" were contrary to Christian teaching. However, he neither mentioned nor criticized anti-Semitism. He was succeeded in 1939 by **Pius XII**, who learned by 1942 of the murders in the camps and elsewhere. His public statements, though, were limited to expressions of sympathy for sufferers of injustice and pleas for humane conduct of the war. Although Jewish leaders did not get from the pope a requested specific condemnation of Nazi anti-Semitism, the Jews of Rome did gain refuge in Vatican buildings during the Nazi occupation of the city. Some historians believed that the pope's public silence was a sign of anti-Semitism within the Church. Others claim that his silence was due to a genuine fear that, if he spoke out, European Catholics might themselves be subjected to a "final solution."

The Catholic Church in Germany did little to oppose Nazi anti-Semitism and was alleged to have given documents to authorities in order to detect people of Jewish origin. One of the very few clergymen to denounce the mass murders of Jews was **Bernard Lichtenberg**. Throughout Western Europe, Catholic clergy often spoke out against persecution of Jews and aided in rescue work. Indeed, many convents and monasteries protected young Jewish children by converting them temporarily to Catholicism. In Eastern Europe, however, Catholic officials were less willing to take a strong public stance and in some cases actually cooperated with the Germans.

Orthodox leaders in some Eastern European nations were more responsive, heeding the pronouncement by the **Patriarch of Constantinople**. He urged his bishops to help Jews and to proclaim in their churches that to conceal Jews was a sacred duty.

The response by Protestant churches was generally mixed. In many German Protestant congregations, there were Nazi supporters who acquiesced in anti-Jewish legislation and other measures. Rarely did any church protest against the persecution. Christians who had converted from Judaism were excluded from some churches but were protected by others. Within German-occupied nations, the position of Protestant communities varied. In Denmark, France, Holland, and Norway, there were examples of local churches and indi-

Main Idea:
Some historians believed that the pope's public silence was a sign of anti-Semitism within the Church. Others claim that his silence was due to a genuine fear that, if he spoke out, European Catholics might themselves be subjected to a "final solution."

vidual clergymen issuing public protests when deportations of Jews started. Few such protests were made in Austria, Belgium, Finland, Poland, and the Soviet Union.

Christian Rescuers—The "Righteous Among the Nations"

Christians who sought to help Jews during the Holocaust did so at great risk. Their efforts took several forms, such as smuggling weapons, arranging hiding places, and organizing rescues. They acted for reasons of friendliness, compassion, and their view of humane Christian teachings about helping those in need. For their actions, such individuals were honored by the state of Israel with the title "righteous among the nations." Their names and deeds are documented in the major Holocaust study center in Israel, the Yad Vashem Martyrs' and Heroes' Memorial Museum, built in 1953. Some of those so honored, including Wallenberg, Sugihara, and de Susa Mendes, were the following:

Anne Frank (1929–1945), German Jewish diarist.

- In France, **Mother Maria** of Paris produced false identification papers in her convent. She organized an underground network of Orthodox and Catholic clergy who gave shelter to Jews and smuggled many out of Paris. She was subsequently arrested and sent to die in a gas chamber.
- In Amsterdam, Dutch Christians **Jan** and **Miep Gies** hid Jews in an attic. Among those in hiding there from 1942 to 1944 were Otto Frank and his family. A young girl in this family, **Anne Frank**, kept a daily account of her life. Although she was eventually arrested and sent to a concentration camp where she died, her account was published after the war and became internationally famous, with the title *The Diary of a Young Girl*.
- In Germany itself, one of the very few Protestant clergymen who eventually protested against the Nazis was Pastor **Martin Niemoller**. He was arrested and sent to several concentration camps. Somehow, he was able to survive. After the war, he made a revealing statement that shows the danger of apathy (not caring):

> First they came for the Jews. I was silent. I was not a Jew. Then they came for the Communists. I was silent. I was not a Communist. Then they came for the trade unionists. I was silent. I was not a trade unionist. Then they came for me. There was no one left to speak for me.

The efforts of these people, as well as those of Raoul Wallenberg, the Danes, the Swedes and others, were noble and courageous. Yet, such efforts were isolated ones and far too few. The sad fact is that these efforts saved, at most, only a few thousand Jewish lives. The Nazis took six million.

Martin Niemoller (1892–1984), German anti-Nazi Protestant theologian, c. 1946.

THE HOLOCAUST ENDS—
DEFEAT OF NAZI GERMANY IN 1945

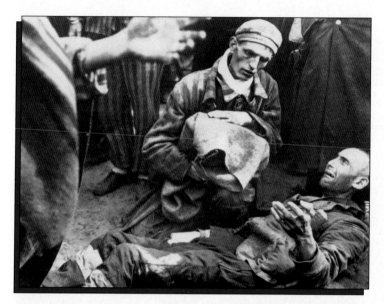

Concentration camp prisoners after the liberation. Photograph, May 1945.

By early 1945, it was clear that the Allied forces were going to defeat the Germans and that the war in Europe would soon end. The horrors of the camps would also come to an end. As the Russians pushed closer on Germany's eastern front, they liberated (freed) the camp at Maidanek in July 1944 and reached Auschwitz the following January. The Germans had already fled, having blown up several crematoria and gas chambers. The destruction had been ordered by Himmler, in an attempt to wipe out evidence of Nazi atrocities. The effects of the atrocities were nevertheless obvious to the Russians, as they initially found hundreds of corpses and eight thousand weak and emaciated survivors. In the main camp alone, there were two hundred starving children your age and younger. The Russian army gave little aid to these survivors, mostly because its chief goal was to reach Berlin.

The Death Marches

Three weeks prior to the Russian discoveries at Auschwitz, the Germans burned thousands of bodies, organized forced marches of more than sixty-five thousand prisoners out of the camp, and shot hundreds who were too sick and lame to walk. The forced movement of prisoners westward toward Germany became rightly known as the **death marches**. Long columns of Jews and others were herded through snow and freezing weather, subject to humiliation and beating by the guards. Those inmates who were unable to keep up were either shot or left to die along the way. The fact that the Nazis continued to murder Jews, even when it was certain that the Allies were going to win the war, is further evidence of the inexplicable malice.

The Death Toll

American and British forces attacking Germany's western front were able to liberate several camps. When they came to places such as Buchenwald and Bergen-Belsen in April 1945, however, they were completely unprepared for what they saw. To view unburied corpses and skeleton-like survivors amidst a horrible stench was enough to cause physical and mental disorders among Allied soldiers. Inmates had to be disinfected and "deloused"; they were unable to digest normal food, having suffered from malnourishment for months, if not years. The American general, Dwight D. Eisenhower, commander of the Allied forces in Europe, was accompanied by U.S. generals George Patton and Omar Bradley on an inspection of the Ohrduf camp in May 1945. They were shocked

Citizens of the city of Landsberg, Germany being forced by American troops to visit the concentration camp to view the gaunt, charred corpses of the prisoners in April 1945.

to find corpses of Jewish inmates scattered throughout the camp. German citizens who lived near camps such as Dachau and Buchenwald, and who claimed to be ignorant of what went on in the camps, were forced to march through them by the Allies and on occasion to bury corpses.

The greatest and most unspeakable horror of that past—the twelve years from 1933 to 1945—was the intentional murder of more than six million innocent people simply because they were Jewish. The approximate numbers of those killed, along with the percentage of the prewar Jewish population they represent are as follows:

Jewish Death Toll in the Holocaust

Country	Deaths	%	Country	Deaths	%
Austria	40,000	20%	Hungary	200,000	50%
Belgium	40,000	67%	Italy	8,000	16%
Czechoslovakia	315,000	88%	Latvia	80,000	84%
Denmark	500	8%	Lithuania	217,000	97%
Estonia	1,500	33%	Luxembourg	700	23%
Finland	8	1%	Norway	760	42%
France	90,000	30%	Poland	2,850,000	88%
Germany	170,000	32%	Romania	425,000	50%
Greece	60,000	80%	Soviet Union	1,252,000	44%
Holland	105,000	75%	Yugoslavia	60,000	80%

Source: Figures are from 36 Questions Asked About the Holocaust (Simon Wiesenthal Center, New York, 1979), p.1.

These numbers stagger the imagination. Even to contemplate the figure of six million is bewildering. It is likely that the greatest number of people you have ever seen together was at a sports complex. Some baseball stadiums and football arenas in the United States can hold a hundred thousand people. It would take sixty Yankee Stadiums to hold every person who died in the Holocaust!

Further examination of these numbers reveals additional shocking conclusions. Almost one and one-half million of the dead were children. Thus, almost an entire generation had been destroyed. And at the other end of the life spectrum, it has been estimated that almost no one over the age of 35 had survived the Holocaust. The continued existence of European Jewry over the previous two thousand years had suffered a terrible blow. This can be seen in the table which shows the number of Jews in Europe in a particular year and the percentage that number represented of all Jews in the world at the time.

Jewish World Population

Year	Number of Jews	Percentage
1840	3,950,000	88%
1900	8,900,000	81%
1939	9,500,000	57%
1946	2,850,000	26%

Source: Figures are from Y. Gutman and C. Schaztket, *The Holocaust and Its Significance* (The Zalman Shazar Center, Jerusalem, 1983), p 228.

With such a loss of life, European Jewish culture faced an uncertain future. Did this mean that the final solution was a success?

CONSEQUENCES AND LEGACIES (1945–2000)

The Nuremberg War Crimes Trials (1945–1949)

What should be done with those Germans who were responsible for planning and carrying out the final solution? This became a challenging question in November 1945, when twenty-two high-ranking Nazi officials went on trial in the city of **Nuremberg** before an international military tribunal (a court with judges from the four major Allied victors—the United States, Great Britain, France, and the Soviet Union). Several charges were brought against them, including committing war crimes and committing crimes against humanity. This last charge was the only one that had some connection with the attempted genocide against the Jews of Europe. Yet, the killing of Jews only because they were Jews was not considered a crime. Rather, the charge of crimes against humanity was applied specifically to acts of violence committed against all civilians of occupied nations—for example, Hungarians, French, Russians, and Poles. However, evidence of genocide was presented to the judges. It consisted of oral testimony, documents, films, and photographs. Some of it consisted of such horrible material that one British official considered the material too terrible to present to the judges. Nevertheless, its presentation was vital in making the world aware of how inhuman were the Nazi actions against Jews and many other people.

The accused Nazis were allowed to hire lawyers and to defend themselves, privileges they had never granted to those they had once accused and victimized. Hermann Göring (Hitler's closest aide and head of the German air force), **Hans Frank** (governor-general of Nazi-occupied Poland), and the other Nuremberg defendants raised several issues in their defense. They knew they could not claim that the Holocaust never happened, and there was too much evidence to prove that it did occur. Yet, two of their issues were pressed strongly upon the judges in an attempt to support their claim of innocence:

One issue was that they were "just following orders." The tribunal rejected this by stating that duty to such basic human laws and laws against murder, enslavement, and extermination take priority over any obedience to nation or government.

Another issue raised by the defense rested upon the *Führer-prinzip* (the Nazi "leadership principal"). This theory held that, since all commands were ordered by Hitler as a dictator and refusal to obey them would be punished by death, therefore only Hitler could be held responsible and all other Nazis were innocent of any wrongdoing. The Nuremberg judges rejected this contention, noting that individuals are responsible for their actions and that ordered acts of brutality and torture cannot be excused, as such acts violate the international law of war.

In October 1946, the court gave its verdict. Of the twenty-two defendants, nineteen were found guilty, three were acquitted. Twelve were sentenced to hang, and seven received varied prison sentences ranging from ten years to life. There were many other trials of Nazi officials, held in Nuremberg as well as in the different parts of Germany under Allied occupation and in countries where

Main Idea:
What should be done with those Germans who were responsible for planning and carrying out the final solution? This became a challenging question in November 1945, when twenty-two high-ranking Nazi officials went on trial in the city of **Nuremberg** before an international military tribunal.

The defendents at the Nuremberg Trials (front row, L – R): Hermann Goering, Rudolf Hess, Joachim von Ribbentrop, and Wilhelm Keitel. (Back row, L – R): Karl Doenitz, Roeder, Baldur von Schirach, Fritz Sauckel, and Alfred Jodl. 1945–1946.

war crimes and civilian atrocities were committed. Placed on trial were those Germans, and their collaborators, responsible for conducting medical experiments and for administering and carrying out evil acts in the death camps, concentration camps, and ghettos.

Searches for Other Criminals Involved in the Holocaust

Veteran Nazi hunter, Simon Weisenthal, 1981. © vario images GmbH & Co. KG

In the years after 1945, it became apparent that many individuals who had been involved in Holocaust-related atrocities were still alive. They had escaped arrest by taking any of several actions: leaving their birthplace for another country, changing their names, blending back quietly into their prewar homes and occupations, and being protected by friends and sympathizers. Searches for such people were conducted both by various nations as well as by private investigators, such as **Simon Wiesenthal**. Among the most publicized hunted-down individuals were Adolf Eichmann (captured by Israeli agents in Argentina in 1961), Josef Mengele (discovered to have drowned in Brazil in 1979), **Hermine Braunsteiner-Ryan** (a guard at Maidanek, deported from the United States in 1973), **John Demjanjuk** (a guard at Sobibor and Treblinka, deported from the United States in 1981).

Remembrance: Preservation of Memory

- *German Agreement to Finance Auschwitz Restoration and to Compensate Holocaust Survivors:* In late 1992, the German government said that it would provide $6 million to restore the Auschwitz death camp and to preserve it as a memorial site. The government also signed an agreement to pay compensation to Holocaust survivors who previously had received little or nothing from the government.
- *Creation by France of a National Day of Remembrance:* In February 1993, French President François Mitterrand signed a decree that established a national day of remembrance to recall the anti-Semitic crimes carried out by the Vichy collaborationist regime and the occupying German forces between 1940 and 1944. The date chosen was July 16, as it was on this date in 1942 that the first of several mass arrests of Jews was made by French police officers. Thousands of those arrested were eventually deported to German death camps throughout Europe.

The Holocaust Museum in Washington, D.C. © Sandra Baker/Alamy.

- *Opening of the U.S. Holocaust Memorial Museum in Washington, D.C.:* On April 26, 1993, this museum was formally opened and dedicated in our nation's capital. The collection of historical items here includes a railroad car that transported Jews to Auschwitz, as well as empty canisters of Zyklon B poison gas. At the dedication were President Bill Clinton, many world leaders, and thousands of Holocaust survivors.

- *Showing of the Holocaust Movie* Schindler's List: In 1993, *Schindler's List* opened in theaters across the United States. It told how **Oskar Schindler**, a German Christian factory owner, tried to protect Jews in Poland from the Nazis. It received favorable reviews and won an Academy Award for best picture in 1994.

Museum of Jewish Heritage, Hudson River Park, Manhattan, New York. © Ambient Images, Inc.

- *Opening of The Museum of Jewish Heritage—A Living Memorial to the Holocaust in New York City:* Dedicated in 1997, this complex stands in an urban region that has the largest number of Holocaust survivors residing in such an area, outside of Israel.

- *The Court Judgment against* **David Irving**: In 1993, an American college Professor, Deborah Lipstadt, wrote a book about people who denied that the Holocaust ever happened. She condemned a British writer named **David Irving** as a Holocaust denier. He sued her for libel in a British court and lost. The judge, deciding the case in 1999, concluded that Professor Lipstadt had proved that Irving's claims were wrong and that he had maliciously and intentionally falsified history. Lipstadt's accusation about him was correct.

LINKS TO TODAY

Remembrance: Preservation of Memory in the Twenty-First Century

In the United States: With each passing year since 1945, the number of living Holocaust survivors has become fewer and fewer. Among those who immigrated to America, the vast majority quickly sought to establish families. Large numbers of their children and grandchildren, to maintain memory, have formed 2G (second generation) and 3G (third generation) groups. Increased awareness of the Holocaust has also come about with the growth of courses in high schools and colleges, as well as web sites. A vast amount of survivor testimony and eyewitness accounts are accessible from the archives of the Shoah Foundation Institute for Visual History and Education. Begun by movie producer Steven Spielberg, this project has become a valuable educational resource. (*Shoah* is the Hebrew name for the Holocaust.)

The honoring of non-Jews as Righteous Among the Nations has continued. In August 2006, Professor Clara Ambrus-Bayer was given this well-deserved Yad Vashem designation at a ceremony in New York City at the office of the Israeli Consulate General. As a pediatrician now living as an American citizen in Buffalo, New York, she lived in Budapest,

Hungary, during the Holocaust. As a teenager, she hid Jews in her parents' textile factory as well as in her home. In later years, she made this reminiscence: "We opened our doors to all who asked asylum there . . . we developed elaborate hiding places and managed to share our meager food supplies so that we all survived the war."

The Holocaust has remained as a topic for the film industry. Examples of twenty-first century Holocaust-related films are *Paper Clips* and *The Pianist*.

In Germany: In May 2005, Germany's Holocaust memorial was officially opened in Berlin. At the inauguration ceremony, attended by all senior members of the government, the president of the German Parliament stated: "Today we are opening a memorial that commemorates the worst, the most atrocious of the crimes committed by Nazi Germany, the attempt to destroy a whole people. The horror touches the limit of our comprehension." He further noted that the structure will serve "as a place of memory "for future generations, helping them "to face up to the incomprehensible facts."

Around the World: On January 27, 2006, the United Nations observed its first ever Holocaust Remembrance Day ceremonies. This date is the anniversary of the liberation of the Auschwitz death camp. The vote establishing this commemoration also called on UN member states to include study of the Holocaust in their educational curriculums.

Two trips by **Pope Benedict XVI** had enormous significance. In August 2005, he visited a synagogue in Cologne, Germany. He was received with great emotion by hundreds of people, especially as this Jewish house of worship was destroyed during Kristallnacht in 1938 when eleven thousand Jews lived in the city. The structure was rebuilt in 1959; Jews now number five thousand in Cologne. Then in May 2006 he traveled to Auschwitz. While there, he condemned the Nazi regime as a group of "vicious criminals." He further stated that "the place where we are standing is a place of memory." The first papal trip to Auschwitz was made in 1979 by Pope John Paul II.

Holocaust Memorial in Berlin.© Juergen Henkelmann Photography/Alamy.

Lingering Issues: Although the specific events of the Holocaust ended in 1945, their consequences have raised challenging issues. Here a few recent ones.

1. *The fight over a suitcase.* Pierre L. was a French Jew who was deported by the Germans to Auschwitz in 1943. As part of their big lie practices, the Germans told all rounded–up Jews to bring suitcases as they would be taken by train to a labor camp—not a death camp. Records show that Pierre arrived in Auschwitz July 1943 with his suitcase. Yet, there is no further record of him, and it is not known how or when he died. Soon after the war, this suitcase was one of many that were put on display in the new Auschwitz-Birkenau State Museum. In 2004, the museum agreed to lend the suitcase to a Paris foundation until June 2005 for an exhibit on the Holocaust. During a visit to the Paris exhibition, Michel L., Pierre's son, saw the suitcase. (As a young boy in 1940, Michel was sent by his father to live with a farmer in order to avoid capture by the Germans.) Michel identified the suitcase as his father's, as the suitcase had Pierre's name, last home address, and Auschwitz prison reference number. Although Michel recognizes the importance of the museum's retaining the suitcase for historical display purposes, he nevertheless feels that the suitcase should stay in Paris and be in his possession. In January 2006, a French court issued a temporary order, preventing return of the suitcase to Poland. How would you decide this case? For Michel or for the museum?

2. *A proposed change of name.* Another Auschwitz-related issue, although somewhat less challenging than the suitcase dilemma, concerns the name of this infamous death camp. Poland has asked the United Nations to change the organization's official name of the site from "Auschwitz Concentration Camp" to the "Former Nazi German Concentration Camp of Auschwitz." Should this be done? Why did Poland want the name change? What would be the German reaction to this request? What would be the effect, if any, of a name change?

Suitcases of Jews brought to Auschwitz Birkenau death camp on display in the nearby Auschwitz museum.
© Philip Wolmuth/Alamy.

3. *The controversy over distributing money from Holocaust settlements.* In the years just after 1945, Holocaust survivors began making monetary claims against both European governments and private organizations that had benefited from the persecution of Jews during the Holocaust. Most of these claims, known as restitution concerning lost money and property, were negotiated by the New York-based Conference on Jewish Material Claims Against Germany (the Claims Conference). By 1998, settlements of billions of dollars had been reached. These were, for example, from Swiss banks that had unclaimed bank accounts held by those murdered, from Germany and German companies for using slave laborers, and from insurance companies that never paid off the policies of the dead. Although monies have begun to be distributed to those individuals, heirs, and organizations deemed eligible, controversies have arisen in recent years over these and future payments. Here are some examples: (1) A federal judge in New York decided that most of the money in a fund set up as part of the Swiss banks settlement should go to hard-pressed, poor survivors in the former Soviet Union rather than to those in the United States. His decision rested on the fact that the first group did not have such help programs as Medicare, although he did recognize the fact that about 25 percent of survivors in America live below the poverty line. (2) In another settlement, the Claims Conference agreed to a formula giving 80 percent of funds for health and social services for survivors and 20 percent for Holocaust education and research. One prominent survivor in the United States disagreed, stating that such monies, also known as reparations, should go to survivors and that education and research should be the responsibility of all Jewish organizations. Yet, another prominent survivor in the United States argued that it is fair to use some reparation dollars for publishing books, training teachers, and so on, so that future generations will know about the Holocaust. How would you decide the two situations described above? If you know any survivors or members of their families, would you pose these situations to them? Why or why not?

4. *France and its railroad system may have to pay for more than transportation costs.* In August of 2006, the families of almost seven hundred Holocaust victims, as well as over one hundred survivors, demanded $162 million from the government of France and from SNCF, the national railroad. According to their lawyer, the claims were for reparations due to the suffering and pain experienced by victims and survivors who were imprisoned in French camps and then transported by French rail eastward. Several ultimately went to their deaths. The claimants were very hopeful of winning, mainly because a French court in June ordered the state and the national railroad to pay $80,000 to a Jewish family whose members were transported to and held in the Drancy camp near Paris. The court concluded that the state did nothing "when it had a chance to" and that the railroad did not object and had actually billed the state for third-class travel even though it used freight cars and cattle cars.

CHAPTER SUMMARY

The official actions taken by France and the United States (national day of remembrance and establishment of Holocaust Museum) serve as powerful reminders of one of the worst instances in history of man's inhumanity to man. Such thoughts and remembrances about the Holocaust will also lead us to bear in mind the tragedies suffered by other groups of people because of prejudice. Examples include the racism against blacks in South Africa and during slavery in the United States, the attempted genocides committed by the Turks against Armenians and by the Sudanese against people living in the Darfur region of that country. There are lessons to be learned, with implications for all of us, from remembering and studying bias-related actions against any ethnic or racial group of people. Knowledge of the Holocaust makes very vivid these lessons and their consequences.

- *Dehumanization*: To reduce any group to something less than human is to consider them unworthy of respect and, ultimately, unworthy of life itself. Isn't this what happened in the gas chambers?
- *Apathy*: Not caring about the persecution of others will encourage the tormentors and can destroy hope in the persecuted. It can also affect one's own sense of morality and guilt. Finally, its full meaning becomes frightfully clear when those who are apathetic find themselves to be targets of persecution and have no one to lift a helping hand or raise a voice in protest. The story of Pastor Martin Niemoller comes to mind.
- *Individual responsibility*: People must think about the consequences and results of their actions; otherwise, they are responsible for what may come to pass. Nazi desk clerks who arranged for Jews to be crowded in transports as well as scientists who manufactured Zyklon B gas are not free of guilt for the deaths in the camps.
- *Wrongful use of science and technology*: Advances in knowledge about the natural world and in the ability to control it have the potential for good as well as evil. Germany was well-known, prior to the Holocaust, for its scientific and industrial achievements. Yet, scientists and industrial concerns abused their talents by seeking to destroy life instead of trying to preserve it.
- *Individual courage*: The willingness of some non-Jews to act as rescuers has much to tell us. Their actions, amidst severe dangers, showed their ethical priority in putting human life ahead of concerns about status, personal safety, profit, and submission to wrongful authority. Recent research on such people revealed that they shared a spirit of independence, as well as empathy, compassion, and intolerance for injustice.

The history and lessons of the Holocaust are instructive. The uniqueness of this man-made tragedy rests in a combination of events, personalities, and factors that had never occurred previously. It is hoped that they will never occur again, to Jews or to any group, anywhere in the world. This hope will be realized through education, awareness, respect for human rights, and a consistent willingness to maintain safeguards against all forms of prejudice and bias. These tasks will not be easy, for as President Bill Clinton, in speaking at the Holocaust Memorial Museum's dedication in 1993, commented, "How fragile are the safeguards of civilization." Can we maintain these safeguards? Will we?

Lastly, we need to remember the words of Israeli Professor Yehuda Bauer, a noted Holocaust scholar:

Events happen because they are possible. If they are possible once, they are possible again. In that sense, the Holocaust is not unprecedented, but a warning for the future.

IMPORTANT PEOPLE, PLACES, AND TERMS

KEY TERMS

Holocaust	Aryan	Warsaw Ghetto
holocaust	boycott	Uprising
genocide	SS	ZOB
annihilation	Gestapo	spiritual resistance
apathy	Nuremberg Laws	sanctuary
anti-Semitism	*anschluss*	death marches
prejudice	Evian Conference	Nuremberg War
deicide	Kristallnacht	Crimes Trials
"blood libel"	akitonen	gas chambers
stereotype	"big lie"	"final solution"
ghetto	*Judenrein*	"Righteous Among the
secular	death camps	Nations"
pogrom	*Judenrat*	deportation
scapegoat	Wannsee Conference	kapos
Reformation	Einsatzgruppen	Sobibor Revolt
Mein Kampf	concentration camp	"Arbeit Macht Frei"
Nazi	crematory	collective guilt
Third Reich	euthanasia	collaborator
master race	Zyklon B	partisan

PEOPLE

Adolf Hitler	Januscz Korczak	Deborah Lipstadt
John Donne	Herschel Gryznszpan	Pope Benedict XVI
Martin Luther	Raoul Wallenberg	Sempo Sugihara
Richard Wagner	King Christian X	Aristide de Susa
Josef Goebbels	Pope John XXIII	Mendes
Heinrich Himmler	Anne Frank	Tuvia Bielski
Reinhard Heydrich	Martin Niemoller	Patriarch of
Josef Mengele	Dwight D. Eisenhower	Constantinople
Emmanuel Ringelblum	Adolf Eichmann	

PLACES

Warsaw Ghetto	Holland	Nuremberg
Spain	Russia	Evian
Poland	Germany	France

Vilna	Buchenwald	Ottoman Empire
Lithuania	Mauthausen	Sweden
Lake Wannsee	Palestine	Thereisenstadt
Berlin	Britain	Cologne
Auschwitz	New York	Yad Vashem
Hungary	Denmark	Budapest
Treblinka	Israel	
Dachau	Kielce	

CHAPTER 11

MULTIPLE-CHOICE QUESTIONS

Select the number of the correct answer.

1. After World War II, a new word was used to describe the planned destruction of a group of people as a result of its religion, race, or national background. This word is

   (1) suicide
   (2) patricide
   (3) deicide
   (4) genocide

2. In history, the specific term "The Holocaust" refers to the

   (1) nuclear bombing of Hiroshima and Nagasaki, Japan.
   (2) planned execution of Armenians.
   (3) execution of European Jews as part of the Nazi Final Solution.
   (4) September 11, 2001, attack on the World Trade Center and the Pentagon.

3. Hostile actions specifically directed against Jewish people only because they are Jews are described as

   (1) nationalism
   (2) anti-Semitism
   (3) propaganda
   (4) ethnocentrism

4. Which statement is true about anti-Semitism prior to Hitler and Nazi Germany?

   (1) Anti-Semitism had a long history in Europe with both religious and secular examples.
   (2) Christian churches have consistently spoken out against anti-Semitism.
   (3) Prejudice against Jewish people was for the most part unknown in Europe until Adolf Hitler became head of the Nazis.
   (4) Historically anti-Semitism was found primarily in the Mediterranean countries and in the Scandinavian countries.

5. During the 1300s the European Jewish population was blamed for the

   (1) failure of the Crusades
   (2) development of the Protestant Reformation
   (3) spread of the disease known as the Black Death
   (4) patriotic music of Richard Wagner

6. The Nazi philosophy of the concept of the master race encouraged the idea that

   (1) the Nazis would be able to change non-Germans into productive citizens
   (2) Germans of the "Aryan race" were superior to all other peoples in physical strength and mental abilities

(3) any German family who had fought in previous wars for Germany would be given a privileged status before the law

(4) as long as the military was composed of Aryans, the Nazis would be able to thrive, and society as a whole would be unchanged

7. "Jews forbidden to marry non-Jews"
   "Jews forbidden to own dogs"
   "Jews forbidden to enter certain restaurants"

   The legal measures described above are examples taken from
   (1) the Martin Luther Bible
   (2) the plans for the *anschluss*
   (3) the Nuremburg Laws
   (4) Weimar Republic constitution

8. In the history of Nazi Germany, the events of Kristallnacht, November 9, 1938, have been remembered as

   (1) a night of horror, death, and destruction for Jewish people in Germany
   (2) an opportunity for German Jews to prove that they were patriotic citizens
   (3) a time when German Jews were deliberately removed to Poland
   (4) the last time Jews living in Germany would be allowed to peacefully leave the country

9. The Nazis organized the Jewish population of Germany and occupied countries in ghettos in order to

   (1) allow for traditional Jewish occupations and schooling to occur
   (2) control the movement of Jews and to limit their activities
   (3) demonstrate to their wartime allies that life within Germany was essentially unchanged since the war began
   (4) prevent unnecessary deaths and violence in the Jewish communities

10. The main purpose of the Wannsee Conference near Berlin in 1942 was to

    (1) organize Nazi military plans against their Allied enemies
    (2) determine how to train Jewish workers for production of military needs
    (3) strengthen propaganda techniques throughout the Third Reich
    (4) agree on a comprehensive plan to eliminate all Jews in Germany and the occupied countries

11. Place the following events in Holocaust history in the correct chronological order

    A. Nazi extermination camps such as Auschwitz and Treblinka were built in Poland.
    B. The Dachau concentration camp opened near Munich, Germany.
    C. Kristallnacht, or the night of broken glass.
    D. The Warsaw Ghetto was created.

    (1) B, C, D, A   (3) C, D, B, A
    (2) B, D, A, C   (4) A, B, C, D

12. "Arbeit Macht Frei" (Work Will Make You Free) is an example of

    (1) a Nazi campaign slogan
    (2) the big lie technique
    (3) the code name for building the concentration camps
    (4) an accurate promise made to camp inmates

13. Which statement is an opinion about the Jewish resistance to the Holocaust?

    (1) A small number of Jews felt that their suffering was God's will.
    (2) The Jews did not receive any serious help from any of the countries that were fighting the Nazis.
    (3) Jews at this time were generally isolated from contact with the rest of the world.
    (4) If the Jews had shown strong leadership, they would have been able to resist the horrors of the Holocaust.

14. Treblinka, Sobibor, and Auschwitz are all examples of camps that

    (1) experienced revolts by inmates
    (2) closed years before the end of World War II
    (3) were primarily work camps for women
    (4) were located within Germany

15. A government enforced method of identifying Jewish citizens during the Nazi years was

    (1) that all men over 18 had to serve in the army
    (2) adults and children wore yellow stars on their clothing
    (3) no Jew was allowed to leave his own home
    (4) Jews had attendance taken when they attended services at their synagogues

16. What explains the lack of world effort to help the Jewish situation?

    (1) Many world leaders blamed the Jews for starting the war
    (2) It would have been too costly to become involved in an additional war in Europe
    (3) Some government officials and private citizens refused to believe that such terrible events as the Holocaust were actually occurring
    (4) The Japanese were causing so many problems in the Pacific that Allied troops could not be sent to Europe

17. Christian churches in Europe generally took what position toward the Holocaust?

    (1) Ministers and priests spoke out directly against the Nazi laws.
    (2) The Pope led the Catholics to fight strongly against the wrongs that were being committed in the name of national pride.
    (3) Most ministers encouraged Jewish rabbis to remain silent in the face of oppression.
    (4) There was mixed reaction by organized Christian groups to the Holocaust but very little was accomplished to help the Jews.

18. "Then they came for me. There was no one left to speak for me." Martin Niemoller

    The excerpt above refers to the fact that
    (1) many people chose to be activists and to fight the Nazis
    (2) every Jew in Europe had been killed by the end of the war
    (3) many people decided to look out for themselves before worrying about what was happening to other people
    (4) Germans encouraged their citizens to practice freedom of religion

19. The victorious American army was so shocked by what it found in the liberated camps that it

    (1) set the camps on fire immediately to destroy them
    (2) buried the dead victims but refused admittance to the press
    (3) seized the valuables from the camps immediately to help pay for the extended war effort by the Allies
    (4) forced German citizens living near the camps to march through them to see what had been taking place

20. Which defense was found to be not acceptable at the Nuremburg War Crimes Trials?

    (1) The defendants claimed that they were only following orders.
    (2) Nazis protested that the Holocaust had never happened to the extent that they were being blamed.
    (3) Accused Nazis were forbidden to have lawyers speak in their defense.
    (4) Nazi generals said that they did not follow the "leadership principle" as ordered by Hitler and therefore couldn't be blamed.

THEMATIC ESSAY

Directions: Write a well-organized essay that includes an introduction, several paragraphs addressing the task below, and a conclusion.

Theme: Human Rights

The era of the Holocaust in Global History was a time of a loss of human rights for millions of people. Those who caused the Holocaust justified their actions to themselves and their nation. Some others attempted resistance, and many others were unable or unwilling to do so.

Task

- Identify the era of the Holocaust in Global History.
- Identify two individuals who justified their role in the Holocaust and explain exactly what that role was.
- Identify any individual, group, or country who attempted to resist the Holocaust and explain the actions of that person or group.

You may use any examples from your study of the Holocaust. Some suggestions you might wish to consider are Adolf Hitler, Josef Mengele, Joseph Goebbels, Raoul Wallenberg, residents of the Warsaw Ghetto, and some inmates at Treblinka or Sobibor.

You are *not* limited to these suggestions.

Guidelines

In your essay, be sure to

- develop all aspects of the *Task*
- support the theme with relevant facts, examples, and details
- use a logical and clear plan of organization, including an introduction and a conclusion that are beyond a restatement of the theme
- introduce the theme by establishing a framework that is beyond a simple restatement of the *Task* and conclude with a summation of the theme

---

DOCUMENT-BASED ESSAY QUESTION

This question is based on the accompanying documents (1–8). It is designed to test your ability to work with historical documents. Some of the documents have been edited for the purpose of the question. As you analyze the documents, take into account the source of each document and any point of view that may be presented in the document.

Historical Context

During Nazi Germany's Third Reich the Holocaust occurred which deprived millions of people of justice and basic human rights.

Task

Using information from the documents and your knowledge of global history, answer the questions that follow each document in Part A. Your answers to the questions will help you write the Part B essay in which you will be asked to

- describe how people were deprived of basic human rights during the Holocaust
- discuss two short-term results of the Holocaust and two long-term results of the Holocaust and include in your answer the impact of the term and plan, "The Final Solution"

Part A: Short Answer Questions

Directions: Analyze the document and answer the short answer questions that follow each document.

Document 1   The following statement is from Reinhard Heydrich, SS Chief Heinrich Himmler's head deputy and head of the Reich Main Security Office following the Wannsee Conference held to discuss the implementation of the "Final Solution."

"Under suitable supervision, Jews shall be . . . taken to the east," Heydrich announced, "and deployed in appropriate work . . . Able-bodied Jews, separated by sex, will be taken to those areas in large work details to build roads, and a large part will doubtlessly be lost through natural attrition. The survival remnants . . . will have to be treated appropriately . . ."

Questions

1. a. According to Reinhard Heydrich's statement, what job was to be assigned to able bodied Jews?
   b. What is also suggested in the statement as likely to happen to other Jews?

Document 2

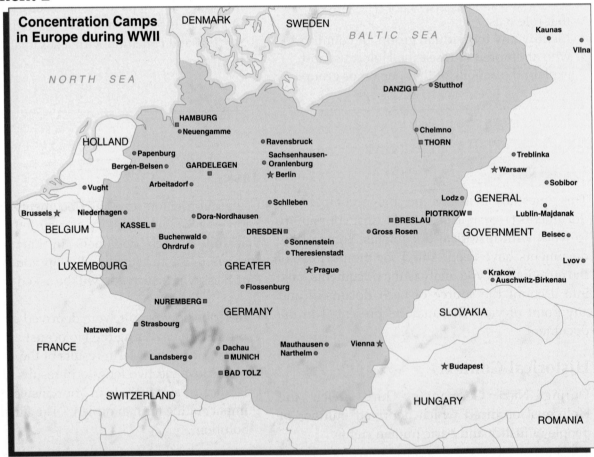

Question

2. Develop a generalization about the location of the concentration camps in Europe during World War II.

Document 3

Question

3. From the Nazi viewpoint why would the map opposite be extremely useful to the completion of at least one of their goals?

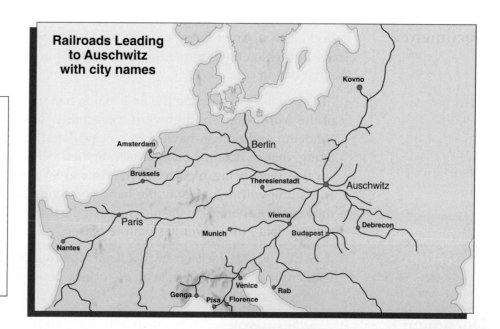

Railroads Leading to Auschwitz with city names

Kovno · Amsterdam · Berlin · Brussels · Theresienstadt · Auschwitz · Paris · Vienna · Debrecon · Nantes · Munich · Budapest · Venice · Rab · Genga · Pisa · Florence

Document 4

The picture was taken on May 5, 1945 by the United States Army. It shows thousands of wedding rings removed near the Buchenwald concentration camp.

Question

4. Why would the Nazis remove the wedding rings from their victims in the concentration camps?

Document 5

Questions

5. a. What does this photograph tell you about a goal of this group?

b. What does it also suggest about a possible problem for the group?

Jewish partisan group new Vilna.

Document 6

Question

6. Why would American soldiers force Germans to view this scene at a liberated concentration camp?

Germans viewing bodies at a concentration camp.

Document 7 Robert Jackson, Chief Prosecutor for the United States at the Nuremberg Trials, addressed the International Military Tribunal on November 20, 1945, the first day in court:

> "The privilege of opening the first trial in history for crimes against the peace of the world imposes a grave responsibility. The wrongs which we seek to condemn and punish have been so calculated, so malignant, and so devastating, that civilization cannot tolerate their being ignored, because it cannot survive their being repeated. That four great nations, flushed with victory and stung with injury, stay the hands of vengeance and voluntarily submit their captive enemies to the judgment of the law, is one of the most significant tributes that Power ever has paid to reason."

Questions
7. a. Why does Mr. Jackson say the Trial at Nuremberg has been called?
   b. Identify one of the European victorious nations that Mr. Jackson is referring to in his statement.

Document 8

Question
8. What is Holocaust survivor Wiesel saying about what actions individuals should take even years after the Holocaust?
a.   b.

a. "I swore never to be silent whenever and wherever human beings endure suffering and humiliation. We must always take sides. Neutrality helps the oppressor, never the victim. Silence encourages the tormentor, never the tormented."

—Elie Wiesel

b. "I decided to devote my life to telling the story because I felt that having survived I owe something to the dead, and anyone who does not remember betrays them again."

—Elie Wiesel

Part B: Essay

Directions: Write a well-organized essay that includes an introduction, several paragraphs, and a conclusion. Use evidence from *at least five* documents in your essay. Support your response with relevant facts, examples, and details. Include additional outside information.

Historical Context

During Nazi Germany's Third Reich the Holocaust occurred, which deprived millions of people of justice and basic human rights.

Task

Using information from the documents and your knowledge of global history, answer the questions that follow each document in Part A. Your answers to the questions will help you write the Part B essay in which you will be asked to

- describe how people were deprived of basic human rights during the Holocaust
- discuss two short-term results of the Holocaust and two long-term results of the Holocaust and include in your answer the impact of the term and plan, "The Final Solution"

Guidelines

In your essay, be sure to

- develop all aspects of the *Task*
- incorporate information from *at least five* documents
- incorporate relevant outside information.
- support the theme with relevant facts, examples, and details
- use a logical and clear plan of organization, including an introduction and conclusion that are beyond a restatement of the theme

ERA VII

CONCLUDING THE TWENTIETH CENTURY AND ENTERING THE TWENTY-FIRST CENTURY

INTRODUCTION

After World War II, many areas of the world that had been European colonies experienced independence movements. These independence movements and the accompanying growth in nationalism were fueled by the fact that the colonial powers were generally weakened as a result of the war. Independence leaders in Africa and Asia had often received their education in European universities and frequently surprised the Europeans with their abilities to inspire a desire for change within their homelands. Some former colonies such as India gained independence peacefully. Others such as Vietnam were involved in a long struggle to gain independence. Newly emerging nations struggled with a wide variety of problems to achieve their independence and have achieved varying degrees of success in attaining their goals.

The chapters in ERA VII will help you understand the many political, economic, and cultural changes that have happened in the last sixty years or so since the end of World War II. Decolonization, nationalism, justice, power, cultural diversity, interdependence, urbanization, and scarcity are some of the key concepts that are essential to your work on this time period.

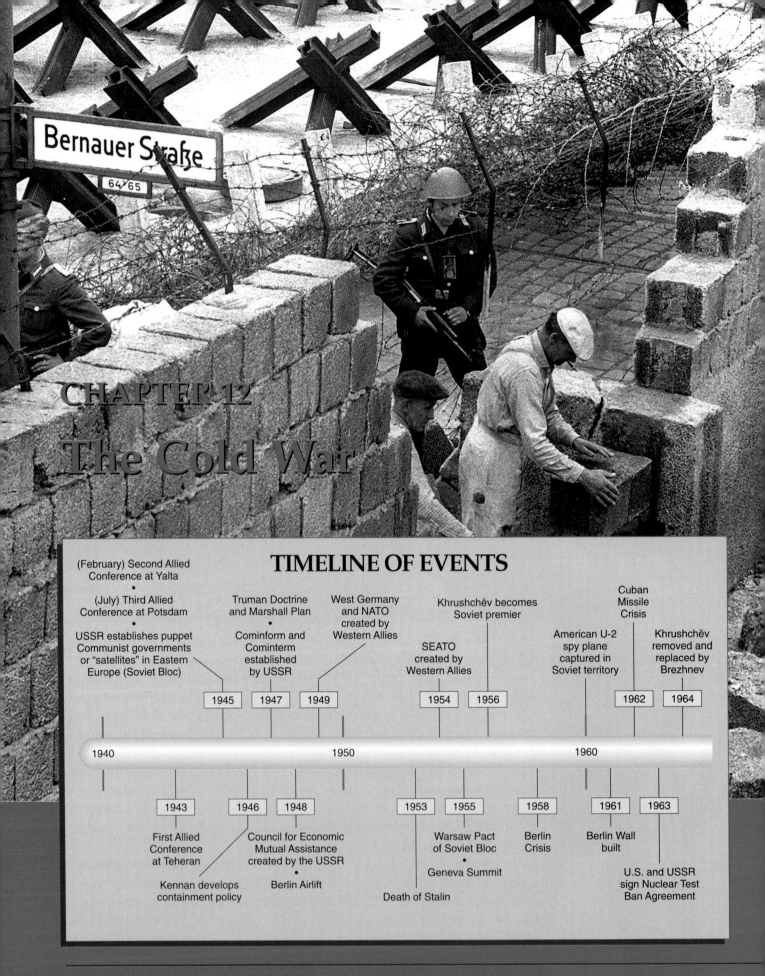

CHAPTER 12
The Cold War

TIMELINE OF EVENTS

(February) Second Allied Conference at Yalta

(July) Third Allied Conference at Potsdam

USSR establishes puppet Communist governments or "satellites" in Eastern Europe (Soviet Bloc)

Truman Doctrine and Marshall Plan

Cominform and Cominterm established by USSR

West Germany and NATO created by Western Allies

Khrushchëv becomes Soviet premier

SEATO created by Western Allies

Cuban Missile Crisis

American U-2 spy plane captured in Soviet territory

Khrushchëv removed and replaced by Brezhnev

| 1945 | 1947 | 1949 | 1954 | 1956 | 1962 | 1964 |

1940 — 1950 — 1960

| 1943 | 1946 | 1948 | 1953 | 1955 | 1958 | 1961 | 1963 |

First Allied Conference at Teheran

Council for Economic Mutual Assistance created by the USSR

Warsaw Pact of Soviet Bloc

Geneva Summit

Berlin Crisis

Berlin Wall built

U.S. and USSR sign Nuclear Test Ban Agreement

Kennan develops containment policy

Berlin Airlift

Death of Stalin

In 1945, the victorious Allied leaders were faced with creating a lasting peace. From the start, mistrust between the Soviet Union and the West made this difficult. This mistrust grew into hostility, but it never "heated up" into another conflict such as World War II. Yet, this "cold" struggle between East and West was no friendly rivalry. The **Cold War** was a battle of words and propaganda, involving competition in science and weapons, and in seeking allies among the emerging nations of Africa, Asia, and Latin America. It was a war in every way. The two new superpowers, the United States and the Soviet Union, had conflicting ideologies about politics, economics, and human rights. The nations of Europe were divided between them, and the rest of the world became the arena in which these two sides would wrestle for influence and control.

AGREEMENTS AFTER WORLD WAR II (1943–1945)

The Mistrust Between the Allies

Although they were allies, the great mistrust between the Soviet Union and the United States and Great Britain made them uneasy partners against the Axis powers. The reasons were mainly philosophical, political, and historical:

1. Communist theory viewed the capitalist nations as enemies, claiming that communism would one day spread over the earth.
2. Since the Communists came to power in 1917, the leaders of the Western capitalist democracies viewed them as threats and said so.

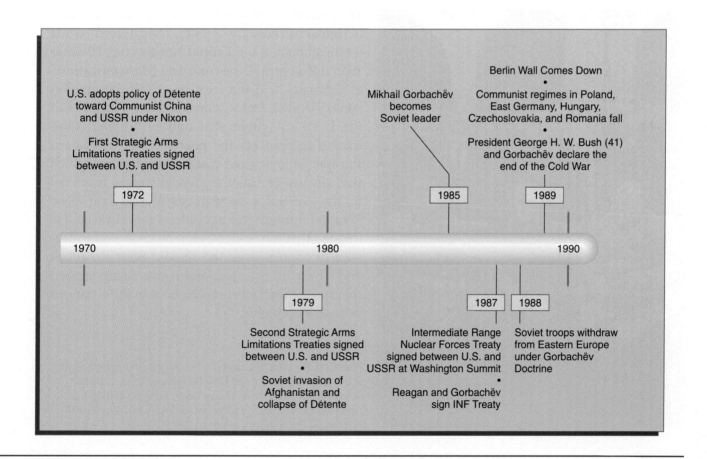

3. The Allies supported the **White Army** during the **Russian Civil War** (1918–1921). The United States and Great Britain had landed troops on Russian soil during the conflict, thus adding to the Soviet fear of invasion.
4. The United States did not recognize the U.S.S.R. until 1933.
5. The dictatorial, police-state policies of the U.S.S.R. contrasted with the democratic ideals of the Western nations.

Opposition to Nazi Germany was the only bond that held them together. Once that was gone, the old suspicions reappeared. The decisions made during the peace settlements in the years immediately after World War II laid the groundwork for the Cold War by dividing Europe into two specific spheres of political influence (Communist and democratic).

The Teheran Conference (1943)

The first conference took place in **Teheran (Iran)** in 1943 between the Soviet dictator **Joseph Stalin**, American President **Franklin Roosevelt**, and British Prime Minister **Sir Winston Churchill** (see Chapter 9 in this volume). At that meeting, Stalin agreed to bring the U.S.S.R. into the war against Japan after the defeat of Germany, and the United States and Great Britain agreed to open a second front in France, forcing the Nazis to divide their army. Stalin rejected a proposal that they open another front in Eastern Europe, which would have given the British and Americans greater influence in the region.

The Yalta Conference (February 1945)

The second conference took place at **Yalta (Crimea)** in February of 1945. They agreed on the establishment of the **United Nations** (see Chapter 10 in this volume), the complete "**denazification**" of Germany, and the creation of four occupation zones (United States, Great Britain, France, and the U.S.S.R.) within that nation, but the Allies soon disagreed on the postwar fate of **Eastern Europe**. Stalin argued that Eastern Europe, which was already occupied by Soviet troops, was vital to the U.S.S.R.'s security as Russia had been invaded through these countries for centuries. He insisted that the Soviet Union be given some measure of control over the region. Both Roosevelt and Churchill objected, and it was finally agreed that free general elections be held in these nations as soon as possible.

Winston Churchill, Franklin D. Roosevelt, and Joseph Stalin at the Yalta Conference at Livadia Palace, Yalta, Crimea. Standing left to right: Anthony Eden, Edward Stettinius, Alexander Cadogan, Vyacheslav Molotov, and W. Averell Harriman. Photograph, February 1945.

The Potsdam Conference (July 1945)

Allied leaders on the terrace of Castle Cecilienhof during the Potsdam Conference. From left: the newly elected British prime minister Clement Attlee, the American President Harry S. Truman, and the Soviet head of state Joseph Stalin. Photograph, August 1945.

The last meeting of the three allies took place in **Potsdam** (**Germany**) in July of 1945. At this conference, the only original member left was Stalin, as Roosevelt had died and Churchill had lost that year's election in Britain. The United States was represented by the new president, **Harry Truman**, and Great Britain by its new Prime Minister **Clement Attlee**. Once again, they agreed on matters concerning Germany, but Eastern Europe was still a sensitive issue. The vague assurance of free elections in the near future was all that the Western Allies could obtain from Stalin.

THE RISE OF THE COLD WAR (1946–1972)

The Descent of the Iron Curtain

With the spirit of cooperation already disappearing after the Potsdam Conference, Stalin ignored the previous agreements for free elections and forced Communist dictatorships on the Eastern European nations of **Poland**, **Romania**, **Bulgaria**, and **Hungary**. Independent local Communist regimes had established themselves in **Yugoslavia**, **Czechoslovakia**, and **Albania**, initially appearing as friendly to the U.S.S.R. The Allies were infuriated at the creation of these Soviet **satellites** (smaller nations controlled by a larger one). Truman denounced the new governments, and Churchill added a new term to the political vocabulary when he warned of an **"iron curtain"** dividing a free and democratic West from an East under totalitarian rule. Stalin retaliated by calling the Western democracies the enemies of communism. While not all the Eastern European Communist leaders were obedient to Stalin, their nations nevertheless became known as the **Soviet bloc**, or **Eastern bloc**. This grouping, also called the **Communist bloc**, was to stand in contrast to the **Western bloc**, or the **Free-World bloc**.

The Division of Berlin

The breakdown of cooperation was felt most strongly in Germany, which was still divided into zones of occupation. **Berlin**, the former German capital city, which was within the Soviet zone, was itself divided into four occupation sectors. Access to the individual sectors was only through the Soviet zone. In 1947, the British, French, and American zones joined together for economic reasons. With this union, the Western powers took the first steps toward establishing West Germany (see Chapter 9 in this volume).

The Policy of Containment

Main Idea:
Developed in 1946 by American diplomat **George Kennan**, the containment theory argued that only through determined and continued resistance could the advance of Soviet power be stopped.

After the war in Europe, Communist rebels captured northern **Greece** with the assistance of the Albanians and Soviet backing, leading to the **Greek Civil War** (1945–1948). Similar rebellions took place in **Turkey** and **Iran**. In response to these acts of Soviet expansionism, President Truman announced the **Truman Doctrine** in 1947. This was a policy to support any free nation trying to resist being forcibly taken over by another power. As a result of this, the United States sent military and economic aid to assist those countries fighting Communist forces. The Truman Doctrine was part of a new American policy known as **containment**. Developed in 1946 by American diplomat **George Kennan**, the containment theory argued that only through determined and continued resistance could the advance of Soviet power be stopped. Communism, he believed, had to be "contained" to where it already existed and not be allowed to spread any further. Communism and Soviet power were viewed, in a sense, as a contagious disease. The disease had to be contained before it "infected" other parts of the globe.

The containment policy was further pursued with the **Marshall Plan** later that year. Proposed by the American Secretary of State **George Marshall**, the Marshall Plan was a broad program of economic assistance to help Europe recover from the devastation of the war. Marshall feared that if economic conditions became bad enough in Western Europe, successful Communist revolutions might occur there. Both the Truman Doctrine and the Marshall Plan were highly successful. By 1948, the Communist rebellions in Greece, Turkey, and Iran had been defeated and the Western European nations underwent a remarkable economic recovery.

Cominform and the CEMA

In 1947, as a way of countering U.S. economic involvement in Western Europe, the Soviet Union established the Communist Information Bureau or **Cominform**. This was an organization designed to better coordinate the policies of the Soviet Union and the nations of Eastern Europe. In reality it was a restoration of the **Cominterm** or Communist International, which worked for world revolution. The following year, a Soviet version of the Marshall Plan, the **Council for Economic Mutual Assistance**, was created. In reality, these policies merely tightened the U.S.S.R.'s grip on its Eastern European satellites.

The Division of Germany

As tensions in Germany grew greater, the Soviets cut off all access routes between Berlin and the Western occupation zones in June of 1948. This trapped the Westerners living in the city and was called the Berlin Blockade. In response, the United States established the **Berlin Airlift**, which flew food, fuel, and supplies to the Western sectors. With the Berlin Airlift making the blockade ineffectual, the Soviets decided not to escalate the crisis and reopened the access routes in May of 1949. A month later, the Western Allies established the **Federal Republic of Germany** or West Germany as it came to be known. The Soviets responded by creating an East Germany, the **German Democratic Republic**, in their zone.

The Creation of NATO

The mounting tension between the East and West gradually led to military alliances. In April of 1949, representatives of twelve Western nations signed the **North Atlantic Pact**. This was a mutual defense agreement (if one nation is attacked, the others will come to its aid) between the **United States, Great Britain, France, Belgium**, the **Netherlands, Luxembourg, Denmark, Norway, Iceland, Canada, Italy**, and **Portugal**. In 1952, **Greece** and **Turkey** joined followed by **West Germany** in 1955. The **North Atlantic Treaty Organization** (**NATO**) was established to coordinate the activities of the alliance and be ready to respond to any acts of Soviet expansion in Europe.

The Creation of the Warsaw Pact

The Soviets responded to West Germany's joining of NATO with the creation of the **Warsaw Pact**. This was a military alliance of the **Soviet Union** with **Albania, Bulgaria, Czechoslovakia, East Germany, Hungary, Poland**, and **Romania**. **Yugoslavia**, under the independent Communist leader **Tito**, refused to join. (In 1961, Albania left both the Warsaw Pact and the Soviet bloc.)

The Arms Race

Both alliances now began to stockpile huge quantities of arms. They enlarged their armed forces, increased military spending, and sent spies into each other's member nations. Thus, as the 1950s came to a close, it appeared that a frightening repetition of history was occurring. The two military alliances were reminders of the "two armed camps" of the alliances that existed before World War I (see Chapter 7 in this volume). Both the **Triple Alliance** and **Triple Entente** claimed to be merely defensive in purpose. That is, each would fight only if attacked by the other. A similar policy was echoed by NATO and the Warsaw Pact. Yet, the existence of these two groupings made the world more alarmed than was the case with the earlier alliances.

> **Main Idea:**
> The two military alliances were reminders of the "two armed camps" of the alliances that existed before World War I.

1. NATO and the Warsaw Pact had many more member nations, spanning three continents, than earlier alliances.
2. Their armed forces were larger.
3. Their weapons were newer and more deadly. Air forces, intercontinental missiles, and atomic power came to be possessed by both sides.
4. Fear and distrust on both sides was enormous. The West was upset with the U.S.S.R.'s post-World War II expansion into Eastern Europe, Stalin's treachery, and the messianic belief of the Communists that spoke of inevitable world domination. The Soviets claimed that the Western Powers were "ganging up" on them. NATO was seen as a Western threat, reminiscent of two previous invasions of Russia from the West (Napoleon in 1812 and Hitler in 1941). Amidst such tensions, we should not be surprised to find their effect on many other global areas.

The Creation of SEATO

The rise of Communist regimes in **China** under **Mao Zedong** and **North Korea** under **Kim Il-Sung** in 1949 created panic in the West. These nations were friendly with the U.S.S.R., taking a similar anti-Western and anti-American stance. When North Korea attacked South Korea in 1950, United Nations forces, led by the United States, went to war. The conflict became known as the **Korean War** (1950–1953). An armistice brought the fighting to a temporary halt. However, no peace treaty formally ending the war was ever signed. North Korea received weapons from the U.S.S.R., as well as both arms and manpower from Communist China. Yet, the North Koreans failed to take the South. This was considered a successful application of the containment policy by the United States and its allies as it had stopped Communist expansion and reestablished the **status quo** (existing state of affairs) before the war.

The United States, in the forefront of having successfully protected a nation from Communist domination, became more convinced of the importance of practicing containment. In 1954, U.S. President **Dwight Eisenhower** expanded the Western anti-Communist alliance system with the creation of the **Southeast Asia Treaty Organization** (**SEATO**). This included the **United States, Great Britain, France, Australia, New Zealand, the Philippines, Thailand,** and **Pakistan.**

The Policy of Peaceful Coexistence

In 1953, Stalin died and control of the government went to much more moderate leadership. The new Soviet leader, **Nikita Khrushchev** (r. 1956–1964), adapted a doctrine called **"Peaceful coexistence."** This was a policy of peaceful competition between the East and the West that would be based on greater achievement as a means of influencing non-allied nations. In the U.S.S.R., Khrushchev had begun several reforms in domestic policy and had a reputation for being a reformer (see Chapter 13 "The Decline and Collapse of Communism . . .").

In July of 1955, President Eisenhower, British Prime Minister **Anthony Eden**, and French Premier **Edgar Fauré** met with Khrushchev in **Geneva** (**Switzerland**). Known as the **Geneva Summit**, it was the first breakthrough in Soviet-Western relations since the start of the Cold War in 1945.

The Berlin Crisis (1958)

U.S. Air Force U-2 reconnaissance plane, c. 1950s.

The tension soon returned, however, as Khrushchev began a campaign to demilitarize and neutralize West Berlin in November of 1958. He demanded that the Western powers pull out all military personnel and equipment from Berlin in six months or he would turn the city over to the East Germans (a government the West did not recognize). When the Western powers refused to give in, Khrushchev let the deadline pass, ending the **Berlin Crisis of 1958**. This event was viewed internationally as an embarrassment to the Communists. The Soviet premier agreed to meet with Eisenhower at a summit in Paris in 1960, but the capture of an American U-2 spy plane carrying out surveillance operations over Soviet territory resulted in its cancellation.

In early 1961, Khrushchev renewed his pressure on the Western powers about West Berlin. In August, the Soviets and East Germans closed the border between East and West Berlin and began the construction of a wall that divided the city. The **Berlin Wall**, which was built to prevent East Germans from escaping to the West, became a symbol of Communist oppression in Eastern Europe. The crisis subsided, but relations between East and West began to deteriorate.

The Cuban Missile Crisis (1962)

When the revolutionary leader **Fidel Castro** took power in **Cuba** in 1959, he was at first welcomed as a relief to the military dictatorship of **General Fulgencio Batista**. By 1960, however, Castro had made it clear that he was clearly within the Communist camp and strengthened his ties with the U.S.S.R. and Communist China. Seeing Castro as a threat to American security, the United States responded by arming and preparing a military force composed of Cuban exiles to overthrow the regime. The failure of this group at the **Bay of Pigs** in 1961 drove Castro to seek assistance from the Soviet Union. The Soviets provided Castro with conventional arms but also began to construct missile launching pads for intermediate-range missiles. American President **John Kennedy** demanded that the missiles be dismantled. He ordered a blockade to prevent Soviet ships from bringing further equipment to Cuba. After tense negotiations, Khrushchev removed the missiles. Kennedy pledged not to invade Cuba and to pull NATO missiles out of Turkey.

Detail of the front page of *The New York Times* for October 29, 1962, announcing the agreement of the Soviet Union to remove its guided missiles from Cuba.

After the **Cuban Missile Crisis of 1962**, the **Washington-Moscow hotline** (telephone that linked the U.S. president with the premier of the U.S.S.R.) was established in case of another crisis. Following the crisis, the U.S. and U.S.S.R. signed the first **nuclear test ban** in July of 1963, which agreed to stop the testing of nuclear weapons in the air. This was the first agreement of its kind, indicative of the changes the Cuban Missile Crisis had created. In October of 1964, however, the reform-minded Khrushchev was removed from office and replaced with the hard-line Communist **Leonid Brezhnev** (see Chapter 13 in this volume). This resulted in a return to a more antagonistic Soviet foreign policy and a renewal of strained relations between the two superpowers.

THE DECLINE OF THE COLD WAR (1972–1989)

The Policy of Detente

As the decade progressed, there was an improvement in East-West relations. Beginning in the presidency of **Richard Nixon**, a "thaw" in the Cold War began. Relations improved between the United States and its Western allies, and the Soviet Union. A policy of **Detente (understanding)** was adopted, and new conferences on arms control followed. In 1972 and 1979, two **Strategic Arms Limitations Treaties** (**SALT I** and **SALT II**) were signed, which put limited restrictions on weapons production.

Detente declined in the early 1980s due to the Soviet invasion of Afghanistan in 1979 and the imposition of a military government by the Soviet

U.S. President Richard Nixon visiting Moscow in 1972.

Union on Poland in 1981. To the West, these actions seemed to be a return to the expansionist policies of Stalin's rule. However, both policies met with great resistance within the Soviet bloc. The war in Afghanistan cost thousands of lives and became very unpopular in the U.S.S.R., sparking desertions in the army and protests at home. The crackdown in Poland only served to unify the Polish people in their opposition to Soviet domination (see Chapter 13 in this volume).

The End of the Cold War

After **Mikhail Gorbachev** (r. 1985–1991) became the Soviet leader in 1985, relations with the West, particularly the United States, improved. Gorbachev's policies of **Glasnost** (openness) and **Perestroika** (restructuring) brought political and economic reforms that were viewed with admiration in the West (see Chapter 13 in this volume). In December of 1987, American President **Ronald Reagan** and Gorbachev signed the **Intermediate Range Nuclear Forces Treaty (INF)** at the **Washington Summit**. This was an agreement to destroy all American and Soviet missiles within a range of 315 to 3,125 miles within three years. It was the first American-Soviet agreement to actually reduce the level of arms.

In 1988, Gorbachev began to pull out Soviet troops from Eastern Europe (the **Gorbachev Doctrine**). This was followed by the fall of the Berlin Wall in 1989 and with it almost all the Communist regimes of Eastern Europe (see Chapter 13 in this volume). With the collapse of the Soviet bloc in Eastern Europe, the need for the NATO alliance disappeared. In December of 1989, American President **George H. W. Bush** and Gorbachev officially declared the end of the Cold War at the **Malta Conference**. The struggle that had divided both Europe and the world for forty-five years was finally over.

CHAPTER SUMMARY

The Cold War had divided the post-World War II world into hostile camps for almost half a century. The fear, suspicion, and hatred this struggle created has left three legacies. The first is a vacuum of power as the nations once dominated by the U.S.S.R. become independent. Much ancient hatred has resurfaced as the common enemy that controlled them has gone. The second is the excess supply of arms, including nuclear weapons that are available to these warring nations as well as others throughout the world. The last is the environmental, economic, and psychological damage done to the individual nations on both sides. The ideological struggle of the Cold War has been replaced by nationalism, on the one hand, and a desire for greater global cooperation on the other. The military alliances created during the Cold War were not designed to handle the new conflicts that have arisen throughout Europe and the world in recent years. Creating a new order will be an enormous challenge for leaders in the future.

LINK TO TODAY

One of the most enduring creations of the Cold War is the fictional character of secret agent 007, James Bond. This character, who became the subject of a series of novels and an even longer group of films, was the brainchild of British novelist Ian Fleming. During World War II and the early part of the Cold War, the author was himself in the service of British Intelligence. The character of Bond was in part based on people Fleming knew, as well as himself. The stories, although highly exaggerated, reflected the dangers and hardships faced by secret operatives during the Cold War. Agent 007 faced increasingly larger-than-life villains and impossible situations.

When the popular novels were adapted for the movies, the character of James Bond became more glamorous than in the novels. Fantastic inventions and equally extraordinary villains were featured. As the Cold War came to an end in the early 1990s, Agent 007 began working with his former Russian and Chinese enemies to defeat power-hungry villains, bent on world conquest. With the release of the twentieth James Bond feature film, *Casino Royale,* and the debut of the sixth actor to play Agent 007, the series shows no signs of ending anywhere in the near future. It is increasingly difficult for younger fans to appreciate Bond's Cold War origins as new threats, such as international terrorism, present themselves in the post-9/11 era.

Ian Fleming (1908–1964), English novelist, on the set of "From Russia With Love" with Sean Connery in 1963.

KEY TERMS

Cold War	Berlin Airlift	Washington-Moscow
White Army	North Atlantic Pact	Hotline
Russian Civil War	North Atlantic Treaty	nuclear test ban
denazification	Organization (NATO)	Détente
United Nations	Warsaw Pact	Strategic Arms
iron curtain	Triple Alliance	Limitation Treaties
satellite	Triple Entente	(SALT)
Greek Civil War	Southeast Asia Treaty	Glasnost
Truman Doctrine	Organization (SEATO)	Perestroika
Containment	Korean War	Intermediate Range
Marshall Plan	peaceful coexistence	Nuclear Forces (INF)
Cominform	Berlin Crisis	Treaty
Cominterm	Berlin Wall	Gorbachev Doctrine
Council for Economic	Cuban Missile Crisis	Washington Summit
Mutual Assistance		Malta Conference

PEOPLE

Joseph Stalin	Mao Zedong	John Kennedy
Franklin Roosevelt	Kim Il-Sung	Leonid Brezhnev
Winston Churchill	Dwight Eisenhower	Richard Nixon
Harry Truman	Nikita Khrushchev	Mikhail Gorbachev
Clement Attlee	Anthony Eden	Ronald Reagan
George Kennan	Edgar Fauré	George H.W. Bush
George Marshall	Fidel Castro	
Tito	Fulgencio Batista	

PLACES

Teheran	Greece	Italy
Yalta	Turkey	Portugal
Eastern Europe	Iran	West Germany
Potsdam	Federal Republic of	Soviet Union
Poland	Germany	East Germany
Romania	German Democratic	China
Bulgaria	Republic	North Korea
Hungary	United States	Australia
Yugoslavia	Great Britain	New Zealand
Czechoslovakia	France	Philippines
Albania	Belgium	Thailand
Soviet bloc	Netherlands	Pakistan
Eastern bloc	Luxembourg	Geneva
Communist bloc	Denmark	Cuba
Western bloc	Norway	Bay of Pigs
Free-World bloc	Iceland	
Berlin	Canada	

CHAPTER 12

MULTIPLE-CHOICE QUESTIONS

Select the number of the correct answer.

1. A basic reason for mistrust of the United States and Great Britain by the Soviet Union after World War II was that

   (1) communists claimed that they could work peacefully with capitalists
   (2) during the Russian Civil War the Allies sent troops to support the White Army
   (3) the Soviets were recognized by the United States as the legitimate government at the end of the Russian Civil War
   (4) the Soviets were willing to accept the political viewpoints of Western capitalist democracies

2. The Teheran Conference in 1943 brought together the leaders of which three countries?

   (1) Soviet Union, Italy, Japan
   (2) Great Britain, France, Poland
   (3) United States, Soviet Union, Great Britain
   (4) France, Japan, Russia

3. At the Yalta Conference, months before World War II was even over, the participants agreed to form four occupation zones in what country?

   (1) Japan   (3) Soviet Union
   (2) Italy   (4) Germany

4. How was the Potsdam Conference different from the previous wartime conferences?

   (1) Both the United States and Great Britain had new leaders.
   (2) The postwar government of Eastern Europe was no longer an issue.
   (3) Germany was no longer a topic at the conference table.
   (4) Differing viewpoints on governments of some war-torn countries were not considered significant.

5. The term "iron curtain" was first used by

   (1) Josef Stalin
   (2) Harry Truman
   (3) Clement Attlee
   (4) Winston Churchill

6. The term "iron curtain" described

   (1) a wall that was built between Eastern and Western Europe
   (2) a political boundary that existed between democratic and totalitarian governments in Europe after World War II
   (3) a plan to divide the Soviet bloc of nations
   (4) a geographic division between the rich and poor countries of Europe following World War II

7. At the end of World War II, the city of Berlin

   (1) was no longer the capital of Germany and had been divided into four sections
   (2) remained the capital of Germany under Soviet control
   (3) was too badly destroyed during the war to be of any interest to the rest of the world
   (4) was the economic center of modern Germany

8. The Truman Doctrine was an effort of the U.S. government to

   (1) send military and economic aid to countries fighting communism
   (2) rebuild hospitals and schools in Western European countries damaged by the war.
   (3) teach nuclear power programs to other victorious nations
   (4) spread American technology in Eastern Asia

9. Postwar Europe was a place for the United States to practice its policy of containment which meant that

   (1) Europe would begin to use only American currency
   (2) the United States would attempt to stop the spread of communism before it spread elsewhere
   (3) the defeated European countries would all be the site of future American military bases
   (4) the former Allied powers were united in their struggle against new democracies in Eastern Europe

10. Western European democracies after World War II were aided by the Marshall Plan because the United States

    (1) had made large sums of money while fighting the war
    (2) felt responsible for the damage done to major cities during the war
    (3) wanted to make those countries strong enough economically to resist the threat of communism
    (4) was held responsible for problems that occurred with Eastern Europe by the democratic leaders of Western Europe

11. A sign of the desire of the Soviets to increase their control of parts of Eastern Europe was their

    (1) refusal to join the United Nations
    (2) acceptance of the Marshall Plan in Eastern Europe
    (3) isolation of all parts of the city of Berlin
    (4) admission into NATO

12. The original purpose of the formation of the North Atlantic Treaty Organization was

    (1) to study ecological postwar concerns in the Atlantic Ocean
    (2) to build new universities to teach about democracy
    (3) a free-trade agreement between all member nations
    (4) a mutual defense agreement whereby if one member is attacked, the others will come to its defense

13. The Soviet Union responded to the development of the North Atlantic Treaty Organization by

    (1) forming the Warsaw Pact
    (2) ending the Berlin Blockade
    (3) forcing Yugoslavia to become Communist
    (4) conducting military maneuvers near Great Britain in the Atlantic

14. Tensions increased between Communist and non-Communist nations over which world event in 1950?

    (1) The Berlin Blockade
    (2) The Chinese invasion of Korea
    (3) The North Korean invasion of South Korea
    (4) The formation of SEATO

15. When Nikita Khrushchev came to power in the Soviet Union in 1953 he introduced a policy called

    (1) isolationism
    (2) détente
    (3) militarism
    (4) peaceful coexistence

16. Place the following events of the Cold War in correct chronological order:

    A. Bay of Pigs incident defused
    B. Fidel Castro assumes leadership of Cuba
    C. First Nuclear Test Ban Treaty is signed
    D. Cuban Missile Crisis averted

    (1) A, B, C, D   (3) C, B, A, D
    (2) B, D, C, A   (4) B, A, D, C

17. Which president of the United States experienced a "thaw" or period of detente during the Cold War?

    (1) Dwight Eisenhower
    (2) John F. Kennedy
    (3) Richard Nixon
    (4) Jimmy Carter

18. Soviet Premier Mikhail Gorbachev surprised the United States with his policy of "glasnost" which meant

    (1) restructuring
    (2) openness
    (3) imperialism
    (4) aggression

19. The Berlin Wall divided the city of Berlin in eastern and western sectors from

    (1) 1961 to 1989
    (2) the end of World War II until the end of the Berlin Airlift
    (3) the end of the Korean War until the Cuban Missile Crisis
    (4) 1953 to 1980

20. A valid conclusion about the Cold War would be that it

    (1) was a period of almost constant warfare between democratic and Communist nations
    (2) divided the world into two major groups based on theories of governmental practice for almost half a century
    (3) enabled Eastern European nations suffering from the aftermath of World War II to rebuild strong economies based on capitalism
    (4) strengthened ties between the United States and the Soviet Union

THEMATIC ESSAY

Directions: Write a well-organized essay that includes an introduction, several paragraphs addressing the task below, and a conclusion.

Theme: Conflict and Political Systems

The period after the end of World War II was known as the Cold War because it was characterized by a series of events that caused tension between democracies and Communist governments.

Task

Select three events that occurred during the Cold War and, for each,

- describe the nature of the event and identify the nations involved in the event
- discuss the resolution of the event, giving both a short-term and long-term result of the event
- explain why the event would be considered a factor in the Era of the Cold War

You may use any examples from the period of the Cold War. Some examples you might wish to consider include the division of Berlin, the creation of new German nations, the Cuban Missile Crisis, the Korean War, and the Soviet invasion of Afghanistan.

You are *not* limited to these suggestions.

Guidelines

In your essay, be sure to

- address all aspects of the *Task*
- support the theme with relevant facts, examples, and details
- use a logical and clear plan of organization, including an introduction and a conclusion that are beyond a restatement of the theme
- introduce the theme by establishing a framework that is beyond a simple restatement of the *Task* and conclude with a summation of the theme

DOCUMENT-BASED ESSAY QUESTION

This question is based on the accompanying documents (1–8). The question is designed to test your ability to work with historical documents. Some of the documents have been edited for the purposes of this question. As you analyze the documents, take into account the source of each document and any point of view that may be presented in the document.

Historical Context

Conflict is a clash of ideas, interests, or wills that result from incompatible opposing forces. World cultures have come in conflict many times in global history and this was true at the end of World War II.

Task

Using information from the documents and your knowledge of global history, answer the questions that follow each document in Part A. Your answers to the questions will help you write the Part B essay in which you will be asked to

- identify a reason for conflict between the United States and the Soviet Union after World War II
- describe two specific events that occurred because of this conflict
- discuss two viewpoints offered on resolving the conflict

Part A: Short-Answer Questions

Directions: Analyze the documents and answer the short-answer questions that follow each document.

Document 1

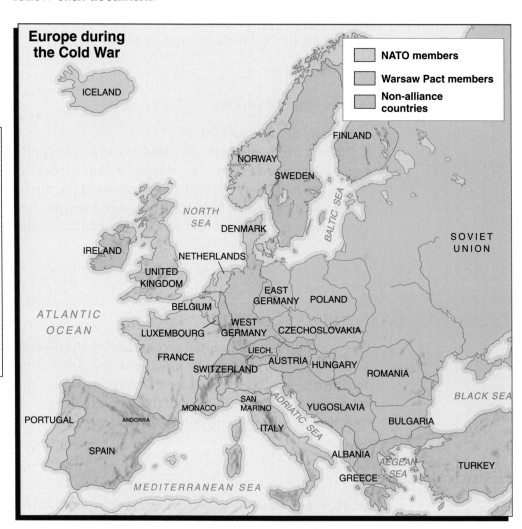

Questions

1. According to the map
   a. identify one member of the Communist Bloc.
   b. identify one member of the NATO alliance in 1955.

Document 2

Berlin Wall memorial crosses.

Question

2. From the picture and caption, what do the crosses show?

Document 3

In considering the requirements for the rehabilitation of Europe, the physical loss of life, the visible destruction of cities, factories, mines, and railroads was correctly estimated, but it has become obvious during recent months that this visible destruction was probably less serious than the dislocation of the entire fabric of European economy. For the past ten years conditions have been abnormal. The feverish preparation for war and the more feverish maintenance of the war effort engulfed all aspects of national economies. Machinery has fallen into disrepair or is entirely obsolete. Under the arbitrary and destructive Nazi rule, virtually every possible enterprise was geared into the German war machine. Long-standing commercial ties, private institutions, banks, insurance companies, and shipping companies disappeared through loss of capital, absorption through nationalization, or by simple destruction. In many countries, confidence in the local currency has been severely shaken. The breakdown of the business structure of Europe during the war was complete. Recovery has been seriously retarded by the fact that two years after the close of hostilities a peace settlement with Germany and Austria has not been agreed upon. But even given a more prompt solution of these difficult problems, the rehabilitation of the economic structure of Europe quite evidently will require a much longer time and greater effort than has been foreseen.

Excerpt from a speech by Secretary of State George C. Marshall, June 5, 1947.

Question

3. According to Secretary Marshall, what were three problems that existed in Europe at the end of World War II?
   a.
   b.
   c.

Document 4

From Stettin in the Baltic to Trieste in the Adriatic, an iron curtain has descended across the Continent. Behind that line lie all the capitals of the ancient states of Central and Eastern Europe. Warsaw, Berlin, Prague, Vienna, Budapest, Belgrade, Bucharest, and Sofia, all these famous cities and the populations around them lie in what I must call the Soviet sphere, and all are subject in one form or another, not only to Soviet influence but to a very high and, in many cases, increasing measure of control from Moscow.

Excerpt from a speech by Winston Churchill, Westminster College, Fulton, Missouri, March 5, 1946

Questions

4. a. What does Churchill mean about an "iron curtain" in this speech?
   b. Identify two cities that he says are behind this "iron curtain."
   c. Who does Churchill say exerts the strongest influence on these cities?

Document 5

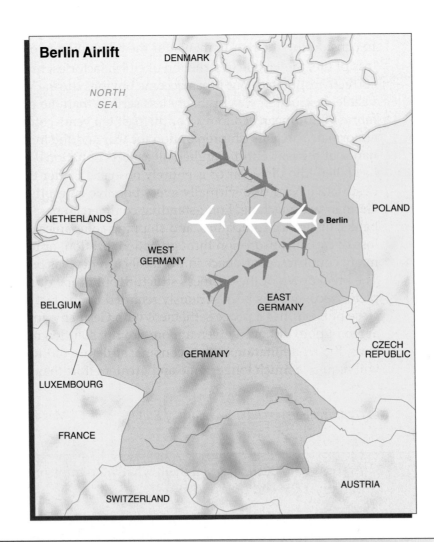

Berlin Airlift

DENMARK

NORTH SEA

NETHERLANDS

POLAND

Berlin

WEST GERMANY

BELGIUM

EAST GERMANY

GERMANY

CZECH REPUBLIC

LUXEMBOURG

FRANCE

AUSTRIA

SWITZERLAND

Questions

5. a. What event is shown in the map?
   b. What happened to Berlin that caused the Airlift?

Document 6

In the light of the above, it will be clearly seen that the Soviet pressure against the free institutions of the western world is something that can be contained by the adroit and vigilant application of counter-force at a series of constantly shifting geographical and political points, corresponding to the shifts and maneuvers of Soviet policy, but which cannot be charmed or talked out of existence. The Russians look forward to a duel of infinite duration, and they see that already they have scored great successes. It must be borne in mind that there was a time when the Communist Party represented far more of a minority in the sphere of Russian national life than Soviet power today represents in the world community.

Excerpt from "The Sources of Soviet Conduct" 1946 by George Kennan

---

Question

6. What is George Kennan suggesting the western world do to stop Soviet pressure against its free institutions?

Document 7

"Surely, God on high has not refused to give us enough wisdom to find ways to bring us an improvement in relations between the two great nations on earth."

Quotation from Soviet Leader Mikhail Gorbachev

Questions	7. a. Who are the two great nations in Gorbachev's quotation?
	b. What does he say is necessary to bring to these two nations?

Part B: Essay

Directions: Write a well-organized essay that includes an introduction, several paragraphs, and a conclusion. Use evidence from *at least four* documents in the body of the essay. Support your response with relevant facts, examples, and details. Include additional outside information.

Historical Context

Conflict is a clash of ideas, interests, or wills that result from incompatible opposing forces. World cultures have come in conflict many times in global history and this was true at the end of World War II.

Task

Using information from the documents and your knowledge of global history, answer the questions that follow each document in Part A. Your answers to the questions will help you write the Part B essay in which you will be asked to

- identify a reason for conflict between the United States and the Soviet Union after World War II
- describe two specific events that occurred because of this conflict
- discuss two viewpoints offered on resolving the conflict.

Guidelines

In your essay, be sure to

- address all aspects of the *Task* by accurately analyzing and interpreting *at least four* documents
- incorporate information from the documents in the body of the essay
- incorporate relevant outside information
- support the theme with relevant facts, examples, and details
- use a logical and clear plan of organization
- introduce the theme by establishing a framework that is beyond a simple restatement of the *Task* or *Historical Context* and conclude with a summation of the theme

CHAPTER 13

The Decline and Collapse of Communism in the Soviet Union and Eastern Europe

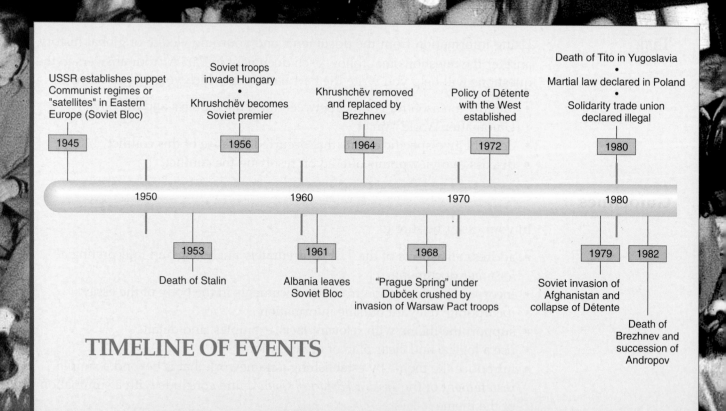

USSR establishes puppet Communist regimes or "satellites" in Eastern Europe (Soviet Bloc)

1945

Soviet troops invade Hungary
•
Khrushchёv becomes Soviet premier

1956

Khrushchёv removed and replaced by Brezhnev

1964

Policy of Détente with the West established

1972

Death of Tito in Yugoslavia
•
Martial law declared in Poland
•
Solidarity trade union declared illegal

1980

1950   1960   1970   1980

1953

Death of Stalin

1961

Albania leaves Soviet Bloc

1968

"Prague Spring" under Dubček crushed by invasion of Warsaw Pact troops

1979

Soviet invasion of Afghanistan and collapse of Détente

1982

Death of Brezhnev and succession of Andropov

TIMELINE OF EVENTS

The Soviet Union emerged from World War II as a superpower. Even though Stalin's successors tried to reduce repression after his death, the U.S.S.R. remained a totalitarian state. Involved in the Cold War with the West, the Soviet and Eastern European Communist systems proved unable to maintain their military machine and improve the standard of living for their people. By 1989, being a world power was too costly for the Soviet Union to continue indefinitely. It was also becoming clear that communism in the Soviet Union was a failure. In 1991, after seventy years of communism in Russia and forty-five years of Soviet domination in Eastern Europe, the Communist system behind the Iron Curtain collapsed. That this occurred with little violence or bloodshed is remarkable. However, enormous damage had been done. Even though the country was polluted, technologically backward, economically damaged, and politically inexperienced, the people under the former Communist regimes in Eastern Europe now began to stumble forward towards democracy and capitalism.

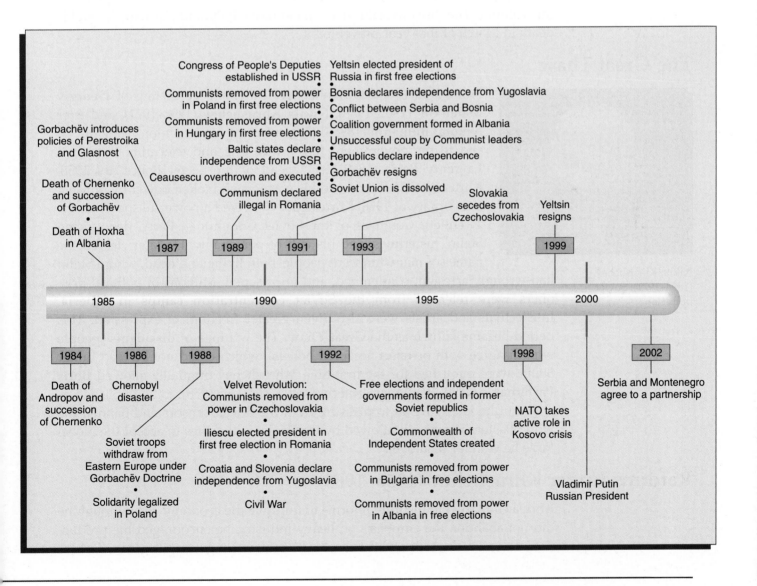

THE DECLINE AND COLLAPSE OF THE SOVIET UNION (1945–1991)

The U.S.S.R. After World War II

After World War II, the U.S.S.R. gained control over most of Eastern Europe. This brought greater territory for the Soviet empire, as well as larger strains on its devastated economy. The cost of maintaining troops in the Eastern European nations and keeping a strong military made it necessary for emphasis to continue to be placed on the development of heavy industry. Consumer goods and housing were neglected, and food shortages were common. The new series of **Five Year Plans** continued to promote industrial production primarily for military expansion.

As **Joseph Stalin**'s dictatorship (r. 1925–1953) wound down to its last years, the Soviet Union remained a police state. Intellectuals and artists were prevented from free expression. Stalin developed a **cult of personality**, by which he was officially worshiped through government propaganda. In early 1953, it appeared that he was about to launch another **Purge** (see Chapter 8 in this volume "The Rise of Totalitarianism in Russia, Italy, and Germany"), but his death in March of that year prevented it.

The Great Thaw

Nikita Khrushchev (1894–1971). Soviet politician.

From 1953 to 1958, a collective leadership consisting of **Georgiy Malenkov** (1902–1988), **Nikita Khrushchev** (1894–1971), and later **Nikolai Bulganin** (1895–1975), ruled the Soviet Union. They put an end to the government terror, arresting and executing the hated **Lavrenty Beria** (1899–1953), head of the Secret Police. By 1958, Khrushchev had removed his partners and taken power by himself. In February of 1956, Khrushchev delivered a powerful speech at the Twentieth Congress of the Soviet Communist Party, denouncing Stalin, his crimes, and his cult of personality. He later cleared the names of many innocent people, both living and dead, whom Stalin had wrongly arrested, condemned, and imprisoned. Millions of political prisoners were released from the Soviet **concentration camps** in **Siberia**. Intellectuals and artists were also given greater freedom of expression. This period became known as the **Great Thaw**. The writings of **dissidents** (people who disagree with or reject accepted beliefs), which could not be read under Stalin, were published for the first time. Khrushchev originally allowed **Boris Pasternak**'s (1890–1960) masterpiece, *Doctor Zhivago* (1958), to be published as well, but he later gave in to pressure from the Soviet censors and banned the work. Pasternak was not allowed by the Soviet authorities to accept the Nobel Prize he won for the novel.

Reforms Under Khrushchev (1958–1963)

Khrushchev tried to institute reforms to improve the economy. Even though he did not abandon the emphasis on heavy industry, he encouraged the production of consumer goods and the construction of housing. Despite great efforts to

Brezhnev at a White House meeting with President Richard Nixon, 1973.

catch up with Western production, the Soviet economy began to lag during the 1960s. In an effort to increase agricultural production, Khrushchev combined collective farms into larger units, hoping to improve efficiency. He also initiated the **Virgin Lands Program**, which tried to cultivate semi-arid land in western Siberia and central Asia. Despite some early successes, a series of droughts turned the area into a desert, and the Virgin Lands Program was an embarrassing failure.

Most of the Soviet Union's resources went into an **arms race** (competition to build weapons) along with space research. In the autumn of 1957, the Soviets launched *Sputnik I*, the first artificial earth satellite. This landmark achievement was followed by the successful sending of a rocket to the moon in 1959. In April of 1961, the first manned orbital flight was made by **Yury Gagarin** (1934–1968). Although these accomplishments brought great prestige to the U.S.S.R., they were an expense the Soviets could not afford. Khrushchev's foreign policy shifted from one of reconciliation with the West to an aggressive attitude that led to serious confrontations (see Chapter 12 in this volume "The Cold War").

Opposition to Khrushchev gradually increased within the Soviet leadership. He was criticized for his failures in agriculture and foreign policy. Viewed by many as a "rude peasant" who was incompetent, Khrushchev was removed from his position in October of 1964. **Aleksei Kosigin** (1904–1980) replaced him as premier and **Leonid Brezhnev** (r. 1964–1982) became general secretary of the Communist Party. By 1977, Brezhnev became dominant in the Soviet government, taking on the title of President (1977–1982).

The U.S.S.R. Under Brezhnev (1964–1982)

Brezhnev ruled the U.S.S.R. with a strong hand. His leadership was a period of great stagnation. Stubbornly, and without much regard for his people's welfare, Brezhnev refused to depart from the traditional Soviet goals or methods of rule. For intellectuals and artists, it was a return to repression. All literature and art were censored, and human rights were abused openly. An underground dissident movement began that included writers, poets, journalists, clergy, professors, students, and scientists. Publishing their works in underground presses known as **Samizdat**, they exposed the injustices of the Soviet system and protested their continuation.

The Dissidence of Solzhenitsyn and Sakharov

The most famous figures of this movement were the dissident writer **Aleksandr Solzhenitsyn** (1918–) and the eminent scientist **Andrei Sakharov** (1921–1989). Under Stalin, Solzhenitsyn had been imprisoned in a Siberian labor camp, which he wrote about in a short novel, *One Day in the Life of Ivan Denisovich*

Alexander Solzhenitsyn (1918-), Russian writer. Three photographs taken during the period of his imprisonment in the Soviet Union, 1945–1953.

(1962). His subsequent works were banned under Brezhnev and only published in the West or by Samizdat. Like Pasternak, he was not allowed to accept his Nobel Prize for literature in 1970. When he completed a massive three-volume history of the Siberian camps, the *Gulag Archipelago* (1974), it was banned. Its publication in the West resulted in Solzhenitsyn's expulsion from the Soviet Union the following year. Andrei Sakharov was a prominent physicist and "father of the Soviet hydrogen bomb." He also joined the ranks of the dissidents with the publication of his book, *My Country and the World* (1974), in which he called for greater freedom of expression and the reform of the political system. In 1975, he was awarded the Nobel Prize, but he was also not allowed to accept it. Sakharov's contacts with Western journalists resulted in his internal exile in the city of Gorky, which was not open to foreigners. In 1987, Sakharov was released and allowed to return to Moscow, where he was elected a member of the **Congress of People's Deputies** and died in 1989.

Economic Decline

Main Idea:
The increased contact with the West due to **Detente** made the Soviet consumers aware of how poor their standard of living was compared with nations in the West and the United States.

In economic affairs, the Brezhnev years were a period of decline and decay. Although more consumer goods and housing became available, the quality was poor, and the output could not keep up with the growing population. The levels of agricultural production declined, and the U.S.S.R. was forced to depend on imports from the United States and the West. The increased contact with the West due to **Detente** (see Chapter 12 in this volume "The Cold War") made the Soviet consumers aware of how poor their standard of living was compared with nations in the West and the United States. Most people had to stand on long lines for hours to get the most basic items. A privileged class of Communist Party elites had also developed under Brezhnev. They lived a luxurious lifestyle, able to get any product they wanted, including much sought after Western goods, in "special" stores with no lines. This antagonized many Soviet citizens further. Finally, the repressive nature of the Brezhnev regime and the inefficiency of the Soviet system made them both angry and cynical. The Soviet invasion of **Afghanistan** in 1979 further angered the population, especially the young (see Chapter 12 in this volume).

Andropov and Chernenko (1982–1985)

Following Brezhnev's death in 1982, there was a succession of leaders with brief administrations. **Yury Andropov** (r. 1982–1984) became seriously ill after taking power. He tried to institute basic economic reforms, but his sudden death in February of 1984 prevented any serious changes from being implemented. His successor, **Konstantin Chernenko** (r. 1984–1985) was a reactionary who wished to continue the policies of Brezhnev. Already declining in health when he took Andropov's place, he died in March of 1985.

Soviet Head of State and Communist Party leader Mikhail Gorbachev visiting the United States in 1987. Photographed alongside American President Ronald Reagan at a podium in front of the White House, Washington, D.C., December 1, 1987.

Reform Under Gorbachev (1985–1989)

With the rise of **Mikhail Gorbachev** (r. 1985–1991), a younger generation of Soviet leaders took control. Even though he wanted to begin reforms, Gorbachev was hesitant at first. The meltdown of the nuclear reactor at **Chernobyl** in 1986 made the need for reform clear. The accident was a major disaster that contaminated whole areas of the Ukraine, poisoning thousands of people and animals. It greatly reduced the capability of one of the world's most fertile regions to produce crops. The slow reaction of the government to the disaster and its clumsy attempt to cover it up angered the population. This gave Gorbachev the excuse he needed to seek reforms. He immediately introduced two new radical programs: **Glasnost** and **Perestroika**.

Glasnost

The policy of Glasnost (openness) was aimed at reducing the intellectual, political, and cultural repression that had been part of the Soviet system. The media (newspapers, radio, and television) were given more freedom in their reporting. For the first time, dissenting opinions could be expressed openly. Glasnost also led to the publication of books that had been banned, such as Pasternak's *Doctor Zhivago*. Gorbachev also released dissidents who were imprisoned or in exile, including Sakharov. He even invited Solzhenitsyn back to the U.S.S.R.

Perestroika

Perestroika (restructuring) was created to promote greater productivity in both industry and agriculture. It also was designed to improve the quality of Soviet goods. Gorbachev began by reforming the U.S.S.R.'s **command economy** (a system in which government planners make all economic decisions). Gorbachev decentralized Soviet industrial and agricultural management by giving factory and farm managers greater control over determining both the production and the distribution of profits. Worker incentives, such as a pay increase for greater individual productivity, were adopted. The goal was to make factories and farms independent, self-sufficient, and profitable so that they would no longer need government **subsidies** (money to make up losses). The Law of Cooperatives of 1987 allowed Soviet citizens to set up private businesses (free of state controls) and keep the profits. This was intended to encourage more production of better products and services, beginning a system of individual enterprise. The Agricultural Reform Law of 1988 broke up the state and collective farms, replacing them with a private leasing system. Individual farmers were able to own and profit from their farms once they paid off a long-term lease. The goal of this reform was to promote greater productivity through the private ownership of land. Clearly, the changes described here, although commonplace in our own society, were monumental for the U.S.S.R. The reason was that they completely violated traditional Communist theory. Yet, Gorbachev was willing to try such "violations" if they could result in a more productive economy for the Soviet Union.

The Gorbachev Doctrine

Politically, Perestroika reduced the direct involvement of the Communist Party leadership in the day-to-day governance of the country and increased the authority of local government agencies. This angered the nomenklatura or ruling group of the Communist Party. Religious freedoms were also granted, and the **Russian Orthodox Church** celebrated its millennium (one-thousandth anniversary) with the support of the government. Jews were permitted greater freedom, with an increasing number allowed to migrate to other countries. In foreign affairs, Gorbachev implemented the **Gorbachev Doctrine**, a policy of noninterference in Eastern Europe and the world. By autumn of 1988, he began to reduce the number of Soviet troops in some of the satellite nations, encouraging the collapse of the Communist regimes in those nations a year later.

The Decline of the Communist Party of the Soviet Union

Faced with growing opposition from a number of older bureaucrats, military leaders, and Party officials, Gorbachev took the title of president and removed his opponents from positions of power in 1988. In 1989, he instituted a Soviet Parliament, the **Congress of People's Deputies**. Members would be chosen by free elections, a new procedure for the Soviet Union. Despite enormous advantages and influence over the election process, a number of prominent Communists were nevertheless defeated. The majority of representatives were, however, Communists who ran unopposed. Yet, this panicked Gorbachev. Despite being dedicated to reform, he feared that if this trend continued, the dominance of the Communist Party would slowly disappear. The election of dissidents, such as Sakharov, and officials who were openly critical of the regime, such as **Boris Yeltsin**, was seen by Gorbachev as a threat to the survival of the system. Yeltsin had risen to power by promoting Russian nationalism and downplaying the Soviet Union. The population, which had always seen the two as the same, took a new pride in their nation and directed their anger directly at the Soviet government. Gorbachev, who never understood this, continued to remain a strong supporter of communism and became as unpopular as the system he defended. He also came under heavy criticism from conservative hardline communists for allowing the election.

> **Main Idea:**
> The election of dissidents, such as Sakharov, and officials who were openly critical of the regime, such as **Boris Yeltsin**, was seen by Gorbachev as a threat to the survival of the system.

Gorbachev's Retreat from Reform (1989–1991)

Main Idea:
By February of 1991, Gorbachev was calling himself "a dedicated Communist" and criticizing many former allies as "radicals."

In March of 1989, the Baltic Sea satellite nations of **Lithuania** and **Estonia** declared their independence. Neighboring **Latvia** followed later in the year. These declarations were encouraged by the withdrawal of Soviet domination in Eastern Europe that was taking place under the Gorbachev Doctrine. That same month, the Congress of People's Deputies repealed the Communist Party's monopoly of political power. This meant that the Communists could no longer be the only political party allowed by law. At the **May Day** celebration on May 1 (the traditional day of celebration worldwide for all Socialists and Communists), Gorbachev and the other Soviet leaders were jeered at by protesters. At the Communist Party Congress in July, Boris Yeltsin resigned dramatically from the party. With the resignation of foreign minister Eduard Shevardnadze in December, Gorbachev began to back down from his reforms. By February of 1991, Gorbachev was calling himself "a dedicated Communist" and criticizing many former allies as "radicals."

The Union Treaty of Republics

With Yeltsin's election as president of the **Russian Republic**, the largest nation among the fifteen republics that made up the U.S.S.R., Gorbachev now had a rival. Soon strains between the Russian and Soviet governments appeared. In July, Shevardnadze also quit the Communist Party, founding a movement for democratic reform. Totally overwhelmed by the turn of events, Gorbachev agreed to sign a union treaty with the heads of ten republics that gave them greater autonomy. His agreement to the new arrangement frightened conservatives into calling on the military to "save the country."

The Russian Revolution of 1991

In August, while Gorbachev was on vacation in the Crimea, a military *coup d'état* (an unexpected seizure of power) took place. Gorbachev was put under house arrest, and martial law was declared. Lacking any public support, including the military, the coup was unsuccessful and collapsed after three days.

Yeltsin delivering a speech on top of a tank in Moscow during the attempted military coup. August 19, 1991.

Main Idea:
The failed overthrow discredited the Communist Party and the KGB. This turn of events became known as the **Russian Revolution of 1991.**

Yeltsin, who had appeared on the steps of the Russian Republic's government building and defied the illegal takeover, became a national hero. Gorbachev returned, and the leaders of the coup were disgraced. Some were arrested, while others committed suicide.

Rumors soon began that Gorbachev had actually planned the takeover as a way of undoing his reforms before the Communist Party leadership had completely lost power. Although these accusations were never proven, the coup had made him appear very weak and incompetent. The failed overthrow discredited the Communist Party and the KGB. This turn of events became known as the **Russian Revolution of 1991**. Disregarding the previous unsigned union agreement, Yeltsin declared Russia an independent state. One by one, the other republics also claimed independence. Gorbachev tried desperately, but unsuccessfully, to stop the swift breakup of the Soviet Union. On December 25, 1991, he resigned from the presidency of an empire that no longer existed. That evening, the Soviet flag was lowered from the Kremlin for the last time. This historic episode now meant that communism in both Russia and the Soviet Union was over. The revolution that had shook the world seventy years earlier ended not with a bang, but a whimper.

The Commonwealth of Independent States (1991–)

With the U.S.S.R. disbanded, each republic held its own elections and established its own independent government. Russia, as the largest and most populous of these states, took a leadership position in creating a new union of autonomous nations, the **Commonwealth of Independent States (CIS)**. The United Nations recognized each new nation, giving each nation its own representatives.

Some republics did not make a smooth transition. Civil war flared up in **Georgia** between the newly elected government under **Eduard Shevardnadze** and rebels who refused to recognize it. Fighting between the Christians of **Armenia** and the Muslims of **Azerbaijan** also began. This conflict had started in the last years of Gorbachev's rule but grew worse without the Soviet government to mediate.

Russia tried to assume the role of leader of the new Commonwealth, but the other republics were still fearful of once again being dominated by them. This was especially true in the **Ukraine**, where strong feelings of nationalism had risen. In 1992 and 1993, Russia and the Ukraine negotiated a compromise over the **Black Sea Fleet** in the Crimea, an area in the southern Ukraine that was a very important naval base for the Russians. The two nations finally agreed that it would belong to the Ukraine, but the Russian fleet would be allowed its use.

The Conflict Between Yeltsin and Parliament

In the fall of 1993, President Yeltsin dismissed the Congress of People's Deputies. Composed mainly of Communists from the Gorbachev period, this former Soviet Parliament had blocked all of his efforts to reform the Russian economic system into a capitalist free market. Yeltsin demanded that new elections be held. He pointed out that most of the Parliament's deputies had never really been elected by the people as they ran unopposed in most cases in the first elections of 1989. Realizing that they probably would not be returned to

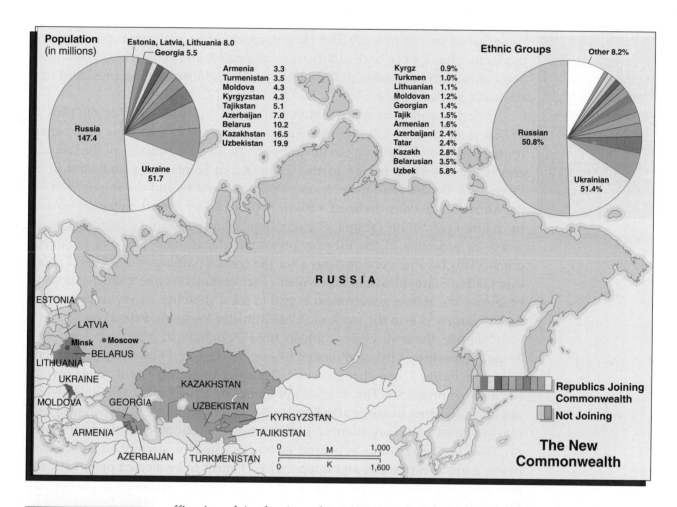

Population (in millions)

Estonia, Latvia, Lithuania 8.0
Georgia 5.5

Armenia	3.3
Turmenistan	3.5
Moldova	4.3
Kyrgyzstan	4.3
Tajikstan	5.1
Azerbaijan	7.0
Belarus	10.2
Kazakhstan	16.5
Uzbekistan	19.9

Russia 147.4

Ukraine 51.7

Ethnic Groups

Other 8.2%

Kyrgz	0.9%
Turkmen	1.0%
Lithuanian	1.1%
Moldovan	1.2%
Georgian	1.4%
Tajik	1.5%
Armenian	1.6%
Azerbaijani	2.4%
Tatar	2.4%
Kazakh	2.8%
Belarusian	3.5%
Uzbek	5.8%

Russian 50.8%

Ukrainian 51.4%

RUSSIA

ESTONIA
LATVIA
Minsk • Moscow
BELARUS
LITHUANIA
UKRAINE
MOLDOVA
GEORGIA
ARMENIA
AZERBAIJAN   TURKMENISTAN
KAZAKHSTAN
UZBEKISTAN
KYRGYZSTAN
TAJIKISTAN

Republics Joining Commonwealth
Not Joining

The New Commonwealth

0 — M — 1,000
0 — K — 1,600

Main Idea:
Realizing that they probably would not be returned to office in a fair election, the majority of representatives refused to stop meeting and barricaded themselves in the Parliament building.

office in a fair election, the majority of representatives refused to stop meeting and barricaded themselves in the Parliament building. After a brief standoff between the Parliament and their supporters, Yeltsin ordered troops to retake the Parliament building and arrest the rebellious deputies. These decisive actions were successful and added to his popularity. Yeltsin also took steps toward creating a new constitution wherein the presidency would gain greater power. While this move was seen by some as the first step to a dictatorship, others saw it as necessary to push through economic reforms. Not surprisingly, in a nation that has only known autocracy throughout its history, Yeltsin's bid for greater power had given many Russians new confidence in him as a strong leader. Yet, the enormous suffering that the economic transformation brought created new problems that threatened the development of democracy in Russia. This became evident in the national elections of December 1993, when ultra-nationalist **Vladimir Zhirinovskiy** and his party won an impressive number of seats in the new Russian Parliament or **Duma**.

The Yeltsin Presidency (1994–1999)

The national election of 1994 confirmed popular support for both Yeltsin and the new Constitution within the year; however, the Russian Army's inability to put down rebellion in **Chechnya** (republic within Russia), a rise in government corruption and organized crime, and the hardships created by economic reforms overwhelmed the Yeltsin presidency. Despite these problems, Yeltsin

---

campaigned successfully in 1996 on a platform of commitment to reform and moderate choice over both right-wing nationalist and old-style Communists. Soon after both his health and popularity faded, the struggling president continuously shifted ministers.

Yeltsin seemed to recover both physically and politically at the start of 1997. A peace treaty in Chechnya and mild improvements in the economy helped restore public confidence in the government. In July, the remains of the last czar and his family were buried in the Cathedral of Saints Peter and Paul in St. Petersburg. By late 1997, the economy declined steadily, and the standard of living for most Russians declined with it. Popular anger forced Yeltsin to remove the reformers from his cabinet. The economic relapse continued into 1998, made worse by a decline in the Russian president's health and a rise in organized crime. (This became very obvious after the contract killing of the liberal politician **Galina Starovoitova** in November.) Facing staggering economic and social problems, the Yeltsin government began to see a slow but steady improvement in 1999 largely due to the work of Prime Minister **Yevgeniy Primakov.**

Despite these successes, Yeltsin fired Primakov in May and appointed **Sergei Stepashin** as prime minister. In August, Yeltsin replaced Stepashin with **Vladimir Putin**. These changes created further resentment and anger toward the Russian president. This was compounded by government scandals involving the laundering of money by Russian banks. On January 31, Yeltsin resigned, making Putin acting president until the national elections scheduled for March of 2000. The resignation appeared to be designed to strengthen his current prime minister's position and improve his chances to be elected president. The new support Putin received from politicians in January 2000 seemed to confirm the wisdom of Yeltsin's action.

The Putin Presidency (1999–)

In the election of March 2000, Putin was elected president with a strong popular mandate. His platform of ending corruption in government and opposing the **oligarchs** (government insiders who took illegal advantage of their position to gain control of newly privatized industries, becoming enormously wealthy and influential) gave him enormous public support. His KGB background gave Putin the image of a strong decisive leader who would both strengthen internal security against terrorism and restore Russia's declining military power. The election also saw a significant drop in support for the Communist Party, the Ultra Nationalists, and other extreme parties that had done fairly well in the last election due to anger over the economy.

Despite Putin's authoritarian style in implementing his reforms he has remained popular. Since 2000, Putin has increased the strength of the national government. He greatly weakened the power of local government by stripping the eighty-nine governors of the Russian Federation of their seats in the Federation Council and creating seven new supra-regional governors appointed by the president. Putin also obtained legislation allowing the president to remove any regional leader accused by federal authorities of wrong doing. He gained greater influence over the Duma by creating federal requirements for political parties.

Putin placed restrictions on the Russian media's ability to criticize the government. Many people, especially outside Russia, saw this control of much of the media as censorship of free speech, but it gave the president surprising popular support. Exposure of the corruption and responsibility of the oligarchs for the 1998 economic collapse has given Putin the political mandate to make needed economic reforms. In 2001, Putin designed a new land code allowing the purchase and sale of land in Russian cities for the first time since the Bolshevik Revolution of 1917. It generated a new housing market attracting both domestic and foreign investment. The expansion of privatization and free enterprise resulted in the development of stock exchanges to provide investment capital throughout Russia in the 1990s. The lack of regulation, however, as well as the problems the government experienced in tax collecting, resulted in the creation of a small aggressive class of wealthy entrepreneurs, often tied to organized crime, with government connections. Most ordinary Russians, with low-paying jobs, and the elderly, dependent on small pensions, became extremely resentful of the rise of this group. Social ills, such as crime, prostitution, and alcoholism, combined with high unemployment and government corruption, led to disillusion with the new system and the flight of many young people to the West in search of economic opportunities. Upon coming to power, Putin took steps to correct these problems by reducing taxes, implementing reforms to curb corruption within the government bureaucracy, cracking down on organized crime, and waging a war on the oligarchs in which the government seized control of their industries.

> **Main Idea:**
> Despite Putin's use of authoritarian means, which resulted in strong criticism from both within and abroad, by 2002 it appeared that the Russian economy had stabilized.

Despite Putin's use of authoritarian means, which resulted in strong criticism from both within and abroad, by 2002 it appeared that the Russian economy had stabilized. The government's budget showed a surplus and Russia had paid all of its foreign debts in full for the first time since 1991. Putin's strong action restored public confidence in the economy, which revived foreign investment. The government's seizure of control of the oil and gas industries from the oligarchs contributed greatly to the economic recovery because of the high prices being paid for energy on the international market. Finally, the successful humbling of the oligarchs created greater confidence in the government and opened up new opportunities for small independent entrepreneurs. Even though government corruption and organized crime remain a problem, the Putin administration has put the Russian economy on a forward track.

Russian Foreign Policy Under Putin

The NATO military intervention on the side of the ethnic Albanians of Kosovo and the bombing of Serbia in the spring of 1999 created further strains in the relations between Russia, and the West and the United States. Russia supported Serbia and was highly critical of the NATO actions in the Yugoslav province. It's role in ending the conflict and the involvement of Russian troops in the peacekeeping force resulted in further tensions and mutual suspicions.

Terrorist attacks in Russian cities during the summer of 1999 were blamed on Chechen separatists. This resulted in a full-scale Russian military invasion of Chechnya that autumn. By the winter, Russian troops had captured much Chechen territory and forced thousands of refugees to flee. The international community, including the United States, was critical of Russia's harsh reaction to the terrorist attacks. Yeltsin responded that it was an internal matter and that it was hypocritical of the West to criticize Russia's actions after NATO's military interference in Kosovo and the bombing of Serbia.

On coming to power in 2001, Putin escalated Russian military action in Chechnya. The campaign was successful in crushing rebel resistance and recapturing the Chechen capital city of **Grozny** as well as most of the lowlands, but it devastated both the country itself and the economy. By 2002, the costs of the war and the continuation of Chechen terrorism within Russia forced Putin to rethink his strategy. Working with the pro-Russian Chechen President **Aslan Maskhadov** to end the fighting, they adopted a compromise that would allow Chechnya autonomy while it remained part of Russia. Even though the compromise has resulted in a considerable decline in violence, the problems are far from resolved, and the threat of a new conflict continues.

As the new millennium began, new tensions between Russia and both the nations of the CIS and the West were becoming apparent. Each was still struggling to solve its economic problems, especially Russia, in order to make a smooth transition to capitalism and the free market. At the same time, strong nationalist movements within these nations and popular anger over poor economic conditions brought on by the transitions may limit or even prevent the success of their economic reforms. This may very well decide the extent to which these countries will become and/or remain democracies.

THE RISE AND FALL OF COMMUNISM IN EASTERN EUROPE (1945–1992)

Soviet Domination (1945–1988)

The end of World War II brought a considerable extension of Soviet power in Eastern Europe. It imposed Communist-dominated governments on the **Baltic States** (**Estonia**, **Latvia**, and **Lithuania**), **Poland**, **Romania**, **Bulgaria**, **Hungary**, and **East Germany**. In **Czechoslovakia**, **Yugoslavia**, and **Albania**, local Communist governments took control and worked an accommodation with the Soviets (see Chapter 12 in this volume).

The End of Soviet Domination (1988–1990)

With the announcement of the Gorbachev Doctrine in 1988 and the withdrawal of the Soviet presence in Eastern Europe, the Communist regimes began to fall. The first signs were in Poland and Hungary where dissatisfaction with the regimes had reached crisis proportions. The loss of Soviet economic and political support forced these governments to begin backing down. By the end of 1989, most of those nations had already or were in the process of overthrowing the governments placed there by the Soviets. Yugoslavia and Albania, the two countries whose Communist governments had not been imposed by the Soviet Union, would undergo political change a year later.

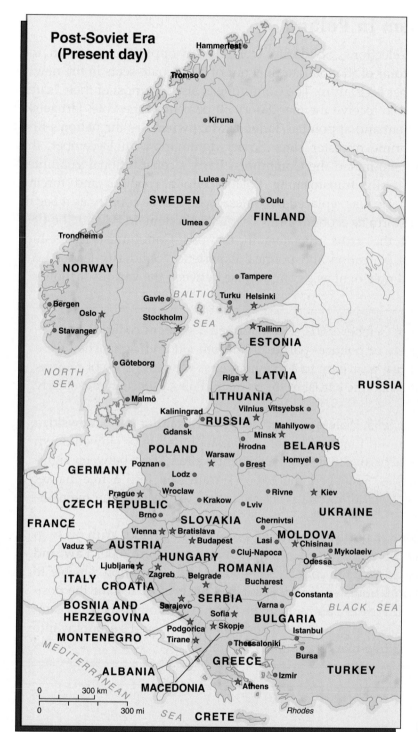

Post-Soviet Era (Present day)

East Germany

The **Berlin Wall,** the hated symbol of Communist domination and the Cold War, was torn down as the East German regime under **Eric Honecker** was overthrown. East Germany's reunification with the West in 1990 marked the end of the Communist era in Eastern Europe and the start of a turbulent period of reorganization (see Chapter 9 "World War II" in this volume).

Poland

When Poland regained its independence after World War I, it became a Democracy. Such was its political status until 1926, when an authoritarian regime began under Marshal **Joseph Pilsudski**. In 1939, the nation was invaded and occupied by Nazi Germany. This marked the beginning of World War II in Europe. In 1945, with Soviet forces driving the Nazis out, Poland came under Stalin's control. A Soviet-supported Polish Communist regime was placed over the country. Poland now became a satellite of the U.S.S.R.

The Rise of Solidarity

In 1980, the anti-Communist labor union **Solidarity** began to challenge the authority of the Polish Communist government under **General Wojciech Jaruzelski**. Solidarity's leader, **Lech Walesa**, led the union in an eight-year struggle against the regime, despite the fact that it was officially banned in 1981. In the summer of 1988, strikes throughout the nation forced Jaruzelski to agree to negotiations with the workers of the still illegal trade union. The government agreed to legalize Solidarity and hold partially free elections that would divide power in the Polish Parliament between the Communists and their opposition.

The Collapse of Communism in Poland

In the June 1989 elections, Solidarity won all the opposition seats in the Parliament (35 percent of the total) and 99 out of 100 Senate seats in the newly created two-chamber legislature. The Communists also lost most of their "safe" seats as they failed to receive the mandatory 50 percent of the vote. Jaruzelski was elected president and appointed **Tadeusz Mazowiecki** as the nation's first non-Communist prime minister since Soviet domination. In December, the Polish Parliament eliminated the Communist Party's constitutional guarantee of leadership, officially transforming Poland into a republic and forcing Jaruzelski to resign. He was replaced by Walesa, who led his country as it began its struggle to transform its economy into a capitalist system. In Poland, the 1990 elections revealed the great divisions in the post-Communist leadership. Despite his lack of education and political experience, Solidarity leader Lech Walesa was elected president as a compromise between the various factions.

POLAND SINCE 1991

After the election of October 1991, Walesa formed a series of coalition governments with a variety of political parties from both left and right. They were unable to make a real transition to a free market as the rapid pace of reforms had created great economic hardship for so many Poles, especially the elderly and farmers.

In November 1995, Walesa was replaced by **Alexander Kwasniewski**, a moderate who believed that the economic transition had to be slowed down and monitored. Successive Polish governments, alternating between right- and left-wing parties, managed the nation's transition into a free-market economy. By 2004, Poland had been accepted for European Union membership.

In 2005 **Lech Kaczynski** was elected president of Poland. With his twin brother **Jaroslaw**, he had formed a new political party in 2000, **Law and Justice**, aimed at ridding the country of scandal and corruption. Unable to work with the prime minister, Kaczynski asked his brother to take the position in 2006. Fervently anti-Communist, the Kaczynski brothers began a campaign to end corruption in government and transform Poland's economy into a thriving capitalist free-market economy.

Hungary

After World War I, Hungary lost two-thirds of its land and population in the peace settlements. The Habsburg monarchy was replaced by a military dictatorship under Admiral **Nicholas Horthy,** who sided with Germany in World War II in hopes of regaining its lost territories. After the war, the Soviet Union installed a Moscow-trained dictator. Hungary became a satellite of the U.S.S.R. The Hungarian people never accepted this imposition. Stalin's death in 1953 gave Hungary and the nations of Eastern Europe the false impression that they could develop independently.

The 1956 Hungarian Revolution

In 1956, **Imre Nagy**, a Hungarian communist, became Party leader. In an atmosphere of great nationalism, Nagy announced that Hungary would reestablish a multiparty system and pursue a neutral foreign policy. This would mean abandoning its connection with the U.S.S.R. Such a striking announcement angered the Soviets. They responded by mounting an invasion of the country in October. Nagy was removed from power and later executed. This harsh policy of not permitting independent actions by Soviet satellites became known as the **Brezhnev Doctrine**.

The Collapse of Communism in Hungary

Janos Kadar was installed as Hungary's new Communist dictator. Kadar ruthlessly suppressed dissent, but he also gradually introduced reforms that permitted limited private economic enterprise and greater cultural expression. In May of 1988, Kadar fell from power and was replaced by **Karol Grosz**. He began to democratize the nation and introduce reforms to revitalize its economy. A year later, the Hungarian government dismantled the barbed-wire fence on the German border that had come to symbolize the Iron Curtain. It had long prevented many East Germans, who were tired of the harsh government control and poor living standards in their country, from crossing through Hungary to the West. In an act of defiance, refugees were allowed through.

The Establishment of Democracy in Hungary

In September of 1989, as a multiparty system began to appear, negotiations were held between the Communist leaders and representatives of the new political parties that had formed to ensure an orderly transition of power. It was decided that Hungary would become a democratic republic with a one-chamber legislature elected by **universal suffrage** (all citizens may vote), and a weak presidency. In the October elections, despite a change in name to the Hungarian Socialist Party, the Communists were badly defeated. In December, the Parliament dissolved itself. New elections in 1990 swept the remaining Communists from power. The new Parliament ended the Communists' control through legislation and put Hungary on the path to a fully capitalist economy. In June of 1990, Imre Nagy was reburied with honors as a hero of the failed 1956 Hungarian Revolution.

HUNGARY SINCE 1991

Throughout the 1990s Hungary made enormous progress toward transforming itself into a fully capitalist economy. By 2004, Hungary had qualified for membership in the European Union. Despite shifting policies between right-wing, left-wing, and centrist parties, Hungary continues to develop its economy, which remains one of the strongest in Eastern Europe.

Czechoslovakia

Czechoslovakia, the union of Bohemia, Moravia, and Slovakia, was created at the end of World War I from the Austro-Hungarian Empire. It was the only Eastern European nation to maintain a parliamentary democracy from 1918 to 1938. The Czech experiment with democracy ended in 1938, due to the attack by Nazi Germany (see Chapter 9, "World War II"). In retaliation, the Czech government expelled 2.5 million ethnic Germans in 1945, after Germany's defeat. With strong support from the Soviet Union, the Czech Communist Party was able to gain 38 percent of the vote and some key government positions in the 1946 elections. In February 1948, working with the Soviet Union, the Communists seized power from the Czechoslovakian president and began Stalinist purges of dissidents. By the end of the year, Czechoslovakia was a Soviet satellite. Its people were severely distressed, as a result of coming under Soviet control.

The Prague Spring

After twenty years of Communist rule, discontent reached a crisis level. This resulted in the removal of the president and party leader **Antonin Novotny**. He was replaced by **Alexander Dubcek**, who immediately initiated a reform program. From January to August of 1968, Dubcek abolished censorship, allowed greater cultural and intellectual freedom, began to improve relations with the West, and discussed further democratization. Calling his policies, "Socialism with a human face," the brief period of Dubcek's rule became known as the **Prague Spring** (Prague was the capital of Czechoslovakia). This meant that the Dubcek reforms were seen in Czechoslovakia as a welcome change, just as spring is enjoyed after winter. Fearing they were setting a bad example, the Soviets ordered the leaders to limit the reforms. When they refused, the Soviet Union invaded Czechoslovakia with Warsaw Pact troops. Dubcek was forced out of office, to the dismay of the Czechoslovakian people. His successor, **Gustav Husak**, restored strict Communist control over the nation. Husak remained in power until **Milos Jakes** replaced him in December of 1987.

The Velvet Revolution

Twenty years after the Soviet invasion, the deteriorating economy in Czechoslovakia and events in other Soviet satellites, most notably Poland and Hungary, encouraged dissent. The violent reaction of the police to student demonstrations and the arrest of the popular dramatist, political essayist, and human rights advocate **Vaclav Havel** in 1989, sparked even greater waves of protest. Havel was the cofounder of the **Charter 77** reform movement, a group based on a document developed by the **Helsinki Conference**. This is an international organization that monitors and reports on human rights violations. He was released within five months due to public pressure. By that summer, student demonstrations had started again.

In November, their numbers reached 25,000, and the authorities reacted by clubbing the students off the streets. Two days later, a demonstration of hundreds of thousands filled Wenceslas Square in Prague. It brought together the two largest groups opposing the Communist government—the Czech Civic Forum (led by Havel) and the Slovak Public Against Violence in Slovakia. After several days of equally huge demonstrations, the Jakes government resigned. This was the beginning of what became known as Czechoslovakia's **Velvet Revolution**. Starting in December, the Communist-dominated Parliament voted to shift to a free-market economy and a Western-type parliamentary system, hoping to maintain their power in the face of widespread dissatisfaction. Dubcek was named chairman of the National Parliament, and Havel was elected interim president of Czechoslovakia, the first non-Communist leader in over forty years. In June of 1990, Havel was reelected president, and the Communists were swept out of power in the national elections. They received only 13 percent of the vote. The new government began the transition from a command economy to a free market. It also had to undo forty years of economic mismanagement and environmental damage from heavy industrialization without pollution controls.

Czechoslovakia Becomes Two Nations

By 1991, there was discontent in Slovakia. The Slovak people, who had long felt dominated by the Czechs, became resentful of Havel's intention to wind down Slovakia's chief industry, the production of arms. The Slovak Prime Minister **Vladimir Meciar** announced that the republic would continue to sell arms without seeking the national government in Prague's approval. A national hero in the Czech republics of Bohemia and Moravia and a respected figure internationally, Havel became highly unpopular in Slovakia, largely due to Meciar. Adopting a nationalist doctrine, Meciar mounted a campaign to promote Slovak secession from Czechoslovakia. Slovak opposition leaders in the capital of **Bratislava**, including Dubcek, called for his resignation. Despite a fierce battle, Meciar succeeded in gaining a vote for independence in the summer of 1992. Havel resigned as president in disgust, warning against the division of the nation. On January 1, 1993, Czechoslovakia legally separated into the nations of the **Czech Republic** and **Slovakia**. With the wisdom of the split still in question on the part of many Slovaks as well as Czechs, the two countries face an uncertain future.

THE CZECH REPUBLIC SINCE 1993

After the separation, the Czech Republic was able to make the transition to a free-market democracy with relatively few problems. Under successive governments ranging from left to right and center, state control of the economy gradually diminished and was replaced by a growth of private industry, employment, and social stability. In 2004, the Czech Republic was accepted for membership in the European Union.

SLOVAKIA SINCE 1993

In contrast to the Czech Republic, Slovakia became increasingly conservative and nationalistic. Under Meciar (1993–1998) privatization and the transition to a free-market economy was slowed down as he built up his own personal power base. His attempts to censor the free press greatly damaged Slovakia's world image as a developing democracy. Meciar's nationalistic policies hurt both the economy (because they discouraged badly needed foreign investment to build industries) and relations with Slovakia's neighbors (because of the harsh treatment of its large Hungarian minority). By 1998, Slovakia's health and education systems were bankrupt, the economy was on the verge of collapse, and privatizations, which had failed as state enterprises, were sold to Meciar's political appointees at bargain prices.

In the elections of September 1998, Meciar and his nationalist party were voted out. New democratic and pro-Western parties dominated successive governments that took Slovakia in a different direction. The nationalist policies of the Meciar era were abandoned, and greater efforts were made to develop a free-market economy by encouraging foreign investment, increasing privatization, ending corruption in government through reforms, and increasing democratic participation by amending the constitution to provide for direct popular election of the president. By 2001, Slovakia officially applied for membership in the European Union. In 2006, the first left-wing government under **Robert Fico** and his Smer (Direction) Party took power. While moderating the nationalistic policies of Meciar and the successive right wing governments that followed him, Smer's socialist policies may hurt the efforts at privatization and hinder Slovakia's entry into the European Union.

Romania

The nation of Romania, combining Wallachia, Moldavia, Bessarabia, and later Transylvania, was formed in the early nineteenth century. It gained independence from the Ottoman Empire in 1878. After World War I, the Romanian monarchy supported a fascist dictatorship under Marshal **Ion Antonesçu**. He joined his nation to the Axis powers in World War II. Toward the end of the war, Romania became disgusted with the Nazis and made a separate peace with the Allies. Subsequently, Romania became an independent constitutional monarchy under **King Michael V**. The monarchy lasted from 1945 until 1948, when a Soviet-supported Romanian Communist Party took control of the government. The Communists ousted the king and established a harsh dictatorship under **Gheorghe Gheorghiu-Dej**.

The Dictatorship of Ceausesçu

After Gheorghiu-Dej's death in 1965, **Nicolae Ceausesçu** replaced him as leader of the Communist regime. While he appeared to be a reformer, Ceausesçu was in reality a brutal dictator. Although Romania seemed to enjoy a measure of independence from the Soviet Union, he secretly cleared all his actions with Moscow. Under his rule, Romania's economy and environment were seriously damaged through waste, incompetence, and corruption. His racist dreams of creating a dominant Romanian people inspired anticontraceptive and antiabortion policies. These resulted in a high infant mortality rate and cruel and unsanitary state orphanages that often sold children to foreigners. The extravagant and wasteful lifestyle of Ceausescu further antagonized the Romanian people. They were upset with the dictator's image abroad as a reformer and independent Communist leader. Pressure for reform finally exploded in December of 1989 when the Ceausescu regime was violently overthrown. Ceausescu and his wife were arrested, tried, and then executed on Romanian national television.

The National Salvation Front

The new government, called the National Salvation Front, was composed of ex-Communists. The new interim president, **Ion Iliescu**, was formerly a close associate of Ceausescu. The new government outlawed Communism, disbanded the Romanian secret police, and began the privatization of collective farms. In Romania's first free elections in May of 1990, Iliescu was reelected president by an overwhelming majority. During the campaign, however, antigovernment demonstrators were brutally suppressed, and opposition leaders were physically attacked. There was also a question of possible fraud in the election itself. By 1991, there was growing dissatisfaction with the government, which many saw as a thinly disguised continuation of the Ceausescu regime. Protests and demonstrations forced the National Salvation Front's vice president to resign, charging that the government was protecting former Communists because of the existence of information that could associate the leaders with Ceausescu.

> **Main Idea:**
> During the 1990s the Romanian government struggled to provide democratic and free-market reforms while making very slow progress.

Dissatisfaction with the Iliescu government continued into 1996 when a reformist coalition was elected. Disputes within the coalition, corruption within the democracy, and the prime minister's inability to provide strong leadership resulted in a sharp decline in the economy. The elections in 1998 resulted in a reformist coalition. Efforts to implement free-market reforms led to strikes by miners; other groups were also adversely affected. As crime and the economy worsened, a disillusioned population brought former leader Ion Iliescu and his right-wing party to power in 2000. While supporting Romania's integration with the Western European democracies and free-market reforms in general, he also pledged to end corruption in government and crime. President Iliescu and his prime minister **Adrian Nastase** soon encountered the same problems trying to balance the need for free-market reforms with the economic hardships. Since 2001, Romania has made slow progress achieving these goals and has applied for membership in the European Union.

Bulgaria

Bulgaria was created in 1878 as a result of the Russo-Turkish War. In both world wars, it sided with Germany in hopes of regaining control of territories lost during the Second Balkan War of 1913 (see Chapter 4, Section 2, in this volume). In 1944, Soviet troops entered the country and installed a Communist-dominated coalition. A brutal Communist regime under **Georgi Dmitrov** ruled Bulgaria until 1954.

The Zhivkov Regime

Dmitrov was replaced by **Todor Zhivkov**, who attempted to divert the growing discontent with the Communist system by emphasizing Bulgarian nationalism. During the 1980s, Zhivkov persecuted the Turkish minority in Bulgaria, forcing them to adopt Bulgarian names and culture or face deportation. Despite a massive campaign that appealed to Bulgarian history and culture, the Communist dictator did not succeed. The continuing decline of the economy combined with the persecution of minorities created unrest throughout the country. Anticipating an overthrow, Zhivkov abruptly resigned in November of 1989 as both head of state and Communist Party leader.

The Collapse of Communism in Bulgaria

In 1990, the Bulgarian parliament, the **National Assembly**, agreed to end the constitutionally granted dominance of the Communist Party of the Bulgarian government. The Communists also lost their control over the armed forces. A new premier appointed a cabinet and a new all-Communist government. The National Assembly passed laws permitting ethnic Turks to reassume their Islamic names and the practice of their faith. The Communist Party, renamed the Bulgarian Socialist Party, won control of the new parliament after elections were held. Despite their strong showing, the Socialists faced growing opposition. A new coalition government was formed by the Socialists and the **Union of Democratic Forces**, a group made up of nineteen political parties in favor of establishing a democratic government. The Union of Democratic Forces was divided into two internal groups, one promising slow gradual economic reform, while the other favored faster paced reforms. In the summer of 1991, a new constitution was created. Yet, the former Communists remained the dominant political force in the nation.

BULGARIA SINCE 1991

From 1991 to 1997, governments consisting of ex-Communists ruled Bulgaria. Public dissatisfaction with corruption in the bureaucracy and economic stagnation led to the election of the nation's first real reformers of 1997. A coalition government began a program of economic reforms to transform Bulgaria into a free-market economy. Crime was reduced, foreign investment began, privatization was implemented, economic productivity rose, and the private sector grew for the first time in the post-Communist era. Despite these gains, the standard of living for the average Bulgarian had stagnated. The transition to a free market had been particularly difficult for the urban populations, especially the elderly, who depended on pensions.

In 2001, the former Bulgarian King **Simeon II** of Saxe-Coburg-Gotha, and his Simeon National Movement Party seemed to offer a "third way" between the reforms and the Socialists who wanted to reverse the reforms. Winning a majority on the June elections, Simeon became prime minister, forming a government that included many returning Bulgarian émigrés who had been educated in the West. This led to a growth in foreign investment and efficiency in government due to experienced ministers trained outside Bulgaria. Bulgaria has made greater progress toward its transition to a free-market economy and officially applied for membership in the European Union.

Albania

Albania was ruled by the Ottoman Empire from the fifteenth century until 1912, when it was established as an independent nation after the First Balkan War (see Chapter 4, Section 2, in this volume). A nation with a Muslim majority, it was ruled by an Eastern Orthodox Christian monarch, **King Zog**, as a compromise with the other nations surrounding Albania. In 1939, fascist Italy invaded the country, ousting the king and establishing a military dictatorship. After World War II, Albania became a satellite of the Soviet Union under the independent and hard-line Communist dictator **Enver Hoxha** (1908–1985).

Albania Under Hoxha

Under Hoxha, Albania suffered under a brutal and destructive regime. Albanian Communist rule forced the tiny nation into political and economic exile from the rest of the world. All religion was savagely repressed, and the country had the worst living standards of all the Eastern European nations. A dedicated **Stalinist**, Hoxha thought the Soviet dictator's successors were far too liberal and mild. Disillusioned with the U.S.S.R., Albania broke its ties with the Soviet bloc and became allied with Communist China and its equally hard-line leader **Mao Zedong** in 1960.

The Collapse of Communism in Albania

Following Hoxha's death in 1985, the Communist domination of Albania slowly began to crumble. Hoxha's successor, **Ramiz Alia**, was forced to begin political and economic reforms in March of 1990, as he saw the rest of Eastern Europe abandoning the Communist system. Faced with internal unrest and economic collapse, Alia slowly began to decentralize the economic system. In March of 1991, Europe's poorest state finally ended its isolation by establishing diplomatic ties with the European Community, the United States, and the Soviet Union. The government also legalized labor strikes and ended the ban on religious practice. In addition, Albania held its first multiparty elections since the Communist takeover.

While the Communists won with a two-thirds majority in a questionably run election, the unpopular government was forced to step down. A multiparty coalition was formed to temporarily run the nation. In the spring of 1992, new elections were held in which the Communists were removed from power. The new government began to make economic and political reforms to transform Albania, one of the poorest nations in the world, to a functioning free-market economy and democracy. The popular government's involvement in a disastrous

> **Main Idea:**
> In the spring of 1992, new elections were held in which the Communists were removed from power.

investment scheme ("Pyramid Scandal") cost thousands of Albanians their life savings in 1996 and created a scandal that resulted in riots and rebellion. By 1997, a state of civil war existed between forces loyal to the government and those who opposed it. Forcing thousands of Albanians to flee, the fighting brought an international peacekeeping force to restore order. UN-monitored elections were held in April 1998, bringing to power a coalition of Socialist parties.

Main Idea:
The infusion of foreign money helped the nation deal with the cost of the refugees, stimulated economic productivity, and raised the standard of living, especially in cities.

National elections were held once again in the fall of 1998. The new Albanian government faced enormous domestic problems in trying to undo the damage of the previous governments. **Pandeli Majko** became Prime Minister. A member of the new post-Hoxha generation, he enjoyed great popularity, especially among younger people. He faced enormous opposition from a coalition of parties determined to prevent reform toward a free market. Committed to ending government corruption and ending crime, the Majko government found itself overwhelmed as thousands of refugees flooded Albania from Kosovo in the spring of 1991.

The Albanian majority in the Yugoslav Province of Kosovo had been at odds with the Serbian government since the breakup of Yugoslavia began. The crisis had an unexpected economic positive effect as the arrival of UN troops, foreigners, and Western aid created new employment in the construction and humanitarian service industries, especially in the Albanian capital city of Tirana. The infusion of foreign money helped the nation deal with the cost of the refugees, stimulated economic productivity, and raised the standard of living, especially in cities. This allowed the government to pursue privatization and reforms toward a free-market economy and to strengthen Albania's ties to Western Europe. In the elections of 2000, the Socialists won a majority in the Albanian Parliament, allowing the government to pursue its goal of reforming the economy, fighting organized crime, ending government corruption, and ending civil fighting within Albania. Succeeding annual elections have strengthened this mandate.

Yugoslavia

Unlike the other nations of its region, Yugoslavia was a mixture of nations and religions. It emerged as a nation after World War I, known as the *Kingdom of the Serbs, Croats, and Slovenes* (the three Slavic peoples it united). In 1929, it was renamed the *Kingdom of Yugoslavia* (Southern Slavs). It was ruled by the Serbian monarchy until World War II, when the Germans ousted the king and established a military dictatorship. A similar fascist regime was created by the Nazis in Croatia. After the war, the Soviet Union occupied the nation, where the Yugoslavian Communists, under **Josip Brodz,** known as Marshal **Tito** (r. 1945–1980), had already seized power.

Yugoslavia Under Tito

Tito divided Yugoslavia into the republics of **Serbia**, **Croatia**, **Slovenia**, **Montenegro**, **Macedonia**, and **Bosnia-Hercegovina**, with the two autonomous (self-governing) provinces of **Vojvodina** and **Kosovo**. In March of 1948, Tito, who did not owe his power to the Soviets as other Eastern European communist regimes did, left the Soviet Bloc. Under Tito, Yugoslavia became a Communist dictatorship that was free of Soviet control. Tito ruled Yugoslavia until 1980, using a combination of force, the development of a Yugoslavian nationalism, and limited capitalism. The nation's ability to remain independent of the Soviet Union was beneficial.

The Disintegration of Yugoslavia

After Tito's death, the forces of local nationalism began to resurface. The dictator's personal appeal and use of force had prevented the various nationalities that composed Yugoslavia from traditional territorial disputes. Many Serbians felt that the Croatian-born Tito had deliberately broken up the Serbian population, which was numerically larger, into many independent Yugoslav republics in order to weaken their political influence.

War in Slovenia and Croatia

By 1990, the nations of Croatia and Slovenia declared themselves independent. Trying to prevent the disintegration of the country, the Serbian-dominated Yugoslav government and military sent troops into Slovenia and Croatia. The well-organized Slovenian government was able to successfully repulse the government troops with its volunteer army. The Yugoslav government was forced to recognize Slovenia's independence. However, in Croatia, it was a different situation. Croatia's declaration of independence prompted a violent response from its sizable Serbian minority. The Serbians and Croatians became involved in local conflicts, which grew larger when the Yugoslavian Army interfered in support of the Serbian minority. While outwardly claiming that they were trying to prevent Croatia's break from the Yugoslav union, it soon became clear that the Serbian-dominated army had taken sides in what had become an ethnic war between Serbs and Croats. Acts of violence and brutality were committed on both sides, with the term **"ethnic cleansing"** (killing with the intention of wiping out a whole race of people) being used to describe the extent of the violence there.

Conflict in Bosnia-Herçegovina

As a truce was finally reached between Croatia and Serbia in 1991, conflict broke out between Serbians and Muslims of **Bosnia-Herçegovina**, a heavily Muslim republic with large Serbian and Croatian populations (Muslims are the largest group, but no group is over 50 percent). This was the result of the Bosnian government's declaration of its independence from Yugoslavia. The Serbs of Bosnia-Herçegovina feared the Muslim-dominated government and wanted union with the other Serbian areas of Yugoslavia. The Bosnian Serbs soon were supported by Yugoslav army units sent to stop the fighting and prevent Bosnia-Herçegovina from leaving Yugoslavia. As in Croatia, it soon became an ethnic war between the Serbs and Bosnian Muslims. The Croatians soon became involved with the Croatian army units that were invading parts of Bosnia-Herçegovina. By 1993, Serbia and Croatia controlled large parts of Bosnia-Herçegovina.

The conflict soon became a three-way ethnic war between Bosnia's Serbs, Croats, and Muslims, with the Yugoslav and Croatian governments arming their Bosnian kinsmen. The war was also encouraged by national politicians (Serbian President **Slobodan Milosevic**, Croatian President **Franjo Tudjman**, and Bosnian President **Alija Izetbegovic**). In late 1992, the former Yugoslav Republic of Macedonia declared independence, leaving only the Republics of Serbia and Montenegro. The killing in Bosnia continued despite the efforts of the United Nations and the European union to resolve the conflict.

In 1995, the **Dayton Peace Conference** divided Bosnia-Herçegovina into a Serb republic and a Croatian/Bosnian Muslim state. Even though the **Dayton Accord** reduced the conflict, it did not end it, and an international peacekeeping force remains in Bosnia-Herçegovina. In 1997, U.S. air strikes against military positions in violation of the cease-fire agreement further helped to keep the peace.

Conflict in Kosovo

In 1998, conflict erupted in the Yugoslav Province of Kosovo between the Yugoslav police and Albanian separatists demanding union with Albania (known as the **Kosovo Liberation Army** or **KLA**). In April 1999, NATO began a massive air campaign against Serbia. This led to a new wave of ethnic cleansing by Milosevic using the Yugoslav military to drive out the Albanian population from Kosovo. Although NATO claimed that the action was only to stop the ethnic cleansing in Kosovo, the bombing of civilians and foreign embassies in the Serbian capital city of **Belgrade**, as well as Albanian refugee convoys, raised questions about the role of NATO in this conflict. The Yugoslav government and some nations, especially Russia and China, viewed the military action against Serbia as a violation of national security. The countries of NATO and other nations saw the military interference as a stand against ethnic cleansing and the violation of human rights. The United Nations, while condemning Milosevic's actions, resented NATO's unilateral action as it undermined the UN's authority.

YUGOSLAVIA SINCE 1999

The aftermath of the NATO military intervention in 1999 in Kosovo severely weakened Milosevic politically. Economic decline in Serbia and growing political opposition led to his defeat in the elections of September 2000. Despite his efforts to contest the election results, public anger against him made it clear his thirteen-year rule was over.

Vojislav Kostunica became the new Serbian president. In an attempt to maintain good relations with the West, he sent Milosevic to The Hague for trial in the International Court for his role in the war crimes during the Yugoslav civil war. This turned out to be a decision that divided the Serbian population. Kostunica also worked to keep Kosovo as part of Serbia. Finally, he was determined to prevent Montenegro from leaving what was left of Yugoslavia.

Kostunica's preoccupation with keeping Serbia's borders and the division over Milosevic prevented him from dealing with the growing domestic problems. Economic assistance from the West in order to prevent further problems in Serbia helped the Kostunica government to spur economic growth.

In 2002, Serbia and Montenegro agreed to a partnership that would keep them allied, but allow each one domestic autonomy (self-rule). Serbia also came to an understanding with the other former Yugoslav states. Serbia and Montenegro continue to face challenges as they make the transition to free-market democracies.

CHAPTER SUMMARY

The violence and disorder in Eastern Europe following the collapse of the Soviet Union and its satellite regimes presents new challenges to the world community. The need for international attention to solve local as well as global problems demands a new attitude and outlook on the part of all nations. The countries of Eastern Europe may have to find their own solution in the creation of a union similar to that of the European community. Before that can occur, however, they must solve their historic internal and regional problems. The Communist regimes were only able to suppress these conflicts. Their failure to solve them has left Eastern Europe with an old legacy of resentment and hatred in addition to the economic and environmental destruction that the Communists created in the name of "progress." In their newly found freedom, these countries face enormous obstacles and problems that will require all their resources to solve.

LINK TO TODAY

On April 23, 2007, Boris Yeltsin, the first elected president of Russia, died of heart failure. As you read in this chapter, President Yeltsin served from 1991 until 1999. His death drew international attention. Former U.S. President George H. W. Bush and former U.S. President Bill Clinton both attended the funeral in Moscow along with dignitaries from many nations. It was the first Russian Orthodox Church-sanctioned (approved) funeral for a Russian head of state in more than a century. Thousands of Russians viewed Boris Yeltsin's coffin in the Cathedral of Christ the Savior in Moscow. What makes this church especially interesting is that this cathedral was destroyed by Josef Stalin during the Soviet antireligious era. While Yeltsin was president, the cathedral was rebuilt. Soviet leaders have traditionally been buried in Moscow's Red Square outside of the Kremlin wall, near Lenin's tomb. Yeltsin was buried in a Russian cemetery near the cathedral, which has been the burial place of some of Russia's literary giants and also some famous Russian musicians. Even in death, Boris Yeltsin was able to be part of change as Russia continues in its transition from communism to democracy.

KEY TERMS

Cult of Personality
Purge
Five Year Plans
concentration camps
Great Thaw
dissidents
arms race
Sputnik
Samizdat
Détente
Afghanistan War
Glasnost
Perestroika
Congress of People's Deputies
Gorbachev Doctrine
command economy

subsidies
Russian Orthodox Church
May Day
coup d'état
Russian Revolution of 1991
Union Treaty of Republics
Duma
oligarchs
Berlin Wall
Solidarity
Law and Justice
Brezhnev Doctrine
universal suffrage
Prague Spring

Charter 77
Helsinki Conference
Velvet Revolution
Bulgarian National Assembly
Union of Democratic Forces
Cold War
ethnic cleansing
Dayton Peace Conference
Dayton Accord
Kosovo Liberation Army (KLA)
Balkanization

PEOPLE

Joseph Stalin
Boris Yeltsin
Eduard Shevardnadze
Vladimir Zhrinovskiy
Galina Starovoitova
Vladimir Putin
Yevgeniy Primakov
Sergei Stepashin
Aslan Maskhadov
Eric Honecker
Simeon II
King Zog
Enver Hoxha
Mao Zedong
Ramiz Alia
Pandeli Majko
Joseph Pilsudski
General Wojciech Jaruzelski
Lech Walesa
Georgiy Malenkov
Nikita Khrushchev

Nikolai Bulganin
Lavrenty Beria
Boris Pasternak
Yury Gagarin
Aleksei Kosigin
Leonid Brezhnev
Alexsandr Solzhenitsyn
Andrei Sakharov
Yury Andropov
Konstantin Chernenko
Mikhail Gorbachev
Tadeusz Mazowiecki
Alexander Kwasniewski
Lech and Jaroslaw Kaczynski
Nicholas Horthy
Imre Nagy
Janos Kadar
Karol Grosz

Antonin Novotny
Alexander Dubcek
Gustav Husak
Milos Jukes
Vaclav Havel
Vladimir Meciar
Robert Fico
Ion Antonescu
Michael V
Gheorghe Gheorghiu-Dej
Nicolae Ceausescu
Ion Iliescu
Adrian Nastase
Georgi Dmitrov
Todor Zhivkov
Tito
Slobodan Milosevic
Franjo Tudjman
Alija Izetbegovic
Vojislav Kostunica

PLACES

Siberia	Chechnya	Bratislava
Chernobyl	Grozny	Czech Republic
Lithuania	Russia	Slovakia
Estonia	Baltic States	Vodina
Latvia	Poland	Kosovo
Russian Republic	Romania	Serbia
Commonwealth of	Bulgaria	Croatia
Independent States	Hungary	Slovenia
(CIS)	East Germany	Montenegro
Georgia	Czechoslovakia	Macedonia
Armenia	Yugoslavia	Bosnia-Herçegovina
Azerbaijan	Albania	Belgrade
Ukraine	The Balkan Peninsula	

CHAPTER 13

MULTIPLE-CHOICE QUESTIONS

Select the number of the correct answer.

1. The U.S.S.R. promoted a series of Five Year Plans with the intention of

   (1) developing new highways and train stations
   (2) producing cheaper consumer goods
   (3) encouraging industrial production for military expansion
   (4) strengthening educational systems for college preparation

2. When Nikita Khrushchev gained complete control of the Soviet government in the 1950s he surprised the country by

   (1) speaking out against many of the actions of Joseph Stalin
   (2) promoting the former head of the secret police to be his assistant
   (3) tightening government control on many political prisoners
   (4) allowing Boris Pasternak, the author of the novel *Doctor Zhivago*, to receive a Nobel Prize for literature

3. Aleksandr Solzhenitsyn was exiled from the Soviet Union because he

   (1) sold nuclear secrets to the West
   (2) wrote a book about life in the Siberian prison camps
   (3) tried to be appointed to a government position
   (4) participated in Russian space explorations

4. By the 1980s some Russians were becoming aware that their standard of living

   (1) far surpassed that of the West
   (2) was given more attention in their country than industrial growth
   (3) had shown tremendous growth during the Brezhnev years
   (4) lacked even some basic necessities that Western Europe took for granted

5. The Enterprise Law of 1987, the Law of Cooperatives of 1987, and the Agricultural Reform Law of 1988 were all examples of

(1) Yeltsin's theories of communist practices
(2) Gorbachev's policy of Perestroika
(3) Andropov's policy of nonalignment
(4) Sakharov's work after election to the Politburo

6. The year 1991 was a turning point for the Soviet Union because

(1) Gorbachev came into a leadership position
(2) U.S. President Reagan declared an end to the Cold War
(3) Russian Orthodox churches were permanently closed
(4) Yeltsin declared Russia an independent state

7. By the early 1990s, the former Communist Soviet Union had become

(1) the Commonwealth of Independent States
(2) the site of a major civil war between Russia and Ukraine
(3) one nation named Russia
(4) an economically strong democratic union of democratic states

8. Boris Yeltsin's term as president was characterized by

(1) a long period of solid economic growth
(2) a gradual return to Communist restrictions
(3) an effort to improve ties with the West
(4) a refusal to recognize the other newly independent members of the former U.S.S.R.

9. A method used by Russian President Vladimir Putin to strengthen his control was to

(1) remove power from local-level leadership
(2) encourage renewed membership in the Communist party
(3) practice total freedom of the press
(4) allow the increased development of private enterprise

10. Chechnya has been a continuing problem for Russia because it wants

(1) Russia to take over its economic development
(2) to become part of Ukraine
(3) to become a separate sovereign nation
(4) the United States to give it military support

11. The end of communism in the Soviet Union was a cause of

(1) increased problems in foreign relations with Western nations
(2) the decline of Communist governments in Eastern Europe
(3) a quickly improved economy for the CIS
(4) new interest in environmental issues

12. Lech Walesa led a reform movement known as Solidarity in

(1) East Germany
(2) Georgia
(3) Poland
(4) Hungary

13. Czechoslovakia split into two nations in 1993 primarily to allow

(1) the Czech Republic to remain communist and Slovakia to become a democratic republic
(2) each country greater freedom of choice within their own governments
(3) both countries to strengthen their ties to the Warsaw Pact nations
(4) each country to return to individual command economies

14. In the 1980s and 1990s, Romania's efforts at becoming a democracy were hindered by

    (1) a series of leaders who appeared to be reformers but really were more interested in personal gain
    (2) political demonstrators who made the government unstable
    (3) the unwillingness of the Romanians to support reforms
    (4) interference from foreign governments, especially the United States

15. As a Communist dictator, Marshal Tito had a different situation than other Eastern European nations in that he

    (1) had only one ethnic group to govern
    (2) allowed citizens more personal freedoms
    (3) encouraged the broad development of Western-style capitalism
    (4) did not owe his power and position to the Soviets

16. The Dayton Peace Conference attempted to solve difficulties in Bosnia-Herçegovina by

    (1) strengthening the power of the Serbian leader Milosevic
    (2) dividing the area into two separate countries
    (3) totally ending the practice of ethnic cleansing
    (4) enforcing the rule of the Muslim dominated government

17. The incident at Chernobyl was of worldwide concern because it

    (1) demonstrated the widespread effects of a nuclear accident
    (2) resulted in an expansion of communism in Eastern Europe
    (3) allowed the Warsaw Pact nations greater voice in economic decision making
    (4) confirmed the Soviets as capable of making nuclear bombs

18. The headline below could have correctly appeared in what country in the spring of 1968: "Alexander Dubcek Puts a Human Face on Socialism"

    (1) Yugoslavia
    (2) Romania
    (3) Bulgaria
    (4) Czechoslovakia

19. Which of the following is a result of the other three?

    (1) Communist policies were enforced in most of Eastern Europe for more than thirty years following World War II.
    (2) Corrupt dictators controlled many of the nations of Eastern Europe for many years after World War II.
    (3) Eastern Europe in the twenty-first century continues to lag behind Western Europe in economic development.
    (4) Military goals were more important in post-World War II Eastern Europe than the production of consumer goods.

20. What would be a valid conclusion about post-World War II Eastern European nations?

    (1) The former Soviet Union has continued to be a strong governmental influence on these nations.
    (2) Military governments in most countries have managed to establish stable command economies.
    (3) These nations have been satisfied to remain separate from the industrialization of Western Europe.
    (4) Most Eastern European nations have struggled to become democracies and desire to achieve a higher standard of living for their citizens.

Directions: Write a well-organized essay that includes an introduction, several paragraphs addressing the task below, and a conclusion.

Theme: Change Within Nation-States

The nations of Eastern Europe and the Soviet Union have witnessed major economic and political changes since the end of World War II and into the twenty-first century.

Task

Use the Soviet Union and one other country to complete the following:

- describe the political and economic situation of each country at the end of World War II and at the end of the twentieth century
- discuss two changes that have occurred in each country and explain the reasons for each change

You may use the Soviet Union and any other Eastern European nation. Some suggestions you might wish to consider include East Germany, Poland, Czechoslovakia, Hungary, or Yugoslavia.

You are *not* limited to these suggestions.

Guidelines

In your essay, be sure to

- develop all aspects of the *Task*
- support the theme with relevant facts, examples, and details
- use a logical and clear plan of organization, including an introduction and a conclusion that are beyond a restatement of the theme
- introduce the theme by establishing a framework that is beyond a simple restatement of the *Task* and conclude with a summation of the theme

DOCUMENT-BASED ESSAY QUESTION

This question is based on the accompanying documents (1–6). The question is designed to test your ability to work with historical documents. Some of the documents have been edited for the purposes of this question. As you analyze the documents, take into account the source of each document and any point of view that may be presented in the document.

Historical Context

A challenge for nation-states is to establish a form of political system that can meet both the needs and wants of its people. This has been especially true in Eastern Europe and the Soviet Union since World War II.

Task

Using information from the documents and your knowledge of global history, answer the questions that follow each document in Part A. Your answers to the questions will help you write the Part B essay in which you will be asked to

- discuss one way in which a political system's decisions about economic needs and wants may be impacted by geography.
- describe how a specific country in Eastern or Central Europe has dealt with economic decision making in recent years.
- identify a political leader in Eastern or Central Europe or Russia and describe his impact on the government and/or economy of his nation in recent years.

Part A: Short Answer Questions

Directions: Analyze the documents and answer the short answer questions that follow each document.

Document 1

Questions

1. a. Identify any three landlocked countries on this map.
   b. Identify a country on the Baltic Sea.
   c. Identify a country on the Black Sea.

Document 2

"I believed it would succeed. It was Polish Solidarity and its victory that put an end to the old era when what mattered were borders and rival blocs."

"I made the right decisions. I set everything on the right course, the reforms are going in the right direction."

Quotations from Lech Walesa, Polish trade union activist 1990s

Question	2. What is Walesa referring to in the terms "old era" and "rival blocs"?

Document 3

"Not least the very significant strides Romania and Bulgaria have made to strengthening democracy and human rights in their countries. Just as every Romanian and every Bulgarian citizen traveling to, or working, or studying in another EU country can enjoy fundamental rights and freedoms, so every British citizen and all EU citizens know that those same rights will be respected and democratic values shared in Romania and Bulgaria.

But today I want to concentrate on the strong economic reasons for the UK's unwavering support for Enlargement. There are three important groups who will benefit by the events of 1 January 2007:

• Firstly, Romania and Bulgaria.
• Secondly, British businesses who will have new trading partners.
• And thirdly, by its enlargement, the EU can respond better to the challenges of globalization.

"My colleagues from Romania and Bulgaria have my warmest congratulations. They also have my sincere admiration. It is no easy task to meet the standards for EU membership. And it is easy to forget how very far Romania and Bulgaria have come in a short period of time.

We can all remember the dying days of Communism. Romania under Ceaucescu probably suffered more than any other Eastern European country. We can remember the revelations of the greed of the Ceaucescu elite. And the social cost of that greed. The children abandoned to orphanages because their parents could not afford them. The food queues and lack of basic commodities like soap and washing powder.

In the 1930s Romania was known as the Paris of the East. Yet this proud European country was practically brought to its knees by Communist economic planning.

Romania is firmly back on its feet. I salute Minister Vladescu. Because dealing with the enormous challenge of establishing a functioning market economy is not easy. Up until 2000, Romania was seen as one of the worst performing economies in Eastern Europe. About 36% of the population was poor, inflation was running at 54% per year, and the budget deficit was virtually out of control…"

Excerpt from a speech by Lord Triesman in London marking the acceptance of Bulgaria and Romania into the European Union, 2007

Questions

3. a. Who are two groups that Lord Triesman says will benefit from the admission of Romania and Bulgaria into the EU?

b. What are two problems Lord Triesman notes that Romania has suffered in the recent past?

Document 4

"My sacred duty is to bring together the Russian people, unite the people around clear tasks. We have one Fatherland, one people, and a common future."

—Vladimir Putin

"Nobody and nothing will stop Russia on the road to strengthening democracy and ensuring human rights and freedoms."

—Vladimir Putin

Question

4. What seem to be two major goals for Putin?

Document 5

"Let's not talk about Communism. Communism was just an idea, just pie in the sky."

"It is especially important to encourage unorthodox thinking when the situation is critical: At such moments every new word and fresh thought is more precious than gold. Indeed, people must not be deprived of the right to think their own thoughts."

Quotations from Boris Yeltsin, Russian Leader 1990s

Question

5. How do the quotations from Boris Yelstin show that the leader of a former Communist nation was accepting change in his nation?

Document 6

a.
POLAND
Economy Overview:

Poland has steadfastly pursued a policy of economic liberalization since 1900 and today stands out as a success story among transition economies. Even so, much remains to be done, especially in bringing down the unemployment rate —still the highest in the EU despite recent improvement. The privatization of small- and medium-sized state-owned companies and a liberal law on establishing new firms has encouraged the development of the private business sector, but legal and bureaucratic obstacles alongside persistent corruption are hampering its further development. Poland's agricultural sector remains handicapped by surplus labor, inefficient small farms, and lack of investment. Restructuring and privatization of "sensitive sectors" (e.g., coal, steel, railroads, and energy), while recently initiated, have stalled. Reforms in health care, education, the pension system, and state administration have resulted in larger-than-expected fiscal pressures. Further progress in public finance depends mainly on reducing losses in Polish state enterprises, restraining entitlements, and overhauling the tax code to incorporate the growing gray economy and farmers, most of whom pay no tax.

Excerpt from the World Fact Book

b.
CZECH REPUBLIC
Economy Overview:

The Czech Republic is one of the most stable and prosperous of the post-Communist states of Central and Eastern Europe. Growth in 2000-05 was supported by exports to the EU, primarily to Germany, and a strong recovery of foreign and domestic investment. Domestic demand is playing an ever more important role in underpinning growth as interest rates drop and the availability of credit cards and mortgages increases. The current account deficit has declined to around 3% of GDP as demand for Czech products in the European Union has increased. Inflation is under control. Recent accession to the EU gives further impetus and direction to structural reform. In early 2004 the government passed increases in the Value Added Tax (VAT) and tightened eligibility for social benefits with the intention to bring the public finance gap down to 4% of GDP by 2006, but more difficult pension and healthcare reforms will have to wait until after the next elections. Privatization of the state-owned telecommunications firm Cesky Telecom took place in 2005. intensified restructuring among large enterprises, improvements in the financial sector, and effective use of available EU funds should strengthen output growth.

Excerpt from the World Fact Book

| Questions | 6. a. According to the World Fact Book what is a current problem for the Polish economy and what is an example of success for the Polish economy? |
| | b. What are two examples of positive economic change that have occurred in the Czech Republic? |

Part B: Essay

Directions: Write a well-organized essay that includes an introduction, several paragraphs, and a conclusion. Use evidence from *at least four* documents in the body of the essay. Support your response with relevant facts, examples, and details. Include additional outside information.

Historical Context

A challenge for nation-states is to establish a form of political system that can meet both the needs and wants of its people. This has been especially true in Eastern Europe and the Soviet Union since World War II.

Task

Using information from the documents and your knowledge of global history, answer the questions that follow each document in Part A. Your answers to the questions will help you write the Part B essay in which you will be asked to

- discuss one way in which a political system's decisions about economic needs and wants may be impacted by geography
- describe how a specific country in Eastern or Central Europe has dealt with economic decision-making in recent years
- identify a political leader in Eastern or Central Europe or Russia and describe his impact on the government and/or economy of his nation in recent years

Guidelines

In your essay, be sure to

- address all aspects of the *Task* by accurately analyzing and interpreting *at least four* documents
- incorporate information from the documents in the body of the essay
- incorporate relevant outside information
- support the theme with relevant facts, examples, and details
- use a logical and clear plan of organization
- introduce the theme by establishing a framework that is beyond a simple restatement of the *Task* or *Historical Context* and conclude with a summation of the theme

CHAPTER 14
Modern Western Europe

TIMELINE OF EVENTS

Margaret Thatcher
first female
Prime Minister of UK

1979

Angela Merkel first female
Chancellor of Germany

Switzerland
joins the UN

2002

1980   1985   1990   1995   2000   2005

1992

European Union is established
by signing of the Maastricht Treaty

2004

Socialist government
by the signing of the
Maastricht Treaty
comes to power in Spain

Terrorists kill 100's in
Madrid train bombing

In the early years of the twenty-first century, **Western Europe** has been strongly influenced by important economic and political developments that have radically changed the course of world and European history. The end of communism in the former Soviet Union and Eastern Europe in 1989 and the on-going creation and development of the **European Union** (EU) beginning in 1992 have led to greater political and economic integration. Today there is no longer an emphasis on military issues and plans designed to meet the challenges posed by the Soviet Union and Communist nations of **Eastern Europe**. There is more of an emphasis on furthering the political and economic unification of European nations.

THE END OF THE COLD WAR

The military focus of Western European nations changed dramatically after the fall of the Iron Curtain in 1989. The end of the Communist governments in the Soviet Union and Eastern Europe allowed the countries of Western Europe to concentrate on other issues that have led to greater overall European economic and political unity. Today the differences and separation of European nations into two rival blocs—the western democratic and eastern Communist nations that existed in Europe during the Cold War—are no longer relevant. The peaceful reunification of the Federal Republic of Germany and the Democratic Republic of Germany symbolizes the new Europe of the twenty-first century. The military alliances, NATO, and the Warsaw Pact, which were formed to prepare the competing blocs for a possible inter-European nation have changed focus or ended. NATO still exists, but its purpose has shifted to that of an alliance to protect European security concerns. The Warsaw Pact no longer exists.

Today the goals of European countries are political integration and economic unity. The "Old Europe" has ceased to exist, and a "New Europe" has become increasingly real. In geographic terms, there are European nations still classified as being in Western Europe. However, the New Europe puts into question whether Western Europe will continue to exist as a separate political or economic entity as the twenty-first century progresses.

THE EUROPEAN UNION

The European Union (EU) was formally established in 1992 after the approval of the **Maastricht Treaty**. However, dating back to 1951, many of the economic aspects of the EU were created in a series of common market agreements. Today the European Union has become an intergovernmental and super-national union of twenty-seven democratic countries or member states. Other European nations are candidates for membership. In the coming years, nations such as Croatia and Serbia will be admitted to the growing EU. As of 2008, Turkey is also seeking EU membership although its geographic location, mostly outside of Europe, and large Islamic population may lead to the rejection of its candidacy.

The EU has given Western European nations and, now, a growing number of Eastern European countries a common single economic market. In the EU,

Main Idea:
Today the European Union has become an intergovernmental and supernational union of twenty-seven democratic countries or member states.

there is a customs union and a unified trade policy regulating increasingly freer trade among member countries. The EU nations share responsibilities for maintaining a single currency, the euro, which is managed by the European Central Bank. There is a European Court of Justice, European Parliament, and even a common EU passport. All these developments have furthered the idea of European citizenship and political integration.

An apparatus and structure for a unified central government is developing in the EU designated capitol, **Brussels, Belgium**. Several elected and rotating presidencies have been created: the European Council, the European Commission, and the Council of the EU. These organizations are intended to give the member nations a united position on important issues and resolve disputes. The countries of the European Union have transferred to the Brussels-based central government considerable sovereignty, that is powers that each

European Union

individual country exercised. In certain ways, the EU has taken on the character of a federation or confederation. Nevertheless, the individual nations and peoples of the EU still retain the rights and privileges of nationhood and citizenship of their countries. In addition, cultural differences such as language still exist. There is no plan to develop a common European culture or language.

In the following sections of this chapter you will read about the recent histories of several Western European nations and about their changing political, economic, and social conditions in the twenty-first century.

France

France was a founding member of the European Union. It has been in the forefront of the nations seeking to exploit the momentum of economic and political union. France has sought to provide the EU with leadership and direction. French governments, both Socialist and Center-Right, have supported the goal of a capable European Union based on the mutual economic, political, social, and security needs of the member nations. President **Jacques Chirac** was a strong proponent of further EU political integration. However, the French electorate voted against the ratification of the European Constitutional Treaty in May 2005.

> **Main Idea:**
> The popular vote in France against further efforts to create a stronger central European government is a reflection of the growing concerns that French people have about certain political, economic, and social issues and problems.

The popular vote in France against further efforts to create a stronger central European government is a reflection of the growing concerns that French people have about certain political, economic, and social issues and problems. The French people are reluctant to grant a central government outside of their nation control of the political developments within their country. There are also concerns and fears about the consequences relating to increased economic and political unification and globalization. Many French people believe this will lead to even more unemployment and an erosion of the social security benefits and net that protects French workers and people in general. French people are also increasingly worried about the growing social problems that relate to the large number of immigrants, particularly those who come from Islamic nations, residing in and claiming benefits and seeking jobs in their nation.

What is happening in France is in many ways a mirror of the issues and problems that affect the people in other nations of Western Europe. In the presidential election of 2007, the majority of the French voted for **Nicholas Sarkozy**, who promised change and to assemble a diverse cabinet. It then must decide about whether to lead the country on a path of even greater European unity and integration or to pull France back and to stress its own individual sense of nationalism regarding political, economic, and social issues.

Jacques Chirac (1932 –)

Spain

Jose Luis Rodriguez
Zapatero.

Since the end of the Franco dictatorship in 1975, **Spain** has become a more politically democratic and economically developed nation. From 1978 to the present, Spain has undergone significant political change and experienced rapid economic development and growth, which has made it one of the leading nations of the European Union.

The "Partido Popular" governed the nation from 1996 to 2004 under the leadership of **Jose Maria Anzar**. In 2004, a socialist government once again came to power under the leadership of **Jose Luis Zapatero**. The socialist victory came after the Anzar government falsely accused the Basque separatist movement of responsibility for a terrorist attack on commuter trains in **Madrid,** which caused hundreds of deaths and injuries. The terrorist attack was later linked to an Islamic group, which had ties to Al-Qaida.

In the early years of the twenty-first century, Spain needs to find solutions to pressing problems. There are growing calls for greater autonomy and even separation and independence from the Basque and Catalonian regions. There is the possibility that as Europe pursues greater political and economic integration, the wealthiest Spanish regions may become completely autonomous or even independent. Spain also has an immigration problem similar to that of France. In Spain, radical fundamentalists are calling for the establishment of a new Islamic nation in the southern area of the nation, which up to 1492 was called Granada.

Germany

> **Main Idea:**
> Despite the economic and social costs, Germany remained the world's third leading economy into the twenty-first century.

During the 1990s, the Christian Democratic Union (CDU) led by **Helmut Kohl** governed the united German federal republic. Chancellor Kohl and the **CDU/CSU** (Christian Social Union) political coalition worked to further the development of the European Union. In addition, Germany, Europe's wealthiest and largest economy, had to shoulder the financial costs of integrating the people of the German Democratic Republic into the nation's capitalist economic system. There were enormous problems in integrating a previously Communist nation with a Socialist economic system into one that thrived on entrepreneurial industrial production, exports, and free enterprise ideas. The East German people had grown up within a Socialist system and a cushion of state-supported benefits. Despite the economic and social costs, Germany remained the world's third leading economy into the twenty-first century. During this time period, Germany continued to be a strong supporter of promoting further European integration, including the establishment of a monetary union and the creation of the Euro currency.

In 1998, **Gerhard Schroeder** and the Social Democratic Party (SDP) won the national elections. Chancellor Schroeder continued the growth of industrial production and increased globalization of trade. He also strengthened the social benefits and protections given to the German workers. In his foreign policy, Schroeder supported ideas for a strong and expanded European Union. Schroeder came into conflict with the United States because of this refusal to support the Iraq War, which began in 2003. Chancellor Schroeder and the SDP remained in power until 2005.

Angela Merkel and Jacques Chirac.

Starting in 2003, the conservatives began to make gains in state elections. In 2005, under the leadership of **Angela Merkel,** a coalition of conservative parties (the CDU/CSU) narrowly won the federal elections held in September 2005. However, the conservative coalition did not have a clear majority. After negotiations between the conservative CDU/CSU and the Socialist SDP, a grand coalition was announced. Angela Merkel was sworn in as the first woman and the first East German to become a chancellor of Germany. Merkel faces a number of difficult issues to resolve. They include a high rate of unemployment, resentment over the number of Islamic immigrants, and an economy that provides workers with social benefits, which decrease the nation's ability to compete in a world where economic globalization is increasing.

Italy

Since the end of World War II, **Italy** has changed from an agricultural economy to one based on industrialization. It was a founding member of the European Union and is ranked as the world's fifth largest industrial economy. Currently Italy, like other members of the EU, is recovering from an economic downturn that occurred after the September 11, 2001 attacks on the United States. Labor Union membership impacts about 40 percent of Italian workers, and the unions have played an important role in national social and economic issues.

Italy is an active participant in United Nations peacekeeping efforts. It sent troops to Afghanistan in support of the U.S. mission called Operation Enduring Freedom in 2003. Italy works closely with the EU and NATO on common defense and security issues in light of growing world terrorism. Italy and the United States have also worked closely on the Middle East peace process, the worldwide illegal drug trade, and assistance to Russia and the new independent states of the former Soviet Union.

United Kingdom

Margaret Thatcher, English Prime Minister from 1979–1990.

The **United Kingdom** (U.K.) is composed of England, Wales, Scotland, and Northern Ireland. It is an island nation that historically has been one of the most powerful countries in Europe, and through much of the twentieth century, in the world. Its island location encouraged the area to develop what was to become the world's largest and most powerful navy.

Queen Elizabeth II is the chief of state in a constitutional monarchy. She has reigned since 1952. After a period of time in the 1990s when the British public questioned the role of the monarchy, the Queen again continues to enjoy great popularity. In 1979, the United Kingdom made political history as **Margaret Thatcher** became the first female prime minister as head of the Conservative Party. Thatcher was a strong leader who developed very close ties to a fellow Conservative, the American President Ronald Reagan. As the British economy declined at the end of the 1980s, Thatcher too lost power and left office. In 1997, the Labour Party led by **Tony Blair** took control of the government, and Blair became prime minister. Blair has been a strong ally of the United States and especially of President George W. Bush in his war on terror and military presence in Iraq.

The United Kingdom is a member of the EU but has not adopted the common currency. Recent polls show that public support for the euro currency is lacking. The U.K. is one of five permanent members of the UN Security Council and was a founding member of NATO. Its major political issue currently is that of its relationship with the **Republic of Ireland** and Northern Ireland. See Chapter 15 in this volume for a detailed explanation of this situation. London's subway system was bombed in 2005 by Islamic terrorists. In 2006, the actions of extremists within the United Kingdom caused their arrest for a plot to destroy multiple aircraft as they were in the air between the United Kingdom and the United States. It is likely that the threat and the reality of terrorism will continue for the British for some time to come.

Republic of Ireland

As already noted, Ireland's current political situation is described elsewhere, but it is important to note that the country has experienced unprecedented economic growth especially in the last two decades. What was once a primarily rural and agriculturally based economy now has a large manufacturing sector. It is home to many international companies, partly due to its geographic location on the edge of the Atlantic Ocean.

Ireland has recorded a 6% rate of growth in the last ten years alone and its average per capita (per person) growth rate for GDP (Gross Domestic Product) is 40% higher than the usually highest nations in Europe in economic production (Great Britain, Germany, France, and Italy). It is generally considered the fastest growing economy in Europe today.

Switzerland

In 2002, **Switzerland,** a nation famous for its historic policy of neutrality, became a member of the United Nations for the first time. Its conservative government though has remained strongly opposed to Switzerland becoming a member of the European Union. The Swiss constitution supports the role of private enterprise and local government. Since Switzerland is a very modernized and Westernized nation, it is interesting to note that women did not get the right to vote until 1971. It did not take women too long to catch up within the government though, as in 1999 Switzerland elected its first woman president who also happened to be its first Jewish president.

The Netherlands

Among European nations, the **Netherlands** has very liberal social policies. Prostitution is legal, and in 2000 the Netherlands became the first nation in the world to legalize same-sex marriage.

The Netherlands has also been a member of the EU since the 1950s, and in general the country enjoys a typical Western European high standard of living. It does have the distinction of being one of the world's leading donors of foreign aid. This foreign aid is given through the United Nations as well as EU programs and private aid organizations. The country was particularly generous in the aid it gave in the 2004 tsunami relief efforts. The country is also a major contributor to international programs against narcotic drugs. In addition, the Dutch are concerned about a small but growing number of Islamic jihadists, one of whom murdered Theo Van Gogh, a well-known film producer and descendant of the famous painter, in 2004.

The Scandinavian Nations

Norway

In 1994, **Norway** voted against joining the EU, but it does enjoy free trade with EU nations in industrial sectors of the economy. In the 1970s, Norway emerged as a major producer of oil and gas. Their trade in these commodities since that time has helped the Norwegian economy enormously. Today it is one of the richest countries in the world based on per capita distribution. Unemployment is very low, and growth possibilities continue to be encouraging.

In the area of foreign relations, Norway supports international cooperation and the peaceful settlement of disputes as an active member of NATO. The nation is active in encouraging democracy throughout the developing world and also in protecting human rights.

Sweden

Sweden is a highly industrial country that did not become a member of the EU until 1995. It had cooperated in economic efforts with the EU since the 1970s but had always resisted joining for fear of endangering its status as a neutral nation. In 2002, Sweden decided to take a more active stand against threats to peace and security but continued to maintain a policy of nonparticipation in military alliances. The end of the Cold War plus the September 11, 2001 attacks are at least somewhat responsible for the change in policy. Sweden is an active member of the U.N. specialized agencies and also participates actively in NATO as well as international peacekeeping operations. Sweden joined the EU with a provision to allow it not to participate in any future EU defense alliance. When the vote was taken on whether to join the EU, over 83 percent of the population voted, and over 52 percent voted for union.

Denmark

Denmark occupies a strategic location at the entrance to the Baltic Sea, which has made it a center for American and other groups having interests in the Baltic area. Denmark is a member of both the EU and NATO and a strong supporter of world peacekeeping efforts. It has also participated in UN and U.S. efforts in Iraq and in Afghanistan since 2003. Early in 2006, a Danish publication printed political cartoons depicting the prophet Mohammed. Violent protests, riots, and demonstrations over the cartoons occurred in several Muslim countries because some Muslims believed that the cartoons portrayed Muslims as supporting terrorism. Any illustration of Mohammed is forbidden by Islamic practice, as such illustrations are considered to be a form of idol worship.

CHAPTER SUMMARY

The nations of Western Europe recovered from the devastating effects of World War II. Most are highly industrialized and enjoy very high standards of living. Their governments are a variety of types of democracies, but some still retain constitutional or limited monarchies. For their common benefit, the majority of the area has formed mutual defense pacts like NATO and unions to improve trade and economic growth like the European Union.

These nations are determined to prevent further world wars and participate in the United Nations peacekeeping efforts. Some have supported the U.S. invasion of Iraq and Afghanistan and others have not, but all maintain some level of positive relationship with the United States. The end of the Cold War has brought most of these countries closer to the nations of Eastern Europe and Russia for their combined benefit. The threat of global terrorism such as the attacks the United Kingdom and Spain experienced in the first years of the twenty-first century is an ongoing concern. Other concerns for most of these countries have to do with environmental issues, the threat of nuclear power in less stable areas of the world, and the growing minority or immigrant issue within Western Europe.

LINK TO TODAY

Early in 2008, it is interesting to note that, for the first time in the history of the United States, there is a serious and viable female candidate for president from a major party. Western Europe has experienced a range of attitudes toward women and the political world in the last few decades. Remember it was only in the 1970s that women received the right to vote in Switzerland, and they have already had a female president. Margaret Thatcher rose to political power in the 1970s, and when she attended meetings of the economic Group of 7 (now 8) she was pictured with a group of all male leaders from the other member nations. In the summer of 2006, the world watched while Angela Merkel represented Germany at meetings of that same group in St. Petersburg. As the twenty-first century progresses, it will be interesting to observe the continuing and changing role of women in world politics.

IMPORTANT PEOPLE, PLACES, AND TERMS

KEY TERMS

bloc	euro	NATO
Maastricht Treaty	Customs Union	terrorism
sovereignty		

PEOPLE

Jacques Chirac	Helmut Kohl	Queen Elizabeth II
Jose Maria Anzar	Gerhard Schroeder	Margaret Thatcher
Jose Luis Zapatero	Angela Merkel	Tony Blair

PLACES

Western Europe	Madrid	Denmark
European Union	Germany	Switzerland
Eastern Europe	Italy	The Netherlands
Brussels, Belgium	Great Britain	Norway
France	Republic of Ireland	
Spain	Sweden	

CHAPTER 14

MULTIPLE-CHOICE QUESTIONS

Select the number of the correct answer.

1. From the middle of the twentieth century to the end of the twentieth century, which pair of terms best describes the general shift in European thinking?

   (1) From colonialism to imperialism
   (2) From militarism to conquest
   (3) From confrontation to cooperation
   (4) From nationalism to totalitarianism

2. The major physical symbol of the Iron Curtain or the Cold War in Europe was

   (1) the English Channel
   (2) the Swiss Alps
   (3) Red Square in Moscow, Russia
   (4) The Berlin Wall, Germany

3. Which European organization no longer exists?

   (1) NATO
   (2) Warsaw Pact
   (3) European Union
   (4) European Central Bank

4. The letters NATO stand for

   (1) North Atlantic Treaty Organization
   (2) New Association Treaty Office
   (3) North American Treaty Organization
   (4) National Advancement of Tourist Offices

5. When a nation or group decides on a type of currency, it is deciding on its

   (1) money   (3) passport
   (2) flag   (4) language

6. In which nation would the following headline most likely appear? "Basque Separatists Agree to a Cease-Fire"

   (1) United Kingdom
   (2) Italy
   (3) Sweden
   (4) Spain

7. Several European nations in the twentieth century are concerned about the growing strength of

   (1) existing monarchies and royal families
   (2) the Islamic European population
   (3) American tourists
   (4) Communism in the former Eastern bloc countries

8. German Chancellor Gerhard Schroeder came into conflict with the United States because of his refusal to

   (1) continue free-trade alliances
   (2) attend meetings of the Group of 8 summit
   (3) support the Iraq War
   (4) allow women to hold public office

9. Since German unification in 1989, Angela Merkel was the first person from East Germany to

   (1) cross the fallen Berlin Wall
   (2) become chancellor of a united Germany
   (3) criticize the high rate of unemployment
   (4) be elected to the government from the liberal party

10. Italy's actions of sending troops to Afghanistan, helping to found the European Union, and giving assistance to the new nations of the former Soviet Union are all examples of

    (1) fascism
    (2) totalitarianism
    (3) international cooperation
    (4) isolationism

11. Although Queen Elizabeth is the reigning monarch of the United Kingdom, her powers are limited by

    (1) the prime minister
    (2) tradition
    (3) the Royal family
    (4) the British constitution

12. In 2002, Switzerland departed from its long-held policy of neutrality in order to

    (1) elect its first woman president
    (2) join the European Union
    (3) send troops to the Iraq War
    (4) become a member of the United Nations

13. Norway has not joined the European Union, but it is permitted

    (1) free trade with member nations
    (2) to request foreign aid
    (3) the use of the euro
    (4) to apply for help in its unemployment crisis

14. Which nation took the strongest stand against military participation when it joined the European Union?

    (1) Spain   (3) Italy
    (2) The Netherlands   (4) Sweden

15. Global terrorism is an increasing threat in the twenty-first century to Western Europe because

    (1) all of the Western European nations supported the Coalition Forces and the United States in the War in Iraq
    (2) terrorists from many different causes recognize that terrorist acts attract significant attention to their cause
    (3) the United States has decided to stop its own war against terrorism
    (4) Western European countries do not have a sufficient military or police force to investigate all of the terrorist organizations

16. Identify the leader that is correctly matched with his or her nation.

    (1) Nicholas Sarkozy . . . France
    (2) Gerhard Schroeder . . . Norway
    (3) Angela Merkel . . . Switzerland
    (4) Jose Luis Zapatero . . . Italy

17. Brussels, Belgium, has the distinction of being the

    (1) largest city in Europe
    (2) capital of the European Union
    (3) first city to allow legal same-sex marriages
    (4) the center of the Basque movement

18. Former British Prime Minister Tony Blair exhibited very close ties to U.S. President George Bush during what world crisis?

    (1) The formation of the European Union
    (2) The expansion of terrorists in France
    (3) The deployment of troops in the Iraq War
    (4) The success of the conservative party in the United Kingdom

19. Some European nations have been slow to join the European Union as a result of a fear of

  (1) loss of national identity
  (2) the return of communism
  (3) absolute leaders that remain in some European countries
  (4) an economic slowdown based on trade shortages

20. Which change have the many European countries experienced since the end of World War II?

  (1) Population growth has been very rapid.
  (2) Democracies are now totalitarian states.
  (3) Agrarian economies became industry-based economies.
  (4) Neutral nations are increasingly isolationist.

THEMATIC ESSAY

Directions: Write a well-organized essay that includes an introduction, several paragraphs addressing the task below, and a conclusion.

Theme: Places and Regions

Geography places a major role in any nation's foreign relations and economic decision making. The nations of Western Europe are in the same geographic place in the world and form an important political and economic region.

Task

Select any three nations in Western Europe and, for each,

- describe a current economic or political issue
- briefly discuss how the country has dealt or is dealing with the issue
- describe the relationship of the nation to any one other European nation or world organization

Note: Do not repeat information used for one country in your answer for another country.

You may use any countries in Western Europe. Some suggestions you might wish to consider include Spain, France, Germany, Sweden, and Switzerland.

You are *not* limited to these suggestions.

Guidelines

In your essay, be sure to

- address all aspects of the *Task*
- support the theme with relevant facts, examples, and details
- use a logical and clear plan of organization, including an introduction and a conclusion that are beyond a restatement of the theme
- introduce the theme by establishing a framework that is beyond a simple restatement of the *Task* and conclude with a summation of the theme

This question is based on the accompanying documents (1–8). The question is designed to test your ability to work with historical documents. Some of the documents have been edited for the purposes of this question. As you analyze the documents, take into account the source of each document and any point of view that may be presented in the document.

Historical Context

The desire of cultures to retain their own identities while dealing with diversity is as old as global history itself and as current as twenty-first century Western Europe. Currently the area is struggling with issues of identity and diversity.

Task

Using information from the documents and your knowledge of global history, answer the questions that follow each document in Part A. Your answers to the questions will help you write the Part B essay in which you will be asked to:

Select two aspects of life in twenty-first century Western Europe that are experiencing change with regard to identity and diversity. For each area or topic

- explain the specific issue of identity or diversity
- discuss how some part or all of Western Europe is dealing with the issue
- describe the current status of the situation

Part A: Short-Answer Questions

Directions: Analyze the documents and answer the questions that follow each document.

Document 1

"We may have lost the fear of the bomb in this post cold-war era, but many have not lost the fear of what the future will hold. As someone said to me recently, 'The fuure isn't what it used to be.'"

—Eva Burrows

Question	1. According the statement, what do you think the speaker means by the "fear of what the future will hold"?

Document 2

Question

2. According to the map identify the two Mediterranean nations that are current members of the European Union?

Document 3

Question

3. What does this photograph show about human reaction to the fall of the Berlin Wall?

Document 4

AFTER 40 YEARS, SEPARATISTS IN SPAIN DECLARE CEASE-FIRE
By Renwick McLean

SEVILLE, March 22—The militant Basque separatist group ETA, which has killed more than 800 people and terrorized Spain for nearly 40 years, announced a permanent cease-fire today, saying that it would turn its attention to achieving independence for the Basque region through politics.

A permanent cease-fire, which the group said would take effect on March 24, has been the paramount objective of successive Spanish government since the establishment of democracy here in 1977.

Politicians and victims groups said it was important to treat the announcement with caution, saying that ETA had a history of deceit and unfulfilled promises.

But the overriding tone of most comments suggested that much of the country was allowing itself to contemplate a future that was finally free of the threat of ETA violence.

ETA, which was founded in the 1950s during the dictatorship of General Francisco Franco, first announced the cease-fire this morning in a statement to Radio Euskadi, a Basque radio station. Three of its members, whose faces were hidden by white veils, later read the statement during an appearance on a television station operated by the Basque regional government.

"The objective of our decision is to advance the democratic process," the statement said, "in order to construct a new framework that will recognize the rights that we as a people deserve."

"At the end of the process, the Basque citizens should have the final word and decision about their future."

ETA has killed more than 800 people, about half of them civilians, during its effort to create an independent Basque state encompassing sections of northern Spain and southern France.

It has not killed anyone since May of 2003, and speculation has been growing for months that the group was contemplating a permanent cease-fire.

Ever since the March 11, 2004, train bombings in Madrid, an attack thought to be carried out by Islamic radicals in which 191 people were killed, investigators and politicians have speculated that the group was reassessing whether it should continue with terrorist attacks.

The group, already widely despised in Spain, even inside the Basque region, would have triggered an unprecedented level of outrage from the public if it continued with terrorist attacks after the March 11 bombings, these officials say.

Source: Excerpt from "After 40 Years, Separatists in Spain Declare Cease-Fire." The New York Times. *Article dated March 22, 2006.*

Questions

4. a. According to the article what was the purpose of the announcement by the Basque separatist group?
   b. How did some politicians and victim's groups feel about the news?

Document 5

The flag is that of the European Union (EU). There are twelve stars because the number twelve is traditionally the symbol of perfection, completeness, and unity. The flag therefore remains unchanged regardless of EU growth.

Questions

5. a. According to the caption with the flag why are there twelve stars?
   b. What will happen to the style of the flag if more members join the EU?

Document 6

—*Euro coins*

The Eurosystem, which consists of the European Central Bank (ECB) and the national central banks of the 13 countries belonging to the euro area, has the exclusive right to issue euro banknotes. All decisions on the designs, the denominations, etc., of the euro banknotes are taken by the ECB.

Question

6. According to the caption, who has the exclusive right to issue euro banknotes?

Document 7

A Guide to the European Union
Frequently Asked Questions
VISA/PASSPORT REQUIREMENTS

Common information for Schengen Visa Applicants

If you intend to transit through or visit several Schengen states (Germany, Austria, Belgium, France, Greece, Italy, Luxembourg, Netherlands, Portugal, Sweden, Spain, Denmark, Finland, Iceland, and Norway) for up to 90 days for tourist or business purposes you have to obtain your Schengen visa from the Consulate of the country of your main destination.

Schengen lane (= the Schengen area, the Schengen countries):

In 1985, five EU countries (France, Germany, Belgium, Luxembourg and the Netherlands) agreed to abolish all checks on people travelling between them. This created a territory without internal borders which became known as the

Shengen area. (Schengen is the town in Luxembourg where the agreement was signed.)

The Schengen countries introduced a common visa policy for the whole area and agreed to establish effective controls at its external borders. Checks at the internal borders may be carried out for a limited period if public order or national security make this necessary.

Little by little, the Schengen area has been extended to include every EU country plus Iceland and Norway, and the agreement has become an integral part of the EU treaties. However, Ireland and the United Kingdom do not take part in the arrangements relating to border controls and visas.

You do not need a visa for travelling within the Schengen area if you are a citizen of one of the Schengen countries. If you have a visa for entering any Schengen country it automatically allows you to travel freely throughout the Schengen area, except Ireland and the United Kingdom.

Source: http://www.delaus.ec.europa.edu/eu_guide/faqschengenvisas.htm

Questions 7. a. According to this information guide what are "Schengen countries"?
b. How did this area get its name?

Document 8

IMMIGRATION EUROPE: CRISIS OR DENIAL?

Until the mid to late 20th century, Switzerland was neatly divided into four groups that, despite cultural variations, all shared very "Swiss characteristics" and lived in relative harmony in the same small country. In their characteristics, the Swiss German, Swiss French, Swiss Italians and Swiss Latin-Romans were united: They were neutral and peaceful, reserved, polite, very precise, hard working, clean, and criminal activity was virtually unheard of among them. The same is true today and the Swiss have been stereotyped as "too perfect," and even "boring" because of it. The Swiss, though, naturally think this is the only way to be, and generally expect all others to be this way. In this regard they can be a bit naïve. And this explains why the cultural diversity and unfortunate increase in crime that have accelerated with immigration, have sent shock waves through this most unprepared-for-immigrants of all European countries.

Switzerland is now one of the most favored of all European destinations for immigrants, who make up a steadily increasing 20% of this alpine country's population, and this alarms the Swiss. The populous recently voted to cut the ratio of foreigners back to 18%, which means the expulsion of thousands of legal residents is imminent. Like the rest of Europe, and in particular those countries in the European Union (which Switzerland is not), Switzerland is scrambling to cut back on immigration, both legal and illegal. But is it the right thing to do?

"Last year," Romesh Ratnesar of *Time* reports, "the 16 million legal immigrants in Western Europe earned more than $460 billion." In the European Union, the number of self-employed foreigners has risen by some 20% in less than a decade. In some countries, immigrants make up a substantial portion of the labor force, or even have higher average household incomes. All of that equates quite simply to spending power. But the notion that a certain amount of immigration is a good thing, has yet to catch on in Europe. Entry is being blocked more and more, leading to a lucrative underground world of illegal smuggling. The Dover incident prompted E.U. officials to review and possibly ease immigration and asylum policies for those with legitimate refugee claims.

Although it has signed various agreements for work exchange with the E.U., Switzerland insulates itself from the larger picture, to some extent, by remaining independent. At the moment, Italian, French and German borders of Switzerland are not substantially secure, and as the rest of Europe relaxes borders, those in Switzerland may be reformed in the opposite direction.

This despite a U.N. report released this year which stated that an aging population and downward spiraling birthrates will result in a labor deficit that will call for an influx of 35 million adult immigrants by the year 2025 to stabilize labor and economic conditions.

Right now, today, most of Western Europe is suffering from a lack of labor for low-paying jobs, as well as a gap in the technology pool. Foreigners can help fill these slots. Unless Europeans start having a lot more babies, right now, experts find it difficult to imagine how the need for immigration might diminish.

Although some strides have been made, proposals such as the one in Ireland, to bring in some 200,000 skilled laborers over the next seven years, are just too modest to make any tangible difference. Other programs like those in Germany, designed to approve residency permits to 20,000 techies over the next 3 years, are meeting with tremendous resistance.

Source: Article from http://immigration.about.com/library/weekly/aa071700a.htm

Questions

8. a. According to the excerpt from the article "Immigration Europe: Crisis or Denial," why might it be helpful for Europeans to welcome immigrants?
   b. Which European country according to the article is working to cut back on the number of its immigrants?

Part B: Essay

Directions: Write a well-organized essay that includes an introduction, several paragraphs, and a conclusion. Use evidence from *at least five* documents in the body of the essay. Support your response with relevant facts, examples, and details. Include additional outside information.

Historical Context

The desire of cultures to retain their own identities while dealing with diversity is as old as global history itself and as current as twenty-first century Western Europe. Currently the area is struggling with issues of identity and diversity.

Task

Using information from the documents and your knowledge of global history, answer the questions that follow each document in Part A. Your answers to the questions will help you write the Part B essay in which you will be asked to

- select two aspects of life in twenty-first century Western Europe that are experiencing change with regard to identity and diversity
- explain the specific issue of identity or diversity
- discuss how some part or all of Western Europe is dealing with the issue
- describe the current status of the situation

Guidelines

In your essay, be sure to

- address all aspects of the *Task* by accurately analyzing and interpreting *at least five* documents
- incorporate information from the documents in the body of the essay
- incorporate relevant outside information
- support the theme with relevant facts, examples, and details
- use a logical and clear plan of organization
- introduce the theme by establishing a framework that is beyond a simple restatement of the *Task* or *Historical Context* and conclude with a summation of the theme

CHAPTER 15

The End of European Imperialism: Independence and Decolonization

Jomo Kenyatta, the first leader of independent Kenya.

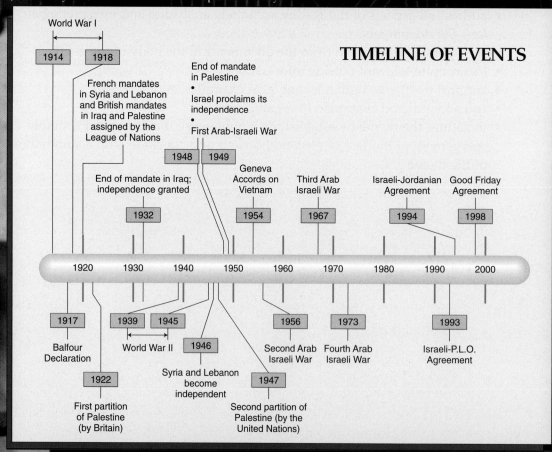

TIMELINE OF EVENTS

World War I

1914 — 1918

French mandates in Syria and Lebanon and British mandates in Iraq and Palestine assigned by the League of Nations

End of mandate in Palestine

Israel proclaims its independence

First Arab-Israeli War

1948   1949

End of mandate in Iraq; independence granted

1932

Geneva Accords on Vietnam

1954

Third Arab Israeli War

1967

Israeli-Jordanian Agreement

1994

Good Friday Agreement

1998

1920   1930   1940   1950   1960   1970   1980   1990   2000

1917

Balfour Declaration

1939   1945

World War II

1946

1956

Second Arab Israeli War

1973

Fourth Arab Israeli War

1993

Israeli-P.L.O. Agreement

1922

First partition of Palestine (by Britain)

Syria and Lebanon become independent

1947

Second partition of Palestine (by the United Nations)

hat's in a name? There's plenty—especially if you trace the end of European **imperialism** in this century in both Africa and Asia. Consider the following. If you compared two maps of Africa in the twentieth century, one drawn between 1900 and 1945, and one drawn at the end of the century, you would see several contrasts. The first map would show the colonies of the Gold Coast, Rhodesia, and the Belgian Congo, as well as the cities of Leopoldville and Salisbury. On the more recent map, you would not find these names. Instead, you would find the nations of Ghana, Zimbabwe, and Zaire, and the cities of Kinshasa and Harare. On contrasting maps of Asia, you would find that the cities of Batavia and Saigon have been replaced by Djakarta and Ho Chi Minh City.

These changes can be explained as decisions made by people who became free from colonial domination. A free people may wish to change names that were given to them and their land without their consent. Such changes can be interpreted as a rejection of an imperialistic era in their history. On the other hand, a free people may wish to retain certain features of their colonized past. The nation of Singapore retained its colonial name, and Malaysia has a name similar to its colonial name of Malaya. Pakistanis adapted so well to the British sport of cricket, introduced during the British colonial era, that they are said to have a better team today than Britain itself has!

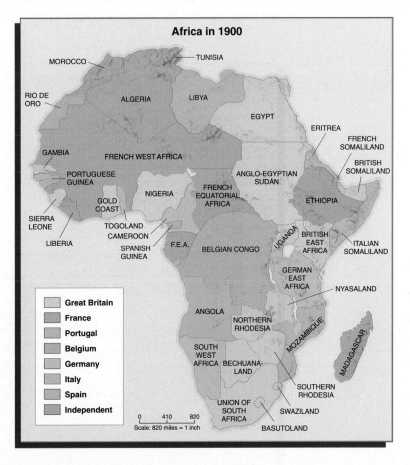

To see a map of Africa today, turn to page 478.

World War II lasted from 1939 to 1945. The period after the war was a time when many African and Asian nations emerged from their colonial status to become free peoples. Therefore, the post-World War II period can be called a time of **decolonization**. In this chapter, we will learn why decolonization occurred in Africa and Asia. In addition, we will evaluate the positive and negative aspects of imperialism.

GENERAL REASONS FOR DECOLONIZATION AND THE GROWTH OF INDEPENDENCE

In the years after World War II, over fifty nations in Africa and Asia became independent. For some of them, the transition from a colony to a free, sovereign nation was peaceful. For others, the transition was marked by violence and bloodshed. There were many general reasons for the end of imperialism since 1945.

1. Nationalist movements in the colonies had become very powerful. Some of these movements had even started before World War II. They gained support from native people as well as from some people in the mother country (the imperial nation itself). Ironically, the native leaders of several independence movements were educated in European countries and the United States. Some of them would become the heads of the newly formed nations.

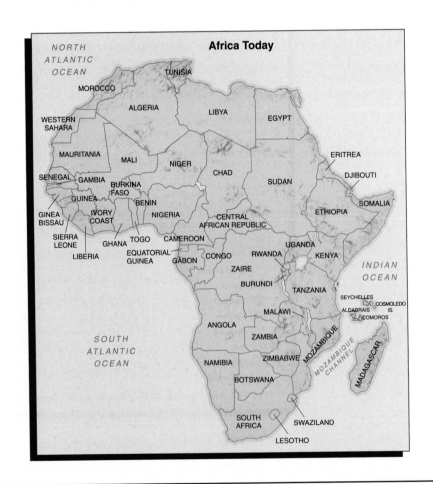

2. The Western European nations were weary after fighting World War II. The tremendous loss of life and property among both winners and losers in this war contributed to a weakening of the desire to maintain colonial empires. Some of the victorious nations that had colonies questioned whether they could afford the money and military power needed to keep their possessions.

3. The Western concepts associated with democracy were powerful arguments for promoting independence. The ideals of freedom and self-determination, prized by Western democracies in their wartime struggle against Nazi Germany, fascist Italy, and imperial Japan, became goals aspired to by people in the African and Asian colonies. Indeed, if such ideals were features of "superior" societies, then, argued nationalist leaders, why shouldn't they all be applied to colonized people. These leaders also pointed to the countless soldiers from several colonies that fought in the armies of the mother countries during the war. Not only did soldiers from, for example, Algeria and India shed blood for France and Britain, but they were also told that they were fighting for noble democratic values. For them to claim these values for their own societies after the war seemed only natural.

4. The United Nations came into being. A fourth reason to explain the post-World War II surge in independence was related to the values and ideals mentioned earlier. To advance and foster them, as part of an effort to achieve world peace, the United Nations was created in 1945. The existence of the UN furnished colonized peoples with yet another source of hope for seeking a change in their political status.

As we now move to examine these changes in different geographic locales, we should be aware that some changes occurred faster than others. It was not until 1975, thirty years after the war ended and the UN was formed, that the vast majority of colonies had attained freedom. A primary reason for this long and uneven transition to independence rests with the different policies of the colonial powers (see Chapter 6 in this volume for full explanations of these policies).

DECOLONIZATION IN AFRICA

In 1945, there were only four independent nations in **Africa—Egypt**, **Ethiopia**, **Liberia**, and **South Africa**. The rest of the continent was part of the colonial empires of European nations. Those with the largest possessions were **Britain**, **France**, **Portugal**, and **Belgium**.

Great Britain

Britain's policy of indirect rule permitted rulers to retain some power. In addition, it enabled selected Africans to receive a British-style education in Britain. One of these was **Kwame Nkrumah**, who became the first head of **Ghana** in 1957. In many cases, a native elite or special few people were ready to take over control as the British departed. Thus, Britain had made modest preparations for self-government in its colonies. Throughout the 1950s and 1960s, as the British flag was lowered over its African colonies, the transfer of power was accomplished peacefully in almost all instances.

Jomo Kenyatta (c. 1894–1978), President of Kenya. Photographed in 1971 in Nairobi, Kenya.

Photo credit: Erik Falkensteen/The Granger Collection, NYC.

Ruins of Great Zimbabwe, 1200–1400. No mortar was used.

Main Idea:
The only exceptions to a peaceful transfer to power were in British East Africa (now **Kenya**) and **Rhodesia** (now Zimbabwe).

The only exceptions to a peaceful transfer to power were in British East Africa (now **Kenya**) and **Rhodesia** (now Zimbabwe). In the former, many British settlers owned large amounts of land and came to Kenya to live out their lives and have their children inherit the land. This "**settler mentality**" was at odds with the desire of Kenyans to own land and to become independent. Violence over these issues began in the 1950s, caused by a Kenyan group known as the **Mau Mau**. Although the British were able to put down the Mau Mau Rebellion, it was only after thousands of lives, mainly African, had been lost. The Mau Mau leader, **Jomo Kenyatta**, who had been imprisoned by the British, became the first leader of independent Kenya. Independence came in 1963.

Violence also took place in Rhodesia. It came about because of the action taken by the white minority headed by **Ian Smith**, who ran the colonial government. In 1965, the white government, fearing eventual black rule that had been promised by the British, declared its independence from Britain. Britain was upset with this decision, as were the black Rhodesians. A civil war broke out, with the black Rhodesians, headed by **Robert Mugabe** and **Joshua Nkomo**, fighting Ian Smith's government. Eventually, a cease-fire was reached. Free elections, held under British supervision in 1979, resulted in Robert Mugabe becoming prime minister. In 1980, the name of the nation was officially changed to **Zimbabwe**. This was the name of the site of a former African kingdom in the region, prior to the arrival of **Cecil Rhodes** and the area becoming a British colony.

The British Commonwealth of Nations

As we have seen, decolonization was achieved in both violent and nonviolent ways. Several former colonies retain ties today to their former foreign rulers. Many of Britain's colonies, after achieving independence, voluntarily chose membership in the **British Commonwealth of Nations**.

This is an organization with forty-nine members. It includes Great Britain and most of its former colonies in Africa, Asia, North America, Central and South America, the West Indies in the Caribbean region, Australia, New

Main Idea:
Many of Britain's colonies, after achieving independence, voluntarily chose membership in the **British Commonwealth of Nations**.

Zealand, and scattered islands in the Mediterranean Sea, Indian Ocean, and Western Pacific Ocean. The Commonwealth was created with passage of an act by the British Parliament, called the **Statute of Westminster**, in 1931. It provided that Britain and those former colonies that were independent as of that year—Australia, Canada, South Africa, and New Zealand—were equal partners in the organization. Membership would be voluntary, without any interference by Britain in the affairs of the other members. Each member would, however, declare loyalty to the British Crown and recognize its cultural links to Britain. Membership increased in the post-World War II era, as new nations chose to become part of the Commonwealth.

Into the 1990s, Commonwealth members would usually meet once a year to discuss matters of mutual interest. The organization also provides some economic privileges for its members. There are scientific and educational exchanges of information as well as sporting and cultural events. Critics of the Commonwealth claim that it has little purpose, saying the membership is too large and represents too many diverse geographical areas and conflicting political and economic interests. Canada, Australia, and New Zealand—original Commonwealth members—are still active. Two former British possessions, **South Africa** and **Ireland**, however, chose not to remain as members.

Canada

Although once held by France, **Canada** came under British rule in 1763 after the French and Indian War. A revolt against the British was put down in 1837. As more and more English people migrated to Canada, and as a wave of democratic reforms were taking place in the mother country itself during the first half of the nineteenth century, Canada was to experience important political changes. The **Durham Report** of 1839, written by Lord Durham of Britain, recommended self-government for the Canadians. The recommendation was adopted in 1867, with passage of the **British North America Act**. Canada became a dominion. This meant that it enjoyed self-government but remained part of the British Empire. A governor-general from Britain represented the monarch and, in theory, had a veto power. This was hardly used, however. Canadians consider 1867 as their year of independence.

Australia and New Zealand

A continent in itself, **Australia** became a British possession in 1770 with the arrival of Captain **James Cook**. Up until 1840, it was used by Britain as a place to send debtors and criminals. The discovery of gold in 1851 spurred immigration there. It received dominion status, as in the case above of Canada, in 1901. **New Zealand**, to the southeast of Australia, was also explored and settled by Captain Cook. It became a dominion in 1907.

James Cook (1728–1779). Oil on canvas (detail), 1776, by John Webber.

South Africa

Nelson Mandela (1918 –). South African president, 1994–1999, and Black political leader. Photographed in 1999.

This southernmost region of Africa had become a dominion in 1910. It joined the Commonwealth in 1931. Although greatly outnumbered by blacks, the white population owned vast amounts of land, controlled the nation, and discriminated against blacks. The policy of **apartheid**, keeping the races apart, was an example of this discrimination. Within the white population were both English-speaking people and **Afrikaans**-speaking people. They were descendants of Europeans who had begun arriving there in the seventeenth century. The **Afrikaners**, mainly of Dutch extraction, won control of the government in 1948. In 1961, subjected to harsh attacks on its apartheid policies from other Commonwealth members, South Africa withdrew from the Commonwealth. It declared itself to be a republic. Into the 1980s, the government continued its discriminatory practices against blacks. However, in the early 1990s, as a result of worldwide condemnation of these practices such as boycotts, and of protests by black South Africans, the government began to make some changes. Apartheid laws were relaxed, interracial marriages were allowed, the ban on the black-controlled **African National Congress** political party was removed, and greater political participation for nonwhites was granted. In 1992 and 1993, President **Frederik W. de Klerk** and black African leader **Nelson Mandela** met frequently to consider a further easing of tensions and more political involvement of blacks in the nation's government.

These efforts resulted in a historic agreement, reached without violence, announced in November 1993. Signed by the major political groups in the nation, this agreement spelled out a death warrant for apartheid. Its major features were as follows:

1. A new constitution, guaranteeing equal rights for all citizens, became the supreme law of the land until such time as an elected legislature writes a permanent version. Discrimination by race was forbidden.
2. Free elections for a legislature, to be called the parliament, were scheduled for April 1994. The parliament would consist of an assembly and a senate.
3. The office of a president, who is to be chosen by the assembly, was designated.

Although the agreement was not signed by extreme white separatist groups, most South Africans appeared ready to support it. As expected, historic parliamentary elections were held in 1994 in a peaceful atmosphere. Mandela was chosen the nation's president.

Southwest Africa

The early 1990s witnessed another political change in southern African affairs. This involved the nearby territory once known as **Southwest Africa**. Southwest Africa had been a German colony from the late nineteenth century until the end of World War I in 1918. After the war, the League of Nations made it a mandate under South Africa. South Africa exploited the region and imposed its apartheid laws there. Facing criticism from the United Nations and frequent raids from a resistance movement, the South-West Africa People's Organization, South

Africa finally agreed to grant independence to the region in March 1990. The new nation changed its name to **Namibia**, with **Sam Nujoma**, a former head of the resistance movement, as its president.

France

Leopold Sedar Senghor (1906–2001). Senegalese statesman and writer.

France's policies of direct rule and assimilation established close links with its African colonies. These policies were to provide some basis in preparing for self-government. The colonies sent many soldiers to fight under French General **Charles de Gaulle** in World War II. They were also allowed, unlike the British colonies, to elect representatives to the French legislature in Paris. However, independence movements arose. Often, they were led by Africans who were educated in France and who eventually would become leaders of new nations. These included **Felix Houphouet-Boigny (Ivory Coast)** and **Leopold Senghor (Senegal).** In the 1950s, the North African colonies of **Tunisia**, **Morocco**, and **Libya** achieved independence peacefully. In 1960, twelve new independent nations were peacefully formed from French territories in West Africa and Equatorial Africa.

The only nonpeaceful transition to independence occurred in **Algeria**. Many French people had settled there and developed the kind of settler mentality we have previously described. They viewed Algeria as if it were part of France. So did the French government. Unwilling to give up Algeria, the French

> **Main Idea:**
> Unwilling to give up Algeria, the French were faced with a bloody rebellion led by **Ahmed Ben Bella.**

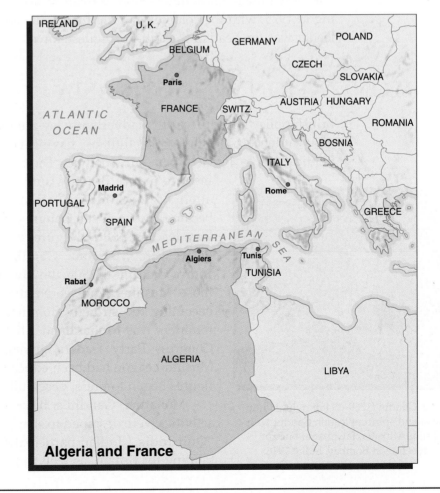

Algeria and France

were faced with a bloody rebellion led by **Ahmed Ben Bella**. From 1954 to 1962, a colonial war enveloped France and Algeria. Peace and independence finally came in 1962, with Ben Bella as the new nation's leader.

The French Community

France wished to create a relationship with its former colonies, similar to the British Commonwealth of Nations. Accordingly, in 1958, the French Community was established. Several new African nations joined, under provisions that treated them as equals with France, and aimed at consultations on various economic and defense policies. However, as many members began to withdraw, the organization ceased to function. Nevertheless, France still gives economic aid and provides military support upon request when it feels it is necessary. For example, French troops were sent to the African nations of Chad and Gabon in the late twentieth century and Cote d'Ivoire in this century. These actions were done to suppress armed opposition to the governments there.

Portugal

Portugal's policy of paternalism viewed colonies as though they were children. Portugal did very little to prepare them for independence. As was true of France in regard to Algeria, Portugal looked upon its African possessions in **Angola**, **Mozambique**, and **Guinea** as if they were parts of Portugal. Consequently, it was unwilling to grant independence freely. Colonial wars thus broke out, ending in 1975, with the colonies gaining their independence. Mozambique's first leader was the head of the anti-Portuguese forces, **Samora Machel**.

DECOLONIZATION IN SOUTH ASIA

British policy in India was to inadvertently lay the seeds for growth of a strong independence movement. The Indians, having been taught to value British political values, learned them only too well. The first organized political movement to reduce Britain's authority began in 1885 with creation of the **Indian National Congress**. It eventually became known as the **Congress Party**. In the twentieth century, leading political figures associated with the Congress Party were **Mahatma Gandhi**, **Jawaharlal Nehru**, and **Indira Gandhi**. In 1906, the **Muslim League** was created by those Muslims who feared that the Congress Party was becoming too strongly dominated by Hindus. One of its founders was **Mohammed Ali Jinnah**. As was true of the Congress Party leaders, Jinnah and the leaders of the Muslim League had been educated in England. All of these figures began to press, peacefully, for independence.

Mahatma Gandhi's boycotts and other nonviolent activities were designed to shame the British and have them **"Quit India."** Indian participation in World Wars I and II, fighting for Britain, as well as Parliament's passing legisla-

Mohandas Gandhi (1869–1948), right, Hindu nationalist and spiritual leader. Gandhi with Indian Prime Minister, Jawaharlal Nehru, during a meeting in Bombay, India, 1946.

Indira Nehru Gandhi (1917–1984). Indian political leader.

tion to increase local self-rule, raised hopes for independence. With the end of World War II, Britain moved more quickly to make these hopes a reality. However, even though the British had aimed to leave behind them a single united country, there was much tension between Hindus and Muslims. The Congress Party and the Muslim League were unable to solve all their political differences over the future of India. Britain had hoped that the huge colony of India would be transformed into the nation of India. Many Muslims, fearing that such a nation would have a Hindu majority and might act against their interests, talked of having a nation of their own.

The differences between the two groups led to much bloodshed and numerous migrations of people throughout the subcontinent. Each group sought to be where its members were in a majority. Civil war loomed as a distinct possibility if there was no agreement on a partition or division of the colony. Finally on August 15, 1947, independence came with the creation of two nations, India and Pakistan, formed by a partition of what had been the British crown colony of India. Pakistan would be divided into a West Pakistan and an East Pakistan, separated by India. Consequently, one of the greatest and bloodiest migrations in history now gained increased intensity. Many more Hindus now traveled to live in India, while many Muslims now traveled to live in Pakistan. Horrific bloodshed often occurred between the groups. This interreligious antagonism is known as communalism. India with a majority of Hindus, chose Nehru as its first president. Pakistan became a Muslim-dominated nation with Jinnah as its first head. A further partition in the subcontinent took place in 1971, when **East Pakistan** separated from **West Pakistan** due to political and economic disputes. East Pakistan mounted a successful rebellion, helped by India, and became a new nation known as **Bangladesh**.

Another area of tension was in **Kashmir**. The current Indian state of Kashmir is the larger part of a region that was taken over by India after the 1947 partition of the subcontinent. Although most Kashmiris are Muslim, the ruler at that time was a Hindu and wanted to link himself with India. India and Pakistan have fought over Kashmir. As the result of a UN cease-fire arrangement in 1949, a third of the entire region came under Pakistani control. The Pakistani part is known as **Azad Kashmir**. The

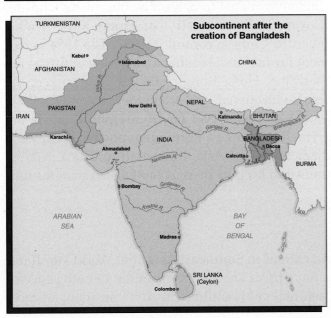

remaining two-thirds part is under Indian control and is known simply as Kashmir. Tension remained between both nations, however, and has continued up to the present (see Chapter 16 in this volume).

DECOLONIZATION IN EAST AND SOUTHEAST ASIA

World War II witnessed a temporary halt in European control in East and Southeast Asia. The halt was the result of conquests by Japan. Japanese imperialism replaced Western imperialism as Japan's forces defeated British, French, and American troops wherever the Westerners had possessions. These lands were eventually retaken, as Western forces and their Asian allies pushed Japan back to its homeland territory. The Japanese surrender in 1945 ended the war and left open the issue of whether or not Western colonial control would resume.

East Asia

China's struggle against Japanese occupation in World War II was helped by Britain and the United States. By war's end, **China** had become an ally of the Western nations and one of the prominent nations in the United Nations. It thus regained, with two small exceptions, all territories that had been taken as colonies or spheres of influence prior to the war. One of these exceptions was **Hong Kong**, where Britain retained its colonial control. This control had begun after the Opium War (see Chapter 6, "Imperialism"). China, under the nationalist rule of **Chiang Kai-shek** in the late 1940s, was not very concerned about the retention of Hong Kong as a colony. It was much more concerned with fighting off the Chinese Communists in a civil war.

Chiang Kai-shek (1887–1975), Chinese general and statesman, with his wife during the early part of World War II.

The Communists were victorious in 1949, led by **Mao Zedong**. The new leaders objected to continued British control over what they considered to be Chinese land. From 1982 to 1984, Britain and China negotiated to determine the colony's future. It was finally decided that Hong Kong would revert to Chinese control in 1997. The 1984 agreement further declared that for a period of fifty years thereafter, Hong Kong could continue to keep its legal, educational, and economic systems. The 1997 reversion led to great celebration in China. Not far from Hong Kong is the Portuguese colony of **Macao**. Having become a Portuguese possession in 1557, it is the oldest European settlement in East Asia. It reverted to China in 1999, under an agreement that permits it to keep its present capitalist system for fifty years.

Southeast Asia

The emergence of independent nations in **Southeast Asia** after World War II followed a pattern similar to that in Africa. There were examples of both peaceful and violent transitions from **colonial subjugation**. The first transition, a peaceful one, occurred with recognition of **Philippine** independence by the United States in 1946. The other Western nations that gradually loosened their imperial ties were the Netherlands, Britain, and France.

The Netherlands

With the Japanese surrender in 1945, the people of the Netherlands East Indies proclaimed their independence from Holland and declared their new government to be the **Republic of Indonesia**. The Dutch refused to accept this state of affairs and sent troops to regain control. From 1945 to 1949, bitter warfare took place. The Indonesians were led by **Achmed Sukarno**, a Dutch-educated engineer. With intervention by the United Nations, a cease-fire was put into effect. In December 1949, the Dutch formally recognized Indonesian independence. Sukarno became the new nation's first head of state.

Great Britain

The end of British rule in Southeast Asia was characterized by nonviolence. With its decision to withdraw from nearby India and without any wish to remain in Burma, Britain recognized **Burma** (now **Myanmar**) as a free nation in 1948. Britain retained its authority in Malaya after the war, and was able to defeat a Communist-led rebellion. The colony attained sovereignty peacefully in 1963, taking the name **Malaysia**. It was controlled by its major ethnic groups, Malays. Worried about such a situation, **Singapore**, inhabited mainly by people of Chinese extraction, broke away from Malaysia to become a separate nation in 1965. The final curtain call for British colonialism in Southeast Asia came with the granting of independence to the small oil-rich kingdom of **Brunei** in 1984.

France

The French exit from its colonies in Southeast Asia was made only after a bitter and long war (1946–1954). **French Indochina**, taken by Japan during the war, consisted of the present-day countries of **Laos**, **Vietnam**, and **Cambodia**. In Indochina, as in other regions ruled by Japan, native leaders formed a resistance group to fight for independence. **Ho Chi Minh** was the head of such a group, the **Viet Minh**. After the war, he declared Vietnam to be an independent country. France disregarded this, seeking to regain control and subjugation in Indochina. In 1946, the Viet Minh, an openly Communist organization, began fighting the French. This conflict was to become the bloodiest colonial war in Asia.

Leaders of the Viet Minh, including Ho Chi Minh (center, facing camera) and General Vo Nguyen Giap (right), receiving advice from communist China during the French-Indochina War (1949–1954). On the wall are portraits of Mao and Ho Chi Minh.

By 1954, with French public opinion torn over the struggle, and with major victories by the Viet Minh such as at **Dien Bien Phu**, France agreed to negotiations for peace. The Geneva Accords, ending the war, were signed in 1954. They resulted in independence for the countries of Laos and Cambodia. Vietnam was to be divided into two independent parts: a Communist-led North Vietnam and a South Vietnam under the anti-Communist leaders. A vote was scheduled to be held in 1956 to decide on a single government for the two Vietnams. This never took place.

By the early 1960s, widespread fighting had broken out in South Vietnam. This resulted from discontent of some of its citizens as well as attempts by the North Vietnamese to establish one unified nation. Fighting against the South Vietnamese government were the **Viet Cong** (South Vietnamese Communists) and ultimately the army of North Vietnam. The Viet Cong and the North Vietnamese received material assistance from China and the Soviet Union. The South Vietnamese received help from the United States in the form of equipment as well as over 500,000 combat troops. In 1973, President **Richard Nixon** withdrew American forces in the hope that North and South Vietnam could work out their differences peacefully. The South Vietnamese government, under President **Nguyen Van Thieu**, grew weak and very unpopular. Fighting resumed, resulting in a North Vietnamese takeover in 1975 and the proclamation in 1976 of a unified country. **Hanoi** became the country's capital, while Saigon, the former capital of South Vietnam, had its name changed to Ho Chi Minh City. In 1993, the first year of President **Bill Clinton's** administration, the United States and Vietnam began to consider the possibility of establishing diplomatic relations. In 1994, tourism and economic contacts were promoted. Vietnam also turned over much information on American servicemen killed or missing in the war. Full diplomatic relations between the United States and Vietnam came about in 1995.

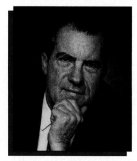

Richard M. Nixon (1913–1994). Detail, oil on canvas, 1968, by Norman Rockwell.

THE MIDDLE EAST

The **Middle East** is a geographic term that refers mostly to the areas of Southwest Asia and Northeast Africa. European contact with these areas has been ongoing for thousands of years, examples being the periods of the Punic Wars, Alexander the Great, the Roman Empire, the Byzantine Empire, the Crusades, and the Ottoman Turks. The major European imperialistic involvement in modern times was within the last 120 years. It is this time period that we will now study. Our study will only concern the Asian portion of the Middle East, as we have already "traveled" to the African portion (see Chapter 6 in this volume).

Among many factors that made the Middle East a target for European imperialism were two specific ones:

1. The Middle East was a strategic location as the crossroads of three continents—Europe, Africa, and Asia. With completion of the **Suez Canal** in 1869, the Middle East became a vital link in the water route between Europe and Asia.
2. The Middle East was also a source of oil. The world's greatest oil reserves are in the Persian Gulf area.

Over a period of time, these lands and other regions of the Middle East had become part of the **Ottoman Empire** (1453–1918). The empire gradually weakened during the 1800s, becoming known as the "sick man of Europe" (see Chapter 4, Section 2, in this volume). The ruling Ottoman Turks were corrupt, inefficient, and unresponsive to the needs of the many different peoples under their authority. The final blow to the empire came in 1918 with the end of World War I. The Turks had fought on the side of Germany and Austria-Hungary and lost the war. Consequently, the Middle Eastern lands that belonged to the empire and that were mainly inhabited by Arabs were taken away. They were placed under the control of the newly formed League of Nations. From 1920 onward, the League created mandates in **Palestine**, **Iraq**, and **Syria** among others. A mandate was permission given to a nation to rule over a region temporarily, until the region was considered ready for independence. Mandates in the Middle East were given to Britain and France.

Great Britain

Britain received mandates over Iraq and Palestine. Although the mandate in Iraq did not begin officially until 1922, Britain had already developed contact with this region. It had obtained concessions for oil in Iraq, as well as in present-day **Kuwait** and **Iran**. This arrangement permitted Britain to explore for and produce oil, while sharing the profits with the region's local rulers. At the time of such arrangements, prior to World War I, the British were well aware that the native Arabs did not like being under the authority of the Ottoman Turks. As a result, Britain befriended the Iraqis by supporting their anti-Turkish sentiments. As long as Britain was able to extract profits from oil, it made little attempt to impose its culture on the Arabs in Iraq. Indirect rule was the policy. The mandate ended in 1932, although British advisers continued to maintain a role in Iraqi political and economic affairs.

The Balfour Declaration and the British Mandate in Palestine

Main Idea:
The British mandate in Palestine proved to be very troublesome, presenting serious problems not found in the mandate in Iraq.

The word "Palestine" refers to a geographical area, not to a nation. There has never been a nation or state called Palestine. Therefore, a Palestinian is a resident in the area but not a citizen of any nation called Palestine. The British mandate in Palestine proved to be very troublesome, presenting serious problems not found in the mandate in Iraq. This was because both Jews and Arabs had wanted to create nation-states in the region. During World War I, British forces defeated the Turks and took over Palestine. Britain made territorial promises to both Jews and Arabs and issued an important document in 1917 called the **Balfour Declaration**. Named after Lord **Arthur Balfour**, the English statesman, the document proposed that Great Britain would view "with favor the establishment in Palestine of a national home for the Jewish people, . . . it being understood that nothing shall be done which may prejudice the civil and religious rights of . . . non-Jewish communities." **Zionists**, those Jews who pressed for some part of Palestine as a Jewish homeland, saw hope in the Balfour Declaration. Arab nationalists wanted the land for their own, and were against giving any part to Zionists. Fighting broke out between both groups, mostly on

Balfour Declaration, 1917. The letter written by British Foreign Secretary Arthur James Balfour to Lord Rothschild on November 2, 1917, setting forth British support for the establishment of a national home for the Jewish people in Palestine.

the part of Arabs attacking Jews, as well as between each group and the British. In 1922, Britain single-handedly partitioned Palestine, taking about 77 percent of it and establishing this as the Arab kingdom of Transjordan. To carve out such a large area for a new Arab nation was a surprising decision, especially as no Jewish homeland was established. Transjordan was given limited freedom and was promised eventual independence by the British. This promise was fulfilled in 1946, with the region to take the name of Jordan. The British stayed on good terms with the Jordanians, helping to train an armed force known as the Arab Legion.

The United Nations Partition Plan for Palestine

In 1922, the remaining 23 percent of Palestine, lying to the west of Transjordan, along the Mediterranean Sea, was still a mandate under British control. It remained so until 1947, without any Jewish homeland being created. By that time, fighting between all three groups had increased and Britain decided to let the new international organization, the United Nations, resolve the political status of the region. The United Nations decided to partition this remaining portion of Palestine, only 23 percent of the original British mandate, in November 1947. It gave a part to the Zionists as a Jewish state and a part to be a Palestinian Arab state on the **West Bank** of the Jordan River. The city of Jerusalem, holy to both Jews and Muslims, was to be under UN supervision. Jews accepted the partition plan and declared the state of Israel in May 1948. This declaration fulfilled the hopes of early Zionist leaders such as **Theodore Herzl**. The British mandate in Palestine had come to an end. The United States, the Soviet Union, and most of the rest of the world gave full diplomatic recognition to Israel. However, Arabs in Jordan and in other Arab nations rejected the partition plan. In May 1948, twenty-four hours after Israel declared its independence, six Arab nations declared war on Israel. This was a tragic development, especially in light of Israel's clearly announced hope for peace as stressed in its Proclamation of Independence that May: "We extend our hand to all neighboring states and their peoples in an offer of peace." The Arab world's refusal of this offer plunged the region into a cycle of bloodshed that would continue for over fifty years.

The Four Major Arab-Israeli Wars

THE WAR FOR INDEPENDENCE (1948–1949)

Although the combined Arab forces were larger and better equipped, they were unable to accomplish their goal of destroying Israel. A truce arranged by the UN ended the fighting temporarily.

Dome of the Rock in Jerusalem.

Israel was then, and still is, the only democracy in the Middle East. Although it was established as a Jewish state, it has always permitted religious freedom to all peoples in its borders. Nevertheless, during the 1948–1949 war, over 700,000 Palestinian Arabs fled from Israel to Arab lands, thus becoming refugees. Some of these people fled because they feared the fighting. However, the Arab governments and armies urged the people to leave and promised to let them return once the expected victory over Israel had been achieved. Yet, a large number of Arabs remained in the new Jewish state. (They and their descendents have been treated respectfully and now make up almost twenty percent of Israel's population.)

This first Arab-Israeli War also affected the status of Jerusalem. The Israelis gained control of the western part of the city while the Jordanians seized East **Jerusalem**. East Jerusalem, also called the "old city," contains several sites holy to Jews, Christians, and Muslims. Jordan initially promised equal access to these sites, but it did not permit Jews to visit their holy sites such as the Western Wall. This was a violation of the UN Partition Plan. **Jordan** also seized and occupied the West Bank. This occupation was illegal and also violated the Partition Plan. This area, under the plan, was supposed to become an independent Palestinian state. The Jordanian occupation received international condemnation and was never recognized by any Arab nation. It was to last for nineteen years.

THE 1956 WAR

Under its president, Gamal Abdel Nasser, Egypt took over the Suez Canal from England in 1956 and prohibited Israel from using it. In addition, terrorist raids into Israel, supported by Egypt and other Arab nations, caused the deaths of many Israeli men, women, and children. As a result, Egypt and Israel went to war again. Israel defeated the Egyptian army in the Sinai Desert and occupied the region. The UN arranged a cease-fire, ending this second Arab-Israeli War. Egypt kept the Suez Canal. Israel gave back the **Sinai Desert**, hoping that in return Egypt would recognize her and agree to peace. As Egypt refused recognition and maintained a hostile attitude, the UN sent an emergency force of soldiers (the UNEF) to keep peace on Israel's borders.

THE SIX-DAY WAR (THE JUNE WAR, 1967)

Egypt and the other Arab nations continued to refuse recognition of Israel and stepped up their terrorist attacks, threats of annihilation, and anti-Semitic propaganda. The Egyptians built up their forces in the Sinai Desert with Russian aid, forbade Israeli use of the Suez Canal, and closed the Gulf of Aqaba to Israeli shipping. It also ordered the UNEF to leave the border areas with Israel. These

Israeli soldiers at the Wailing Wall after the capture of Jerusalem during the Six-Day War, June 1967.

measures foreshadowed an all-out Egyptian military campaign, leading Israel to strike at Egypt in early June 1967. As Egypt and other Arab nations were now engaged in fighting Israel, the third Arab-Israeli War occurred. Arab armies that attacked Israel from the north, east, and south were thrown back, and Israel took over large amounts of land—the Sinai Peninsula and **Gaza** (from Egypt), the West Bank of the Jordan River and East Jerusalem (from Jordan, which had illegally taken these areas in the 1948–1949 War and was asked by Israel not to attack her in 1967), and the **Golan Heights** (from Syria). The war lasted for six days. Israel annexed East Jerusalem and the Golan Heights, making them parts of Israel. Israel offered to negotiate with the Arabs over the newly won territories if the Arabs would sign a peace treaty and recognize Israel's right to exist. Israel had fought a defensive war and did not seek to expand its borders. The West Bank contained a very large Arab population, and Israel now designated the area politically by the ancient territorial names—Judea and Samaria.

As thousands of people fled the fighting, the number of Arab refugees in Judea, Samaria, and Arab nations such as Jordan, Lebanon, and Syria increased. Many of these refugees were forced by their Arab host nations to live in various camps and regions that had poor health and housing facilities and that served as training grounds for terrorist activity against Israel. In November 1967, the UN passed Resolution 242. This document called for all warring nations to recognize one another and make peace and for Israel to withdraw from some of the seized lands. The Arab nations continued their nonrecognition policy toward Israel. Israel, consequently, refused to return territory until it received Arab recognition.

THE YOM KIPPUR WAR (1973)

The fourth Arab-Israeli War was begun by Egypt on Yom Kippur, October 6, 1973. The Egyptians knew that Yom Kippur is the holiest day of the year for Jews and, thus, purposely made a surprise attack across the Suez Canal on that day. The Israeli government, under Prime Minister **Golda Meir**, was not prepared for such an assault on such a holy day. The war, which the Egyptians called The October War, lasted almost a month. Egypt gained at first a small amount of land in the Sinai, but was eventually beaten back onto its own land, and almost had its Third Army group totally destroyed. Syrian troops attacked Israel on the

Golda Meir (1898–1978), Israeli stateswoman, addressing the General Assembly of the United Nations in New York while Foreign Minister of Israel, October 2, 1963.

Golan Heights but were beaten back. Several other Arab countries sent troops to fight. The Soviet Union increased its arms shipments to the Arabs, hoping to avoid another victory by Israel. To counter the Soviets, the United States sent military equipment to Israel. Oil-rich Arab nations, such as Saudi Arabia, pressured the United States not to help Israel and began an oil embargo (a refusal to sell oil). Once again the UN arranged a cease-fire to end the fighting. The UN also passed Resolution 338, calling for "negotiations . . . between the parties concerned . . . aimed at establishing . . . peace in the Middle East."

Developments Between 1973 and 2000

In 1977, Egyptian President **Anwar Sadat** visited Israel to begin peace talks. He was the first Arab leader to visit Israel. Later in the year, Israeli Prime Minister **Menachem Begin** visited Egypt. These exchanges led to meetings and agreements at Camp David, near Washington, D.C., between these two leaders and U.S. President **Jimmy Carter**. The Camp David Accords paved the way for the historic Israel-Egypt Peace Treaty, signed in Washington, D.C., on March 26, 1979, by Begin and Sadat. The treaty provided that (1) Egypt and Israel would recognize each other and exchange ambassadors; (2) the state of war that existed between them from 1948 to 1979 was over; (3) Israel would return the Sinai Peninsula to Egypt in stages between 1979 and 1982, and a UN peacekeeping force would be reestablished on the border; and (4) negotiations would begin on the status of the Palestinian Arabs. Many Arab nations and Islamic extremists were angry at Egypt's actions. This anger reached a deadly peak in 1981, when Muslim extremists assassinated Sadat. **Hosni Mubarak** became the new Egyptian president.

Main Idea:
The Camp David Accords paved the way for the historic Israel-Egypt Peace Treaty, signed in Washington, D.C., on March 26, 1979, by Begin and Sadat.

Anwar Sadat, Jimmy Carter, and Menachem Begin at the White House, 1979, after signing Mideast peace treaty.

The year 1982 witnessed stability on Israel's southern border in contrast with instability on her northern border. In the south, it kept its promise to finish the reversion to Egypt of the Sinai Peninsula. In the north, however, Israel found it necessary, as a matter of self-defense, to respond to repeated terrorist attacks from Lebanon by the **PLO (Palestine Liberation Organization)**; the Lebanese government was unable or unwilling to stop these attacks. The PLO was formed in 1964 by Arabs from the Palestinian areas who wanted to destroy Israel and to create a Palestinian state. With its leader, **Yasir Arafat**, the organization issued propaganda against Jews and against Israel, while carrying out murderous attacks against Israeli civilians. The PLO claimed to speak on behalf of all Palestinian Arabs and was supported by most Arab nations. By 1984, the PLO was forced to leave Lebanon, as Israeli troops moved as far north as Beirut. The Israeli army then pulled out except for a small "security zone" in southern Lebanon.

In 1987, an armed uprising by Palestinians in the West Bank and the Gaza Strip began. This uprising, known in Arabic as the *intifada*, and led by the PLO, was a protest against Israeli control of the lands won in war. Many Palestinians supported the PLO in its goals of overthrowing Israel and establishing a Palestinian state. However, the PLO was branded as a terrorist group by Israel because it was one of several Arab organizations that continued to carry out unprovoked deadly attacks on civilians in the Middle East and elsewhere in the world. Consequently, the Israeli government refused to negotiate with the PLO over land issues. Yet, in September 1993, a change took place in Washington, D.C. With U.S. President Bill Clinton presiding, Israeli Prime Minister **Yitzhak Rabin** and PLO Chairman Yasir Arafat signed an agreement providing for mutual recognition by both sides. Furthermore, the PLO would renounce violence against Israel, Israel would withdraw from specific parts of the West Bank (a "land for peace" idea), and talks would begin on the future of a Palestinian state. These provisions

Yitzhak Rabin, Bill Clinton, and Yasir Arafat in Washington, D.C. at the 1993 agreement signing.

had originally been negotiated at Oslo, Norway, and thus became known as The Oslo Accords or Declaration of Principles. As promising as these accords sounded, they did not prove to be fulfilling. Continuing violations by Palestinian terror groups such as **Hamas**, as well as anti-Semitic teachings in Palestinian schools doomed the accords.

Two other agreements affecting the region did make for peaceful arrangements that exist until the present day. One was the signing in Jerusalem, in 1993, of an accord between Israel and the Vatican, whereby diplomatic relations would be established for the first time. The Roman Catholic Church would now recognize the state of Israel, reversing its prior policy. In 1994, Jordan became the second Arab nation to recognize Israel when Prime Minister Rabin and Jordan's **King Hussein** signed a peace treaty. If other Arab nations follow the examples of Egypt and Jordan and recognize Israel, hopes for settlement of what has become known as the Arab-Israeli dispute may be eventually realized.

France

> **Main Idea:**
> French authority was easy to impose because of the various religious and ethnic groups in Syria and Lebanon, including the Kurds, Maronite Christians, Druze, and diverse Muslim groups.

In 1920, France was given mandates in Lebanon and Syria. However, French involvement in these regions goes back to the sixteenth century. France's commercial and cultural ties to the region became so strong that, by 1900, her economic involvement in the area was the greatest of any European power. In addition, the Ottoman rulers had let France become the protector of all Catholics in the regions; the French language was also widely spoken.

Nevertheless there was resistance to French mandatory control in Syria and Lebanon. An independence-seeking movement was put down by French troops in the 1920s. Consequently, France established overall colonial control of both Syria and Lebanon. The two regions, sometimes referred to as **The Levant**, became part of the French Empire. All education in public schools was conducted in French. French was substituted for Arabic as the official language. Under the French-controlled economy, Beirut became a prosperous city. French authority was easy to impose because of the various religious and ethnic groups in Syria and Lebanon, including the Kurds, Maronite Christians, Druze, and diverse Muslim groups. The French befriended each of these, thus following a policy of "divide and conquer" as well as "divide and rule."

Health services, transportation, and communication were improved with the French presence. Yet, the desire for independence lingered into the 1940s. In 1946, France granted independence to both colonies. Factors leading to this situation included the impact of World War II (1939–1945) on a weary France, the wishes of the colonized peoples, and pressure from the United Nations and France's allies.

Other Political Developments in the Middle East

IN IRAN—ISLAMIC FUNDAMENTALISM AND THE WAR WITH IRAQ

The Shah (ruler) of Iran, **Mohammed Riza Pahlavi**, introduced several Western and modern practices into his country during the 1960s and 1970s. However, many religious leaders felt that traditional Islamic customs were threatened by these Western ideas. These leaders were Islamic fundamentalists, who wanted to keep Islam pure and strict, without any alleged "contamination" from the outside world. Known also as Islamists, they opposed the Shah and were also upset with the harsh dictatorial manner in which he ruled. Riots and demonstrations against the Shah forced him to leave Iran in 1979. In his place, the country was run by an Islamic Revolutionary Council, led by Ayatollah **Ruhollah Khomeini**. This Iranian Revolution, also known as the Islamic Revolution, caused concern in other Muslim nations in the Middle East. The Ayatollah's government was anti-Western and held fifty-two Americans as hostages from 1979 to 1981. Although Khomeini died in 1989, the new rulers have followed similar foreign and domestic policies.

In 1980, war between Iran and Iraq broke out when Iraq, under its leader, **Saddam Hussein**, attacked Iran. Known as the Iran-Iraq War, this conflict had several causes. These included political causes: each nation wanted to dominate the Persian Gulf area, Hussein and Khomeini frequently criticized each other, and there were unresolved border disputes; social causes: Iraq feared the "export" of the Iranian Revolution, and there were great religious differences between the **Sunni Muslims** of Iraq and the **Shi'ite Muslims** of Iran; economic causes: the oil fields of the Persian Gulf area are very valuable, and the Persian Gulf itself is the most important route for transporting oil from the Middle East. The fighting ended in 1988 under a UN-supervised agreement, but it caused hundreds of thousands of casualties and hurt the economies of both nations. The war ended as a stalemate.

LEBANON—CIVIL WAR AND SYRIAN OCCUPATION

A civil war broke out in Lebanon in 1975 and lasted until 1990. It can be explained by examining the country's political and religious history. When the French mandate in Lebanon ended in 1943, a government was created that was supposed to strike a balance between Lebanese Christians and Muslims. Since the Christians were then the majority group, it was decided that most of the top government positions would go to Christians. From the 1940s to the 1970s, Lebanon prospered economically and was peaceful. However, Muslims became the majority group and they wanted changes in the political structure so as to give them more power. It was also in this period that Palestinian refugees, including PLO leaders, settled in Lebanon as a result of the Arab-Israeli wars. From these settlements and refugee camps, many Palestinians made terrorist raids into Israel. Frequently, Israeli forces attacked these settlements and refugee camps in retaliation. Lebanese Christians, represented by the Phalange, a political party, were against the Palestinian presence in Lebanon.

> **Main Idea:**
> Although Syria's purpose was to restore order and peace, at various times the Syrians supported different militias in Lebanon.

In 1975, Muslims and Christians began to fight each other. In addition, different Muslim groups began to fight one another and different Christian groups began to fight one another. Each of the groups formed its own army or militia. In 1976, Syria, under President **Hafez al-Assad**, sent in troops as requested by the Arab League (an organization of Arab nations in the Middle East). Although Syria's purpose was to restore order and peace, at various times the Syrians supported different militias in Lebanon. By 1990, there were forty thousand Syrian soldiers in Lebanon and President Assad began to drop hints of incorporating and adding Lebanon into a "greater Syria."

Other Middle Eastern nations, such as Iran and Libya, also supported one or more of the warring groups. Some of these groups, such as **Islamic Jihad**, carried out terrorist attacks against foreigners and other Lebanese in order to focus world attention on their political goals. These terrorist activities included taking citizens of France, the United States, Germany, and the former Soviet Union as hostages and sometimes killing them, and hijacking a TWA airplane and other airliners, thus making air travel very unsafe. Tragically, there was no single government in Lebanon acceptable to all of its people and able to bring stability to the nation by crushing the terrorist groups and various militias. The civil war resulted in separated enclaves (closed-in areas) in Beirut and elsewhere under the control of whatever militia proved to be the strongest. The Lebanese economy was ruined by the war.

A long series of negotiations led to an agreement that helped to bring the conflict to an end in 1990. This agreement, The National Reconciliation Pact, provided for a new government in which Muslims and Christians would share power equally. The Lebanese army regained control of most of the country. Many Lebanese now returned to their country, having fled during the long war. Electricity and basic services were restored as the economy began to prosper. Yet, Syria kept its forty thousand soldiers there and significantly influenced major government policies. These policies did little to meet the needs of the Lebanese population. A 1991 agreement between both nations spoke of cooperation on political and economic issues, primarily favoring Syrian objectives. For this and other reasons, many Lebanese, especially the Christians among them, wanted Syria to end its occupation. Syria refused to do this until 2005 (see Chapter 16 in this volume).

WAR IN AFGHANISTAN (1979–1989)

In 1979, a Marxist pro-Soviet government came to power in Afghanistan. It faced opposition by the majority of Afghan people, who began an armed struggle against it. The Soviet Union invaded Afghanistan, claiming that it was responding to a request of the Afghan government. However, many observers believe that the real reasons for the Soviet actions were to gain access to oil and gas deposits in Afghanistan and possibly to reach through Iran into the Persian Gulf. The Soviets may also have been afraid of the impact of Islamic fundamentalism in Afghanistan and Iran on Muslim communities in the Soviet Union. The Soviet military action was condemned by nations around the globe and caused controversy in the Soviet Union itself. The Afghan fighters, the Mujahadeen, were supplied by the United States and were able to deny the Soviet Union a victory. In 1989, the Soviets retreated from Afghanistan with severe military and political losses.

LIBYA AND STATE-SUPPORTED TERRORISM

Ever since Colonel **Muammar Qaddafi** came to power in 1969, Libya had supported terrorist groups. These groups carried out actions mainly against Israeli and U.S. interests. In 1986, U.S. bombers raided Libya for violence directed against Americans in Europe and the Middle East. The worst incident of terrorist violence involving Libya concerned its unspeakable and outrageous bombing of Pan Am flight 103, an American aircraft, as it flew over Lockerbie, Scotland, in 1988. The death toll numbered all 259 passengers and crew members, allegedly the work of agents trained in Libya. Libya refused to release the subjects to U.S. authorities. In 1998, however, under international pressure, Libya finally agreed to release two suspects to stand trial. One of them was found guilty in a trial in 2001.

The Libyan government's connection with such bloody and inhuman, unprovoked acts toward innocent people of other nations is an example of "state-supported terrorism." This term refers to a government policy that supports, trains, finances, and protects organizations that engage in terrorist activities. Besides Libya, other Middle Eastern nations that have provided such support are Iran, Syria, Iraq, and Yemen. Examples of groups that have received their assistance have been Islamic Jihad, Hamas, and the PLO. American officials were concerned about any links between Middle East terrorists and the 1993 bombing of the World Trade Center in New York City.

OPERATION DESERT STORM—THE PERSIAN GULF WAR OF 1991

This war lasted from January 18, 1991 to February 27, 1991. The conflict, whose chief adversaries were Iraq and the United States, had its roots in the Iraqi invasion of Kuwait in August 1990. Iraq, which wanted to take over Kuwait's rich oil fields and have greater access to the Persian Gulf, would probably have sought to take over Saudi Arabia eventually. Such actions would have given Iraq control over 40 percent of the world's oil reserves. Saddam Hussein refused to leave Kuwait despite UN requests and its eventual imposition of trade sanctions and threat to use force.

George H. W. Bush (1924–): Contemporary American Engraving.

As Iraqi troops killed, tortured, and raped thousands of Kuwaitis, destroyed much property, and were poised for an attack on Saudi Arabia, U.S. President George H. W. Bush assembled a multinational force of 500,000 troops from twenty-nine countries. This coalition, under the command of American General Norman Schwarzkopf and containing 450,000 U.S. troops, went into action in January under the authority of a UN Security Council resolution when Iraq failed to meet a deadline for withdrawing its troops from Kuwait. With the use of high-tech weaponry, the U.S.-led coalition forces defeated the Iraqis and freed Kuwait in five weeks.

The chief consequences of the war were as follows: (1) Saddam Hussein remained in power, still in possession of a large army. He frequently failed to cooperate with the UN teams that frequently visited Iraq, under UN orders, to check out his weapons systems. (2) The ecology of the Persian Gulf area was severely upset by Iraqi soldiers. They burned oil wells and released large amounts of petroleum into the Gulf waters. (3) A major split among Arabs occurred. Egypt, Saudi Arabia, Syria, and Kuwait sided with the United States. In support of Iraq, although not sending in any fighters, were Jordan, Yemen, Tunisia, Algeria, and the PLO. (4) Kurdish people in Iraq were treated very harshly by Saddam Hussein. Their attempt to break away from Iraqi rule was suppressed, and many were killed or forced to become refugees. Thousands were given "safe-haven" areas in northern Iraq under the protection of the United States and the United Nations.

Ireland

The Irish Question has been a source of controversy between Ireland and Britain for centuries (see Chapter 16 in *Global History, Volume One* and Chapter 3 in this volume). By 1600, Protestant England had gained control over Catholic Ireland. From that time until the twentieth century, British imperialist treatment of the Irish had been cruel and harsh. When Oliver Cromwell ruled England in the seventeenth century, many Irish were killed by his forces; in addition, Protestants from England and Scotland took over large areas of land in Northern Ireland. Until the 1800s, Irish Catholics could not hold political office and were taxed to support the Anglican (Protestant) Church.

Division of Ireland

In 1905, the **Sinn Fein** (meaning in Gaelic "ourselves alone") party was formed as a nationalist group to press Britain for Irish independence. Its leader was **Eamon de Valera**. It was during World War I that these nationalists got aid from Germany and mounted an armed uprising in Dublin against British rule.

Although this **Easter Rebellion** in 1916 was unsuccessful, with many rebel leaders executed, the Sinn Fein continued its campaign for home rule and independence. This campaign was conducted peacefully as well as through guerilla warfare against British forces. In 1921, the southern four-fifths of the island of Ireland became a free nation known as the Republic of Ireland. The remaining one-fifth, Northern Ireland, also known as Ulster, decided to remain as part of the United Kingdom (the official name for the united nation of England, Scotland, Wales, and Northern Ireland). The division of the island was completed in 1922. In 1949, the Irish Republic ended its membership in the British Commonwealth.

Political and Sectarian Strife

Catholics in Northern Ireland wanted the area to be united with the Irish Republic to the south, as did the new Republic of Ireland itself. These requests were turned down by Britain, particularly because the majority of Ulster citizens were Protestants and wanted to stay under the British crown. Extremist groups, both Catholic and Protestant, began to fight an undeclared civil war in Northern Ireland. This kind of religious conflict is known as **sectarian strife**. This violence escalated in 1969 and continued into the 1990s. The **Irish Republican Army (IRA)**, along with its political component, the Sinn Fein, spoke for many **Ulster** Catholics and demanded a united Ireland. Militant Protestants, headed by the Reverend **Ian Paisley**, were against unification. British troops were sent to Ulster in 1969 to help maintain peace and stop the killings and terrorist actions of both sides. Most of the violence, often directed against civilians, was carried out by the IRA and a Protestant group, the **Ulster Freedom Fighters** (UFF). British efforts to reduce the violence were not very successful.

Attempted Solutions

A political solution to what had been called "the Troubles" was attempted in 1985 with the **Hillsborough Agreement**. This provided for greater cooperation against extremist groups, stopping discrimination toward the Catholic minority in the north, and giving the Republic of Ireland some involvement in the governing of Northern Ireland. The agreement had mixed results and was criticized by both Catholics and Protestants. For Protestants, the agreement went too far. For Catholics, it did not go far enough.

In 1992, another political solution was attempted as officials from Britain, Ireland, and Northern Ireland met in the Irish capital of **Dublin**. They hoped to stem the violence and terrorism that had taken over three thousand lives during the previous twenty-three years. Lives were lost in Ulster, as well as in Britain itself. One hopeful sign for peace in Dublin was the presence at the talks of a leader from one of the major Protestant political parties of Northern Ireland for the first time since 1922. That party, the Ulster Unionist Party, was nevertheless in favor of continuing the region's link to Britain. This contrasted with the wish of Ulster Catholics for more say in the Ulster government and eventual unification with Ireland, as well as the Irish government's wish for unification of the island. Neither the IRA nor the Sinn Fein was invited to the Dublin talks, as they refused to give up their campaign of violence to end British rule in the north. The 1992 talks in Dublin were suspended, however, as little progress was made on the issues. Violence continued on both sides in 1993, thus hampering the chances

Gerry Adams, right, after cease-fire in East Belfast.

of holding further talks. An additional troublesome item concerned a request made by Protestant political leaders. They said they would not attend any talks until the Irish government promises to change its constitutional claim of sovereignty in the north. The Irish government, in turn, has said that this can only be accomplished as part of an overall negotiated agreement.

In 1994, another relevant item made the news. As a result of talks between **Gerry Adams**, president of Sinn Fein, and **John Hume**, head of a Catholic political party in Northern Ireland, a plan was considered whereby the Sinn Fein would be allowed to take part in peace negotiations if it promised to halt acts of violence by the IRA. Yet, it was obvious that such a plan would have to be weighed carefully and agreed to by other key figures: Irish Prime Minister **Albert Reynolds**, British Prime Minister **John Major**, and Ulster leaders such as Reverend Paisley. These efforts, as well as other ones, progressed very slowly from this point until 1998. In that year, however, thanks to the assistance of a U.S. Senator, **George Mitchell**, a peace plan was reached on the Good Friday religious holiday. This was on April 10, 1998. This accord, known as the **Good Friday Agreement**, established a timetable whereby the British would withdraw and a government made up of representatives of both the Protestant Unionists and the Catholic Nationalists, including Sinn Fein, would share power and the decision-making process.

Approval of the Good Friday Agreement by the political parties of Northern Ireland was slow in coming about, particularly as extremists on both sides found objections. In 1999, the whole process temporarily stopped over the issue of the IRA disarming before the new power-sharing executive was set up. By the autumn of 1999, due to the effort of Unionist leader **David Trimble** and Nationalist Gerry Adams, the Good Friday Agreement appeared to be back on track. Despite good intentions, implementation of the Good Friday Agreement proved to be difficult from 1999 to 2005. Yet in 2005, hopes for peace in Northern Ireland increased when the IRA officially gave up its armed struggle and agreed to hand in its weapons (known as **decommissioning**). Furthermore, a crucial meeting was planned for October of 2006 in Scotland. It would include Sinn Fein leader Gerry Adams, Democratic Unionist leader Ian Paisley, as well as

Main Idea:
Despite good intentions, implementation of the Good Friday Agreement proved to be difficult from 1999 to 2005.

Prime Minister Tony Blair of Britain and his counterpart, Bertie Ahearn of Ireland. Its purpose was to establish a power-sharing arrangement for Northern Ireland among its various political parties. Failure to do this by November would result in a reversion to direct rule by Britain over Northern Ireland.

EVALUATION OF IMPERIALISM

European Imperialism had both positive and negative effects for those nations who acquired land overseas. On the positive side, it was obvious that the growth of an empire gave a nation prestige, wealth, and a way to spread its culture. The mother country's standard of living improved, while careers in the military and foreign service were made available. Investors and business leaders were furnished with raw material and expanding markets.

On the negative side was the reality that imperialistic ventures could draw nations into wars. These might be with rival colonial powers or with the colonies themselves. Taxpayers in the mother country would have to pay for wars and imperialistic consequences.

The effects of imperialism upon the colonized regions were also a mix of the positive and negative.

LINK TO TODAY
Place Names with a History

What's in a name? This was a question we posed at the start of this chapter. We raise it again now, as we end our discussion of imperialism. The legacy of imperialism can be seen in an unexpected name change in Africa in the late twentieth century and also in a controversy over an expected name change in Europe in the early twenty-first century. Let us go first to Africa. It was there in 1842, that France established a protectorate in a coastal part of West Africa. This protectorate was called by a French name, Côte d'Ivoire. With independence in 1960, the name was changed to Ivory Coast. Yet, in 1985, under the leadership of a conservative pro-Western president who had close ties with France, Felix Houphouet-Boigny, the name was changed back to Côte d'Ivoire. Even though he died in 2003, the French name is still used.

A different kind of naming situation occurred in the southwest of Ireland in 2006. In that region is a town named Dingle. That was an English name given to the town in 1824, when the British controlled Ireland. Dingle became well-known as one of Ireland's most famous tourist destinations. Yet, in an attempt to preserve Gaelic, the native Irish language, a government official in 2004 ordered over 2,300 communities to adopt Irish/Gaelic names. Dingle would thus be known as Daingean. The town's inhabitants were upset about this situation. In October 2006, they voted overwhelmingly to adopt a bilingual name: Dingle

Daingean Ui Chuis. They felt that Dingle was a valuable commercial name, even though it had been imposed by the British, and that its prosperous tourist industry would be hurt with visitors being confused, for example, with unfamiliar names on road signs and maps. The government official, Eamon O Cuiv, is a grandson of one of Ireland's founding fathers, Eamon de Valera. As was true of his grandfather, Mr. O Cuiv is a strong supporter of the Irish language. He claimed that the vote in Dingle could not revoke his order. Here now is a moment when history, tradition, and commerce give rise to a dilemma. The past and the present meet head on. A conflict also now exists between local and national power. Will there be a lawsuit? How should this issue over the name of a town be resolved?

CHAPTER SUMMARY

So we have come to the end of an era of European history. The impact of European nations on the world has changed. The end of World War II saw the end of colonialism. France and Great Britain were too weakened to try to keep control of their possessions. The movement into independence was very uneven. There was some relationship between the manner in which the colonies were treated and how independence was achieved. The newly emerging nations from rule by Britain and France, for example, generally made a smoother transition and kept up relationships with their former rulers. Those colonies controlled by Belgium and Portugal had a far more difficult time.

On the Asian continent, there were more difficulties. When the Indian subcontinent split into two nations, with Pakistan and India divided on religious lines, bloodshed resulted. The religious difficulties continue to exist. The Chinese underwent a civil war that resulted in a Communist victory. The United States became involved in a land war in Southeast Asia when it involved itself in a long, drawn-out conflict in Vietnam.

The Middle East of today bears effects of European imperialism. These are not as pronounced, however, as they are in Africa and other parts of Asia. The main reason for this contrast is that European colonialism in the Middle East came later and ended sooner than was the case elsewhere. The decline of European colonialism in Asia, as well as in Africa, was most evident in the years following World War II. In almost all instances, this decline was accomplished peacefully. It was not marked by widespread outbreaks of violent rebellion, as was true of the American Revolution, when the thirteen colonies fought against British rule in the eighteenth century. In the twentieth century, the struggle against various forms of imperialism, along with the emergence of new, independent nations, was a crucial turning point in world history.

There are still problems to be resolved. The ongoing problem of Ireland is still with us, like a festering sore that may be healing slowly. The relations between the Catholics and Protestants in the north have improved, thus making possible some kind of political solution.

This chapter's last section was an evaluation of the period of colonialism. Did the European nations benefit? Did the African or Asian people benefit? What do you think?

IMPORTANT PEOPLE, PLACES, AND TERMS

KEY TERMS

imperialism
decolonization
"settler mentality"
Mau Mau
British Commonwealth
  of Nations
Statute of Westminster
Durham Report
British North American
  Act
apartheid
Afrikaans
Afrikaner

Indian National
  Congress
Congress Party
"Quit India"
colonial subjugation
Viet Minh
Viet Cong
Ottoman Empire
Balfour Declaration
Zionists
Palestine Liberation
  Organization
Hamas

Sunni Muslims
Shi'ite Muslims
Sinn Fein
Easter Rebellion
sectarian strife
Irish Republican Army
  (IRA)
Hillsborough
  Agreement
Good Friday
  Agreement
decommissioning

PEOPLE

Kwame Nkrumah
Jomo Kenyatta
Ian Smith
Robert Mugabe
Joshua Nkomo
Cecil Rhodes
James Cook
Frederik W. de Klerk
Nelson Mandela
Sam Nujoma
Charles de Gaulle
Felix Houphouet-
  Boigny
Leopold Senghor
Ahmed Ben Bella

Samora Machel
Mahatma Gandhi
Jawaharlal Nehru
Indira Gandhi
Mohammed Ali Jinnah
Chiang Kai-shek
Mao Zedong
Achmed Sukarno
Ho Chi Minh
Richard Nixon
Nguyen Van Thieu
Bill Clinton
Arthur Belfour
Theodore Herzl
Golda Meir

Anwar Sadat
Menachem Begin
Jimmy Carter
Hosni Mubarak
Yasir Arafat
Mohammed Riza
  Pahlavi
Ruhollah Khomeini
Saddam Hussein
Muammar Qaddafi
Eamon de Valera
Ian Paisley
Gerry Adams
George Mitchell

PLACES

Africa
Egypt
Ethiopia
Liberia
South Africa
Ghana
Kenya
Zimbabwe
Ireland
Canada
Australia

New Zeland
Southwest Africa
Namibia
Ivory Coast
Senegal
Tunisia
Algeria
Morocco
Libya
East Pakistan
West Pakistan

Bangladesh
Kashmir
Azad Kashmir
China
Hong Kong
Macao
Philippines
Southeast Asia
Netherlands
Republic of Indonesia
Burma

Myanmar	Hanoi	Jerusalem
Malaysia	Middle East	Jordan
Singapore	Suez Canal	Sinai Desert
Brunei	Palestine	Gaza
French Indochina	Iraq	Golan Heights
Laos	Syria	Ulster
Vietnam	Kuwait	The Levant
Cambodia	Iran	Dublin
Dien Bien Phu	West Bank	

CHAPTER 15

MULTIPLE-CHOICE QUESTIONS

Select the number of the correct answer.

1. World War II had which impact on European colonies?

   (1) It strengthened their desire for continued protection by the European countries.
   (2) It lessened the desire for democracy in those colonies.
   (3) It caused native peoples to struggle to achieve the goals of freedom and self-determination.
   (4) Colonialism was made stronger by the defeat of Nazi Germany and fascist Italy.

2. What would be a valid conclusion about the process of independence in the European colonies.

   (1) In all colonies there was a unified approach to applying for independence.
   (2) The process of gaining independence varied from peaceful to violent among the colonies.
   (3) European nations had a renewed sense of colonial power after World War II and resisted any efforts at independence.
   (4) The process of independence was a swift one and occurred within fifteen years of the end of World War II.

3. The African nations of Kenya and Zimbabwe had similarities in their struggle for independence in that

   (1) they lacked strong national leaders
   (2) Great Britain willingly gave each area its independence
   (3) foreign countries helped to finance their independence movements
   (4) both countries experienced periods of violence over several years

4. The Statute of Westminster, an act of the British Parliament, created

   (1) independence for the Republic of South Africa
   (2) the United Nations
   (3) the British Commonwealth of Nations
   (4) the union of several islands in the West Indies

5. The position of the governor general in Canada still exists and is a direct representative of the

   (1) British monarch
   (2) Canadian prime minister
   (3) secretary general of the United Nations
   (4) House of Lords in the British Parliament

6. The policy of apartheid in South Africa was an example of discrimination between

   (1) the black and white populations of the area
   (2) Christians and Muslims in South Africa
   (3) the wealthy landowners and the urban populations
   (4) those of Dutch heritage and those of British heritage

7. Nelson Mandela made history in 1994 by

   (1) being chosen the first black president of South Africa
   (2) leading a major demonstration against apartheid
   (3) receiving the support of even the major white separatist groups
   (4) being released from prison

8. In the struggle for Indian independence from Great Britain, who became famous for leading nonviolent protests and boycotts of British goods?

   (1) Indira Gandhi
   (2) Mohammed Ali Jinnah
   (3) Jawaharlal Nehru
   (4) Mohandas Gandhi

9. When India and Pakistan were divided into separate independent countries, the division was based primarily on

   (1) geography
   (2) type of government
   (3) religion
   (4) foreign alliances

10. At the end of the twentieth century, Hong Kong and Macao made headlines because both

    (1) joined together to form an international trade and banking center in Asia
    (2) were surrendered to Chinese control by their former colonial rulers
    (3) joined the United Nations
    (4) were sites of violent revolutions against independence

11. When the French colony of Vietnam wanted to gain its independence, it

    (1) was forced to accept a Communist form of government
    (2) fought France in a war that lasted nine years
    (3) formed a union with Laos and Cambodia
    (4) asked for and received assistance from the United States

12. Israel traces its foundation as a nation to

    (1) The Balfour Declaration of 1917
    (2) the end of World War II
    (3) its own declaration of independence in May 1948
    (4) the 1922 establishment of the Arab kingdom of Transjordan

13. For the first twenty-five years that Israel was an independent nation, it experienced

    (1) major discoveries of oil resources in its territory
    (2) substantial foreign aid
    (3) a policy of neutrality and disinterest from the United Nations
    (4) a series of wars with its Arab neighbors

14. Overall, the Soviet Union's attempts to control Afghanistan during the 1980s resulted in

    (1) a failure for the Soviets
    (2) a civil war in Afghanistan
    (3) the involvement by United Nations troops
    (4) the Afghan Mujahadeen gaining control of the government

15. One of the most serious examples of "state-supported terrorism" during the 1990s occurred in Europe when

    (1) the World Trade Center was bombed in 1993
    (2) Iran seized American hostages in Teheran
    (3) private citizens were killed randomly on a Mediterranean cruise ship
    (4) Pan Am flight 103 was bombed as it flew over Scotland

16. The cause of the Persian Gulf War of 1991 was

    (1) repeated Arab attacks on Israel
    (2) the invasion of Kuwait by Iraq
    (3) the nationalization of the Suez Canal by Egypt
    (4) the failure of Iraq to comply with a United Nations resolution

17. What is the best description of the Irish Republican Army and Sinn Fein?

    (1) the IRA is the official army of the Republic of Ireland, and Sinn Fein is its accepted leader
    (2) the IRA is a terrorist organization without government support, and Sinn Fein is a political party that represents its views
    (3) the IRA acts with the approval of Sinn Fein to promote Irish nationalism
    (4) Ian Paisley has been at different times leader of both groups

18. The second half of the twentieth century was a time across the globe for a shift from colonialism to

    (1) imperialism   (3) totalitarianism
    (2) militarism   (4) independence

19. Which independence leader is matched correctly with his own nation?

    (1) Jomo Kenyatta and Nigeria
    (2) Achmed Sukarno and the Philippines
    (3) Theodore Herzl and Israel
    (4) Ho Chi Minh and Hong Kong

20. Which event could be best considered a cause of the other three?

    (1) Europeans seized colonies across the globe for their own benefit.
    (2) Europeans built schools, roads, and hospitals in their colonies.
    (3) Colonists improved their standard of living and desired independence.
    (4) Educated leaders who gained support from the native populations worked for national sovereignty.

THEMATIC ESSAY

Directions: Write a well-organized essay that includes an introduction, several paragraphs addressing the task below, and a conclusion.

Theme: Nationalism

Nationalism has been a powerful force for areas around the world since the end of World War II.

Task

Define the term *nationalism* and then select two nations and, for each,

- describe how nationalism played a role in that nation since the conclusion of World War II
- identify one key individual in the country of your choice and describe what that person did to encourage nationalism
- discuss at least one problem that the person or country experienced in its effort to achieve nationalism or independence

You may use any nations from your study of global history. Some suggestions you might wish to consider include the Republic of South Africa, Kenya, India, Vietnam, Israel, and Ireland.

You are *not* limited to these suggestions.

Guidelines

In your essay, be sure to

- address all aspects of the *Task*
- support the theme with relevant facts, examples, and details
- use a logical and clear plan of organization, including an introduction and a conclusion that are beyond a restatement of the theme
- introduce the theme by establishing a framework that is beyond a simple restatement of the *Task* and conclude with a summation of the theme

DOCUMENT-BASED ESSAY QUESTION

This question is based on the accompanying documents (1–7). The question is designed to test your ability to work with historical documents. Some of the documents have been edited for the purposes of this question. As you analyze the documents, take into account the source of each document and any point of view that may be presented in the document.

Historical Context

Just as individuals have distinct identities, so, too, do individual world cultures. Throughout global history, various cultures have impacted the iden-tity of other cultures, sometimes positively, some-times negatively.

Task

Using information from the documents and your knowledge of global history, answer the ques-tions that follow each document in Part A. Your answers to the questions will help you write the Part B essay, in which you will be asked to

- select any three examples in global history in which two cultures have come in contact
- describe, in each case, if the contact was posi-tive or negative and give specific reasons for your answer

Part A: Short Answer Question

Directions: Analyze the documents and answer the short answer questions that follow each document.

Document 1

Queen Victoria (1819-1901)
Queen Victoria chose Ottawa as Canada's capital in 1858. Nearly forty years later, a monument to Queen Victoria, intended as part of a lavish celebration of the Queen's Diamond Jubilee, the sixtieth year of her reign, was proposed for the Hill.

The competition for this monument was only open to Canadian sculptors. Louis-Philippe Hébert, a sculptor from Quebec, won the contract. Before being placed on Parliament Hill, the statue was first displayed at the Universal Exposition in Paris in 1900.

Queen Elizabeth II
Depicted on her horse Centenial—the former RCMP (Royal Canadian Mounted Police) horse officially presented to Her Majesty in 1977—Queen Elizabeth has reigned as Canada's monarch since 1952.

The monument was unveiled as part of Canada's 125th anniversary celebrations. Jack Harman and his staff of ten worked for two years to create this monument.

Question	1. How can you explain the presence of the above statutes?

Document 2

Excerpt from a tour book about Hong Kong

Because of these dazzling contrasts, Hong Kong offers visitors something unique – the chance to experience a vibrant Chinese city without sacrificing the comforts of home. To be sure, much of Hong Kong's Western fabric comes from the legacy left by the British, who ruled the colony until 1997, when it was handed back to China as a Special Administrative Region (thus the SAR abbreviation you'll see there and throughout this book). British influence is still evident everywhere, from Hong Kong's school system to its free-market economy, from its rugby teams to its double-decker buses, and from English pubs and tea in the afternoon to (my favorite) orderly queues. But though the city was molded by the British, it has always been, at its heart, Chinese, with Chinese medicine shops, street vendors, lively dim sum restaurants, old men taking their caged birds for walks in the park, and colorful festivals. Indeed, for the casual visitor, Hong Kong seems little changed since the 1997 handover. No doubt some visitors remain oblivious to even the most visible sign of that change: the replacement of the Union Jack and old flag of the Crown Colony of Hong Kong with the red, starred flag of China and the new red Hong Kong flag with its emblem of the bauhinia flower.

Source: Excerpt from a tour book about Hong Kong
(http://www.frommers.com/destinations/honkong/0078010001.html)

Question	2. According to the excerpt above, identify three things that show that Hong Kong had ties to Great Britain.

Document 3

FOUR GREEN FIELDS

"What did I have?", said the fine old woman
"What did I have?", this proud old woman did say
"I had four green fields, each one was a jewel
But strangers came and tried to take them from me
I had fine, strong sons, they fought to save my jewels
They fought and died and that was my grief", said she

"Long time ago", said the fine old woman
"Long time ago", this proud old woman did say
"There was war and death, plundering and pillage
My children starved by mountain, valley and sea
And their wailing cries, they shook the very heavens
My four green fields ran red with their blood", said she

"What have I now?", said the fine old woman
"What have I now?", this proud old woman did say

"I have four green fields, one of them's in bondage
In strangers hands that tried to take it from me
But my sons have sons, as brave as were their fathers
My fourth green field will bloom once again", said she.

Source:
http://www.pintraderscorner.100megsfree5.com/stpats/fourgreenfields.htm

In this song by Tommy Makem, the old woman represents Ireland and the four fields are the four provinces of Ireland.

Questions	3. a. According to the caption and song lyrics, Four Green Fields, does the old woman say what has happened in history to her "fields"?
	b. What does she mean when she says that one of her fields is in "bondage"?
	c. What does she predict will happen that has happened before?

Document 4

SIGNIFICANT NAME CHANGES

The following list shows acts of geographical renaming that have been of international importance or significance.

- Beijing – named Peiping from 1927 to 1949, during which time Nanking was the national capital. In English-speaking countries, Beijing was generally known as Peking before its name change, but following the Communist takeover, the pinyin transcription scheme was introduced, and Beijing was adopted
- Benin – formerly Dahomey
- Burkina Faso from Upper Volta in 1984
- Ethiopia – historically known as Abyssinia as well as Ethiopia
- Ghana – formerly the Gold Coast
- Ho Chi Minh City – formerly Saigon, changed in 1975 after the fall of South Vietnam
- Iran – known as Persia before 1979 (both names were used in the mid-20th century)
- Ireland (republic) – before 1937 the Irish Free State. Since 1949 commonly referred to by the official description Republic of Ireland, apart from in treaties, etc. State does not include all of the island of Ireland.
- Istanbul since March 28, 1930 – formerly Byzantium (under Greek rule) then Constantinople (under Roman and Ottoman rule)
- Jordan – formerly Transjordan
- Mumbai – from Bombay in December 1995 by right wing Hindu nationalist Shiv Sena-BJP coalition government
- Myanmar, in 1988 the military junta changed the name but Burma is still widely used in English (see explanation of names of Burma/Myanmar)

- Namibia – formerly South-West Africa
- New York City was once New Amsterdam
- Nizhny Novgorod was Gorky during the time of the Soviet Union
- Western Sahara –formerly Spanish Sahara
- Zimbabwe – part of Rhodesia until 1910; then known as Southern Rhodesia until a year before it declared independence in 1965; known as **Rhodesia** until 1979, then became Zimbabwe-Rhodesia until it assumed the current name in 1980; Numerous cities and towns in Zimbabwe were also changed in an attempt to eradicate symbols of British colonialism and white minority rule (such as Salisbury to Harare)

Source: http://en.wikipedia.org/wiki/Geographical_renaming

Question

4. Select any two examples from the list above and explain why the name changes mentioned in the list occurred.

Document 5

SPEECHES AND ARTICLES BY U.S. CONSUL GENERAL JAMES B. CUNNINGHAM

Remarks by U.S. Consul General James B. Cunningham
Independence Day Reception in Macau
Mandarin Oriental Hotel
July 6, 2006

(As prepared for delivery)

Chief Executive Ho, distinguished guests and friends, I am pleased to join you in Macau in celebration of the 230th anniversary of the signing of the Declaration of Independence, the bold document that created the United States. Although we may be far from home, we Americans enjoy coming together to celebrate the ideals of our forefathers, including the right to "Life, Liberty and the Pursuit of Happiness." All across America, my countrymen celebrate Independence Day with picnics, parades, and fireworks.

Our Independence Day is an occasion to look back at our history and development. I'm especially pleased to be in Macau as one could say this was one of the starting points of U.S. engagement in Asia. On July 3, 1844 – the day before our Independence Day – my country signed its first treaty with China. The Treaty of Wanghsia was negotiated and signed right here in Macau by U.S. Minister Caleb Cushing and Viceroy of Canton Ki Ying. A replica of the stone table they used for the signing ceremony is still in one of the terraced gardens of Guan Yin Temple, not far from where we are gathered tonight. Macau then became an important destination for the original American business community in China, which brought their families to Macau to live. Among them were the grandparents of our great president, Franklin Delano Roosevelt, whose mother spent part of her childhood here.

The American business community in Macau is again growing with increased U.S. investment and presence. It is therefore fitting to bring together our Macanese friends and my countrymen, including the American Chamber of Commerce's Macau committee. Such receptions are only a small part of our interaction. The U.S. Consulate General has an active presence here in the form of the American Corner for U.S.-related exhibits, talks by Consulate staffs, and video conferences. The Corner also provides teaching and reference materials for anyone interested in the United States. And we will be looking at ways to expand our contacts in the coming year.

This past year, Macau welcomed the first U.S. scholar under the Fulbright program, one of the world's largest academic exchanges. Fulbright grants allow Americans to study and lecture abroad; and foreign nationals to study in the U.S. Next fall, an American "junior scholar" will begin a ten-month research grant here. We are encouraged by this progress and hope to give many more American scholars the opportunity to discover your academic institutions.

Source: http://hongkong.usconsulate.gov/cg_jc2006070601.html

Question

5. According to the speech by U.S. Consul General Cunningham, how did the culture of Macau come in contact with American culture?

Document 6

EXCERPT FROM THE CAMP DAVID ACCORDS

**THE CAMP DAVID ACCORDS
THE FRAMEWORK FOR PEACE IN THE MIDDLE EAST**

Muhammad Anwar al-Sadat, President of the Arab Republic of Egypt, and Menachem Begin, Prime Minister of Israel, met with Jimmy Carter, President of the United States of America, at Camp David from September 5 to September 17, 1978, and have agreed on the following framework for peace in the Middle East. They invite other parties to the Arab-Israel conflict to adhere to it.

Preamble

The search for peace in the Middle East must be guided by the following:

- The agreed basis for a peaceful settlement of the conflict between Israel and its neighbors in United Nations Security Council Resolution 242, in all its parts.
- After four wars during 30 years, despite intensive human efforts, the Middle East, which is the cradle of civilization and the birthplace of three great religions, does not enjoy the blessings of peace. The people of the Middle East yearn for peace so that the vast human and natural resources of the region can be turned to the pursuits of peace and so that this area can become a model for the coexistence and cooperation among nations.

- The historic initiative of President Sadat in visiting Jerusalem and the reception accorded to him by the parliament, government and people of Israel, and the reciprocal visit of Prime Minister Begin to Ismailia, the peace proposals made by both leaders, as well as the warm reception of these missions by the peoples of both countries, have created an unprecedented opportunity for peace which must not be lost if this generation and future generations are to be spared the tragedies of war.
- The provisions of the Charter of the United Nations and the other accepted norms of international law and legitimacy now provide accepted standards for the conduct of relations among all states.
- To achieve a relationship of peace, in the spirit of Article 2 of the United Nations Charter, future negotiations between Israel and any neighbor prepared to negotiate peace and security with it are necessary for the purpose of carrying out all the provisions and principles of Resolutions 242 and 338.
- Peace requires respect for the sovereignty, territorial integrity and political independence of every state in the area and their right to live in peace within secure and recognized boundaries free from threats or acts of force. Progress toward that goal can accelerate movement toward a new era of reconciliation in the Middle East marked by cooperation in promoting economic development, in maintaining stability and in assuring security.
- Security is enhanced by a relationship of peace and by cooperation between nations which enjoy normal relations. In addition, under the terms of peace treaties, the parties can, on the basis of reciprocity, agree to special security arrangements such as demilitarized zones, limited armaments areas, early warning stations, the presence of international forces, liaison, agreed measures for monitoring and other arrangements that they agree are useful.

Source: Excerpt from the Camp David Accords (taken from www.jimmycarterlibrary.org/documents/campdavid/accords.phtml)

Questions

6. a. According to the Introduction and Preamble to the Camp David Accords, who specifically met with President Jimmy Carter?
  b. Briefly explain two goals of the Preamble.

Document 7

EXCERPT FROM A TRAVEL GUIDE ABOUT JERUSALEM

It is in the midst of these two contrasting halves that the Old City is to be found: with the exception of the museums on the western edge of town, most of Jerusalem's main sights are found here. Into this small area of land, less than one square kilometre (200 acres), is crammed a labyrinth of streets enclosed within walls of limestone dating back to the 16th century and the reign of the Ottoman ruler Suleiman the Magnificent. This, the focus of all Jerusalem's historical and religious divisions, is where the majority of visitors to the city will spend most of their time. The Old City is divided into quarters, named after the four communities that inhabited it during the Middle Ages: Arab, Jewish, Christian and Armenian. Its network of winding streets offers the chance to step back almost literally in time to savour the feel of cheek-by-jowl Middle Eastern Life. Within yards, you may wander from the hustle and bustle of an Arab souk into the quiet calm of an Armenian…

Excerpt from a travel guide about Jerusalem (taken from http://www.cityguidetravel-guides.com/city/59/city_guide/Middle-East/Jerusalem.html)

Question	**7.** According to the excerpt what religious groups have influenced the city of Jerusalem?

Part B: Essay

Directions: Write a well-organized essay that includes an introduction, several paragraphs, and a conclusion. Use evidence from *at least four* documents in the body of the essay. Support your response with relevant facts, examples, and details. Include additional outside information.

Historical Context

Just as individuals have distinct identities, so, too, do individual world cultures. Throughout global history, various cultures have impacted the identity of other cultures, sometimes positively, sometimes negatively.

Task

Using information from the documents and your knowledge of global history, answer the questions that follow each document in Part A. Your answers to the questions will help you write the Part B essay, in which you will be asked to

- select any three examples in global history in which two cultures have come in contact
- describe, in each case, if the contact was positive or negative and give specific reasons for your answer

Guidelines

In your essay, be sure to

- address all aspects of the *Task* by accurately analyzing and interpreting *at least four* documents
- incorporate information from the documents in the body of the essay
- incorporate relevant outside information
- support the theme with relevant facts, examples, and details
- use a logical and clear plan of organization
- introduce the theme by establishing a framework that is beyond a simple restatement of the *Task* or *Historical Context* and conclude with a summation of the theme

CHAPTER 16

Newly Emerging Nations in Africa and Asia

The victory of Ghana President Kwame Nkrumah in Accra, Ghana, 1961.

After World War II, independence movements successfully ended European imperialism in Africa and Asia. The newly emerging nations varied from region to region, each one interpreting nationhood in a different way. Under colonialism, many colonial citizens had served in the European imperial armies or worked in colonial bureaucracies. Others acquired new skills working in cities or studying in European schools. They became influenced by Western European ideas, particularly nationalism. These groups began to imagine unified nations, transferred their loyalties from traditional authorities, and formed elite groups that would lead the independence movements to form new governments.

Successful independence movements in Asia had encouraged Africans to create their own nations. Some nationalists adopted the nonviolent tactics of Gandhi in India and used passive resistance, while others employed violence using guerilla warfare. The Europeans, who were recovering from World War II, could not afford a long struggle to maintain their African possessions. They began to prepare their colonies for independence.

In 1957 Ghana (formerly the Gold Coast) was the first to gain its independence. By 1977, with over forty independent nations in **Africa**, European colonialism ended. The colonial legacy left problems for the newly independent nations to resolve. Most of these countries were based on the artificial borders created by the Europeans. Ethnic groups and tribes were often divided into two or more "nations" by the arbitrary divisions made by the colonial powers. This resulted in rivalries between the many ethnic and religious groups within many new countries. Many nations had hundreds of languages, customs, religions, and ethnic groups within their borders.

Some African leaders tried to resolve these problems by outlawing all but one political party as a means of unifying the diverse populations. This was not viewed as undemocratic but as a way of including everyone in creating a stable government. In other nations, elections were corrupt and failed to produce any real national consensus. This led to bitter and often bloody conflicts between rival groups. In many African nations, the military overthrew the government and established a dictatorship. These often proved brutal, corrupt, and ineffective and were later overthrown by rival military leaders. These bloody civil wars between military leaders frequently devastated African nations.

In 1960, there was a call for **Pan-Africanism**. This movement was an attempt by various leaders to join all African peoples together in order to improve economic, political, and social conditions throughout the continent. Nationalism, however, often proved a stumbling block to this goal. In 1963, the **Organization of African Unity (OAU)** was created to foster cooperation and unity between African nations in order to achieve progress. It was disbanded in 2002 and replaced by the **African Union (AU)**, a far more effective organization with a membership of fifty-three nations. Despite these efforts, many African nations witnessed regular periods of violent conflict, sometimes resulting in **genocide** (the deliberate attempt to exterminate a people or group). The proliferation of weapons since the end of the Cold War (1989) has expanded conflicts throughout the continent, destabilizing regions even further.

> **Main Idea:** Successful independence movements in Asia had encouraged Africans to create their own nations.

European decolonization had very different results in Asia, the home of many ancient civilizations and empires. The various Western philosophies of capitalism, secularism, socialism, communism, and, of course, nationalism have been influential throughout the continent.

Ataturk's legacy of nationalism and secularism has continued in Turkey, although it has come under increasing criticism in recent years. The policies of persecution and legal harassment of the majority of Turkey's non-Turkish Christian minorities, the recent government war against the Muslim Kurds, and the occupation of the island of Cyprus, further advanced the nationalist agenda of the succeeding Turkish governments under the direction of the military. Popular protest, support for pro-Islamic parties, the inability of these governments to reform the economy, and Turkey's failure to join the European Union, have indicated a weakening of nationalist appeal and a growing awareness among the population of the need for change.

In the Middle East, the Arab-Israeli conflict, in particular the Palestinian situation, has created wide divisions and high tensions in the region. The rise in terrorism by Islamic fundamentalist groups has greatly benefited from the Palestinian problem, which has served as propaganda to create Arab hatred for Israel and the United States. The terrorists, funded in the past by Arab states such as Saudi Arabia, have now started to pose a threat to those regimes as well. Further complicating the situation is the U.S. occupation of Iraq, whose feuding groups are making a transition to democracy difficult, while Iran is funding terrorism and trying to gain nuclear weapons.

South Asia's traditional conflicts among religious (Hindus, Muslims), ethnic (Tamils, Sinhalese), and national (Indonesians, East Timorese) groups have limited economic growth and political stability.

The nations of Southeast Asia, on the other hand, are recovering from the wars and genocides of the recent past. Vietnam is struggling to transform its economy from a Communist to capitalist system while trying to maintain its authoritarian political structure. Cambodia, however, has rid itself of its Communist past with the final defeat of the Khmer Rouge and is slowly modernizing under a constitutional monarchy.

In East Asia, China is trying to become a capitalist economic giant but remains limited by its large population and totalitarian government. Japan's miraculous postwar economic growth has been slowed down and frustrated by changing world markets, growing competition, limited resources, and changes in Japanese society. South Korea continues to develop a strong economy, but the North, under the brutal dictatorship of Kim Jong Il, remains an impoverished military state whose nuclear ambitions are being increasingly viewed as a threat to regional stability and world peace.

Central Asia's newly independent nations have developed in different ways. Kazakhstan, Kyrgyzstan, and Uzbekistan are developing capitalist economies and democratic societies with varying degrees of success, but Tajikistan is still hampered by an ongoing struggle with Islamic fundamentalists, while impoverished Turkmenistan has become a brutal dictatorship.

Finally, in Transcaucasia, religious and civil conflicts have greatly hampered these nations' efforts to modernize into capitalist democracies. The con-

Main Idea: European decolonization had very different results in Asia, the home of many ancient civilizations and empires.

Main Idea: Kazakhstan, Kyrgyzstan, and Uzbekistan are developing capitalist economies and democratic societies with varying degrees of success, but Tajikistan is still hampered by an ongoing struggle with Islamic fundamentalists, while impoverished Turkmenistan has become a brutal dictatorship.

tinuing war in Nagorno-Karabakh has greatly limited the development of both Armenia and Azerbaijan into prosperous modern states, despite the latter's potential oil wealth. Georgia's battles with rebellious regions has also had a negative effect on that nation. The leadership of its American-educated president has, however, improved internal stability and diplomatic relations with the rest of the world.

SECTION 1

Africa

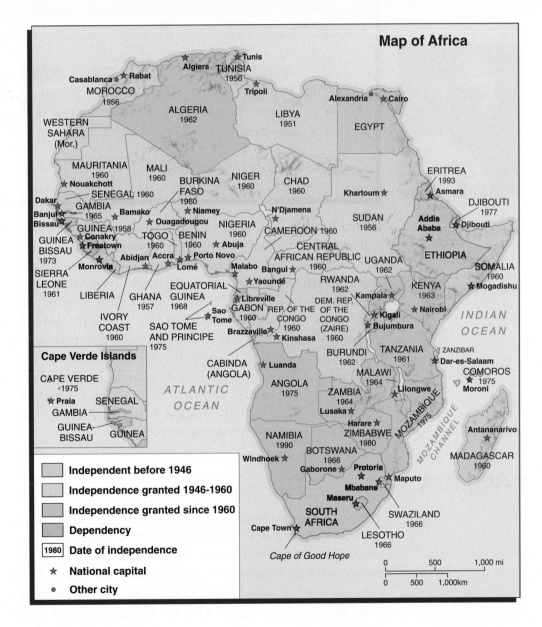

Map of Africa

Independent before 1946

Independence granted 1946-1960

Independence granted since 1960

Dependency

1980 Date of independence

★ National capital

• Other city

GHANA

TIMELINE OF EVENTS

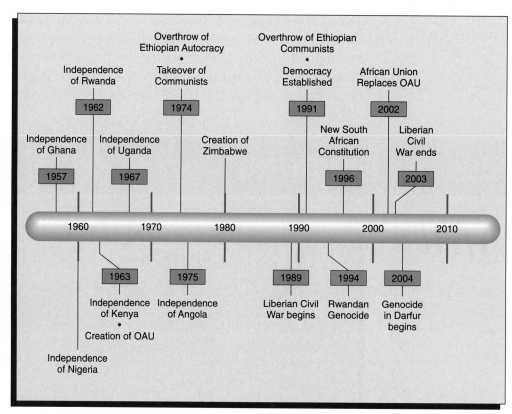

Overthrow of Ethiopian Autocracy
•

Overthrow of Ethiopian Communists
•

Independence of Rwanda — **1962**

Takeover of Communists — **1974**

Democracy Established — **1991**

African Union Replaces OAU — **2002**

Independence of Ghana — **1957**

Independence of Uganda — **1967**

Creation of Zimbabwe

New South African Constitution — **1996**

Liberian Civil War ends — **2003**

1960   1970   1980   1990   2000   2010

1963

1975

1989

1994

2004

Independence of Kenya

Independence of Angola

Liberian Civil War begins

Rwandan Genocide

Genocide in Darfur begins

• Creation of OAU

Independence of Nigeria

Kwame Nkrumah, Ghanaian politician, addressing the plenary meeting of the United Nations' Assembly in New York City, September 1960.

Ghana became a republic in 1960. President **Kwame Nkrumah** built hospitals and schools while promoting developmental projects. He ran the country into debt, however, and jailed his opponents when accused of corruption. Nkrumah was given dictatorial powers in 1964 and created a one-party Socialist state. In 1966, he was overthrown by the military. This was followed by a series of military coups. Several of these were led by **Jerry Rawlings**, who eventually assumed dictatorial powers. He suspended the constitution and instituted programs that decreased the deficit over the next ten years. In 1992, Rawlings returned the country to civilian rule, and elections were held. Rawlings was elected president in 1992 and 1996. In 2000, **John Agyekum Kufuor** was elected president, setting up the **National Reconciliation Commission** to review human rights abuses during military rule.

NIGERIA

In 1960, **Nigeria** was granted independence by the British government. Almost immediately, regional and ethnic differences led to conflict. The northern region, which had the largest population, consisted of the **Hausa** and **Fulani** people who took control of the Federal government. This led to much resentment by the **Ibo** people in the southeast and the **Yoruba** in the southwest. In 1966, there was a coup, led by Ibo military officers and violent persecutions against the Ibo people living in the north were led by Hausa soldiers. **General Ojukwu**, leader of the Ibo, declared eastern Nigeria the independent **Republic of Biafra**. This led to a civil war in which over one million Biafrans died as a result of Nigerian invasion.

From 1970 to 1989, the country was ruled by various military dictators. In 1989, the incumbent president, **General Ibrahim Babangida,** again allowed political parties to register. When elections were held in the summer of 1993, the results were voided by Babangida. After much turmoil and protest, he resigned, and a provisional government was created. That government was overthrown the same year. In 1999, Nigeria returned to civilian government with democratic elections. **Olusegun Obasanjo**, promising reforms, was elected president. The popular leader was reelected in 2003 despite his failure to keep his promises. The government has faced increasing violence in the northern states as Muslim fanatics have tried to impose Islamic law on the region and continue to persecute the Christian minority there. In addition, the Hausa-Yoruba tribal conflict has threatened to destabilize other regions in the nation.

SIERRA LEONE

In 1961, **Sierra Leone** became an independent republic. It was a functioning democracy until 1978 when a one-party state was created. Protests against the government by students and public employees from 1984 to 1985 led to riots and the restoration of multiparty elections.

In 1991, Sierra Leone was attacked by murderous rebels, calling themselves the **Revolutionary United Front (RUF)**. By July of 1999, the RUF had taken over half the country including diamond mines, which they looted and marketed through Liberia. In May of 1997, the army briefly overthrew President **Ahmad Tejan Kabbah**, who was restored to power by a coalition of Nigerian-led West African troops. The coalition then assisted Kabbah against the RUF. In 2000, the RUF was defeated. In 2001, the Parliament with United Nations and British support extended Kabbah's term for six months, while the RUF was disarmed with the help of UN troops. While some RUF rebels continued to fight in the East, the Civil War had ended, and Kabbah was overwhelmingly reelected in May of 2002.

RWANDA

In 1962, **Rwanda** became an independent nation. Plagued by conflict between the **Tutsi** people, who had established a powerful monarchy in the fifteenth century, and the **Hutus**, whom they had forced into serfdom, Rwanda's history is one of violence and vengeance. Under European rule (first Germany and then Belgium), Tutsi domination continued until the 1950s, when they resisted Belgium's attempts to implement democratic institutions. In 1959, the Hutus revolted against the monarchy in a bloody civil war, which led to a mass exodus of Tutsis. In 1961, the Hutus won a UN referendum, which granted them full autonomy. In July, Rwanda became an independent state. In 1990, Tutsi refugees from Uganda fought with its army to return to Rwanda. By 1993, over one million people had been displaced, and a cease-fire and amnesty paved the way for political reform. A new Rwandan constitution, allowing for a multiparty democracy went into effect in June of 1992. A proposal was signed to merge the Hutu armies of the government and the Tutsi **Rwandan Patriotic Front** in 1993.

In April of 1994, the Hutu president of Rwanda was killed, and civil war was renewed. The Hutu Army of Rwanda and Hutu militias were driven into neighboring countries by the Tutsi Patriotic Front. The Hutus reportedly slaughtered over 500,000 as they were driven out. By the time a Tutsi-dominated multiethnic "government of national unity" was established, over a million people were dead and three million were refugees. This became known as the **Rwandan genocide**. Despite the efforts of the government to maintain unity, reprisal killings by Tutsis followed.

In 1996, the government in neighboring Zaire collapsed, and its military began to expel the Tutsi community of 400,000 that had been there since the eighteenth century. The Tutsi resisted and gained support from the Rwandan government, which resulted in a war between Rwanda and Zaire. Five hundred thousand Hutu militia men and other refugees fled Zaire back to Rwanda. Blaming the Tutsis for their refugee status, the Hutu militia men began slaughtering Tutsis in Rwanda. By 1999, the Hutu rebellion was defeated by the Rwandan government. In April of 2000, **Paul Kagame** was elected the first Tutsi president of Rwanda; he was reelected in 2003. Despite the efforts of the Kagame government to maintain peace and unity, tensions remain high between the two groups. Several UN-sponsored tribunals to investigate the Rwandan genocide and punish those responsible for it, have had little success.

Main Idea:
By the time a Tutsi-dominated multiethnic "government of national unity" was established, over a million people were dead and three million were refugees.

KENYA

President of Kenya in Nairobi, Kenya in 1971.

In 1963, **Kenya** was granted independence. The following year it became a republic in the British Commonwealth of nations, and **Jomo Kenyatta** became its first president. The various ethnic groups in Kenya (the **Kikuiu**, the **Luo**, the **Masai**, the **Kalenjin**, and others) had many traditional animosities between them. Kenyatta, a Kikuiu, urged his people to forget their ethnic loyalties and accept a principle he called **harambee** ("pulling together"). Kenyatta died in 1975 and was succeeded by **Daniel Arap Moi**. Kenya's political parties represented major ethnic groups, which served to prolong the ethnic rivalries. In 1982, the nation was declared a one-party state with the only legal political organization being the **Kenya African National Union (KANU)**.

In 1991, a constitutional amendment established a multiparty system. This resulted in factionalism and frequent fraud during elections. Moi, elected to his fourth term in December of 1992, dissolved the multiparty legislature in January of 1993. He was reelected in 1999 but was prohibited by the constitution to run in 2002. The opposition leader, **Mwai Kibaki**, won the election by promising to end corruption, but he has made little progress toward that goal. The government has been unable to control local ethnic conflicts within Kenya, and the nation is considered one of the top human rights violators in the world.

UGANDA

Idi Amin Dada.

In 1967, a new constitution proclaimed **Uganda** an independent republic. Its first president **Milton Obote** was overthrown in 1971, by **General Idi Amin Dada,** who established a military dictatorship. Declaring himself "president," Amin dissolved the parliament and assumed absolute powers. In 1972, he expelled Uganda's Asians (people of Indian and Pakistani descent), who controlled most of the country's small businesses. Most other nations including the United States, broke off diplomatic relations with Uganda in 1973. In 1976, Amin declared himself "President for Life." His eight-year rule was marked by extreme violence, and the persecution of political and tribal opponents (as many as 300,000 may have been killed between 1971 and 1979). The country's prosperous agricultural, mining, and commercial economy was destroyed. Its infrastructure, which included an excellent road and rail network built by the British, fell into ruins. Amin's personal behavior, which included sadistic practices and cannibalism, marked him internationally as a madman. In 1978, Amin, with the aide of Libyan troops, invaded Tanzania, which countered by invading Uganda. Supported by the vast majority of Ugandans who hated Amin, Tanzanian forces defeated and drove Amin into exile in 1979.

In January 1986, **Yoweri Museveni** organized a new government, which restored order. With help from the World Bank and the International Monetary Fund (IMF), he began to rebuild Uganda's economy and society. Museveni was reelected in 1996, and Uganda became one of the fastest growing economies in Africa. In June 2001, Museveni was reelected again. Since 2002, the Ugandan government has fought against the **Lord's Resistance Army**, a militia largely made up of the **Acholi tribe** led by **Joseph Kony** seeking to establish a theocracy based upon the Ten Commandments. His methods though have included mass kidnapping, rape, and murder.

ANGOLA

Jonas Malheiro Savimbi (1934–2002) led UNITA, an anti-Communist rebel group that fought against the MPLA in the Angolan Civil War until his assassination in 2002.

In 1975, **Angola** was granted independence by Portugal. A civil war between several independence groups led to the victory of the **Movement for the Liberation of Angola (MPLA)** in 1976, which organized a Marxist state with Soviet funding and Cuban technical and military support. Large portions of the country remained in the hands of the **National Union for the Total Independence of Angola (UNITA)**, which continued the civil war through the 1980s with Chinese and American support. Cuban troops withdrew from Angola between 1989 and 1991 and a cease-fire between the government and UNITA was concluded in 1991. In September 1992 Angola held its first elections since 1975.

The victory of the MPLA candidate and the refusal of UNITA's leader **Jonas Savimbi** to accept the results led to renewed fighting. Despite efforts by UN peacekeepers, the conflict continued until 2002, taking over one hundred thousand lives. Savimbi's death in February 2002 resulted in an end to the long civil war and the demobilization of UNITA.

ZIMBABWE

Robert Mugabe, second President of Zimbabwe.

Main Idea:
Mugabe's unpopular leadership has decimated the nation's economy and has become in reality a dictatorship.

In 1980, the newly created state of **Zimbabwe** held its first elections. The **Zimbabwe African National Union (ZANU)** won a clear majority, and its leader **Robert Mugabe** became prime minister. As Mugabe began a program of national reconstruction, opposition leader **Joshua Nkomo** and his **Zimbabwe African Peoples Union (ZAPU)**, continued to engage in sporadic warfare against the government. The elections of 1985 increased ZANU's majority in parliament, and in 1987 the constitution was amended strengthening the presidency and ending the separate seats held for whites in government. After elections, the new parliament lacked any white representation, and guerillas began attacks on white-owned farms. In December of 1987, Mugabe and Nkomo agreed to merge their political parties, creating a one-party state under Mugabe. Opposition grew as inflation and unemployment rose to over 50 percent. In 2000, voters rejected a new constitution that would grant Mugabe twelve more years and the right to seize white-owned farms without compensation. Ignoring the government, black squatters, often criminals, began occupying white-owned farms and driving out the owners. The government's policy of encouraging the illegal seizure of white-owned farms resulted in the decline of the nation's tobacco harvest, which further hurt the economy. In the elections of 2000, the opposition gained enough seats to block any new legislation, but Mugabe continued to encourage the seizure of white-owned farms and the arrests of political opponents.

In March of 2002, Mugabe won a highly questionable victory over his principle opponent **Morgan Tsuangirai**. The army tortured and raped thousands of Tsuangirai supporters, preventing many from voting. Mugabe's policies led to the worst famine in sixty years. Over three hundred members of the opposition were illegally arrested, which led to an unsuccessful general strike in June 2003. Completely destroying any opposition, Mugabe easily won reelection in April of 2005, which was followed by a violent crackdown against thousands of poor people in the cities. Mugabe's unpopular leadership has decimated the nation's economy and has become in reality a dictatorship.

SOUTH AFRICA

Nelson Mandela (1918–), South African President (1994–1999) and Black political leader.

Unlike the other nations of Africa, South Africa, Ethiopia, and Liberia are older established nations that did not have the same experience with European imperialism. Their development was different from those nations that were artificially created by colonialism.

In May of 1996, **South Africa** completed the transition to full democracy when it approved a permanent constitution, which created a strong central government, an independent judiciary, and a Bill of Rights with one of the widest guarantees of freedom in the world. The South African Bill of Rights includes the right to adequate food, housing, water, health care, and education. During the **apartheid era**, there had been legal separation of races in South Africa.

In June of 1999, South Africa held its second post-apartheid election. The **African National Congress (ANC)** won a huge victory, taking the majority of

Thabo Mvuyelwa Mbeki
(1942 –), President of the
Republic of South Africa.

Haile Selassie
(1892–1975), Emperor of
Ethiopia from 1930 to
1974.

Malnourishment in
Ethiopia.

seats in the national assembly. **Thabo Mbeki**, who replaced Nelson Mandela as ANC party chief, was elected the new president of South Africa. The 2004 elections reelected the ANC with an even larger majority, despite the government's involvement in several scandals and its reluctance to approve a bill that would provide free drugs to AIDS sufferers. The Mbeki government continues to try to balance the conflicting needs of South Africa's various racial, ethnic, and political groups as well as address the enduring effects of the apartheid era.

ETHIOPIA

In 1941, **Ethiopia** was liberated from Italian control and **Emperor Haile Selassie** returned to his throne. Civil unrest erupted in February of 1974, and in September Selassie was deposed. A coalition of urban elites and the armed forces took over, abolishing the monarchy in 1975. The power of the Ethiopian Orthodox Church was limited. Land reform was instituted, and a socialist state was proclaimed. In 1977, Ethiopian Communists under the leadership of **Colonel Mengistu Haile Mariam** seized power and established a provisional military council. From 1977 to 1978 a period of **"Red Terror"** followed as thousands of the regime's opponents were arrested and executed. In 1976, Ethiopia and the U.S.S.R. began a military alliance. In 1977, Somalia invaded Ethiopia trying to reclaim certain disputed areas of the country. With strong Soviet support and Cuban troops, the Somalis were expelled by March of 1978. Mengistu continued to repress the population brutally in order to prevent any uprising against his unpopular regime. Like Stalin in the 1930s, he used man-made famine as a means of exterminating the independent farming class and crushing any future opposition by the populace. Mengistu outlawed all forms of religion and vigorously persecuted the Ethiopian Church.

The province of **Eritrea,** which had been part of the Ethiopian Empire since 1962, had started to reclaim its independence after Selassie's overthrow. By 1991, Eritrean forces had gained control of all its traditional territory, including Ethiopia's outlets to the sea. Another rebel group, the **Ethiopian People's Revolutionary Democratic Front (EPRDF)**, which wanted autonomy for **Tigre**, a northern region between Ethiopia and Eritrea, launched a major offensive in 1991 as well. This forced Mengistu to flee the country, allowing the rebel forces to enter the country unopposed in May.

The years of civil war and famine had destroyed Ethiopia economically and socially. A transitional government was installed to create a new constitution in July of 1991 recognizing Eritrean independence. In June of 1992, the country's first multiparty elections were held. They were so badly mishandled that many political groups withdrew from the government. By June of 1994, the EPRDF won a vast majority in the Ethiopian Parliament, and its leader, **Meles Zenawi** became premier. A small border war with Eritrea in May–June 1998 had become a major conflict by 1999. It only ended in June of 2000 when the International Court restored the 1998 borders between the two nations. In May 2005, charges of fraud in the elections led to violence and tarnished the government's image.

LIBERIA

Main Idea:
By early 1999, Taylor had been condemned by most of the international community for his repressive rule and aiding rebels in Sierra Leone. In return for his support, the rebels shared the profits from their illegal diamond trade.

In its first 100 years of independence, **Liberia** succeeded in protecting its borders from British and French attempts to expand on their territory. Although the descendants of freed American slaves are a minority in Liberia's diverse population, they have consistently dominated the country's political life. **William V. S. Tubman** was elected president in 1944 and served until his death in 1971, successfully steering Liberia through the post-war era of African nationalism and decolonization. He was succeeded by **William R. Tolbert, Jr.**, who was overthrown in a military coup led by **Master Sergeant Samuel K. Doe**. Doe suspended the constitution and imposed martial law. Presidential elections were held in October 1985 under the terms of a new constitution, which allowed universal suffrage for the first time. Doe and his party won a landslide victory in November and the **Second Republic** under the new constitution began in January 1986.

In December 1989, antigovernment guerillas of the **National Patriotic Forces of Liberia** (NPFL), led by **Charles Taylor**, crossed the border from the Ivory Coast and began a huge ethnic war. A peacekeeping force of the **Economic Community of West African States** (ECOWAS) landed in the Liberian capital city of **Monrovia** in August to mediate the cease-fire and prepare for free elections. In September, Doe was killed, but a cease-fire was finally agreed upon in November of 1990.

From 1990 to 1992, Charles Taylor strengthened his power over Liberia despite the establishment of a democratic government by the West African States. By 1993, the government and ECOWAS forces succeeded in containing Taylor's forces. An interim coalition government was established, but elections were never held because extensive fighting continued until late 1996. Up to this time, over 150,000 had died in the civil conflict. In early 1997, ECOWAS restored order. In the elections of July 1997, Taylor won a landslide victory but then attempted to arrest an opposition leader, which led to fighting in the capital city. By early 1999, Taylor had been condemned by most of the international community for his repressive rule and aiding rebels in Sierra Leone. In return for his support, the rebels shared the profits from their illegal diamond trade.

In August 2003, Taylor was forced into exile by ECOWAS and international pressure. An interim government was set up, but elections were not held until late 2005.

GENOCIDE IN SUDAN AND DARFUR

Since 1989, when **Lieutenant General Omar Ahmed el-Bashir** seized power, the nation of Sudan has been involved in a civil war that has led to the genocide of both minorities and independent farmers. A heavily Sunni Muslim country (70 percent), the government has continually tried to impose Islamic law **(Sharia)** on the entire country, including the south, which practices Christianity and traditional African religions (30 percent). This is further complicated by the fact that, even though most of the Sudanese population is mixed racially, the culture of the north is Arab, whereas in the south (including the southern Muslims of **Darfur**), it is black. Despite attempts by the United Nations and the international community to mediate a peace, the Bashir government continued to use its military superiority to kill thousands who opposed the imposition of Islamic law.

In 2004, the Sudanese government began a war with the people of the Darfur region, arming and encouraging Darfuri Arab tribal militiamen to attack Darfuri farming villages. Even though both sides were Muslim, it was clear by 2005 that the Bashir regime was using genocide as a means of crushing the traditional independence of the Darfur region. Despite calls for an end to the genocide by the United Nations, a number of human rights groups, and the international community, the killing in Darfur continues as there is reluctance on the part of the world community to send military forces to resolve the situation. Thousands of refugees have left their homes in search of safety in temporary camps. The situation in the camps is very difficult with concerns about food shortages, medical care, sanitation, and security.

SECTION 2

Middle East

TURKEY

TIMELINE OF EVENTS

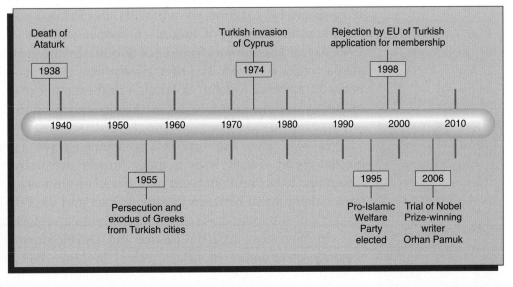

Kemal Ataturk (1881–1938), Turkish soldier and statesman. In uniform as the Supreme Commander of the Turkish Armed Forces, 1922.

After **Ataturk's** death in 1938, **Turkey** remained a republic controlled by the military. After World War II, it became a major recipient of American aid under the **Truman Doctrine** and **Marshall Plan** (see Chapter 12, "The Cold War"). Turkey became a member of **NATO** and remained staunchly anti-Communist. In 1955, a violent persecution of the Greek population in the cities of western Turkey, in particular **Istanbul**, led to the forced exodus of most of the Hellenic community, which had been there from ancient times. This was followed by near conflict with Greece when the Greek majority on the island of **Cyprus** tried to annex themselves to mainland Greece. (A UN-sponsored agreement, guaranteeing the

Main Idea:
Turkey also forced the resettlement of Greek and Turkish Cypriots as well as bringing settlers from the mainland to expand the Turkish population. These actions were condemned by the international community and are one of the reasons that member nations will not accept Turkey in the European Union.

rights of the Greek majority and Turkish minority, made the island an independent nation in 1960). In 1974, Turkish troops invaded Cyprus, occupying the northeastern 40 percent of the island. They justified this action by claiming they were responding to an attempted overthrow of the government by Greek nationalists. The United States cut off military aid to Turkey in 1975, and the UN condemned the invasion, refusing to recognize the puppet state Turkey had established in northern Cyprus. Turkey also forced the resettlement of Greek and Turkish Cypriots as well as bringing settlers from the mainland to expand the Turkish population. These actions were condemned by the international community and are one of the reasons that member nations will not accept Turkey in the European Union.

Throughout the postwar period, Turkey alternated between civil and military governments. Martial law was imposed in 1978 as a result of mounting protest and violence. The military ruled Turkey from 1980 to 1983. Even though Turkey supported the United States in the **Persian Gulf War in 1991**, it continued to persecute its **Kurdish** population in the north. This led to serious violence between Kurdish nationalists and the Turkish government in 1992–1993. Under **Tansu Ciller**, Turkey's first-ever woman prime minister elected in 1994, military operations against Kurdish rebels intensified, including an attack into Iraq by fifty thousand Turkish troops. This nationalist policy was popular in Turkey; nevertheless the economy continued to decline.

In December 1995, the Ciller government collapsed in a corruption scandal and elections put the pro-Islamic **Refah (Welfare) Party** in power. After months of unsuccessful coalition governments, the Refah leader **Necmettim Erbakan** became prime minister of Turkey's first openly pro-Islamic government in June 1996. A year later he was forced out of office by the Turkish military, which created a fragile coalition. The new government closed some Islamic schools and banned traditional Muslim clothing. A further source of tension was the rejection of Turkey's application to enter the **European Union** in 1998. In 1999, that government fell due to corruption charges, and an interim government was formed.

In May 2000, the Turkish Parliament elected a new president, **Ahmet Necdet Sezer**. Faced with a mass hunger strike by political prisoners in December 2000, President Sezer announced an amnesty plan to release 72,000. A personal argument between President Sezer and the Prime Minister in 2001 led to a serious economic crisis that forced foreign investors to pull out of Turkey.

Main Idea:
The Turkish government continues to face external pressure over its human rights record, while pursuing entry into the European Union and internal pressure over its struggling economy and the growing influence of pro-Islamic political parties.

In November 2002 the **Justice and Development Party** formed the first majority government in fifteen years. In June 2003, in an attempt to win European Union approval, the Turkish Parliament voted to allow limited civil rights for the Kurds and granted amnesty to former Kurdish nationalist fighters. In June 2004, however, sporadic violence between Kurdish nationalists and the Turkish troops began again. In 2006, the world-famous Turkish writer **Orhan Pamuk**, who had acknowledged the **Armenian genocide** of 1915 and other massacres that successive Turkish governments had committed, was arrested for "anti-Turkish propaganda." His trial attracted international attention and extremely negative press, forcing the Turkish court to acquit him. The Turkish government continues to face external pressure over its human rights record, while pursuing entry into the European Union and internal pressure over its struggling economy and the growing influence of pro-Islamic political parties.

TIMELINE OF EVENTS

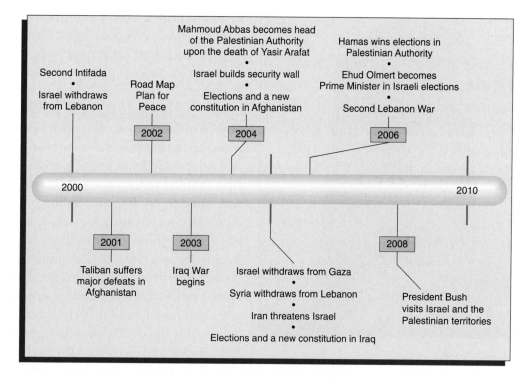

Mahmoud Abbas becomes head of the Palestinian Authority upon the death of Yasir Arafat
•
Israel builds security wall
•
Elections and a new constitution in Afghanistan

Hamas wins elections in Palestinian Authority
•
Ehud Olmert becomes Prime Minister in Israeli elections
•
Second Lebanon War

Second Intifada
•
Israel withdraws from Lebanon

Road Map Plan for Peace

| 2002 | 2004 | 2006 |

2000   2010

| 2001 | 2003 | 2008 |

Taliban suffers major defeats in Afghanistan

Iraq War begins

Israel withdraws from Gaza
•
Syria withdraws from Lebanon
•
Iran threatens Israel

President Bush visits Israel and the Palestinian territories

Elections and a new constitution in Iraq

A second **intifada** emerged in 2000, similar to the one begun in 1987. This showed continued Palestinian resentment against Israel and its perceived occupation and settlement policies. The resentment was seen in deadly terrorist attacks on Jewish civilians. These attacks on innocent people were carried out by **homicide bombers** (often labeled in the media as **suicide bombers**). One Israeli countermeasure was the construction of a barrier, started in 2004, known as the **security wall** or **separation barrier.** This was designed to stop penetration of homicide bombers from the West Bank. It has had much success in reducing

murderous acts. The Israelis also claim that it was necessary since the Palestine Authority has failed to disarm terrorist groups and to prevent their attacks. However, its erection caused bitterness in the Arab world and harsh criticism from several nations outside of the Middle East. Critics condemned it as illegal. However, other nations have constructed similar barriers for various protective purposes and were not widely criticized. Examples are Saudi Arabia, India, Kuwait, Uzbekistan, Botswana, South Korea, England, and the United States.

Jerusalem, the Old City.

New York headquarters of the United Nations.

A more hopeful sign of calm was a **"Roadmap Plan for Peace,"** formulated in 2002. This plan grew out of the **Oslo Accords** of 1993. The plan was to be guided by the United States, Russia, the United Nations, and the European Union. Their goal, as agreed to by Israel and the Palestinians, was to plan for a future Palestinian state. The Palestinians, in the meantime, in turn would adopt democratic reforms, end terrorist actions, and halt the vicious anti-Semitism that was promoted and prevalent in mosques and schools. Israel would stop settler buildups and withdraw from specific areas in the occupied territories. Unfortunately, from 2004 to 2008, the roadmap did not appear to be succeeding. The ruling Palestinian Authority took very little action to prevent armed terrorist groups from committing atrocities against Israelis. Israel, in response to Palestinian violence, carried out house searches, made arrests of suspected terrorists, closed down border crossings, and targeted assassinations of militant leaders. The cycle of attacks and counterattacks resulted in the deaths of many people. The preaching and teaching of anti-Semitism throughout the occupied areas, as well as in most of the Arab world, continued unabated. In the last several years, a number of events have occurred in the Middle East that may likely influence the course of future relations between Israel and the Muslim peoples in the Middle East.

The death of Syrian President **Hafez al-Assad** in 2000 had little effect on the situation. He permitted dangerous radical Arab terrorists within his country. His place was taken by his son, **Bashir al-Assad**, who has shown a slightly more willing attitude in working toward better relations with Israel. Yet, he refuses to grant recognition to Israel and has demanded that Israel return the **Golan Heights** to Syria. He also has allowed terrorist organizations to remain in his country.

The death of **Yasir Arafat** in 2004 had many consequences. As the most significant figure among Palestinians, he was involved in high-level negotiations with Israel, the United States, and many other nations in an attempt to create a Palestinian state and to better the lives of his people. By the time of his death, he had failed to accomplish these goals, as he was not seen as trustworthy by the Americans and the Israelis. His place as head of the Palestinian Authority was taken by **Mahmoud Abbas**. He faces acute challenges in trying to unify his people and in disarming violent militant groups who want to destroy Israel.

Under a decision by Prime Minister **Ariel Sharon**, Israel arranged for the removal of all the over eight thousand Jewish settlers from the **Gaza Strip** in 2005. This entire area would now have limited self-rule under the Palestinian Authority, with the hope of one day becoming part of a Palestinian state. Although some Israelis were against Sharon's decision to evacuate Gaza, the vast majority of the population supported it and hoped it would be seen as a step toward peace by the Palestinians and their supporters in the Arab world and elsewhere. Their hopes were dashed. Palestinian militants have fired rockets

Main Idea: Mahmoud Abbas faces acute challenges in trying to unify his people and in disarming violent militant groups who want to destroy Israel.

from 2005 onward into Israel, causing deaths, severe property damage, and frequent evacuations of school children. The Palestinian Authority appeared to be more interested in maintaining hostility toward Israel than in improving the daily lives of the people it ruled. Examples could be seen in the rocket attacks, the kidnapping of an Israeli soldier, the smuggling of arms from Egypt through tunnels, as well as the failure to build schools, hospitals, and sanitation facilities.

Main Idea:
In November 2005, Iran's President **Mahmoud Ahmadinejad** called for the eradication and destruction of Israel by any means possible.

In November 2005, Iran's President **Mahmoud Ahmadinejad** called for the eradication and destruction of Israel by any means possible. This was seen as a very dangerous pronouncement and a violation of the United Nations Charter. Although no Middle East Arab nation condemned the threat, it was denounced by the United States and many other nations. It was also criticized by then United Nations Secretary-General **Kofi Annan**, who canceled a previously planned trip to Iran. Iran is thought to possess nuclear weapons and has been very reluctant to permit any UN-supervised inspection of its nuclear facilities. It has also supported radical Islamist groups who have carried out homicide bombings in Israel, Argentina, and elsewhere. In the summer of 2006, Iran was condemned as the arms supplier to **Hizballah**, as that Islamist group waged attacks on Israel.

The early months of 2006 witnessed some major developments affecting Arab-Israeli relations. In January, the elections held in the Palestinian territories were won by **Hamas**. This victory was seen, however, as a severe hindrance to the peace process. Labeled as a terrorist group by the United States and the European Union, Hamas staged several homicide bombings over the years that have killed innocent Israelis and some Westerners. Hamas rejects any negotiations with Israel, refuses to recognize any Israeli land claims, and vows to destroy Israel. Hamas has not been willing to recognize Israel, renounce violence, and accept previous agreements. Hamas also presents a problem in the search for unity among all Palestinians. Led by **Ismail Haniya**, Hamas is an Islamic fundamentalist organization that has not gotten along well with the Palestinian **Fatah Party**. Fatah is more of a secular, less religious-oriented party, whose head, Mahmoud Abbas is the President of the Palestinian Authority. He has frequently disagreed with Haniya and has threatened to call for new elections. Yet, Haniya was warned that such a threat could lead to a civil war. This would not be a surprising development, as shootings and killings between the two Palestinian groups have occurred throughout 2006. This disunity among Palestinians is one reason why Israel feels it has no "peace partner" with whom it can deal. January was also a crucial month for Israel, as was March. Early in January, Prime Minister Ariel Sharon was hospitalized with a severe stroke. He was thus unable to run for office in the national elections scheduled for March. In his place, **Ehud Olmert**, the former mayor of Jerusalem ran for Prime Minister and won. He has stated that he is willing, if Hamas continues its antagonistic policies, to unilaterally fix Israel's eastern border in the near future. This means that Israel would take action by itself to decide a location in the West Bank where it would establish a border. However, the consideration of such action receded into the background in late 2006, as Israel was more concerned with the fighting that broke out in the summer. This has been called, among other names, the **Second Lebanon War**.

Main Idea:
Shootings and killings between the two Palestinian groups have occurred throughout 2006. This disunity among Palestinians is one reason why Israel feels it has no "peace partner" with whom it can deal.

The Second Lebanon War lasted for thirty-four days, July to August 2006.

It has been labeled a "second war" because Israel had previously, in 1982, fought in Lebanon. However, to call each of these struggles a "Lebanon War" is misleading. The governments of Israel and Lebanon did not go to war against each other. No shots were fired between soldiers of the two nations. Yet, most of the fighting occurred in Lebanon. Why was this so? It was because Israel in 2006 was attacked by Hizballah, an Arab terrorist group dedicated to Israel's destruction, and based in Lebanon. Hizballah forces had also crossed into Israeli territory and kidnapped two Israeli soldiers whom they refused to return.

Main Idea:
In 2008, President Bush made a historic trip to the region, hoping to promote peace efforts.

Hizballah launched thousands of rockets into Israel from various locations in Lebanon. It had obtained weapons and help from Iran, but it did not represent the government of Lebanon nor the majority of the Lebanese people. Yet, the Lebanese government could not and made no attempt to stop Hizballah from its actions. Consequently, Israel retaliated by attacking those specific areas in Lebanon where Hizballah had weapons and soldiers. This was a matter of self-defense. Israel's army went into Lebanon, and its warplanes bombed known Hizballah strongholds. The damage to Hizballah-occupied regions was severe, especially as Hizballah refused to release the captured soldiers and to stop firing rockets on Israeli cities. Thousands of Israelis had to be evacuated from parts of Northern Israel. Ironically, Israeli Arabs suffered 40 percent of the fatalities in that section of Israel.

Sheik **Hassan Nasrallah**, Hizballah's leader, sought to blame Israel for the war and for damage, deaths, and disruption in Lebanon. In reality, he and his extremist group caused the crisis and were criticized by other Arabs. At an **Arab League** meeting, Saudi Arabia and Jordan were seconded by Egypt and others in denouncing Hizballah's "unexpected, inappropriate, and irresponsible acts." Iran also received condemnation for arming and supporting Hizballah. The major Egyptian newspaper, *Al-Ahram*, went so far as to state that "all Iran wants is to extend its hegemony [control and power] over the eastern Arab countries, and is trying to use Hizballah as a Trojan horse to achieve this aim." Blame was also heaped on Hizballah by several countries, such as the United States, Russia, and Britain, and by the UN Security Council. One key factor for such blame, noting the words of the Arab League condemnation, was the lack of any firm reason for Hizballah's belligerence. Its attacks from Lebanon were "unexpected" because Israel no longer had any involvement in Lebanese affairs.

In 2000, Israel removed its forces from Lebanon after vanquishing the PLO. Hizballah's violation of an internationally recognized border was an act of war and was thus the chief reason for denunciation by the United Nations. This denunciation was evident in Security Council Resolution 1701. This resolution brought a halt to the fighting. It put the blame on Hizballah, made an Israeli with-

Saddam Hussein (1937–2006).

U.S. soldiers in Iraq.

Main Idea:
Dissatisfaction about the course of the war among Americans was considered to be a major reason for the success of the Democratic Party in the elections. Democrats were able to gain control of both houses of Congress.

drawal from Lebanon conditional on the behavior of Hizballah, and mandated the disarming of Hizballah and an embargo (stoppage) on arms shipments to Hizballah. To enforce this last provision, the UN authorized a multinational force to patrol the waters off Lebanon as well as Lebanon's border with Syria.

In March 2003, the United States attacked Iraq. Although not supported by the United Nations, but with some help from coalition partners such as Great Britain, the United States was able to defeat the forces of **Saddam Hussein** in less than two months. Saddam Hussein was arrested in December 2003, put on trial in 2005, and executed in 2006 after a trial by jury.

The invasion of Iraq was said to be for several reasons: Iraq's possession of **WMDs** (**weapons of mass destruction**) and its refusal to comply with demands and requests by UN inspectors over a number of years after the 1991 **Persian Gulf War**, Iraq's support of terrorist organizations such as **Al Qaeda** and its leader, **Osama bin Laden**, and Iraq's possible links to the **September 11, 2001** attacks on the World Trade Center in New York and the Pentagon in Washington, D.C. Yet, in the immediate four years after Iraq's defeat, several investigations expressed doubts about the WMD issue as well as any link to Al Qaeda and the 9/11 attack. During those years, the United States and its coalition partners faced increasing isolated fighting from small groups of insurgent Iraqis and other Arabs who slipped into Iraq and were known as **jihadists**.

Although the United States lost over three thousand troops during this time, it tried to achieve unity among Iraq's different ethnic groups and to promote democratic reforms in the country as well as better living conditions. A new constitution was written, and elections were held to select a governing body. Traditional tensions between **Sunni Muslims**, **Shi'ite Muslims,** and **Kurds** often made these goals difficult to achieve. The sectarian violence between them caused hundreds of deaths of innocent civilians. In late 2005, the United States began to consider the start of gradual troop withdrawals. As these considerations gathered momentum in 2006, the plan was that U.S.-trained Iraqi soldiers and police could help preserve safety and stability. Inside the United States, controversy grew about the American presence in Iraq. The question of whether to send more troops was frequently debated, as was the issue of whether the United States should stay in or leave Iraq. U.S. President **George W. Bush** maintained that the American role in Iraq was vital in the war against global terrorism. He and his aides were in frequent contact with Iraqi Prime Minister **Nuri al-Maliki**. In the November 2006 American Congressional elections, the Iraq war became a significant campaign issue. Dissatisfaction about the course of the war among Americans was considered to be a major reason for the success of the Democratic Party in the elections. Democrats were able to gain control of both houses of Congress.

The war in Afghanistan is a struggle against global terrorism, which was also a factor responsible for American forces fighting in Afghanistan, according to President Bush. Control of that country by the **Taliban**, beginning in the 1990s, continued into the 2000s. As Islamic fundamentalists, the Taliban government claimed to be anti-American and protected the terrorist group Al Qaeda.

Al Qaeda was held responsible by the United States for the attacks in New York, Washington, D.C., and Pennsylvania on September 11, 2001. The United States viewed this unprovoked aggression as an act of war and sent military forces to Afghanistan. The goal was to overthrow the Taliban (which had refused to shut down Al Qaeda and give up its leader, Osama bin Laden), destroy Al Qaeda, and capture its leaders. With the defeat of the Taliban in December 2001, the United States helped anti-Taliban Afghans create a government headed by **Hamid Karzai**. The year 2004 became noteworthy upon his election as president and the writing of a new constitution. Nevertheless, scattered fighting and homicide bombings by Taliban terrorists continued. These were being met by the remaining American forces, supported by troops from some NATO countries and from Pakistan. The hunt for Osama bin Laden continued, however, as he was thought to be hiding in the rugged mountainous region surrounding the Afghan-Pakistani border. By the end of 2006, the Taliban were regaining strength in Afghanistan.

Syria had been condemned by the United States for continuing to permit terrorist groups to stay in the country. Limited sanctions were applied to Syria by the United States in 2004, as a result of the Syria Accountability Act of 2003. These were designed to affect Syria's economy and reduce its trade with America. The United States was also concerned with the flow of Arab terrorists and jihadists (those claiming to fight a holy war) who crossed from Syria into Iraq. As Syria was not seen as being cooperative enough to stem this flow, American and Iraqi soldiers stepped up their military operations on the border in 2005. Syria was also accused by the United States as well as the United Nations of being responsible for the 2005 assassination of Lebanese Prime Minister **Rafiq Hariri**. Under international pressure, Syria was willing to consider some form of cooperation with the United Nations in an investigation of the killing. International pressure also resulted in Syria finally removing its thirty thousand troops from Lebanon in 2005, after being there since 1976.

President George W. Bush declared his wish to see change and transformation in the Middle East, with moves toward democratic rule. He claimed that the region as well as the rest of the world would be safer with the success of such movement. With the exception of Israel, there are no democratic nations in the Middle East. Although it is recognized that democracy, with its emphasis on open elections and protection of freedom and civil rights, cannot develop overnight, there were nevertheless some small advances made during the years 2004–2006. Evidence could be seen in the major elections held in Afghanistan and Iraq under American occupation, as well as in the Palestinian territories and Lebanon, and to a lesser degree in Egypt and Saudi Arabia.

Main Idea:
The goal was to overthrow the Taliban (which had refused to shut down Al Qaeda and give up its leader, Osama bin Laden), destroy Al Qaeda, and capture its leaders.

Main Idea:
Although it is recognized that democracy, with its emphasis on open elections and protection of freedom and civil rights, cannot develop overnight, there were nevertheless some small advances made during the years 2004–2006.

South Asia

INDIA

TIMELINE OF EVENTS

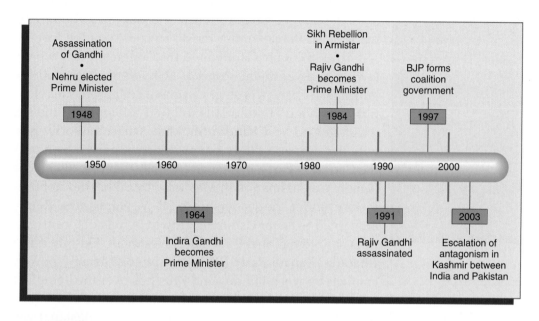

Assassination of Gandhi
•
Nehru elected Prime Minister

1948

Sikh Rebellion in Armistar
•
Rajiv Gandhi becomes Prime Minister

1984

BJP forms coalition government

1997

1950   1960   1970   1980   1990   2000

1964

Indira Gandhi becomes Prime Minister

1991

Rajiv Gandhi assassinated

2003

Escalation of antagonism in Kashmir between India and Pakistan

Indian Prime Minister Nehru addressing the General Assembly of the United nations in New York City on October 3, 1960.

After the division of India and Pakistan, **India** continued to be troubled by disputes with its neighbors and separatist movements within its borders. Almost immediately, fighting began between Hindu and Muslim refugees being repatriated to India or Pakistan. In addition, conflict began in **Kashmir**, where Muslim separatists, encouraged and armed by Pakistan, demanded an end to Indian rule. In the Punjab region, **Sikh** separatists also rose up demanding the formation of an independent state of **Khalistan**. These problems, which have resulted in years of war and thousands of deaths, have still not been resolved to the present day.

Mohandas Gandhi's assassination by a Hindu extremist, who blamed him for partition, in January of 1948 greatly aggravated an already tense situation. Under Prime Minister **Jawaharlal Nehru**, Gandhi's successor, India assumed a role of leadership in the world movement of nonaligned nations and followed that policy in international affairs. Nehru's death in 1964 and his succession by his daughter, **Indira Gandhi**, in 1966 split the Congress Party into "old" and "new" wings. By 1975, after the New Congress Party was convicted of voting fraud,

Indira Nehru Gandhi (1917–1984). Indian political leader.

Mrs. Gandhi declared a state of emergency, imposing censorship and arresting thousands for political offenses. An opposition coalition, led by the **Janata Dall Party (JDP)**, won a massive victory in 1977. Gandhi was driven from office. In 1980, Mrs. Gandhi and the New Congress Party returned to power, and she resumed the prime ministership. She continued to be repressive and antagonized many groups within the nation, in particular, the Sikhs. In 1984, after an army attack on the Sikh's **Golden Temple** in Amritsar, Gandhi was assassinated by Sikh bodyguards in October. She was succeeded by her son, **Rajiv Gandhi**, who placed Punjab under the direct control of the federal government.

Main Idea:
In 1980, Mrs. Gandhi and the New Congress Party returned to power, and she resumed the prime ministership. She continued to be repressive and antagonized many groups within the nation, in particular, the Sikhs.

In 1989, Rajiv Gandhi and the Congress Party were voted out of office following a government scandal. They were succeeded by **V. P. Singh** and the Janata Dall Party, whose government collapsed after eleven months over a dispute involving Hindu plans to build a temple on the site of a Mosque. Singh was followed by **Chandra Shekhar,** whose minority government only served with the support of the Congress Party. Angered by a parliamentary boycott by the Congress Party, instigated by Rajiv Gandhi, Shekhar quit in March of 1991. Gandhi's assassination in May (also by Sikhs) did not prevent a Congress Party victory under the leadership of **P. V. Narasimha Rao.** The Rao government attempted to foster economic growth by relaxing centralized planning and controls on international trade and investment. Despite this, the opposition Hindu **Bharatiya Janata Party (BJP)** became increasingly powerful as a result of new conflicts between Hindus and Muslims over the demolishing of a mosque built over an earlier sacred Hindu site in December of 1992. An increase in violence in Kashmir also brought new tensions with Pakistan. Even though the Rao government's economic policies produced good results, the internal religious conflicts had hurt political stability. The Congress Party was defeated in the elections of May 1996, replaced by a weak coalition government that was itself defeated in the elections of 1997. The BJP was able to form a coalition government under Prime Minister **Atal Behari Vajapyee** in March 1998. The BJP coalition asserted India's claims in Kashmir and carried out underground tests of five nuclear devices as a means of making India's nuclear power a deterrent. Despite a rise in attacks against Indian forces in Kashmir by Muslim insurgents, India retaliated forcefully, and peace was restored in July of 1999.

Main Idea:
By 2003, the Kashmir crisis had escalated, and Britain and the United States intervened diplomatically. By 2004, serious talks between both nations were occurring regularly, and tensions had somewhat diminished.

In December of 2001, an attack on the Indian Parliament by five Pakistan-based terrorists revived tensions between India and Pakistan. To make matters worse, Hindu mobs killed Muslims while attacks on Muslims, particularly in Kashmir, increased. By 2003, the Kashmir crisis had escalated, and Britain and the United States intervened diplomatically. By 2004, serious talks between both nations were occurring regularly, and tensions had somewhat diminished. In the elections of 2004, the BJP was voted out and replaced by the **United Progressive Alliance (UPA)**. Under the leadership of **Manmohan Singh**, the first Sikh to be the head of Indian government, the United States formally agreed to provide India with nuclear power expertise.

PAKISTAN

TIMELINE OF EVENTS

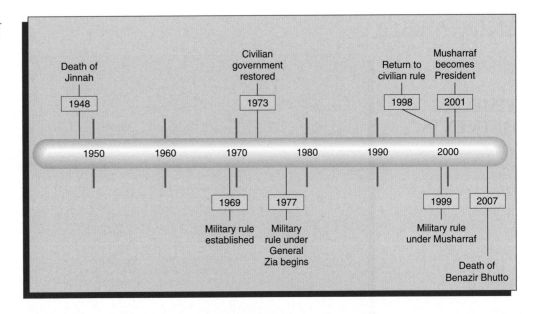

Death of Jinnah — 1948

Civilian government restored — 1973

Return to civilian rule — 1998

Musharraf becomes President — 2001

1950 — 1960 — 1970 — 1980 — 1990 — 2000

1969 — Military rule established

1977 — Military rule under General Zia begins

1999 — Military rule under Musharraf

2007 — Death of Benazir Bhutto

Main Idea: From 1988 to 1999, parliamentary power shifted between Bhutto and the **Pakistan People's Party (PPP)**, and **Nawaz Sharif**, leader of the **Muslim League**.

The assassination of Benazir Bhutto in 2007 heightened tensions and anti-Musharraf feelings.

After the separation with India, **Pakistan** became an independent nation under the leadership of its founder **Muhammed Ali Jinnah**. His sudden death in 1948 resulted in power struggles between political parties until the military suspended the constitution and declared martial law in 1958. Pakistan was ruled by **General Muhammed Ayub Khan**, who was elected president in 1960 and 1965. After Khan's resignation in 1969, a new government was formed under **General Yahya Khan**, and martial law was reinstated. By 1970, civil war erupted as East Pakistan unsuccessfully attempted to achieve independence. Pakistanis elected **Zulfikar Ali Bhutto** president. In 1971, the Bengalis (East Pakistanis) were successful and formed the new nation of **Bangladesh**. In July of 1977, Bhutto was overthrown by the military under **General Muhammed Zia ul-Haq**. He was convicted of involvement in a 1974 political murder and hanged in April of 1979. Under General Zia, Pakistan implemented Islamic law in parallel with the constitutional law of Pakistan's parliamentary system. In 1986, Bhutto's daughter **Benazir Bhutto** organized opposition parties against Zia, which led to widespread protest and rioting. In August of 1988, Zia was killed in an airplane crash.

From 1988 to 1999, parliamentary power shifted between Bhutto and the **Pakistan People's Party (PPP)**, and **Nawaz Sharif**, leader of the **Muslim League**. Each continually attacked the other with propaganda during which time there was enormous tension with India over Kashmir. The tensions with India led to the nuclear test rivalry between the two nations in May of 1998. In July of 1999, Sharif agreed to withdraw support for the Muslims in Kashmir, which resulted in his overthrow by the military under **General Pervez Musharraf**. Sharif was tried on corruption charges and sentenced to life imprisonment in 2000. Despite promises to return civilian rule, Musharraf appointed himself president in June of 2001 and has continued to rule Pakistan. Under Musharraf, Pakistan has maintained a difficult foreign policy of supporting the United States against the Taliban in Afghanistan while refusing to give in on Kashmir and suppressing extremist Muslims in his own country. Surviving a December 2003 assassination attempt, Musharraf agreed to step down as the army chief but promised to remain as president until the 2007 elections.

INDONESIA

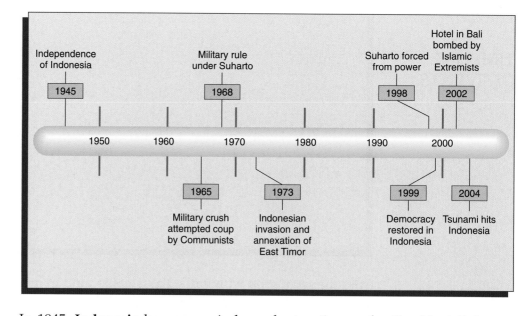

In 1945, **Indonesia** became an independent nation under President **Sukarno**, founder of the **Indonesian Nationalist Party (PNI)**. While under Sukarno, Indonesia took a leading role in international affairs among the Third World, but his politics became increasingly leftist as he developed hostility towards the Western powers and became friendly with Communist China. In 1965, the army crushed an attempted takeover by the **Indonesian Communist Party (PKI)**, which set off popular unrest in which several thousand people were killed as suspected Communists. Sukarno was removed and **General Suharto** became president in 1968. Under Suharto, the economy and foreign investment grew rapidly while the PKI was banned and Indonesian policy shifted in favor of the West. Suharto's policy of a **transmigration**, which was to move farmers from overcrowded to underdeveloped areas, had mixed success. In 1975, Indonesia invaded an annexed **East Timor**, during which over 100,000 people in the region were killed. Suharto became the head of the **Golkan** or **United Front Party**. Despite the repressive nature of his regime, Suharto was reelected five more times, the last in 1997. By 1998, however, continuing unrest in East Timor, and growing public disillusionment, with corruption in Suharto's family and close associates, and the financial crisis that swept through Asia led to strikes and riots that forced him to resign in May.

Vice President **Habibie** became president in new elections in 1999. The June elections, however, brought a parliamentary majority led by Sukarno's daughter, **Megawati**. A vote by the people of East Timor for independence from Indonesia resulted in new conflict and the sending of UN peacekeeping troops. In October of 1999, the assembly approved East Timor's independence and elected Muslim cleric **Abdurrahman Wahid** as president with Megawati as his vice president. The aging and incompetent administration of Wahid forced him to turn power over to Megawati in 2000. In July 2001, Wahid was formerly impeached and replaced by Megawati as president. In August 2002, the assembly amended the constitution and established direct election of the president,

> **Main Idea:** Despite the repressive nature of his regime, Suharto was reelected five more times, the last in 1997.

abolishing the military's thirty-eight seats in the assembly. The bombing of an Indonesian resort in **Bali** in 2002 by Islamic extremists created new concerns for the moderate Muslim Indonesians. In December, the rebellious population of the **Aceh Province** reached an agreement that established peace in the area. Megawati's decision to impose martial law in Aceh only led to renewed violence and rebellion. In the July 2004 elections, Megawati was defeated by **Suseilo Bamband Yudoyono**. Under the new president, a formal peace treaty was reached with Aceh's rebels in August 2005. He also kept the nation together during the devastating **tsunami** (an unusually large and destructive sea wave) in December 2004, which claimed the lives of well over 100,000 people. The tsunami impacted hundreds of thousands of people across the coastlines of South and Southeast Asia destroying homes, businesses, and entire villages. Financial aid poured into the area from all over the world in an effort to assist in the recovery process.

SRI LANKA

TIMELINE OF EVENTS

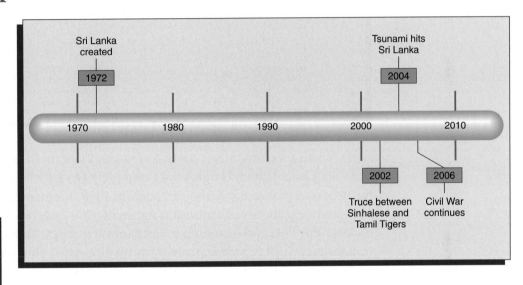

> **Main Idea:**
> From its creation in 1972, the **Republic of Sri Lanka** has been destabilized by the long struggle between the **Tamils** and **Sinhalese**.

From its creation in 1972, the **Republic of Sri Lanka** has been destabilized by the long struggle between the **Tamils** and **Sinhalese**. The mostly Hindu Tamil minority became a politically powerful middle class under British rule, which was resented by the mostly Buddhist Sinhalese majority. After independence, Tamil power and rights declined. The **Tamil Tigers**, a group dedicated to complete independence for the Tamil areas of Sri Lanka, was created the same year as the nation. Despite several cease-fires, the Tigers fought a civil war with the government for Sri Lanka. By 2001, the Tigers had grown stronger, and their military successes brought a negotiated truce in 2002. Despite a period of peace, which included the tragedy of the 2004 tsunami, which killed over 30,000 people, fighting began again in August 2006.

Southeast Asia

VIETNAM

TIMELINE OF EVENTS

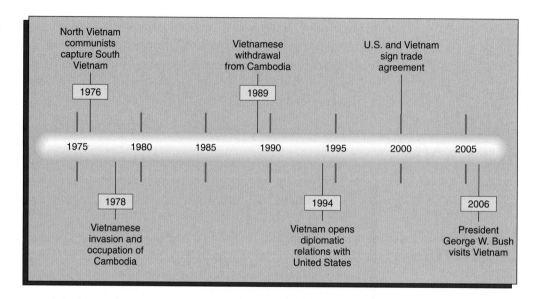

North Vietnam communists capture South Vietnam

1976

Vietnamese withdrawal from Cambodia

1989

U.S. and Vietnam sign trade agreement

1975 1980 1985 1990 1995 2000 2005

1978

Vietnamese invasion and occupation of Cambodia

1994

Vietnam opens diplomatic relations with United States

2006

President George W. Bush visits Vietnam

After North Vietnam seized control of South Vietnam in July 1976, a Communist state was established. **Saigon** was renamed **Ho Chi Minh City,** and a Soviet naval base replaced the American base. In 1978, Vietnamese troops invaded and occupied neighboring **Cambodia**, removing the government of the murderous dictator **Pol Pot**, and installing a Vietnamese puppet, **Heng Samrin**, as premier. In February 1979, China launched an unsuccessful attack over its border with Vietnam in retaliation for the invasion of Cambodia and the treatment of ethnic Chinese in that nation. In 1989, fearing future conflict with China, Vietnam removed its troops from Cambodia.

Vietnam's Communist government was run through a Central Committee, which had no strong leaders to dominate it. Its economy, hampered by excessive **collectivization** (government control of production and the economy), steadily declined. With the collapse of the U.S.S.R. and loss of desperately needed Soviet financial aid, the government was forced to allow private enterprise. By 1992, collectivization was quietly being abandoned, and foreign investment was encouraged. Using the return of American Prisoners of War (POWs) and information about Missing In Action (MIAs), Vietnam opened diplomatic relations with the United States in 1994. By July 1995, American firms were operating in Vietnam, and its first-ever national **Civil Code** under the Communist government was established. In July 2000, the United States and Vietnam signed their first trade agreement. In April 2001, a new secretary general, **Nong Duc Mahn**, was appointed with the aim of modernizing the economy and ending corruption. In December of that year, Vietnam signed a trade agreement with the United States that granted private investors equal access to bank credit with the public sector. The government has taken many steps toward modifying their economic system, but the Communists had no intention of losing their political control as their party continued to dominate "elections" to the National Assembly. In June 2005, Prime Minister **Phan Van Khai** became the first Vietnamese leader to visit the White House since the end of the Vietnam War. This was reciprocated in November 2006 by American President George W. Bush who became the second American president to visit Vietnam since the Communist takeover.

Main Idea:
With the collapse of the U.S.S.R. and loss of desperately needed Soviet financial aid, the government was forced to allow private enterprise. By 1992, collectivization was quietly being abandoned, and foreign investment was encouraged.

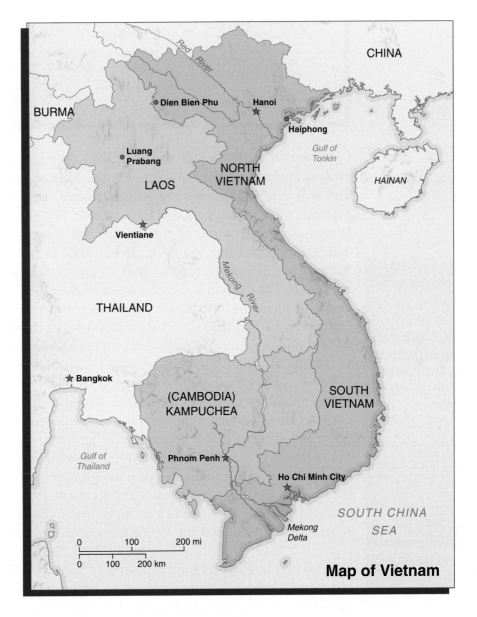

Map of Vietnam

CAMBODIA

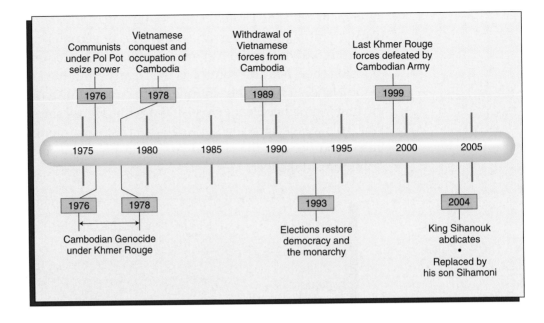

Communists under Pol Pot seize power — 1976

Vietnamese conquest and occupation of Cambodia — 1978

Withdrawal of Vietnamese forces from Cambodia — 1989

Last Khmer Rouge forces defeated by Cambodian Army — 1999

1975 1980 1985 1990 1995 2000 2005

1976 — 1978
Cambodian Genocide under Khmer Rouge

1993
Elections restore democracy and the monarchy

2004
King Sihanouk abdicates
•
Replaced by his son Sihamoni

Main Idea: Renaming the nation **Kampuchea**, the government tried to impose drastic social and economic changes on Cambodian society between 1975 and 1978. The results of these policies were the near destruction of the economy and the needless slaughter of innocent people.

Civil war and invasions have plagued Cambodia since 1970, when Prince **Norodom Sihanouk** was overthrown. The military dictatorship that overthrew him was unable to defeat the **Khmer Rouge**, a Communist force backed by Vietnam, which took control of the nation in 1976. Under its leader, Pol Pot, the Khmer Rouge government was brutal and repressive, committing genocide against the population and killing thousands of people. Renaming the nation **Kampuchea**, the government tried to impose drastic social and economic changes on Cambodian society between 1975 and 1978. The results of these policies were the near destruction of the economy and the needless slaughter of innocent people. These events were the basis of the film *The Killing Fields*. Pol Pot's actions angered Vietnam, and, with Soviet assistance, Vietnam conquered Cambodia in 1978. A puppet Vietnamese government headed by **Hun Sen** was installed. This government was forced to form a coalition with the Khmer Rouge and other groups in 1989 as the Vietnamese withdrew their forces.

A United Nations-supervised cease-fire agreement that provided for a UN peacekeeping force and internationally monitored elections was signed in 1991. The elections of May 1993 produced the 120-member National Assembly, which created a new constitution and provided for the return of Sihanouk as king. In September 1993, Sihanouk became the monarch of Cambodia, and his new government immediately opened relations with the United States. The Khmer Rouge, which boycotted the 1993 elections, began armed resistance against the new government the following year. By 1999, the last Khmer Rouge troops had surrendered and leaders were captured. In January 2001, the National Assembly approved a United Nations international tribunal to try the mass murderers of the Khmer Rouge. Sihanouk abdicated in 2004 and was replaced by his son, **Norodom Sihamoni**.

SECTION 5

East Asia

CHINA

TIMELINE OF EVENTS

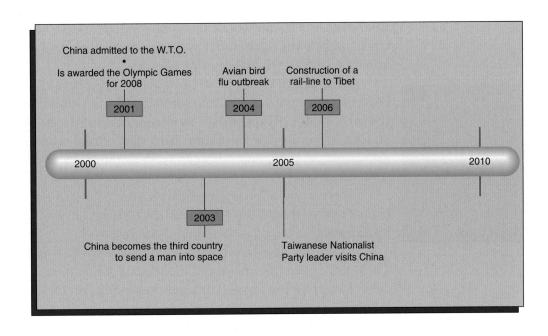

China admitted to the W.T.O.

Is awarded the Olympic Games for 2008

2001

Avian bird flu outbreak

2004

Construction of a rail-line to Tibet

2006

2000   2005   2010

2003

China becomes the third country to send a man into space

Taiwanese Nationalist Party leader visits China

> **Main Idea:**
> By 2020, China is expected to overtake Japan as the world's second largest economy. In fact, to most people's surprise, Japan imports more from China than it does from the United States.

With the dawn of the current century, **China**'s status on the world stage in terms of economics and diplomacy has grown remarkably. Its influence is rising. Trading statistics provide an important clue to understanding vital changes. For example, to judge from China's recent economic growth, her economy by 2010 will be twice that of Germany's. Germany as of 2005 was the world's third largest economy. By 2020, China is expected to overtake Japan as the world's second largest economy. In fact, to most people's surprise, Japan imports more from China than it does from the United States. In addition, China has emerged as the largest trading partner of South Korea, the world's twelfth major economy. Accordingly, these developments have caused Japan and South Korea to realize that China is now vital to their well-being. Consequently, they are more willing to support China in various policy issues even if this means positioning themselves against the United States. Unlike the international politics of the twentieth century, both the United States and China are seen as major powers in Asia. A good example can be seen in the talks concerning North Korea's nuclear status, wherein South Korea and Japan have given support to some Chinese policy stances as opposed to some of those championed by the United States.

A sixty-year period of hostility between the Chinese Nationalist Party and the Chinese Communist Party ended in 2005 when the Taiwanese Nationalist

Party leader, **Lien Chan**, visited China. The visit in April 2005 to Beijing was historic. He met with China's president and Communist Party leader **Hu Jintao**. The last time the heads of these two parties had met was in 1945. It was then when Nationalist **Chiang Kai-shek** and Communist **Mao Zedong** failed in an attempt to achieve a cease-fire during the Chinese Civil War. The 2005 meeting led to a discussion on reducing tensions between the two Chinas, if the Nationalists should regain control of Taiwan in the near future. The Nationalists, who controlled Taiwan until 2000, control the legislature, but they lost the presidency then to the Democratic Progressive Party. Its leader, **Chen Shui-bian,** is a proponent of Taiwanese independence and was angered by Lien Chan's trip to the mainland. On the domestic scene, several issues have gained attention in the early twenty-first century.

> **Main Idea:**
> On the domestic scene, several issues have gained attention in the early twenty-first century.

Some health issues have caused alarm throughout China. HIV/AIDS has been increasing at a rapid rate. In 2002, China suffered an outbreak of **SARS (Severe Acute Respiratory Syndrome)**. Hundreds died as a result. In 2004–2005, episodes of **avian bird flu virus** worried medical officials. Thousands of birds and chickens were slaughtered in an effort to contain the contamination.

Space exploration was evidenced by a major achievement. In August 2003, China became the third nation, after the United States and Russia, to send a man into space.

Industrial disasters have accompanied China's economic advancement. These have been due mainly to inadequate regulation, corruption, and human error. Examples can be seen in a gas well explosion in South Central China that killed 233 people. In 2005, a benzene runoff polluted a river near **Harbin** in the north; it left millions without drinkable water for several days.

China's treatment of two large minority groups has raised issues of prejudicial and abusive treatment. **Tibetans** came under Chinese occupation in 1951, with a Communist government being installed in 1953. The Buddhist religion was repressed, as 100,000 Tibetans fled to India with their spiritual leader, the **Dalai Lama**. In July 2006, China finished building the world's highest railway line. It runs for over seven hundred miles, often at over sixteen thousand feet above sea level, from Beijing to the Tibetan capital city of **Lhasa.** Although its construction is a significant engineering accomplishment, it has caused concern

Chiang Kai-shek (1887–1975), Chinese general and statesman c. 1930.

about its bringing additional Chinese into the area and the effect this will have on Tibet's people and culture. Sinkiang Province in the northwest has a large Muslim population. They fear crackdowns on their rights and freedoms and have considered separating themselves from China.

Censorship continues to be a firm policy of the government. Evidence can be seen in restrictions on use of the Internet as well as on the content of newspapers and official government publications.

In the area of science and mathematics education, China has made great strides. Increasing numbers of students are majoring in various scientific and mathematical areas, as well as in related fields such as engineering. Several American observers of these trends are wary of the perceived growing gap between American and Chinese education in these and other disciplines. One such observer, *New York Times* reporter Thomas Friedman, has noted that 59 percent of undergraduates in China receive degrees in science and engineering, while the number in the United States is 32 percent. He also predicted that in a few years the number of Chinese who can speak English will exceed the entire population of the United States.

The status of women has undergone a slight change. This can be seen in an increasing divorce rate, usually initiated by women, and a changing view of marriage. Although these trends are found mainly in urban areas, they are typical for developing countries that are rapidly modernizing, gaining affluence, and being exposed to Western influences. In the area of international relations, the post-2000 period has been marked by numerous developments.

Relations with Russia have been improving. In November of 2005, Russian President **Vladimir Putin** announced that Russia would build a pipeline carrying oil into China. Russia is the world's second largest oil exporter, after Saudi Arabia. Russian trade with China was approaching record levels in 2006.

Chinese pride was bolstered in 2001 by two noteworthy international acts of recognition. China was admitted into the **WTO (World Trade Organization)** and was awarded the Olympic Games for the year 2008.

China has taken a larger diplomatic role with regard to situations on the Korean peninsula. China has hosted talks and acted as an intermediary on issues relating to North Korea's nuclear weapons program.

To feed its enormous growing energy needs, China has sent emissaries to oil-rich areas such as Venezuela, the Middle East, and Africa to promote imports. Relations with those African nations who have great oil production potential have grown. For example, China has signed over forty oil agreements with various nations and is providing free equipment and drugs to help fight AIDS and malaria.

With reference to Japan and the frequent talk about its gaining a seat on the United Nations Security Council, China has taken a very dim view. It is not likely that China would vote for Japan's admission. One reason rests with Chinese dismay over the content in Japanese history textbooks. The Chinese claim that these books distort and falsify Japanese actions in China during the twentieth century, particularly in what both Chinese and Japanese refer to as the **Pacific War** (1931–1945).

Main Idea: Censorship continues to be a firm policy of the government. Evidence can be seen in restrictions on use of the Internet as well as on the content of newspapers and official government publications.

Main Idea: China has signed over forty oil agreements with various nations and is providing free equipment and drugs to help fight AIDS and malaria.

JAPAN

TIMELINE OF EVENTS

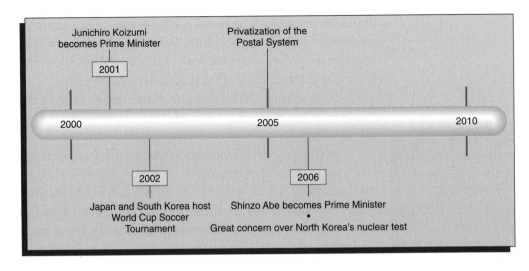

Junichiro Koizumi becomes Prime Minister

2001

Privatization of the Postal System

2000   2005   2010

2002

Japan and South Korea host World Cup Soccer Tournament

2006

Shinzo Abe becomes Prime Minister

Great concern over North Korea's nuclear test

Main Idea:
These visits showed an increasing concern by Japan to seek closer ties with these two neighbors.

The first major domestic development in **Japan** at the start of the current century occurred in April 2001. The leader of the **LDP (Liberal Democratic Party)**, **Junichiro Koizumi**, became prime minister. His hold on power, and that of the LDP, was confirmed in the elections of November 2003 and of September 2005. These election victories for Koizumi's ruling party led to a wave of optimism among investors. The Nikkei stock index jumped more than 1 percent in early trade. The 2005 election results gave the 63-year-old LDP leader a clear mandate for economic, social, and political reform. Adding to the air of economic enthusiasm were revised figures from the government showing that the world's second-largest economy was growing at an annualized rate of 3.3 percent. The LDP had won 296 of the 480 contested seats in a major triumph. That is the second-largest figure in the LDP's fifty-year history.

September 2006 witnessed another peaceful change in Japan's political scene. True to a promise he had made months ago, Koizumi stepped down from his post as prime minister. He was succeeded by **Shinzo Abe**. Within two weeks of taking office, he made visits to China and South Korea. These visits showed an increasing concern by Japan to seek closer ties with these two neighbors. These visits were also significant for these two reasons: (1) The visit to China was the first made by a Japanese prime minister in five years. Both China and South Korea had refused to hold such summit meetings with former Prime Minister Koizumi because of his pilgrimages to the Yasakuni Shrine in Tokyo. (2) Mr. Abe's China trip broke a tradition whereby a Japanese leader's initial overseas visit would be to the United States.

Another political development concerned the emperor. A historic change in regard to the role of the emperor may be forthcoming. In 2005, Prime Minister Koizumi announced that he wanted to have a law passed that allows a woman to become emperor. This was because a male royal baby had not been born in Japan from 1965 until September 6, 2006, when Prince **Hisahito**, grandson of Emperor **Akihito**, was born. His name means virtuous, calm, and everlasting in Japanese. Now that this male heir has been born, changes to the laws may still occur to allow the children of a female emperor to be heirs to the throne. The law may also guarantee that an emperor's first-born child will be first in line to the throne, regardless of its sex. These changes may also be postponed as they seem less important now to many Japanese.

Main Idea:
The *Tokyo Shimbun* newspaper reported that 84 percent of Japanese back the changes.

Opponents of the proposals have already voiced their concerns. Many strongly disagree with the idea that a woman can be emperor. They believe God wants only men to be head of the royal family. They argue that a male emperor is an essential and sacred part of Japanese history and culture. They also want the return of former imperial family members who left royal life after World War II. These relatives could make sure a male becomes emperor. The public strongly supports Koizumi's plans. The *Tokyo Shimbun* newspaper reported that 84 percent of Japanese back the changes.

On the economic front, it was during the 1980s that Japan experienced a **bubble economy.** This means that due to speculation the value of land and stocks became extremely overpriced. Many banks lent money to help people meet high prices. Yet, scores of borrowers were unable to pay back the loans. In the early 1990s, the Japanese economy crashed. Although Japan still enjoyed a huge trade surplus with the United States, land and stock prices collapsed and a number of banks folded. Between 1989 and 2002, Japan's stock market (the **Nikkei**) fell from 39,000 to 8,500. The state of the economy rebounded somewhat in the early years of the twenty-first century. Despite its recent troubles, Japan's economy is still one of the most powerful in the world and a critical force in maintaining global economic stability. In October 2005, Prime Minister Koizumi achieved a stunning economic victory in the Diet. His plan to privatize the nation's $3 trillion postal system and thus create the world's largest bank was approved. Up to this point, as run by the government, the system received tremendous amounts of money from the Japanese population as a form of savings. Politicians, however, would frequently use some of these monies to fund unnecessary and wasteful public works projects (i.e., highways) in order to please their constituents. Koizumi's hope was that the funds would be used more productively. In the field of international relations, Japan has been the focus of many closely watched developments.

In November 2003, after the American attack on Iraq, the Japanese cabinet approved the deployment of over five hundred noncombatant troops to aid reconstruction efforts in that country. This was the first time that Japanese soldiers were sent to a combat zone since World War II. The move provoked controversy in Japan as some feared this might lead to a military right-wing resurgence. Prime Minister Koizumi defended the move as one that was needed to show Japan's

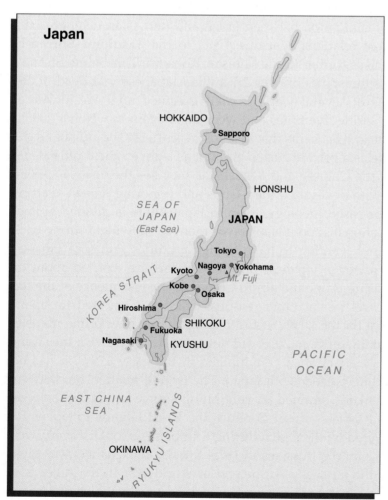

Main Idea:
Article IX of the Constitution limits Japan's use of its armed forces, causing contoversy.

importance as a major nation and global power player. Conservatives supported the move and also spoke of rescinding Article IX. Their efforts received some recognition as a result of the harsh military stance taken by North Korea. That nation has claimed to have nuclear capabilities and has threatened Japan. Very alarming was the firing by North Korea of a missile over Japan in August 1998 and a missile shot into the Sea of Japan in May 2005. Prime Minister Koizumi hinted at some form of retaliation should a North Korean missile actually hit Japan.

Main Idea:
Japan's relationship with China has improved greatly since the end of World War II.

Japan's relationship with China has improved greatly since the end of World War II. However, because China's recent economic growth encourages closer economic ties with Japan, Japan finds itself caught between its security alliance with the United States and the need to maintain friendly relations with China. China perceives itself as a potential target of American and Japanese military cooperation in East Asia. The Chinese are concerned that the large American military presence in Japan might be used against China in the event that American-Chinese hostilities erupt. The Chinese are also upset, as are the Koreans, about the alleged misrepresentations in Japanese history school textbooks about Japan's role in East Asia during World War II. The war, also called the Pacific War in Asia, is not accurately described, as narrations about it fail to mention many of the Japanese atrocities that took place in China and Korea between 1931 and 1945. Chinese demonstrations against the publication of these government approved books can seriously affect Japan's relations with China. Still another bone of contention between Japan and her Asian neighbors that could affect economic relations concerns visits to the **Yasukuni Shrine** by Japanese officials such as former Prime Minister Koizumi. This Shinto Shrine is in Tokyo and honors the spirits of over 2.5 million Japanese war dead. It also includes the remains of several war criminals executed after World War II. Koizumi visited the shrine five times and went there again in October 2005 to offer respect to the dead. He claims that his most recent visit should not be criticized as it was made as a private citizen and not as a government official. Yet, such visits infuriate the Chinese and Koreans as they see the visits as paying homage to soldiers who devastated their lands and honoring Japan's wartime expansionist emperor-based ideology. Even in Japan there is divided opinion about these visits. Nationalist politicians favor them as showing a strong backbone to China and not wanting to have foreign attitudes influence Japanese internal decisions. However, Japanese business leaders are worried about the future of their increasing economic ties to China. As a consequence of the flap over these visits as well as for other reasons, China has objected to Japan's attempt to gain a seat on the UN's Security Council. The new prime minister, Shinzo Abe, upon taking office in 2006, did not say if he would visit the shrine.

Main Idea:
Japanese business leaders are worried about the future of their increasing economic ties to China. As a consequence of the flap over these visits as well as for other reasons, China has objected to Japan's attempt to gain a seat on the UN's Security Council.

Although Russia abandoned communism in the early 1990s, it has not become a major trading partner with Japan. The overall relationship between Japan and Russia remains strained. A continuing source of tension between Japan and Russia is Russia's refusal to return the **Kuril Islands** to Japan. The Kuril Islands, discovered by the Dutch during Europe's Age of Discovery, were ceded to the Japanese by the Russians in 1875. Russia, in exchange, was given **Sakhalin Island** by the Japanese. At the end of World War II, the Allies gave both Sakhalin and the Kurils to the Soviet Union, the name by which Russia and several other small republics under Russian control used during the era of Communist rule (1917–1991). When the Soviet Union broke up in 1991 and its Communist government collapsed, Russia, as the dominant power within the former Soviet Union, retained the international rights and obligations previously held by the Soviets. These rights included possession of Sakhalin and the Kurils. Japan today still seeks the return of the Kuril Islands, which Russia refuses to cede. Nevertheless, in spite of these tensions, in November 2005, Japan was given a promise by Russian President Vladimir Putin to construct a pipeline that would carry Siberian oil to the Sea of Japan. As Japan has no oil resources, such a promise bodes well for her future energy needs.

One positive development affecting Japanese and Koreans occurred in 2002. Japan and South Korea cohosted the international soccer competition known as the **World Cup**. Previously, Japan had been recognized as the site for international sports competition. Japan had hosted the Winter Games on three occasions. In 1964, Tokyo was host to the Summer Games. Osaka, while never hosting Olympic competition, was host to EXPO '70, the 1970 world's fair. This was the first time that a world exhibition was held in Asia.

KOREA

TIMELINE OF EVENTS

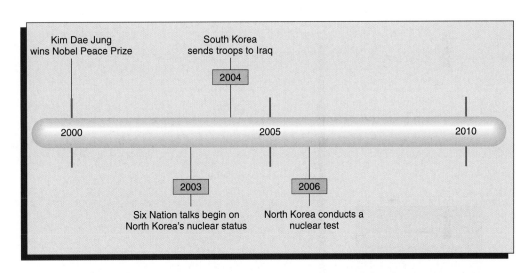

The twenty-first century began on a high note for **South Korea**. Its president, **Kim Dae Jung**, met **North Korean** leader **Kim Jong Il** in June 2000. At this unprecedented meeting in Pyongyang, North Korea's capital, they agreed to seek reconciliation and unification for their countries. In October of that year, President Jung was awarded the Nobel Peace Prize. The peaceful election in December of a new president, **Roh Moo Hyun**, was yet a further sign of democratic stability in South Korea. To support the U.S. military role in Iraq, South Korea sent three thousand troops there in 2004. Although South Korea's military is mainly concerned about the actions of North Korea, President Roh's government was less fearful of future hostility from North Korea than was the United States. The South's **"Sunshine Policy"** toward the North and its attempt to relieve food shortages there by sending shipments of grain and other goods were examples. The United States would adopt a stronger stand toward the North and was more worried about North Korea's potential for nuclear aggression.

In 2002, President George W. Bush of the United States accused North Korea, along with Iran and Iraq, of being a member of the **"Axis of Evil."** By using this term, he linked these nations as a threat to world peace. In that same year, North Korea admitted to maintaining a secret nuclear weapons program. Such activity was a violation of past agreements. In the following year, North Korea withdrew from the **Nuclear Non-proliferation Treaty**. The United States then insisted that the North dismantle its nuclear weapons program, but the North demanded a nonaggression treaty and economic aid from the United States. Six-nation talks sponsored by China, beginning in 2003, have failed to result in any agreement on the nuclear weapons issue. In October 2006, North Korea tested a nuclear device. The test received worldwide condemnation. The Security Council of the United Nations passed a resolution barring the sale of certain military and consumer goods to North Korea from other nations. Yet, a problem remained concerning the means of enforcing this resolution. China and Russia disagreed with the United States on the best way to ultimately respond to North Korea's testing. Japan, meanwhile, immediately imposed a ban on imports and ships from North Korea. South Korea condemned the test but initially did not support the United States call for a total economic blockade of North Korea.

Main Idea:
Six-nation talks sponsored by China, beginning in 2003, have failed to result in any agreement on the nuclear weapons issue.

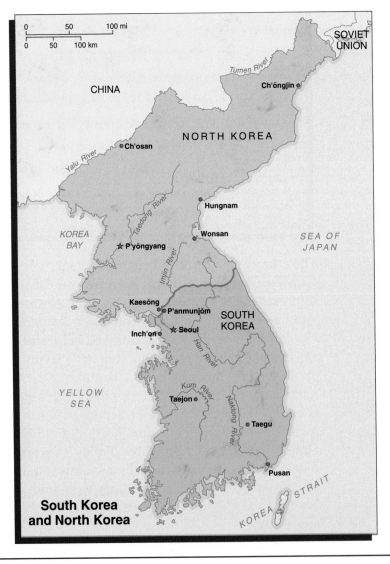

South Korea and North Korea

Central Asia

TIMELINE OF EVENTS

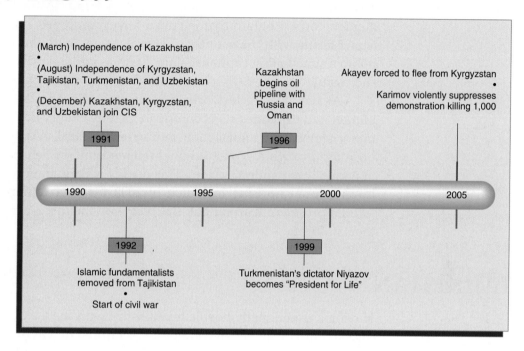

(March) Independence of Kazakhstan

(August) Independence of Kyrgyzstan, Tajikistan, Turkmenistan, and Uzbekistan

(December) Kazakhstan, Kyrgyzstan, and Uzbekistan join CIS

1991

Kazakhstan begins oil pipeline with Russia and Oman

1996

Akayev forced to flee from Kyrgyzstan

Karimov violently suppresses demonstration killing 1,000

1990 — 1995 — 2000 — 2005

1992

Islamic fundamentalists removed from Tajikistan

Start of civil war

1999

Turkmenistan's dictator Niyazov becomes "President for Life"

KAZAKHSTAN

Main Idea:
Kazakhstan's economic future is dependant on its enormous, untapped gas and oil reserves.

Kazakhstan became independent in March 1991 and joined the **Commonwealth of Independent States (CIS)** in December. From the start, it pursued closer economic, but not political, ties with Russia and Belarus. The last remaining Soviet-era nuclear missile was detonated underground in May 1995. The last missile silo was torn down in September 1996. In 1998, the capital was moved (for security reasons) from **Almaty** to the remote city of **Akmola**, which was renamed **Astana** ("capital" in Kazakh).

In December 1991, Kazakhstan held its first presidential election, electing Kazakh Republic President **Nursultan Nazarbayev**, the only candidate, as the new nation's first leader. In April 1995, a referendum canceled the 1996 election and extended Nazarbayev's term to 2000, followed by a new constitution giving the president control of the Supreme Court and the power to dissolve the Parliament at will. During the following years, Nazarbayev solidified his control of the government and made several lucrative energy deals. Kazakhstan's economic future is dependant on its enormous, untapped gas and oil reserves. Beginning in April 1996, Kazakhstan, Russia, and the Arab state of **Oman** established a consortium with eight oil companies to build a nine hundred-mile pipeline linking the **Tengiz** fields with Russia's Black Sea port and that of **Novorossiyak**. Despite the lack of democracy under the Nazarbayev regime, the potential prosperity through Kazakhstan's energy sources may keep him in power indefinitely.

KYRGYZSTAN

In August of 1991, **Kyrgyzstan** joined the other Central Asian republics of the U.S.S.R. in declaring its independence. In December of 1991, it also joined the Commonwealth of Independent States. The president of the Soviet Republic, popular reformer **Askar Akayev**, was elected as the nation's new leader. With assistance from the **International Monetary Fund (IMF)**, he began a radical economic reform program that included lowering wages, raising prices, and abolishing tariffs with the country's Central Asian neighbors in order to transform it into a functioning capitalist state. Despite initial hardships, the reforms were successful.

Akayev was reelected in 1995. In 1996, Kyrgyzstan joined The Common Market and expanded its economy to include energy development, transportation systems, and information industries. In 2000, Akayev won a third term, pushing through a "constitutional referendum" in February of 2003 that gave him greatly expanded powers. This made his regime repressive and unpopular, leading to an uprising in March of 2005 that forced him to flee the country. Interim president **Kurmanbek Bakiyev** won the July elections, taking charge as the nation's new leader.

TAJIKISTAN

Having a traditionally hostile relationship with the U.S.S.R. and the lowest living standard of all the Soviet Republics, **Tajikistan** was one of the first to declare its independence in August of 1991. Former Communist Party leader **Rakhmon Nabiyev** became the new nation's first president. Six months later, Islamic fundamentalists armed by Iran and Afghanistan overthrew the Nabiyev government, establishing a fundamentalist Muslim state. In early 1992, pro-Communist forces launched a successful counterattack, removing the fundamentalists and establishing an interim government. In the November 1994 elections, a new constitution with strong presidential powers was adapted, and **Emonali Rakhmonov** was elected president. The war between the new government and Islamic rebels continued despite United Nations attempts to mediate a cease-fire in 1994 and 1995. In 1999, a constitutional referendum was approved allowing opposition Muslim parties and extending the presidential term to seven years. Rakhmonov was also reelected for a second term.

TURKMENISTAN

The most remote of the former Soviet republics, **Turkmenistan** did not become involved in democratic or economic reforms after it became an independent nation in August of 1991. The Communist party still controls the country's politics under the direction of its president **Saparmurat Niyazov**. Elected as the Soviet republic's president in 1990, he was elected as the president of the new nation in 1991 and then reelected in 1994. Niyazov developed a Soviet-style authoritarian regime that became a repressive dictatorship. Eliminating all opposition, Parliament and the **People's Council** were under his direct control. In 1999, the Parliament unanimously elected him "President for Life."

Since 2000, a cult of personality has grown around Niyazov with his pictures and statues prominently displayed everywhere. In addition to schools, institutions, stadiums, and public works, the month of January was renamed after him in 2002. While Niyazov is suspected of embezzling huge sums from state revenues, his hold on power has silenced any domestic criticism. With vast oil and gas reserves, outside powers are reluctant to become involved in Turkmenistan's internal affairs.

UZBEKISTAN

As was the case with the other Central Asian Soviet republics, **Uzbekistan** declared its independence in August of 1991, elected its republic president as the nation's leader, and joined the CIS in December. President **Islam Karimov** began to reduce the country's dependence on Russia by banning the use of the ruble, making trade agreements with its neighbors, and encouraging the nation's large ethnic Russian population to leave. Karimov and his **Democratic Party** became popular, winning reelection and majority control of the first Uzbek Parliament in 1994. The country made a slow but steady economic recovery. Karimov's rule became extremely repressive, however, regularly violating civil and human rights. Due to the Karimov regime's cooperation with the United States in allowing American military bases in 2002, these violations were largely ignored. In May of 2005, the government violently suppressed a demonstration, killing over 1,000 people. When the United Nations assisted fleeing refugees, Karimov blamed the United States and ordered its troops to leave. With limited industry and resources, the present government may not be able to hold back the growing domestic opposition to Karimov's abusive rule without alienating itself from the international community and outside sources of economic aid.

The leaders of 11 ex-Soviet states (left to right) Leonid Kuchma of Ukraine, Imomali Rakhmonov of Tajikistan, Askar Akayev of Kyrgyzstan, Eduard Shevardnadze of Georgia, Haydar Alyev of Azerbaijan, Vladimir Putin of Russia, Alexander Lukashenko of Belarus, Robert Kocharyan of Armenia, Nursultan Nazarbayev of Kazakhstan, Petru Lucinschi of Moldova and Islam Karimov of Uzbekistan sit during a news conference in Minsk on December 1, 2000.

Transcaucasian Nations

TIMELINE OF EVENTS

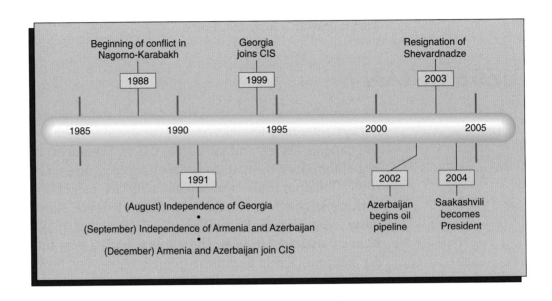

ARMENIA

Even before the Soviet republic of Armenia declared itself independent in September of 1991, there had been conflict with neighboring **Azerbaijan** over **Nagorno-Karabakh,** an Armenian Christian area in Muslim Azerbaijan. Since 1988, when the 180,000 ethnic Armenians demanded that the region become part of Armenia, fighting between the two has been an ongoing conflict.

Despite joining the CIS in December, Armenia's preoccupation with Nagorno-Karabakh has hurt its economy by limiting trade and frightening away foreign investment. In September of 1991, **Levon Ter-Petrossian** was elected as the president of the newly independent Armenian nation. In 1995, a new constitution, giving greater power to the president, was passed. Petrossian was reelected in 1996 but resigned in February of 1998 due to an argument over national policy in Nagorno-Karabakh with his hardline premier **Robert Kocharian**, who was elected president in March.

In October of 1999, gunmen entered the Armenian Parliament, assassinating Premier **Vazgen Sargissian** and seven others. Kocharian appointed the assassinated premier's brother **Aram Sargissian** to replace him. In March 2003, Kocharian was elected to a second term. Trying to build the nation's economy, which has been devastated by the conflict in Nagorno-Karabakh, is a challenge the Kocharian government must continue to face.

Main Idea: Despite joining the CIS in December, Armenia's preoccupation with Nagorno-Karabakh has hurt its economy by limiting trade and frightening away foreign investment.

AZERBAIJAN

As with neighboring Armenia, the Soviet republic of Azerbaijan's chief concern was the war in Nagorno-Karabakh. In response to attacks on Communist party buildings and Armenians starting in 1988, a brutal Soviet army intervention to restore order occurred in January of 1990. The first secretary of the Azerbaijan Communist Party was replaced by **Ayaz Mutalibov**, who was elected president of the Soviet republic in September 1991. Azerbaijan declared independence in October and joined the CIS in December. In 1992, Mutalibov was forced from office, as was his successor, by armed rebels angry after the fighting in Nagorno-Karabakh had shifted in favor of Armenia. He was replaced by a former Communist Party boss, **Heydar Aliyev**, in 1993.

Surviving two attempted overthrows of his government and popular anger over Azerbaijan's continuing losses in the war, Aliyev took advantage of the country's wealth in natural resources and signed a $7.4 billion deal with Western oil companies to develop oil fields in the Caspian Sea in 1994. Reviving the sagging economy, Aliyev and his **New Azerbaijan Party** (**NAP**), won the 1996 elections. That same year he negotiated with Russia to create an oil pipeline from the Caspian to the Black Sea. Angry over corruption and abuses by the Aliyev government, opposition parties boycotted the 1998 elections. Despite criticism by European monitors, Aliyev was reelected. By 2002, Aliyev was seriously ill, and the construction of the oil pipeline had begun; the secessionist ethnic Armenians in Nagorno-Karabakh elected a president. In 2003, Aliyev appointed his son **Ilham Aliyev** to replace him.

Aided by new growth in the economy due to Azerbaijan's growing oil industry, Ilham Aliyev won the November 2003 elections for president. In 2005, he was reelected, but international monitors reported that fraud and abuse were widespread. As it becomes increasingly likely that Nagorno-Karabakh will become independent, if not part of Armenia, the Aliyev government continues to secure its political power and exploit the new wealth brought by the nation's natural resources.

> **Main Idea:** Aliyev took advantage of the country's wealth in natural resources and signed a $7.4 billion deal with Western oil companies to develop oil fields in the Caspian Sea in 1994.

GEORGIA

The extremely nationalistic Georgians became involved in conflicts, both from within and outside their borders, while still a republic of the U.S.S.R. Throughout the period of Soviet domination, they fought the concept of "One Soviet People," which they correctly saw as an attempt to force an atheistic Communist Russian identity on them. From 1998, during the period of Glasnost, Georgians openly demanded independence. They were one of the first republics to proclaim it after the failure of the August coup of 1991.

While Georgians struggled to create their own nation, the mostly Muslim provinces of **Abkhazia**, **Adzharia**, and **South Ossetia**, began fighting for their independence from Orthodox Christian Georgia. The greater conflict is in Abkhazia, the home of **Zviad Gamsakhurdia**, Georgia's first president after independence. Elected in May of 1991, while Georgia was still a Soviet republic, he was ousted in December. Fighting between the Georgian army and troops loyal to Gamsakhurdia continued from 1991 to 1993, resulting in over two thousand deaths, including Gamsakhurdia himself.

Gamsakhurdia was replaced by **Eduard Shevardnadze**, a former Soviet official who persuaded Parliament to give him emergency powers to end the fighting. By 1994, Shevardnadze had restored order and consolidated his political power. He began to renew relations with Russia, and Georgia finally joined the CIS. In 1995, the Georgian Parliament overwhelmingly approved a new constitution, giving the president more power. Shevardnadze easily won the 1995 elections. Despite continued fighting in the rebellious provinces, the presence of Russian troops in Georgia, and several assassination attempts on his life, Shevardnadze was once again reelected in 2000. That same year, Georgia joined the World Trade Organization, thanks in great part to his economic reforms. In November of 2001, he brought American troops to train the Georgian army. Even though the Shevardnadze government had many successes, the president's autocratic style angered many Georgians. Growing protests led to his resignation at the end of 2003.

In 2004, American-educated **Mikhail Saakashvili**, leader of the **National Movement Party (NMP)**, was elected president, beginning a series of economic, social, and constitutional reforms. The removal of the pro-Russian Shevardnadze, however, resulted in a worsening of relations with Russia. Throughout 2005–2006, Georgia and Russia accused each other of sending spies, creating great tensions between the two nations. Despite Saakashvili's successful reforms, which improved the economy, the general quality of life, and further democratized Georgia, the threat of conflict with Russia, as well as the continuing fighting with the rebellious provinces, poses great challenges for his government and the nation.

CHAPTER SUMMARY

As you have seen, over the last sixty plus years, since the end of World War II in 1945, the map of the world has changed dramatically. Nationalism has been a driving force for independence movements throughout Africa and Asia. Internal domestic conflicts and international conflicts between two or more nations have changed the course of history for the nations involved. Just as individuals may struggle to achieve personal success, some nations have had to struggle for success at unity and peace and financial and governmental stability, while others have achieved it with less difficulty. In each new nation, certain individuals can be identified as crucial to its success. As you have read, there has not been just one single form of government adopted or one economic system accepted by all nations. Many of them are still struggling for recognition within the world community and to attain the standard of living achieved by the western world. It will be up to each new nation to face the challenges of the twenty-first century.

LINK TO TODAY

The countries you have read about in this chapter are still in the process of evolving. Today the United States is a democracy that has stood the test of well over two hundred years. The United States has survived many challenges including foreign attacks and wars, a major civil war, presidential impeachments, and constitutional crises. The same is true of many of these new struggling governments. Each is attempting to solve its national and international crises by using the form of government that its leaders and/or its people have chosen. Just as young people today face some challenges that are different from what their parents faced, these new young countries are facing challenges of the twenty-first century. These challenges include worldwide terrorism, the sale of illegal weapons, the widening development of nuclear power, environmental issues, and new health issues. You will read more about these concerns and challenges in Chapters 18 through 20 in this volume.

IMPORTANT PEOPLE, PLACES, AND TERMS

KEY TERMS

Pan-Africanism
Organization of African Unity (OAU)
African Union (AU)
genocide
National Reconciliation Commission
Revolutionary United Front (RUF)
Rwandan Patriotic Front
Rwandan genocide
harambee
Kenya African National Union (KANU)
Lord's Resistance Army
Movement for the Liberation of Angola (MPLA)
The National Union for the Total Independence of Angola (UNITA)

Zimbabwe African National Union (ZANU)
Zimbabwe African Peoples Union (ZAPU)
apartheid era
Nelson Mandela's African National Congress (ANC)
Red Terror
Ethiopian People's Revolutionary Democratic Front (EPRDF)
Second Republic
National Patriotic Forces of Liberia (NPFL)
Economic Community of West African State (ECOWAS)
Sharia law
Truman Doctrine
Marshall Plan
NATO
Persian Gulf War

Refah (Welfare) Party
European Union
Justice and Development Party
Armenian genocide
intifada
homicide bomber
suicide bomber
security wall
separation barrier
Roadmap Plan for Peace
Oslo Accords
Fatah Party
Second Lebanon War
Arab League
Weapons of mass destruction (WMD)
Persian Gulf War
Al Qaeda
September 11, 2001
jihadists
Bharatiya Janata Party (BJP)

United Progressive
Alliance (UPA)
Pakistan People's Party
(PPP)
Muslim League
Indonesian Nationalist
Party (PNI)
Indonesian Communist
Party (PKI)
transmigration
Golkan
United Front Party
tsunami
collectivization
Civil Code

severe acute respira-
tory syndrome
(SARS)
avian bird flu virus
World Trade
Organization (WTO)
Pacific War
Liberal Democratic
Party (LDP)
bubble economy
Nikkei
Yasukuni Shrine
Sunshine Policy
Axis of Evil
Nuclear Non-prolifera-

tion Treaty
Commonwealth of
Independent States
(CIS)
International Monetary
Fund (IMF)
Common Market
People's Council
Democratic Party
New Azerbaijan Party
(NAP)
National Movement
Party (NMP)

PEOPLE

Kwame Nkrumah
Jerry Rawlings
John Agyekum Kufuor
Hausa
Fulani
Ibo
Yoruba
General Ojukwu
General Ibrahim
Babangida
Olusegun Obasanjo
Ahmad Tejan Kabbah
Tutsi
Hutus
Paul Kagame
Jomo Kenyatta
Kikuiu
Luo
Masai
Kalenjin
Daniel Arap Moi
Mwai Kibaki
General Idi Amin Dada
Yoweri Musevini
Acholi tribe
Joseph Kony
Robert Mugabe
Joshua Nkomo
Morgan Tsuangirai

Thabo Mbeki
Emperor Haile Selassie
Colonel Mengistu Haile
Mariam
Meles Zenawi
William V. S. Tubman
William R. Tolbert, Jr.
Master Sergeant Samuel
K. Doe
Charles Taylor
Lieutenant General
Omar Ahmed el-
Bashir
Kemal Ataturk
Kurdish
Tansu Ciller
Necmettim Erbakan
Ahmet Necdet Sezer
Orhan Pamuk
Hafez al-Assad
Bashir al-Assad
Yasir Arafat
Mahmoud Abbas
Ariel Sharon
Mahmoud
Ahmadinejad
Kofi Annan
Hizballah
Hamas

Ismail Haniya
Ehud Olmert
Hassan Nasrallah
Saddam Hussein
Osama bin Laden
Sunni Muslims
Shi'ite Muslims
Kurds
George W. Bush
Nuri al-Maliki
Taliban
Hamid Karzai
Rafiq Hariri
Sikh
Jawaharlal Nehru
Indira Gandhi
Rajiv Gandhi
V. P. Singh
Chandra Shekhar
P. V. Narasimha Rao
Atal Behari Vajapyee
Manmohan Singh
Muhammed Ali Jinnah
General Muhammed
Ayub Khan
General Yahahya Khan
Zulfikar Ali Bhutto
General Muhammed
Zia ul-Haq

Benazir Bhutto	Norodom Sihanouk	Roh Moo Hyun
Nawaz Sharif	Khmer Rouge	Nursultan Nazarbayev
General Pervez Musharraf	Hun Sen	Askar Akayev
	Norodom Sihamoni	Kurmanbek Bakiyev
Sukarno	Lien Chan	Rakhmon Nabiyev
General Suharto	Hu Jintao	Emonali Rakhmonov
Habibie	Chiang Kai-shek	Saparmurat Niyazov
Megawati	Mao Zedong	Islam Karimov
Abdurrahman Wahid	Chen Shui-bian	Levon Ter-Petrossian
Suseilo Bamband Yudoyono	Tibetans	Robert Kocharian
	Dalai Lama	Vazgen Sargissian
Tamils	Vladimir Putin	Aram Sargissian
Sinhalese	Junichiro Koizumi	Ayaz Mutalibov
Tamil Tigers	Shinzo Abe	Heydar Aliyev
Pol Pot	Prince Hisahito	Ilham Aliyev
Heng Samrin	Emperor Akihito	Zviad Gamsakhurdia
Nong Duc Mahn	Kim Dae Jung	Eduard Shevardnadze
Phan Van Khai	Kim Jong Il	Mikhail Saakashvili

PLACES

Africa	Gaza Strip	Sakhalin Island
Ghana	India	South Korea
Nigeria	Kashmir	North Korea
Republic of Biafra	Khalistan	Kazakhstan
Sierra Leone	Golden Temple	Almaty
Rwanda	Pakistan	Akmola
Kenya	Bangladesh	Astana
Uganda	Indonesia	Oman
Angola	East Timor	Tengiz
Zimbabwe	Bali	Novorossiyak
South Africa	Aceh Province	Kyrgyzstan
Ethiopia	Republic of Sri Lanka	Tajikistan
Eritrea	Vietnam	Turkmenistan
Tigre	Saigon	Uzbekistan
Liberia	Ho Chi Minh City	Armenia
Monrovia	Cambodia	Azerbaijan
Darfur	Kampuchea	Nagorno-Karabakh
Turkey	China	Georgia
Istanbul	Lhasa	Abkhazia
Cyprus	Japan	Adzharia
Golan Heights	Kuril Islands	South Ossetia

CHAPTER 16

MULTIPLE-CHOICE QUESTIONS

Select the number of the correct answer.

1. Which of the following was a cause of the other three?
   (1) Ethnic African groups and tribes were divided by foreign powers
   (2) Colonizing nations changed existing place names
   (3) Europeans took native lands for themselves
   (4) Many languages existed within an area's borders

2. The attempted formation of the Republic of Biafra was a result of the persecution of the Ibo people in
   (1) Nigeria   (3) Ivory Coast
   (2) Ghana   (4) Rwanda

3. The Rwandan genocide refers to the period of ethnic warfare between
   (1) the Ibo and the Hausa tribes
   (2) the Tutsi and the Hutu tribes
   (3) the Yoruba and the Fulani tribes
   (4) the Rwandans and the Kikuiu tribe

4. During most of the 1970s, which African nation was under the control of military dictator Idi Amin?
   (1) Kenya   (3) Ghana
   (2) Ethiopia   (4) Uganda

5. During the decade of the 1990s the Republic of South Africa made history by
   (1) electing a woman president
   (2) legally ending the practice of apartheid
   (3) providing free medicine to AIDS victims
   (4) requesting the return of the former British government

6. Liberia has had the distinction of having a number of its leaders of government be
   (1) descendants of American slaves
   (2) trained as Communist spokesmen
   (3) previous European politicians
   (4) entirely from military backgrounds

7. "University Students Demonstrate to Draw Attention to Darfur Crisis." Given the above headline, what specific crisis in Darfur are students demonstrating about?
   (1) illegal trapping and murder of endangered wildlife
   (2) the results of environmental pollution
   (3) racial genocide and starvation
   (4) a worldwide terrorist organization

8. A minority group that continues to have difficulty in achieving justice and civil rights in Turkey are the
   (1) Muslims   (3) Palestinians
   (2) Kurds   (4) Sikhs

9. Mahmoud Abbas replaced what long-time Palestinian leader in 2004?
   (1) Hafez al-Assad   (3) Yasir Arafat
   (2) Kofi Anan   (4) Ariel Sharon

10. A major reason that the United States attacked Iraq in 2003 was the
    (1) Iraqi invasion of Kuwait to control its oil fields
    (2) treatment of Kurds living in Iraq
    (3) belief of President Bush that Iraq possessed weapons of mass destruction
    (4) request for its assistance by an international coalition

11. After several years of American troop involvement in Iraq, fighting between which two groups has escalated into what some have called a civil war?
    (1) Kurds and Hizballah
    (2) Hamas and Sunni Muslims
    (3) Al Qaeda and Palestinians
    (4) Shi'ite Muslims and Sunni Muslims

12. The group known as the Taliban is best described as

    (1) anti-American Islamic fundamentalists based in Afghanistan
    (2) Afghani President Karzai's elected Parliament
    (3) highly trained American Iraqi military police
    (4) a well-organized group of Iraqi and Afghani female protestors

13. In 2004 much of South and Southeast Asia was impacted by a major natural disaster called

    (1) a typhoon
    (2) an earthquake
    (3) a hurricane
    (4) a tsunami

14. Place the following events in Vietnamese history in the correct chronological order

    A. President George W. Bush makes an official visit to Vietnam
    B. North Vietnam seizes control of South Vietnam to form one country
    C American firms began to operate in Vietnam
    D. The Vietnamese withdrew from their occupation of Cambodia

    (1) C, D, B, A
    (2) B, A, C, D
    (3) D, C, A, B
    (4) B, D, C, A

15. In the twenty-first century China has been forced to deal with which new domestic medical issues?

    (1) SARS and avian bird flu
    (2) Smallpox and HIV/AIDS
    (3) Polio and typhoid fever
    (4) Malaria and measles

16. As Chinese development continues to increase rapidly, the country is actively seeking to trade for additional supplies of

    (1) wood products
    (2) oil
    (3) coal
    (4) automobile parts

17. A source of controversy in twenty-first century Japan to those interested in politics concerns the

    (1) role of the prime minister
    (2) development of new political parties
    (3) possibility of a female being allowed to become the emperor
    (4) existence of a favorable trade relationship with the United States

18. A current major world concern exists over North Korea's

    (1) improving alliance with South Korea
    (2) trade balance with Japan
    (3) growing domestic democratic movement
    (4) nuclear weapons program

19. What do Kazakhstan, Kyrgystan, and Tajikistan have in common?

    (1) They are all part of the Pacific Rim nations.
    (2) They were all part of the former U.S.S.R.
    (3) They have all made peaceful transitions from Communist states to democracies.
    (4) They are all primarily Muslim states.

20. The Commonwealth of Independent States is composed of

    (1) former members of the Union of Soviet Socialist Republics
    (2) countries that have not been allowed to join the British Commonwealth
    (3) any member of the world community that is independent
    (4) only countries that belong to the Security Council of the United Nations

THEMATIC ESSAY

Directions: Write a well-organized essay that includes an introduction, several paragraphs addressing the task below, and a conclusion.

Theme: Political Systems and Power

A political system in any nation addresses basic questions of government. Each system determines what its powers are and what functions of government it will perform.

Task

Since the end of World War II, many new countries were formed from what were previously colonies in Africa and Asia. These new nations were formed in a variety of ways, and they have adopted an assortment of types of political systems. Some were formed fairly easily, while others experienced some difficulties determining who would control the power in the new nation.

Select *one* African and *one* Asian nation that has been formed since the end of World War II and, for each,

- describe the actual process by which the country gained its independence

- describe the form of political system the country has adopted
- explain how it was determined who would control the power in the new nation
- describe the part at least one person played in the independence movement

You may use any two examples from your study of global history and geography. Some suggestions you might wish to consider are Nigeria, Ghana, Kenya, India, Pakistan, and Vietnam.

You are *not* limited to these suggestions.

Guidelines

In your essay, be sure to

- develop all aspects of the *Task*
- support the theme with relevant facts, examples, and details
- use a logical and clear plan of organization, including an introduction and a conclusion that are beyond a restatement of the theme
- introduce the theme by establishing a framework that is beyond a simple restatement of the *Task* and conclude with a summation of the theme

---

DOCUMENT-BASED ESSAY QUESTION

This question is based on the accompanying documents (1–6). The question is designed to test your ability to work with historical documents. Some of the documents have been edited for the purposes of this question. As you analyze the documents, take into account the source of each document and any point of view that may be presented in the document.

Historical Context

Power refers to the ability of people to compel or influence the actions of others. In global history and current events people who have gained power have used it for good and for evil.

Task

Using information from the documents and your knowledge of global history, answer the questions that follow each document in Part A. Your answers to the questions will help you write the Part B essay in which you will be asked to

- select two leaders and describe how they have used power
- evaluate whether each leader is regarded as having used power in a positive or negative manner either to his own people or in the rest of the world community

---

Part A: Short Answer Questions

Directions: Analyze the documents and answer the short answer questions that follow each document.

Document 1   "Power tends to corrupt, and absolute power corrupts absolutely."

—Lord Acton, *Letter to Bishop Mandell Creighton, 1887*

Question   **1.** Explain in your own words the quotation from Lord Acton.

Document 2   Sunday, 5 November, 2000, 17:17 GMT

HAILE SELASSIE LAID TO REST

Ethiopia's last emperor, Haile Selassie, has finally been laid to rest in Addis Ababa's Trinity Cathedral, more than 25 years after his mysterious death.

Priests in lavish robes, elderly warriors with lions' manes on their heads and dreadlocked Rastafarians joined the funeral procession for the man some believe to be a living god.

But the crowds were much smaller than expected, several thousand-strong, not the hundreds of thousands predicted by the organisers, the Emperor Haile Selassie I Foundation.

. . .

His body has now been laid to rest at the cathedral where other members of the Ethiopian Imperial family have been buried.

After prayers attended by members of the former royal family, the Patriarch of the Ethiopian Orthodox Church, Abune Paulos, paid tribute to the emperor, stressing his "remarkable contribution to Ethiopia, the church, Africa and the entire world."

"Although they killed you and threw your body in an unmarked grave, they could not tarnish your image," said an Orthodox priest during the mass.

. . .

Haile Selassie ruled Ethiopia for 45 years before he was overthrown by the Marxist dictator Mengistu Haile Mariam in 1974.

. . .

More than 25 years have passed since his death, but his legacy still lives on. Haile Selassie is one of the founding fathers of the OAU and is viewed by many as the figurehead of African independence, for his defiance against the Italian colonial invasion in the 1930s.

. . .

Ras Lumumba, a Sudanese Rastafarian who came to settle in Ethiopia three years ago, says the Emperor is their Messiah or Jah.

"Haile Selassie is King of Kings, Lord of Lords, and the conquering lion of the Tribe of Judah. He is everything to us Rastafarians and we will never accept that he is dead."

Source: Excerpt from http://news.bbc.co.uk/1/hi/world/africa/1007735.stm

Question   **2.** According to the BBC news article, why was Haile Selassie given such an impressive funeral?

Document 3

1900s

2003

Question

3. Based on the pictures above, what appears to have happened to Saddam Hussein over the time these pictures were taken?

Document 4

Friday, 14 April 2000, 13:59 GMT 14:59 UK

POL POT: LIFE OF A TYRANT

Pol Pot's death in April 1998 heralded the end of the brutal career of a man responsible for overseeing one of the worst genocides of the 20th century.

Between 1975 and 1979 his regime claimed the lives of more than 1m people —through execution, starvation and disease— as the Khmer Rouge tried to turn Cambodia back to the middle ages.

For many survivors of that era, the joy of his demise will only be tempered with the regret that he was not called to account for his crimes against humanity. The "people's tribunal" at which his former colleagues sentenced him to life imprisonment last year was widely regarded as little more than a show trial.

Ideologue

Many precise details of Pol Pot's life remain shrouded in mystery.
He is thought to have been about 72 when he died, although the exact date of his birth is not clear.

. . .

Pol Pot officially retired as leader of the Khmer Rouge at the end of the 1980s. Following a bloody power struggle inside the Khmer Rouge he was arrested by his former colleagues in July 1997, and charged with treason.

After a "people's tribunal" sentenced him to life under house arrest he gave an interview two months later in which he declared: "My conscience is clear".

Source: Excerpt from
http://news.bbc.co.uk/1/hi/world/asia-pacific/78988.stm

Question

4. According to the BBC news article what kind of a leader was Pol Pot?

Document 5

North Korea: A secretive society and its strange leader
Updated Tue. Oct. 10 2006 1:54 PM ET

CTV.CA NEWS STAFF

The world doesn't quite know what to make of North Korea's diminutive leader, Kim Jong-il.

He is considered to be a ruthless dictator who stands accused of heinous crimes, maintains a million-man army (the world's fifth-largest military) and hasn't backed down from his nuclear ambitions in the face of global opposition.

. . .

After his father passed away in 1994, he took over as leader of the ruling Korean Workers' Party—the position he still holds.

His status as a cult figure has been established among North Korea's 23 million people. They refer to him as "Dear Leader" and celebrate his birthday every year with a designated holiday.

However, even the mildest acts of dissent can lead to punishment.

Defectors have connected him to terror activities around the world, including the bombing of a Korean Airlines jet in 1986 that left more than 100 people dead.

He reportedly also masterminded a 1983 terrorist bombing in Myanmar that killed 17 South Korean officials.

North Korean spy An Myung Jin told the BBC that terrorism isn't considered a crime under Kim Jong-il's regime but is looked at as "an essential tool for completing the revolution."

He said tactics included blowing up targets, kidnapping generals, members of parliament and students from South Korea — all with the goal of bringing both Koreas under communist rule.

There have also been reports of torture, public executions, slave labour, and forced abortions and infanticides.

. . .

Aid agencies estimate that anywhere from two million to three million people have died since the mid-1990s as the result of food shortages brought on by natural disasters and economic mismanagement.

While the country exists in almost hermit-like seclusion from the rest of the world, with all media tightly controlled by the state, it has relied heavily on foreign aid to feed millions of its own people.

*Source: Excerpt from http://www.ctv.ca/servlet/ArticleNews/story/CTVNews/ 20060705/NorthKorea_FactFile_*

Question

5. According to the CTV news article, how is the North Korean leader, Kim Jong-il, viewed by many of those outside of North Korea?

Document 6

Leader of the All India Muslim League, Muhammed Ali Jinnah, with Mohandas Gandhi in Bombay, India, September 9, 1944.

Mausoleum of Mohammad Ali Jinnah (1876–1948) in Karachi, Pakistan. Jinnah was a lawyer and politician who fought for the cause of India's independence from Britain, then moved on to found a Muslim state in Pakistan in 1947.

Questions

6. a. Based on the picture, what seems to be the relationship of the two leaders?
   b. From studying the photograph, what can you determine about how Pakistan Muslims felt about Jinnah?

Part B: Essay

Directions: Write a well-organized essay that includes an introduction, several paragraphs, and a conclusion. Use evidence from *at least four* documents in the body of the essay. Support your response with relevant facts, examples, and details. Include additional outside information.

Historical Context

Power refers to the ability of people to compel or influence the actions of others. In global history and current events people who have gained power have used it for good and for evil.

Task

Using information from the documents and your knowledge of global history, answer the questions that follow each document in Part A. Your answers to the questions will help you write the Part B essay in which you will be asked to

- select two leaders and describe how they have used power
- evaluate whether each leader is regarded as having used power in a positive or negative manner either with his own people or in the rest of the world community

Guidelines

In your essay, be sure to

- address all aspects of the *Task* by accurately analyzing and interpreting *at least four* documents
- incorporate information from the documents in the body of the essay
- incorporate relevant outside information
- support the theme with relevant facts, examples, and details
- use a logical and clear plan of organization
- introduce the theme by establishing a framework that is beyond a simple restatement of the *Task* or *Historical Context* and conclude with a summation of the theme

CHAPTER 17

Political, Economic, and Social Change in Latin America and the Caribbean

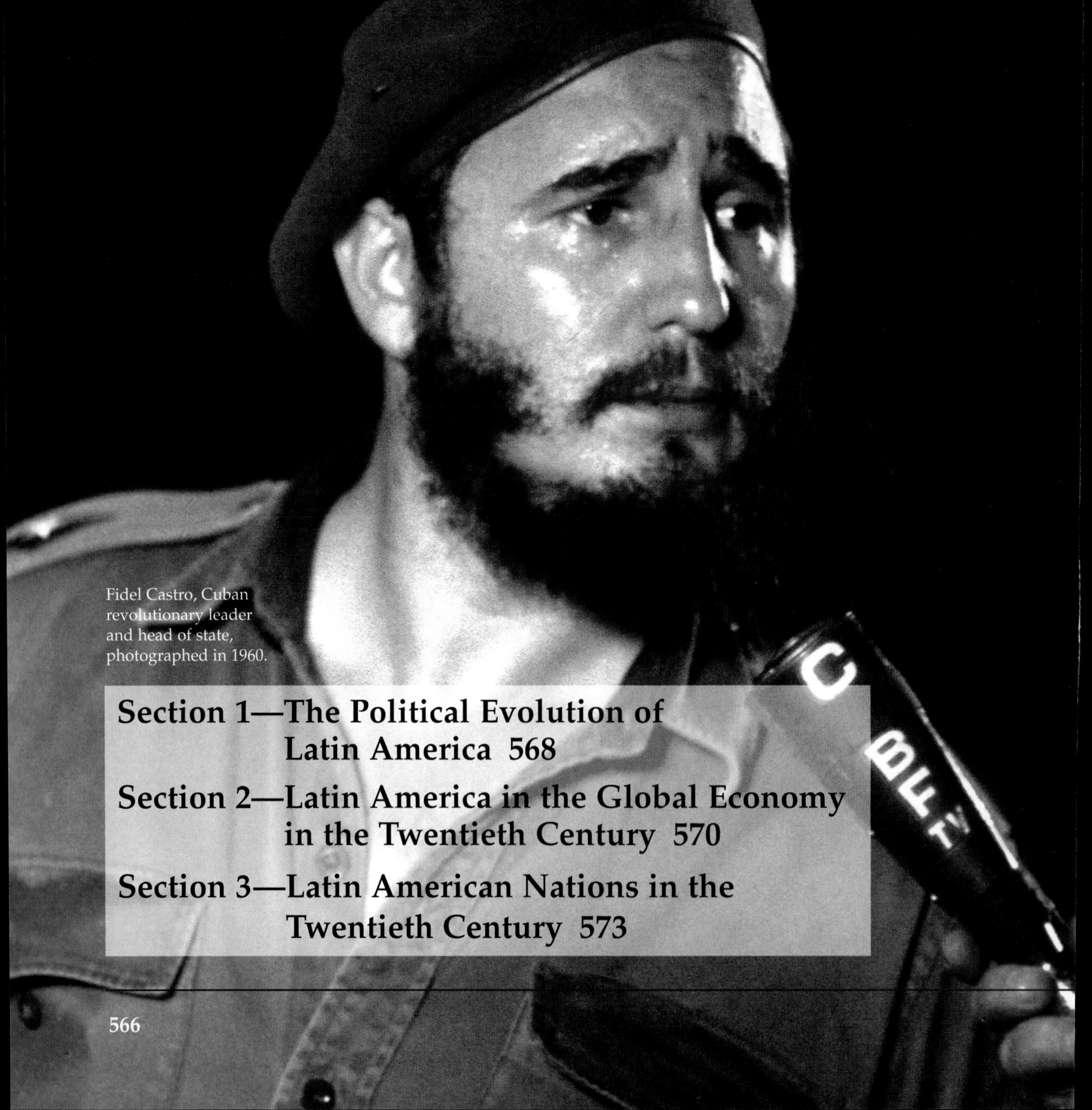

Fidel Castro, Cuban revolutionary leader and head of state, photographed in 1960.

Latin American nations underwent a series of far-reaching political, economic, and social changes in the twentieth century. For long periods in the 1900s, dictatorial or military governments ruled most nations of **Latin America**. Rich people who represented the interests of the upper classes controlled the governments and economies throughout the region. These elite groups—the wealthy landowners, merchants, bankers, and military leaders—dominated national and regional politics and the local economies. However, by the end of the century, the political systems in most Latin American nations began to change and became more democratic. As the century progressed, the middle and lower classes had an increasing influence on political events, particularly when elections took place.

In addition, in the 1900s the economies of Latin American countries became more integrated into the growing global trading system. Most Latin American nations, particularly countries with export economies based on agricultural or mineral resources, were dependent on the more developed nations for industrial goods and investment capital. This meant that the nations of Latin America supplied the industrial nations with agricultural and ranching products and raw materials and produced limited industrial goods. In the 1900s, this economic dependency was basically a continuation of the subservient or dependent role that Latin America played throughout the Colonial Era and during the first century of national independence. However, as the 1900s progressed, some nations such as Brazil, Cuba, and Venezuela increased their efforts to achieve economic independence.

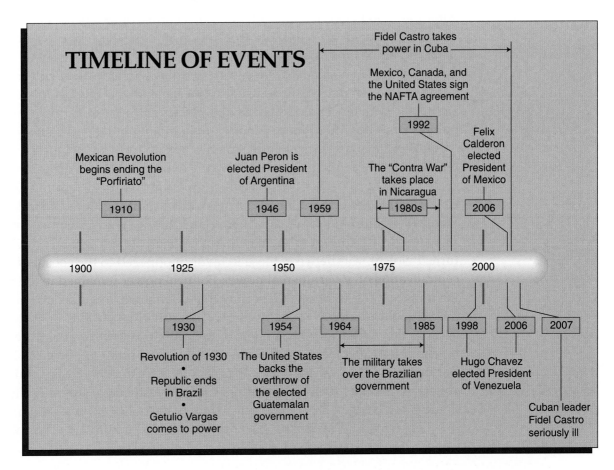

Political, Economic, and Social Change in Latin America and the Caribbean **567**

During the 1900s, Latin American nations continued to be linked by many cultural and social traditions. However, these shared commonalities of language, religion, and Spanish culture became increasingly integrated with other influences. In the twentieth century, the cultural and social heritage that the Latin American nations shared after the Wars of Independence gave way to individual differences among the countries and peoples of the region. This led to the development of distinct national identities throughout Latin America.

The Political Evolution of Latin America

POLITICS PRIOR TO THE TWENTIETH CENTURY

After the Colonial Period and into the first century of independence, the upper classes continued to politically control their countries. The wealthy elites remained at the top of the economic and social order. The leaders of the national independence movements were most often large landowners, rich local merchants, some religious figures, usually priests, and aspiring middle-class professionals. With few exceptions, the upper-class elites took over political control in most countries after independence and held onto power well into the 1900s.

After independence in Latin America, the political life of most nations was marked by a struggle for power between two upper-class parties who represented wealthy people. The two competing political groups were the Conservative and the Liberal parties. These elite groups included large landowners, important merchants, and the other wealthy members of society. They fought for control of the new nations. The political struggle, which often turned violent, was between those in favor or opposed to the consolidation and centralization of governmental power. Political power remained in the hands of the upper-class groups of each society that dominated and most benefited from the nation's economy. Usually, the conservatives won the political battles because they often had the support of the military. However, the development of communist ideology in Cuba after Fidel Castro came to power in 1960 and the overall affects of the Cold War led to armed conflicts in many Latin American nations, such as Argentina, Chile, Brazil, Peru, Uruguay, Nicaragua, El Salvador, Guatemala, and elsewhere where the political, economic, and social problems could no longer be easily contained and controlled. The rule of the upper classes began to be increasingly challenged.

POLITICS IN THE TWENTIETH CENTURY

By the end of the nineteenth century, most of the Latin American nations had stable political boundaries. Central governments became more powerful as national armies grew in importance. As the national governments became stronger, their political power became more far-reaching into the different areas of the country. However, despite growing centralization, and the old-style political bosses, the caudillos, who were often large landowners, still exercised regional or local influence. In the twentieth century, rulers in many Latin American nations were civilian dictators or military officers who held onto political power as long as they effectively controlled the nation's armed forces. As the twentieth century progressed, the military more often seized political power. Military rule peaked in the second half of the 1900s and then gradually declined. Democratically elected governments became the rule rather than the exception by the end of the century. In some nations such as Peru, Nicaragua, and Venezuela, Socialist and Communist ideas found a receptive audience among the poorer groups in society and their defenders.

THE RISE OF THE MIDDLE CLASS

In the first decades of the twentieth century, the middle class was still small in number in almost every nation and lacked political influence. However, as the 1900s progressed, in many countries, middle-class groups grew in percentage of the population and became more involved and influential in national politics. The middle classes took advantage of educational and economic opportunities and became upwardly socially mobile. They often found their livelihoods in national organizations such as the military, mainly the army; government bureaucracies including educational institutions; small business; and the legal profession.

In some countries, such as Argentina and Uruguay, the middle class formed political parties and ultimately gained political power in a democratic manner. In other countries, such as Venezuela, Colombia, and Brazil, middle-class groups aligned themselves with the upper classes to form political alliances and share political power. Almost always, middle-class groups shared the upper classes' fear and dislike of the poorer segments of society.

THE LOWER CLASSES LACK POLITICAL POWER

In the 1900s, the lower classes of Latin American nations, people who were mostly "mestizos," mulattos, blacks, poor whites, and Native Americans (or Indian) continued to be the majority of the population. Upward social mobility was most always not very easy for people who came from the lower classes. They lacked educational and economic opportunities. Therefore, during the 1900s, the vast majority of the lower classes remained poor and continued to struggle for their livelihood. Throughout Latin America, the lower classes of society were denied access to political power. Even in cases when and where political power was seized in the name of the lower classes such as Bolivia, Guatemala, and Cuba, the real rulers of the nation remained essentially well-educated upper- or middle-class people.

SECTION 2

Latin America in the Global Economy in the Twentieth Century

THE ECONOMIC HERITAGE OF LATIN AMERICA

In the Colonial Period, Spain and Portugal imposed the rules of mercantilism on their Latin American colonies. After national independence in the 1800s, the economies of the Latin American countries were no longer controlled by Spain and Portugal. However, through World War I, another European nation, Great Britain, dominated the trade with Latin American countries and made the largest investments in capital. As the nineteenth century progressed, the Latin American nations found themselves increasingly integrated into the world economy. Trade with and investment by the United States and other developed European nations continued to increase. It was difficult to break the economic ties of cash crop dependency that existed from the earlier pre-independence period.

DEPENDENCY AND INTEGRATION OF LATIN AMERICAN ECONOMIES IN THE 1900s

After the First World War, the United States began to replace Great Britain as the leading trading partner and investor in Latin American countries. The United States had a long economic relationship with Latin America dating from the colonial period when much illegal trade took place. The United States and Latin American nations trading relationships grew throughout the 1800s. By the turn of the twentieth century, the United States began to play more of a controlling role in the affairs of Latin American nations particularly in times of political crisis and revolution. The Spanish American War in 1898 brought the United States into direct control of Latin American lands in the Caribbean region. During the first decades of the 1900s, the United States continued to politically intervene in Latin American nations, particularly in the Caribbean region and Central

America as it became more economically involved in Latin America. During this period, the United States followed a foreign policy called dollar diplomacy, which meant that what was good for American business was good for Latin America.

As the twentieth century progressed, U.S. investment throughout Latin America increased enormously. Some nations, particularly in the Caribbean region and Central America, became heavily dependent on the United States in terms of trade. For example, Honduras and Nicaragua were referred to as banana republics because they were monocultural agricultural economies that were economically dependent on the United States as a market for their crops, particularly bananas. Latin American countries became more economically dependent and integrated into the economies of the United States and other developed nations.

For example, Cuba, until Fidel Castro led a successful revolution in 1959, sold most of its sugar and tobacco crops to the United States, which controlled its economy. Brazil and Colombia were the leading coffee-producing nations; however, the marketing and pricing of this food commodity was controlled in London, England. Chile became known for its copper mines; Bolivia had tin mines; Peru sold guano, a fertilizer; and Venezuela exported cacao. In return for exporting these food products or raw materials to the developed industrial nations, these and other Latin American countries were markets for finished goods and investment capital.

ECONOMIC NATIONALISM AND THE ISSUE OF OIL

During the twentieth century, some nations in Latin America tried to develop more economic independence. After the Mexican Revolution of 1910, the Constitution of 1917 was passed; it included a provision that sought to protect the Mexican nation's subsoil resources from foreign exploitation. The revolutionary leaders wanted to safeguard their subsoil mining rights that had been given away to foreign companies during the Porfirio Diaz period. This desire to protect Mexican natural resources, particularly oil, led to an ongoing conflict with the United States, which threatened invasion on several occasions to protect American business interests.

During the 1930s, Lazaro Cardenas nationalized the Mexican petroleum industry and created a state-owned and -directed company, Petroleos, Mexicanos, PEMEX, to manage the oil industry. President Franklin Roosevelt was willing to accept this nationalization because the United States foreign policy toward Latin America changed from the Big Stick Policy and Dollar Diplomacy to that of the Good Neighbor Policy.

In the 1930s, Brazil, Latin America's largest and most populous nation, began to support ideas favoring its economic self-interests or economic nationalism. President Getulio Vargas, backed by the military leadership, wanted to make Brazil more self-sufficient economically and less dependent on agricultural export products, particularly coffee. Brazil began to develop its own industries, especially its ability to mine iron and process it into steel. In 1937, the Estado Novo was created, and a new constitution was adopted. This constitution sought to guarantee the rights of the Brazilian people and nation to control their own economy and led to efforts to develop national industries. Although Brazil is now more integrated into the global economy, the nation has continued to develop its national economic interests, particularly with the support of the Brazilian military.

In the 1930s, Argentina also tried to reduce its economic dependency on foreign nations. Argentina's economy was primarily based on the production and exportation of agricultural and ranching products and the importation of finished goods, mainly from Europe. This economic dependency dated back to the nineteenth century and the development of refrigerated ships, which were capable of transporting Argentinean beef and wheat without spoilage. Under the government of Juan Peron, Argentina tried to pursue a more independent economic path and promote its own industrial growth. During the time of Juan Peron, from the mid-1940s to his fall in 1955, Argentina had a greater control over the workings of the nation's economy.

THE PULL OF THE INTERNATIONAL ECONOMY IN THE TWENTIETH CENTURY

In the 1900s, some Latin American nations sought to promote their own national economic interests. However, for the most part, Latin American countries became more integrated into the global trading system and dependent on the more developed industrial nations, particularly the United States. This economic integration grew because Latin American nations became increasingly dependent on international lending organizations, particularly foreign banks for investment capital. By the 1980s, many Latin American countries were heavily indebted and subject to economic demands by the International Monetary Fund and World Bank.

In addition, most of the Latin American economies continued to be export-oriented. They were dependent on the sale of foodstuffs and raw materials. Even countries, which had surplus energy resources of oil and gas, could not escape the pull of and dependency on the more developed industrial nations. For example, Mexico and Venezuela earned huge profits from the export of petroleum products. Nevertheless, the profits earned from oil exportation were not used by these nations to develop more independent national economies. With the exception of Brazil, which became one of the world's largest economies, Latin American nations remained exporters of agricultural crops and raw materials and very dependent on the global trading system for the importation of industrial goods.

> **Main Idea:**
> By the 1980s, many Latin American countries were heavily indebted and subject to economic demands by the International Monetary Fund and World Bank.

Latin American Nations in the Twentieth Century

In this section, you will read about the political, economic, and social histories of the Latin American nations. In the 1900s, Latin American countries continued to develop their individual national histories and cultures. Despite commonalities in Latin American history and culture, there were differences in the way that countries developed in the second century of national independence.

MEXICO

The Mexican Revolution (1910–1940)

Emiliano Zapata (1879–1919), Mexican revolutionary.

The Mexican Revolution of 1910 lasted well into the second decade of the twentieth century. In the 1900s, the Revolution of 1910 was very important in determining the history of **Mexico.** The revolution, which first started as a battle between the dominant upper classes of society for political power, soon involved the middle and lower classes in a violent struggle. In this section, you will read about many of the famous names that are associated with the first phase of the **Mexican Revolution** (1910–1940); Francisco Madero, Victoriano Huerta, Venustiano Carranza, Emiliano Zapata, Pancho Villa, Alvaro Obregon, Plutarco Calles, and Lazaro Cardenas.

After the assassination of **Francisco Madero**, who was the opposition candidate against **Porfirio Diaz** in 1910, the Mexican Revolution broke out. The uprising against the Diaz regime soon spread to other parts of the country. Diaz was forced into exile. **Victoriano Huerta**, a general, took control of the government. **Venustiano Carranza**, who now led the revolutionary forces, opposed him. Two revolutionaries, **Emiliano Zapata** and **Pancho Villa**, both interested in agrarian reform and the rights of the lower classes, were the military leaders of the rebel forces. By 1914, Huerta, who had political problems with the United States, was forced to give up power and went into exile. Carranza, who was a wealthy landowner, took control of

Mexican Revolution, 1910. A battle between federal forces and Zapata followers. Zinc engraving by Jose Guadalupe Posada.

the Mexican government. However, he soon fell out with Zapata and Villa over the issue of agrarian reform. Carranza, the leader of the Constitutionalists, was able to hold onto power with the help of his key military leader **Alvaro Obregon**. During his presidency, the famous Constitution of 1917 was passed. The Constitution, which continues to exist today, empowered the government to redistribute land, subjected the church to new regulations, allowed labor to organize, and gave the Mexican nation subsoil rights to mineral wealth. In 1919, Zapata was assassinated, and Villa's northern military forces were defeated. By 1920, Carranza was forced from power, and Obregon became president.

President Cardenas (right) with his ministers at a meeting in Mexico, 1938.

Three Revolutions. Fragment from Diego Rivera's mural "History and Perspective of Mexico" at the National Palace, Mexico City.

During President Obregon's term, needed reforms were made, which expanded rural education and created a limited land distribution program. A government-supported labor movement was established. Obregon also came to an agreement with the United States that resulted in American diplomatic recognition in return for protection of foreign oil interests. In 1924, Obregon peacefully transferred the presidency to **Plutarco Callas,** a northern political leader. During his term, he stabilized the political system and put down a rebellion led by Catholic Church reactionaries. Callas continued to secularize Mexico after the defeat of the "Cristeros," a catholic priest led rebellion of mostly poor religiously minded peasants.

Obregon was reelected in 1928 but was soon assassinated. Callas became the leader behind the political scene and selected the next presidents. A new political party was created, the **Partido Nacional Revolucionario (PRN)**. In 1934, **Lazaro Cardenas** was elected president and began an ambitious land distribution program known as the communal land ownership system, or *ejido*. Cardenas also nationalized the Mexico petroleum industry into a state-owned system called PEMEX. The nationalization of the foreign oil interests was done under the famous Article 27 of the Constitution of 1917. Lazaro Cardenas maximized the social and economic goals and reforms associated with the Mexican Revolution.

The Revolution also unleashed a great deal of creative energy in the arts and literature. Paintings, particularly public murals, by a trio of gifted artists, **Diego Rivera**, **David Sequeiros**, and **Jose Orozco**, were works of art and social messages to the masses of illiterate Mexicans. The self-portrait paintings of **Frieda Kahlo** also gained an international reputation. In literature, there was a commitment to "Indianism" in the books of important Mexican writers such as **Carlos Fuentes** and **Mariano Azuela**.

The Mexican Revolution Comes to an End (1940–2000)

In 1940, starting with the election of **Manuel Avila Camacho**, the Mexican Revolution turned more conservative. Presidents of Mexico continued to be nominated by and elected from the ruling party, the PRM, later to become the *Partido Revolucionario Institucional (PRI)*, for the remainder of the century. Radical social and political goals were no longer pursued. Thereafter, the presidents and party leaders sought to work more with business and industry leaders and control what was in effect a one-party political system for their own personal benefits. The basic goals of Cardenas's successors became political stability and economic growth with social controls through party-dominated organizations.

In 1968, students, workers, and their intellectual supporters sought to reignite the spirit of the Mexican Revolution. The government used soldiers and police to crush the reform movement. The massacre of **Tlateloco** for a time ended hope that the PRI could be democratically forced to give up its monopoly on power.

During the decades after World War II, Mexico's economic relationship with the United States grew. The value of products imported from and exported to the United States increased. Mexican workers, both legal and illegal immigrants, in the United States played an ever-larger role in the American economy. In 1992, during the presidency of **Carlos Gotari Salinas**, Mexico, the United States, and Canada joined together in the **North American Free Trade Agreement** designed to further integrate their economies. NAFTA is an example of a modern international trade agreement.

In the last decades of the twentieth century, Mexico experienced severe economic and social problems. These unresolved problems led to continuous demands for a real political restructuring. By the end of the century, the population of Mexico more than doubled to over 100 million. There wasn't enough work for all Mexicans at home in industry and agriculture. This led to increasing immigration, both legal and illegal, to the United States. In addition, the issue of narcotics trafficking became increasingly troublesome. Drug trafficking led to more corruption in Mexican government, particularly among the police and military, because of the huge profits that could be earned. The last president of Mexico in the twentieth century, **Ernesto Zedillo**, recognized the growing political impasse and allowed a more freely contested presidential election.

The result of the first really free presidential election resulted in the defeat of the PRI candidate and election of the *Partido Accion Nacional (PAN)* candidate, **Vincente Fox** in 2000. President Fox ruled Mexico for six years (2000–2006), and during his term in office he faced enormous economic and social problems. An economy that offered too few jobs to a growing population led to increased immigration to the United States. Economic and social inequities, drug trafficking and its corrupting influences, and other problems continued to plague Mexico. In 2006, **Felix Calderon**, also of the PAN, was elected president in a hotly contested election. Mexico is the United States' major economic partner in Latin America and overall its most important concern because of the long border and interconnected political, economic, and social history that both nations share.

Main Idea:
Economic and social inequities, drug trafficking and its corrupting influences, and other problems continued to plague Mexico.

CENTRAL AMERICA: PANAMA, GUATEMALA, EL SALVADOR, HONDURAS, NICARAGUA, AND COSTA RICA

In the twentieth century, the economies of the **Central American** nations were mostly based on the export of commercial plantation crops and import of industrialized goods. During the 1900s, the expression "banana republic" was used to describe the Central American nations. This meant that these nations were essentially monoagricultural, and their economies depended on one particular cash crop. Honduras, Costa Rica, and Panama had mostly banana plantations, whereas Nicaragua, El Salvador, and Guatemala were mainly coffee-producing countries.

During the 1900s, political systems of Central American countries reflected the hierarchical organization of society. For their own economic and social benefits, the upper classes ruled over the vast majority of people, who were mostly landless and poor. In all of these nations, the wealthy landowning families controlled almost all the good agricultural land. The rich landowners and merchants exploited the growth and export of the banana and coffee crops. The rural poor worked as farm laborers for low wages on commercial plantations to produce the export crops. Agricultural laborers lived in poverty and had few political rights. The urban working class was very small in Central America because of a lack of industrial development. Middle-class groups existed in all nations but were also small in number.

In the twentieth century, the overall political and economic influence of the United States was very strong throughout Central America. During the Cold War, the United States militarily intervened whenever it considered its economic and political interests threatened. This was particularly true in Nicaragua, Panama, and Guatemala. The United States also used its political influence and military and intelligence capabilities to support the economic interests of large American corporations with investments in Central America. For example, U.S. foreign policy in the region backed the economic interests of the United Fruit Company (UFCO), which had a virtual monopoly on the production and sale of bananas. Throughout the twentieth century, the United States remained the Central American nations' largest trading partner.

In the 1960s, the **Central American Common Market (CACM)** was formed to stimulate industrial development by promoting free trade among member nations and common tariffs to protect infant industries. Only Panama did not join because of its special status with the **Panama Canal**. The CACM met with some limited success in the development of local industries. The lack of investment capital and urban working class were handicaps to economic diversification. The population remained largely rural, although the capitol cities experienced growth because of internal migration.

> **Main Idea:**
> In the 1960s, the **Central American Common Market (CACM)** was formed to stimulate industrial development by promoting free trade among member nations and common tariffs to protect infant industries.

Panama

Panama was originally a part of **Colombia.** The United States was instrumental in the establishment of the Panamanian nation in 1903. Panama became an independent country after the United States decided to build an interocean canal across the Isthmus of Panama and thereby connect the Atlantic and Pacific

Oceans. Colombia's refusal to accept the United States' demands led to the American recognition of Panama. Until then, Panama was a province of Colombia. The **Hay-Bunau-Varilla Treaty**, which guaranteed the independence of the newly recognized Panama, authorized the United States to build the canal and establish a canal zone in perpetuity. The United States received the right to administer the Canal Zone and manage the Canal. The Canal Zone effectively divided the nation in two for most of the twentieth century.

Boats on the Panama Canal shortly after its opening in 1914.

After independence, the United States intervened in Panamanian politics and prevented any change in the Panama Canal's status. In the 1960s, rising Panamanian nationalism eventually led to an agreement with the United States. A new treaty was negotiated; it called for the sovereignty of the canal including the Canal Zone to be returned to Panama in 1999. At that time, Panama took over the responsibility of managing and securing the safety of the canal. Since then, Panama has turned over the Panama Canal's management to a private Chinese company.

Guatemala

Jacobo Arbenz Guzman (1913–1971), photographed while President of Guatemala.

Guatemala had a long history of dictatorial rule throughout most of the twentieth century. In Guatemala, social class divisions between the **Mayan** and **mestizo** majority and the upper-class Ladino population remained strong throughout the 1900s. The upper-class wealthy landowners had large homes in the capital, Guatemala City, and the countryside and controlled the economy, which was largely based on agricultural production. The Guatemalan military backed the interests of the upper class. Most of the Mayans lived in rural villages and were engaged in small subsistence agriculture to feed their families. They worked seasonally for the large landowners on plantations to earn their livelihoods.

During the 1950s, the government of **Jacobo Arbenz** sought to bring about a social revolution accompanied by a land reform program. In 1954, Arbenz was overthrown in a military coup supported by the American **Central Intelligence Agency (CIA)**. The U.S. government supported the interests of the United Fruit Company. For the next decades, revolutionary activity resulted in a harsh military repression and high death toll among the rural Mayan population. By the 1980s, more democratic governments were elected, and some respect for human rights and constitutionally guaranteed liberties were slowly restored. In the 1990s, the vast majority of the lower class socioeconomic groups remained very poor, and immigration out of the nation continued to increase.

El Salvador

A small aristocracy of wealthy landowners politically controlled **El Salvador** for most of the twentieth century. The economy was based largely on coffee production. The vast majority of people were poor farm laborers. They were economically exploited and lacked political representation, human rights, and constitutional liberties. Throughout the 1900s, the farm laborers rose up in rebellion to improve their socioeconomic situation. They were always brutally repressed by the military, which protected the interests of the wealthy landowners. The landowners refused to agree to any type of agrarian or democratic reforms. They lived a comfortable and protected life in **San Salvador,** the capital.

> **Main Idea:**
> By the 1990s, El Salvador, a small nation of about 1.5 million inhabitants, opened its political system and made it more democratic.

In the 1970s, another attempt at land reform failed. Soon after, a violent revolution led by the **National Liberation Front** (**NLF**) broke out. The armed forces sought to wipe out the NLF, but the fighting continued into the 1980s. Eventually the armed conflict in the rural countryside came into the urban areas. Peace finally came after the NLF was able to bring the fighting into San Salvador and penetrated to where the upper and middle classes lived. By the 1990s, El Salvador, a small nation of about 1.5 million inhabitants, opened its political system and made it more democratic. Political parties competed for leadership in elections. Poverty and the lack of opportunity for the largely landless lower class remained problems. Immigration out of the nation became an outlet for many poor Salvadorians.

Honduras

Honduras, a large nation in terms of territory with a relatively small population, was considered a stereotypical banana republic throughout the 1900s. The wealthy landed upper class, who exploited the vast majority of landless peasants, owned all of the good agricultural land. The military in Honduras consistently supported the rights of the wealthy landowners and oppressed the poorer groups in society. The Honduran armed forces historically has had strong ties to the U.S. military and supported American foreign policy interests in Guatemala, Cuba, and, more recently, Nicaragua. In the 1990s, immigration out of Honduras was increasing because of growing crime, repression, and lack of economic opportunity.

Nicaragua

For much of its history, **Nicaragua** has been influenced by nations that have intervened in its political affairs. From the 1850s, when Great Britain and the United States concluded a treaty about a possible interocean canal, into the twentieth century, Nicaragua has been invaded and at times occupied. In the early twentieth century, the United States repeatedly intervened in Nicaraguan internal politics. In the 1930s, the United States foreign policy toward Latin

America shifted from that of a **"Big Stick"** to that of a **"Good Neighbor."** At that time, the United States trained a national guard to act as a domestic police force and help maintain order in the nation. **Anastasio Somoza** was chosen as the leader of the national guard.

During the 1930s, a Nicaraguan nationalist, **Augusto Sandino** was assassinated and became a martyred national hero. Sandino wanted to bring his nation more political autonomy and a democratic electoral system. Thereafter, until a successful revolution caused the Nicaraguan government to collapse in 1979, the nation was ruled by the Somoza family and their associates. Throughout their over four decades of rule, the Somoza family became extremely wealthy because they controlled the national economy for their personal benefit. In the 1960s, a revolutionary movement, the Sandinista National Liberation Front, began a long violent military struggle. By the late 1970s, the Sandinistas took power after the Somoza regime collapsed.

At first, the United States under President Carter accepted the outcome of the revolution. However, after the Nicaraguan government accepted Cuban assistance, the United States turned against the Sandinista-led government because of what it believed was the Sandinista Marxist orientation. During the 1980s, a civil war, the **Contra War**, broke out. The Sandinistas who controlled the Nicaraguan military fought against a counterrevolutionary army of Nicaraguan exiles based mostly in Honduras. The American government led by President Reagan openly supported the Contras.

By the late 1980s, the war became a stalemate. The Sandinista government, faced with a severe economic crisis and no hope for a decisive military victory, agreed to elections. In the 1990 presidential election, **Violeta Chamorro**, a moderate, defeated the Sandinista candidate, **Daniel Ortega**. Chamorro declared an end to the fighting and a general amnesty. In the 1990s, Nicaragua continued to promote national reconciliation and develop as a democracy. However, solutions to economic problems and political corruption still needed to be found; the government's inability to find answers led to increasing outward immigration. After Chamorro left office, the next presidents did little to help the vast majority of Nicaraguan people. In 2006, the former Sandinista leader Daniel Ortega was elected president of Nicaragua.

> **Main Idea:**
> In the 1990s, Nicaragua continued to promote national reconciliation and develop as a democracy.

Costa Rica

After World War II, under the political leadership of Jose Figueres, **Costa Rica** developed a constitutional democracy. Costa Rica benefited from having a small population and a racially and socially homogeneous society. Agriculture, particularly coffee production, was the principal mainstay of the economy. However, in the last decades of the 1900s, Costa Rica was able to attract foreign investment because of its stable political situation. Some industrial development and growth took place. In addition, Costa Rica became an international tourist attraction and retirement center for those seeking a warm and friendly year-round environment. In the 1900s, Costa Rica was the exception to the general rule in Central America and offered continued prospects for future development and opportunity.

THE CARIBBEAN BASIN: CUBA, THE DOMINICAN REPUBLIC, HAITI, AND PUERTO RICO

Cuba

From the time of Spanish colonization in the early 1500s until 1898, Cuba's historical development was very influenced by its geographic location, agricultural potential, and slavery. After the era of Latin American independence ended in the 1820s, **Cuba** remained a Spanish colony until 1898. In the nineteenth century, Cuba was a major producer of agricultural crops: sugarcane, tobacco, and coffee. The commercial plantation economy was based on the exploitation of slave labor. The exportation of commercial agricultural crops was very profitable for the Spanish government and wealthy upper-class landowners and merchants.

In the last decades of the 1800s, the Spanish government tried to stamp out a growing independence movement in Cuba. The Spanish military used harsh measures of suppression. During this period, **Jose Marti**, a revolutionary poet, fought with other Cuban nationalists for independence. They wanted to establish a Cuban government, which was free of foreign interference and control. However, American political and economic interests pushed for U.S. intervention in Cuba. Ultimately, after the sinking of the **battleship *Maine*** in Havana Harbor, the United States declared a war on Spain. As a result of the **Spanish American War** in 1898, Cuba was given its independence. However, after the war the United States gained control of a naval base in Cuba, in **Guantanamo Bay**. The United States took political control of Cuba for several years. After granting the island nation its independence, the United States openly declared its right to intervene in Cuban affairs.

Jose J. Marti (1853–1895), Cuban patriot. Detail. Oil on canvas, 1891, by Herman Norman.

From the early 1900s until the **Cuban Revolution** led by **Fidel Castro** in 1959, the United States dominated Cuban political and economic affairs to protect U.S. business interests. In the 1930s, when Franklin Roosevelt's Good Neighbor Policy went into effect, the United States helped **Fulgencio Batista**, a military noncommissioned officer rise to power. Batista became the leader of the Cuban National Guard, which made him the real ruler of the country. From 1934 to 1959, Batista controlled Cuba and either directly governed the nation as president or ruled from behind the political scene through politicians he controlled.

The United States' economic interests increased enormously during the Batista years. American investment grew particularly in the sugar, tobacco, and alcohol, mostly rum, industries. Prior to 1959, many Americans lived all over Cuba, particularly in Havana, where they enjoyed a privileged life. During the decades of Batista's dictatorship, Cuba became a safe haven for criminals, or "gangsters," from the United States.

Cuba was an island of multiple racial types. The vast majority of the Cuban population was poor and worked in the agricultural sector. Poverty was widespread; however, the black population was the least well off. Into the mid-1950s, Batista was able to keep the nation and people under his tight control through the use of his secret police and army. During the 1950s, Fidel Castro, a young Cuban of middle-class origins and a good education, began a revolution to overthrow the Batista regime. By the late 1950s, despite earlier failures, Castro

Cuban students serving in the militia using an anti-aircraft gun against the C.I.A. backed invasion force of anti-Castro exiles at the Bay of Pigs, April 17, 1961.

became a serious threat to the Batista government. Castro operated from mountain bases and his revolutionary forces benefited enormously from popular support. By 1958, Castro was able to take the war more to the urban areas, and Batista's army collapsed. Batista lost support of the United States and fled the country on New Year's Eve. In early 1959, Castro triumphantly entered Havana and, with his fellow revolutionaries, took political power. Castro at this time was most likely motivated by reformist Socialist and liberal political, economic, and social ideas.

At first, the United States accepted the political change in Cuba. However, after Cuba became more anti-American and pro-Soviet Union, the United States' foreign policy toward the Castro government changed. The United States accused Castro of turning Cuba into a Communist regime. During the first years of Castro's rule, the Cuban government enacted a radical land reform program, which eliminated private property. The Castro-led government also made other radical reforms including the nationalization of private banks and businesses. The radical reforms led to a mass immigration of the upper and middle classes mostly to the United States.

In 1961, during the Kennedy presidency the United States tried to remove the Castro-led government by backing the unsuccessful **Bay of Pigs invasion** of Cuban exiles. Shortly thereafter, the United States and the Soviet Union almost went to the brink of nuclear war over the issue of Russian missiles being placed in Cuba. Fortunately, the Soviet Union agreed to remove the missiles thereby averting a possible nuclear confrontation. Since that time, the Fidel Castro government has remained in power. However, the United States instituted an economic boycott. In 1989, the collapse of the Soviet Union, Cuba's greatest economic helper and protector, led to increased economic hardship in Cuba. Since taking power in 1959, the Castro government has never allowed democratic elections and has used political repression, including jail time and exile for opponents, to keep its hold on political power. Fidel Castro has ruled Cuba for over forty years. In 2007, he became seriously ill. Castro deserves credit for much of what has been done in Cuba to educate people and to develop a low-cost national health system. However, Cuba under Castro's dictatorial rule has become a nation where electoral democracy is severely limited and political freedom and human rights are violated.

Hispaniola: The Dominican Republic and Haiti

The Dominican Republic

The **Dominican Republic** shares the island of **Hispaniola** with **Haiti**. During the Colonial Period, the future Dominican Republic was a colony of Spain. France gained control of the western part of Hispaniola from Spain and colonized the territory, which would become Haiti. In 1804, after its long struggle for independence, Haiti took control of the Spanish side of the island and ruled over all of Hispaniola for several decades. The memory of this time period when Haiti ruled the entire island of Hispaniola still arouses anger between the two countries.

In 1844, the Dominican Republic gained its independence and became a nation. For the remainder of the century, the ruling landowning class fought a series of "caudillo wars," or military disputes for political power. These wealthy upper-class landowners were the descendents of the Spanish colonial elite. They ruled over a black population of poor and exploited rural peasants. The commercial agricultural economy was based on sugarcane production. The landowners exploited the labor of the rural peasantry.

In the 1900s, the United States used its military to intervene in and at times occupy the Dominican Republic to restore order or enforce debt collection. In the 1930s, the United States assisted the Dominican Republic to set up a national guard and police force. The American goal was to help the upper class retain political and economic control. From the 1930s until 1961, the United States continued to exercise political influence and safeguard its economic investments through its support of the national-guard leader and dictator, **Rafael Trujillo**.

Rafael Trujillo held onto power until his assassination in 1961. After Trujillo's death, **Juan Bosch** was elected president in 1962. Bosch's election was opposed by most of Dominican upper-class and middle-class groups. They feared that a Socialist-type government similar to what was developing in Cuba was in the making. Fighting broke out, but a civil war was averted when the U.S. militarily intervened. Working through the **Organization of American States (OAS)**, the United States supported the military occupation of the Dominican Republic to separate the combatants and arrange for new elections. The political crisis led to increased Dominican immigration to the United States. Immigration served as a political safety valve and offered Dominicans a hope of greater economic opportunity.

In 1966, **Joaquin Balaguer**, a former Trujillo government official, was elected president and held onto power into the late 1970s. In the 1980s, the presidency changed hands when other parties were allowed to run for and assume office. The Dominican military supported this political opening. However, in the elections of 1990 and 1994, Balaguer returned to office. He was backed by the military and continued the traditional political and economic policies that favored the upper and middle classes.

In 1996, **Leonel Fernandez Reyna** won the next presidential election and promised more economic opportunities for an increasingly poverty-stricken majority of Dominicans. **Hippolito Mejia** succeeded Fernandez Reyna as president in 2000, but as with his predecessor, despite similar promises to the Dominican people, the Dominican government was beset by socioeconomic problems that proved difficult to resolve. Fernandez Reyna, who lived in New York City as a youth and attended schools into high school, was reelected to office in 2004.

> **Main Idea:**
> Continuing into the twenty-first century, the Dominican government is beset by socioeconomic problems that are proving difficult to resolve.

Haiti

In 1804, after a slave revolt, Haiti won its independence from France after over a decade of constant warfare. In the early 1800s, Napoleon tried and failed to regain control of the former French colony. Thereafter, throughout the nineteenth century into the twentieth century, Haiti experienced repeated political turmoil. Groups of upper-class light-skinned mulattos, who were a prosperous minority of wealthy landowners and merchants, fought among themselves for political control.

Main Idea: In Haiti the extreme poverty led to chaotic political conditions.

In the 1930s, the United States, seeking to protect its business interests, assisted Haiti in forming a national guard and police force to preserve order. With the assistance of these armed forces, the Haitian mulatto upper class continued to dominate the political and economic life of the nation. However, in the 1940s, the black population backed by the Haitian National Guard, ousted the mulatto president and put a black president in power. In 1957, **Francis "Papa Doc" Duvalier**, seized power and elected himself president. The tyrannical Duvalier regime controlled Haiti through the special police known as the Tontons Macoutes. The Tontons Macoutes were a particularly brutal group; they instilled fear in the population. Papa Doc exploited the Haitian people and drove most of the mulatto class into exile. Duvalier engineered the succession of his son, **Jean Claude "Baby Doc" Duvalier**, who took power upon his death. The new president-for-life lasted in power until 1986, when he fled the country. The Duvaliers only worsened the economic well-being of the nation and its people. In the years that followed, political turmoil continued with a series of military-style governments. Haiti became the poorest nation in the region during the Duvalier years.

In 1990, **Jean–Bertrand Aristide**, a radical priest, was elected president but was not allowed to take power by the military who considered him to be Communist inspired. Aristide finally was brought to power in 1996 and was reelected in 2000. However, he was forced from office in 2004 and went into exile. Haiti's economic situation remained desperate throughout Aristide's years in office. The extreme poverty led to chaotic political conditions. In 2006, **Rene Preval** was elected president. Today the United Nations plays an important role in trying to help Haiti overcome its enormous problems.

Puerto Rico

Puerto Rico became part of the United States as a result of the Spanish American War in 1898. In the late nineteenth century, the Spanish government agreed to give Puerto Rico some local autonomy. However, after the war with Spain was won, the United States decided to retain Puerto Rico as a colony and repressed all attempts by Puerto Ricans to initiate local self-rule. U.S. foreign policy changed in the 1890s. The American nation became more interested in developing its international strategic interests and pursued an expansionist foreign policy. Puerto Rico fit into United States' strategic plans for the future of the Caribbean region. Puerto Rico was not offered independence.

In 1917, Puerto Ricans were granted American citizenship; however, the idea of independence was discouraged. In 1947, the United States did grant Puerto Rico the right to some local self-government and commonwealth status. The United States sought to economically develop the island after World War II through Operation Bootstrap. **Luis Munoz Marin**, the dynamic governor, worked with U.S. government officials and business interests to make Puerto Rico a showcase for industrial investment in Latin America. Puerto Rico's polit-

Main Idea:
Puerto Ricans
continue to
benefit from a
privileged status
as American
citizens. They are
more interested in
economically
improving their
lives than they are
in separating from
the United States.

ical situation remained stable and orderly with the development of a two-party system. The key political issue that the two parties disputed was what type of relationship with the United States that was best for Puerto Rico. The **Popular Democratic Party (PDP)** advocated continued commonwealth status, whereas its rival for power, the **New Progressive Party (PNP)**, argued for statehood.

There were some Puerto Ricans who favored nationalism and independence even prior to the American presence on the island. However, despite some local and international support, the independence movement never became a major factor in Puerto Rican politics or led to the development of a widely popular political party. In the post-World War II period, a nationalist movement did develop. There were attempts by some nationalists to advocate and use violence to achieve their aim of independence, but the vast majority rejected this course of action. Puerto Ricans continued to benefit from a privileged status as American citizens. They were more interested in economically improving their lives than they were in separating from the United States.

In the 1950s, Puerto Rican immigration to the U.S. mainland began to increase. Despite the efforts to improve the island's economy, there were not enough jobs for the growing population. In the closing decades of the twentieth century, Puerto Ricans continued to be primarily interested in issues relating to the island's economic development and local political issues. In the 1990s, a growing trend of retirees immigrating back to the island began to take place.

SOUTH AMERICA: BRAZIL, ARGENTINA, URUGUAY, PARAGUAY, COLOMBIA, VENEZUELA, PERU, ECUADOR, BOLIVIA, CHILE

Brazil

The Brazilian Republic (1889–1930)

In 1889, **Brazil** became a republic after **Emperor Pedro II** was deposed by a military coup. From 1889 to 1930, the country was a constitutional democracy with an elected president. During the republic, the presidency alternated for the most part between the two states that dominated Brazil's political and economic life, Sao Paulo and Minas Gerais. The political agreement between these two key states was referred to as "coffee and milk."

During the republic, agriculture, ranching, and mining continued to be the most important economic pursuits. Brazil mainly exported agricultural, ranching, mining, and forest resources and imported industrial products. By the mid-nineteenth century, coffee had become Brazil's major export crop. **Sao Paulo** was Brazil's largest coffee producer and, due to its exports, became its wealthiest state. Minas Gerais also produced coffee and in addition, had a mining industry and ranching economy. Another major export revenue earner was rubber, extracted from the rubber tree, which helped spur the development of the **Amazon River region.**

Brazil's shift to a republican form of government attracted many European immigrants, particularly Italians and Germans. This European immigration had a large impact on the population of the nation. It brought to Brazil mainly European peoples who settled in cities such as Sao Paulo or the then national capital **Rio de Janeiro**. Many of the European immigrants joined the urban working class or became agricultural workers in the coffee fields. The immigrants also concentrated in the southern-most states of Santa Catarina, Parana, and Rio Grande do Sul, where they became the majority of the population and pursued agricultural and ranching livelihoods.

In the 1920s, Sao Paulo became the increasingly dominant partner of the coffee and milk political coalition. In 1926, Sao Paulo refused to rotate the office of the Brazilian presidency. The "Paulistas" based their political position on the economic idea that their state was Brazil's major earner of export revenues. They believed that the state's economic wealth gave it the right to remain in power. Sao Paulo also had its own state militia, which rivaled the national army. By 1930, those opposed to Sao Paulo's political control of the nation's presidency began a revolution. A successful military coup supported by a coalition of states led to the defeat of Sao Paulo and the end of the republic.

Populism and Development (1930–1964)

Getulio Vargas (1883–1954), Brazilian statesman, giving a radio address, mid-20th century.

The Revolution of 1930 brought **Getulio Vargas** to power as president. Vargas was a populist and became the most important and influential political figure in Brazil from 1930 to 1954. A populist is someone who supports solutions to political, social, and economic issues and problems that are important to all the people. In 1930, after taking political control, Vargas assumed dictatorial powers. Until he was forced out by the military in 1945, Vargas controlled all the successive Brazilian governments either as dictator or elected president. Vargas was a populist and sought to enact programs that he believed favored Brazil and most of its people. During the 1930s, he limited the powers of the agricultural and rural elites, helped new industrial leaders establish themselves, particularly in the urban centers of Sao Paulo and Rio de Janeiro, and promoted policies that favored economic nationalism and an independent foreign policy.

In 1937, Vargas established the *"Estado Novo,"* which was a form of government that resembled fascism or corporatism. However, in World War II he allied Brazil with the United States and allowed the nation to be used as a base for the invasion of North Africa. In 1945, Vargas was forced to give up the presidency, but he remained politically active and was elected as a senator from his home state. In 1951, he was once again reelected as president of Brazil. Vargas committed suicide three years later in 1954. In a farewell letter to the nation, he blamed foreign and antieconomic nationalism interests for this final act of desperation.

From 1954 to 1964, democratically elected presidents ruled Brazil. During this period, Brazil presidents supported programs that were nationalistic, populist, and developmental. A new national capital, **Brasilia,** was built in the center of the country in order to encourage economic development by having more people move inland and away from the coastal cities. In the 1960s, the economic situation in Brazil deteriorated as inflation and social unrest in the cities increased. From 1961 to 1964, President **Joao Goulart** sought to initiate economic and social reforms. His policies angered the Brazilian elite and threatened U.S. and Western economic and political interests. In 1964, Goulart was overthrown, and the military seized political power. The United States backed the coup supporters, and there is evidence that the CIA and American ambassador were involved "behind the scenes" in the military takeover. This type of intervention was the modern-day way that the United States sought to control political events in Latin America.

Military Rule (1964–1985)

From 1964 to 1985, military officers ruled Brazil. The military regime was particularly harsh in the first years that the officers ruled the nation. The military governments assumed arbitrary powers. Civil rights were suspended, and many politicians were denied the right to seek elected office or went into exile. During **General Medici's** years in power, the military dictatorship undertook a ruthless campaign of repression. Their aim was to eliminate all political opposition suspected of being revolutionary or moderately leftist. At first, the military benefited from what was called an economic miracle in the 1970s. For a time, the economy improved, inflation was kept under control, and the middle and working classes began to feel more optimistic about their financial situation and ability to earn a livelihood.

However, by the 1980s hyperinflation returned, and the foreign debt mounted. As the worsening economic situation intensified, the military sought international monetary help to ease the debt payment crisis. To gain financial support, the military government accepted an **International Monetary Fund (IMF)** imposed austerity program. The austerity program led to increased misery and suffering for the middle and working classes as prices of food skyrocketed. There were increasing demands that the military step aside. By the mid-1980s, the military began to prepare for a democratically elected government.

Redemocratization

In 1985, **Trancedo Neves** was elected president as the nation returned to civilian rule. Neves died after the election, and Vice-President **Jose Sarney** became president. Sarney cooperated with the military and moved slowly in the direction of free elections. In 1989, **Fernando Collor** became the first president elected by popular vote after the military regime. However, he resigned from office because of a corruption scandal. In 1994, **Fernando Henrique Cardoso** was elected president and held office for two terms. He was able to guide Brazil through a number of financial crises but could not find a solution for Brazil's most severe problem, the highly unequal distribution of wealth and income.

Main Idea:
The overall goal of the Lula government was to improve the lives of the majority of Brazilians who live in conditions of poverty.

The harsh socioeconomic contradictions of a nation with a small very wealthy elite and a vast majority of poor landless peasants and workers led to the election of **Luiz Ignacio da Silva**, "**Lula**," in 2002. Lula won the election based on his campaign promising social change and his identification with the leftist labor union movement. In his first years in office, President da Silva proved to be a pragmatic leader. He sought to continue the financial policies of his predecessor and reduce national expenditures for costly social programs. He also initiated a Zero Hunger program designed to give each Brazilian three meals a day. The Lula-led government also promised to develop policies that favor the nation's long-term economic interests. Brazil reduced its national debt and dependency on international lending institutions. Brazil initiated economic decisions that favored the development of local industry. The overall goal was to improve the lives of the majority of Brazilians who live in conditions of poverty.

In 2005, Lula's government was accused of political corruption. Despite the accusations of corruption, Lula was reelected president of Brazil in 2007 and promised to continue with socioeconomic programs to help the vast majority of Brazilians who are very poor.

The Rio de la Plata Region: Argentina, Uruguay, and Paraguay

Argentina

By the turn of the twentieth century, **Argentina** seemed destined to become a politically stable and economically prosperous nation. From 1890 to 1914, the agro-export sector experienced rapid economic growth. Argentine beef and wheat were among the valuable agricultural and ranching exports that were grown and raised on the fertile **Pampas** and exported through **Buenos Aires**, the capital and major port of the nation. The country had a developing middle class and a large number of urban workers. They were mostly recent European immigrants who were wage laborers. In the early 1900s, an agreement between the upper class and middle class provided for an expanded electorate and more democratically contested elections. The Radical Civic Party (UCR), which represented middle-class interests, became a force in national and local politics. This led to increased political stability and a sense of economic well-being for an increasing number of Argentines who moved up into the ranks of the middle class.

Main Idea:
During the 1920s, the economic downturn continued and only accelerated after the start of the worldwide Great Depression in 1929.

In the post-World War I period, Argentina's economic prospects began to diminish as the European nations recovered from the long destructive war. There was a declining demand for Argentine foodstuffs. During the 1920s, the economic downturn continued and only accelerated after the start of the worldwide Great Depression in 1929. Argentina's economy was very tied to the world trade system and foreign, particularly British, banking finance and investment. The wage laborers, who were very well organized in unions, particularly in Buenos Aires, were increasingly discontent as the economic crisis worsened. Argentine unions were very influenced by European socialist and anarchist ideas.

In 1930, a coalition of wealthy conservative landowners and merchants and officers in the Argentine military ousted the elected Radical Party President Yrigoyen and created a provisional government. Thereafter, into the 1980s, the military intervened in Argentine politics. The military often stepped into the political arena to arbitrate or even take over the government whenever they believed national or their own personal interests were in danger. A long period of political instability and economic crises entered into the lives of the Argentine people from the 1930s through the 1990s. Argentines continued to be divided along class and political lines even in periods of economic prosperity. The three social groupings were the small but wealthy upper class of landowners and merchants, the middle class made up of small business owners and professional and government workers, and the urban workers who were wage laborers and very well organized in unions, particularly in Buenos Aires. There was no real organized class of agricultural laborers in Argentina. These sharp socioeconomic class differences continually led to bitter political contests for the control of the national government.

During the 1940s, **Juan Peron**, an army officer, became part of the military-backed totalitarian type of government. By using his position as Labor Minister, Peron's popularity grew as he championed the cause of the Argentine labor unions and urban workers. In 1946, Peron was elected president of Argentina. His wife, **Eva Peron**, called Evita, helped him enormously because of her popularity among the working class. Peron's program was based on the idea of social justice. He tried to find nationalistic and populist solutions for Argentina's economic problems. As president, Peron raised wages and promoted an economic policy that gave the state a monopoly over the export of key agricultural crops. In his first years in office, Peron's economic program was successful. However, the wealthy landowners and foreign interests, particularly the United States, opposed Peron. The anti-Peron forces worked to undermine Peron's economic program. After Evita's death in 1952, Argentina's economic problems mounted. Peron was forced out of power and went into exile from 1954 to 1973.

Main Idea:
In 1983, the military was forced to give up political power, and a civilian government was elected.

Nevertheless, Peron continued to influence Argentine politics even though a Peron-inspired political party was not allowed to participate in the electoral process. Argentines in support of Peron and his social justice program were always in opposition and hoped for his return. The Radical Civic Party (UCR) or military governments held power from 1954 to 1973. In 1973, Peron was allowed to return and he was again elected as president, but he died shortly thereafter in 1974. His wife **Isabel**, who was the vice president, became the nation's president. By 1976, as the overall political and economic situation in the nation worsened, the military once again took control of the government. In the late 1970s, the military conducted a deadly campaign to suppress left-wing political opposition. More than 10,000 Argentines were tortured, died, or escaped into exile.

In the 1980s, the military-led government sought to reclaim the **Falklands Islands** from Great Britain. The Falklands, a small group of islands in the South Atlantic, are called the Malvinas by Argentina. The Argentine military campaign to take over the Falklands led to war and ended in disaster. In 1983, the military was forced to give up political power, and a civilian government was elected. For the remainder of the century, Argentina wrestled with the problems of a declining economy, crippling inflation, devaluation of its currency, and the need for national reconciliation concerning the tragic military repression.

In 2003, **Nestor Kirchner** was elected president of Argentina. Kirchner has sought to stabilize the deteriorating socioeconomic situation in the nation and has instituted economic policies that are in Argentina's self interest.

Uruguay

In the first decade of the 1900s, President **Jose Batlle y Ordonez** set the pattern for **Uruguay**'s twentieth-century development. During his administration, important political, social, and economic reforms, including a welfare program, were enacted. The government began to participate more actively in many aspects of the economy. These reforms were to a large measure carried on by his successors. Until the 1950s, Uruguay's export economy provided the government with revenue to support its government-financed programs. Uruguay's export of ranching and agricultural products, particularly beef and wheat, created a favorable balance of trade. Many Uruguayans worked for the government and had generous pensions and other social benefits. **Montevideo**, the nation's capital, was the country's urban and cultural center.

Main Idea:
In the election of 2004, public opinion turned against free-market economic policies.

In the 1950s, Uruguay's economy changed as international demand for its exports decreased. Economic problems, including high unemployment and inflation, led to a sharp decline in the standard of living. In the early 1960s, an urban leftist guerilla movement, the **Tupamaros**, developed; it led to increasing political instability. The Tupamaros sought to help the poorer groups in society by robbing banks, undertaking political kidnappings, and attacking the nation's military and police forces. The government reaction was extremely harsh. With the help of the United States, Uruguayan police, military forces, and intelligence units began a systematic crackdown on the Tupamaros and their supporters. Civil liberties were suspended. The armed forces took over the government. The military dictatorship lasted to 1984, when massive protests led to the reestablishment of civilian rule.

In 1985, **Julio Maria Sanguinetti**, the Colorado Party leader, won the presidential election. In his first administration, he implemented economic reforms and consolidated the nation's return to democratic rule. He also was responsible for the enactment of an amnesty for military leaders accused of human rights violations during the repression. **Luis Alberto Lacalle**, of the National Party, followed as the next president. Lacalle's reforms furthered the liberalization of the economy by opening the nation's ports to international trade and joining a regional trading bloc. Uruguay joined the **Southern Cone Common Market (MERCOSUR)** in 1991.

Sanguinetti was reelected in 1994 and served as president until 2000. Growing economic problems led him to form a coalition government between the Colorado and National Parties. In the election of 2004, public opinion turned against free-market economic policies. **Tabare Vasquez** was elected president and promised an economic program that was centered on developing national solutions to the problems of unemployment and poverty.

Paraguay

Paraguay has always had a tradition of upper-class-dominated political rule. The competing political parties, Colorado and Liberal, have controlled national politics from the 1880s to the present day. In 1904, the Liberal Party gained the presidency and held power until 1940. From the 1930s into the 1950s, Paraguayan politics were defined by the Chaco War against Bolivia, military dictatorships, and civil war.

In 1954, General **Alfredo Stroessner** ended the period of political instability and took power. He was reelected seven times and ruled with the support of the Colorado Party and military. Stroessner pursued policies of national security and anti-communism. He also sought to assimilate the Native American peoples, the Guarani, who were forced to be more sedentary. They were required to live in fixed places, generally on land owned by large landowners. In 1988, Stroessner was overthrown in a military coup led by General **Andres Rodriguez**, who under the Colorado Party banner became the next president.

In 1993, a Colorado civilian candidate was elected president, but political instability developed when the military once again intervened to force him out of office. A struggle between the military and civilian elite eventually led to a political settlement and the selection of another civilian president. In 2003, **Nicanor Duarte Frutos** was elected and sworn in as president. Today, the vast majority of the population, mestizo and **Native American Guarani**, continue to live in poverty and are engaged in agricultural pursuits.

The Andean Nations: Colombia, Venezuela, Peru, Ecuador, Bolivia, and Chile

The **Andean nations** form a subregional group within Latin America. The Andean classification is largely based on these nations' physical characteristics, which make the **Andes Mountains** an important geographical feature in these countries.

Colombia

In the twentieth century, Colombia continued to be affected by Conservative Party versus Liberal Party rivalries for political power. These violent struggles for control of the nation's government based in the capital, **Bogota**, often led to military-backed dictatorships. The vast majority of Colombians remained poverty stricken particularly in the rural areas where large landowners were powerful. Attempts to enact land reform were not successful.

In the post-World War II era, growing rural and urban dissatisfaction led to the "Bogotazo" uprising known as *la violencia*, which was ruthlessly suppressed. The violence began in 1948, after the assassination of the leftist Liberal leader, **Jorge Gaitan**. Estimates are that up to 300,000 Colombians, mostly peasants, were killed before the government reestablished civil order. Military dictatorships continued to govern into the 1950s. In 1957, General **Rojas Pinilla** was ousted from power and replaced by a conservative and liberal coalition civilian government. The Conservative and Liberal Parties continued to compete for power but in a more democratic manner. The political leadership of these parties still represented the upper classes and some middle-class groups. Colombia's agricultural economy, based particularly on coffee exportation, began to recover and foreign investment increased.

> **Main Idea:** Colombia's agricultural economy, based particularly on coffee exportation, began to recover and foreign investment increased.

Starting in the 1970s and lasting until the present day, Colombia has been plagued by a number of interrelated problems. Leftist revolutionary guerilla movements, such as the **Revolutionary Armed Forces of Colombia (FARC)**, and the **National Liberation Army (ELN)** established bases in some rural and mountainous areas. In some regions, the guerilla movements were able to gain control of and intimidate the local populations. Also, Colombia became a center for the production and exportation of narcotics. Narcotics trafficking became a multimillion dollar business. The growth of **drug cartels**, particularly in Medellin and Cali, which were aligned and supported by revolutionary movements, destabilized politics and life in general. Drug production was stimulated by the fact that so many poor peasants could only earn a decent living growing coca and marijuana plants. The drug-related violence became very problematic because it created a climate of fear and insecurity even in wealthy urban areas. Private militias supported by landowners and businessmen were also a growing problem. In 2002, **Alvaro Uribe Velez**, a hard-line right-wing politician, became president and promised a crackdown on the leftist revolutionary movements and drug traffickers and to disband the right-wing militias. Uribe Velez was reelected president in 2006 and promised a continued crackdown of narcotics trafficking and revolutionary guerilla groups.

Venezuela

From 1908 to 1935, Juan Vincente Gomez dominated Venezuelan politics. The Venezuelan military backed General Gomez's authoritarian rule. Gomez was able to end almost a century of the caudillo rule and wars by suppressing all potential revolts.

Starting in 1935, **Venezuela** began to pursue a path toward representative democracy and elections. In 1958, the Venezuelan military withdrew from politics. For the remainder of the twentieth century, the two major Venezuelan political parties, **Accion Democratica (AD)** and the **Social Democratic Party (COPEI)** competed for political power through the election process.

Starting in the 1920s, Venezuela began to benefit from a **petroleum industry** boom. By the 1930s, Venezuela had a capable labor force and acquired the technology to develop its petroleum industry. Oil revenues became the major factor in the nation's economic life, earning more than 70 percent of the export total. Venezuela became the largest oil exporter in Latin America. The development of the petroleum industry made Venezuela Latin America's leading nation in terms of per capita income. Cocoa and coffee were the main products of the rural agricultural economy.

> **Main Idea:**
> Chavez became the key figure in Venezuelan politics in the early twenty-first century when in 1998, he was elected president of Venezuela.

Despite the oil revenues and development of a middle class, mainly based in the capital Caracas, the gap between rich and poor widened in Venezuela into the 1980s. The two major political parties, AD and COPEI, primarily represented the interests of the upper and middle classes. Starting in the 1980s, political scandals and corruption and a worsening economic situation caused by heavy foreign debt, led to increasing unrest in Venezuela and demands for change. In the 1990s, a young military officer, **Hugo Chavez**, tried to overthrow the existing government and was imprisoned.

Chavez became the key figure in Venezuelan politics in the early twenty-first century when in 1998, he was elected president of Venezuela. Despite the opposition of the traditional political parties who were supported by the upper and middle classes and the United States, Chavez has been able to consolidate his presidential rule. In 2004, he was successful in his campaign to bring about constitutional reform. In 2006, Chavez was reelected and stated he intended to turn Venezuela into a Socialist nation. Chavez wants to change the nation's dependent economic role as a supplier of petroleum and agricultural products in exchange for imported manufactured goods. He has called for the nationalization of key industries and institutions. Using the Socialist model, Chavez wants to initiate economic, social, and educational programs that assist the vast majority of Venezuelans who live in conditions of poverty. Chavez's goal is to offer all Venezuelans a real hope of increased economic opportunity and social equality. An important question is whether President Chavez can create a system of democratic socialism in Venezuela without resorting to totalitarian methods.

Peru

By the early 1900s, **Peru** was able to achieve a measure of political stability after almost eighty years of conservative versus liberal disputes, authoritarian rule, and a disastrous war with Chile, The War of the Pacific (see Chapter 5 in this volume). During these years, the ruling "Civilista" Party passed social, political, and economic legislation. The agricultural and industrial sectors of the economy experienced renewed growth. This economic revival led to more internal migration to the coast, the rise of a middle class, and the growth of a labor movement, particularly in the capital, **Lima.** Peru's economy remained based on a combination of developing industry and agricultural exports of cotton, sugar, minerals, and fishmeal.

> **Main Idea:**
> In the early years of the twenty-first century, the vast majority of the Peruvians, in the urban and rural areas, still continue to live in substandard economic conditions.

In the 1920s, a new political party, led by Victor Haya de la Torre, the *Alianza Popular Revolucionaria* (APRA), developed. APRA sought to represent the interests of the urban middle and working classes. Thereafter, APRA presented a political alternative to the ruling oligarchy and the armed forces. Although APRA was legalized after World War II, the ruling oligarchy and military remained in power until the 1960s. In 1963, a new political party, *Accion Popular* (AP), led by Fernando Belaunde Terry, won the nation's presidential election and promised economic reforms to help the vast majority of Peruvians who lived in conditions of poverty. However, the Belaunde Terry government was not able to find solutions for the increasing rural and urban worker poverty and increased internal migration from the mountainous areas to the coastal region, particularly to Lima. Alan Garcia, the APRA candidate, won the presidency in the mid-1980s. In the 1970s and 1980s, despite governments that were Socialist and reform minded, Peru's economic situation continued to deteriorate, and the poverty of most Peruvians worsened.

Starting in the 1960s, a particularly violent rural-based and Maoist-inspired group, the **Shining Path** (*Sendero Luminoso*, or SL), began to play a deadly role in Peruvian politics. By the 1990s, the *Sendero Luminoso* was finally suppressed with the capture and imprisonment of its leader **Abimael Guzmann.** President **Alberto Fujimori** ruled Peru from 1990 to 2000. Fujimori is credited with eliminating the SL, reviving the viability of the Peruvian economy, and encouraging renewed foreign investment. In 2000, he was forced to resign because of political corruption scandals and went into exile. In the early years of the twenty-first century, the vast majority of the Peruvians, in the urban and rural areas, still continue to live in substandard economic conditions.

Ecuador

For most of the twentieth century, **Ecuador** was ruled by a series of authoritarian political leaders who represented the interests of the landed oligarchy and military forces. Jose Velasco Ibarra, who held the presidency for a number of

---

terms from 1944 to 1972, is the best example of this type of elitist authoritarian ruler. The vast majority of people, primarily Native Americans, were engaged in subsistence agriculture or the growing of commercial export-oriented crops—bananas, coffee, and cacao. Their economic situation continued to be marginal, and internal migration and immigration increased in the last decades of the 1900s.

The discovery of petroleum in the Amazonian region made oil Ecuador's leading export. The issue of the ownership of oil resources rekindled a long-term border dispute with Peru for control of an area of the Amazon. Both nations claimed the same large area of Amazon territory. After a number of military confrontations, the dispute was finally settled in 1998 through international arbitration. As Ecuador entered the twenty-first century, the nation's political situation remained unstable with few presidents finishing their term of office. The vast majority of Ecuadorians continue to live in difficult economic conditions.

Bolivia

Bolivia's loss of its nitrate-rich seacoast during the War of the Pacific (1879–1883), further isolated the already politically unstable and caudillo-dominated nation. In the twentieth century, **Bolivia** continued to be ruled by a series of authoritarian political leaders who represented the interests of the landed and mine-owning upper class and armed forces. In the 1900s, silver and later tin brought a measure of prosperity and political stability to Bolivia. The laissez–faire capitalist policies enriched the political and social elite. The vast majority of people, Native Americans, continued as always to live in difficult poverty-stricken conditions.

Starting in 1951, under the leadership of Victor Paz Estenssoro, the National Revolutionary Movement (MNR), sought to gain power democratically and bring about reforms. Paz Estenssoro held the presidency for twelve years until 1964. During his presidency, he promoted public education and sweeping land reform and nationalized the mining industry. A strong union movement representing miners and teachers developed. In 1964, Paz Estenssoro was overthrown by the military. Military-backed governments held power until 1993.

Starting in 1993, more democratically elected political leaders pursued a policy of economic liberalization as they sought to further integrate Bolivia into the international trading system. At the turn of the century, most Bolivians still lived in poverty in rural areas. The agricultural situation remains complicated because of the development of narcotics trafficking. The Native Americans, Quechua and Aymara, have since pre-Columbian times chewed on coca leaves to fight hunger and cold. This leaf, which is grown in the lowland regions of Bolivia, is the source of the paste base of cocaine and has become a major export. Efforts to eradicate coca leaf production have met resistance from poor farmers who depend on the sale of this revenue-producing crop for their livelihoods. In 2005, **Evo Morales** of the **Movement Towards Socialism (MAS) Party** won the presidential election. Morales's election was the first time in Bolivian history that a president who was elected by the people actually represented the interests of the overwhelming majority of the Native American, or Indian, population.

Main Idea: Morales's election was the first time in Bolivian history that a president who was elected by the people actually represented the interests of the overwhelming majority of the Native American, or Indian, population.

Chile

General Augusto Pinochet (left) photographed with President Salvador Allende of Chile, August 23, 1973, nineteen days before he would lead the military coup that overthrew Allende's government.

Main Idea:
Allende called for programs that included nationalization of most remaining private industries and banks, massive land expropriation, and collectivization.

From the early years of the twentieth century, Chilean political history evolved more democratically than the other Andean nations. Chile's historical and cultural differences led to the rise of middle and working classes, which were powerful enough to influence elections. In Chile, reformist-minded presidents alternated with conservative leaders for political power. By the 1930s, after a period of military governments, constitutional rule was restored and a strong middle-class party, the Radical Party, came into power. The Radicals were able to remain in office until 1952. During their years in power, the role of the state in the economy increased. From 1952 to 1964, Chilean politics shifted to the right, and two military-minded and conservative presidents were elected to office.

In 1964, the Christian Democratic Party's candidate, Eduardo Frei, was elected and began another period of major social and economic reform. Frei sought to promote programs for education, housing, and agrarian reform, including the unionization of agricultural workers. By 1967, Frei ran into increasing opposition from leftist groups, who found his reforms to be inadequate, and conservatives, who found them excessive. Chilean politics became very polarized between those who supported either the leftist or rightist positions. The center or middle position of gradual moderate reforms no longer attracted a majority.

In 1973, **Salvador Allende**, the Socialist Party candidate, gained the presidency as part of a broad coalition called the Popular Unity (UP). Allende called for programs that included nationalization of most remaining private industries and banks, massive land expropriation, and collectivization. Immediately after Allende's election, the United States expressed its disapproval with the results and put in place some economic sanctions. The United States reaction was consistent with its position during the Cold War to oppose any reform government as Socialist or Communist influenced. The polarization of Chilean society along political lines worsened. In September 1973, a military coup took place during which time Allende died.

The military coup was led by General **Augusto Pinochet**. A period of harsh repression followed the military coup and thousands of people, including foreigners who had come to Chile to support Allende, were either killed or disappeared. Chile experienced a period of severe military rule under Pinochet's dictatorial leadership. In 1988, Pinochet was rejected by the Chilean people in a plebiscite when he asked for a second term of eight years as the candidate of the military junta, a group of leading military officers. Thereafter, Chile returned to democratic rule.

During the Pinochet military regime, the junta started a program of economic liberalization and privatization. The market economy policies were designed based on the ideas of Dr. Milton Friedman of the University of Chicago. Chile became a showcase for economic **globalization** in Latin America. The economy grew rapidly from 1976 to 1981 fueled by private foreign loans; however, income distribution became less equal. Increasing numbers of Chileans faced poverty while the upper 5 percent of the population received 75 percent of the total national income. The Chilean small and medium businesses also were ruined by the junta economic policies. Multinational corporations and the Chilean oligarchy of wealthy businessmen, large landowners, and high-level military officers profited the most during the Pinochet years.

After the Pinochet electoral defeat in the 1988 plebiscite, the constitution was amended. A transition to democracy began. In 1989 Patricio Alywin, a Christian Democrat, was elected as part of a coalition of major political parties. Alywin soon released a report on human rights violations committed during the military dictatorship. In 1993, Eduardo Frei, another Christian Democrat, was elected for a six-year term under the banner of the *Concertacion* coalition. Alywin and Frei continued the liberal economic policies begun in the 1970s but also worked to safeguard Chilean democratic traditions.

In 1999, the presidential election was a contest for office by candidates from the major political parties. Ricardo Lagos Escobar of the Socialist Party and Party for Democracy led the *Concertacion* coalition to victory and held office from 2000 to 2006. During his years in office, unsuccessful attempts were made to put Augusto Pinochet on trial for his overall responsibility for the crimes committed in the years of military dictatorship. In 2006, the Socialist leader **Michelle Bachelet** was elected. Bachelet promised economic reforms that would benefit the middle and working classes.

TWENTY-FIRST CENTURY ECONOMIC AND SOCIAL ISSUES

By the end of the 1990s, the increasing globalization of world economy had not brought Latin American nations the prosperity they needed to improve the lives of the vast majority of their populations. In the twenty-first century, Latin American nations have to find solutions for difficult issues to resolve economic, political, and social problems if their people are to have greater hope and more opportunities for a better life. In this section, you will read about the important issues that Latin American nations are facing today.

Trade and Investment

From colonial times to the present, Latin American nations and peoples have lived under the influence of external economic forces and institutions. From the colonial period to recent times, the economic influence of European nations and the United States led to the development of economies that were dependent on markets and capital investment they did not control. These economies were based on the export of agricultural and ranching products and raw materials, such as precious metals, and the importation of finished goods.

In the twentieth century, even after the United States replaced Great Britain as Latin America's most important trading partner and investor, Latin America's overall global trading relations and dependency on the developed industrial nations remained basically the same. The Latin American countries continued to export foodstuffs and raw materials to, and import finished products from, the United States and European nations. In the last decades of the 1900s, Asian nations—Japan, South Korea, and, increasingly, China—developed trade relations with Latin American countries. A familiar pattern of economic dependency was created. Latin American countries sold foodstuffs and raw materials and bought manufactured goods.

In the 1900s, there were increased foreign, particularly American, investments in Latin American nations. These public and private investments further increased the region's dependency on international capital and financial organizations. Throughout the twentieth century, the international markets for the region's agricultural products and raw materials were still controlled by nations and institutions outside of the region. International financial institutions, such as the IMF and World Bank, required countries wanting assistance with debt payment or in need of loans to make economic decisions that often increased local prices for foodstuffs and energy.

Landownership

Today, throughout Latin America, the best agricultural and ranching lands remain, as they have always been, in the hands of a small and wealthy landowning upper class. Most large landowners are engaged in commercial agriculture or ranching pursuits. They primarily produce for an export market. The ownership of large tracts of land offers political influence and a high social status. Wealthy merchants also benefit from a system of landownership that leads to the export of agricultural and ranching products and other raw materials and import of manufactured goods.

In Latin America, similar economic situations exist in the mining industries. The mine owners and operators receive most of the profits and exploit mineworkers who labor for low wages and in dangerous conditions. A wealthy class of industrialists also exists in some nations, such as Brazil, Mexico, and Chile, where national industries have been able to develop. There are also national businesses and banking institutions in all Latin American countries, which provide good income for a small group of upper- and middle-class people who are well educated.

Socioeconomic Conditions

Throughout Latin America, a relatively small percentage of the population, the wealthy upper class and in some countries a developing middle class, enjoy a good lifestyle. They can provide their families with good housing, health care, education, and, in general, a quality of food, entertainment, and recreational activities not available to other groups in society.

Rising Economic Nationalism

By the late 1990s, some Latin American nations became increasingly critical of how economic globalization was affecting their countries' trade, national industries, and people. The critics of the trend toward greater globalization claimed that the changing world economy resulted in increased poverty and hardship for most of their population. They argued that globalization created an even greater economic dependency on markets and institutions outside of their countries. These nations sought to decrease, if not end, the economic dependency and control of their countries' resources that foreign countries and international institutions exercised.

The Latin American nations are increasingly supporting economic policies that are designed to benefit their countries and people as opposed to satisfying the financial demands of more developed areas of the world such as the United States, the European Union, and international monetary organizations. It is not clear whether the leaders of the Latin American nations will be successful in ending the centuries-old pattern of economic dependency. Nevertheless, in the early years of the twenty–first century, there is an increasing awareness in Latin America that there is a great need to enact economic policies that will decrease the percentage of the population who live in conditions of poverty.

LINK TO TODAY

In the United States today, there are over forty million people who can trace their origins to a Latin American nation or commonwealth. If we look at how our nation has changed in terms of population in the past fifty years, we can see that the largest number of immigrants have come from Latin American countries. There are many reasons why people from Latin American nations want to immigrate to the United States. The main reason is that they are hoping to find greater economic opportunities here. Latin American immigrants want to provide themselves and their families with a decent livelihood. For whatever reason people come, they bring their culture with them and influence life here in the United States by making us a more multicultural nation.

Our multicultural society has changed for the better because of the contributions made by the many Latin Americans who live in the United States today. Music, literature, dance, theater, television, spoken language, and other cultural mediums have all been greatly influenced by our nation's growing immigration from Latin American nations. If we look to the future, it is clear that these intercultural connections and influences will continue to expand. Today in the United States, we can see that our nation has profited enormously from its Latin American connections and heritage.

CHAPTER SUMMARY

In the twentieth century, the nations of Latin America evolved as they became more integrated into the growing global trading system and developed their own national histories. At the beginning of the 1900s, we can see that almost all Latin American countries experienced many of the same political, economic, and social problems. These issues were a carryover from the first century of nationhood. Most nations were ruled by dictators who usually had close ties with the military. Large landowners were the local political leaders, or caudillos, who exercised great power in their regions. The vast majority of people were poor agricultural workers who had little if any of their own land and limited political rights.

As the 1900s progressed, the political power and reach of the national governments increased in almost all nations. Although the local elites, or wealthy landowners, still had the highest social status, they lost their arbitrary political power and became more subject to the national governments. Dictatorial civilian and military rulers continued to dominate politics well into the twentieth century, but changes took place in all Latin American nations. Democratically elected governments became the rule rather than the exception. When the twentieth century ended, all Latin American countries, with the exception of Cuba, had democratically elected governments where at least two political parties competed for power.

During the 1900s, the economic situation also evolved. The nations of Latin America began the twentieth century in a state of economic dependency on the more developed nations, particularly the United States and Western Europe countries. At the turn of the twenty-first century, Latin American nations were increasingly tied to the global trading system, and a number of countries had developed a level of economic independence. Brazil developed one of the top ten economies of the world and in part became a nation where industrial production was significant. Venezuela gained an increasing measure of independence because of the value of its petroleum resources. Mexico entered into a trading agreement with the United States and Canada, as a partner. Other nations whose economies remained mainly based on the export of agriculture or minerals gained a measure of economic independence as developed nations in Asia, Japan, and China, offered trade options for their resources.

There was also a changing social situation in almost all Latin American nations. There was increased migration from the countryside to the city, particularly to the national capital. In some nations, immigration also rose significantly, particularly from Central American nations affected by armed conflict or conditions of poverty. Mexico also experienced a constant flow of immigrants to the United States and Canada. Although most people remained poor and had difficulty in earning a livelihood, the lower classes became increasingly aware of their political rights. Through the power of the vote, Brazil, Venezuela, Bolivia, Peru, Chile, Mexico, and other nations elected leaders more responsive to their needs. The wealthy landowners, bankers, industrialists, and merchants still retained the greatest percentage of the nation's riches and income; however, middle-class groups were developing in many nations.

IMPORTANT PEOPLE, PLACES, AND TERMS

KEY TERMS

Mexican Revolution	Central American	Central Intelligence
Partido Revolucionario	Common Market	Agency (CIA)
Institutional (PRI)	(CACM)	"Big Stick"
North American Free	Hay-Burau-Varilla	"Good Neighbor"
Trade Agreement	Treaty	Sandinista National
(NAFTA)	Mayan	Liberation Front
	mestizo	Contra War

battleship *Maine*	International Monetary Fund (IMF)	petroleum industry
Spanish American War		Shining Path
Cuban Revolution	Tupamaros	globalization
Bay of Pigs invasion	Southern Cone	Dollar Diplomacy
Organization of American States (OAS)	Common Market (MERCOSUR)	Economic Dependency
	drug cartels	Foreign Investment

PEOPLE

Francisco Madero	Daniel Ortega	Juan Peron
Victoriano Huerta	Juan Peron	Eva Peron
Emiliano Zapata	Fidel Castro	José Batlle y Ordonez
Pancho Villa	Fulgencio Batista	Isabel Peron
Alvaro Obregon	Francis "Papa Doc" Duvalier	Nestor Kirchner
Plutarco Callas		Tabare Vasquez
Lazaro Cardenas	Claude "Baby Doc" Duvalier	Native American Guarani
Diego Riviera		
Frieda Kahlo	Jean-Bértrand Aristide	Alvaro Uribe Velez
Manuel Avila Camacho	Luis Munoz Marin	Hugo Chavez
Vincente Fox	Emperor Pedro II	Alberto Fuljimoro
Felix Calderon	Getulio Vargas	Evo Morales
Augusto Sandino	Luis Ignacio da Silva, "Lula"	Salvador Allende
Violeta Chamorro		Augusto Pinochet

PLACES

Latin America	Guantanamo Bay	Falkland Islands
Mexico	Dominican Republic	Uruguay
Central America	Hispaniola	Montevideo
Panama Canal	Haiti	Paraguay
Panama	Puerto Rico	Andean nations
Colombia	Brazil	Andes Mountains
Guatemala	Sao Paolo	Bogota
El Salvador	Amazon River region	Venezuela
San Salvador	Rio de Janeiro	Peru
Honduras	Brasilia	Lima
Nicaragua	Argentina	Ecuador
Costa Rica	Pampas	Bolivia
Cuba	Buenos Aires	Chile

CHAPTER 17

MULTIPLE-CHOICE QUESTIONS

Select the number of the correct answer.

1. By the twentieth century how did many of the economies of Latin American nations change?

    (1) More natural resources were produced for European nations.
    (2) These economies became more integrated into the global trading system.
    (3) Many nations became more dependent on the former colonial powers.
    (4) Mineral resources and agricultural production declined.

2. Through much of the nineteenth and twentieth centuries which group held most of the political power in the newly independent Latin American countries?

    (1) Wealthy elites with good educations
    (2) Military leaders
    (3) Kings or queens from royal families
    (4) Roman Catholic church leaders

3. As the twentieth century progressed, which statement could be made about the middle class in most Latin American countries?

    (1) The middle class lacked the ability to organize or to gain any political power.
    (2) The middle class joined with the poorer segments of society in a struggle for equality.
    (3) The middle class took advantage of educational and economic opportunities and became upwardly socially mobile.
    (4) The middle class continued to remain poor and continued to struggle for their livelihood.

4. What is the most accurate description for the term "banana republics"?

    (1) Countries that import large quantities of fruit
    (2) Countries that primarily trade a variety of manufactured goods with the United States
    (3) Countries that grow primarily a single cash crop for export to the United States
    (4) Countries with the rights to open a popular clothing store chain

5. During the 1900s, several Latin American nations tried to become more economically independent. Which natural resource available in many of these countries should have enabled them to accomplish this goal?

    (1) Petroleum
    (2) Uranium
    (3) Cattle
    (4) Silver

6. From the end of the nineteenth century through the beginning of the twenty-first century, which list of governmental types best describes the order in which they appeared in Brazil?

    (1) constitutional monarchy, military dictatorship, Communist
    (2) republic, fascist state, a democracy, military rule, democracy
    (3) democracy, constitutional monarchy, Communist, military rule
    (4) dictatorship, military junta, absolute monarchy, democracy

7. From 1910 through 1940 the Mexican government was characterized by which type of activities?

   (1) efforts to follow the Communist revolution in Russia
   (2) extremely conservative leadership controlled by the wealthy
   (3) a series of violent revolutions to increase Church control
   (4) a progression of reformer presidents who struggled to improve the daily lives of Mexicans

8. During the end of the twentieth century and continuing today, which topic has become an increasing problem between Mexico and the United States?

   (1) the sale of agricultural products
   (2) immigration
   (3) the development of nuclear weapons
   (4) the rise of fanatical religious groups

9. Which grouping of nations could all be described as part of Central America?

   (1) Honduras, Costa Rica, Panama, El Salvador
   (2) Guatemala, Mexico, Venezuela, Chile
   (3) Nicaragua, Costa Rica, Colombia, Mexico
   (4) Panama, Brazil, Argentina, Peru

10. The United States has maintained a very active interest in the government of Panama as a result of its

    (1) rich oil reserves
    (2) association with Cuba's Communist leader, Castro
    (3) inter-ocean canal
    (4) plentiful fishing banks

11. In Nicaragua, the election of 1990 was especially significant because

    (1) moderate female candidate, Violeta Barrios de Chamorro, defeated the Sandinista candidate, Daniel Ortega

    (2) the Somoza family regained power after losing it in the 1960s
    (3) the United States used the Good Neighbor Policy to conduct elections
    (4) President Reagan continued to support the Contra War

12. Review the events in Cuban twentieth century history and place them in the correct chronological order.

    A. The United States is involved in the Bay of Pigs invasion.
    B. Fulgencio Batista benefited from American investments in Cuba.
    C. Fidel Castro gained control of an increasingly anti-American Cuba.
    D. The United States forces a showdown with the Soviet Union over missiles placed in Cuba.

    (1) C, A, B, D   (3) C, B, A, D
    (2) B, C, D, A   (4) B, C, A, D

13. Which title given below would be appropriate for an article about the Dominican Republic and Haiti in the twentieth century?

    (1) Island Nations Enjoy Prosperity Under Communist Rule
    (2) Island Neighbors Endure Revolutions and Political Instability
    (3) Foreign Powers Succeed in Controlling Nations of Hispaniola
    (4) American Good Neighbor Policy Highly Successful

14. During the twentieth century, citizens of Puerto Rico were different from citizens of most other Caribbean nations because they were

    (1) struggling to gain independence from Spain
    (2) trying to revolt against a Communist government
    (3) unwilling to emigrate to other countries
    (4) granted American citizenship

15. To many observers, Argentina at the beginning of the twentieth century had a more promising future than at the beginning of the twenty-first century. Which statement best explains this situation?

(1) Argentina had a booming economy in the early 1900s but suffered setbacks under a series of military and civilian leaders during the twentieth century.
(2) By the middle of the twentieth century, Argentina had become a Communist nation.
(3) Argentina lost the Falkland Island War with Great Britain.
(4) Agricultural laborers had organized into such a strong labor union that they demanded too many benefits from the government.

16. Venezuela, Peru, Chile, and Bolivia share which geographic feature?

(1) The Pacific Ocean
(2) The Atacama Desert
(3) The Andes Mountains
(4) The Caribbean Sea

17. Which nation is the largest exporter of oil in Latin America?

(1) Brazil
(2) Colombia
(3) Chile
(4) Venezuela

18. Which leader is paired correctly with his nation?

(1) Juan Peron—Brazil
(2) Augosto Pinochet—Chile
(3) Alberto Fujimori—Venezuela
(4) Hugo Chavez—Peru

19. In what area have Latin American immigrants to the United States most influenced American cultural development?

(1) with their advanced technological skills
(2) by taking roles of major political leadership
(3) in music, literature, dance, and theater
(4) with traditional ideas about family relationships

20. Which generalization could correctly be made about Latin America during the twentieth century and into the twenty-first century?

(1) The vast majority of nations had a democratic form of government.
(2) Most countries were still isolated economically.
(3) The Roman Catholic Church was the only significant religious influence in the area.
(4) Few Latin Americans showed any sign of interest in leaving their native homelands.

THEMATIC ESSAY

Directions: Write a well-organized essay that includes an introduction, several paragraphs addressing the task below, and a conclusion.

Theme: Economic Nationalism and Political Systems

Latin American nations in the twentieth century have struggled with forms of governments that would encourage their economic growth.

Task   Select any *one* Latin American nation *and* Cuba, and for each,

> • identify the country and describe its type of economy and government
> • explain why the country adopted the type of economic system and government that it has
> • evaluate the success each country has had reaching its economic goals

> You may select any two countries from your study of global history and Latin America. Some countries you may wish to consider include Mexico, Brazil, Venezuela, Argentina, and Chile.

> You are *not* limited to these suggestions.

Guidelines

In your essay, be sure to

> • address all aspects of the *Task*
> • support the theme with relevant facts, examples, and details
> • use a logical and clear plan of organization, including an introduction and a conclusion that are beyond a restatement of the theme
> • introduce the theme by establishing a framework that is beyond a simple restatement of the *Task* and conclude with a summation of the theme

DOCUMENT-BASED ESSAY QUESTION

This question is based on the accompanying documents (1–8). The question is designed to test your ability to work with historical documents. Some of the documents have been edited for the purposes of this question. As you analyze the documents, take into account the source of each document and any point of view that may be presented in the document.

Historical Context

The nations of Latin America, like all other world nations are influenced by their geography and natural surroundings. It has become an increasing challenge for nations to meet their economic needs and wants in a modern way while at the same time using the environment in a way that is not harmful.

Task   Using information from the documents and your knowledge of global history, answer the questions that follow each document in Part A. Your answers to the questions will help you write the Part B essay in which you will be asked to

> • identify and describe three different types of products being produced by Latin American nations currently
> • describe at least two ways in which the demands of international trade have an impact on Latin America

Part A: Short Answer Section

Directions: Analyze the documents and answer the short-answer questions that follow each document.

Document 1

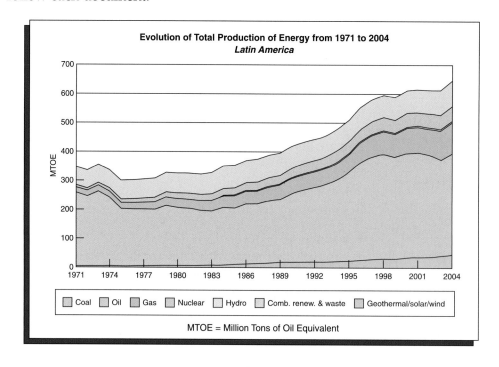

Evolution of Total Production of Energy from 1971 to 2004
Latin America

MTOE = Million Tons of Oil Equivalent

Question

1. What does the graph provided illustrate about oil production in Latin American countries since the 1970s?

Document 2

Questions

2. a. According to the photograph, is the scene in an urban or rural area?
   b. What is the product being harvested?
   c. What is one problem there might be in getting the product to market?

Document 3

NORTH AMERICAN FREE TRADE AGREEMENT

PART ONE: GENERAL PART

Chapter One: Objectives

Article 101: Establishment of the Free Trade Area
The Parties to this Agreement, consistent with Article XXIV of the General Agreement on Tariffs and Trade, hereby establish a free trade area.

Article 102: Objectives
1. The objectives of this Agreement, as elaborated more specifically through its principles and rules, including national treatment, most-favored-nation treatment and transparency, are to:

   a) eliminate barriers to trade in, and facilitate the cross-border movement of, goods and services between the territories of the Parties;

   b) promote conditions of fair competition in the free trade area;

   c) increase substantially investment opportunities in the territories of the Parties;

   d) provide adequate and effective protection and enforcement of intellectual property rights in each Party's territory;

   e) create effective procedures for the implementation and application of this Agreement, for its joint administration and for the resolution of disputes; and

   f) establish a framework for further trilateral, regional and multilateral cooperation to expand and enhance the benefits of this Agreement.

Source: Excerpt from the North American Free Trade Agreement (taken from http://www.sice.oas.org/trade/nafta/chap-01.asp)

Question   **3.** Based on the document what are two goals of the North American Free Trade Agreement?

Document 4

Question

4. According to the photograph, what activity is taking place in the rain forest?

Document 5

Selected Nations in Rank Order of Real Growth Rate of GDP

Rank among world nations	Country	GDP – real growth rate (%)
19	Venezuela	8.80
32	Cuba	7.50
51	Peru	6.50
56	Panama	6.30
109	Chile	4.80
146	U.S.A.	3.40
154	Brazil	3.10

Source: CIA—The World Factbook (taken from https://www.cia.gov/publications/factbook/rankorder/2003rank.html)

Questions

5. a. According to the chart which Latin American country has the fastest growth rate?

b. Of the countries shown on the chart, how many have a faster growth rate than the United States?

Document 6

Note: The document for this question appears on the facing page.

Questions

6. According to the chart showing the Principal Commodities Shipped through the Panama Canal,
   a. identify any two categories of products
   b. identify a product that is shipped in a greater quantity northward than southward

---

Principal Commodities Shipped through the Panama Canal
Fiscal Years 2004 through 2006

(Thousands of Long Tons*)

TABLE NO. 7

South (Atlantic to Pacific)			COMMODITIES	North (Pacific to Atlantic)		
FY 2004	FY 2005	FY 2006		FY 2006	FY 2005	FY 2004
2,464	285	107	Canned and Refrigerated Foods:	5,015	5,389	8,273
20	15	43	Canned Foods:	46	37	104
-	5	-	Fish	40	36	54
20	7	-	Fruit	3	-	19
-	-	-	Milk	-	-	-
-	-	-	Vegetables	-	-	24
-	3	42	Other and unclassified	4	2	7
2,443	271	64	Refrigerated Foods:	4,968	5,352	8,169
182	12	5	Bananas	3,174	3,385	3,126
23	-	-	Dairy products	-	-	-
909	136	37	Fish	525	571	485
59	9	16	Fruit, excluding bananas	883	962	1,082
5	-	4	Meat	16	74	119
1,266	114	1	Other and unclassified	370	360	3,358
8,177	8,954	8,377	Chemicals and Petroleum Chemicals:	5,350	4,473	2,077
5,063	2,956	4,847	Chemicals:	4,298	3,610	1,701
416	336	181	Caustic soda	242	72	16
4,356	2,421	2,964	Chemical Miscellaneous	3,800	2,972	1,150
150	-	-	Ethanol	-	-	110
35	15	19	Methanol	117	236	138
-	-	-	Mtbe	-	-	5
107	51	180	Sulfuric Acid	95	325	281
3,113	5,998	3,530	Petroleum Chemicals:	1,053	863	376
49	23	-	Benzene	513	470	293
1,074	-	-	Styrene	-	-	-
587	634	177	Toluene	11	-	-
397	741	247	Xylene	-	5	-
1,006	4,598	3,105	Other and unclassified	508	387	84
5,922	4,231	1,924	Coal and Coke (Excluding petroleum coke):	3,804	5,204	6,337
5,426	3,282	1,924	Coal	3,164	2,706	3,416
496	949	-	Coke	640	2,498	2,920
30,967	24,908	34,400	Grains:	2,256	1,775	2,444
248	-	-	Barley	60	101	163
13,539	4,843	17,840	Corn	233	40	205
20	32	20	Oats	1	-	-
467	580	482	Rice	403	567	385
1,889	4,267	5,732	Sorghum	151	162	-
10,845	10,445	8,492	Soybeans	32	134	128
1,990	637	774	Wheat	1,265	242	1,360
1,969	4,102	1,060	Other and unclassified	111	529	204
1,948	1,687	1,584	Lumber and Products:	4,284	4,255	3,143
8	236	207	Boards and planks	120	352	784
3	-	-	Plywood, veneers, and composition board	475	289	138
1,222	728	989	Pulpwood	2,198	1,641	1,555
714	723	388	Other and unclassified	1,491	1,972	667
1,519	1,470	1,289	Machinery and Equipment:	3,275	3,362	2,741
762	919	994	Automobiles, Trucks, Accessories And Parts	2,707	2,476	1,936
47	49	9	Agricultural Machinery And Implements	38	15	30
561	203	54	Construction Machinery And Equipment	122	512	627
25	69	67	Electrical Machinery And Apparatus	59	102	24
6	5	2	Motorcycles, Bicycles And Parts	22	-	-
118	225	162	Other and unclassified	326	257	124

* Data given in thousands is subject to rounding differences. Tonnages less than 500 long tons are not shown.

Department of Corporate Planning and Marketing (PMXR)

TABLE NO. 7

(continued on following page)

Principal Commodities Shipped through the Panama Canal
Fiscal Years 2004 through 2006

(Thousands of Long Tons*)

TABLE NO. 7

South			COMMODITIES	North		
Atlantic to Pacific				Pacific to Atlantic		
FY 2004	FY 2005	FY 2006		FY 2006	FY 2005	FY 2004
3,405	3,346	2,726	Manufactures of Iron and Steel:	4,591	3,037	2,415
170	69	20	Angles, Shapes And Sections	4	71	77
1	-	-	Nails, Tacks And Spikes	-	-	-
1,287	149	157	Plates, Sheets And Coils	1,391	539	892
137	158	179	Tubes, Pipes And Fittings	555	581	368
441	695	582	Wires, Bars And Rods	727	974	393
1,370	2,275	1,789	Other and unclassified	1,914	872	685
588	115	120	Minerals, miscellaneous:	4,658	5,356	5,947
419	-	-	Asbestos	-	-	-
-	-	-	Borax	104	184	199
-	-	-	Infusorial earth	-	-	-
25	39	21	Salt	3,988	4,791	4,685
120	57	80	Soda and sodium compounds	230	118	514
24	19	20	Sulfur	336	263	550
8,822	8,392	5,585	Nitrates, Phosphates and Potash:	731	566	923
579	1,296	-	Ammonium compounds	-	9	1
-	-	-	Fishmeal	-	-	139
119	-	-	Nitrate of soda	89	73	191
1,204	972	614	Phosphates	69	16	10
147	39	45	Potash	35	-	109
6,773	6,085	4,926	Fertilizers, Miscellaneous	538	468	473
5,800	3,344	3,475	Ores and Metals:	11,139	8,590	8,240
2,059	1,227	1,410	Ores:	4,750	5,048	5,359
879	78	131	Alumina/Bauxite	583	136	401
-	77	111	Chrome	-	4	30
75	193	135	Copper	1,623	1,811	1,511
612	176	760	Iron	916	727	359
43	112	84	Lead	62	125	63
172	443	9	Manganese	141	286	189
-	-	-	Tin	-	-	-
15	59	79	Zinc	979	1,262	929
263	88	101	Other and unclassified	446	699	1,877
3,741	2,117	2,065	Metals:	6,389	3,542	2,881
497	197	365	Aluminum	52	66	66
58	41	60	Copper	1,673	1,365	1,567
875	1,154	1,406	Iron	4,359	1,786	496
37	-	-	Lead	-	21	24
2,158	670	146	Scrap	124	145	84
1	-	-	Tin, including Tinplate	4	22	-
14	-	5	Zinc	156	124	450
102	56	82	Other and unclassified	22	11	195
769	868	661	Other Agricultural Commodities:	1,826	1,799	3,379
101	113	61	Beans, Edible	95	83	109
10	-	-	Cocoa And Cacao Beans	71	31	45
-	-	-	Coffee, Raw And Processed	-	5	3
-	-	-	Copra And Coconuts	-	-	4
-	-	-	Cotton, Raw	-	-	-
40	-	-	Molasses	-	483	757
60	40	-	Oilseeds	-	1	106
2	-	-	Peas, Dry	-	-	338
9	-	-	Rubber, Raw	80	7	122
122	346	176	Skins And Hides	-	34	-
426	369	425	Sugar	1,580	1,154	1,895
-	-	-	Wool, Raw	-	-	-

* Data given in thousands is subject to rounding differences. Tonnages less than 500 long tons are not shown.

TABLE NO. 7

Department of Corporate Planning and Marketing (PMXR)

Document 7

Questions

7. a. Based on your study of the given map, which two countries do not have seaports?
  b. Which country has the longest Atlantic Ocean coastline?

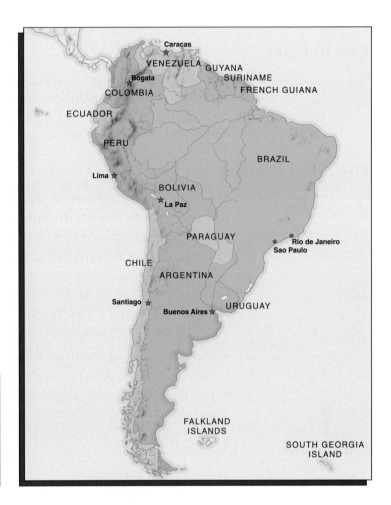

Document 8

Question

8. From your study of the map below, why was the Canal between the Caribbean Sea and the Pacific Ocean constructed in Panama?

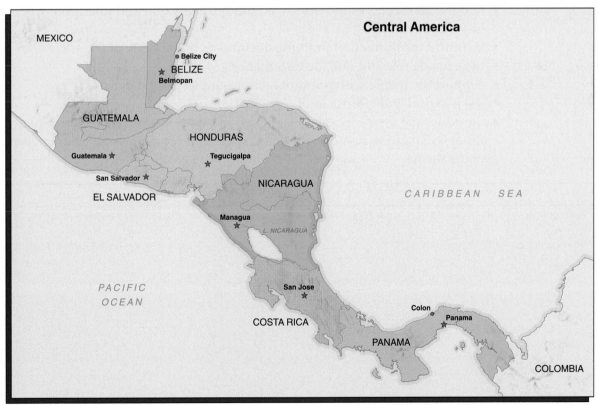

Part B: Essay

Directions: Write a well-organized essay that includes an introduction, several paragraphs, and a conclusion. Use evidence from *at least five* documents in the body of the essay. Support your response with relevant facts, examples, and details. Include additional outside information.

Historical Context

The nations of Latin America, like all other world nations are influenced by their geography and natural surroundings. It has become an increasing challenge for nations to meet their economic needs and wants in a modern way while at the same time using the environment in a way that is not harmful.

Task

Using information from the documents and your knowledge of global history, answer the questions that follow each document in Part A. Your answers to the questions will help you write the Part B essay in which you will be asked to

- identify and describe three different types of products being produced by Latin American nations currently
- describe at least two ways in which the demands of international trade have an impact on Latin America

Guidelines

In your essay, be sure to

- address all aspects of the *Task* by accurately analyzing and interpreting *at least five* documents
- incorporate information from the documents in the body of the essay
- incorporate relevant outside information
- support the theme with relevant facts, examples, and details
- use a logical and clear plan of organization
- introduce the theme by establishing a framework that is beyond a simple restatement of the *Task* or *Historical Context* and conclude with a summation of the theme

ERA VIII

SOME CHALLENGES OF THE TWENTY-FIRST CENTURY

INTRODUCTION

I n this unit we will learn about our world, nations, and people as the twenty-first century begins. If we ever learn anything from history it is time to realize that nations and people have to put aside hatred and settle their differences without going to war. With nuclear weaponry, a wide-scale war might well mean the end of life, as we know it. We must also learn that hatred within a country, or neighbor against neighbor, is self-destructive and will not lead to the solution of economic, political, or social problems. Political and economic leaders, scientists, and educators need to work together to create common goals in order to find solutions for many existing problems.

Many believe that the single greatest problem facing us is the rapid increase in world population that has taken place. With a fixed amount of natural resources and an increasing number of people to share them, a decent standard of living is now more competitive in the nations of our globally interdependent world. In other areas of the world, most notably in many African, Asian, and Latin American nations, there is a great need for economic development to help poor and hungry peoples so that they can have a better quality of life. Food shipments from the agriculturally advanced nations are a humanitarian effort but not the long-term answer.

In this unit, we will also look at global environment issues. Today we realize that the growing damage to and destruction of the environment concerns us all and threatens our future and that of our children.

While we have these problems, not all is gloom and doom. We are living in a world where a global culture is developing. Hopefully this global culture, which combines elements of music, art, literature, film, and other cultural media that will bring future generations closer together.

CHAPTER 18

Global Economic Issues

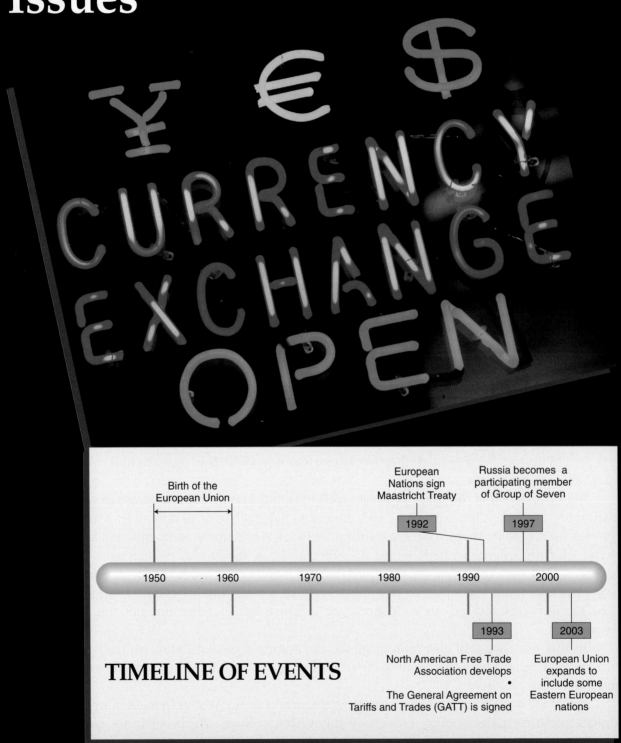

European
Nations sign
Maastricht Treaty

Birth of the
European Union

Russia becomes a
participating member
of Group of Seven

1992

1997

1950   1960   1970   1980   1990   2000

TIMELINE OF EVENTS

1993

2003

North American Free Trade
Association develops

•

The General Agreement on
Tariffs and Trades (GATT) is signed

European Union
expands to
include some
Eastern European
nations

When people shop today, they often have many different choices to select from before purchasing the item they want. This is true of automobiles, clothing, electronic equipment, and most other products. In many countries, there are an increasing number of foreign-made goods in the stores. Think about the products that your family buys. Is the clothing you are wearing manufactured here or in another country? Was the stereo equipment that you have at home produced in China, Japan, Korea, India, the United States, or elsewhere? Will your family buy an American-made automobile or an import from an Asian or European nation the next time a car is purchased?

THE GROWING INTERDEPENDENCE OF THE GLOBAL ECONOMY

The marketplace today has become increasingly global. In this chapter, you will examine many of the important global economic developments. In the last decades, the world has become more economically interrelated. Industrial production and financial institutions are increasingly global in terms of their outlook and reach. For example, many banks have opened branches in countries beyond their home country. Factories often produce goods for home and foreign consumption. These developments are also, in part, a direct result of the scientific and technological progress that has led to a growing **global interdependence**. Communication and transportation networks have improved dramatically in recent decades. Computerization has brought the world economically closer together.

No longer are nations or even regions self-sufficient in terms of their economic needs. The standard of living of almost any country depends on its involvement in the global financial, manufacturing, and trading system. Nations can no longer completely safeguard their economic independence and financial systems if they are interested in participating in the global marketplace. There are too many international factors that affect a nation's economy once that country becomes part of the global trading network. These influential economic factors include the cost of energy and other raw materials in world markets, the cost of labor in the home country and elsewhere, and the nation's ability to resolve technological, transportation, and communication issues.

THE GROWTH OF NEW CENTERS OF INDUSTRIAL PRODUCTION

The economic dominance that the United States, Japan, and some Western European nations, such as Germany, France, and England, exercise over the global economy and other nations' economies is increasingly being challenged. In recent decades, countries whose economies are rapidly developing are making important economic progress because of their ability to produce goods cheaply and sell them to other countries. Often these products are sold to industrialized nations, which previously controlled the manufacture and sale of the

Factory workers from China.

same goods. Today nations such as China, India, Korea, Taiwan, and Brazil are playing a greater role in the developing **interdependent global economy**. In the twenty-first century, the development of economies in nations that were considered nonindustrial countries during the twentieth century will continue at a rapid pace and present new challenges for the developing global economy.

More countries have become more involved in the expanding network of world trade as producers of manufactured goods. There is also a greater competition for available raw materials, particularly energy resources. Prices of raw materials, such as petroleum and minerals, have increased greatly. In addition, the competition to sell manufactured goods, such as automobiles, airplanes, and electronic devices has led to international economic disputes. Trade barriers, multinational corporations, aid to developing nations, the value of national currencies, the interrelated world stock markets, and foreign investment are among the concerns of the expanding global economy. The drug and arms trade are also important issues for the world economy.

New York Stock Exchange.

INTERNATIONAL TRADE AND ECONOMIC COOPERATION

The growth of international trade in the second half of the twentieth century was phenomenal. In the twenty-first century, global trade continues to develop at a rapid rate. All nations are now more than ever dependent on the global trading network to improve the standard of living of their citizens. This is an example of global interdependence. During the twentieth century, some of the industrialized nations, such as the United States, Germany, and Japan, possessed advantages that gave them enormous power in the world trading system. Today, this is less true because even those nations with the largest and most dynamic economies increasingly depend on other countries for raw materials, markets for their products, and factories to produce goods that are sold in their home market.

REGIONAL TRADING ASSOCIATIONS: THE EUROPEAN UNION

There is a growing trend to form mutually beneficial regional trading blocs. In Europe in the post-World War II era, the idea of a common economic community took root. A French banker, **Jean Monnet,** had a vision of a European common market. Monnet envisioned one enormous European market in which there would be no trade barriers among the continent's diverse nations. Beginning in the 1950s, six European countries joined together to form an economic community. In 1992, member nations of the **European Union (EU)** voted to complete the last steps of economic integration. In Maastricht, Holland, the EU member nations agreed to further reduce trading barriers, eventually create a common European currency, and give more of each nation's control of its economy to the central EU governing body, which is based in Brussels, Belgium. Each nation put the **Maastricht Treaty** to a vote for approval or rejection.

The vote on the Maastricht Treaty sparked strong debates in EU member nations, particularly in France, Denmark, Germany, and Great Britain. Those people who argued for the treaty's approval stated that only if Europe united economically would it become able to effectively compete in the changing world markets. Proponents for a yes vote claimed that European production would ultimately become more efficient and less costly. Those against approval argued that their nations would lose control of their economies. Some economic constituencies, such as French farmers, believed they would be negatively affected by increased lower cost agricultural production. Ultimately, the arguments in favor won out and the treaty was approved.

The treaty is a concrete step toward and a model of regional economic cooperation. For example, it is now possible for a member nation such as Germany to manufacture automobiles and sell them in the markets of European Union countries without any import duties or other trade restrictions being imposed. The agricultural and industrial products of EU member nations have an advantage over the same type of goods produced elsewhere. Elimination of import duties means that it is often cheaper to buy and sell agricultural produce, raw materials, and finished goods within the trading community than it would be to sell them outside. The creation of a common currency and a central bank to regulate the monetary system made the European Union a competitive rival of the United States and Japan.

Using a slow but steady approach, European nations slowly developed and expanded the economic influence of the EU **trading bloc**. The European Union has continued to add new members. In 2003, a group of eastern European nations were allowed to join the EU. This regional trading community is now one of the world's leading economic blocs. These nations removed many of the troublesome trading barriers that existed among the nations of Europe. They have developed inter-European Union trade and present a unified position on matters relating to global economic issues.

The creation of a powerful European trading community had an important influence on the development of other regional trading associations. Other

> **Main Idea:**
> The European Union is now one of the world's leading economic blocs.

trading blocs also developed. For example in the western hemisphere in 1993, the United States, Canada, and Mexico joined together to form the **North American Free Trade Association,** referred to as **NAFTA.**

GENERAL AGREEMENT ON TARIFFS AND TRADE

Main Idea:
In 1993, the world's leading trading nations reached a compromise on trade issues. The outcome of negotiations for a **General Agreement on Tariffs and Trade (GATT)** resulted in an agreement for big cuts in tariffs on most goods.

More open global trade permits nations to specialize in the manufacture of products or the extraction and sale of raw materials to maximize profit. The idea is that freer trade with reduced tariffs conflicts with the fact that within a trading bloc such as the EU or NAFTA, member nations often offer lower prices and advantages to their manufacturers and consumers. Also, if a country seeks to go it alone, and then competes in the global trading system against organized regional economic associations, that country is economically hurt by competition and lower pricing. Therefore, the idea of freer trade in the global marketplace has become more important if nations are to overcome trade restrictions that economic blocs impose on non-member-nation's goods and natural resources.

The United States, Japan, China, the Western European nations such as Germany and France, India, and Brazil have the greatest volume of trade. These nations have industrial economies in which many people earn enough money to buy large quantities of goods. They are all concerned with the conflicting issues of having access to other regional markets and safeguarding their own national production. In 1993, the world's leading trading nations reached a compromise on trade issues. The outcome of negotiations for a **General Agreement on Tariffs and Trade** (GATT) resulted in an agreement for big cuts in tariffs on most goods. The United States and the European Union agreed, on average, to cut tariffs in half on each other's goods. Tariffs on goods from the rest of the world were cut less. In addition, a schedule to reduce tariffs on agricultural productions was included in the agreement. The attempt to place tariffs on agricultural crops has proven to be difficult to implement. Some countries, including the United States and France, seek to protect their nation's farmers by means of subsidies and minimum-price supports.

The first GATT signing took place in Havana in 1947. Twenty-three nations including the United States signed the original trade agreement. The GATT has added new members since then and has been renegotiated a number of times. The latest version of the GATT is called the Doha Development Round, but these trade negotiations have stalled because of disagreements between developed nations such as the United States and Japan and developing nations. The agreement is expected to stimulate business and investment activity by opening markets. It also tries to encourage countries that specialize in growing agricultural products, the extraction of raw materials, and the production of manufactured goods to have more open markets and efficient economic practices. To a large measure, the GATT has stimulated more trade and reduced existing tariffs in certain markets.

However, today there are still agricultural issues and other unresolved problems relating to property rights concerning movies and software, and in the field of financial services. In addition, there is more concern in some nations that there is an imbalance and unfairness regarding the way global trade has been liberalized and has developed in recent years. There have been many protests against economic globalization. The results of recent elections in Venezuela, Bolivia, and Ecuador are examples of nations that are increasingly questioning the value of economic globalization for their countries and people. Nevertheless, there still is a strong belief that the GATT is crucial for the future of more open trade among the industrial nations and the developing countries of the world.

MULTINATIONAL CORPORATIONS

Multinational corporations are companies that operate and have investments in more than one country. These companies manufacture and market products in more than one country to help link the world-trading network together. Multinational corporations control an expanding volume of trade in all global regions. These businesses are very competitive and seek to penetrate new markets whenever an economic opportunity presents itself. For example, General Motors, the Sony Corporation, Toyota, and Volkswagen are corporations that began respectively in the United States, Japan, and Germany, but that now have become multinational because they operate and invest in other nations. Multinational companies can have positive and negative effects within the global economy and in individual nations.

Advantages of Multinational Corporations

Multinational corporations often have access to enormous financial resources, such as bank loans and stock issues, which allow them to invest in costly industrial expansion and technology. These companies bring new manufacturing facilities to developing countries that do not have sufficient national funding to increase their industrial production. Jobs are created, workers earn and spend salaries, and the standard of living rises, especially for those people involved in the employ of these companies. Another benefit is the use of a nation's natural resources in the multinational corporations' factories. An improved transportation and communication network generally results from these companies' need to have reliable connections to the global market.

Disadvantages of Multinational Corporations

The national industries of developing countries can suffer when forced to compete with multinational corporations. And, the exploitation of raw materials can have a negative ecological impact if national regulations or safeguards are not present. Furthermore, the outflow of capital (money that leaves a nation) to foreign-based corporations is another serious problem. Corporations often send profits abroad in dollars or in other currencies, such as the Japanese yen or European euro. This can lead to a major devaluation (or loss in value) of a nation's currency if too much money leaves the country. Multinational companies often act in their own self-interest, particularly regarding the remittance of profits (the sending of money abroad).

Even economic blocs, such as the European Union, cannot completely control multinational companies. The international business outlook of corporations that have ventured beyond their original national borders makes them increasingly independent, self-sufficient, and adaptable to changing conditions. International companies can evade import restrictions by investing in manufacturing to produce their product within a market that penalizes the importation of goods.

The European automobile market is an example of what is now happening. Germany, Italy, France, and Great Britain are all major European automobile producers. Within the EU, these nations are no longer subject to import restrictions. Therefore, production by an EU member or nonmember in any EU country opens the markets to all EU nations.

For example, in Great Britain, there is growing Japanese corporate investment in automobile plants to produce Toyotas, Mitsubishis, and other cars. The European-made Japanese automobiles are not considered foreign exports and therefore are not subject to the usual import restrictions that limit imports and raise their prices. These cars differ from Japanese automobiles made in Japan and sold in Europe, which are considered imports and are subject to taxes and other restrictions. The excellent quality of Japanese cars produced in Great Britain and their competitive prices make them an increasing threat to the European Union's automobile industry. The U.S. automobile market has also suffered from this type of economic penetration.

In the 1990s, there was the danger that multinational corporations serving their own interests could ignite a trade war that would be disastrous for the global economy. The inability to control international companies can have long-term negative economic consequences for many nations. The identification of multinational corporations with particular countries can cause rifts that have economic repercussions. For example, the environmental disaster in **Bhopal, India,** in 1984 at the Goodyear-operated plant caused severe strains between that nation and the United States. In Bhopal, a chemical plant owned by a multinational company, the Union Carbide Corporation, whose headquarters is based in the United States, leaked a large quantity of poisonous gas, which killed 2,000 people and severely injured 150,000 others. The Indian government sued the Union Carbide Corporation for damages. However, the fact that Union Carbide operated in India through a subsidiary (or company that controlled another company) complicated the case and involved the United States.

Toyota automobile production.

Multinational companies because of the lack of effective international controls sometimes cause problems. This can lead nations to take economic measures designed to hurt countries that are the home country of the multinational corporation. This action is called an economic reprisal or revenge. Ultimately, it can pit one trading bloc against another and depress world economic growth. This means that unless some international agreement is made about the way multinational corporations invest and operate, global manufacturing and trade could even decrease. This is true of the competition to sell airplanes in the international market between the Boeing and Aero-Spatial Corporations, which has brought the United States and the European Union into conflict about issues relating to state subsidies and fair trade.

PRESENT AND FUTURE ECONOMIC ISSUES

Most nations are still trying to meet the basic needs of their citizens in a world that has become more economically interdependent. One important long-range issue is the growing economic gap between the limited number of rich nations and the much larger group of poor countries. During the 1980s, poorer nations, particularly those dependent on the sale of raw materials to earn foreign exchange, found themselves increasingly in debt to richer nations, private banks, and international lending agencies. Investment capital was needed. Many developing nations borrowed heavily, and national debt levels increased.

Main Idea:
One important long-range issue is the growing economic gap between the limited number of rich nations and the much larger group of poor countries.

There is also the important issue of debt relief for many of the nations in the developing world. This is particularly a difficult problem to resolve throughout Africa and in many nations of Latin America, Asia, and Eastern Europe. Nations such as Brazil and Mexico have learned that huge borrowing to finance infrastructure projects and basic facilities, such as power plants and communication systems, led to enormous debt. The debt owed was difficult to ever repay without severely damaging national interests. The repayment of the debt principle and servicing of the debt interest is too great of an economic burden for many poor nations. These countries are often required to take economic measures by the World Bank, **International Monetary Fund (IMF)**, and private lenders that led to hardships for their citizens who are faced with higher costs of living because prices rise and subsidies are removed by governments who have to satisfy lender demands. The best solution for developing nations would be the forgiveness or cancellation of this crushing debt or another form of debt relief by lending nations and international banks.

Another issue is the unstable political climate in developing nations, which leads to negative economic conditions for investment and operating businesses. Political instability makes a nation more of a risk for investment. Also, sometimes poor nations invest borrowed money in worthless large-scale projects. These status projects such as large government buildings and glamorous residential-type palaces for government leaders do little to improve the overall economic conditions of the nation or people. This misuse of investment capital has discouraged banks, corporations, and individual investors in more stable and wealthier countries from investing. Corruption and outright thievery has occurred too often. For example, in some African nations, these types of problems have occurred even after political leaders who promised economic change and reforms were successful in obtaining capital to develop their economies.

The road to a more diversified economy, one more varied in terms of goods produced and a higher standard of living, is long and difficult. The negative impact of a large national debt (money owed by a country) is the loss of economic independence to international financial institutions. Private banks and other lending institutions want to be repaid. Their pursuit of repayment can place restrictions on the debtor nation, which can adversely impact the people and overall economy of that nation. To make the necessary economic transformation and repay debt, nations often require funding from outside international sources. The IMF, World Bank, private banks, and industrial nations can supply the financial assistance to support attempts by developing nations for economic diversification. However, economic assistance comes with demands made on the nation to change how the economy functions. For example, the IMF often asks borrowing nations to eliminate price supports, which can lead to internal uprisings against the sudden rise in the cost of living.

In Europe, the collapse of communism in the Soviet Union and Eastern Europe resulted in a widening of the economic gap within the region. Western Europe's economic growth and cooperation was in sharp contrast to the former Communist bloc nations' shattered economies. Huge investments have become necessary in Poland, Hungary, Russia, Ukraine, and elsewhere if these countries are to develop diversified economies and raise the standard of living of their people.

The danger of failing to develop the economies of the poorer European nations is enormous. There is the risk of a massive migration from the developing nations of Eastern Europe, where desperate workers who cannot find employment in their own countries will seek a brighter economic future in the industrialized nations of Western Europe. Germany, France, Great Britain, and Italy all confront this problem.

Unemployment is a complicated issue. There is an increasing problem of finding work for all of the people in the countries of the EU who are legal residents and the increasing numbers of illegal immigrants who are arriving. For example, in the fall of 1993, in Germany, Volkswagen changed the schedule of a number of automobile plants to a four-day workweek to increase the total number of jobs for workers. There is also the problem of workers from other nations who were invited by EU countries to come and work in jobs that could not be filled in the 1970s and 1980s. They have worked for a number of years and now find that they are less in demand and no longer welcome. Often these workers have brought their families to the host country and cut ties to their countries of origin. There are also many immigrants who are living without proper documents. This is a growing problem particularly since integration has proven to be increasingly difficult especially with workers and families whose origins are in Islamic nations.

Most of the nations in developing global regions are facing growing economic problems. As the twenty-first century begins, many poor nations find it ever more difficult to attract investment capital. There is little capital available in these nations. This means people lack the money needed to start or expand a busi-

Main Idea:
The road to a diversified economy, one varied in terms of goods produced and a higher standard of living, is long and difficult.

ness to improve their lives and employ others. These poor nations of Africa, Asia, Latin America, the Caribbean basin, and the Middle East face competition from Eastern Europe and the countries of the Commonwealth of Independent States for international funding and general economic support. Unless these nations are assisted and develop economically, the issues of improving the national standard of living, unemployment, and illegal immigration cannot be remedied.

THE INTERNATIONAL FINANCIAL SYSTEM

The 1980s and 1990s were decades of growing international financial cooperation by the wealthier nations. The **Group of Seven** (the leading industrial countries) increasingly worked together as a financial community to control the international monetary system. These nations—the **United States**, **Japan**, **Germany**, **France**, **Canada**, **Great Britain**, and **Italy**—coordinate their monetary policies because they consider cooperation to be essential for their mutual economic health. The Group of Seven now meets whenever there is a need to resolve a critical monetary issue that affects the global economy. In recent years, **Russia** has been invited to meetings, and the organization has become an economic **Summit of Eight**. In the future, it is obvious that the nations of China, India, Brazil, and Korea will have to be given a greater voice in the deliberations and decisionmaking concerning monetary policies in the increasingly interdependent global economy.

> **Main Idea:**
> Each member nation of the Summit of Eight sends representatives of its national bank to international meetings to try to keep **currency fluctuations** (changes in the value of money) within reasonable limits.

One issue of concern is how to support the value of a particular national currency, that is, how much it should be worth. The Summit of Eight supports the idea of determining the value of a nation's or bloc's money by the market conditions of supply and demand. This means that a **currency** is allowed to float. The decline in value of a currency can have a dramatic impact on trade. For example, a cheaper dollar makes it easier for other nations to buy more American products. However, the export of products to the United States becomes more difficult because foreign goods are then more expensive. Therefore, each country sends representatives of its national bank to international meetings to try to keep **currency fluctuations** (changes in the value of money) within reasonable limits. In recent years, the value of some Asian currencies, particularly that of China, has presented a problem for nations that allow their money to be determined in an open market. China fixes the value of its currency at an unrealistically low exchange rate, which gives its products an advantage in international markets.

INTERNATIONAL ECONOMIC PROBLEMS

The Global Drug Trade

Drug trafficking is an international economic concern. In addition to the severe political, social, and health problems caused by the widespread and growing use of illegal narcotics, the global financial system is negatively affected by the vast sums of money that are earned by the international **drug cartels**. Cartels are business associations that are monopolistic in their actions. It is estimated that the United States alone has more than a multibillion-dollar annual market for drugs such as cocaine, heroin, and marijuana. The long-term negative economic and health consequences for the United States, European Union, and other major drug-consuming nations are enormous and growing.

Main Idea:
The drug traffickers control large transportation and communication networks and have gained entrance into the international financial system.

The drug cartels have become powerful international business organizations. The drug traffickers control large transportation and communication networks and have gained entrance into the international financial system. Huge sums of money are laundered, and made clean, and seemingly legal, by investing in legal businesses. The banks that accept deposits from drug traffickers are corrupted by associating with these people as well as by the profits earned in these financial transactions. The drug cartels control tremendous sums of money. This illegally earned wealth poses political and social problems for all nations involved in the narcotics network. For example, in **Colombia**, **Mexico**, and Afghanistan, the consequences of drug production and trafficking have led to more violence and political instability. It is difficult to ask poor farmers to produce agricultural crops for a subsistence type of existence or even to grow non-drug-related cash crops for the market when they can grow drug-related crops such as opium, coca, or marijuana for profit. Poor farmers want to not only survive but also offer better lives and opportunities for their families, and drug money often provides a better income. This is a complicated issue, which will require drug-producing and -consuming nations to cooperate.

Also some political organizations often make alliances with drug traffickers to earn money for their revolutionary activities. In addition, the problem is complicated by police officers and the military leaders who are bribed to look the other way or stage meaningless headline-producing raids.

In South America, the struggle against the powerful drug cartels demonstrates that a local or regional approach will not work to reduce or eliminate drug production. It is obvious that increased international cooperation is needed to fight what has become one of the world's most serious economic problems—the global drug trade.

The Arms Trade

The sales of weapons to nations that can ill afford to waste needed financial resources expanded enormously during the 1990s and continues today. The competitive **arms trade** has been estimated to be worth more than $50 billion annually. The United States, France, Russia, and Great Britain are the world's largest sellers of weapons. However, these nations are not the only producers of arms for export. Developing nations such as Brazil, China, and Israel possess large weapons industries that earn foreign exchange for other economic needs.

The breakup of the Soviet Union and the political changes in Eastern Europe have complicated the arms problem. There is now a terrible danger that sophisticated military technology to make missiles, fighter planes, and even nuclear weapons will become increasingly available. Government officials and military leaders in Russia, Ukraine, and elsewhere have sold military technology and equipment for needed cash to any nation that can pay for them. Some of this weaponry has a nuclear, chemical, and biological destructive capability.

The Gulf War in 1991 was proof of what can happen if advanced military technology falls into the wrong hands. The former Soviet Union built up the Iraqi military to the point where the leader of this nation, **Saddam Hussein**, became an international threat. In addition to the Soviet Union, during the 1980s, the United States, France, and other nations also sold **Iraq** military technology and equipment. Iraq's invasion of **Kuwait**, motivated by the desire to gain control of that nation's oil resources, led to a war between Iraq and an international and United Nations-sanctioned military force led by the United States. Saddam Hussein made a huge investment in his military forces but lost to the combined UN force in the Gulf War. The price paid in lives lost and property destroyed was enormous.

The use of financial resources to purchase weapons by poor nations has a negative impact on the people of these countries. The economic consequences of such misguided actions leave less money available in nation's budgets for education, public health, housing, and the creation of jobs. The wealthier nations, such as the United States, France, and Great Britain often justify the arms trade as an economic necessity. For the United States, arms production has been an integral part of the American economy since the Cold War began. In the 1990s, the United States and other Western nations faced the need to make some economic adjustments because there was no longer as great a need to build up an arms supply in the event of a war with the Communist bloc nations. They looked for and found other markets for their weaponry in developing nations, which led to an increase of even more deadly warfare.

The collapse of the Soviet Union and other Eastern European Communist countries eliminated the menace of war between the superpowers and their respective allies. In the first decade of the twenty-first century, the menace of international terrorism particularly after the September 11, 2001, attack on the United States led to a revival of the arms industry and the development of new types of weaponry and means of surveillance. This has only been reinforced by the war that has developed in Iraq after the ouster of Saddam Hussein from power.

The real cost of arms sales can be seen in the political instability in a growing number of developing nations in Africa, Asia, and Europe. The problem is compounded by the sale of weapons by private arms dealers to terrorist organizations and revolutionary groups. Unless the weapons-exporting nations and the increasing number of developing countries show greater international cooperation and restrain nations that participate in the destructive arms trade, this problem will continue well into the twenty-first century.

> **Main Idea:**
> The real cost of arms sales can be seen in the political instability in a growing number of developing nations in Africa, Asia, and Europe.

LINK TO TODAY

If we look at the world today, we can see that the nations and people of our globe are increasingly economically interdependent. It is not possible for a nation to isolate itself and remain outside of the global trading network and, at the same time, guarantee most of its citizens a decent standard of living. For a nation to be economically successful, there is a need for that country to understand the needs and workings of the changing global marketplace and trading system. The political and economic leaders must plan and prepare that society to take part in the global economy. This economic planning includes so many important factors. There is a need to think in terms of long-term economic goals, to develop leadership, to administer and manage businesses, to have an educated workforce, to provide for capital investment, to maintain a stable currency, and to have access to natural resources.

In the first stages of the Industrial Revolution, only a few nations were able to put all of these factors together and offer most of their people an opportunity for a better life and standard of living. These nations were Great Britain, France, Germany, and several other Western European countries, the United States, and Japan. In the post-World War II period, many nations gained their political independence and began to develop their own economies for the benefit of their own society. By the late twentieth century, an increasing number of nations reached the stage of assembling the necessary factors to develop and advance their economies.

Today, we see that the world has grown enormously in terms of economic development and interdependence. There is more economic competition today among nations that produce finished goods for the international market. Here in the United States and elsewhere in Western Europe and Japan, there is a growing realization that the globalization of the world economy means that other nations want to share in the benefits of industrialization. This means that more manufacturing will take place in countries that have better skilled and educated workers whose labor costs less. It also means that the nations that sell natural resources, particularly energy and minerals, can sell at higher prices because there are more buyers and a greater need and use of their raw materials.

Today, we must reevaluate what the United States is doing and where our economy is heading. If we are to continue to offer most people in our country the opportunity for a decent standard of living, we have to continually adjust to the changing nature of the interdependent global economy. We can no longer take it for granted that just because we are living in the United States and are Americans that we are guaranteed a bright economic future. Global economic interdependence has led to greater competition and the need to constantly rethink and adjust our national and personal economic goals.

CHAPTER SUMMARY

No nation can isolate itself from the rest of the world and hope that its people can prosper economically and benefit from production and services available in other countries. For example, as you look around your house, you may note that many of the goods you enjoy have come from overseas. Your standard of living is directly tied to international trade. Yet, we cannot continue to increase our debt through a negative balance of trade. We must increase our exports to the nations we import from. This affects jobs here. It is a complicated problem with complex solutions.

Globally, economic problems remain that need to be solved. For example, the imbalances caused by the global trading system, the outsourcing of jobs, and industrial currency fluctuations pose important problems for the United States. We live in an economically interdependent world. A frost in Brazil raises the price of a cup of coffee; a stronger yen in Japan raises the prices of our automobiles. Our elected leaders will be facing these real challenges to policy. What should the role of the United States be? What should the role of other nations be as their economies develop?

IMPORTANT PEOPLE, PLACES, AND TERMS

KEY TERMS

global interdependence	General Agreement on	Group of Seven
interdependent global	Tariffs and Trade	Summit of Eight
economy	(GATT)	currency
European Union (EU)	Computerization	currency fluctuations
Maastricht Treaty	multinational	drug trafficking
trading bloc	corporation	drug cartels
North American Free	International Monetary	arms trade
Trade Association	Fund (IMF)	
(NAFTA)		

PEOPLE

Jean Monnet

PLACES

Bhopal, India	Japan	Mexico
Russia	Germany	Afghanistan
China	France	Iraq
India	Canada	Kuwait
Brazil	Great Britain	
United States	Colombia	

CHAPTER 18

MULTIPLE-CHOICE QUESTIONS

Select the number of the correct answer.

1. A major factor in the success of countries whose economies are rapidly developing and making economic progress is their ability to

    (1) pay their workers a high salary
    (2) produce goods cheaply and sell on the world marketplace
    (3) encourage traditional forms of domestic handicrafts
    (4) rely on single-crop agriculture

2. Global interdependence can best be described as

    (1) the reliance of a nation on other nations to gain products that will enable its citizens to achieve a higher standard of living
    (2) the ability of a country to be completely self-sufficient in the production of energy resources
    (3) the willingness of world nations to accept as trading partners only those nations that share a common political philosophy
    (4) world trade agreements enforced by the United Nations

3. The European Union used which technique to help the area become an economic competitor of such countries as Japan and the United States?

    (1) approved a common language for all participating nations
    (2) removed all national borders to encourage easier and quicker trade
    (3) created a common currency
    (4) increased tariffs among the member nations

4. GATT or the General Agreement on Tariffs and Trade is an attempt to

    (1) encourage trade among the most industrialized nations of the world
    (2) increase the divide between the richest and the poorest of the world's nations
    (3) eliminate agricultural trading between nations
    (4) prevent any nation from negatively impacting the economy of another nation

5. The Volkswagen Corporation of Germany is an example of a multinational company because

    (1) it has offices in every world nation today
    (2) many people like to drive Volkswagen cars to conserve energy
    (3) it plans to expand beyond Germany sometime in the future
    (4) the Volkswagen company operates and invests in other world nations for its own advantage

6. Developing nations may be hurt by which action of a multinational company?

    (1) the sale of manufactured products in the developing country
    (2) the hiring of native workers
    (3) the construction of bridges and roadways
    (4) the return of the profits of production or sales to the home country of the multinational company

7. A consumer living in a European Union nation who wishes to purchase an automobile produced by another EU country has an advantage over consumers living in many other parts of the world because

   (1) there are no longer import restrictions for that consumer
   (2) auto makers offer a wider selection to Europeans
   (3) European cars are considered by consumers to be superior to those produced elsewhere
   (4) the taxes are higher than the taxes charged on non-European imports

8. A current serious long-range economic issue is the

   (1) growing number of nations that practice traditional agricultural techniques
   (2) increasing gap between the very rich countries and the larger group of poor nations
   (3) number of developing nations that are turning to communism as the answer to their economic difficulties
   (4) desire of more nations in Africa and Asia to be entirely self-sufficient

9. When a nation has a diversified economy, that nation

   (1) depends primarily on several strong agricultural products for foreign trade
   (2) encourages its citizens to invest in other nations
   (3) usually has a higher standard of living and produces a wide variety of consumer and industrial goods
   (4) borrows heavily from foreign banks to strengthen the development of natural resources

10. Within modern Europe there is a wide economic gap between

    (1) Italy and France
    (2) Germany and the rest of the continent
    (3) Eastern European nations and Western European nations
    (4) Great Britain and all of continental Europe

11. From an economic viewpoint, immigrants and foreign workers have posed a growing problem in several European countries in recent years as a result of the fact that

    (1) they are unwilling to learn the language of the host country
    (2) there are far fewer job opportunities and there is growing unemployment
    (3) their cultures are so different from the European country that they have difficulty blending into the society
    (4) the immigrants want to open their own factories, and the European countries will not allow them to do that

12. In economic terms, capital means

    (1) the largest city in a developing country
    (2) the ability to attract and keep foreign investment
    (3) the point at which a country controls its own economic future
    (4) money for investment in new businesses

13. Which concept has encouraged world nations to work together for their mutual advantage?

    (1) nationalism
    (2) imperialism
    (3) socialism
    (4) interdependence

14. Since the 1990s as Eastern European nations began to move toward private ownership of businesses, they were moving away from

    (1) a free enterprise system
    (2) a traditional economy
    (3) a command economy
    (4) a market economy

15. What would be the best explanation for the headline that follows:

    "Economic Group of Seven Expands to Allow Russia to Become Eighth Member"

    (1) Changes in the Russian government and economy improved Russia's standing among industrialized nations.
    (2) The other nations did not want to exclude a large Communist nation from their meetings.
    (3) Russia was requesting large amounts of foreign aid.
    (4) Russia was the only Asian nation to be excluded from the meetings.

16. When countries set the value of their currency at a very low exchange rate, what occurs?

    (1) Other countries cannot afford to buy their products.
    (2) Other countries lower the value of their currencies.
    (3) The products of that nation have an advantage in the international marketplace.
    (4) The country will be forced to continually adjust their currency rate upward.

17. Which of the following is a cause of the other three?

    (1) increased street crime and domestic violence
    (2) growing global drug trade
    (3) political instability and support for revolutionary activities
    (4) police and military officers accepting bribes for political favors

18. A negative aspect of the sale of weapons on the international market is that

    (1) developing nations spend money on weapons that could be better spent on the immediate needs of their citizens
    (2) the sale of weapons improves the economies of some of the richest countries in the world
    (3) all developing countries are unable to compete in the production of missiles and fighter planes
    (4) most nations will be able to produce nuclear weapons themselves in the very near future

19. Which statement expresses an opinion about international trade in the twenty-first century?

    (1) Bad weather or natural disasters in one part of the world may cause shortages of some products in another part of the world.
    (2) To avoid the economic problems of developing countries, a wise government may decide to isolate itself from foreign trade.
    (3) Wealthy countries benefit from trade with developing countries.
    (4) Economic competition will continue to occur between nations that produce similar items for sale.

20. A trading bloc is best defined as

    (1) nations with similar economic goals and one language
    (2) countries in one area of the world that are industrialized
    (3) places with common types of governments
    (4) nations that have agreed to remove barriers to foreign trade with each other

THEMATIC ESSAY

Directions: Write a well-organized essay that includes an introduction, several paragraphs addressing the task below, and a conclusion.

Theme: Interdependence

The world community of nations has become increasingly interdependent in recent years. Developed nations and those in the process of development recognize that each group needs each other.

Task

Select a nation that is considered economically well developed or industrialized and another that is considered a developing nation.

For each nation you have selected

- explain why each nation fits the category you have chosen for it
- discuss the impact of the world drug trade and the world arms trade on each of the nations
- describe how each nation you have chosen might view the other nation in economic terms

You may use any examples from your study of global history and geography but *do not use the United States.* Developed nations you might wish to consider include Japan, Great Britain, Germany, or France. Developing countries you might wish to consider include Mexico, any Eastern European nation, India, or Nigeria.

You are *not* limited to these suggestions.

Guidelines

In your essay, be sure to

- address all aspects of the *Task*
- support the theme with relevant facts, examples, and details
- use a logical and clear plan of organization, including an introduction and a conclusion that are beyond a restatement of the theme
- introduce the theme by establishing a framework that is beyond a simple restatement of the *Task* and conclude with a summation of the theme

DOCUMENT-BASED ESSAY QUESTION

Document-based questions for Chapters 18, 19, and 20 appear at the end of Chapter 20.

CHAPTER 19

Global Environmental and Social Issues

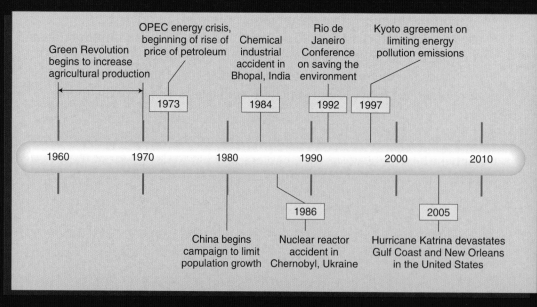

TIMELINE OF EVENTS

Green Revolution begins to increase agricultural production

OPEC energy crisis, beginning of rise of price of petroleum — 1973

Chemical industrial accident in Bhopal, India — 1984

Rio de Janeiro Conference on saving the environment — 1992

Kyoto agreement on limiting energy pollution emissions — 1997

1960　1970　1980　1990　2000　2010

China begins campaign to limit population growth

Nuclear reactor accident in Chernobyl, Ukraine — 1986

Hurricane Katrina devastates Gulf Coast and New Orleans in the United States — 2005

Globalization has made us more aware of the world around us. There are environmental and social issues of increasing concern because of the problems now taking place or others that will happen in the future. Examples of these problems are **global warming**, depletion of natural resources, lack of enough clean fresh water, and destruction of the environment. We need to be more concerned about these problems because of the consequences for our lives today and in the future. Some of these environmental and social problems such as global warming and pandemic diseases need immediate attention because they no longer can be ignored. Atmospheric pollution and its affect on global warming need to be addressed because rising global temperatures will affect the lives of millions of people in all parts of the world. These are also social problems that are not limited to any one country, people, or continent. Among these social issues are poverty, hunger, pandemic and other diseases, racial and religious prejudice, availability of medications, and illegal immigration.

In this chapter, you will read about and examine many of the environmental and social issues that are important to all of us. You will learn that there are often conflicting opinions about the causes of and solutions to problems resulting from these issues. These differences in opinion have led to controversies among respected politicians, educators, scientists, and others interested in studying about and resolving these issues. The people concerned about the environmental and social problems do not necessarily agree about the causes and proposed solutions. The environmental and social issues and their proposed solutions are worth learning about and discussing in your classes and with your friends and family. Sharing facts, ideas, and opinions will help you understand the environmental and social issues that determine how you live today and in the future.

There are important words and expressions that people use when talking about these issues and problems. In this chapter you will learn the definition of many of these words and expressions relating to environmental and social issues. For example, you will read words and expressions concerning topics such as global warming, Green Revolution, **pandemic diseases** (an epidemic over a wide geographic area), climatic change, sexually transmitted diseases, **ecosystems**, population control, and **greenhouse effect**. It is important to understand these words and expressions if you are to think about and discuss these important issues.

Main Idea:
You will read words and expressions concerning topics such as global warming, Green Revolution, **pandemic diseases** (an epidemic over a wide geographic area), climatic change, sexually transmitted diseases, **ecosystems**, population control, and **greenhouse effect**.

WORLD POPULATION GROWTH

There was an explosive growth of world population during the twentieth century. The estimated global population of 1.5 billion at the end of the nineteenth century is now calculated to be more than 6 billion. The 400 percent increase in the number of human beings inhabiting the earth in about a century is directly related to many of the environmental and social problems that confront us today. Population growth in some parts of the world has strained the ability of many countries to adequately feed the inhabitants of these lands. Nations are also finding it more difficult to safeguard their resources for future generations. Today some nations are facing a situation predicted by **Thomas Malthus**.

In China, the nation with the largest population, the government sought to restrict the birth rate by decreeing a policy that allowed one child per family.

Writing at the end of the seventeenth century, Malthus stated that when the world population increased beyond a certain point, food production would not keep pace with population growth thereby causing increasing poverty. He wrote that there would be too many people to adequately feed, house, clothe, and provide for in a humane manner. Malthus could not foresee the **Green Revolution**, which greatly increased the food supply in places such as **India** and **Pakistan**. However, he was correct in predicting that it would be very difficult to resolve the twin problems of poverty and hunger.

People who study population growth predict the world population will continue to expand in future decades. At the present rate of growth, the population of the earth is expected to top ten billion by the third decade of the twenty-first century before it levels off. Today, most people are able to live longer than people did in past generations. The control of deadly diseases, including smallpox, tuberculosis, and polio through vaccines and effective medical treatment, have allowed more children to survive into adulthood. The declining infant mortality rate, measured by the number of deaths per thousand infants, and the corresponding high birth rate have led to a doubling of population every twenty to thirty years in many developing countries. This population growth has resulted in increasing environmental and social problems in these developing countries. Food supplies, housing, schools, and jobs are needed to maintain and improve the standard of living of the rising populations. Unfortunately, in too many developing nations, considerable obstacles exist to meet even the basic needs of these growing populations.

Main Idea:
The highest rate of rapid population growth is taking place in Asia, Africa, and Latin America.

The highest rate of rapid population growth is taking place in Asia, Africa, and Latin America. The explosion in population and lack of available land to grow food crops has forced many people to abandon rural areas and flock to cities. Urban centers in developing nations are threatened because overpopulation has resulted in slum conditions for larger numbers of people. For example, a Peruvian farmer who comes to Lima, the capital, to escape horrible economic conditions in the countryside can find life in the big city to be dehumanizing, unhealthy, and deadly in other ways. The slums of the cities in developing nations often lack sewers, toilets, and safe drinking water. This has led to increased immigration, often illegal, into other areas of the world, notably Western Europe and North America, by people in search of a better quality of life.

The goal of controlling the birth rate often conflicts with religious ideas and traditional social customs. For example, the Roman Catholic Church, Protestant churches, Islamic religious organizations, and some Orthodox Jewish groups are very opposed to abortion and any ideas that would limit birth other than by abstinence. Parents in rural areas who need more hands to help work the land and want a guarantee that there will be someone to care for them in old age frequently prize a large family. Religious leaders with large followings often prevent family planning programs from successfully working and vehemently oppose all efforts to legalize abortions. The concept of birth control remains a controversial issue because many religious leaders and their congregations believe that population control and abortion are against the teachings of their religion.

Main Idea: The goal of controlling the birth rate often conflicts with religious ideas and traditional social customs.

In China, the nation with the largest population, the government sought to restrict the birth rate by decreeing a policy that allowed one child per family. The struggles **China** faced is an example of how difficult it is to establish an effective birth control program. In the 1980s, the population of China was estimated to be between 900 million and 1 billion. Parents who violated the official limit faced community pressures and heavy penalties. Despite some early successes, families that refused to settle for one child, particularly if it was a girl, violated the imposed limit. China's growing population is once again threatening to wipe out gains made in food production and health services. Today, the population of China is estimated to be close to 1.5 billion! The hope in China is that the rapidly expanding economy will provide enough work for everyone and raise the standard of living. In India, the country with the world's second largest population, the desire to have a male child, which can now be predicted by technological means, has led to the reduction of female births. This might have been a limiting factor in population growth; however, in India economic growth has accelerated and led to greater longevity, rising expectations for a better life, and a continued high birth rate.

In Europe, particularly in the EU countries, population growth has been less rapid because of industrialization and the shift from an agricultural to a highly urban society. Nations such as France, Germany, Italy, and Great Britain have lower birth rates and aging populations. A growing number of people in these countries believe that having too many children reduces the quality of a family's life. These countries have more advanced industrial economies and have become population magnets for people who want to work and have a better life. This has led to increased illegal immigration into these Western European nations. Problems relating to illegal immigration are also confronting the United States.

Overall, rapid population growth continues to be an issue that must be addressed. Our future existence is threatened unless solutions are found to the environmental and social problems arising from this increasing human population. We have to learn to better utilize the earth's land and resources. We need to safeguard the global environment from the ravages of pollution and find a way to reverse the trend towards global warming. The dramatic **climatic**

changes caused by greenhouse gases such as carbon dioxide, the heating of the earth's atmosphere by industrial pollution, uncontrolled forest burnings, and other causes will be a major concern for future populations in the twenty-first century. If the earth's atmosphere continues to heat up and the ozone layer is increasingly depleted, some land areas may no longer be habitable.

THE ISSUE OF WORLD HUNGER

Hunger and **malnutrition** still exist in many parts of the world. Despite the gains made in food supplies due to the Green Revolution, many nations do not produce enough food to adequately feed their expanding populations. There are a number of factors at work that make the solution to the world hunger problem more complex. Political instability often aggravates the problem of malnutrition. Revolutionary warfare, religious conflict, and tribal strife have caused a decrease in food production in many developing nations, particularly in Africa. For example, there has been an ongoing war in the **Sudan** for the last thirty years. This war between the Arab Islamic population in the northern part of the country and other Sudanese who are from Christian or animist tribes from the southern and western parts of the country has led to much hardship and suffering. Constant warfare has limited the ability to grow food-producing crops, which has resulted in hunger and malnutrition.

Changing climatic conditions have also added to world hunger. In Africa, the **Sahel**, a semiarid belt south of the Sahara, has expanded because of drought conditions and the consequences of **deforestation** and overgrazing of available land. The increasing desertification has made it very difficult to grow crops or raise herding animals. In **Mali** and **Niger**, drought conditions caused by insufficient rainfall and deforestation have resulted in reduced food production and increased hunger. Other regions in Africa are also suffering from the effects of a long period of little rainfall. Dry conditions cause people to dig deeper wells, thereby lowering the water table. Furthermore, because wood is the main source of fuel for cooking, many Africans also burn the available trees and other vegetation. This causes erosion of arable land, land that can be tilled and planted with seed. Overgrazing by herds of cattle, goats, and sheep in many marginal areas compounds the erosion problem.

Main Idea:
Food-deficient nations need more direct aid and financial credit to meet the basic nutritional requirements of their people.

Food-deficient nations need more direct aid and financial credit to meet the basic nutritional requirements of their people. United Nations agencies and food-exporting countries, such as the United States, Canada, and France, are donating food supplies and offering technical assistance to stimulate agricultural production. Private aid organizations, such as CARE, help coordinate the distribution of food and provide some health services. Nevertheless, corruption, the lack of adequate transportation networks, and other regional problems often hamper the distribution of food supplies.

A related problem is the lack of financial resources to invest in improving agricultural production. Many developing countries concentrate investment in the industrial sector. They do not have sufficient funds to industrialize and at the same time invest in improved seed varieties, chemical fertilizers, pesticides, and farm machinery. In addition, the burden of borrowing at high interest rates has added to the cost of modernizing farming technology. Faced with a choice of modernizing industry or agriculture, many developing nations have opted to invest in costly urban and industrial projects. These projects may be well intentioned, but they have little immediate affect on the need to augment food production in order to feed hungry populations.

HEALTH ISSUES

Advances made in public health services and medicines have lengthened life spans. In addition, world health organizations that operate through the United Nations and other private and public agencies seek to provide preventative and curative health care to peoples in need. Nevertheless, despite all the good intentions, there are diseases and health conditions that are ravaging whole populations in certain parts of the world such as Africa below the Sahara. Some diseases, such as **acquired immune deficiency syndrome (AIDS)** and malaria are still devastating many developing nations. AIDS, a disease that came to world attention in the 1980s, continues to spread. In some African countries, such as **Botswana** and **Zaire**, the percentage of affected individuals is alarmingly high. In Africa, traditional social customs that permit polygamy (having more than one wife) and the migration of men to cities to find work aggravate the spread of AIDS and other sexually communicable diseases. Women and children are particularly vulnerable in regions where environmental factors such as drought have led to widespread malnutrition and lower resistance to disease. AIDS is also spreading rapidly in some Asian nations such as India and **China**. In Europe and the United States, the illegal use of injected drugs such as heroin has facilitated the spread of this deadly disease, which destroys a person's immune system. Despite advances in medications and treatments, AIDS and malaria are a continuing threat to the present and future populations of many nations.

Main Idea:
There are diseases and health conditions that are ravaging whole populations in certain parts of the world.

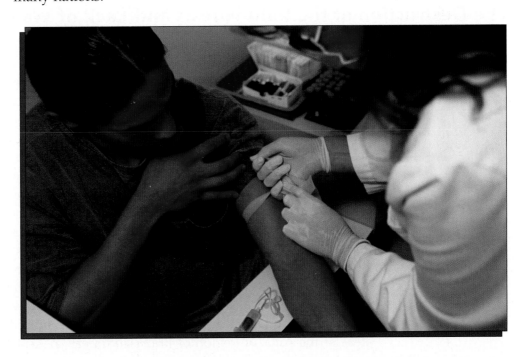

Advances made in public health services and medicines have lengthened life spans.

There are new medications that work to contain the AIDS virus. There also are medicines to control malaria. However, poorer nations have less access to these new and costly medications. Often, even if there are medicines available, these drugs are improperly used or beyond the reach of poor people. The lack of adequate health care systems in countries adds to the devastating effects of these diseases. Unless there is more funded research to find medical cures and if changes do not occur in traditional social behavior, the death rate from diseases such as AIDS and malaria will continue to grow.

Cholera, tuberculosis, chronic diarrhea, and other diseases also continue to devastate vulnerable malnourished populations in Africa, Asia, and Latin America. A lack of a safe water supply, raw sewage, and polluted rivers add to the problem of controlling these diseases. In parts of Eastern Europe and the Commonwealth of Independent States, the inefficient health care system and a lack of medical supplies threatens to increase the death rate from previously controllable diseases such as viral pneumonia.

There is also the possibility that a pandemic flu outbreak may take place in the twenty-first century. This is a very real concern and must be prepared for in advance. The world health organizations may not be as prepared as they need to be to face a potentially disastrous pandemic health threat. If we do not take this threat seriously, millions could die as happened during the flu epidemic in 1918. In the twenty-first century, nations will have to invest more heavily in their public health systems if they are to insure present and future populations of a better chance for healthier and more productive lives. Adequate preventative health care can save lives. Public health programs can also better use their funding if fewer people will have to be treated for diseases that can be prevented and treated before illnesses are very advanced.

ENVIRONMENTAL CONCERNS

The Destruction of the Rain Forests and Lack of Water Resources

The continued destruction of the world's rain forests is also a cause of great concern. The increasing exploitation of tropical rain forests has led to the clearing of large zones in Latin America, Asia, and Africa for farmland, timber, mineral resources, and land to graze cattle. Population pressures have resulted in the decline and extinction of numerous plant and animal species. Population pressures in Africa, Latin America, and Asia are a major cause of the growing destruction of the world's irreplaceable rain forests.

In Brazil, the widespread conversion of primal Amazonian tropical forests to farms and cattle ranches has caused the annual loss of thousands of acres of primary forestland. In the **Amazon Basin** and elsewhere, complicated ecosystems (an environment of animals and plants) have been wiped out. This means that a multitude of plants and animal life have been destroyed forever. Presently, we can only estimate the ultimate cost of the deforestation of the world's tropical regions. However, it is certain that unless the destruction of these vital forests is halted soon, the consequences for humanity will be devastating.

The wholesale clearing and burning of the humid, densely overgrown areas of the Amazon region of Brazil and areas in Asia such as **Sumatra** and

Borneo contribute to a worsening world air quality. The enormous combustion of trees and plants adds to the carbon dioxide in the atmosphere. This ever-larger amount of carbon dioxide in the air works to increase the warming trend known as the greenhouse effect. If allowed to continue unchecked, this will eventually lead to an alarming rise in average world temperatures. The loss of thousands of acres of vegetation reduces the ability of earth to cleanse its atmosphere by releasing oxygen and recycling water back to the earth in the form of rainfall. Some rain forest and other types of land areas are now drought stricken, and formerly useful land has become desert-like. Both Italy and Spain have experienced these new phenomena in parts of their countries. Even in some rain forest areas there is evidence of increasing desertification.

Sea levels are also beginning to rise as the earth's climate gets warmer. This greenhouse effect causes glaciers and ice sheets to melt in formerly frozen parts of the world. Glaciers are retreating throughout Europe and North America. Even the enormous ice sheets in Greenland are breaking down, and huge portions of ice are breaking off and melting freshwater into the oceans. Some islands and low-lying coastal lands are threatened with disappearance into the ocean. In the Pacific Ocean, there are already island chains that will be completely submerged in the coming decades. This will result in resettling ever-larger numbers of people.

We are already seeing some of the devastating effects of the continuing climate warming. There have been more powerful hurricanes in the **Caribbean Basin** because the sea temperature has risen by a degree or more in recent years. The numbers of hurricanes have increased, and some hurricanes are now quickly becoming much stronger and devastating. In 2005, there were more category 4 and 5 storms than ever before. Hurricanes are categorized by their wind speeds in gradations of 1 to 5. We are now seeing some hurricanes that start out as a category 1 or 2 storm quickly becoming a category 4 or 5 storm.

Funding solutions to halt the destruction of rain forests and other forest-lands and compensating for insufficient rainfall will depend on international cooperation in the twenty-first century. Allowed to continue at its present pace,

<aside>
Main Idea:
The increasing exploitation of tropical rain forests has led to the clearing of large zones in Latin America, Asia, and Africa for farmland, timber, mineral resources, and land to graze cattle.
</aside>

It is certain that unless the destruction of these vital forests is halted soon, the consequences for humanity will be devastating.

the clearing of rain forests and other heavily wooded areas will eventually destroy one of the earth's most vital natural resources. There also isn't enough water for people in some regions such as the Middle East. We have to hope that all nations, including the United States and China, will ultimately sign and uphold the principles set forth at the United Nations Conference on Environment and Development held in **Rio de Janeiro, Brazil**, in 1992. This conference led to the drafting and signing of a treaty in 1997 on global warming and the reduction of greenhouse gas emissions, called the **Kyoto Treaty**.

Pollution

Uncontrolled **pollution** has caused heavy damage to the earth, its atmosphere, and the life that inhabits our planet. The growth in world population and increase in industrialization have resulted in an enormous amount of pollution and waste. The sheer volume of garbage and industrial waste produced in the affluent developed nations has led to serious questions about how to dispose of such large amounts of material. In the United States, the average American is responsible for more than 1,400 pounds of trash per year. This figure does not include waste and trash produced by industry, agriculture, and business. The trash goes into local dumps, is burned, or is taken by boat to be dumped into the sea. Landfills in the United States are overflowing and are shutting down. Dangerous chemicals are leaking into the groundwater systems from barrels and cans that have corroded. The incineration of huge amounts of garbage adds to atmospheric pollution, and the constant dumping of sludge and other waste-containing poisonous chemicals has killed plant and fish life and contaminated seafood. Emissions from the use of gasoline and oil in vehicles such as cars and trucks only worsen the pollution crisis.

Many nations have even worse pollution and water disposal problems than the United States. In Eastern Europe, the failure to properly dispose of waste and build industrial facilities with even a minimal concern for pollution control has devastated vast areas of the **Czech Republic, Slovakia, Romania**, and **Poland**. The **Danube**, which flows through Eastern Europe, is just one of the many rivers in Europe that have been badly contaminated and no longer supports plant or animal life in some areas.

Radioactive contamination resulting from the partial meltdown in 1986 of the nuclear power plant in **Chernobyl, Ukraine**, poisoned a wide area of previously habitable and arable land. The growing threat of more nuclear accidents at poorly constructed and maintained atomic plants threatens the security and health of people in nations that can no longer afford to safeguard and refurbish their nuclear technology sites. In Sweden, an affluent, industrialized European country, a total ban on the use of nuclear power to generate energy has been declared, and in the United States, the construction of nuclear plants has practically ended. However, in the twenty-first century, the rising cost of energy, particularly oil, will most likely once again re-ignite the debate about using nuclear energy for peaceful purposes. The poisonous chemical gas leak in **Bhopal, India**, in 1984, and the nuclear accident in Chernobyl are examples of how important it is to have safeguards to prevent chemical and nuclear industrial waste and pollution disasters.

Main Idea:
The growth in world population and increase in industrialization have resulted in an enormous amount of pollution and waste.

The cleanup of toxic dumpsites and bodies of water that have been poisoned is a worldwide concern. Industrialized nations, such as the United States, the Netherlands, and Germany, have large ecology-oriented groups that are working to influence government policy in favor of safeguarding and cleaning up the environment. Nations are becoming more aware of the necessity of working together to solve some of the more threatening environmental problems caused by pollution. The international agreement of eighty-six nations in 1989 to ban chlorofluorocarbons used in refrigeration and air conditioning appliances is a reaction to the growing concern over the depletion of the ozone layer in the polar regions of the earth. The destruction of the ozone layer, a form of oxygen, by man-made chemicals, if allowed to continue, would eventually eliminate the natural protection against the sun's ultraviolet rays. Unless the major producers of these and other chemicals strictly comply with the ban, the menace of increased cases of cancer and even the destruction of vital polar ecosystems is possible by the early twenty-first century.

Main Idea: Nations are becoming more aware of the necessity of working together to solve some of the more threatening environmental problems caused by pollution.

The worldwide growth of industry has dramatically added to the problems of industrial pollution and waste. China, which has rapidly become one of the leading industrial economies of the world, faces enormous pollution and waste problems after only a few decades of modernization. China's failure to properly dispose of industrial pollution and waste has caused severe environmental damage and devastating human health problems. Rivers, which formerly served as sources of freshwater, are now poisonous health hazards. There are growing freshwater shortages caused by the dumping of toxic industrial wastes into the world's rivers and lakes. In some areas of China, the sun always seems to be partially or totally hidden behind clouds of pollution. These types of industrial waste and pollution conditions are true of other nations in Asia and elsewhere.

In Europe and North America, industrial pollution of the atmosphere has led to the destruction of forestlands and plant and animal life in freshwater lakes and ponds. The long-term effects of acid rain, which is a direct result of burning coal as a source of energy in Europe, North America, and in other continents, demonstrate that the world's forests and freshwater resources are in grave danger. Industrial pollution of freshwater sources will be an increasing problem for nations in areas where there is competition for the use of water. Freshwater, which is not polluted, will be an increasingly needed and valuable resource in this century.

The Extinction of Animal Life

The growing destruction of the earth's environment has led to the **extinction** of numerous species of animal life. The world's largest land and sea mammals are increasingly endangered. Certain species of whales are on the verge of becoming extinct, and the once vast herds of African elephants have drastically declined because of the value of these animals' precious ivory tusks. Rhinoceroses, hunted for their horns, which are valued in Asia for medicinal purposes, have all but disappeared in most of their natural habitats. Whole species of frogs are disappearing because rising global temperatures are resulting in the development of more bacteria and fungi, which are causing their extinction.

Main Idea:
Unless more is done to preserve the habitat of the world's wildlife, future generations will only know about most animals by looking at pictures in books or by visiting zoos.

The need to protect and conserve the wildlife of the earth has led to the efforts of international, national, and private organizations to reduce the slaughter. There is now an international agreement to restrict whaling. The use of drift nets by the tuna fishing industry is under attack because of the destruction their use causes to all sea life, particularly dolphins. Ivory importation has been restricted worldwide to protect elephants. Wildlife protection groups are also campaigning against the wearing of furs taken from such endangered species as leopards and tigers. In an effort to save endangered gorillas and other primates, stricter animal reserves policies are being enforced. The value of protecting animals for tourism programs that earn good profits is being encouraged in Africa and South America. Many African wildlife species may only survive if the park reserves where they live are turned into tourist eco-adventure areas, which provide revenues for local populations.

The choice is clear. Unless more is done to preserve the habitat of the world's wildlife, future generations will only know about most animals by looking at pictures in books or by visiting zoos. Greater international cooperation is needed to protect ecosystems that are the homes of irreplaceable animal and plant species.

Energy and Mineral Issues

The major industrialized nations consume the lion's share of the earth's energy and mineral resources. For example, the United States, possessing less than 5 percent of the world's population, consumes about one-quarter of its petroleum. This enormous use of oil to generate energy and other petroleum by-products results in a huge amount of nitrogen oxides and carbon dioxide emissions. Besides being wasteful, these emissions contribute heavily to polluting the environment and heating the atmosphere. The United States is not alone in terms of its vast energy and mineral needs and wasteful practices. Western European and Asian nations also have similar energy and mineral needs and problems.

Main Idea:
In recent years because of growth of the worldwide industrial economy, an increasing number of nations are competing for what in reality is a limited supply of petroleum.

There has been rising concern over the environmental damage caused by energy pollution. The energy crisis involves not only the mining of fuels and minerals and how their use damages the environment but also the consequences of exhausting the earth's reserves. In 1973, the industrialized nations learned how dependent they were on imported oil. The **Organization of Petroleum Exporting Countries (OPEC)**, via an embargo, made people aware of the fact that the oil-importing nations would have to pay more for this precious commodity. Second, the oil crisis clearly revealed that the world's petroleum reserves would someday be exhausted. Since the 1970s, the cost of energy and minerals continued to rise.

In recent years because of growth of the worldwide industrial economy, an increasing number of nations are competing for what in reality is a limited supply of petroleum. In the first decade of the twenty-first century, the price of a barrel of oil reached $70 in 2005. China, India, and other Asian nations have developed industrial economies and require increasing amounts of energy and minerals to fuel and build their economies. This means that we can look forward to paying ever-higher prices for energy and minerals because the predictions are that the worldwide industrial economy will continue to grow and develop.

The end of cheap energy, which started in the 1970s, is leading to many changes. The higher cost of energy affects the economies of all oil-importing nations and the industrialized countries. These nations are now forced to become more conservation conscious of these nonrenewable resources. Nations also have to think about planning for alternative sources of energy to meet their growing needs. For example, fuel efficient automobiles are becoming increasingly popular. In addition, standards for the control of automobile emissions have become a major concern in the United States and elsewhere. In Brazil and other developing countries, programs for gasoline substitution have been introduced. The use of sugarcane to produce an **alternative fuel** called ethanol, a mixture of gasoline and alcohol, is becoming more widespread. The vast deposits of shale, an oil-bearing rock, may someday become another source of petroleum products if the price of energy continues to rise.

Main Idea:
We cannot live without energy and minerals and maintain the modern quality of life that we have gotten accustomed to.

Researchers are seeking new ways to turn the enormous amount of garbage into energy. Solid waste, garbage, and the remains of other materials are more than ever being utilized to produce inexpensive fuels. Throughout the world, the search for cheaper and cleaner sources of energy has increased. There are research programs to better utilize the enormous potential of the sun and wind for power to run factories and provide energy for homes. Experiments with solar heating panels continue to demonstrate that the sun will become a viable source of energy if its potential can be harnessed. Other research involves the study of ocean tides and thermal springs as energy sources.

Today, we have to realize that the earth's energy and mineral resources are not inexhaustible. Petroleum, which is our major source of energy, will eventually not be available to meet our industrial and social needs. This is why we all have to think about conserving energy and minerals and developing new sources for these needs. We cannot live without energy and minerals and maintain the modern quality of life that we have gotten accustomed to. However, nations and individuals can do a better job in terms of conservation of energy and minerals and disposal of their wastes.

LINK TO TODAY

In 2005, the United States experienced an increased number of powerful hurricanes. One of these hurricanes, called Katrina, was particularly devastating because it practically destroyed one of America's largest cities, New Orleans. People throughout our nation and the world were shocked by the severity of Hurricane Katrina. This wind and rainstorm caused widespread flooding as levees broke down, damaging billions of dollars worth of property and killing many people.

Looking at the future, we have to ask ourselves if the hurricane season of 2005 was just unusual and unlucky or if it is a predictor of things to come. It is possible that Hurricane

Katrina is an example of how devastating storms may become as the earth continues to heat up. The issue of global warming is something that we have to think about today and plan for if we are to avoid the consequences of future hurricanes that reach a category 4 or 5 stage. There are also other phenomena that are happening that are gradually affecting our natural environment. These changes may seem slow and gradual, but they are happening and their consequences should cause us concern. We need to do more research and plan for these changes.

For example, many of the nations of Western Europe have a relatively moderate climate when compared to areas in Canada, which are on the same latitude. We know that the Gulf Stream current, which flows deep in the ocean along the European coastline, is the cause of this moderating climatic factor. We also know that as the greenhouse effects warm the earth's climate zones, glaciers and ice sheets are increasingly melting and releasing enormous amounts of freshwater into the oceans. There is the real possibility that someday the Gulf Stream current may be affected, and as a consequence many European nations will experience winters that are much more severe. The message that nature is telling us is becoming increasingly clear. Unless nations and individuals start to pay more attention by researching natural phenomena and planning for changes and consequences, we will live through more catastrophic events like Hurricane Katrina.

CHAPTER SUMMARY

In June 1992, the United Nations sponsored a worldwide conference in Rio de Janeiro to decide on the fate of the earth's environment. Thousands of concerned representatives met to consider two themes that are in many ways incompatible with current economic and social systems: the well-being of the environment and the prosperity of all humankind. Worldwide, there is a growing awareness that environmental deterioration and widespread human poverty will lead to future disasters. Representatives from the nations that attended the Rio de Janeiro conference could not agree on a united plan of action to resolve the many environmental issues facing an increasingly interdependent world. Self-interest dictated how some nations responded to the challenges set forth at the Rio conference. However, there was a worldwide agreement to continue working on problems that threaten the environment and our future on the planet earth. One result of this commitment was the Kyoto Agreement of 1997.

Environmental and social issues are not easy to resolve. For reasons we have now seen, they have caused great concern to humankind in this century; in certain ways, they are more problematic than in previous centuries. The need to resolve the problems caused by these issues requires increasingly greater cooperation among nations. Such cooperation, along with each person's awareness and concern, may make the world more livable in future years.

KEY TERMS

globalization	malnutrition	Organization of
global warming	deforestation	Petroleum Exporting
pandemic diseases	acquired immune	Countries (OPEC)
ecosystem	deficiency syndrome	alternative fuel
greenhouse effect	(AIDS)	Kyoto Treaty
Green Revolution	extinction	pollution
climatic changes	conservation	

PEOPLE

Thomas Malthus

PLACES

China	Mali	Caribbean Basin
India	Sahara Desert	Rio de Janeiro, Brazil
Pakistan	Niger	Chernobyl, Ukraine
Sudan	Sudan	
Sahel	Amazon Basin	

CHAPTER 19

MULTIPLE-CHOICE QUESTIONS

Select the number of the correct answer.

1. Since the beginning of the last century, the world population has

   (1) remained about the same
   (2) decreased slightly as a result of world wars
   (3) increased about four times in size
   (4) suffered from too many natural disasters to accurately be counted

2. Infant mortality rate is measured by

   (1) the number of deaths per thousand infants born
   (2) calulating the total death rate of an area's population
   (3) studying the number of infants who live to adulthood
   (4) dividing the size of the adult population by the number of infants

3. In the twenty-first century, the areas of the world with the greatest population growth rates are

   (1) North America, South America, and Asia
   (2) Asia, Africa, and Latin America
   (3) Africa, Europe, and Asia
   (4) North America, Europe, and the Middle East

4. Efforts to limit family size and to allow abortions are most frequently opposed by which group?

   (1) religious leaders
   (2) the government of China
   (3) medical professionals
   (4) urban dwellers

5. Which generalization is most true about population growth in industrial societies?

   (1) Family size in industrial areas tends to be large to supply factory workers.
   (2) The infant mortality rate is high due to pollution.
   (3) Industrial societies have a population growth rate that is similar to that of traditional agricultural societies.
   (4) Industrial societies generally have lower birth rates and smaller families.

6. Drought, deforestation, and overgrazing in parts of Africa have caused a serious problem of

   (1) air pollution
   (2) widespread hunger and malnutrition
   (3) an increase in the rate of literacy
   (4) urbanization

7. Polygamy, malnutrition, and illegal drug use can all be considered major contributing factors in the continuing growth rate of which disease?

   (1) polio
   (2) cholera
   (3) AIDS
   (4) smallpox

8. Deforestation, practiced in Latin America, Africa, and Asia is best described as

   (1) government programs to protect endangered species
   (2) a desire to limit population growth in urban areas
   (3) the destruction of widespread acreage of rain forest
   (4) efforts to control air pollution in rain forests

9. Bhopal, India, and Chernobyl, Ukraine, can both be described as

   (1) research facilities for the prevention of global warming
   (2) model industrial complexes for environmental safety
   (3) examples of the problems of global warming
   (4) the sites of chemical and nuclear disasters

10. Currently, a popular and effective method of protecting animals in the wild and in danger of becoming extinct is to

   (1) capture them and bring them to zoos in industrialized countries
   (2) develop tourist eco-adventure areas as places to observe without endangering the lives of the animals
   (3) allow them to continue to roam freely in their natural habitats
   (4) enable each country to form its own policies relating to the hunting, sale, or preservation of endangered species

11. A major concern that all humans are beginning to appreciate with regard to energy and mineral resources is the fact that

   (1) these resources are not inexhaustible
   (2) alternative fuels have been developed to substitute for existing resources
   (3) the decline of industrialization will solve the problem of resource shortages
   (4) increasing awareness of environmental issues decreases the need for alternative fuels

THEMATIC ESSAY

Directions: Write a well-organized essay that includes an introduction, several paragraphs addressing the task below, and a conclusion.

Theme: The Environment

Human activities are influenced by the earth's physical features and climatic conditions, and human activities impact the environment in a variety of ways.

Task

Identify two ways in which humans interact currently or have interacted in the last forty years with the environment. For each example identified,

- explain the nature of the interaction
- describe whether the interaction had a short-term or long-term impact
- evaluate the impact on the environment

You may use any examples from your study of global history and geography. Do not use the United States in your answer. Some examples of interaction you might wish to consider include changing African climatic conditions, deforestation in Latin America or elsewhere, industrial pollution, and the extinction of certain forms of animal life.

You are *not* limited to these suggestions.

Guidelines

In your essay, be sure to

- address all aspects of the *Task*
- support the theme with relevant facts, examples, and details
- use a logical and clear plan of organization, including an introduction and a conclusion that are beyond a restatement of the theme
- introduce the theme by establishing a framework that is beyond a simple restatement of the *Task* and conclude with a summation of the theme

DOCUMENT-BASED ESSAY QUESTIONS

Document-based questions for Chapters 18, 19, and 20 appear at the end of Chapter 20.

CHAPTER 20

The Global Impact of Scientific, Technological, and Cultural Issues

The Impact of Science and Technology

The Post-Industrial Era, which began after World War II, marked the start of a new phase in human development. It is now taking shape in the twenty-first century. The period after 1945 was the beginning of a new revolution in science and technology that would transform the industrialized nations while greatly impacting the rest. These changes have accelerated global independence and communication. While facilitating **globalization** and the **"shrinking of the world"** in some respects, they have also created new conflicts and controversies. These advances have had an impact on the work patterns, lifestyles, and standards of living of all people and societies throughout the world.

ARTIFICIAL INTELLIGENCE

In 1940, the first machine with **artificial intelligence** (**AI**) was introduced. Known as the **Electronic Numerical Integrator and Computer** (**ENIAC**), the device became commonly known by the complicated mathematical calculations done in less time and with greater accuracy than humans.

ENIAC, a computer developed at the University of Pennsylvania. Photograph c. 1946

Main Idea:
Computers revolutionized communication, making it possible to send large amounts of information long distances in seconds.

In the 1970s, the tiny low-cost chip was introduced. It has brought the greatest change to human communications since the printing press. The **microchip** stores thousands of **transistors** (devices that conduct electric signals). It made it possible for computers to store huge amounts of information and perform as many as eight million calculations a second. Its tiny size ended the need for a large computer, making the **PC** or **personal computer** possible (before that computers were huge machines that could do less than a modern calculator).

Computers revolutionized communication, making it possible to send large amounts of information long distances in seconds. This allowed investors, stock markets, producers, manufacturers, and customers to communicate instantaneously, bringing transactions to new speeds. By 1990, the production and sale of information was producing half the GNP of the United States, and almost 50 percent of all jobs were information related.

The **information superhighway** by computers was further expanded by the introduction of the **Internet**, which links personal computers throughout the world into one network. This facilitates shopping, trading, researching, sharing information, and communication for the general public. **E-mail** or **electronic messaging** is quickly replacing standard letters as the chief written means of communication. Individual computers were originally linked by modems or devices that converted the digital system computer signals into funds that were processed by the telephone equipment. These are being replaced in the twenty-first century by direct lines and satellites, which provide faster service.

SATELLITE TECHNOLOGY

Satellite technology has further revolutionized the world. Satellites are used to transmit television and radio programs around the globe as well as monitor and predict weather conditions. They can also be used for observations, which aid mapmakers, navigators, and environmentalists, as well as scientists and astronauts. Satellites can also be used for military purposes. These include spying, providing early warning in case of an attack, and guiding unmanned weaponry. For example, satellites both detected Soviet missiles in Cuba in 1962 and guided missiles in the recent invasion of Iraq (2003).

Main Idea:
The greatest impact of satellite technology has however been in the area of communication.

The greatest impact of satellite technology has however been in the area of communication. **Mobile** or **cellular telephones** have become a standard means of communication throughout the world. In many places, they have already replaced the standard "land line" services. The phones themselves have also added such features as cameras, calculators, and direct access to personal computers. Recently the cell phone has adopted greater computer technology, creating "Blackberries" or units that are a combination telephone, camera, calculator, calendar book, and computer. Even traditional land lines have been adapted for digital technology (fiber optics) for improved service.

SPACE EXPLORATION

Main Idea:
In the 1990s, construction of the International Space Station (ISS) by sixteen nations began.

Satellite technology also advanced the exploration of space. Important information about other planets has and continues to be received from satellites. They are also instrumental in communications with and controlling ships and equipment in space from earth. Beginning in the 1960s, the U.S. space program worked toward putting humans in space and learning more about the universe. In 1969, Americans were the first to walk on and explore the moon. In the 1970s, the focus shifted to building orbiting space stations and exploring the rest of the solar system. Reusable space shuttles were built to transport astronauts to these space stations on a regular basis. In the 1990s, construction of the International Space Station (ISS) by sixteen nations, including the United States, members of the European Union, Russia, Japan, the United Kingdom, and Canada began. It will be used to conduct experiments on human reactions to the space conditions, such as the law of gravity, as well as a means of expanding human knowledge on the universe. The exploration of Mars, Jupiter, and Saturn has given scientists valuable information. This was accomplished through the unmanned vehicles and robots taking samples and images that have given humans a closer look at these planets than ever before. In 2006, scientists announced that Pluto was too small to be a planet, reducing the number of planets to eight.

MEDICAL TECHNOLOGY

In the late twentieth and early twenty-first centuries, cancer, heart disease, lung cancer, and **AIDS** were the focus of most health research. Progress has been made in better understanding these diseases and controlling them with early detection, but they remain global threats to human life. **Alzheimer's disease**, which is a debilitating loss of memory, also became a focus of attention in the twenty-first century. The development of a capsule that is inserted directly into the brain and produces a brain hormone called **Nure Growth Factor** (**NGF**) has given hope to millions of sufferers. It is believed that a lack of NGF is the cause of Alzheimer's disease.

Main Idea:
Even though biotechnology and genetic engineering hold much promise for future medical advances, many see these as a threat if they fall into the wrong hands.

In the 1990s, the laser became important to health care. Because of its great precision, the laser became a new and less damaging means of removing or repairing internal parts. It can also be used to detect the exact location of a problem.

The development of **genetic studies** has also transformed medicine. Upon discovering that **mutations** (errors in the coding of **genes**) were responsible for most hereditary diseases, and that human **DNA** holds the genetic instructions to make and operate humans, biologists began the **Human Genome Project** (**HGP**) in 1990. Using **genetic script** or **genome**, this group has decoded much of the information found in DNA (basic genetic material). This has helped scientists and physicians find the causes of and treatments for many diseases. This has also led to genetic treatment (using genes as drugs) for diseases such as cancer, diabetes, and cystic fibrosis.

The need for genes as treatment of diseases led to **cloning** (recreating living organisms) through **genetic engineering** (the manipulation of DNA). This process allowed scientists to change traits in the organisms they produced, avoiding diseases and weaknesses. It also provided organs and genetic materials to be used in fighting diseases. The first clone of an adult animal was in 1997 when a sheep named Dolly was created from only one parent without fertilization. This made the genetic structure of Dolly exactly the same as her parent. The Scottish scientists who created Dolly hoped this would begin an era of medical advance, but it instead created a new controversy. Many people opposed cloning on religious, moral, and ethical grounds. Others feared scientists might use cloning to create superhumans and realize Hitler's dream of a "superior race." These fears grew greater in 2004 when South Korean scientists announced they had cloned human embryos and harvested their **stem cells** (the first cells to develop in the embryos, they are capable of becoming any of the cell types that make up the human body). Scientists believe embryonic stem cells may hold the cures to spinal cord injuries and diseases like diabetes, Parkinson's, and Alzheimer's. As with cloning, there was enormous opposition especially in the United States. The George W. Bush administration severely restricted funding for stem cell research, whereas other nations have been more supportive.

Even though biotechnology and genetic engineering hold much promise for future medical advances, many see these as a threat if they fall into the wrong hands. The ability to alter human genes and control an individual's makeup raises real ethical questions. The cost and availability of these medical advances to people throughout the world raises further issues.

THE GREEN REVOLUTION

The needs of developing nations to increase their agricultural production to keep up with population increases led to new and creative means of getting more out of the land already under cultivation and the expansion of farming into previously unproductive land. Known as the **Green Revolution**, these improvements began in the 1970s as **agronomists** (agricultural scientists) began developing high-yielding plant varieties. These needed more water as well as chemical fertilizers and pesticides to protect them from diseases and insects. New farming techniques, which enabled farmers to get more out of their land, were developed as well. Finally, low-cost farm machines that are useful in small areas had to be developed and made available to farmers. All this was expensive, requiring strong government support. Often international funding, as well as volunteers to train farmers to use new technology, were needed. Critics of the Green Revolution claim that very poor farmers are not getting the new technology and the chemicals being used are polluting the atmosphere. Yet, figures show that overall the Green Revolution has been successful in many places. India is often recognized as one of the places that has made successful efforts at practicing techniques of the Green Revolution.

> **Main Idea:**
> Figures show that overall the Green Revolution
> has been successful in many places.

Global Cultural Patterns

In the late twentieth century, Western civilization, in particular that of the United States, was exported throughout the world. This process continues now into the twenty-first century. In great part due to the Cold War (see Chapter 12 in this volume), American culture and values were promoted through American products around the globe. Combined with the development of a more interdependent world economy through multinational companies, this growth of the common global cultural standard became known as globalization.

GLOBALIZATION

Globalization is the development of a common culture and economy worldwide. Globalization, based on Western institutions and values, primarily those of the United States, was in great part responsible for the collapse of most Communist states by the end of the twentieth century (see Chapter 13 in this volume).

Main Idea:
Globalization is the development of a common culture and economy worldwide.

As the sole victor of the Cold War, the United States became a model for most nations. Using its vast military to try to keep world order, the United States became a global policeman as well. Desiring to attain the same high quality of life enjoyed by most Americans, nations began to imitate the American system.

Capitalist free-market economies developed throughout most of the former Communist world. The growth of continent-wide associations, such as the **European Union (EU)**, the **North American Free Trade Agreement (NAFTA)**, and the **African Union (AU)** are examples of this movement to promote Western-style economic reforms and democracy. Even "Communist" nations such as China and Vietnam are allowing capitalist economic reforms to avoid isolation and the collapse of their domestic economies.

The expansion of American business into the rest of the world quickly caused the growth of multinational corporations. This led to the growth of a global economy, in which the production, distribution, and sales of goods took place on a worldwide scale.

Modern technology, transportation, and communication have interwoven human activities as never before. Consumer goods, including perishable ones, can be moved great distances in a very short time. This has made it possible to buy almost any product at any time of the year. For example, children in developing nations have jerseys of popular American football players, and McDonald's restaurants and Disney theme parks have been built all over the world.

American companies have found it profitable to **outsource** jobs (give them to foreigners) to equally skilled workers outside of the United States who are willing to work for less money. This has been particularly true in the computer services industry. Even though it has created resentment among Americans, outsourcing has helped to build up the economies of other nations, particularly developing ones. Companies have also found it economical to incorporate in other countries where tax rates are lower and inexpensive local labor is also available.

The need for inexpensive labor also affected the movements of populations as immigrants from all over the developing world began to move to more industrialized nations, especially Western Europe and the United States. Predominantly male at first, these populations provided inexpensive labor for industrial and post-industrial nations. As they grew into large urban minority communities, in some nations, such as the United States, the majority assimilated. In the other nations, they have not assimilated, partly due to prejudice and partly due to the lack of higher educational opportunities. An unwillingness by immigrants to assimilate for religious or ethnic reasons exists in some countries. These immigrants, mostly Muslims, have become the recruiting targets of fundamentalist and terrorist groups.

The exporting of American businesses and products to the rest of the world has resulted in the creation of international organizations such as the **World Bank,** the **International Monetary Fund (IMF)**, and the **Organization of Petroleum Exporting Countries (OPEC)**. There are also regulating bodies such as the **World Trade Organization (WTO)**, which maintains the rules of trade between nations. The vast majority of WTO members are also part of the **General Agreement on Tariffs and Trade (GATT)**, which set policies to govern international trade in goods. Nations also belong to **regional trade agreements (RTAs)** that further regulate economic relations among its members. By 2006, there were over three hundred RTAs.

Multinational corporations probably exercise the greatest influence in the globalization process, controlling a significant percentage of the world's economic assets. For example, the combined revenues of the world's largest automobile manufacturers exceed the **GNP (Gross National Product)** of all of Sub-Saharan Africa.

There is much debate over globalization. Critics argue that the poor, especially in developing nations, do not benefit from globalization. They claim it is only the multinational corporations and a small elite in each country that profit from this. Critics believe globalization takes away jobs in industrial and post-industrial nations but does not give the same work to the poor in developing countries, whom it exploits. Often losing jobs to mechanization, they blame the multinationals for using it as a means of expanding corporate power and profits. Population shifts create poverty, prejudice, and conflict, while pollution increases. Supporters argue that globalization has actually given new opportunities for developing nations to improve and expand their economies. They believe that outsourcing has given skilled workers in developing countries employment and experience in their fields. Supporters claim globalization efficiently produces and exposes populations to consumer goods, promotes industrialization, and creates jobs. They claim that the overall economic expansion brought by it benefits all nations eventually. The more consumers purchase, the more production is needed, and the more jobs are created.

Main Idea: Multinational corporations probably exercise the greatest influence in the globalization process, controlling a significant percentage of the world's economic assets.

GLOBAL CULTURAL PATTERNS

Globalization has also brought the growth of common cultural patterns. For example American popular music now has a worldwide audience. Teenagers around the globe try to imitate their American counterparts in dress, habits, and even speech (American slang expressions are used internationally). The international availability of American films and television programming are in great part responsible for this. The availability of satellites and popularity of television and DVD players have created a huge international market for American products. They also provide advertising for American productions. The values and practices advocated in American films are often at odds with local ones. This has resulted in the modification or abandonment altogether of traditional values and practices. For example, women in cultures that are traditionally repressive toward them have found that American films and TV shows provide models for alternative ways of living. These images can also be negative, especially to the young people, as excessive violence and brutality may be depicted in some films. Generally the American lifestyle, which is perceived as one of wealth and personal freedom, is what attracts the most followers.

> **Main Idea:**
> The availability of satellites and popularity of television and DVD players have created a huge international market for American products.

The presence of American-style restaurants (McDonald's), stores (The Gap), and entertainment centers (Disney World) further reinforces the cultural bond with the United States. American clothing or products are viewed as status symbols. For example, perfumes and cologne were unheard of in most of the world until recently and are used worldwide today, especially by the youth, despite their expense. Clothing with designer labels can be seen anywhere, even in developing nations. American hairstyles and the wearing of body jewelry by both genders are also widely imitated.

English has increasingly become the international language. Learning it is viewed as a necessity if the individual is to "get ahead." It is understood that for any career in business or economics, speaking English is almost a requirement. Most schools worldwide teach it as the second language. It is increasingly difficult to find a place in the world where it is not spoken. This is reinforced by the popularity of American films, television, and music. The American mass media (CNN, FOX), with its ability to broadcast all around the world, is also a source for learning English. As the Greek language once was in the Hellenistic world, English has become the international means of communication.

The dominance of the United States militarily, economically, and culturally throughout the world has grown since the end of World War II. There is no question that a world culture based on American culture is established throughout the world. Although it has brought a certain amount of resentment in the form of anti-Americanism in some places, there are few places in the world that have not been influenced by this new cultural pattern.

A MacDonald's in Dubai.

LINK TO TODAY

Throughout this text the chapters have concluded with a section called "Link to Today." This chapter concludes with the understanding that it has brought you to "Today" and beyond. Because technological changes are constantly occurring, even as you have been studying Global History, it is difficult to imagine what changes the future may bring. It can be both fun and challenging to try to predict how daily life will continue to change in the future.

CHAPTER SUMMARY

The impact of science and technology has been a double-edged sword. There is no doubt that it has brought great advances and the opportunity to end much human suffering due to disease and famine, but there are also problems. The possible damage to the environment, as well as the danger of these advances being used to control people or create a "super-race," are viewed as credible threats by many. As the twenty-first century unfolds, these questions and controversies must be reexamined.

IMPORTANT PEOPLE, PLACES, AND TERMS

KEY TERMS

globalization
"shrinking of the world"
artificial intelligence (AI)
ENEAC
microchip
transistors
personal computer (PC)
information superhighway
Internet
E-mail
electronic messaging
satellite technology
cellular phones
International Space Station (ISS)
AIDS

Alzheimer's disease
Nure Growth Factor (NGF)
genes/genetic studies
mutations
DNA
Human Genome Project (HGP)
genetic script
cloning
genetic engineering
stem cells
Green Revolution
agronomists
European Union (EU)
North American Free Trade Agreement (NAFTA)
African Union (AU)

outsource
World Bank
International Monetary Fund (IMF)
Organization of Petroleum Exporting Countries (OPEC)
World Trade Organization (WTO)
General Agreement on Tariffs and Trade (GATT)
regional trade agreements (RTAs)
multinational corporation
Gross National Product (GNP)

CHAPTER 20

MULTIPLE-CHOICE QUESTIONS

Select the number of the correct answer.

1. Which statement best expresses a fact about the use of computers in the last twenty years?

   (1) Computers have been used to find cures for cancer and heart disease.
   (2) As a result of computers, the speed of business transactions has improved life for consumers but made life more difficult for business owners.
   (3) E-mail is quickly replacing standard letters as the chief written means of communication.
   (4) Computers have become so useful that all American families now own one or more of them.

2. In the twenty-first century, the best example of continuing international cooperation is the

   (1) existence of cellular telephones
   (2) discovery of a cure for AIDS
   (3) solution to oceanic pollution
   (4) International Space Station

3. A magazine article including topics such as cloning, lasers, and genetic studies would most likely be found in a magazine or section of a magazine about

   (1) space study
   (2) medical issues
   (3) high-speed communications
   (4) environmental issues

4. Globalization as a process has received increasing attention in recent years because

   (1) more nations are trying to establish their own cultural identity
   (2) cultural diffusion is not possible in the computer age
   (3) many countries are trying to exert their influence over other countries
   (4) there is a recognition of the development of a common culture and economy worldwide

5. The job of an agronomist is best described as

   (1) an agricultural scientist
   (2) a computer programmer
   (3) a medical researcher
   (4) a space technologist

6. Which pair of nations practices communism but allows for some level of capitalism within their nations?

   (1) India and Pakistan
   (2) Germany and Poland
   (3) Nigeria and Egypt
   (4) China and Vietnam

7. If you live in the United States, have a problem with your computer, call the "Help" telephone number, and are connected to a person in a foreign country, you are probably experiencing what trend in action?

   (1) communism
   (2) outsourcing
   (3) artificial intelligence
   (4) agronomics

8. A function of the World Trade Organization is to

   (1) maintain the rules of trade between nations
   (2) set the rates for foreign currencies
   (3) force nations to become involved in international trade
   (4) elect nations to the Security Council

9. Many students in foreign countries today study the English language because

   (1) most foreign governments require students to do so
   (2) English is spoken and understood in every foreign country
   (3) comprehension of the English language is seen by many in foreign countries as a method of achieving success
   (4) most other languages are considered "dead" languages

THEMATIC ESSAY

Directions: Write a well-organized essay that includes an introduction, several paragraphs addressing the task below, and a conclusion.

Theme: Science and Technology

In the last years of the twentieth century and the early years of the twenty-first century, science and technology have played increasingly important roles in the development of world culture.

Task

Select two areas of science and/or technology and for each

- describe how that area has changed or developed in the last thirty years
- discuss a positive and negative impact the scientific or technological advancement has had on a specific area of the world

You may use any examples from your study of global history and geography. Do *not* use the United States as an area in your answer. Some suggestions you might wish to consider include the use of satellites, medical breakthroughs, the use of computers, and space exploration.

You are *not* limited to these suggestions.

Guidelines

In your essay, be sure to

- address all aspects of the *Task*
- support the theme with relevant facts, examples, and details
- use a logical and clear plan of organization, including an introduction and a conclusion that are beyond a restatement of the theme
- introduce the theme by establishing a framework that is beyond a simple restatement of the *Task* and conclude with a summation of the theme

---

CHAPTERS 18–20 DOCUMENT-BASED ESSAY QUESTION

This question is based on the accompanying documents (1–6). The question is designed to test your ability to work with historical documents. Some of the documents have been edited for the purposes of this question. As you analyze the documents, take into account the source of each document and any point of view that may be presented in the document.

Historical Context

Interdependence means reliance upon others in mutually beneficial interactions and exchanges. Sometimes these interactions do not always have positive results.

Task

Using information from the documents and your knowledge of global history, answer the questions that follow each document in Part A. Your answers to the questions will help you write the Part B essay in which you will be asked to

- discuss two ways in which some members of the world community are attempting to have positive interactions with other members of the world community
- describe one area in which some nations or groups are trying to limit international transactions as a result of their negative impact

---

Part A: Short Answer Questions

Directions: Analyze the documents and answer the questions that follow each document.

Document 1

COMMON PROVISIONS OF THE MAASTRICHT TREATY

ARTICLE A

By this Treaty, the High Contracting Parties establish among themselves a European Union, hereinafter called "the Union".

This Treaty marks a new stage in the process of creating an ever closer union among the peoples of Europe, in which decisions are taken as closely as possible to the citizen.

The Union shall be founded on the European Communities, supplemented by the policies and forms of cooperation established by this Treaty. Its task shall be to organize, in a manner demonstrating consistency and solidarity, relations between the Member States and between their peoples.

ARTICLE B

The Union shall set itself the following objectives:

- to promote economic and social progress which is balanced and sustainable, in particular through the creation of an area without internal frontiers, through the strengthening of economic and social cohesion and through the establishment of economic and monetary union, ultimately including a single currency in accordance with the provisions of this Treaty;
- to assert its identity on the international scene, in particular through the implementation of a common foreign and security policy including the eventual framing of a common defence policy, which might in time lead to a common defence;
- to strengthen the protection of the rights and interests of the nationals of its Member States through the introduction of a citizenship of the Union;
- to develop close cooperation on justice and home affairs;
- to maintain in full the "acquis communautaire" and build on it with a view to considering, through the procedure referred to in Article N(2), to what extent the policies and forms of cooperation introduced by this Treaty may need to be revised with the aim of ensuring the effectiveness of the mechanisms and the institutions of the Community.

The objectives of the Union shall be achieved as provided in this Treaty and in accordance with the condition and the timetable set out therein while respecting the principle of subsidiarity as defined in Article 3b of the Treaty establishing the European Community.

Source: Excerpt from Title I (Common Provisions) of the Maastricht Treaty (taken from http://europa.eu/int/en/record/mt/title1.html)

Questions

1.

a. According to Article A of the Maastricht Treaty, what did the Treaty establish?

b. According to Article B describe two objectives of the Treaty.

Document 2

LIST OF MULTINATIONAL CORPORATIONS

Airbus	Chevron	Hewlett Packard	Pfizer
Altria Group	Citigroup	Hitachi, Ltd.	Philips
American	ConocoPhillips	Honda	Procter &
Express	Daimler-Chrysler	HSBC	Gamble
AOL	Dell	Infosys	Shell
Atari	Epson	Ingersoll Rand	Samsung
AXA	Ernst & Young	Johnson &	Telefonica
Bacardi	ExxonMobil	Johnson	Texas
BASF	Fiat	Krispy Kreme	Instruments
Bayer	Ford Motor	LG	The Walt Disney
Bic	Company	Lockheed Martin	Company
BMW	General Electric	Microsoft	Toshiba
Boeing	General Motors	Monsanto	Wal-Mart Stores,
Bombardier	Gillette	Nestlé	Inc.
BP (British	Google	Nike, Inc.	Xerox
Petroleum)	Halliburton	Nissan	
Cadbury	Hearst	Novartis	
Capital One	Corporation	PepsiCo	

Source: http://en.wikipedia.org/wiki/List_of_multinational_corporations

Questions

2. a. Identify any two companies from the list above that do business in the United States.

    b. Select two companies from the list and identify one product or type of product the company is associated with producing.

Document 3

EDUCATION FOR INNOVATIVE SOCIETIES IN THE 21ST CENTURY
St. Petersburg, July 16, 2006

I. Developing a Global Innovation Society

6. We must generate new knowledge and nurture innovation to sustain long-term economic growth. We will collaborate on creating research networks among higher education institutions, research centers and business, and capitalize on the leading edge technology they produce. We will share best practices on knowledge-based cluster development and public-private ownerships to facilitate global knowledge dissemination and move technologies quickly from the laboratory to the marketplace.

7. We will promote investment in knowledge, research and development. We will also leverage public expenditures strategically to attract private funding in

R&D, including in the education sector. In addition, we will encourage closer cooperation between universities and industry. These actions will generate innovation that improves the lives of our people, the prosperity of our nations and the well-being of the global community.

8. We will develop policies to promote the creation and dissemination of new technologies that encourage innovation and entrepreneurship. We will also make effective use of technological advances and research across businesses, education systems, and nations, while preserving the rights of innovators. We appreciate the contribution made by business and higher education leaders from our countries who met in Moscow on July 11, 2006 to discuss leveraging the resources, ideas and expertise of the public and private sectors to foster greater innovation and meet the education and workforce needs of the 21st century.

Source: Excerpt from a statement released by the Group of 8/Summit of 8 at their meeting in Russia in 2006 (from http://www.g7.utoronto.ca/summit/2006stpetersburg/education.html)

Question	**3.** Identify two goals to achieve long-term economic growth.

Document 4

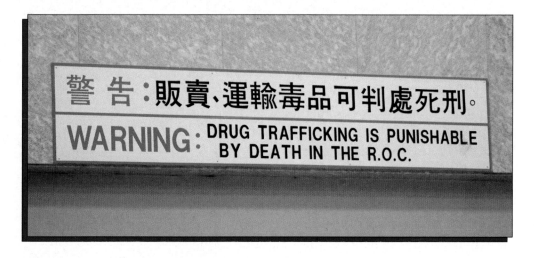

The picture above is of a sign posted at the International Airport in Taiwan.

Question	**4.** According to the sign posted in the International Airport in Taiwan, what activity is strictly forbidden?

Document 5

Small Arms and Light Weapons

Small arms and light weapons fuel civil wars and other conflicts, causing harm to millions of people, particularly in Africa. These small weapons are only part of a larger trade that includes heavier and more lethal weaponry, but light arms are often especially baneful because they are cheap, easy to transport and can be handled by ill-trained rebel soldiers and even chil-

dren. Recent UN reports show how these weapons are illicitly exported, transported with the connivance of government officials in many countries and smuggled into war zones. In some areas, automatic weapons are so cheap they can be bought in exchange for a chicken or a few pounds of rice. This page links to information about the plague of small arms and efforts to block small arms flows.

Source: http://www.globalpolicy.org/security/smallarms/salwindx.htm

Questions

5. a. According to the picture and article above, the trade of what type of product is the United Nations trying to block?
   b. Why has the product become so easy to trade?
   c. Why is the trade of the product causing serious problems?

Document 6

"Being here, living here, is something that I will probably spend the rest of my life striving to find just the right words to try to encompass and convey just a fraction of what makes our endeavors in space so special and essential," said Flight Engineer Peggy Whitson of Expedition 5, who lived six months in space on the station. Backdropped against the Caspian Sea, this full view of the international space station was photographed by a crewmember onboard the Space Shuttle Discovery after the undocking of the two spacecraft. Image credit: NASA

Question

6. What does the picture and comment tell about international cooperation and the ISS?

Part B: Essay

Directions: Write a well-organized essay that includes an introduction, several paragraphs, and a conclusion. Use evidence from *at least four* documents in the body of the essay. Support your response with relevant facts, examples, and details. Include additional outside information.

Historical Context

Interdependence means reliance upon others in mutually beneficial interactions and exchanges. Sometimes these interactions do not always have positive results.

Task

Using information from the documents and your knowledge of global history, answer the questions that follow each document in Part A. Your answers to the questions will help you write the Part B essay in which you will be asked to

- discuss two ways in which some members of the world community are attempting to have positive interactions with other members of the world community
- describe one area in which some nations or groups are trying to limit international transactions as a result of their negative impact

Guidelines

In your essay, be sure to

- address all aspects of the *Task* by accurately analyzing and interpreting *at least four* documents
- incorporate information from the documents in the body of the essay
- incorporate relevant outside information
- support the theme with relevant facts, examples, and details
- use a logical and clear plan of organization
- introduce the theme by establishing a framework that is beyond a simple restatement of the *Task* or *Historical Context* and conclude with a summation of the theme

Index

B

D

F

Falkland Islands, 588
FAO. *See* Food and Agriculture Organization (FAO)
fasci di combattimento, 261
fascism, 54
fascism in Italy. *See also* Italy
    blackshirts, 261
    fasci di combattimento, 261
    fascist rise to power, 261
    Mussolini, Benito, 259–62
    reasons for rise of, 259–60
    timeline of events, 250
Fashoda Incident, 184, 225
Fashoda (town), 184
Fauré, Edgar, 406
Faure, Felix, 86
Fay, Sidney, 228–29
February Revolution (1848), 78–79
Federal Republic of Germany (West Germany), 312–13, 404
Federated Malay States, 209
Feodor, Czar Theodore, 119
Fermi, Enrico, 307
feudalism, 3, 42
Fichte, Johann, 97
Fico, Robert, 438
Field, Cyrus, 16
Fifth Republic (France), 337
Figueres, Jose, 579
Fillmore, President, 203
"Final Solution," 363–64
Finland, 122, 309
First Balkan War, 135
First Opium War, 198–99
First Reich, 104, 267
First Russo-Turkish War, 134
First Socialist International, 41
Five-Year Plans (Soviet Union), 422
Fleming, Ian, 410
flying shuttle, 6
Foch, General Ferdinand, 232
Food and Agriculture Organization (FAO), 334
Ford, Henry, 14
"four-plus-two" negotiations, 314
Fourier, Charles, 40
"Fourteen points," 235, 241, 300
Fourth Republic (France), 337
Fox, Vincente, 575

France
    African imperialism, 188
    Alsace province, 84
    anti-Semitism, 86–87
    Battle of Waterloo (1815), 75
    Bismarck, Otto von, 84
    Blanc, Louis, 79
    Blanqui, Louis Auguste, 80
    Bonaparte, Louis Napoleon, 80–81, 87
    Boulanger, Georges, 86
    Bourbon restoration, 75–76
    Chamber of Deputies, 78, 80
    Charles X, King, 77
    Clemençeau, Georges, 234
    colonies, 83, 182
    Commune of Paris, 84–85
    Communists, 337
    Congress of Vienna, 75
    Crimean War, 82
    de Gaulle, Charles, 297, 302, 336–37, 483
    Dreyfus Affair, 86–87
    Esterazy, Major, 86
    Eugenie, Empress, 82
    European Community, 337
    Fauré, Edgar, 406
    Faure, Felix, 86
    February Revolution (1848), 78–79
    Fifth Republic, 337
    Fourth Republic, 337
    Franco-Prussian War, 83–84
    Giscard d'Estaing, Valery, 337
    Guizot, Francois, 78
    Haussmann, Baron Georges, 81
    Holocaust, 360
    imperialism of, 483–84, 495
    industrialization, 11–12
    July monarchy, 78
    July Ordinances, 77
    June Days of Terror, 80
    laissez-faire ideas, 77
    Legion of Honor, 87
    liberal monarchy in, 77
    Lorraine province, 84
    Louis Philippe, King, 77, 78
    Louis XIV, King, 103
    Louis XVIII, King, 75
    Middle East, 495
    Mitterrand, Francois, 337

    Napoleon III, Emperor, 80, 81, 91, 103
    National Assembly, 337
    Panama Canal, 86
    Pompidou, Georges, 337
    Popular Republic Movement, 337
    post-WW II, 336–37
    protectorate system, 182, 224
    Prussia, peace with, 84–85
    public work projects, 81
    railway system, 12
    Royalists, 85
    Second Empire, 81–84
    Second Republic, 79–81
    Siege of Sebastopol, 82
    Socialists, 337
    Southeast Asia, 209–10
    tariffs, 12
    tenement housing, 34
    textile manufacturing, 11
    Thiers, Adolphe, 78
    Third Republic, 85–86
    timeline of events, 75
    trade barriers, 12
    underground resistance groups, 371
    universal manhood suffrage, 79, 81
    Vichy government, 336
    World War II, 290–91, 295–98, 309, 336–37, 459
    Zola, Emile, 86
Francia, Dr. Jose, 160
Francis (Franz) Ferdinand, Archduke, 226
Franco, Francisco, 285–86
Franco-Prussian War, 83–84, 93, 223–24, 234–35
Frank, Anne, 380
Frank, Hans, 384
Frederick III, Kaiser, 105
free-market pricing, 37
Free-World bloc, 403
French Community, 484
French Indochina, 304, 487
Freud, Sigmund, 50
Friedman, Milton, 594
From Russia with Love (Fleming), 410
Fuentes, Carlos, 574
Fujimori, Alberto, 592
Fulani people, 518
Fulton, Robert, 16
Fundamental Treaty, 312

G

Gabon, 484
Gadsden Purchase, 157
Gagarin, Yuri, 423
Gallipoli (1915), 231
Gamsakhurdia, Zviad, 553
Gandhi, Indira Nehru, 533, 534
Gandhi, Mohandas (Mahatma), 484,
    515, 533
Gandhi, Rajiv, 534
Garcia, Alan, 592
Garibaldi, Giuseppe, 89–90, 92, 94
gas chambers, 368–70, 381
gas mask, 229
gas warfare, 229
GATT. *See* General Agreement on
    Tariffs and Trade (GATT)
gauchos (cowboys), 161
Gauguin, Paul, 52
Gaza Strip, 492, 494, 528
General Agreement on Tariffs and
    Trade (GATT), 616–17, 652
General Relief Committee, 72
genes, 48, 649
genetic engineering, 649
genetics, 48
Geneva Accords, 488
Geneva Summit (1945), 406
genocide
    Africa, 515
    Darfur, 524–25
    Nazi, 304, 353–54, 356, 360, 363,
        375
    Rwandan, 520
    Slovenia and Croatia, 443–44
    Sudan, 376, 524
genome, 649
George, Lloyd, 234
George II, King, 70
George III, King, 70, 197–98
George V, King, 69
Georgia, 122, 517, 553–54
German Confederation, 95, 100–101
German Democratic Republic (East
    Germany), 312–13, 404, 407,
    433
German East Africa, 184, 188
German Empire, 104, 235
Germany. *See also* Nazism in
    Germany
    African imperialism, 188

anti-Catholic legislation, 106
anti-Semitism, 107, 315
Austro-Prussian War (1866),
    100–1
Austro-Prussian War (1870–1871),
    101–4
Battle of Sadowa, 101
Bismarck, Otto von, 84, 99–100,
    103–5, 107, 188, 235, 356
Bundesrat, 104
Carlsbad Decrees (1819), 96
Center Party, 106
Christian Democratic Union, 315
colonies, 105
Congress of Europe, 95
Congress of Vienna, 12, 96
Danish War (1864), 100
denazification of, 402
dictated peace and Hitler, 241
division after WW II, 312–13, 404
economic policies, 106
elections, all-German, 318
Ems Dispatch, 103
Fichte, Johann, 97
First Reich, 104, 267
Frederick III, Kaiser, 105
free-trade area, 13
German Confederation, 95, 100–1
German Empire, 104, 235
Hegel, Georg, 97
Hohenzollern Dynasty, 99, 105,
    239
Holy Roman Empire, 95
imperialism of, 482–83
industrialization, 11–12
iron and coalfields, 12
Kohl, Helmut, 313, 315
kulturkampf (struggle for civi-
    lization), 106–7
Leopold, Prince, 102
Luther, Martin, 106
military restrictions on, 236
Moltke, Helmuth von, 99–100,
    103
Nazi Party, 241
North German Confederation,
    101, 104
occupation, World War II, 309
political policies, 104–5
Prussia, 99–100
railways, 12
Reichstag, 104, 315

reunification, 313–15
Revolution of 1848, 97–98
Rhineland demilitarized, 236
Schleswig-Holstein question, 101
Second Reich, 104, 267
Seven Weeks' War, 100–101
Social Democratic Party, 105–6,
    315
social policies, 106
sphere of influence, 181
Stocker, Adolf, 107
tenement housing, 34
timeline of events, 95
trade barriers, 13
Treaty of Frankfurt, 101
Treaty of Prague, 101
Treitschke, Heinrich von, 97
unification, factors favoring,
    96–97
unification, obstacles to, 96
unification, steps in, 99–104
United Nations, 312
war guilt and reparations, 236
William I, Kaiser Wilhelm, 99,
    101–2, 104–5
William II, Kaiser, 105, 188, 232
World War II, events leading to,
    285–90
World War II, occupation of,
    311–12
Zollverein, 96–97
Gestapo, 267, 359
Ghana, 210, 479, 515, 518
Gheorghiu-Dej, Gheorghe, 438
ghettos, 362, 373
Gies, Miep, 380
Gilbert, Martin, 377
Giscard d'Estaing, Valery, 337
Gladstone, William, 67–68, 70, 73
Glasnost (openness), 425
global cultural patterns, 651–53
global economic issues
    arms trade, 622–23
    drug trade, global, 621–22
    economic issues, present and
        future, 619–21
    European Union, 615–16
    General Agreement on Tariffs and
        Trade (GATT), 616–17
    global economy, growing interde-
        pendence, 613

greenhouse effect, 631
Gross National Product (GNP), 652
Grosz, Karol, 435
Group of 7, 464
Group of 8, 464
Grozny, 432
Grynszpan, Herschel, 361
guano (fertilizer), 155
Guantanamo Bay, 580
Guatemala, 156, 576–78
Guinea, 484
Guizot, Francois, 78
Gulag Archipelago (Solzhenitsyn), 424
Gulf of Finland, 120
Gutenberg, Johannes, 356
Guzmann, Abimael, 592
gypsies, 353, 366
Gysi, Gregor, 313

H

Habibie, Vice President, 536
Habsburg Empire, 131–32, 137, 239
Haiti, 581–83
Hamas, 529
Hamas terror group, 494
Hamid II, Sultan Abdul, 136
Hammarskjold, Dag, 333
Haniya, Ismail, 529
Hanoi, 488
Hard Times (Dickens), 53
Hargreaves, James, 6
Hariri, Rafiq, 532
Harris, Sir Arthur, 316
Harris, Townsend, 203
Hausa people, 518
Hausa-Yoruba tribal conflict, 517
Haussmann, Baron Georges, 81
Havel, Vaclav, 436–37
Hay-Bunau-Varilla Treaty, 577
health, global, 635–36
Hegel, Georg, 97
Heine, Heinrich, 358
Helsinki Conference, 312, 436
Helsinki Pact, 312
Helsinki Watch Committee, 312
hemophilia, 126
heredity, 48
Herzl, Theodore, 490
Heydrich, Reinhard, 361, 363–65
Hillsborough Agreement, 499

Himmler, Heinrich, 359, 363, 368, 372
Hindenburg, Paul von, 266–67
Hindus, 194–95
Hirohito, Emperor, 306, 309
Hiroshima (Japan), 305–6, 353
Hisahito, Prince, 544
Hispaniola, 581
Hitler, Adolf, 263, 265, 267, 285, 287, 297–99, 303
HIV/AIDS, 523, 543, 635–39
Hizballah, 529–31
HMS Beagle, 48
Ho Chi Minh, 487
Ho Chi Minh City, 538
Hobbes, Thomas, 28
Hohenzollern Dynasty, 99, 105, 239
Holland, 3, 371
Holocaust, 107, 266, 303. See also anti-Semitism
  aktionen (planned action), 360
  Allies, failed to act, 377
  apathy about, 390
  Aryan supremacy, 265–66, 358
  Auschwitz camp, 366–67, 369–70, 373, 375, 381, 385
  Belzec camp, 366, 369
  Bergen-Belsen camp, 366, 381
  Bialystok ghetto (Poland), 362, 373
  book burnings of Jewish authors, 358–59
  Buchenwald camp, 366, 381
  camps, concentration, 366
  camps, uprising in, 373
  Catholic Church (Eastern Europe), 379
  Catholic Church (Germany), 379
  Chelmno camp (Poland), 363
  Christian rescuers, 380
  churches, role of, 379–80
  crematories, 368, 370, 381
  criminals, search for other, 385
  Dachau camp, 366
  death camps, 366–67
  death marches, 381
  death toll, 381–83
  definition of, 353
  dehumanization of, 390
  Denmark, 377–78
  Drancy camp, 389
  Eichmann, Adolf, 363, 367, 385

Einsatzgruppen, 365–66
European Jews, deaths, 353–54, 356
Evian Conference, 360
"Final Solution," 363–64
France, 360
Frank, Anne, 380
gas chambers, 368–70, 381
genocide, Nazi, 353–54, 356, 360, 363, 375
ghettos, 362, 373
Goebbels, Josef, 358, 361
Göring, Hermann, 384
gypsies, 353, 366
Heydrich, Reinhard, 361, 363–65
Himmler, Heinrich, 359, 363, 368, 372
Hitler's war against Jews (1933–1939), 357–61
Hitler's war against Jews (1939–1945), 361–70
homosexuals, 353, 366
individual courage, 390
individual responsibility, 390
Jehovah's Witnesses, 366
Jewish resistance to Nazis, 370–80
John XXIII, Pope, 379
Judenrat (Jewish Council), 362–63
Korczak, Janiuscz, 375–76
Krakow ghetto (Poland), 362
Kristallnacht, 360–61
"leadership principle," 384
Lichtenberg, Bernard, 379
Lodz ghetto (Poland), 362
Maidanek camp, 366, 381
master race theory, Nazi, 358
Mauthausen camp, 366
medical experiments, 368–69
Mein Kampf (Hitler), 357
Mengele, Dr. Josef, 367–69, 385
mentally retarded, 366
Nazi Germany, defeat, 381
Nazi Party, 287, 357–58
Nazis, 107, 266, 303
Niemoller, Martin, 380, 390
Nuremberg Laws, 355, 359
Nuremberg War Crimes Trials, 310–11, 361, 383–85
Ohrduf camp, 382
Patton, George, 381–82
physically handicapped, 353, 366
Pius XI, Pope, 379

N

NAFTA. *See* North American Free Trade Agreement (NAFTA)
Nagasaki (Japan), 306, 353
Nagorno-Karabakh war, 517, 552
Nagy, Imre, 435
Namibia, 483
Napoleon III, Emperor, 80–1, 91, 103. *See also* Bonaparte, Louis Napoleon
Napoleonic Wars, 122, 225
Narodniks, 125
Nasrallah, Shiek Hassan, 530
Nasser, Gamal Abdel, 491
Nastase, Adrian, 439
National Assembly, 337
National Day of Remembrance, 385
National Liberation Army, 590
National Liberation Front, 578
National Movement Party, 554
National Patriotic Forces of Liberia, 524
National Reconstruction Commission, 518
National Revolutionary Movement, 593
National Salvation Front, 439
National Union for the Total Independence of Angola, 521
nationalism, 49, 88–89, 223
Nationalist Republic of China (Taiwan), 119, 331, 541–42
nationality, 96, 224
native Guarani population, 161
NATO. *See* North Atlantic Treaty Organization (NATO)
natural law, 46
natural selection, 49, 55
Nazarbayev, President Nursultan, 549
Nazi-Soviet Nonaggression Pact, 290, 295
Nazism in Germany. *See also* Germany
  anti-Semitism, 266–67, 304
  Aryans, 265–66
  concentration camps, 267, 303, 304
  death camps, 267, 303
  denazification, 311
  Enabling Act, 267

fear of Communism, 266
genocide tactics, 304
German nationalism, 265
Gestapo, 267
Hitler, Adolf, 263, 265, 267
Hitler's war against Jews (1933–1939), 357–61
Hitler's war against Jews (1939–1945), 361–70
Holocaust, 107, 266, 303
"inferior human beings," 304
master race theory, 266, 283, 358
Mein Kampf (Hitler), 265
Nazi Party, 241, 287, 357–58
Nazis, 107, 266, 303
Nazis, defeat, 381
Nazis, in power, 266–67
Nazis, rise to power, 265–66
opposition, removal of, 266
propaganda, 266
Reichstag, 264, 266
Third Reich, 263, 267
timeline of events, 250
totalitarianism, 262–63, 269, 294
Treaty of Versailles, 263, 265, 267
Weimar Republic, 263–64, 266
Nehru, Jawaharlal, 484, 533
Nehru Gandhi, Indira, 484
Neo-Fascists, 339
Netherlands, 6, 11, 13, 36, 207–8, 462–63
Netherlands East Indies, 207, 487
Neves, Trancedo, 586
New Azerbaijan Party, 553
new economic theories and ideas
  Adam Smith, economic ideas of, 37, 155
  communism, theory of, 42–43
  criticism of, 36
  economic reform, ideas of, 36, 38–39
  economic theories and ideas, new, 36–45
  food supply and population growth, 37–38
  industrial economy and role of government, 37–39
  liberal reformers, 36
  Marx, Karl, 41–43
  radical revolutionaries, 36
  reform, call for, 36
  socialism, 39–40

  socialism, scientific, 41
  socialism, utopian, 40
  worker movements, beginning, 39
New Granada, Viceroyalty of, 164
New Lanark (Scotland), 40
New Orleans, 641
New York State, 379
New Zealand, 481
Newcomen, Thomas, 8
Newcomen pump, 8
Nguyen Van Thieu, 488
Nicaragua, 156, 571, 576, 578–79
Nicholas I, Czar, 123
Nicholas II, Czar, 126, 137, 231
Niemoller, Martin, 380, 390
Niger, 634
Nigeria, 186, 210, 518–19
Nile River, 187
9/11 attack, 531
Nine Power Treaty, 282, 291
1956 War, 491
Nixon, Richard, 408, 488
Niyazov, Saparmurat, 550–51
Nkomo, Joshua, 480, 522
Nkrumah, Kwame, 479, 518
Nong Duc Mahn, 539
nonliving matter, 48
Normandy, 301
North Africa, 188, 301
North American Free Trade Agreement (NAFTA), 575, 616, 651
North Atlantic Pact, 405
North Atlantic Treaty Organization (NATO)
  creation of, 312, 405
  Kosovo, 431–32, 444
  Serbia, 432
  Turkey, 525
  Western Europe, 335, 461–63
  Yugoslavia, 431
North German Confederation, 101, 104
North Korea. *See also* Korea; South Korea
  emerging nation, 516
  Kim Il Sung, 406
  Kim Jong II, 547
  missile firing and Japan, 546
  nuclear weapons, 548
  timeline of events, 547

Weizsacker, Richard von, 314
Yalta Conference, 302–3
Zhukov, General, 299, 303

X

X-rays, 50

Y

Yale, Elihu, 196
Yalta Conference, 302–3, 330, 402
Yasukuni Shrine, 546
Yeltsin, Boris, 426–30, 432
Yom Kippur War (1973), 492–93
Yoruba (Nigeria), 518
Young Italy Society, 90
"Young Turks," 136, 238
Yrigoyen, President, 587

Yuan Shi-kai, 200
Yudoyono, Suseilo Bamband, 537
Yugoslavia, 131, 242
    Communist regime, 403
    disintegration of, 443
    mass killings, 376
    NATO, 431
    since 1999, 444
    Tito, Marshal, 405, 442–43

Z

Zaire, 520, 635
Zapata, Emiliano, 573–74
Zapatero, Jose Luis, 460
Zedillo, Ernesto, 575
Zemskii Sobor (Council of Nobles), 120
Zenawi, Meles, 523

Zhirinovskiy, Vladimir, 429
Zhivkov, Todor, 299, 303, 440
Zia ul-Haq, Muhammed, 535
Zimbabwe, 480, 522
Zimbabwe African National Union, 522
Zionists, 489
ZOB (Jewish Fighting Organization), 372–73
Zog, King (Albania), 441
Zola, Emile, 86
Zollverein (customs union), 13, 96–97
Zulus (tribal people), 186
Zyklon B (insecticide), 369–70, 385, 390